Columbus, Geo.,

FROM ITS

Selection as a "Trading Town"

IN

1827,

TO ITS

Partial Destruction by Wilson's Raid,

IN

1865.

HISTORY—INCIDENT—PERSONALITY.

PART I—1827 TO 1846.

COMPILED BY JOHN H. MARTIN.

Southern Historical Press, Inc.
Greenville, South Carolina

Additional Errata for History of Columbus, Ga. Book

A correction to misinformation of part one, page 50 under "Died."
In the July 5 entry is found "Samuel Sully, merchant." Mr. Edge
R. Reid, Associate Publisher of The Ledger-Enquirer Newspapers of
Columbus sent the following correction which was discovered after
correspondence from the Isaac Delgado Museum of New Orleans con-
cerning a portrait of Chester Sully, brother to the artist Thomas
Sully, which the Delgado Museum had received. This history by
Martin does contain the notation above concerning the death of
Samuel Sully. However, the microfilm of The Columbus Enquirer
for July, 1834 contains this obituary in the issue of July 12,
1834: "Died, in Columbus, Georgia on the night of the 5th inst.
Chester Sully, merchant in said town. We are informed he has
a wife and a large family of children, in St. Mark's, or Pensacola,
Florida, with whom we sincerely sympathise for their loss..."
This correction will show that Thomas Sully had a brother Chester
Sully who died in Columbus, Ga., and that the painting of Chester
Sully by his brother Thomas Sully is now in the possession of the
Isaac Delgado in New Orleans.

Please direct all correspondence and book orders to:
SOUTHERN HISTORICAL PRESS, Inc.
PO Box 1267
Greenville, SC   29602-1267

Originally printed: Columbus, GA. 1874
New Material Copyright 1988 by:
   Alvie L. Davidson
ISBN #978-1-63914-141-8
Printed in the United States of America

INTRODUCTION.

When the prospectus for this compilation was issued, neither the publisher nor the editor could make any reliable estimate of the size of the volume—not a page of it having then been prepared. We soon discovered that it was impossible to crowd into the space which we at first proposed as a limit, more than half the matter that ought to go into the work, and as the price at which it was offered could not justify the furnishing of a volume of double the number of pages contemplated, we concluded to extend the work and divide it into two parts, each covering the space of about nineteen years. The first part is now presented.

The editor is conscious of many defects and deficiencies. These were unavoidable. The newspaper files, upon which he had mainly to rely, were wholly missing for the years 1835 and 1836, and many numbers were missing from the files of other early years within our reach. We procured a file of the Macon [Georgia] *Messenger* for the years 1835–6, which enabled us to supply many incidents of the Creek war. Old citizens assisted us with their recollections, and though we could not make up a perfect history of that stirring time from these disconnected data, we trust that we have given enough to interest and inform most readers. Of course our chapters for these two years are deficient in minor *local* incidents that the papers of the city would have furnished had they been accessible.

The editor pleads, also, his pressing and unflagging work upon a daily newspaper, as an excuse for the lack of a better arrangement of the facts in this publication, as well as its very plain style. He can say, indeed that he has only had *snatches of time* to devote to it. Some old citizens will no doubt be disappointed because it does not contain incidents worthy of note within their remembrance. But even they might have overlooked some incidents equally noteworthy that aré reported. It would have been impossible for any one person, with the imperfect records at hand, to gather up all the facts deserving mention.

It will be seen that we have not included any *living* persons in the short personal sketches contained in this part, and we have endeavored to avoid any compliment (however deserving) to persons now living. These brief sketches are not brought up as closely as they should properly have been, but omissions in this respect will be supplied in the remainder of the work.

Prior to the year 1389 we had to rely entirely on the newspapers for records of marriages and deaths, and they are deficient. There are records of marriages in the Ordinary's office, commencing with that year, and we have been kindly permitted to use them. But the death roll is still incomplete.

The newspapers for the years over which we have gone devoted little space and paid but little attention to local affairs—much less than they now do. We have been surprised to find that they often contained but very slight mention, and sometimes none at all, of local questions, which, as we learn from allusions in the proceedings of Council, must have much interested the city and its people. As there was a marked improvement in this respect in the newspapers of later date, as the files are more complete, as well as the written records, we can safely promise that there will be fewer omissions in the second part. That part will also conclude with interesting statistics in reference to the factories, churches, &c., at the present time.

With this explanation we submit the first half of our work to the public, hoping that it contains matter that will interest and inform them, with all its imperfections.

THE EDITOR.

ERRATA.

Gen. James N. Bethune informs us that the lot which brought the highest price at the first sale was not the south-west corner of Broad and Crawford streets, as stated on page 12, but "the opposite corner;" also that according to his recollection it was purchased by Henry C. Cook and John Fontaine for $1,875. Our information was derived from another old citizen, as to the location and purchasers. The *Enquirer* states that the price was $1,855.

We have given two dates for the arrival of the first steamboat—one on the authority of the *Enquirer*, the other on that of an old citizen. Subsequent inquiry almost convinces us that the 22d of February, 1828, was the time, and the "Steubenville," the boat.

On page 36 we attribute to Opotheololo a boast that was made by another Indian chief, Pushmataha.

On page 89, "A. B. Rozan" should have been printed A. B. Ragan.

Ou page 107, "Philip T. Schulz" should have been printed Philip T. Schley.

There are no doubt some unavoidable mistakes made in transcribing or printing a few proper names.

ADDITIONAL ERRATA: In the original printing page numbers 93 and 94 were skipped. What is numbered page 95 should have been page 93, et seq. We have followed the original pagination in this reprint.

COLUMBUS, GA.

1827.

A "TRADING TOWN" ESTABLISHED.

The first step towards the establishment of a town on the site on which the city of Columbus now stands, was taken by the Georgia Legislature of 1827. The act of that year was not one of incorporation. It was entitled "An act to lay out a trading town, and to dispose of all the lands reserved for the use of the State near the Coweta Falls, on the Chattahoochee river, and to name the same." This act was "assented to" Dec. 24, (one advertisement says Dec. 22,) 1827. It provided for the appointment by the Governor of five Commissioners to select the most eligible site on the reserve (known as the Coweta Reserve, near Coweta Falls on the Chattahoochee,) to appropriate a square or oblong square of twelve hundred acres for the commons and town, which was to be called and known by the name of COLUMBUS. They were to lay out not less than five hundred building lots of half an acre each, and to make a reservation of one square containing ten acres for the public buildings of the county of Muscogee, with the privilege to the county of selling what was not needed for this purpose.

The Commissioners appointed to execute the trust were,

Ignatius Few, Elias Beall, Philip H. Alston, James Hallam, and E. L. DeGraffenried.

The present site of Columbus was at that time an almost unbroken lowland forest, in some places hardly penetrable through its thick undergrowth, and in others covered by swamps and ponds of water. Where some of the finest buildings now stand there were marshes or ponds. From one block north of where the "Perry House" now stands, all south and east was a muddy swamp, filled with briars and vines and small undergrowth among the large forest trees, so that in many places it was difficult to get through. Upon the present location of the "Perry House," and extending two blocks north, was a pond where wild ducks and geese were often shot. Fish of large size were for some time afterwards caught out of ponds of which no traces now remain. Between Oglethorpe street and the river the land was generally high and dry, interspersed with pretty groves of fine shade trees. But east of Oglethorpe street and all south was mostly wet swamp land.

The few houses that had been erected prior to the first sale of lots by the Commissioners were along a road that crossed the river at a ferry near where the Hospital now is. It was a section of the old "Federal Road." Traces of this river crossing may still be seen on the Alabama bank. The hotel was there and three or four stores, whose principal trade was with the Indians. But when the town was laid off and the lots sold, these settlements, being out of town, eventually had to move up within the space laid out into lots. There were but few comfortable houses up to that time—some small log houses, some board houses or tents, and some Indian houses.

At that time there were a number of springs of excellent water running out of the bluff along the river. There were as many as ten or twelve of them from the "City Mills" location down to the wharf, and they afforded plenty of the best water. Gov. Forsyth, who attended the sale of the lots in 1828, preferred to camp out in a beautiful grove just below the present wharf, and pitched his tent beside one of these springs. With the march of civilization receded the beauties as well as the wildness of Nature, and these fine springs have long since ceased their refreshing flow.

The scenery on the bank of the river was very beautiful, including some of the finest natural groves. The river, too, presented quite a different appearance from the muddy Chattahoochee of this time, with its high water-bed extended by caving to twice its original extent, its banks on both sides precipitous and bare, and those on the Alabama side still falling in with every freshet. The waters were clear and rippling, and the rocks that presented themselves for some distance above the steamboat landing or head of navigation nearly extended across the river in places, with channels or pools between, from which nearly all the varieties of fresh-water fish were taken in abundance. It was interesting and amusing to see the Indians catching shad in the spring of the year. They used dip-nets, made of wahoo bark split up in small strips. The net was fastened to the ends of two large canes, about fifteen feet long. They would arrange themselves in a row, five to fifteen in number, on the edge of the place where they wished to dip. They would then dip their nets in regular order, one net following right after the other. When one caught a fish he would throw it out of his net behind him, and never lose more than one dip. The whole party would yell every time there was a fish caught. But the shad, like the springs, have long since disappeared from our river, and some can hardly believe that they were ever caught here. The clear, fresh water of the Chattahoochee must then have been much more congenial and inviting to these dainty fish than the turbid stream of the present time, muddied by its passage through hundreds of thousands of acres of cultivated ground and polluted by the sewerage filth of the towns and factories on its banks.

An old writer describes the natural beauties of the locality at that time as follows:

"The most fertile imagination could not conceive a place more enchanting than this is in reality. Neither is it deficient in the various natural capacities for the convenient transaction of business.

Standing at the centre, the eye can feast the mind with contemplating the most delightful scenery, which raises a thousand romantic and poetic associations. The river on each side is adorned with forest, as beautiful as nature could make it; and the channel is made rugged and firm by the deposit* of immense heaps of solid rock. The rapids continue for a great distance, sometimes forcing the river down into a narrow channel of great depth and inconceivable swiftness. In the course of the descent of the river through some of these places, the torrent is opposed by rocks of immovable fixture, which throw it up into mountain waves, or dash it away in a wide expanse of beautiful white caps, counter currents, and eddies."

NATURAL ADVANTAGES.

It was apparent that these were great, and though the results that might reasonably have been contemplated have not yet been fully attained, the causes of the failure or delay are also evident, and there is good reason to hope that all the anticipations of the past will yet be fully realized, if not by the agencies originally had in view, by others now progressively at work. The location being at the permanent head of navigation of a fine boatable stream, on the outskirts of continuous white settlement—with a strip of Indian territory sixty miles in width separating it from white civilization and commerce in Alabama, and this Indian country one of known fertility and beauty, whose opening to white settlement was only a question of time—there was good reason to anticipate for Columbus a rapid growth and far-reaching trade. For some time its trade by wagon and by the river was extensive, reaching from Apalachicola to the section of country now including Heard, Carroll and Fulton counties, and embracing nearly all the region between the Chattahoochee and Flint rivers. But railroads came from the east westward, and their general effect has been to carry trade to the east. The river trade has been nearly broken up, and railroads connecting with more eastern cities now traverse nearly all the country from which Columbus formerly derived her distant wagon trade. We may confidently hope for a considerable extension

---

* Either this word does not exactly express the writer's meaning, or the river must then have moved rocks in its course as it moves sand now.

of trade from railroads now in course of construction, which will give us more direct communication with the great West; but unquestionably the safest reliance of Columbus for a steady advance in business and a permanent prosperity are her great advantages for manufacturing. Her princely cotton mills, already finding all over the Union a ready sale for their superior fabrics, are her "jewels," of which she may well be as proud as the Roman matron of her sons; and when we consider that not one-twentieth part of her great water power is yet appropriated, that she is in the very heart of the cotton growing region, with superior facilities both for obtaining the raw material and shipping the fabrics, and that the profits of the factories now in operation are sufficient to satisfy the cupidity of the most exacting capitalist, we cannot fail to see that this is the citadel of our strength—the firm foundation of a progress and prosperity that will yet realize all the expectations ever indulged concerning Columbus. It is not probable that the utilization of this great water power was one of the objects contemplated in the selection of the site of Columbus, and good fortune rather than human sagacity favored the city in this respect.

1828.

INTEREST THROUGHOUT THE STATE.

Much interest was aroused throughout the State by the legislation looking to the establishment of the new town of Columbus, and the anticipated sale of the lots. The advantages of the locality were so apparent as to attract the attention of men of a speculating disposition, as well as of persons desiring to try their fortune in a new settlement with such fine prospects. We find that complaints against the tardy action of the Commissioners, and of the gentleman selected by them to make the surveys and prepare the plan of the town, found their way into the public prints. On the 11th of July, the surveyor, Mr. Edward Lloyd Thomas, defended himself against the charge of failure to return the plan to the Surveyor General's office, stating that he had sent the plan to the Executive Department and to other places.

THE POPULATION.

Before the sale of the town lots the population of the place was very much mixed, as is generally the case in new settlements. It amounted to about three hundred.

THE INDIANS.

During the day there would generally be hundreds, and sometimes thousands of Indians from the Alabama side in town, but they were not allowed to stay on the Georgia side at night. They were generally friendly and harmless while on this side of the river, but sometimes annoying, as they would go to private houses, to the alarm of some of the ladies. But their object was to get something to eat or steal. We find the Creeks called "a remnant of beggars and drunkards" by a writer of that time.

THE COLUMBUS ENQUIRER.

This paper was established by Mirabeau B. Lamar in this year, and the first number was issued during the last week in May. It was a weekly sheet of good size and fair appearance, and its editorial conduct gave ample evidence of the ability which afterwards secured for its accomplished founder high positions and an enduring fame. It is chiefly from its columns that we glean most of the facts that make up what we can give of the earlier history of Columbus.

On the 5th of July, the *Enquirer* said: "Our town offers many advantages to the agriculturalist who may locate near it, as well as to the merchant or mechanic, as our market will afford good prices for all kinds of produce, and *our river* a safe and convenient navigation on which to export the same. Those who may visit this place with a view of purchasing to settle here, will not leave us disappointed. We hear of many strangers who have come to examine the public property before the day of sale arrives."

RIVER IMPROVEMENT.

At that early day this subject engaged the earnest attention of both the State authorities and the new settlers of Columbus. They contemplated not only the improvement of the navigation below the town, but the opening of the river above to regular pole-boat navigation. The latter proposition would seem to us at this time to have been a wild scheme; and yet we find a correspondent asserting on the 9th of August that "the river is navigable for pole-boats 200 miles above the falls; the obstruction to navigation above the town continues for twenty miles, but boats can, in the winter, come within four miles of the town;" and we find in the *Enquirer* of Sept. 13th the official report (dated "Upper Bushy Head Shoal, Chattahoochee, 27th August, 1828,") of "one of the Commissioners of the Chattahoochee Navigation above the Coweta Falls," in which report this Commissioner informs Gov. Forsyth that with the money appropriated by the State for improving the navigation of that part of the river, the Commissioners had bought on the eastern shore of Maryland and at Charleston, S. C., "fifteen likely negro fellows and one woman;" that they had constructed "an excellent three decked boat, sixty feet keel, nine feet beam, well constructed for the accommodation of the hands, overseer, and one Commissioner, also for the safety of the tools and provisions and the storing of powder for blasting." The report goes on to state the operations on the upper river, in the section flowing between Coweta and Carroll counties, announces considerable progress, and expresses hope of the accomplishment of much improvement. Now who shall say that Georgians at that time, and especially frontier Georgians, were not men of enterprise and pluck?

The State Engineer also made a report (published in June) on the practicability of improving the river below the town. He recommended a "wing-dam" about three feet above sum-

mer water at Woolfolk's bar, and an excavation of the channel to the desired depth, expressing the opinion that there
was not the slightest probability of its re-accumulation; also
a wing-dam at Mound Shoal, a little below Woolfolk's bar,
and about half a mile above the mouth of Upatoie creek.

SALE OF THE LOTS.

The first sale of town lots by the Commissioners commenced on the 10th and closed on the 23d of July. The
attendance was large, and the bidding lively. Many tents
were erected by persons attending the sale, and the town presented an animated and bustling appearance. The lot that
sold highest at that sale was the one on the southwest corner
of Broad and Crawford streets, afterwards known as the Columbus Hotel lot. It was bought by Messrs. Nicholas Howard (of Greensboro') and Peter Dudley, who immediately
erected the "Columbus Hotel" on the lot.

The number of half-acre lots in the plan of the town was
632, of which 488 were sold, leaving 144 to be disposed of
at some future period. There were also sold 25 gardening
lots of 10 acres each, and 20 of 20 acres, besides a number of
larger lots outside of the limits of the town. The total proceeds of this sale were $130,991, one-fifth of which was re-
quired in cash. The highest price given was for the lot above
mentioned, $1,855. Many lots were bought with a view to
immediate settlement, and many others by speculators with a
view to an advance.

IMPROVEMENTS.

After the sale of the lots, improvements commenced and
buildings went up rapidly. On the 28th of November the
Enquirer said: "Notwithstanding the great disadvantages
which builders have labored under in procuring lumber, we
can safely say that no place has improved more rapidly than
the town of Columbus. Each holder of a lot or lots seems
intent on improving his property immediately, and there are
now either completed or nearly so, on the half-acre lots,
nearly a hundred good framed buildings. Our mills are now

in better order for supplying lumber than they have ever been before. But one three-story framed house has yet been erected, and but two brick buildings commenced in the town. We should be pleased to see more of this description of building carried on."

About this time the *Enquirer* stated that the population numbered 700 to 1,000 souls, and felt grateful that the health was so good, saying that there had not been more than a half dozen cases of fever during the whole summer, and but four deaths—three whites and one black.

INCIDENTS.

The first person buried in the cemetery was a young man by the name of Thomas—a son of Edward Lloyd Thomas, the gentleman mentioned as the surveyor. He was buried on the hill before the location was fully determined upon, but when determined it included the grave of young Thomas. He was buried in March of this year.

The 4th of July was celebrated in a spirited and patriotic manner for a frontier settlement. Col. Ulysses Lewis was the reader of the declaration, and James Van Ness the orator.

A theater was "erected" for the purpose and opened for a short engagement as early as July of this year, and we find the performances of the company highly complimented. But we suppose the Columbus theatre-goers of that day were hardly so critical or discriminating as those of the present time, and there was some difference between the rough unsuitable hall in which the performance was given and Springer's Opera House with its fine scenery and luxurious furnishing.

The first manufacturing establishment that was built here was a turning lathe, erected on the little branch north of the city, just below where the North and South Railroad now crosses that branch. Nobody thought in 1828, when that little turning lathe was started, that Columbus would ever be the manufacturing place it is now, even; much less did they entertain the hope that it would ever win the appellation, "Lowell of the South."

The first steamboat that came to Columbus was in March, 1828. After she had been here a week or ten days, making some repairs, the Captain arranged for a pleasure excursion down the river as far as Woolfolk's Mound, the next Sunday. Nearly every body went, and a good number of them had to walk back to town on account, as the captain alleged, not being able to raise sufficient steam for the boat to make headway against the river current. The next morning about daybreak the signal gun* of the boat was heard, giving notice of her return.

There were no churches here during this year. There would occasionally be preaching by some missionary to the frontier heathen, or by some traveling minister. Columbus was a pretty "hard" place for a year or two. There was not much execution of law or government of any kind. Every body had to look out for themselves. This being the case, we are not surprised to find the files of the *Enquirer* for those years abounding with reports of duels, impromptu fights, and duelling correspondence.

The following, in regard to the streets and scenery of Columbus, from the *Enquirer* of August 9th, 1828, will still be of interest. The streets remain as originally laid out, but the "romantic walks" and gushing springs are among the things that were:

"The streets running parallel with the river are nine in number, and are all 132 feet wide, except Broad, which is 164 feet wide. This street is one and a half miles long, and is a perfect level the whole distance, except one depression. The cross streets are thirteen in number, and are each 99 feet wide. From the width of the streets an elegant and airy appearance is given to the town. There is a wide expanse left between the town and the river for a promenade, which, after it shall have been properly prepared, will form one of the handsomest and most romantic walks in the State. All along the bank of the river opposite the town, fine, pure water gushes out, which affords not only a great convenience, but a great luxury to citizens."

In October, Henry C. Dawson took charge of the McIntosh

* It was a custom then, and for many years afterward, for boats to carry a small cannon, and on nearing a town or landing to give notice of their approach by discharging it.

House, and Peter Dudley became sole proprietor of the Columbus Hotel.

A new hotel, called "Muscogee Hall," on the corner of Broad and Crawford streets, was opened in November by Nicholas Howard.

At the Presidential election in November, the Jackson electors received 143 votes, and the Adams electors 17.

The first bale of cotton ever sold in the town was brought in November from Gwinnett county, and bought by Robert Maharrey at 12½c.

On the 29th of November the pole-boat Rob Roy, Love owner, arrived from Apalachicola with a full cargo of groceries for J. Fontaine, Maharrey, Love & Co.

A clever local conundrum which we find in the paper is this: "Why is the town of Columbus like modest ladies?" The answer—"Because it is on the reserve."

OFFICERS.

Hon. Walter T. Colquitt was Judge, and Andrew B. Griffin Clerk of the Superior Court this year. The following gentlemen constituted the Grand Jury at the Fall Term: E. E. Bissell, foreman, John R. Page, Samuel B. Head, E. B. Lucus, Stoddard Russell, Robert Daniel, Robt. Henry, Benj. Tarver, Thomas Rogers, Thomas Lang, Samuel E. Buckler, Joseph White, Hillery Triplett, Samuel Koockogy, Thomas Cox, Thos. Sluck, Jona. A. Hudson.

James C. Holland was Sheriff, and P. Robertson Deputy Sheriff.

John Townsend was Clerk of the County Court.

Joel B. Scott was Coroner.

Edwin E. Bissel and G. W. Dillard were Justices of the Inferior Court.

S. J. Cooley was Postmaster until October, when Jas. Van Ness was appointed.

At the October election, Sowell Woolfolk was chosen Senator, and W. D. Lucas Representative.

Mirabeau B. Lamar severed his connection with the *Enquirer* on the 1st of October, 1830. He represented Muscogee county in the Legislature of Georgia in 1829 '30. Shortly after his retirement from the *Enquirer* he removed to Texas, and there received the highest honors within the gift of the people. He was elected President of the young and independent Republic in 1838. He died in Texas in December, 1859. Gen. L. was twice married. His first wife is buried in the cemetery in this city; his second was a daughter of the Rev. John Newland Maffitt.

Walter T. Colquitt was for a number of years the most brilliant (perhaps not the most solid) member of the bar of Columbus. He was noted for keenness of wit and repartee and versatility of talent. As a lawyer, judge, both a representative and senator in Congress, he was equally conspicuous and efficient. He died in Macon, Ga., on the 7th of May, 1855, after a long and painful illness.

MARRIAGES.

July 28.—Col. P. H. Alston and Miss Sarah D. Parks.

Sept. 6.—Maj. Rufus M. Farrington and Miss Sarah, daughter of Gen. Wm. McIntosh.

Sept. 7.—Samuel E. Buckler and Miss Sophia Tomlin.

Sept. 20.—James Brown, of Augusta, and Miss Ann Dukes.

Sept. 28—Samuel R. Andrews and Miss Elizabeth Day.

DEATHS.

July 26.—Elizabeth, infant child of Blake and Lucy Robinson.

Aug. 30.—Wilson (an Irishman) drowned in the river.

Sept. 16.—Mrs. Davis, a native of North Carolina.

Oct. 18.—James B. Crawford, aged 30 years.

Nov. 13.—"Indian Boy," aged 12 years, from a stab in the forehead.

We find the names of the following business and professional men of Columbus during this year:

Merchants—James W. Fannin, jr., Thomas Lang, Phelps & Bonner, Jacob I. Moses & Co., I. Scott, Joel B. Scott, Jona. A. Hudson, Sowell Woolfolk, Farlin & Nafew, Elisha Avery.

Lawyers—Ulysses Lewis, Wm. J. W. Wellborn, Samuel T. Bailey, James Van Ness, Thos. G. Gordon, Julius C. Alford.

Doctors—I. T. Scott, H. C. Phelps, E. L. DeGraffenried, Fitzgerald Bird.

Hotel Keepers—Wm. D. Lucas, Nicholas Howard, Peter Dudley, Henry C. Dawson; *Teacher*—Jno. R. Page; *Barber*—Wm. Woodliff; *Brickmakers*—Winston & Alford, Zoroaster Robinson; *Tailor*—J. W. Radcliff; *Gin Maker, &c.*—Rhoderic Murray.

Latest quotations of prices of merchandise for this year, Dec. 13th: Bacon 12½c., Bagging and Twine 50c., Cotton 7¾c., Corn 50 to 75c., Flour $10 to $15, Molasses 50c., Salt $2 50, Brown Sugar 10 to 12c., Coffee 18 to 20c., Tobacco 25c., Whisky 75c.

1829.

THE TOWN INCORPORATED.

The first act of incorporation of the Town of Columbus passed the Legislature of Georgia in December, 1828, and was signed by the Governor on the 19th of that month. It provided for the election on the 1st Monday in January, 1829, of an Intendant and six Commissioners, and vested the municipal government in them. The election resulted in the choice of Ulysses Lewis as Mayor, and Samuel B. Head, James Van Ness, Ira Scott, Simon L. Smith, George W. Dillard and Thos. G. Gordon as Commissioners. [Another ticket for Commissioners, which associated Messrs. Van Ness and Scott with M. B. Lamar, Fitzgerald Bird, T. T. Gammage and Henry C. Phelps, had previously been nominated by a meeting of citizens; but Messrs. Lamar, Bird and Gammage declined before the day of election.]

On the same day county officers for Muscogee were elected, as follows: Arian Coaker. Tax Collector; James Johnson, Receiver of Tax Returns; E. E. Bissel, Jas. Hitchcock, B. A.

Sorsby, Samuel R. Andrews and W. P. Baker, Justices of the Inferior Court.

R. T. Marks was Clerk of the new city government.

On the 19th of January, "nine fisheries on the Chattahoochee, within the corporate limits of the town of Columbus," were publicly rented out for the year by the Clerk of the Town; but the amounts for which they rented are not published. All other traps were required to be removed within ten days.

In accordance with authority specially delegated by the new charter, the first ordinance of the municipal government was one requiring all houses on the streets and common to be removed, and forbidding all persons to cut down or destroy any tree on the river common.

At this time the "Northern and Southern mail" was carried through Columbus, tri-weekly, accross the Indian Territory, via the Creek Agency in Alabama.

On the 27th day of February, the sale of the remaining half-acre lots in Columbus was closed, having continued six days. The aggregate amount of the sales was $4,585.

The Intendant and Commissioners passed an ordinance to let out to the highest bidder, on the 2d of February, the work of cleaning out of Front, Broad, Oglethorpe, Randolph, and St. Clair streets—the two latter to their intersection with Oglethorpe. Front, Broad and Oglethorpe were to be cleaned entirely of trees, stumps, and bushes, which were to be taken up by the roots, the streets to be grubbed, and all rocks over three pounds in weight to be removed.

We take this order as an indication of the extent to which close occupation of the town had then progressed from the river eastward.

On the 14th of February, the *Enquirer* said:

"Columbus is rapidly advancing in improvements. Building is carried on in a style that would do honor to our populous cities, and with a rapidity scarcely equalled within our knowledge. Such is the progressive style, that we frequently find large two-storied houses and well-cleaned gardens, in various parts of the town, where but a short time previously, we were rambling after game. Ramblers are not unfrequently surprised at finding their hunting ground so suddenly converted from a wilderness into cultivated fields or adorned by the labors of the architect and enlivened by traffic. We have dry goods and groceries in abundance, and all the difficulty in the way of good living is the want of the *wherewith* to purchase the commodities. Few of our citizens having the necessary cash or credit, are often reduced to deplorable straits. The absence of the grand *sine qua non*, however, seems to be no barrier to the growth of the town."

There was much apprehension, this year, of trouble with the Indians. The Legislature passed an act forbidding their crossing the river into Georgia without permits. In July the President of the United States had a thousand stand of arms forwarded to Fort Mitchell for the use of the frontier citizens, and thirty or forty regulars, on their way to the Agency, passed through Columbus in July. But many of the head men of the Indian nation visited Columbus and pronounced the reports of their hostile intentions false. The "Frontier Guards" were, however, ordered out on one occasion.

Politics ran so high this year, that we find an advertisement offering prime cotton for sale by retail to "anti-tariff ladies."

On the 10th of November the Commissioners appointed for the purpose announced that they had laid out a market road from Decatur to Columbus.

The Bank of Columbus was organized this year.

We find the names of the following steamboats that arrived during the year: Fanny, Robert Emmett, and Virginia· The latter was the first arrival of the winter, and did not get up until the 28th of December, so low was the river in the fall and early winter. The Emmett made one trip in 60 hours.

INCIDENTS.

On the —— of January, Mr. Elisha Avery, a native of Connecticut, and four negroes were drowned by the upsetting of a batteau in which they were making a trip from Columbus to Apalachicola. The Mayor, Col. Lewis, Mr. Root, and eight negroes in all were in the boat, but all except those first mentioned escaped.

There was a great rise of the Chattahoochee in February of this year. Back lots (in the lower portions heretofore mentioned) were inundated, and the house of the editor of the *Enquirer* was submerged almost to its windows.

On the 25th of May, the steamer Virginia, a large and fine boat, arrived, having made the run from Apalachicola in 38 hours.

W. A. Spalding, of the firm of Fontaine & Spalding, was drowned in the Chattahoochee on the 1st of June. He was a native of Maryland, and was only 21 years old.

A temperance society was organized on the 1st of August— E. L. DeGraffenried, President; Andrew Harvill and Rob't Jones, Vice Presidents; James Van Ness, Corresponding Secretary; James W. Fannin, Recording Secretary; Thos. W. Cox, Secretary.

On the 8th of August it was announced that Mr. Richard T. Marks had purchased a half interest in the *Enquirer*.

In September, Upatoie post office was established—Simon Manning, postmaster.

At the October election of this year, M. B. Lamar, Senator, and W. D. Lucas, Representative, were elected to the Legislature.

Oct. 17th, the first load of new cotton was brought in by John D. Chambless of Talbot county. It was classed middling, and bought by S. & R. T. Woolfolk at 7c.

The Virginia again arrived on the 28th of December, being the first boat of the winter, after a suspension of navigation in the summer and fall. The Virginia took down 400 bales of cotton for New Orleans.

On the 7th of March 500 shares of the stock of the Bank of Columbus had been taken, and it was anticipated that the Bank would speedily go into operation under favorable auspices.

The Superior Court of the county then took jurisdiction of such offences as fighting in the streets and keeping disorderly houses in Columbus, as we find in the presentments of the Grand Jury at February term.

The town tax this year was 5 per cent. upon the amount paid to the State for the town lots.

We find the names of two Columbus volunteer companies —the "Frontier Guards" and the "Columbus Fencibles" mentioned in June. A. Y. Gresham was Captain, and ——— Marks, Orderly Sergeant of the "Frontier Guards."

The 4th of July was celebrated under an arbor—a large crowd attending. The "Frontier Guards" formed the procession. Prayer by Rev. Mr. Hammill; reading by Nathaniel P. Bond; oration by Capt. A. Y. Gresham; dinner at Howard's Hotel.

MARRIAGES.

Feb. 3.—Capt. James Johnson, of the steamboat Emmett, and Miss Dorothy Coker.

Feb. 10.—Richard T. Marks and Miss Jacintha E. Dawson.

March 10.—Oliver Jeter and Miss Mary Ann Gartrell.

March 12.—Wm. Middleton and Miss Lydia Dobbs.

Aug. 24.—Thos. Slack and Julia Ann Howard.

Dec. 20.—Sowell Woolfolk and Miss Sophia W. Thomas, the latter of Milledgeville.

DEATHS.

June 1.—Matthew Wells, aged 50.

Aug. 2.—Mrs. Judith W. Thornton, consort of Dr. Hudson A. Thornton.

Sept. 5.—Pleasant Robinson, Deputy Sheriff.

Oct. 18.—Wm. Martin, aged 27, a native of Georgia.

Dec. 18.—Benjamin Jepson, sr., a native of Boston, aged 63.

Cotton was quoted, Dec. 26th, $7\frac{7}{8}$ to 8c. No other quotations given.

The following business men (not mentioned in 1828,) advertised in the *Enquirer* in 1829:

Merchants.—A. R. Mershon, Asa Bates, T. H. Ball, M. M. Butt, A. & D. Hungerford, L. J. Davies, Jas. S. Norman, Allen & Powers, John Fontaine, Bird & Sullivan, Wm. Taxley, H. A. & D. Thornton, Shaw & Dean, Wiley, Baxter & Fort, Allen & Powers, M. M. Butt & Co., James Kivlin.

Doctors.—H. A. Thornton; *Lawyers*—John Taylor, Nathaniel P. Bond, Joseph T. Camp; *Tailors*—Radcliff & Roberson; *Saddler*— James S. Norman; *Warehouse*—B. A. Sorsby, S. & R. T. Woolfolk; *Factorage and Commission*—Hodges, Moore & Jones; *Milliners*—Mrs. Jewett and Miss Thweatt; *Teacher*—Mrs. Jane L. Marks.

1830.

IMPROVEMENT AND PROSPERITY.

The frontier settlement had now assumed the proportions and the air of a "trading town" indeed, and its pioneer settlers congratulated themselves on the prospect of realizing their fondest anticipations. An amendment of the charter so as to obtain a "city government" was talked of. On the 27th of February the *Enquirer* said:

"No inland town of the South within our recollection has progressed with more rapidity in the line of substantial and elegant improvements, and none, we are certain, has a fairer prospect of attaining extensive commercial importance. At the time of the sales (July, 1828,) there was but one frame building erected in this town, and there are now seventy-five excellent and permanent frame buildings, all of which, with one or two exceptions, are occupied. There are, also, twelve dry goods and grocery stores, one drug store, and two commodious and extensive hotels. These improvements have all been made while doubt and uncertainty existed in relation to the growth and prosperity of Columbus, and whilst no settled conviction obtained in the minds of any of the actual value of property in which investments were made. But every day is developing the true resources of Columbus, and exhibiting its real claims to the attention and patronage of wealth, industry and talent."

The population, as reported by the Marshal in April, was 1,152 persons; as reported to the *Enquirer* by Dr. DeGraffenried (a State census) in October, it was then 1,261. The population of the county of Muscogee, at the last named count, was 3,507, of whom 2,262 were whites.

The regular navigation of the river was still a question of some uncertainty. A steamboat—the "Steubenville"—had arrived as early as the 22d of February, 1828, being the first steamer that had ever reached "the falls;" but the boats at first run were evidently too large, or of too heavy draught, for navigating the river either early in the fall or late in the spring. The "Baltimore" made a trip this year late in April, and was said by the *Enquirer* to be the only one of the boats in the trade suitable to the navigation of the river so late in the spring. It thought that boats drawing, when loaded, from 30 to 36 inches, could run throughout the year.

The citizens were now solicitous for the removal of the Indians—no doubt speculating views as well as apprehensions of trouble with them influencing the appeals for their removal.

The first fire reported in the town was on the night of the 14th of March, when the kitchen of Mr. Davis was consumed. It aroused some of the citizens to make a call for a public meeting to take into consideration some measures for protection against fire. But, as is usual with the first cry of "wolf," the excitement appears to have subsided without action.

A debating society in full blast this year was one evidence of social and intellectual improvement.

At the municipal election in January, James Van Ness was elected Intendant. R. T. Marks was Town Clerk this year, and John R. Page Treasurer. Moses Butt was acting as Intendant in November. We cannot find the names of the Town Commissioners of this year.

The prospectus for a new paper, to be called the *Democrat*, was out in August.

There was a controversy, during the fall, between Lieut. Clark, of the U. S. Artillery, and the authorities of Columbus, as to whether the Indians were entitled to the west bank of the river and to equal interests in the ferries established over it. The town authorities denied this right and refused to comply with the demand.

INCIDENTS.

The discovery of particles of gold on the river bank, in April, is mentioned. It no doubt created a sensation. As the precious metal appears not to have been found since then, and as we now know that the Chattahoochee and its tributaries cross the gold belt at several points, the probability is that the gold found in 1830 was washed down with the sands from above in some freshet.

A new hotel, called Lafayette Hall, was opened in the spring of this year—John C. Blance proprietor. It was on the corner of Oglethorpe and Bridge streets.

The 4th of July was again celebrated with becoming spirit. The "Frontier Guards" headed the procession. Maj. A. F. Moore was Marshal of the day; the prayer was by Rev. Mr. Moore; Col. Ulysses Lewis was the reader of the Declaration, and M. B. Lamar, Esq., the orator. A public dinner at Howard's Hotel wound up the celebration with a feast of good things, including patriotism and hilarity.

The first load of new cotton was received on the 15th of September. It was from the plantation of Mr. McGehee, of Meriwether county, and was sold to Stewart & Fontaine at 10 cents. The next week several loads were received, and sold at 10¼ to 11 cents. Nearly 100 bales were received on the 28th of October — reported as an unusually large day's receipts.

In July, Mr. Lamar retired from the *Enquirer*, having sold his interest to Mr. James Van Ness. In November, Mr. Marks sold his interest to Messrs. Henry W. Hilliard and James N. Bethune.

In April, some "malicious villain" entered the *Enquirer* office at night and *pied* the forms and cases.

The anniversary of St. John the Baptist was celebrated by the Columbian Lodge of Columbus. The address was delivered by Rev. Barkley Martin. H. R. Taylor was Secretary of this Lodge.

At the county election in October, Sowell Woolfolk was elected Senator, and A. Y. Gresham Representative.

A new pole boat, called the "Mary Jones," was launched by Hodges, Moore & Co., in September.

Pole boats arrived and departed frequently during this year.

The first steamboat arrival of this winter was the "Baltimore," on the 17th day of December, in five days from Apalachicola.

On the 22d December, the steamer Georgian, a new boat built at Pittsburgh for a company of gentlemen of Columbus, arrived in fifteen days from Pittsburgh.

PERSONAL.

The county officers, elected in January, were—Wm. Holland, Sheriff; A. B. Griffin, Clerk of the Superior Court; John Townsend, Clerk of the Inferior Court.

The following gentlemen constituted Muscogee grand jury for the Spring term of 1830: J. W. Fannin, E. C. Alford, Asa Bates, H. R. Taylor, David Dean, William Mullally, David W. Upton, S. R. Andrews, E. L. Lucas, W. D. Lucas, B G. Lucas, H. C. Phelps, A. R. Mershon, E. Jewett, J. R. Lyons, B. Tarver, A. L. Watkins, Neill McNorton, J. P. Jackson, Thomas Davis, Jonathan A. Hudson.

Julius C. Alford did not long remain a citizen of Columbus, but removed in a short time to LaGrange, and while residing there was elected to Congress in 1839. He had notable characteristics and an originality *sui generis*. His impetuous and impulsive style of debate won for him the appropriate name "War Horse of Troup." It is reported of him that while in Congress he startled the House from its propriety by a terrific imitation of the Indian war-whoop, which he did in answer to a Northern member who had defended the Georgia and Alabama Indians and blamed the whites for their warlike demonstrations. He removed to Alabama about the year 1850, settling in Pike County, and died there several years ago.

Ulysses Lewis was a man of characteristics peculiarly fitted to impress and mould frontier society, and no doubt contributed much to the giving of tone to the civilization of both Columbus and Russell county, Ala., to which county he removed with the first wave of white settlement. He was sternly upright and just, with a courage for any emergency, and a fund of hard common sense that made him the very man for leadership in such a country. After his removal to Alabama he was for a number of years Judge of the County (now Probate) Court of Russell, and made one of the best and most satisfactory county officers in the State. He died in August, 1856.

MARRIAGES.

March 11—Dr. Wiley J. Underwood and Miss Mary Ann Bohannon.
April 7—James Kivlin and Miss Louisa Dillard.
April 22—William Hayes and Miss Almina Holland.
April 27—Andrew B. Griffin, Esq., and Miss Caroline Tatom.
July 25—Henry W. Hilliard and Miss Mary Bedell.
July 29—Tuscan H. Ball and Miss Margaret M. L. W. Malone.
Dec. 16—Terrill Brooks and Miss Mary Perry.

DEATHS.

Aug. 20—Mrs. M. B. Lamar, aged 21.

We notice among the business and professional men mentioned, and whose names are not already given, the following:

Merchants—Richards & Manley, Lewis C. Allen, Henry Johnson, Hudson & Thornton, James Hitchcock, T. T. Gammage, Hodges, Moore & Co., M. R. Evans & Co., H. S. Smith & Co., B. Tarver & Co.

Lawyers—A. Y. Gresham, John Taylor, Garrett Hallenbeck, Philo D. Woodruff, Grigsby E. Thomas.

Doctors—J. W. Malone, Scott & Kennedy, Underwood & Mills, A. S. Clifton.

Teacher—Miss Kingsbury; *Auctioneer*—F. E. Bissell; *Clothier and Tailor*—Henry Johnson; *Watchmaker*—William Russell.

Latest quotations of this year, Dec. 18: Cotton $8\frac{1}{4}$ to $8\frac{1}{2}$; Bagging 23; Bacon 9 to $12\frac{1}{2}$; Coffee 15 to 17; Sugar 10 to 12; Flour $8 to $9; Meal 75; Molasses 45.

1831.

Increasing Business—A New Bank and a Fire Company—Presbyterian Church Built—A Year of Sickness, &c.

The year 1831 was one of considerable progress in Columbus, and all that we find on record denotes increasing trade and a steady advance towards the settled social status and public conveniences of older towns.

On the 8th of January the following gentlemen were elected to constitute the municipal government for the year:

Intendant—Sowell Woolfolk.

Commissioners—Fitzgerald Bird, Abraham F. Moore, Wm. D. Hargrove, James Hitchcock, Asa Bates, and Joseph T. Camp.

On Tuesday following the Board was organized, and elected the officers named below:

Clerk—Edm'd Bugg; *Treasurer*—C. E. Mims; *Marshal*—Ephraim Bundy; *Auctioneers*—F. S. Cook and E. E. Bissell; *Clerk of Market*—Patrick W. Flynn.

In June books were opened for subscription to the capital stock of a Bank, to be called the "Farmers' Bank of Chattahoochee." On the 7th of November this Bank was organized by the election of the following gentlemen as Directors: E. S. Shorter, M. Butt, A. Iverson, G. W. Dillingham, and Joel Branham. At a subsequent meeting of directors, E. S. Shorter was elected President, and Edward Carey Cashier.

A fire which occurred at an early hour of the morning of the 21st of May, appears to have fanned the feeling in favor of a fire company to a striking heat, and before the sun went down that day the company was formed and the following gentlemen were elected officers: G. E. Thomas, Chief Engineer; Asa Bates, Captain of the Engine; Robt. Jones, Captain Fire Hook Department; James Daniel, Captain Ladder Department; Joseph T. Camp, Captain Bucket Department; M. W. Thweatte, Captain Safety Department; L. C. Allen, Marshal. At a subsequent meeting of the company held on Tuesday evening following these appointments were made; George Smith, Treasurer; E. Bugg, Secretary.

The house burned was a large dwelling nearly completed for Mr. Stewart, near the river in the upper part of the town. As the building had not been delivered, the loss was divided between Mr. Stewart and the builders—Messrs. Bates and Dibble.

This was a hard year with the Indians across the river,

and increased vigilance to prevent them committing depredations was found to be necessary. They suffered greatly for
the want of food—which was ascribed in part to the failure
of their corn crops and in part to the scarcity of game, and
they were terribly afflicted with the small pox. They were
constantly begging at every house, and subsisted in great
part on roots and the bark of trees. During this year Dr.
DeGraffenried visited the Nation, and on his return advised
general vaccination as a preventive of small pox in Columbus. There were one or two cases in the town, and alarm on
the subject extended to the surrounding country.

On the 15th of October, the building committee of the
Presbyterian Church announced that the house would be
dedicated on the following Sunday, when a collection would be
taken up to assist in paying the sum due on the building.
They also returned thanks to the citizens for liberal contributions towards this church. Mr. J. S. Norman was Secretary.

The local causes of sickness in some parts of the town,
mentioned in the first chapter of this compilation, seem to
have found, during this year, fit conditions for their develop-
ment. On the 20th of October, the *Enquirer* said:

"Our town has suffered much in comparison with other years.
Sickness has been confined almost exclusively to sections of the town
where there are large quantities of standing water, collected by exces-
sive rains which fell in August and September. On Broad street and
some other portions of the town there has been almost perfect health.
The local causes which have produced disease the present season will
be entirely removed before the return of another summer."

November 19—Number of deaths that have occurred in the town
of Columbus from the first day of June, 1831, to this date, taken by
order of the Commissioners: White adults 20; white children 20;
black adults 8; black children 9; total 57.

Out of the above number forty have died of fever, three in child-
bed, and two from intemperance.

Columbus then had a Northern mail daily, via Augusta,
Milledgeville and Macon, and a daily Southern mail via Montgomery and Mobile. There was also a stage line from Columbus to Macon, run via Thomaston and Forsyth, and the fare

was $8 50 to Macon. The stage left Columbus every Friday at 7 a. m., and arrived at Macon about noon on Sunday, traveling only in the day time. There were several other weekly mails, but we are not informed as to their modes of conveyance.

INCIDENTS.

The steamboats, whose arrivals and departures during the year we find noticed were the following: Herald, Plaquemine, Marion, Baltimore, Jenkins, Georgian.

There was great rejoicing over the arrival of the Georgian on the 12th of January, not only because she was owned by a Columbus company, but because she was intended to inaugurate *competition* in boating. A large crowd met her at the wharf, and hailed her arrival by a salute from a cannon, &c. She had on her own decks over 1,000 barrels of freight, and towed the barge Mary Jones with 700 barrels.

The Muscogee Bible Society was in active operation, supplying Bibles to the destitute. There was also a circulating library.

In February, H. W. Hilliard retired from the editorial management of the *Enquirer*.

A new ferry, about one mile below the town, was established in June, by S. M. Ingersoll and Seaborn Jones.

Columbian Lodge celebrated the 24th of June—Garrett Hallenbeck orator.

The 4th of July was again celebrated with cannon, the reading of the Declaration, an address by N. B. Bond, Esq., and a dinner.

The pioneer military company, the "Frontier Guards," disbanded, and in September, the "Columbus Volunteers" were organized, with A. S. Rutherford Captain.

A volunteer military company for temporary service, if needed, in quelling an apprehended outbreak commenced by the slaves belonging to the Indians, was formed in October. It was in command of Jas. C. Hall and E. B. W. Spivey. The outbreak did not occur, or did not reach Columbus.

Cotton came in quite freely in the fall, and was quoted in November 6½ to 7¼c.; in December 6½ to 8c.

In October, Sowell Woolfolk was elected Senator, and Willis P. Baker Representative of Muscogee county.

PERSONAL.

Rev. J. Boring was the Methodist Minister in charge this year, and Rev. A. Hamill P. E. of Columbus District.

The following were grand jurors for Muscogee, at the Spring term, 1831: John McClusky, Geo. W. Elliott, W. H. Alston, J. T. Kilgore, W. D. Lucas, Harvey Hall, Girard Birde, J. Hitchcock, A. R. Mershon, S. M. Ingersoll, J. B. Kennedy, A. F. Moore, J. P. Jackson, G. W. Dillard, H. C. Phelps, H. C. Dawson, B. G. G. A. Lucas.

George W. Dillard was announced in April as the proprietor of the "Globe Tavern."

John G. Prince, a late comer and a merchant of Columbus, was drowned in the river, while bathing, on —th of July. He was from Salem, Mass.

John and Frances Love took charge of the McIntosh Hall, a new hotel, in October.

M. M. Hinch had charge of the Jackson Hotel.

The Columbus *Democrat* was published this year, but we find no reference to the time when it was started.

Latest quotations, Dec. 31st: Bacon 12c.; Bagging 21 to 25c.; Corn 37c.; Cotton 5 to 7¼c.; Coffee 17 to 20c.; Flour $8 to $9; Molasses 50c.; Sugar 9 to 10½c.

We find the following names of business and professional men, not included in previous notices:

Merchants—Manley & Harris, Harvey Hall, Nourse & Clark, Smith & Morgan, R. P. Guayard, Jones & Harper, E. S. Norton, Scott & Kennedy, Dillingham & Tarver, E. Wells & Co., Clifton & Kennedy, Lawhon & Howell, L. C. Allen, Lewis Leon, D. W. Parr, E. Featherton, James Kivlin, Wm. H Harper.

Lawyers—John Taylor, Lemuel Merrell, Alfred Iverson, John Milton, A. S. Rutherford, James H. Shorter, Bailey & Gordon, Allen Lawhon, James A. Berthelot, Grigsby E. Thomas.

Warehousemen—W. H. Kimbrough, Seaborn Jones & S. K. Hodges, M. W. Thweatt.

Doctors.—Broadnax. *Teachers*—Miss Frances Gunby, Garrett Hallenbeck. *Milliner, &c.*—Mrs. Sledge. *Shoe-Maker*—Robt. K. West. *Cabinet-Makers*—Dutton & Stanley. *Dentist*—John A. Cleveland. *Jeweller*—Wm. Russell.

MARRIAGES.

Jan. 27—William Holland and Miss Martha Bilbro.

March 29—Dr. Robt. A. Ware and Miss Margaret C. Ellison.

April 6—Daniel D. Ridenhour and Miss Amelia Bennett.

April 7—Alfred Iverson and Miss Julia Frances, daughter of Hon. John Forsyth (near Augusta.)

Aug. 15—J. A. Hudson and Miss Martha E. Abercrombie.

Aug. 30—Dr. J. C. Sullivan and Miss Josephine Grinage.

Dec. 22—Robert Henry Brown and Miss Sarah Pride.

DEATHS.

Jan. 25—Wm. Walker, sr.

May 7—Garland, infant son of Oliver Jeter.

June 5—Mrs. Mary M. Griffin, wife of A. B. Griffin.

Sept. 19—Mrs. Eleanor Johnson, wife of Robt. G. Johnson.

Sept. 24—Mrs. Martha Lucas, wife of Robert Lucas.

Oct. 1—Edmund Bugg, Town Clerk.

Sept. 29—James M. Hitchcock.

Oct. 10—Martha Caroline, daughter of John and Sophia Warren.

Oct. 4—Adelia Maria ; Oct. 8th, Georgiana Adaline ; and Oct. 14th, Delia—all daughters of Wm. D. and Mary H. Lucas ; and Oct. 9th, Mrs. Mary H. wife of William D. Lucas.

Oct. 14—James Thweatt.

Oct. 13—Mrs. Clarissa, wife of Stoddard Rockwell.

Oct. 16—Caroline Eliza, daughter of Wm. D. Lucas.

Oct. 20—Harris McClesky, son of John McClesky.

1832.

First Bridge Commenced—A Sad and Memorable Duel—Another Bank—Ben Marshall's Reserve (Girard) Purchased—Business Largely Increased—A Mayor's Court Established, &c.

This was an eventful year for Columbus, and one in which the citizens appear to have exhibited more public spirit and enterprise than in any previous year of the settlement. Good navigation continued until late in the spring, and opened again early in November, and large stocks of goods were received and sold. The year was also a healthy one.

In January the following municipal ticket was elected, for the year 1832:

Intendant—Samuel Lawhon.

Commissioners—G. E. Thomas, Charles D. Stewart, G. W. Dillingham, Hiram Nourse, William D. Lucas, Elisha Tarver.

H. C. Phelps was Town Clerk.

One of the first acts of the new Board was to advertise for proposals to build a bridge across the Chattahoochee. The bridge was to be about four hundred feet long, including the abutments, and to be built high and strong and of good materials. During the first week in March, the proposal of John Godwin, of Cheraw, S. C., was accepted; the plan of Ithiel Town's patent to be followed, with stone piers and abutments, for $14,000. Daniel Pratt, of Clinton, furnished the model adopted, and was paid $100 for it. Mr. Godwin, with a large force, commenced work on the bridge in May, but did not finish it this year.

On the 23d of January an event occurred which shocked the community, and made men think more seriously of the sad results likely to follow the many personal quarrels (generally springing from politics) that were then so common. One of these difficulties occurred between Gen. Sowell Woolfolk, then State Senator, and who had represented the county in one branch of the Legislature each year since its organization, and Major Joseph T. Camp, a talented lawyer and popular man. They had had a difficulty, without the use of weapons, at Milledgeville, and had then repaired to Fort Mitchell to settle the affair with pistols, but it was there adjusted temporarily. Then followed some publications in the paper, in which it was made to appear that the concession had been entirely on the side of Camp, and this led to a renewal of hostile correspondence, with the sad result told in the following "obituary" from the *Enquirer:*

"On Monday last, 23d instant, an unfortunate meeting, commonly known by the name of an affair of honor, took place near Fort Mitchell, between Gen. Sowell Woolfolk and Major Joseph T. Camp, which terminated in the death of the former. Gen. Woolfolk was shot through the breast, and expired in a few seconds, and Major Camp narrowly escaped life, being shot through the abdomen, but fortunately for him without entering the hollow.

"The next day the body of Gen. Woolfolk was brought to this city and interred with military and Masonic honors. His remains were followed by the most numerous and respectable concourse of his friends, acquaintances and fellow-citizens which has ever been seen on such an occasion.

"In recording this melancholy occurrence humanity shudders at the reflection that the talents, worth and chivalry of our country should be subject to such a barbarous custom. No matter how high and respectable in society, how surrounded with friends, how closely united and necessary to the peace and comfort—yea, even the necessity of a wife and family—how useful and important to the State—all must bow before the unrelenting tyrant. Gen. Woolfolk was warm, devoted friend, a kind and an affectionate brother, a tender and indulgent husband and father, the idol of his family, and occupied a high position in the influence of his fellow-citizens. But he is no more! His relatives bewail his loss; to his country his talents and usefulness are gone forever. He has frequently represented this county in the Legislature of the State, and by that body was promoted to the rank of a Brigadier-General, and he has never sought in vain the confidence and suffrage of his generous people. But he is gone forever. No more shall his high and buoyant step gladden the heart of his disconsolate wife; no more shall his cheering voice awaken the smile of his infant child. 'Alas! nor wife nor child shall he again behold; nor friends nor sacred home.' "

This being the 100th anniversary of the birthday of Washing, the 22d of February was celebrated with much animation. The Columbus Musketeers, the Masonic fraternity and a large concourse of citizens formed the procession to the new Methodist Church, where, after a prayer by the Rev. Mr. Few, Washington's Farewell Address was read by Dr. John J. Wilson, and an appropriate oration delivered by James Van Ness, Esq. A public dinner followed, as usual, at the Columbus Hotel.

About this time Congress passed an act authorizing the corporation of the town of Columbus to select two acres of land on the Alabama side for the abutment of the bridge across the Chattahoochee; but this grant was to be "subject to the incumbrance of the Indian claim," and no houses were to be erected thereon [by the town authorities] even after the extinction of the Indian title.

Later in the year (June 22d) the *Enquirer* announced the sale of these two acres and other land on the Girard side, as follows:

Great Purchase—By the treaty recently concluded at Washington with the Creek Indians, a reserve of one mile square, situated immediately opposite the town of Columbus, and bounded by the western bank of the Chattahoochee, was granted in fee simple to Benjamin Marshall, a half breed Indian. This reserve from its location on the Chattahoochee, at the head of steamboat navigation, and its contiguity to Columbus, has been supposed to possess many advantages, and to be very valuable. It was purchased of the grantee on the 19th inst., by Col. Daniel McDougald, of Harris, and Dr. Robert Collins, of Macon, for the sum of thirty-five thousand dollars. The lines marking the reserve have not yet been run, but it is supposed will extend from the upper limit of this town to some distance below the center. The bridge now constructing across the Chattahoochee river will rest on this reserve, and possibly the ferry owned by the corporation of Columbus may land within its limits.

We learn from one of the owners that this property has been purchased with a view of establishing a town on the opposite bank of the river, and with the design of enjoying the advantages and facilities afforded by the falls for milling and manufacturing purposes, and those presented by the erection of a bridge.

We may get some idea of the extent of the export trade of Columbus for this year from the following statement of the outgoing commerce of Apalachicola. Exports from Apalachicola for the six months ending July 1st: Cotton, 16,000 bales; hides, 2,528; lumber, 491,000 feet; sugar, 129 hhds.; staves, 40,000; vessels entered 64; cleared 67. Of course all this cotton was not shipped from Columbus, but all the cotton which Columbus shipped that year must have gone to Apalachicola. It is probable that very little of the other articles (except perhaps hides) went from Columbus.

On the 4th of August, the *Enquirer*, noticing the presentation to the three banks of the town of bills to the amount of $93,000, all of which was promptly paid, said:

"Well done, Columbus! Four years ago a howling wilderness; now a handsome town, with a population of 1,800 souls and three banks in successful operation to meet their paper with silver if necessary. In addition to the heretofore rapid growth of our town, we notice on Broad street several large and costly brick buildings growing up, and a very extensive warehouse and other arrangements making to receive the cotton crop of next season. Twice the quantity of goods sold last year are being ordered for the ensuing fall and winter, and every preparation is being made to afford facilities for trade and pay liberal prices for cotton. The corporation is building a splendid bridge across the river, which will add much to the beauty and convenience of our town. We have three churches, a theatre, a book store, and a circulating library, and last, but not least, a handsome public garden, now in successful operation. It is situated at the lower end of the town, along the bank of the river, opposite that very abundant spring called Hansill's spring. This garden, called "Spring Garden," was commenced last winter by Mr. Henry C. Phelps, and by whose industry and scientific taste, it has become a beautiful and pleasant resort for our citizens; at the same time affording a delicious harvest of all the various vegetables and fruits common to this latitude."

The following were the names, and the condition on the 1st December of this year, of the three banks above referred to:

The Farmers' bank, with paid up capital stock of $60,000, had bills in circulation to amount of $91,881; deposits $32,579; silver $70,171 71; gold bullion $18,000.

The Bank of Columbus, with a paid up capital of $120,000, had in circulation $229,972; deposits $13,603 50; silver $132,951 92; gold $301 50.

The Insurance Bank, with capital stock of $150,000, had in circulation $101,299; deposits $7,965 23, gold and silver $70,375 72.

In December the Legislature passed an act to establish a Mayor's Court for the town of Columbus.

INCIDENTS.

A gin factory was started early in this year by Ephraim Brown.

A treaty made with the Indians, this year, by the United States Government, gave great satisfaction to the citizens of Columbus. By this treaty the Creek Nation of Indians ceded to the United States all their lands in Alabama, and were to

be removed to a location west of Mississippi river within five
years. The Choctaws had previously made a similar treaty.
The Creek Chiefs signing this treaty were Opotheoholo (he
who "had no father or mother—thunder and lightning
struck a hollow tree, and out jumped Opotheoholo,") Tuckabatchee Hadjo, Efiematta, William McGilivray, and Benjamin
Marshall.

The receipt of goods in 24 days from New York was considered such a feat of rapid transportation as to call for special
notice at this period.

The Bank of Columbus went into active operation in the
spring. Gen. James C. Watson was President, Burton Hepburn Cashier, and James C. Watson, James Wadsworth,
Daniel McDougald, Lewis C. Allen and Jona. A. Hudson Directors.

On the 4th of July the procession was headed by the Mus-
keteers and the Temperance Society; prayer by Rev. Mr.
Few, reading by James Childers, and oration by James A.
Berthelot.

A female academy, under the superintendence of Misses
Gunby and Grigg, was open in July; it was announced in
December that Rev. John Baker had been employed to take
charge of the male academy. Mrs. E. J. Smith had a music
and painting school. G. J. McClesky had an "infant school."

There was some alarm, this year, about the cholera, which
prevailed in other places, but Columbus escaped.

The first load of new cotton of this year was brought in
on the 27th of September, and on the 28th about 20 bales
were received. Price 9 cents.

At the Presidential election, Columbus gave 252 votes for
the Jackson (or Troup) electors, and 15 for the Clay (or
Clark) ticket.

The *Enquirer* was somewhat "stirred up" by the passage
of three loads of cotton from Harris county through Columbus to Montgomery. Since that time the railroads have regulated this matter better.

Cotton was quoted at 6½ to 8c. in January, 9 cents in September, 10½ cents in November, 8½ to 9⅝ in December.

Steamboat arrivals during the year: Baltimore, Marion, Plaquemine, Georgian, Chattalroochee, Van Buren, Columbus.

PERSONAL.

A. Hamill was presiding elder, and I. A. Few stationed Methodist preacher in Columbus this year.

W. D. Lucas had charge of the Columbus ferry and Marshall's grist and saw mills.

The following served as grand jurors, spring term, 1832:

Jas. Coleman, Wm. Kirk, C. M. Farlan, Hardeman Owens, A. S. Clifton, R. D. Wyche, J. Thornton, G. W. Dillingham, L. J. Davies, L. C. Allen, H. K. Hill, H. S. Smith, J. L. Cunningham, Oliver Jeter, D. B. Nafew, Thomas Davis, Isaac W. Webb, Wm. Rogers.

The Temperance Society appears to have been active and flourishing. The following were the officers of this year:

Rev. I. A Few, President; Rev. John Baker, Vice President, Gen. N. Howard, Secretary; G. E. Thomas, Dr. J. J. Wilson, John Coleman, Hiram Nourse, C. E. Bartlett, James Norman and Wm. Root, Executive Committee.

A Health Committee for this year consisted of Drs. Childers, Clifton, Thornton, Broadnax, and Messrs. C. E. Bartlett, Phil. B. Woodruff, A. B. Davis, and James Kivlin.

In October, W. D. Lucas was elected Senator, and A. J. Thornton and E. W. B. Spivey Representatives.

Thos. M. Dennis was acting Postmaster of Columbus, during the latter part of this year.

Sol. Smith and company filled a theatrical engagement in May.

Wm. D. Hargrove was Sheriff; Wm. Holland, Deputy Sheriff; John Townsend, Clerk Court Ordinary; A. B. Griffin, Clerk Superior Court.

The grand jurors for the fall term were:

Nicholas Howard, foreman; J. W. Fannin, jr., E. B. W. Spivey, James Wodsworth, Charles L. Bass, Matt. R. Evans, E. S. Norton J. L. Cunningham, Wm. Clark, Geo. N. Langford, Stephen Kirvin, J. P. Jackson, S. R. Andrews, Alex. Ligon, Wm. Rogers, John Johnston, Wm. Williamson, Drury Mims.

MARRIAGES.

Feb. 16—Thos. S. Martin, of Columbus, and Miss Mary Springer, of Carroll.

March 29—James G. Godfrey and Miss Laura M. Pride.

April 18—David Lopez and Miss Catharine D. Hinton.

June 26—John Spearman and Miss Mary Ann Butt.

July 18—Geo. W. Dillingham, of Columbus, and Miss Lucy E. Ticknor, of Jones.

July 25—Gen. James N. Bethune, of Columbus, and Miss Frances Gunby, of Columbia County.

Aug. 25—Michael N. Clark and Miss Pamelia Hale.

Dec. 17—Moses Yarbrough and Miss Harriet Harper.

DEATHS.

Feb. 5—James Bosworth, formerly of Augusta.

March 24—Harvey H. Squire, merchant, aged 23, formerly of Massachusetts.

April 5—Mrs. Margaret Jeter, formerly of Lincoln county, aged 40 years.

April 12—Wm. A. Hitchcock, tax receiver, aged 32, son of Col. Jas. Hitchcock.

Oct. 20—Nathaniel P. Bond, Esq., formerly of Savannah.

Nov. 14—James H. Westmoreland.

The following are names of business men or firms, not noticed in the personals of previous years:

Merchants—J. P. Jackson, J. S. Smith & Co., O. W. Bird, Harvey Hall & Jacob I. Moses, Bird & Buckham, Calvin Stratton, Stewart & Fontaine, Wm. Jones & Co., Tarver & Squire, E. Featherston, Lawhon & Howell, Wm. P. Malone, Geo. Grieves, Wm. H. Kimbrough, Hudson & Felton.

Blacksmith—Jona. P. Jackson.

Warehousemen—E. S. Shorter, B. P. Tarver & Jas. H. Shorter, W. H. Harper & Felix Lewis, Morris & Evans, Fontaine, Morgan & Perry, Wm. H. Kimbrough.

Carpenter—Charles M. Sledge; *Lawyers*—John Schley, Milton & Lawhon; *Bookbinders*—Purves & Parham, Van Ness, Bethune & Cline; *Hotel Keepers*—Elisha Tarver, John Love, Pomroy & Montague; *Druggist*—Thomas Lang; *Doctors*—Mills & Chipley, A. P. Manley, David Cooper, Wilson & Childers; *Merchant Tailor*—Thomas Beard; *Dentists*—R. S. Drake, A. L. Keagy, E. H. Macon; *Cotton Buyers*—Smith & Morgan, M. W. Perry; *Auctioneer*—E. S. Norton; *Insurance Agent*—G. W. Dillingham; *Millinery*—Mrs. Sledge, Miss Eleonora McCall; *Livery Stable*—J. Bennett.

1833.

A Year of Health and Steady Business — Another Startling Tragedy.

For the year 1833 we can find very little of change or of remarkable incident on record. Business appears to have moved steadily along, without either check or a great acceleration. Political excitement ran high between the Troup and Clark parties, and occasioned many personal controversies, the sad result of one of which forms the most startling incident in the history of the town for that year.

At the election on the first Monday in January, the following municipal officers were chosen:

Intendant—Allen Lawhon.

Commissioners—Eli S. Shorter, Charles D. Stewart, A. S. Clifton, James D. Lucas, Joseph T. Kilgore, Hampton S. Smith.

Sheriff of Mayor's Court—W. D. Hargrove.

Clerk of Mayor's Court—John Townsend.

Officers elected by Intendant and Commissioners:

Clerk—Henry C. Phelps; *Treasurer*—S. R. Andrews; *Marshal*—James C. Holland; *Clerk of Market*—P. W. Flynn.

On the same day the following gentlemen were elected Judges of the Inferior Court of Muscogee county for the ensuing year:

Ebenezer Torrence, James Hitchcock, Job Rogers, Alexander Scott, and Anderson Speer.

The excitement on the subject of the cholera, which continued its ravages in some parts of the country, was to some extent shared in Columbus. The scourge reached Apalachicola, and its existence in that town, with which Columbus had such direct and indispensable communication, quickened the apprehension on the subject. A meeting of citizens to consider the matter was held in June, and a report submitted by a committee composed principally of physicians was adopted. It recommended the strictest attention to diet, cleanliness, temperance, &c., and the keeping of the Indians out of town; but it did not, recommend a quarantine against Apalachicola, though we find that navigation had not at that time closed for the summer. Columbus escaped the cholera, and we may add that it has escaped during every visitation of this dreadful disease to America.

The tragedy to which we have above alluded, and which for a long time afterwards caused rankling and bitter feelings, occurred on the 14th of August. It was the killing of Maj. Joseph T. Camp by Col. John Milton. They were opposing politicians, Milton being a Troup, and Camp a Clark man, and both were lawyers of ability. The quarrel commenced with a communication signed "Carroll," published in the Columbus *Democrat*, which harshly attacked Milton. The editor of the *Democrat* was Cosam Emir Bartlett, and upon him Milton made a demand for the name of the writer of the communication. Bartlett refused to give the name, but avowed his own personal responsibility. This led to a card from Milton, published in the *Enquirer*, in which he declared that no man of honor could notice Bartlett, because of his "debased condition in society." Milton further said in his card that he was satisfied that he knew the writer of "Carroll," and he proceeded to particularize him in such a way as to show that he understood Camp to be the man. He "ventilated" Camp's previous life, or some reported incidents in his previous life, in a caustic manner. Camp replied in a style equally contemptuous and abusive, neither admitting nor denying that he wrote the communication "Carroll," but contending that Bartlett's assumption of responsibility for it was sufficient on that point. The matter rested here, so far as newspaper controversy was involved, for about three weeks, but old citizens say that insults were exchanged between them occasionally on the streets until the day of the killing of Camp. This event was thus noticed by the *Enquirer* of August 10th:

"On Monday morning last Maj. Joseph T. Camp of this place was killed by Col. John Milton.

"As there had been existing between these two gentlemen for some time a controversy, which has resulted thus tragically, and as we doubt not many and contradictory reports have gone out in relation to it, we presume that our readers are desirous of hearing a correct account of the affair.

"That we may be the better able to give this, we shall confine ourselves to the testimony, which was heard before the examining court.

"Immediately after the occurrence Col. Milton gave himself up to the civil authorities, and was brought before Judge Thomas for examination. Upon the examination, it appeared in evidence that there had been a long standing difficulty between the deceased and Milton ; that Milton had frequently understood recently that the deceased had threatened to shoot him in the street. On Monday morning last, Milton was standing on the street near Gen. Howard's store, and saw Camp coming down the street in the direction of where he was standing—he stept into the store and picked up a double barrel gun and shot Camp, discharging the first barrel into his left breast and the other, as he fell, into his back. Upon the hearing of the testimony, the Court upon application admitted the prisoner to bail. On Thursday the grand jury found a true bill for murder, and on Friday the counsel on the part of prosecution moved to have Milton committed ; upon hearing of argument the court decided he should be admitted to bail."

INCIDENTS.

The territory acquired from the Creek Indians having been divided into counties, in December, 1832, by the Legislature of Alabama, the county of Russell was then formed, and we find that early in 1833 some apprehension prevailed in Columbus that the county seat would be located "on the western bank of the Chattahoochee, immediately opposite Columbus," and that this would be "the first movement towards the establishment of a rival town."

The market house having been burned down (the exact date not appearing,) the Clerk of Council advertised on the 6th of April for proposals to build a new one, "precisely as the old one was, with the exception of a ceiling above, which is to be added."

NOTE.—The files for the months of September and October, as well as occasional numbers in other months of this year, being missing, some incidents worthy of note in the history of the town are no doubt lost to us.

The steamboat Georgia, on her way to Columbus, was snagged and sunk in December, with her whole cargo. The goods on board belonging to Columbus merchants were insured. The boat was raised again, and was running in 1834.

Latest quotations of this year, Dec. 14: Cotton 9½ to 10; Bagging 25 to 30; Bacon 15 to 18; Coffee 15 to 20; Corn 50 to 62½; Molasses 40 to 45; Sugar 10 to 14.

The celebration of Washington's birth-day was again one of interest. The farewell Address was read by R. T. Marks, and the address delivered by Samuel W. Flournoy. John H. Love was Marshal of the day.

PERSONAL.

Samuel R. Andrews was for a long time one of the most useful and trusted citizens of Columbus. No man stood higher for unyielding integrity and an old-time candor and sincerity that commended him to the entire confidence of his fellow-citizens. Besides holding the office of Town Treasurer, he was for years an Alderman and a Justice of the Inferior Court, which position he graced by his impartiality and good sense. He was a builder by occupation, and many edifices whose erection he superintended dot the city. He died in 1862, at a good old age.

Dr. Stephen M. Ingersoll was a man of original views and much business enterprise. He removed quite early to Russell county, nearly opposite Columbus, and for some time gave the city trouble by his litigation for Alabama rights which he claimed for the west bank of the river. He was much liked by the Indians, and, while he was prompt to inform the whites of any hostile demonstrations or intentions by the red men, he always opposed any harsh treatment of the latter. He acquired considerable property in Russell county, and had generally on foot some business enterprise in which the public were interested. He died two or three years ago, at an age not far short of four-score.

Seaborn Jones removed from Milledgeville to Columbus. He was one of the shrewdest and most successful lawyers in

Georgia, well versed in the pleadings, and managing his cases with an adroitness that often surprised opposing counsel. He was elected to Congress, this year, in a contest that greatly divided the vote of Muscogee county—both M. B. Lamar and John Milton opposing him, and Lamar especially taking off many votes that Jones would have received had he not been in the field. He made an able member of Congress, and was again elected in 1844, by a close vote, after a spirited contest with the able Whig candidate, Wm. H. Crawford of Sumter. He died March 18, 1864, in the —— year of his age.

John Godwin, builder of the first bridge across the Chattahoochee, was a native of North Carolina, but removed from Cheraw, S. C., to Columbus after making the contract to build the bridge. He did not reside immediately in the city for any length of time, but went over into Alabama, and lived in the immediate vicinity of Fort Ingersoll, a little military post on the hill upon which the Baptist Church in Girard now stands. A number of business men of Columbus lived there at that time, transacting their business in town during the day, and sleeping across the river at night.

Mr. Godwin was a man of much mechanical skill, and became quite famous as a bridge builder. He was a most useful man in a territory such as this section of Georgia and Alabama was at the time when he removed to it, and though he is now dead, some of his works of public improvement "live after him." He acquired a quantity of valuable land in Russell county, and made some improvements far in advance of those common in the country at that time. He never filled or sought public office. He died in February, 1859, at the age of 61 years.

Ulysses Lewis was a man of characteristics peculiarly fitted to impress and mould frontier society, and no doubt contributed much to the giving of tone to the civilization of both Columbus and Russell County, Ala., to which county he removed with the first wave of white settlement. He was sternly upright and just, with a courage for any emergency, and a fund of hard common sense that made him the very man for leadership in such a country. After his removal to Alabama, he was for a number of years Judge of the County (now Probate) Court of Russell, and made one of the best and most satisfactory county officers in the State. He died in August, 1856.

Sol Smith, with his theatrical troupe, again entertained the citizens, in his own theatre, which, with the lot on which it stood (No. 147) and several other lots, were offered for sale by him in April. Palmer's Theatre and Yeaman's Circus also paid the town a visit.

Gov. Forsyth visited Columbus in May, and was tendered a public dinner, but declined.

On the 4th of July, the Declaration was read by Dr. E. L. DeGraffenreid, and the oration delivered by S. W. Flournoy·

On the 5th of July, Hillery Triplett, (whose name was associated with several personal quarrels during the first year or two of the town,) was killed by —— Cogbill, at the public house of George W. Elliott, in the vicinity of the locality on which the town of Crockettsville (afterwards Crawford) was built.

Col. Hardeman Owens, previously of Columbus, was killed at his residence in the Creek territory, on the 31st of July, by a party of United States soldiers.

The following are the names of steamboats given in the list of arrivals during the year : Chattahoochee, Columbus, Versailles, Georgian, Baltimore, Andrew Jackson, Van Buren. The two first named were new, capacious and elegant boats built expressly for this trade.

Rev. Ignatius A. Few was Presiding Elder of the District, and Rev. Jesse Boring stationed M. E. Minister for Columbus.

In March, Messrs. Van Ness and Cline having withdrawn, James N. Bethune became sole proprietor of the *Enquirer.*

The following persons served as grand jurors at the spring term of Muscogee Superior Court, 1833: Jas. Daniel, M. N. Clark, Henry Lee, John Fontaine, Bartlett Wycks, S. R. Andrews, J. T. Kilgore, Darius Cox, Theo. Sapp, Willis P. Baker, James Riley, B. Massey, Edward Carey, Thos. P. Bryan, Josiah Grimes, E. W. B. Spivey, William Rogers, Chancey Pomeroy, L. J. Davies and S. W. Langston.

Wm. L. Jeter had editorial charge of the *Enquirer* during the latter part of this year.

We find advertisements or other mention of the following business men not hitherto noticed:

Merchants—Jacob M. Johnson, Wm. P. Malone, Wm. Beardsley & Co., Grant & Whittich, E. Bland & H. B. Milliken.

Doctors—Thos. Hoxey, John A. Urquhart, R. W. Carnes.

Lawyers—Samuel W. Flournoy, H. J. Harwell, Alfred Iverson, B. V. Iverson.

Cabinet Makers—Thos. W. Dutton, J. S. W. White: *Jewelers*—J. A. S. Turner & Co.: *Milliner*—Mrs. Guyon: *Merchant Tailors*—Geo. H. & C. A. Peabody: *Mattress Making*—Mrs. Goodall: *Baker*—F. R. Brodee: *Dentists*—Gabriel S. Fisher, I. S. Drake, S. C. Cady: *Clothiers*—Ayer & Smith: *Teachers*—Mr. Peabody, Mrs. E. J. Smith, Mrs. H. Blome: *Druggists*—Geo. W. Fletcher & Co.

MARRIAGES.

Jan. 30.—Rev. Andrew Hamill and Miss Maria A. Torrence.

Feb. 12.—Wm. Pride and Miss Caroline McCall.

March 7.—Richard Owens and Miss Martha Green.

May 30.—Sampson Hall and Miss Helen Sanders.

DEATHS.

Jan. 18.—Mrs. Mary Ivey, wife of McGirt Ivey.

Feb. 15.—Mrs. Catharine Alford.

Feb. 23.—Samuel Goodall.

March 4.—Mrs. Catharine Malone.

July 26.—Dr. Gabriel Fisher, dentist.

1834.

Town of Girard Laid Out—The First Bridge · Dispute—An "Episcopal Association" Formed — A Broken Bank—A Scene of Active Business, &c.

Mention is made among the incidents of a previous year, of the purchase of Marshall's reserve (opposite Columbus in

Alabama) by a Columbus company. We find by an advertisement in the *Enquirer* that this company proposed to sell, on the 2d of June of this year, 500 building lots in the town of Girard, including the lot on which stood the western abutment of the bridge across the Chattahoochee, also a valuable saw and grist mill and lots containing valuable water privileges. We cannot find any report of this sale in the files for June or any other month of the year. But we learn that extensive building in Girard was going on in 1834 and 1835.

In January of this year the Legislature of Alabama passed an act authorizing Daniel McDougald, Robert Collins, James C. Watson and Burton Hepburn, constituting the company above named, to "make and erect all things necessary to the permanent erection of the western abutment of said bridge, (the bridge built by the town of Columbus,) on their own lands opposite the said town," and to receive one half of the tolls accruing from said bridge, upon their payment to the Commissioners of one-half the sum expended in building it. The act also declared that the then existing location of the western abutment of the bridge should be permanent, and prohibited any person or corporation to land a bridge on the Alabama shore or to use a ferry within a space of two miles above or below. The act stipulated that the authorities of the county of Russell and those of the town of Columbus should fix the price to be paid by the company for one-half interest in the bridge, and in the event of their refusal or neglect to do so, then the Commissioners of Roads and Revenue of Russell county should alone determine the value.

This proposition of a divided interest in the bridge was not accepted by the town of Columbus, and we have no record of the action of the Commissioners' Court of Russell county in reference to it. But disputes as to the right of Columbus to both ends of the bridge, and of the right of the State of Georgia to both banks of the river, continued for a number of years, and led to vexatious conflicts of local jurisdiction and personal claims. The controversy assumed the form of litigation; the courts of Georgia decided in favor of the rights of their State and Columbus, and the courts of Alabama decided in favor of that State and its citizens. Finally the Supreme Court of the United States decided, on appeal, that the State of Georgia had jurisdiction to the extent of *high water mark* on both sides of the river.

On the 8th of March the *Enquirer* said:

We now have six boats plying between this place and Apalachicola. They were all built in Ohio and brought round by way of New Orleans. The first attempt to construct a boat in our section has been made within a few months. We understand a substantial light draft boat has recently been launched at Fort Gaines by our enterprising fellow citizen, Captain Guyard. She is called the "Native Georgian," having been built of Georgia timber by Georgia mechanics. We hope this laudable undertaking of Captain G. will be liberally rewarded by a full share of public patronage.

A meeting was held at the house of Dr. E. L. de Graffenried, on the 17th of August, to ascertain the prospects for the establishment of an Episcopal Church. A society was formed styled the "Columbus Episcopal Association," and the prospects were found to be most encouraging. The communication reporting the proceedings of this meeting said:

There are at this time three churches in this place in flourishing condition, and it was remarked by one gentleman present that there were more persons present at the first meeting of this society than the other three churches had at their commencement collectively. This shows that a little exertion on the part of those in favor of this movement is only wanted to insure complete success.

A bill to incorporate this Church was introduced in the Legislature in November.

Two events of this year gave evidence, which would be deemed quite conclusive in our times, that the "trading town" was assuming both the airs and the dimensions of a city. These were the possession of a broken Bank and the opening of a race course. The suspension of the Bank of Chattahoochee, in April, created the flutter usually attending such disastrous events. In a few days thereafter an "arrangement" was made by which the Bank passed into the hands of a new Directorship, composed of Gen. Allen Lawhon, Thomas L.

Jackson, Col. John Milton and Robert W. Carnes, of whom
Gen. Lawhon was President, and R. W. Carnes Cashier. A
satisfactory exposition of the affairs of the Bank was promised
soon, but it remained "suspended." The *Enquirer* attributed
the suspension of this Bank to a change which had been made
in its management.

Business opened in a very lively manner this winter, as is
apparent from the following editorial of December 27th :

Our town the present week has presented quite a business like appearance. Bales of cotton have rolled down one street, whilst up another sacks of salt and coffee, hogsheads of sugar, barrels of strong drink and all manner of merchandise have moved to their places of deposit, on every imaginable vehicle, from the strongest road wagon to the humble wheelbarrow. On Christmas eve we went to the wharf to see the cause of so much ado, and there we found seven beautiful steamboats discharging and receiving their cargoes. Three of these boats are entirely new and on their first visit to Columbus—viz : The Eloisa, the Ellen and the Southron. All are splendid crafts— strong, beautiful and well adapted to the navigation of our river. Close beside these, "all in a row," lay our old acquaintances, the Columbus, Chattahoochee, Versailles and Georgian. All of these have done and are still doing good service. We hail these boats, old and new, as evidences of our prosperity, and shall be glad to see them and many more plying our river."

INCIDENTS.

The new steamer Columbus, Jr., struck a snag on the 23d
of February, and sunk. No lives lost,

This appears to have been the first summer that Columbus
enjoyed the luxury of ice. A "Columbus Ice Company" had
been formed, and in March received seventy tons, which was
stored in its ice-house. Our present venerable and respected
citizen, James Kivlin, was the agent of the company for the
sale of it.

The Siamese Twins exhibited in Columbus in March.

The *Enquirer* commenced this year with bright, new type,
making a handsome appearance, under the management of
M. B. Lamar and W. B. Tinsley. On the 29th of March R.
T. Marks took the place of Mr. Lamar ; and on the 12th of
April Wm. B. Tinsley transferred his interest to W. L. Jeter

and S. W. Flournoy. It was then for some time published by Marks, Flournoy & Jeter.

A three days' cock fight commenced on the 1st of July.

B. A. G. Lucas, a former citizen of Columbus, was shot in his house, in the Creek nation, by an Indian, and killed, on the 29th of May; and on the same day Gen. Edward Featherston, a citizen of Columbus, was waylaid by an Indian, whose gun snapped, and thus the General escaped. Thus the two races drifted towards the war that soon followed.

Rev. John Baker, pastor of the Presbyterian Church, died in Virginia on the 15th of June.

In the 4th of July celebration this year, a procession was formed in front of Bedell & Walker's City Hall, under direction of the following officers: President, E. S. Shorter; Vice Presidents J. S. Calhoun, Dr. Hoxey and Ebenezer Torrence; Marshals of the day, Asa Bates and J. C. Holland; marched to the Methodist church where prayer was offered up by Rev. S. K. Hodges, after which the Declaration was read by E. S. Shorter, Esq., and an oration delivered by Judge W. T. Colquitt. After the oration the company, amounting to three or four hundred, repaired to Messrs. Shorter & Tarver's warehouse where a large barbecue had been prepared by Bedell & Walker.

The "Columbus Merchant Mills" were completed this year, three miles above Columbus, and were run by James Shivers & Co.

In November the *Enquirer* office was set on fire by an incendiary, and narrowly escaped destruction.

The steamboat Van Buren, loaded with cotton, was destroyed by fire, in December, while on her way from Columbus to Apalachicola. The passengers had to swim ashore; but were all saved. The loss was estimated at $45,000.

In December the bill establishing the Mayor's Court of Columbus was repealed.

PERSONAL.

The following were officers of a "State Rights Auxilliary Association" organized this year:

President—Allen Lawhon.

Vice-Presidents—G. E. Thomas, J. S. Calhoun, M. B. Lamar, N. Howard, A. S. Clifton.

Secretaries—R. W. Carnes, Garret Hallenbeck.

Treasurer—Samuel W. Flournoy.

Printing and Corresponding Committee—M. Torrence, E. S. Shorter, W. T. Colquitt, H. J. Harwell, W. B. Tinsley, John Milton, J. N. Bethune.

Committee on Orators—U. Lewis, J. A. Urquhart, C. L. Bass, Wm. P. Malone, Thomas C. Evans, Wm. D. Hargrove, A. K. Ayer, Jos. T. Kilgore, H. A. Thornton, E. L. Wittich.

At the October election, Walter T. Colquitt was elected State Senator, and Wm. L. Wynn and John Woolfolk Representatives.

MARRIAGES.

Feb. 20.—A. C. Bostick and Miss Henrietta C. Macall; Harvey Hall and Miss Jane C. Ives.

March 6.—George Montague and Miss Mary Angeline Parsons.

April 10—Simeon Patillo and Miss Harriet Kirkland.

June 15—Wm. D. Hargroves and Mrs. Woolfolk, widow of Sowell Woolfolk.

Nov. 14—Battle A. Sorsby and Miss Elvira, daughter of James C. Cook.

DIED.

April 2—Mrs. Jane Odom, consort of John Odom.

April 27—Samuel, infant son of Dr. Billing.

May 3—Joseph F. Murray, a native of North Carolina.

June 9—Mrs. Ann Elizabeth Wynn, wife of Wm. L. Wynn.

June 12—Mrs. Martha Hudson, wife of Jonathan A. Hudson.

July 5—Samuel Sully, merchant.

July 11—George S. Shivers, Esq.

July 29—Isaac A. Smith, a native of Connecticut.

Aug. 20—Geo. W. Dillingham, a prominent merchant and citizen, formerly of Massachusetts.

Aug. 14—John W. Stapler.

Aug. 20—Mrs. Martha Ann, wife of Moses Jones.

Sept. 1—Miss Mary Ann, daughter of the late Rev. Elijah Tarver.

Sept. 4—Henry P. Garrison.

Sept. 9—Mrs. Mary Vinson, wife of Peyton Vinson.

Nov. 19—Mrs. Elizabeth Watson, wife of Gen. James C. Watson.

Nov. 5—(In Rutherford, N. C.) Mrs. Harriet Camp, widow of Maj. Joseph T. Camp.

Business men whose advertisements appear for the first time:

Merchants—E. E. Powers, G. B. Terry, A. Dodge, M. B. Milliken & Co., J. B. Green & Co., Code & Mathews, R. Woodruff, Benj. Bonney, Peter Ruse, David H. Garland, E. D. Ledyard.

Doctors—J. M. Early, A. M. Walker. *Lawyers*—Thos. C. McKeen, John T. Lamkin, Josephus Echols; *Tailors*—John Quin, F. A. Fairchild; *Teachers*—H. R. McClintock, Miss Briggs; *Warehouse*—Augustus Heyward; *Dentist*—R. B. Martin.

1835.

More Indian Hostilities—Citizens Organized for Defense—Columbus Guards.

As the files of this year and 1836 are missing from the *Enquirer* office, and we can find only three numbers (Jan. 10 to Jan. 23, 1835, inclusive,) our report of minor incidents and personal intelligence must needs be meagre. We have a file of the Macon *Messenger* for the year 1835, from which we obtain some news of Columbus, and we presume that it would have made some mention of anything important occurring here during that year.

At the January election, the following municipal officers were elected: Intendant, James C. Watson; Commissioners—S. R. Bonner, A. S. Clifton, Asa Bates, J. P. H. Campbell, George W. Dillard, Lewis C. Allen.

During this year the troubles with the Indians increased, and the outrages committed by them kept the whites constantly in a state of excitement and alarm. The Indians had, by a treaty with the Federal Government in 1832, bound themselves to remove from the Alabama territory, opposite

Columbus, to their new homes west of the Mississippi, within five years. But there was a large party (possibly a majority) opposed to the treaty at the time, and as the period allowed by it for their remaining in Alabama drew near its close, they became sullen and refractory, and committed many outrages both upon the whites and upon those of their own race who favored the treaty and its execution.

Among the outrages reported in the *Enquirer* for the few weeks of this year above mentioned, are the following: Rev. Mr. Davis of the Presbyterian Church of Columbus, was riding along the road, a few miles from town, when he was ambuscaded and shot in the right shoulder by a party of Indians. But he escaped death at their hands. "But a few weeks ago (said the *Enquirer* of January 10) an innocent child, son of a respectable farmer of Russell county, was shot and inhumanly butchered by one of these merciless savages. Several others have been shot at and narrowly escaped with their lives. It is high time these bloody-thirsty beings should be hunted up and made to suffer for their crimes."

These and other outrages naturally aroused the citizens to the necessity of organization for the protection of themselves and their neighbors. We find in the Macon *Messenger* the proceedings of a meeting of the citizens of Columbus, held on the 25th of April, 1835, which we copy below:

In consequence of the present hostile attitude of the Creek Indians of Alabama, their numerous aggressions upon the property of citizens of Georgia, and their inhuman massacre of several unoffending individuals, a numerous meeting of the citizens of Columbus, Georgia, convened at the Court House in said town, on Saturday the 25th of April, to adopt such measures as might be deemed proper and necessary to quell the disturbances, and to protect from threatened violation the person and property of the inhabitants of Columbus and the territory in Georgia, adjacent to the Creek tribe of Indians.

On motion of John T. Lamkin, Esq., the Hon. Grigsby E. Thomas was called to the Chair, and James Van Ness appointed Secretary.

The object of the meeting was stated at length by the Hon. Eli S. Shorter, and the meeting farther addressed by Gen. D. McDougald, Rev. Mr. Harris, B. Martin, Esq., and Mr. E. L. Wittich, when the following preamble and resolutions, introduced by the latter gentleman, were unanimously adopted.

Whereas, recent acts of hostility upon the part of the Indians in the Creek Nation have induced the Grand Jury of this County to investigate the subject, to devise means to put the town of Columbus in a more complete state of defence, in case of actual danger and alarm : And whereas the Committee appointed by the Grand Jury and the Columbus Guards have met and consulted upon the best means necessary to be adopted in the present unprotected state of the town, have thought proper to call a meeting of the citizens generally, and propose for their adoption the following resolutions :

Resolved, That the citizens present enroll their names in alphabetical order, and that they be divided into companies of ten each, commencing at the first name on the list—one of whom shall be captain.

Resolved, That it shall be the duty of each company to patrol the town from 9 o'clock at night until daylight in the morning, for one night in regular order, commencing with the first company.

Resolved, That each member when on patrol be required to be armed with a good gun and a sufficient quantity of ammunition.

Resolved, That when an alarm is given by the guard, each citizen repair forthwith to the City Hall, armed for active service.

On motion of J. P. H. Campbell, Esq., the following resolutions were adopted :

Resolved, That a committee of three be appointed for the purpose of submitting the proceedings of this meeting to the citizens of the town who are not present, and request them to enroll their names.

Messrs. E. L. Wittich, E. S. Shorter and M. R. Evans were appointed this committee.

The following resolutions, introduced by the Hon. E. S. Shorter, were adopted :

Resolved, That a committee of three be appointed by the Chair, to correspond with the Governor of Georgia, to apprise him of the actings and of the present state of our Indian relations, and respectfully request him to place a sufficient proportion of the military force of this part of the State in a situation for immediate service, and to place them under orders to resist and punish any aggressions which may be committed by the Indians upon the property, habitations or persons of our citizens, committed within our own limits, and if necessary to pursue them within the limits of Alabama.

Resolved also, That the same commitee be instructed respectfully to request the Governor to correspond with the Governor of Alabama, and to assure him of the perfect willingness of the people and authorities of Georgia to co-operate with the authorities of Alabama in any measures which may be deemed necessary in repelling any and all aggressions of the Indians and punishing the offenders.

Messrs. E. S. Shorter, A. Iverson, and J. P. H. Campbell were appointed to compose that committee.

Gen. Daniel McDougald introduced the following resolution, which was adopted :

Resolved, That this meeting recommend to our fellow citizens of Russell County, Alabama, to organize a force for the purpose of scouring the County, demanding of the Chiefs in the different towns the murderers of those of our fellow-citizens who have been, or may be killed; should any emergency arise requiring additional force, we pledge ourselves to render to them efficient aid.

On motion of Mr. E. L. Wittich, it was—

Resolved, That Gen. D. McDougald be appointed to apportion the citizens enrolled into companies and to take charge of them in case of an emergency.

The Columbus Guards were organized by election of officers previously, but they did not receive their commissions until May of this year. They entered the State service under Major General Daniel McDougald in December, 1835, and were, on the 1st of January, 1836, mustered into the service of the United States, from which they were "honorably discharged" on the 1st of September of the same year. The following is the roll of the officers and privates as mustered into service:

Officers—J. A. Urquhart, Captain; Robt. A. Ware, First Lieutenant; Burton Hepburn, Second Lieutenant; Hines Holt, Third Lieutenant; P. A. Clayton, Fourth Lieutenant; John Jones, First Sergeant ; Samuel M. Jackson, Second Sergeant ; David Hudson, Third Sergeant ; Robt. S. Flournoy, Fourth Sergeant ; H. S. Wimberly, Fifth Sergeant; Henry B. Milliken, First Corporal; Geo. W. Martin, Second Corporal ; Wm. L. Jeter, Third Corporal ; John S. Allen, Fourth Corporal; William Butts, Drummer ; John Thompson, Fifer.

Privates—H. C. Anderson, Allen G. Bass, Chas. L. Bass, Asa Bates, G. W. E. Bedell, Jos. Bender, Ransom Bird, S. R. Cashion, John E. Davis, Alphonso Delauney, M. R. Evans, A. L. Grant, Jos. B. Greene, E. S. Greenwood, J. D. Greenwood, Thos. B. Goulding, Thos. G. Gordon, Thos. P. Grimes, Wm. Harper, Jas. L. Hill, J. P. Hitchcock, Henry Hodges, Jas. R. Houghton, Theobald Houghton, Jas. D. Johnson, Jacob M. Johnson Andrew P. Jones, Geo. W. Jones, Jas. H. Jones, John D. Jordan, Henry P. Lathrop, Q. A. Lawhon, John H. Love, Lewis Livingston, Ben. F. Malone, R. T. Marks, Henry Matthews, B. Matthewson, Allen Mims, Wm. Mitchell, Monroe Mitchell, Jas. S. Moore, Jacob I. Moses, Richard W. Morris, Josiah Morris, E. Sigourney Norton, C. S. Pryor, Henry H. Randall, Jas. H. Reynolds, Francis Ruse, Thacker V. Rutherford, Thomas J. Shivers, Wm. Salisbury, Chas. H. Stewart, John St. John, Thomes E. Taggart, Washington Toney, David E. Walker, John T. Walker, W. C. Williamson.

INCIDENTS.

Two of the fine steamers running the Chattahoochee were lost in January of this year. The first was the new boat Eloisa, which was entirely consumed by fire on her first voyage down the river from Columbus, during the first week in January. Her cargo and furniture were entirely lost. She was laden with cotton, owned by merchants of Columbus and elsewhere, but this was insured. The Eloisa was owned by Messrs. Stewart & Fontaine, J. S. Calhoun, B. Hepburn and Col. D. J. Britt, and was commanded by Capt. Britt.

The second boat lost was the Versailles, which was snagged and sunk, early in January, near Fort Gadsden, a short distance above Apalachicola. As her cargo consisted of cotton, she too must have been on her down trip.

C. E. Bartlett published at this time, at his farm near Columbus, a neat little paper called the *Southern Planter*, devoted to agriculture and domestic economy.

This must have been a winter of unusual severity, as we find that on the 9th of January a man named Blalock was found dead near the bridge, having frozen to death during a snow storm the night previous, and on the same night two Indians, in a state of intoxication, were frozen to death near Columbus.

Proposals to build the Episcopal Church were invited by John Forsyth, jr., agent of the building committee, on the 1st of January. We understand that it was the same church building now standing on Oglethorpe street.

Books were opened in Columbus, in February, by Allen Lawhon, John Townsend and Nathaniel Nuckolls, Esqs., for subscription to the stock of the "Pigeon Roost Mining Company," of Lumpkin county. The *Miner's Record*, referring to the incorporation of this company, said: "We are of opinion that stock taken in it will be far more valuable than in any institution in the United States." A year later, in March, 1836, the Macon *Messenger* mentioned as a curiosity the sight of a bank note or draft issued by "Pigeon Roost Mining Company of Lumpkin county," made payable to A. Lawhon at Columbus, and signed Nicholas Howard, President, B. C. Dimmick, Cashier.

In December of this year there were exciting and well attended races over the course at Columbus. At this meeting Col. Crowell's horse, John Bascomb, won the three-mile race, beating J. J. Harrison's Volney, in quick time. This race won for Bascomb a fame all over the Union. He was shortly afterwards matched against Col. Hampton's fast racer Argyle, Hampton staking $17,000, and Crowell $15,000. The race was run at Augusta, and was won by Bascomb in handsome style. A little later Bascomb ran at New York his celebrated race with the champion of the North (Post Boy we believe,) and won in this match of "the North against the South."

Cotton was quoted in January, at 13c. to 15c.

PERSONAL.

Thomas Samford was the Methodist minister stationed at Columbus, and Charles Hardy P. E. of the District.

Wm. Holland was Sheriff, and Joseph T. Killgore, Deputy Sheriff; Jas. C. Holland, Jailor; Gerard Burch, Clerk of the Superior Court; John Townsend, Clerk of the Inferior Court.

In October, Hepburn was elected Senator. and Bonner and Calhoun Representatives.

MARRIAGES.

Jan. 11.—Isaac McGehee, of Girard, and Miss Martha H. Kennon, of Columbus.

Jan. 18.—Wm. Nichols and Miss Sarah Ann Field.

The following are names of business men mentioned in 1835, and not heretofore found in this compilation:

Merchants—Foster & Fogle, Benj. Bonney, Code & Matthews, E.
D. Ledyard, Wittich, Greenwood & Co., William G. Porter, A.
Dodge, David H. Garland & Co., Allen & Hill, R. Woodruff, Niles &
Richards.

Lawyers—Marshall J. Wellborn, Philip H. Echols; *Doctors*—J. J.
Boswell; *Dentists*—Dr. H. Balsau; *Hotel or Boarding House-Keepers*
—Bedell & Walker, Wheelock & Willard, Isaac Mitchell.

1836.

Indian War—The First City Government.

This was a stirring year for Columbus. The work of removing the Indians in small bodies to their home west of the
Mississippi had been going on for some time, but there was a
large and unruly party among them opposed to removal, and
the presumption is that the members of this party remained
as long as possible and thus acquired greater proportionate
strength and influence. They did not bring the difficulty to a
crisis by making a positive stand against removal, but they
commenced hostilities by aggressions on the whites, some of
which are noticed in a previous chapter, and others occurred
early this year. Then followed local organization to protect
the aggressors or commit other aggressions upon the whites
settled in their territory, and finally raids across the river.
There were undoubtedly grievances of which the Indians
justly complained. White settlers moved too soon into the territory, and Indian reservations were often obtained for a mere
song—sometimes, doubtless, by fraud. The General Government at first endeavored to check these aggressions by the
whites, to restrain their settlement in the Indian territory
before the expiration of the time allowed for the full removal
of the Indians, and to remove the most conspicuous offenders.
This condition of affairs on the border crowded Columbus
with transient residents and visitors. Being the place of great-

est security, as well as the most accessible point along the line, people congregated here for safety, for temporary residence until the troubles were over, and for speculating purposes during the continuance of hostilities, as well as for facilities for rushing into the Indian territory as soon as the Government would permit and securing good land locations.

As our files of the *Columbus Enquirer* for the year 1836 are missing, this chapter must of course be lacking in personal news and minor local incidents. But we have the file of the Macon *Messenger* for this year, and from it we glean much information concerning the striking events of that period.

The first newspaper mention of actual Indian hostilities during this year, which we have been able to find, is in the *Messenger* of February 4th. We copy it entire:

"There has been considerable excitement for a week or two past at Columbus, and in the vicinity, from apprehension of hostile intentions on the part of the Indians of that neighborhood, and rumor has thrown in its usual contribution in making up all that was lacking in fact. On Thursday of last week it was understood that 500 Indians had crossed the Chattahoochee at Bryant's ferry, fifteen miles below Columbus. A detachment of twenty-two men, headed by Mr. John Watson, proceeded to the place to ascertain particulars. They there found forty armed Indians, who were returning to the ferry, who took cover and commenced firing. After some firing on both sides, two white men, Mr. Josiah Johnson and Mr. —— McBride, were killed, and two wounded, and the whites then left the field, and the Indians probably returned home.*

"From all that we can learn from people well acquainted with the Indians, we should not judge that there was a hostile disposition on the part of those Indians generally, but that there are outlaws and marauders who are ready to rob and plunder principally for provisions, and to fight whenever it becomes necessary. This we believe to be the fact, both with regard to these Indians and those residing below."

The above was the fight sometimes called the "battle of Hitchity." The commander of the whites was Col. J. H. Watson, formerly of Columbus.

This affair greatly excited the people of Columbus, and two

---

* We learn verbally from an old citizen that the Indians were retreating when the whites came up and rashly fired upon them. The Indians took cover under a bluff, and being thus protected fought with great advantage on their side.

companies were formed, under the command of Alexander McDougald and J. H. P. Campbell, who left Columbus during intensely cold weather and repaired to the scene of hostilities; but they found no Indians.

The Columbus Guards, organized previous to this outbreak, J. A. Urquhart, Captain, were actively engaged in service during these hostilities, and other companies were formed for the occasion. One was an artillery company under Captain Hoxey; another, the Cadet Rifles, under Capt. T. C. Evans; and another, the Muscogee Blues, under Capt. P. T. Schley. All these companies performed good service, and were honorably discharged when hostilities ceased.

On the 14th of April, the Macon *Messenger* said: "The Creek Indians, below Columbus, are said to be almost without provisions, and in a sullen, discontented mood. They are very much dissatisfied at not being permitted to hunt in Georgia (where game is much plentier than in Alabama,) and declare their intention to do so at any risk as soon as the leaves put out."

From the same paper, May 12th: "Our accounts from Columbus are of a most alarming character. A war has already been commenced, and a number of citizens killed. The Creek Indians, below the Federal Road, are all in arms and killing every white person they have fallen in with. There has been less known of the hostility of those above, but it is most probable that all are combined, and that the movements are simultaneous through the whole Nation. They commenced their general work of slaughter on Monday, the 10th inst. Previous to this, on the 5th of May, Major Wm. B. Flournoy, late of Putnam county, in this State, was killed and scalped a few miles below Fort Mitchell. A letter from Col. Crowell, the Agent at Fort Mitchell, dated the 9th, says that 'four persons have been killed and many negroes taken off within a few days'; that he had sent a messenger to some of the principal chiefs, who had returned him word that their young men were bent on war, and have assembled in the swamp near the Federal Road to attack any troops that might march into the Nation.

"The Indians have taken possession of Hardaway's Ferry, eight miles above Columbus. Word was sent into Columbus by Ben Marshall, a half breed, that the Indians intended to burn that place on Tuesday night. Dr. Ingersoll, an enrolling agent, who was in the Nation, at or near Talladega (not the present town of that name), found them to exhibit so much hostility that he was compelled to leave and come into Columbus. Great numbers of people, supposed to be about 2,000, who reside west of the Chattahoochee, had come to Columbus for protection. A company of about twenty men, who went out of Columbus on Monday a few miles, to protect and bring in some families, returned in safety and effected their purpose. Another company of about one hundred men, on Tuesday, went into the Nation eight miles to the Uchee bridge, on the Federal Road, and brought in some straggling settlers, but did not see any Indians. Fifteen dead bodies were seen by the flying inhabitants, who had been shot by the Indians and were lying in the road, five of which were brought into Columbus. Of course, all is confusion and dismay."

In the month of May following these events, as the steamer Hyperion was heading for Columbus, she was fired upon by a party of Indians from the Alabama shore, opposite Woolfolk's Bend, some eight miles below the city. During this fire the pilot at the wheel, a brother of Capt. Brockway, was shot dead at his post, and the engineer and one or two others were wounded. Fortunately the boat drifted to the Georgia shore and thus escaped capture. The surviving officers and crew came up on the Georgia side to town, and reached here shortly after dark on Sunday night. The news spread rapidly and created a big sensation and terrible scare in Columbus. Rev. Mr. Few received the news while preaching at the Methodist Church. He came quietly out of the pulpit, broke the tidings gently to his congregation and advised all to remain cool and self-possessed. A volunteer company was formed in the church, and the preacher was elected captain. This company was detailed for a special guard of the town during the night, and arrangements were perfected on the spot for stations, posting guards, relief of sentinels, &c. W. B. Mitchell was made night officer. This company remained in this service four or five days and were then disbanded.

In May, also, occurred the attack on the stages, which created a greater sensation throughout the country than any previous act of Indian hostility. Two stages carrying the United States mail, going from Columbus to Tuskegee, Ala., were attacked about eighteen miles from Columbus. The Indians killed Mr. Green, one of the drivers, and two horses, and robbed the mail. The next day a party of fifteen men started to come through to Columbus with two stages. Some of these men were passengers and others volunteers who accompanied the stages to assist in their protection. Among the latter, was young Samuel G. Hardaway, late of Montgomery, Ala. At the same place where the stages had been attacked the day previous, this party was also attacked by a body of Indians who had been following for some distance. The horses took fright at this place, ran out of the road and got entangled, and then the Indians came up and commenced the attack. Two of the men were riding on horseback, and kept on. The others got out of the stages to fight the Indians, but most of them unhitched and mounted the stage horses and ran off. Hardaway and two others, on foot, followed behind. The Indians got ahead of them and fired, killing—McKay and another man, a New Yorker. Hardaway was not hurt, but ran towards a swamp, two Indians following. He shot one and reached the swamp. The other Indian followed, and Hardaway shot and killed him. He remained in the swamp, with the dead Indian, three days, eating only young and green whortleberries. When the buzzards began to swarm around the dead Indian he left the swamp and struck the road where the two white men lay dead. The Indians soon pursued him into the swamp again. The next night he went back into the road, where the two men were lying, scalped, and took the road for Tuskegee. On the outskirts of Tuskegee he was hailed by Gen. Thomas S. Woodward, and hospitably received. The party on horseback came through to Columbus safe.

Sam Hardaway served in the Texan army under Gen. Sam Houston, in the fight for the independence of Texas, and had a number of hair-breadth escapes from Mexicans. He was more recently an officer of the Confederate army, and commanded a company at the first battle of Manassas. He died in Montgomery about two years ago.

The Columbus *Herald* of the 22d of May said that there were in Columbus, on the 20th of that month, about 1,200 troops; also that the Indians had destroyed the property of Paddy Carr and taken away his negroes, seventy-seven in number. It is also stated that Gen. Woodward came through the Creek Nation from Tuskegee to Columbus on the 23d, with only eight Indians and eleven white men, and reported that there were 700 friendly Indians at that place, who were ready to take up arms. Gen. Woodward afterwards returned through the Nation to Tuskegee, with only eight men.

The Oglethorpe House, then not quite finished and not yet opened for a Hotel, was taken possession of, and used as a military headquarters and barracks. In case of an alarm or an attack upon the city, the citizens were requested to repair immediately to the Barracks for safety and protection. A number of families (ladies with their children) would go to the Oglethorpe House and stay at night and return home next morning. This was done for some two weeks.

When the Indians commenced their indiscriminate murder and slaughter of the citizens of Alabama, there was a perfect stampede of the citizens for thirty to forty miles out in that State and some very distressing and exciting scenes. Some neighborhoods hearing of the depredations of the Indians, would unite together and take such as they could of their most valuable effects and start for Columbus. Some of these parties would be attacked on the road, and some of them killed; mothers and children scattered and separated, not knowing who was killed or where they were for days in some cases; and for one day and night, the bridge at Columbus was crowded with the refugees from Alabama, coming in all sorts of style; some in wagons, some on horseback, some on foot— mothers calling for their children, husbands for their wives, and no response to their cries. They were met and cared for by the citizens of Columbus and every assistance rendered that could be under the circumstances.

On the 13th of May, the *Enquirer* gave this account of the situation at that time:

"A large body of Indians, variously estimated at from 500 to 1,500 warriors, have congregated about twenty-five miles southeast from this city, and are scouring the country in all directions from their hiding place, or headquarters, indiscriminately butchering our neighbors, men, women and children, plundering their houses, destroying their stock, and laying waste their farms. On Monday last this city presented a scene of confusion and distress, such as we never before witnessed. Our streets were crowded with wagons, carts, horses and footmen, flying for safety from the rifle and tomahawk of the Indians—many of them having left behind their all of earthly possessions, and some their protectors and friends, husbands, wives and children, who had fallen before the murderous savage. We have been unable to ascertain with any certainty the number of those who have been murdered by these lawless savages. Wm. Flournoy, Hammond, McKissack, wife and overseer, Davis, Hobbs, several negroes, and in all probably many others (we fear Doct. Welborn among them) have been killed, and the Indians are yet pursuing their bloody work."

The *Enquirer* of the next day, (in an extra, we suppose,) contained the following article:

"Previous to our last publication all the settlers below the Federal Road had come in. Since that time the Indians have destroyed a family (Mr. Davis', consisting of seven persons,) a few miles above the Federal Road, and many of the settlers in that neighborhood have fled to town. The plantations below Fort Mitchell have been burned and a few negroes are missing. Several large buildings on these plantations were burned to the ground on Tuesday and Wednesday nights. The bridges also on Big Uchee and Little Uchee have been burned. The furniture of all the deserted houses, which have been visited, is destroyed and cattle killed.

"A scouting party of fifty men went out yesterday, but returned without finding Indians, except a small party of friendly Indians, who were coming in for protection. Last night it was expected that the plantations in Broken Arrow Bend, from three to seven miles below this, would be burned. A party of forty whites and fifteen friendly Indians, repaired to the place, to defend the plantations. They returned this morning. The Indians did not show themselves. This morning a letter was received from Marshall's settlement, fifteen miles above this, containing information that the neighborhood had yesterday embodied themselves, (thirty in number); they had a small brush with about fifty Indians, killed one and wounded several others. So that it is certain that they are hostile above the Federal Road also. From all that we can learn, the Hitchetees, Uchees and Tallassees, are all hostile. This is the opinion of Nea-Micco, the head chief.

The Macon *Messenger* of the 19th of May, (whose editor had just returned from a visit to Columbus) said of the scene here presented:

The city and vicinity of Columbus presents a truly distressing scene. Hundreds, probably a thousand, are encamped—some occupying warehouses, and every description of building that could be furnished, and many others with scarcely any protection from the elements. Most who had the means, or friends within reach, have retired to the country. The corporate authority of Columbus has furnished assistance for the destitute ; but this source is precarious, as a scarcity of provisions must ensue, as forces accumulate to carry on the war.

At that time about three hundred friendly Indians had come in, and were camped on the property of Ben Marshall, on the west bank of the river. Two hundred were at Tuskegee, and fifty at Fort Mitchell.

Gen. Scott was in chief command of the United States troops, and controlled all military operations, with his headquarters at Columbus. Gen. Jessup was also here, second in command to Gen. Scott. Early in June, Gen. Jessup left Columbus with an escort of about 200 men, for Tuskegee, where he was to take command of the Alabama troops. The Georgia troops were then encamped on the west bank of the Chattahoochee. The number of Indian warriors professing to be friendly was estimated at about 1,000. and the hostiles at about 6,000.

The Columbus *Sentinel* at this time published the following
list of Georgia companies that had arrived:

Corps.	Captains.	No. Men.
Harris Drafted Men	Vardeman,	62
Talbot do. do.	Miller,	50
Pike Volunteers (cavalry)	Lynch,	39
Monroe Drafted do.	Stewart,	80
Monroe Volunteers	Flewellen,	74
Houston do.	Dennard,	54
Jasper Drafted	Roe,	54
Jasper do.	Lane,	48
Jones do.	Hardeman,	80
Talbot Volunteers	Rush,	99
LaFayette Cavalry	Stinson,	53
Gwinnett do.	Garmany,	76
Houston Drafted	Smith,	101
Upson do.	Crate,	76
Monroe Infantry	Russell,	48
Bibb Volunteers (cavalry)	McCall	41
Heard Infantry	Dent	44
Columbus Guards	Urquhart	62
Muscogee Drafted	Coleman	67
Muscogee Cadet Riflemen	Evans	70
Muscogee Artillery	Hoxey	52
Troup Drafted	Hardin	95
Morgan Volunteers	Porter	61
Taliafarro do.	Sanford	78
Laurens do.	Troup	56
Marion Drafted	Berry	50
Meriwether Drafted	Sloan	84
Troup Cavalry	Kendrick	73
Gwinnett do.	Read	61
Upson Drafted	Bell	67
Baldwin Cavalry	Gaither	54
Henry do.	Love	66
Henry Infantry	Dobson	71
Butts Drafted	Hendricks	73
Oglethorpe Volunteers	Hill	102
Coweta do.	Anderson	87
Pulaski Drafted	Hodges	32
Greene Volunteers	Dawson	102
Wilkes do.	Toombs	60
Clarke do.	Ligon	100
Twiggs do.	Pearson	88
Covington Blues	Floyd	84
Newton Greys	Loyd	100
Wilkinson do.	Barney	65

The *Enquirer* of June gives the following account of an attack on the steamer Metamora early in that month:

On Saturday an attack was made on the steamer Metamora, Loyd,
Captain, which at that time contained the following companies, viz:
Captain Booth's company, Pike Guards, from Alabama; Captain

Adair's company of Randolph Blues, and Capt. Snelgrove's company from Randolph Co., Georgia. In consequence of the Indians having made frequent attacks on the boat passing up and down the river, these troops, who were at that time in Irwinton, determined to pass up in order to obtain a brush with them. The entire company were not ordered on this duty, but those who came volunteered their services for the purpose. The Pike Guards are a mounted company, but so strong was the belief that the boat would be attacked, that they left their horses in Irwinton, to which place they returned on Wednesday. These troops were marched on board the boat about two o'clock on Saturday morning, during a heavy rain, to the amount in numbers of about one hundred and fifty men.

One third of the Georgia troops at least were without arms or ammunition. The boat got under way from Irwinton about daylight the same morning, and passed on without interruption about five miles above Roanoke, when a fire was opened upon her from the Alabama side of the river. The firing was warm and lasted about ten minutes. It was returned with equal warmth and spirit from the boat, and the boat as soon as practicable run ashore, when the troops embarked and formed upon the bluff above. After the boat landed the firing ceased; it was then determined to march back to the place where we were first assailed, and drive back the Indians; but it was found that the creek would have to be passed before the enemy could be come up with. To pass this creek, covered as it was with thick undergrowths, was deemed to be imprudent. The troops were accordingly again embarked, and the boat again got under way. In this attack a man by the name of Samuel Butler, belonging to the Pike Guards, and one of the boat hands, (name unknown) were severely wounded. The number of Indians killed has not been ascertained with any certainty, but it is believed they lost at least three, who were seen to fall. Report says that fourteen dead bodies were found at the place of the attack. Some five miles above, the boat was again attacked, and a running fire kept up for several miles. The Indians, in this attack, did not appear to be numerous at any one place, but only showed one or two at a time, when they were immediately fired upon from the boat. It is believed that more damage was done the Indians in this attack than in the former. One man, Benj. Owens, of the Pike Guards, was wounded—it is feared mortally—in this engagement. He was shot while standing in the after part of the boat aft of the ladies' cabin.

After this engagement, the boat met no further interruption until she arrived at this place, which she did about 12 o'clock Sunday. The wounded have been removed from the boat to a comfortable room, and every attention necessary has been paid them.

Capt. Booth, in behalf of himself and the company he commands, has desired us to return to the citizens of Columbus his warmest thanks for the attention bestowed by them, and particularly the ladies, upon his wounded.

There were two or three attacks made on the steamers Metamora and Hyperion, during their trips up and down the river, but they resulted in no material advantage to either party.

Some of the acts of Governor Schley, of Georgia, and of Governor Clay, of Alabama, in reference to these Indian depredations, were much condemned in Columbus. The people of Columbus wanted Gen. McDougald in chief command of the troops raised for the defence of the frontier, and Gov. Schley, disregarding their wishes, appointed Gen. Sanford to the command. It was also said that Gov. Schley declared that if Gen. McDougald had crossed the Chattahoochee while he was in temporary command, he (Gov. S.) would have had him arrested. Fault was found with Gov. Clay for restraining the Alabama troops from marching into the Indian Nation, and for proclaiming the war over and the Indians peaceable while they were committing some of their worst acts. Both these Governors, it would appear, had to perform the difficult task of sustaining the policy of the Federal Administration (of which both were supporters) and at the same time satisfying the demands of the settlers on their frontier. The Administration at Washington was desirous of avoiding harsh proceedings against the Indians, and the excited white settlers wanted summary and rigorous measures adopted.

One of the most troublesome and active of the hostile Indians in the neighborhood of Columbus was a half-breed named Jim Henry, who, it was said, pushed his reconnoisances and raids into the immediate vicinity of the town. We find the following notice of him in the Columbus *Herald* of the 31st of May:

" A half-breed, by the name of Jim Henry, at the head of 150, all like himself *choking* for the blood of white men, has been prowling the nation like a hungry wolf, and committing depredations wherever he went. On Saturday last a rumor reached the city, that himself and band were within twelve or fifteen miles of the river. Gen. Mc-Dougald promptly called for volunteers to cross the river, at 11 o'clock at night, and they came forward with alacrity from the Columbus Guards, and Capt. Evans' Rifle corps, to the amount of eighty or one hundred men, who marched into the nation at the hour of midnight in search of the savage foe, and after having traveled all night without being able to discover the enemy, returned to their encampments the next morning. The following night Jim Henry and his gang approached within six miles of town and burned the Uchee bridge, crossed to the Georgia side of the river, and committed depredations by killing and destroying the horses and property of Mr. John Victory, whose plantation is about twenty miles below Columbus."

It early became apparent that it was the purpose of a portion of the Indians, who were opposed to removal west of the Mississippi, to cross the Chattahoochee below Columbus, ravage the Georgia counties, along their route, and cut their way through into Florida, there to join the hostile Seminoles. Others contemplated a similar march across the lower counties of Alabama into Florida. An expedition, under command of Major Thomas Hoxey, was organized at Columbus to join other forces and follow or intercept one of these Indian parties, and, after going as far as Fort Gaines by steamer, struck across the country towards Flint river, following the Indian trail as far as Baker county, where it was lost in a swamp. The expedition returned without encountering the Indians. The party of Indians which they were following was supposed to number about two hundred. They committed great depredations and killed a number of whites on their march.

From the Columbus *Enquirer*, June 4th:

"Since our last publication nothing of much importance has transpired worthy the attention of our readers. Troops are arriving daily, and every preparation seems to be making for an active and vigorous campaign, and we indulge the hope that in a few weeks our savage foe will either be exterminated or made to succumb to the brave and patriotic troops who are anxious to be the avengers of the murdered women and children who have fallen victims to savage barbarity. We have understood that orders have been received to make no treaty with them that does not have for its basis their immediate emigration to their destined homes in the West. We subjoin below such items of intelligence as have come to hand.

"On Thursday morning last Scipio, a negro fellow well known to the citizens, arrived in town having made his escape from the Indians the night previous, he stated that the Indians to the amount of about three hundred were assembled between the Big and Little Uchee, under the notorious Jim Henry, a half-breed, known to have been the leader of the party who attacked and burned Roanoke. They have with them a large quantity of plunder, negroes, money, &c., which they have stolen from the whites. Having glutted their appetite for plunder and burned and destroyed everything that came within their reach, their intention was to leave for Florida as soon as practicable.

"Two other negroes attempted to make their escape with Scipio, one of whom came in with him, the other separated from them, and was probably shot by the Indians who pursued them.

"On Saturday night the Guards and Riflemen, under Col. Bates, crossed the river about 11 o'clock, and proceeded about two miles west of Girard, on the new road. The object of the expedition was to arrest any Indian spies that might attempt to come near Columbus. They were so stationed as to command every pass to this city; but returned on Sunday morning without seeing the least sign of an Indian.

"An express reached here on Sunday morning, that the Indians had crossed the river about one mile of Ft. McCreary, and burned and destroyed the plantations of Mr. Quarles and Mrs. Brewer and murdered the overseer of the former. The express stated that it was evidently their intention to retreat into Florida, and that they could be traced on their march for some distance in that direction. The Upson Cavalry were ordered immediately to march to their assistance, and unite with the troops already there under Major Howard, who will scour the country in all directions.

" Sunday morning three Indians were brought in by a small party of white men, who assisted them on their way to Neah Micco's camp. They professed friendship, and showed a pass given them by Tom Car, but were very properly detained and put under guard. Two Cusseta chiefs and one white man arrived in town the same evening, from the camp of Neah Micco. They state that Neah-ah-Mathla arrived at Neah Micco's just previous to their leaving, and said that he was friendly to the whites—that he left his own camp to prevent his people from killing him—that they were mostly hostile and disposed to fight, but that he was bent on peace. He denies ever having received any message to come in, and said it never was his intention to be hostile. They were examined on Monday by Gen. Sanford and stated that they were sent by the two chiefs as embassadors, to learn in what manner they would be treated should they wish to come in and be friendly. They were sent back with instructions to inform the two chiefs that they must come in immediately—that if they remained where they now are they would be considered as hostile and treated as such.

"We learn from a gentleman, recently from Chambers county, Ala., that most of the Indians in that part of the Nation have come in as friendly. All that are disposed to be hostile have left there and have probably joined Neah-ah-Mathla, or some other hostile chiefs.— He states that parties of volunteers, made up from the settlers, and from Meriwether, Troup, &c., have made frequent incursions into the enemy's country—killed a dozen Indians, in all, given protection to those disposed to be friendly, and driven the hostiles down into the counties below. A letter published in another column, gives a brief account of the different expeditions against the savage marauders. They have been promptly and gallantly met and driven from their strongholds by the whites, who have since returned to their homes, where we trust they may enjoy the peace and security so well earned by their bravery.

" The Indians near this place and Fort Mitchell have destroyed the bridges over all the water courses, and are endeavoring in every way in their power to obstruct the passage of the troops who may be sent to subdue them. On Sunday night they advanced within six miles of Columbus and burned the Uchee bridge."

A spirited and hotly contested engagement, fought on the 9th of June, is thus reported by the *Enquirer:*

" One of the most serious and desperate engagements that has ever happened since the commencement of the present war took place about three miles above Fort Jones, on Thursday last. About forty of the Gwinnett cavalry, under Capt. Garmany, were stationed at the house of Mr. Shepherd, the balance of the company having been detailed for some other service. Capt. G. in the forenoon of that day had promised Col. Jernigan, who was then out on a scouting party, to assist him in case he was attacked. At three o'clock in the evening firing was heard at a distance, which was supposed to be an engagement between the aforementioned scouting party and the Indians. Capt. Garmany immediately set off on foot with his forty men, who, after proceeding about half a mile, discovered several Indians, who retreated towards a branch to their main body, consisting of about 250.

"The whites advanced and attacked them, when a battle of more than two hours ensued. It was evident from the movements of the enemy that their object was to out flank and surround the command of

Capt. Garmany, who ordered a retreat back to the house. The Indians pressed upon his men, keeping up a constant fire, which was returned with the desperate courage of those who were determined to sell their lives as dear as possible. Nothing could have exceeded the bravery of this little band, who though compelled to retreat, disputed every inch of ground, and sent many a tawny savage to his last account. Capt. Garmany, whose name will be remembered for his intrepid and dauntless conduct, slew three of his merciless assailants, after he had retreated to the house—one of them after he himself had been shot down. His men, too, no less brave than himself, kept up a constant fire upon their pursuers, until the arrival of a reinforcement of about twenty men from Fort Jones, who charged the Indians and relieved for the time the exhausted troops that had fought the first hard battle. This reinforcement being, however, too small to contend with the overwhelming force of the enemy, were compelled to retreat, after fighting ten to one for almost half an hour. In these engagements some twenty-five or thirty Indians are said to have been killed. Those who have since visited the battle ground suppose from the sign that was left, that the number slain was much greater. Whatever rumor may say of this fight, there can be no question of one thing, that every man engaged in it did his duty, and fought with a courage rarely equaled and never surpassed, by inexperienced volunteers. Gwinnett and Stewart counties have a right to be proud of their sons, who in the hour of trial, have nobly done and nobly died. J. V. Tate, James H. Holland, Wm. Simms, James M. Allen, Robert Holland, James C. Martin, Henry W. Peden, and Isaac Lacy, of the Gwinnett Cavalry, were killed; Capt. Garmany, Mr. Alexander, Mr. Hunt and Mr. Step were wounded. Of the reinforcement from Fort Jones, Robert Billups, David Delk, Esq., Mr. Irwin, and Mr. Hunter were killed.''

Gen. Jessup, after going through the nation, with his escort, to Tuskegee, organized an expedition there to scour the Indian country for the purpose of intimidating the Indians and capturing their hostile leaders. Gen. Scott, with the Georgia troops, was then on their eastern borders, near Columbus. Gen. Jessup took up his line of March from Tuskegee on the 12th of June, with about 800 effective men and two field pieces. In the evening of the same day Gen. Woodward followed the white troops with between 300 and 400 friendly Indians under the chiefs Jim Boy and Tuckabatchee Harjo. The friendly Indians were so impetuous that they had to be allowed to take the lead. On the 15th, at a place known as

the Big Spring, they captured the noted hostile chief Neah-
Emarthla and his son, and Gen. Jessup sent them to Fort
Mitchell. The next day Jim Boy and some of his warriors
penetrated to Neah-Micco's camp on the Big Uchee. They
found it extending along the swamp for two miles or more,
and richly stored with plunder. (Neah-Micco had previously
gone in and declared himself friendly, but the camp was occupied by hostiles.) One hostile Uchee Indian was killed
here, and twelve taken prisoners. That night Opothlayoholo,
with 1,100 friendly Indians and a few whites, joined Gen.
Jessup's forces. The next day, Neah-Emarthla's camp, in
Hatchechubbee swamp, was entered, but that chief had been
captured. Here Gen. Jessup encamped.

The Georgia troops under command of Major General Sanford, numbering about 2,500 men, took up their march down
the river on the 20th of June, to co-operate with the troops
under Gen. Jessup advancing from the west—it being evidently Gen. Scott's plan to pen in the Indians between the
two armies, and by scouring the intervening country capture
the whole of them.

After these operations and movements of Gen. Jessup, the
white troops and friendly Indians had only fugitive (but
in some instances still predatory) parties of hostiles to
pursue. From the 15th to the 25th of June, about 2,000
Indians had come in and surrendered. At that time it was
estimated that only about 200 remained out, chief among
whom was Jim Henry. On the 1st of July an express arrived at Columbus stating that Jim Henry and about 150 hostile
Indians had been captured near Fort Mitchell. The Governor
of Georgia quickly sent a demand on Gen. Jessup for the delivery of Jim Henry to the State authorities, but the reply
was that he had already been surrendered upon a similar demand to the civil authorities of Alabama.

Jim Henry was committed to jail in Girard, to await his
trial in Russell county. A number of Indians were given up
to the Governor of Georgia for trial for murder, &c.

On the 6th of July Gen. Scott, from his headquarters at Columbus, issued an order through Seymour R. Bonner, Aid-de-camp, to the effect that such Indians as could be fully identified as murderers or depredators, should be surrendered to the proper authorities, and that a demand would be made on the agents conducting the emigration to detain all hostile warriors a sufficient length of time for identification.

Capt. John A. Urquhart, the agent appointed by Gov. Schley for the purpose, demanded and received from the emigration agents a number of Indians charged with the com. mission of capital offences, within the jurisdiction of Georgia. These Indians were reluctantly given up, and were brought to Columbus, lodged in jail and tried by the courts; but the evidence not being deemed sufficient to convict them, they were released and removed to the West. Jim Henry was con- fined in the jail of Russell County, at Girard, but by change of venue moved his trial to Chambers County.

Early in July Gen. Scott left Columbus for Washington, leaving Gen. Jessup in command. Gen. Scott left to demand an inquiry concerning his management of the war—a matter outside of the scope of this publication.

After the operations of Gen. Jessup and the friendly In- dians reported above, the work of collecting and sending off the Indians to their territory west of the Mississippi progress- ed rapidly, and they were removed from Alabama more ex- peditiously than they would have been had no hostilities occurred.

Notwithstanding the opinion that with the capture of Jim Henry the war in the nation was ended, there was a sharp brush with a party of hostile Indians, on the 24th of July, at Quarles' plantation, some twenty-two miles below Columbus. The Indians were supposed to number about 200 men. The white force was ninety-eight men of Major Alford's command. The whites lost six killed and fifteen to twenty wounded; the Indians twelve to fifteen killed and a number wounded. The whites stood their ground until their ammunition was exhausted, and then retreated. This Indian force was believed to be a party making their way to the fugitives in Chick-asawhatchee swamp in Georgia.

The party of Indians that crossed the river in the neighborhood of Roanoke, and made their way into the interior of Georgia, continued to excite uneasiness and anxiety—committing depredations on numbers of the inhabitants of the country, murdering some, and terrifying many more.

The escape of these Indians constituted the chief fault found with the military plan of operations against the Indians. Col. Thomas Beall, commanding a detachment of cavalry, was sent in pursuit, and about the 10th of July a battalion of volunteers, composed of the Artillery, Guards and Cadet Riflemen of Columbus, was sent forward to reinforce him. Of the operations of this force we find the following accounts in the Macon *Messenger*:

COLUMBUS, July 16.

"About three miles below Roanoke we struck the trail of the Indians, and pressed them over hill and dale, through swamp and quagmires, through the lower part of Stewart, Randolph and Lee, and finally to Chickasawhatchee swamp in Baker county, where, after ascertaining their position as well as we could with the aid of our guides, we prepared for the attack the next morning, and leaving a sufficient guard to protect our horses, we dismounted, hauled off our coats, tied up our heads with handkerchiefs, and into the swamp we rushed. After proceeding three or four miles through briers, mud and water, sometimes up to the neck, we came in view of their encampment, situated on an island two hundred yards off, which they occupied as a depot for their goods, wares and merchandise, which they had taken from Roanoke. We commenced the attack by charging through mud and water, and notwithstanding they had the decided advantage of us in point of position, we continued the charge with such spirit and determination that we could not be successfully resisted, and after killing and wounding a number, they dispersed, leaving behind all their ill-gotten plunder. Seven of our small army were wounded, some severely, but one mortally.

"Our friend Major John H. Howard was with us, and was among the first, if not the first. who planted his foot upon the island, and acted with great bravery, as I was certain he would whenever an opportunity presented."

The writer further states it as his impression that the Indians have separated in small parties and fled to Florida.

Another account says:

"After the battle in the swamp, very few Indians have been seen—not more than two or three at a time. It was believed they had left the swamp, and had broken up into small parties of three to five, and that they were endeavoring to make their way to Florida. The swamp was scoured for five days, but no Indians found in it. Several small trails have been traced to the Flint river, and it was believed that the Indians traveled principally in the night. They committed no further mischief after the battle. They must be in an entirely destitute condition, as they were driven from their camp naked, and left all their provisions, plunder and spare ammunition. Maj. Alford's detachment arriving with the three Columbus companies, and thirty or forty Indians under Paddy Carr, Col. Beall's command returned to Columbus. All the drafted and volunteer infantry (except the Columbus companies,) have been discharged. It is believed, according to the calculations of the best informed, that there are about two hundred hostile Indians who have not yet surrendered."

The following official dispatch in reference to this party of Indians gives some more particulars in regard to this expedition:

" HEADQUARTERS, NEAR
            CHICKASAWHATCHEE SWAMP,
                        Baker County. }

Sir:—In obedience to orders I have pursued the Indians to this place, where I find them encompassed in a swamp, said to be twenty-five miles long, and varying from one to four in width. At 12 o'clock A. M., the first instant, I learned that the Indians were encamped within four miles of this place, but was unable to reach them short of sixteen miles march. On yesterday, about 10 o'clock A. M. I made an attack upon the enemy, succeeded in driving them from their camp, with the loss of nine that were left dead, and from the sign of blood, I suppose twenty to thirty killed and wounded. The Indians fled precipitately in every direction, but I was unable to pursue them in consequence of the denseness of the bushes through which they retreated, the exhaustion of our men, and the state of our wounded, having seven of them, and two I fear mortally. I think there is no doubt that the Indians are still in the swamp, and from the most intelligent persons here, I am induced to believe they design remaining.

We need one hundred friendly Indians commanded by Paddy Carr, to pursue the Indians and ferret them out, and shall be gratified to receive them as early as practicable. In consequence of the incessant rains we have had, and having fought in water, we need 3,000 cartridges.

In the meantime I may take the liberty of saying that the expedition will be brought to a close, and as soon as it is, a full report will be made as early as practicable.

[Signed.]   THOMAS BEALL,
                                  Col. Com. 1st Brig.
                                      Mounted Volunteers,
To Maj. Gen. Winfield Scott.

THE FIRST CITY GOVERNMENT.

In accordance with an act of the Legislature amending the charter of the town so as to make it a city, and change the title of its representatives to Mayor and Aldermen, an election was held on Saturday the 2d day of January, 1836, for a Mayor and six Aldermen, which resulted in the choice of John Fontaine as Mayor; and Thomas G. Gordon, George W. Dillard, Hampton S. Smith, E. Sigourney Norton, Thos. C. Evans and Earnest L. Wittich, as Aldermen.

On the 4th of the same month, the Mayor and Aldermen elected the following city officers: Nath. M. C. Robinson, Marshal; John Bethune, Treasurer; Henry C. Phelps, Clerk; Richard Gray, Bridge Keeper; Alex Calhoun, Clerk of the Market; Samuel Paxon, Sexton. Subsequently the office of Deputy Marshal was created, and Wm. McGehee elected.

In January the Mayor and Council made a contract for the erection of a guard-house, appointed a committee to order from the North two fire engines, and another to contract for lighting the streets by means of oil-burning lamps. A city watch was also organized, consisting of a captain, lieutenant, and twenty privates—the captain to receive $30 per month, the lieutenant $25, and the privates $20 per month each. Michael N. Clark was elected Captain, Lem. Jepson, Lieutenant, and the following persons enrolled themselves as privates: James D. Bryant, Morgan Brown, Wm. Terry, Hugh McDaniel, John Williams, John McGehee, David Moore, Giles Ivey, Francis Bosworth, James Calhoun, Richard McCarey, C. Hightower, Wm. Monghon, Jona. Hightower, Jordan Kilgore, Miles M. Vance, Jacob C. Porter, Robt. Patterson, James Bloodworth, Francis B. Kilgore.

Afterwards, the number of Guards was reduced to twelve, and new officers as well as privates appointed.

Later in the year, a committee of the Council was appointed to petition the Legislature for authority to sell a portion of the square set apart for town houses and offices, and with the proceeds to build, in conjunction with the county of Muscogee, a Court-house, City Hall, &c.

A contract was made with Geo. W. Pinhorn for painting and putting up seventy boards designating the names of the streets, at $1 per board.

Thus the dignity of a city government was gracefully assumed, and city "style" at once adopted.

In consequence of the report of several cases of small pox, the Board resolved to elect a physician, to be known as the Health officer, whose duty it should be to examine every case of disease brought to the city, to attend cases sent to the hospital, and the paupers of the city. Dr. Boswell was elected ; salary $200.

Early in April, Dr. Boswell reported that there had then been fourteen cases of small pox in the city, only three of which had died.

A contract was this year made with Wm. L. Wynn, by which the city leased to him, for the term of six years, the larger portion of the south common, at the rate of $3 per acre per annum. Another portion was occupied as the race course, having been leased to M. W. Thweatt, Wm. L. Wynn and T. B. Howard for the term of six years, at $700 per annum.

In November, contracts for the rent of fisheries on both sides of the river, for the term of three years, were entered into. Six fisheries on the east side of the river were rented to D. Walling, James W. Howard, James & Hamner, and M. N. Clark, at prices varying from $4 to $225 per year, and aggregating $374 per year ; and four on the west side were rented to James Y. Godfrey, John Townsend, and Wm. Williamson, at prices varying from $4 to $7 50 per year, aggregating $22 per year—showing that the fisheries were then a good source of revenue.

The Columbus *Sentinel* of Feb. 26th, reports the killing of Mr. James Hill, confectioner of Columbus, by a Mrs. Berry, living a few miles from the city, where Mr. H. and a friend stopped and asked the woman to lend them a tumbler from which to drink some champagne which they had along. She refused, and a quarrel ensued between Hill and her, resulting in his shooting into the upper part of the door, and her shooting him with a shot gun. Hill's body was interred with Masonic honors.

Columbus and Macon were disputing as to which was the best cotton market. The quotations were 15 to 15½c. in February, and 18c. in March.

The Farmer's Bank of Chattahoochee was "resuscitated" in March, the stock having been purchased by J. S. Calhoun, and others; Judge Calhoun, President, Chas. Bass, Cashier.

The steamer Ohioan was burned on the Chattahoochee, eight miles below Ocheesee, early in May. She was freighted with merchandise for Columbus. One servant girl was lost. The boat had fifteen passengers, who escaped. Boat and cargo were valued at $25,000. She was owned principally in Mobile.

Jim Henry was confined in the jail of Russell county, and the grand jury found a true bill against him for negro stealing, the punishment of which was death. His counsel succeeded in changing the venue to another county. The following Indians were convicted at the fall term of Russell Circuit Court: Chilancha, alias John, for the murder of Fannin, Tuscoona Fixico and four others for the murder of Green, the stage driver. They were sentenced to be hung on the 25th of November. Four others were detained in Russell jail, to be tried at the next term. The six condemned Indians, mentioned above, were hung at the appointed time in Girard.

The first bale of new cotton, this year, was received at Columbus on the 23d of August, from the plantation of M. R. Evans, and sold by auction at 41½ cents per pound. The prevailing price in the "interior" markets at that time was 16½ to 17c. The Macon *Messenger* doubted the fairness of this sale, and suggested that cotton was bought in Columbus as land was sometimes—"by paying a high price for it, and then receiving part of the money back again."

Early in November of this year, about two-thirds of the town of Girard, opposite Columbus, was sold, and brought, in the aggregate, about $70,000,—a sum showing that the hope of building up a commercial rival to Columbus was then strong. The area of Girard laid out into town lots was about one mile square.

PERSONAL.

At the October election, Lawhon was elected Senator, and Flournoy and Holland Representatives of Muscogee county.

Judge Eli S. Shorter, one of the most gifted lawyers in Georgia, died in Columbus on the 13th of December.

The Methodist Conference was held in Columbus in December, and the ministers were hospitably entertained by the citizens. George A. Chappell was appointed Presiding Elder of the Columbus District, and L. Pierce stationed minister at Columbus.

The following list of licenses granted by the town authorities for the years 1836-7, gives the names of many of the business men of Columbus at that time :

Dray.—R. P. Spencer, A. B. Baker, E. L. Wittich, Seaborn Jones, Charles E. Mims, E. W. Starr, Philip T. Schley, A. K. Ayer, Walter T. Colquitt, Elijah Rosson, Joseph Bender, M. R. Evans, John S. Allen, John T. Walker, John Code, T. G. Atwood, Allen J. Mims, E. S. Greenwood, Sam'l B. Thomas, Edward Featherston, R. S. Hardaway, S. A. Bailey, Geo. W. Ross, Wm. P. Yonge, John Dillingham, Lovick Pierce, Johnson & Way, Mathew Robertson, Elisha Reid, Albert G. Beckham, George Grieve, James Montgomery, John Southern,

Joseph Jefferson, William Nelms, W. S. Holstead, S. R. Bonner, Toney & Rutherford, Clarke, Tarver & Co., J. T. Niles, T. Pitkin, James R. Butts, R. A. Were.

Retail.—John Johnson, Daniel C. Rarl, I. B. Millen, B. Ferguson, A. Calhoun, F. Riba, Welch & Myrich, Thos. McCantz, C. Norman, Andrew Southmayd, Mims & Ridenhour, G. B. Terry, Geo. Grieve, John N. Copeland, A. P. Jones, Nathaniel Trotter, Daniel J. Reese, Samuel Lytle, S. J. Herron, J. H. Ware, Jacob Williams, Paul H. Tiller, James Kivlin, Wicks & Bize, A. C. Hill, E. D. Nichols, J. B. McFarland, Wm. Walling, John C. Mangham, John Logan, Western Harwell, J. Rousseau & Co., John Whitesides, Wm. H. Fields, Sam'l Owens, Turner Williams.

Auction.—Bethune & Holland, Hayward & Ayer, J. T. Niles & Co., S. K. Hodges & Co., R. Hooper.

The large number of dray licenses is sufficient evidence of a brisk and extensive commercial business.

We suppose that the large number of retail licenses is accounted for by the presence of so many soldiers and other strangers during a portion of the year. Probably it was only during this period that many of the persons named above did business in Columbus.

1837.

The Situation After the War.

This was a year of panic and general bank suspension throughout the United States. Business of every kind was crippled, and commercial failures became so common as to create but little surprise when even the largest and apparently strongest houses "went by the board." Columbus was of course affected by the general depression, and was not exempt from the failures so prevalent elsewhere. But the clearing out of the Indians from the adjacent territory in Alabama and the certainty of its early opening to a large white settlement, brought many prospectors and speculators, who thronged the city as the most convenient standpoint for their explorations and operations. There were thousands of them in Columbus during the year; the hotels were generally crowded; there was demand for all the varied commodities which such a movement required; and trade acquired an activity that would otherwise have been wanting. We are not surprised to find, after the stirring events of 1836, the names of many new settlers and business houses.

The City Government for this year was constituted as follows: Mayor, J. S. Calhoun; Aldermen, S. R. Andrews, E. S. Norton, T. G. Gordon, T. C. Evans, S. R. Bonner, Asa Bates; City Clerk, M. N. Clark; Treasurer, John Bethune; Marshal, M. C. Robinson; Clerk of the Market, Bartley Weeks; Sexton, Thos. Ashley; Bridge Keeper, Wm. Gilbert.

Reports of occasional depredations in Eastern Alabama, by bands of predatory Indians, still caused some excitement, but they did not threaten Columbus, nor were the citizens of Columbus called on to aid in their capture.

The improvement of the Chattahoochee above Columbus was still a question before the people; and some deeming the opening of the river impracticable, advocated the building of a railroad to West Point. So it appears that for over forty years Columbus has been "hammering away" in the effort to secure the trade of the upper river counties by improved commercial facilities, and has not yet completed the links.

The Episcopal Church was completed this year, and opened to public worship in June. The pews were rented for the aggregate sum of $3,100.

From the *Enquirer* of October 26th:

"Our city seems to be reviving. Some activity and life has been exhibited in business circles this week. The health of the place is almost unparalleled in its history, nothing like bilious or malignant fever being known among our citizens. We are in hopes that times are getting better and money matters growing easier. This hope is strengthened by the fact that we daily see large numbers of strangers going West to purchase land and find new homes. The Oglethorpe

House, kept by Wm. P. McKeen, is crowded every night with travelers in search of lands and fortunes. The City Hall, too, under the management of our worthy fellow-citizen, Mr. James, is in a like manner filled with sojourners. This is all indicative of better times, and shows the spirit of enterprise which nothing can subdue in the Southern people. Columbus will soon be. herself again. Cotton is selling at 8 to 9¼, and corn from street wagons at 85c. per bushel.

The census of the city taken this year, showed a total population of 4121—whites 2549, blacks 1572. The white males numbered 1556, and the white females 986.

In December the Legislature passed an act amending the Charter so as to divide the city into six wards, giving each ward two Aldermen.

The stalls in the market this year rented for $226 00—six stalls, averaging $37 66 each. The butchers renting them were Emanuel Ezekiel, Philip Gettinger, Elisha Tarver, Thos. Cunningham, Thos. G. Jordan and Charles Bize.

Council made a contract in March, with James Clark, civil engineer, to make a survey of the city for the purpose of enabling the Street Committee to drain off the stagnant water and level the streets. The price to be paid Mr. Clark for this service was $500.

We make an extract from the report of Mr. Clark, to show the difference in altitude or depression of various sections of the city at that time. Taking as a base the floor of the east end of the bridge, reported to be 35 feet above the surface of the water—(stage of water not designated,) Mr. Clark reported that "the city is from 14 to 35 feet above base, excepting the first step or immediate margin of the river bank which in some places is only 5 feet above. The crest of the second bank, on and in rear of which the greater part of the city is located, is from 6 to 12 feet above the most depressed points of Jackson and adjoining streets parallel therewith, and it is the same with reference to Crawford and Thomas streets, the intersection of which with the former is in the bottom of a large shallow basin, that embraces in its slope nearly the whole city and north-eastern precincts. Into this reservoir the drainings of this extensive area are thrown more rapidly than it can be drawn off by the present drains, so that it is several days after the cessation of rain before it is uncovered, when there is left exposed a large surface of alluvium, which, in combination with the atmosphere, must have a deleterious influence upon the health of those residing in the immediate vicinity. This low ground is from 13.50 to 16.50 feet above base, and gradually rises to 18 and 20 feet in Mercer street, through which it is drained by way of the brick-kiln to the river below the city. The bottom of this main drain at the Irwinton (now Eufaula) road is but $37\frac{1}{2}$ feet below the drain at the corner of Troup and Crawford streets, but at times of high water the surface is not more than six or twelve inches below; consequently that low portion of the city is inundated until the supply is decreased."

The report recommends the enlargement and deepening of the existing drains, also a subterranean drain or sewer from Oglethorpe street, through Thomas or Baldwin, to the river. Mr. Clark preferred the former, because by its construction, the ravine at its end might be filled and its extension prevented. He estimated the cost of this sewer at $8,569. He also recommended a similar sewer through Franklin street to the river, at an estimated cost of $3,681.

The report concludes: "To the city, Nature has bountifully given all the advantages of a level location, with gently rising hills in the rear, and a delightful esplanade in front, extending from the calm sluggish current along the last impetuous cataract of the river. It is but a few years since there was a wilderness where is now a large, flourishing city, the mart of an extensive and rapidly populating territory, abounding with vast agricultural and mineral riches, which, as developed, must greatly augment its commercial importance and prosperity; added to which, the immense and valuable water power within its environs will undoubtedly be appreciated and attract to it a large amount of manufacturing capital and industry. With the knowledge of these resources, and of what has already been accomplished by the enterprise and intelligence of her citizens, we may reasonably anticipate that Columbus will soon earn a rank among the most important and beautiful cities of the Union. As conservatory of her interests, it is highly important that the measures you may now adopt for the improvement of the health and conveniences should be such as would add permanently to this desirable result."

The Council made a contract in May, with Wm. B. Robinson & Co., for the construction of the two sewers above named, at the rate of $10.50 per thousand brick laid. But in 1838 it had part of the excavation for the upper sewer filled again, on account of great caving and washing away of the soil by rains while the work of laying the brick was delayed. Council also altered the plan of the lower sewer so as to have part of it walled with plank. It was very liberal in settling with Robinson & Co.

At a meeting held on the 15th of November, Council passed a resolution declaring that, in accordance with the unanimous wish of the citizens, the water privileges of the city should be put upon the market, and appointing a committee to memorialize the Legislature for authority for laying off and selling the "western commons" at public outcry.

The principal taxes for this year were the following: On every $100 value of town lots, 30c., and the same upon the improvements upon them; each white male between 16 and 60 years, 46c.; each slave between same ages 46c.; each free person of color over 20 and under 60 years, $6; each dog, more than one to each family, $1; on all goods, wares and merchandise sold on consignment by resident merchants, 1 per cent.; itinerant traders, 2 per cent.; on each $100 in value of capital in trade—merchandize, shaving notes, &c., 30c.; each lawyer, physician, and broker, $5.

Messrs. H. S. Smith, John Warren and G. E. Thomas announced to Council in April, that they had opened a "diagonal street from Broad to Oglethorpe," christening it "Warren street," and asked Council to accept and keep it open permanently. This is the short street commonly called "Triangle," and sometimes disrespectfully dubbed "Dog Alley."

The construction of the Western and Atlantic Railroad had commenced, under a charter passed by the Legislature in December, 1836, and Columbus had this year a project to connect with it at its southern terminus. A corporation styled the Chattahoochee Railroad and Banking Company undertook the engineering of this enterprise. Its officers were J. C. Watson, President; Wiley Williams, Cashier; A. G. Bass, Teller; John E. Davis, Book-keeper; J. C. Watson, J. S. Calhoun, J. W. Campbell, N. Howard, W. H. Mitchell, James R. Jones and J. L. Lewis, Directors. A proposition was made this year for the city to issue $750,000 in bonds, to be loaned this Bank, to aid in the construction of the road and "for the relief of the people." We find in the *Enquirer* an address by Wiley Williams, J. L. Lewis and R. A. Ware, committee, in favor of this project. It met a stout resistance from Gen. Bethune and others.

The Council and citizens conjointly took action upon this project on the 31st of October. At a meeting held at 9 o'clock a. m. on that day, Council passed resolutions requesting the Legislature to amend the charter of the "Chattahoochee Railroad and Banking Company" so as to allow further time for the payment of installments of the capital stock subscribed; also resolving that the city should subscribe for 2,000 shares of the stock and issue bonds for the purpose. The citizens, at a meeting held at 10 o'clock, unanimously ratified this action; and the Council at another meeting held at 4 o'clock p. m., appointed committees to canvass the city for subscriptions, and asked the opinion of Seaborn Jones, Esq., as to what further steps were necessary to legalize the acts of Council in this respect. At the next meeting of Council a letter from Col. Jones was read, which does not appear upon the minutes, and Council passed a resolution asking of the Legislature special power to issue bonds.

INCIDENTS.

Washington's birth-day was celebrated with old time spirit. Rev. Dr. Pierce offered an appropriate and patriotic prayer; Lieut. Hines Holt read the Farewell Address; and M. J. Wellborn, Esq., delivered an eloquent and impressive oration.

A. M. Gregory, a citizen, was found in a dying condition on the streets on the morning of the 13th of March, and died next day. He was evidently murdered, but the case was involved in mystery.

The suspension of the Chattahoochee Bank was announced in April.

The spring races were well attended and well contested. The principal winning horses were Betsy Baker, Eclipse, Linwood, Turnbull, and Miss Medley.

The city was again troubled with cases of small-pox.

The steamboat Florence arrived for the first time on the 2d of November. Water very low.

A big robbery occurred on the night of the 28th of November. The store of P. Miedzielski was entered, and $6,000 worth of watches, jewelry, &c., stolen.

Heavy rains occurred about the middle of December, washing away creek bridges in the vicinity, mills, &c. The bridge over the Chattahoochee was severely tested, and stood the strain.

Rev. Dr. Pierce offered prayer, H. L. Benning, Esq., was the reader, and Hon. W. T. Colquitt the orator, at the 4th of July celebration.

The first bales of new cotton noticed, were received on the 23d of August. They were from the plantation of J. W. Cowart of Stewart, and were sold at auction at 10⅛c. per pound, Hooper, Thornton & Livingston purchasers.

Gen. M. B. Lamar, then Vice President of Texas, visited

Columbus in June and July, was complimented with a public dinner on the 4th of July, and made a very fine and eloquent speech. He was received with much enthusiasm.

A "new and fashionable" theatre was opened in October. It was on Crawford street, in the rear of McIntosh Hall, was 40x80 feet in area of hall, and capable of accommodating about 400 persons.

PERSONAL.

At the election on the first Monday in January, the following county officers were chosen : Aaron Odum, Tax Collector; G. W. Short, Tax Receiver; Daniel Walling, Coroner; Messrs. Hitchcock, Carnes, Torrence and Parks, Judges of the Inferior Court.

James Herring was acting Postmaster at Columbus.

Asa Bates was acting as Sheriff.

At the October election, W. T. Colquitt, Esq., was elected State Senator, and J. W. Campbell and J. C. Watson Representatives.

In October, the notorious hostile Indian Chief, Jim Henry, having been acquitted of the offences for which he was tried in Alabama, was brought to Columbus and lodged in jail, to stand a trial for crimes against the State of Georgia.

Hon. Jos. L. Sturges was Judge of the Judicial Circuit, vice Hon. A. Iverson, resigned.

The following names of business and professional men are found in the advertisements of the *Enquirer* during 1837:

Merchants.—Allen & Young, G. W. Buckley & Co., Guayard & Jordan, Thos. McQueen, Howard & Wittich, J. T. Niles & Co., Henry King, Underwood, Torrance & Co., Neil & McNair, Johnson, Nuckolls & Co., Wm. & W. Toney, Smith & Morgan, Smalley, Crandall & Co., Preston & Nelms, B. A. Sorsby, Turner, Morris & Co., E. S. Greenwood & Co., Foster & Fogle, DeGilse & Gorman, Wiley Williams & Brother, Henry Mathews, Wade & Co., Read & Talbot, Wade & Beardsley, Hall & Moses, Cary & Day, J. B. Green & Co., T. R. Gold, Starr & Ruse, H. C. Phelps, Robinson, Williams, & Holcomb, J. C. Plant, Ragan, Colquitt & Grant, J. H. Reynolds, J. B. Peabody, Harper, Thornton & Livingston, A Levison, A. McArn, G. W. E. Bedell, B. F. McDaniel, Smith & Grimes, John E. Bacon & Co.

Warehouse & Commission.—G. W. Ross & Co., Augustus Haywood.
Taylors.—McDaniel & Wilhelm.
Hotel-Keepers.—S. J. Herron, Calhoun & Bass, Wm. P. McKeen.
Doctors.—Holt & Persons, Thomas J. Bugg, Boon Sewell, J. Ellis, H. W. Hill.
Lawyers.—Haralson & Lewis, Colquitt, Holt & Echols, John & James Bethune.
Teachers.—Mrs. Tally, Charles H. LaHatt, Mrs. Leigh.
Dentists.—O. P. Laird.
Auctioneers.—R. Hooper, S. M. Jackson.

MARRIAGES.

June 12.—John C. Gray and Miss Sarah Reid.

Feb. 23.—Capt. Sol. W. Munk and Miss Alsey Purson; Dr. George B. Mackey and Miss Margaret White.

April 15.—Lewis Livingston and Miss Elizabeth R. Bass.

May 9.—Charles L. Bass and Miss Rebecca M. Fluker.

At Lousta, on Miccosuka Lake, Dr. John E. Bacon and Miss Clementina Alston.

July 12.—G. B. Phole and Miss Susan M. Crenshaw.

Aug. 24.—W. H. Owens and Miss Emily R. Vason.

At Dahlonega, Sept 1st., Dr. John A. Urquhart and Miss Mary Jane Shorter.

In Harris County, Nov. 21st, John A. Bilbro, of Columbus, and Miss Ann L. Rutledge.

Nov. 30.—Augustus Lawrence and Miss Elenora McCall; Daniel T. Driggers and Miss Frances Colson.

In Talbot, Dec. 5th, H. F. Wimberly, of Columbus, and Miss Anna C. Wood.

DEATHS.

Jan. 12.—David C. Griggs.

May 30.—Mrs. Ellen Emeline Walker.

June 27.—Mrs. Winnifred, consort of Wiley Williams.

July 6.—Henry L. Richardson.

Aug. 10.—Robt. A. Jones.

Aug. 2.—Mrs. Elizabeth R., consort of Dr. H. A. Thornton.

Sept. 23.—Alfred Smith, a native of New York.

Sept. 24.—Mrs. Elizabeth S., consort of Thos. C. McKeen.

Sept. 28.—Miss Clara Cornelia Harden.

Oct. 24.—Mrs. Sarah Jane Redmon.

1838.

A Year of Steady Business—Factories and Rail Roads on Paper, &c., &c.

We find but little evidence of material change in the business or population of the city this year. The cotton trade was considerable and of growing proportions, and the movement for the settlement of the contiguous territory in Alabama still contributed to the improvement of business.

The first election under the amended charter, dividing the city into six wards, was held on the first Saturday in January this year, and resulted in the choice of the following gentlemen—the elections for Aldermen being made by each ward separately: Mayor, Jas. S. Calhoun; Aldermen—1st Ward— Hiram Read, R. Hooper; 2d Ward—H. S. Smith, S. R. Andrews; 3d Ward—J. L. Lewis, Wiley Williams; 4th Ward— A. B. Davis, R. A. Ware; 5th Ward—W. S. Chipley, L. C. Allen; 6th Ward—M. Brooks, George C. Hodges. At the first meeting of this Council the following appointments were made: Attorney, A. Lawhon; Marshal, N. M. C. Robinson; Treasurer, John Bethune; Clerk, J. L. Roberts; Bridge-keeper, W. Gilbert; Sexton, Wm. Gehee; Health Officer, W. K. Schley.

The citizens in January requested the banks of the city to suspend specie payments—the banks of the country generally being in suspension. The Bank of Columbus suspended in accordance with this suggestion, but resumed before the year was out. The Insurance Bank would not suspend. The Planters' and Mechanics' Bank went into operation this year— Gen. D. McDougald, President; Directors—D. McDougald, H. S. Smith, M. W. Perry, Hiram Read, W. B. Ector, Thomas Berry, John Banks. A. B. Rozan was Cashier, and M. Robertson, Book-keeper.

Another Columbus bank at that time was the "Farmers' Bank of Chattahoochee"—J. S. Calhoun, President; D. Hudson, Cashier.

On the 15th of January the Committee of Ways and Means were instructed by Council to report an ordinance authorizing the issue of city bonds to the amount of $750,000 to be loaned to the Chattahoochee Railroad and Banking Company of Georgia. The Committee reported this ordinance at a meeting of Council held on the 20th of January. The plan, was for the city to loan these bonds to subscribers to the capital stock of the company, after they had paid 25 per cent. of their subscriptions in cash, or had executed to the city mortgages on their real estate to secure the payment. The city, also, was to subscribe for 2,000 shares in her corporate capacity. This ordinance was passed on the 29th January. It was reported to Council in March that a sufficient amount had not been subscribed to the capital stock of the company— the condition being that three times the amount of the city's bonds should be subscribed before they were to be issued. But we find that a few weeks afterwards the city subscribed her 2,000 shares of stock, giving a mortgage on the bridge to secure her payment of 25 per cent. of the same, and turned over to the Railroad and Banking Company the mortgages on real estate given by individual stockholders.

At a meeting of the stockholders held on the 24th of March, it was reported that 10,255 shares had been subscribed, and 8,465 were represented.

In June the Commissioners stated in a letter from New York that they had negotiated $300,000 of the loan at 7 per cent., and the amount wanted could have been had upon the same terms, but it was deemed advisable to delay a negotiation of the remainder until fall.

The city this year issued its change bills or "shinplasters," of denominations from 6¼c. to $2, to the amount of $50,000.

The Court House on its present location was commenced this year, the city paying one-third and the county two-thirds of the cost. The contractors were W. & J. Godwin, and the price $30,000.

By an ordinance adopted on the 14th of April, the Mayor was made a salaried officer, and his salary fixed at $1,000 per annum ; but the Council, at its last meeting in December of this year, repealed that portion of the ordinance making the salary $1,000.

On the 17th of May the City Council voted a donation of $2,000 in aid of the citizens of Charleston, S. C., which city had been afflicted by a very destructive fire. The Columbus Guards also contributed $100, and the citizens several hundred dollars more.

The Sexton reported the number of burials in the city cemetery from the 1st of February to the 8th of August, 46, of which 14 were infants, one drowned, one murdered, one suicide. The Mayor announced in August that the city was entirely healthy, with not a case of fever of any kind within the corporate limits.

A committee appointed to examine certain improvements on Woolfolk's sand bar, made by Col. Asa Bates, State Commissioner, reported to Council in October that in their opinion the improvements were of such a character as materially and permanently to improve the navigation at those points, making them navigable at any stage of water when steamboats of ordinary draught could pass other points of the river heretofore considered much less difficult than they were.

The city authorities were this year having built a new market house at the intersection of Broad and St. Clair streets.

Girard was making a contest with Columbus for the trade of the surrounding country. The people over there had a fine wharf opposite Columbus, and early in April the first steamer (the Frances) discharged one hundred barrels of freight upon this wharf.

An effort was made this year, through the press, to induce capitalists to utilize the vast water power of the Chattahoochee in the manufacture of cotton. A writer signing himself "A Friend to Manufacturers," and who stated that he had seen some stupendous manufactories at the North propelled by water, declared that he had never seen such advantages for this purpose as were to be found in Columbus and within one mile of it. He said :

"I see a great source of wealth looming up to the people of this section, both in the corporate limits and above the city. I was actually astounded in viewing the splendid estate of Mr. James C. Cook, extending one mile on the meandering river, and within that distance it has been actually surveyed by a competent engineer, and that it has a fall of one hundred and seventy-five feet, and to all appearance it cannot be less. Every one hundred feet, by aqueducts which appear to have been forced through the solid granite by some mighty convulsion of nature, a splendid location for factories could be selected. It would well compensate any one to go and behold what nature has done, and what art and the superior genius of man permits to lie idle and waste, except the piscatory pleasures which its hospitable owner occasionally derives in drawing from its pure waters the numerous family of the finny tribe, from the bream, trout and shad to the sturdy rock."

The *Enquirer*, on the 30th of August, made a strong appeal on this subject. It predicted that by engaging in this enterprise Columbus could in ten years be what Lowell then was; that instead of 5,000 she would number her 25,000 inhabitants, supplying the entire South and West with her manufactured goods. Bright dreams of the past! how fervently we wish that the splendid cotton mills which we now have may accelerate a movement which has up to this time fallen short of realizing this prediction, but which the success of the manufacturing establishments now in existence proves to have been reasonable and sagacious.

A proposition to water the city by bringing it in pipes from streams in the locality was submitted to Council this year.

A census of the city completed in August of this year, made the whole number of inhabitants 4,265—a very small gain over the enumeration of 1837.

The health of the city this year was good.

On the 18th of October, Mayor Calhoun, by advertisement, offered a reward of $500 "for the apprehension and conviction of the incendiary, or incendiaries, who fired the Court House and Clerk's Office on the morning of the 15th inst."

We find the following notice of this fire in the *Sentinel and Herald* of Oct. 18th:

" On Monday morning, between the hours of three and four o'clock, the alarm of fire was given, and the lurid flame was seen bursting forth in the direction of the Court-house square. On hastening to the spot we found the Court-house wrapped in flames, as also the offices of the Clerks of the Superior and Inferior Courts, standing on the same lot, some twenty yards distant from the Court-house, and being entirely separate. The old Court-house was but trifling in value, and besides our city authorities are in the act of building a new one; but the great inconvenience and loss consequent upon the fire is found in the fact of the Clerks' offices being destroyed, together with all the books, papers, &c., connected with the offices, and appertaining to the Superior Court, more especially as the fall term of said Court was to have commenced its session on the same day of the catastrophe, namely, last Monday.

"This was doubtless the work of an incendiary—some pitiful, base wretch, who probably stood amenable to the requirements of the law at the present term of Court, either in criminal or civil prosecutions, and who lighted the torch with his own vile hand that he might witness at the dead hour of the night, when vigilance herself had fallen asleep, the consummation of his fiend-like wishes, and have the hellish pleasure of saying to himself *thus perisheth the record!*"

The Superior Court met on Monday morning at the Council room, was organized, and in consequence of the destruction of the Court-house and Clerk's office by the fire, adjourned till the second Monday in December next.

INCIDENTS.

Augustus Owens, of Girard, was killed near the entrance of the race course in Columbus, in February, by a man named Fox.

Dr. S. M. Ingersoll obtained from Council the privilege of washing the loose sands of the Chattahoochee for gold; but the locality being so far from the gold region, no remunerative results are reported.

In April the steamboat DeFlore, on her way to Columbus, sunk below Fort Gaines.

An event which shocked the city, on the 30th of May, was the suicide of Mr. E. Sigourney Norton, mentioned in preceding pages. He cut his throat with a razor—being, it was supposed, under the influence of liquor.

It was announced on the 14th of June that the *Enquirer* would thereafter be published by Flournoy, Marks & Chapman.

A young man named Kernin was drowned, in June, in the river opposite the city.

The receipts of cotton from September 1st, 1837, to June 14, 1838, were 42,453 bales.

The 4th of July was celebrated with the usual spirit. Prayer by Rev. A. T. Mann; Independence Ode by the choir of Trinity Church; Reading by N. L. Howard, Esq.; Oration by J. H. P. Campbell, Esq.

The first bale of new cotton was received on the 23d of August, from the plantation of John Woolfolk, and sold at auction.

A great religious revival in August and September was reported by the *Enquirer*.

By the caving in of a sewer near the market-house, upon which a number of men were at work, one white laborer and two negroes were smothered to death.

A long drought, that had lasted for nearly nine weeks, was broken by rains about the middle of September, but they came too late to save the crops, which were cut very short.

The steamboat Floridian, with a valuable cargo of goods for Columbus, was sunk on the 6th of November about 100 miles above Apalachicola. Loss about $70,000, not insured.

The "Columbus Cotton Factory" was in active operation this year, spinning cotton yarns and carding wool.

James Van Ness was Postmaster.

James Hitchcock, Monoah D. Robison and R. W. Carese were Justices of the Inferior Court.

The steamboat Irwinton, on her downward trip in May, with two hundred bales of cotton on board, was sunk to prevent her total destruction by fire.

Receipts of cotton from 1st October, 1837, to 1st October, 1838, 42,878 bales. Quotations—for Oct. 1st, 1838, 10¼c.; Oct. 11th, 10¾ to 11¼c.

The City Treasurer's report, made on the 9th of October, showed the receipts for the 3d quarter of the year $7,035 96, of which $3,640 was from the issue of city bills, $1,930 from the bridge, and $1,168 91 from taxes. Balance in city treasury, $6,837.

PERSONAL.

The county officers for this year, elected in January, were—James Bethune, Sheriff; Gerard Burch, Clerk of the Superior Court; Jos. D. McLester, Tax Receiver; B. G. Kenney, Tax Collector; J. E. Lamar, Surveyor; —— Nicholas, Coroner.

J. C. Holland and H. C. Sapp were elected Justices of the Inferior Court in August.

At the October election, J. S. Calhoun was elected State Senator, and Thomas C. Evans and J. H. Howard Represent-atives.

Hon. Marshall J. Wellborn was Judge of the Chattahoochee Circuit.

Rev. Samuel K. Hodges was P. E. for the Columbus District, and Revs. Thomas Samford and Alfred T. Mann ministers at Columbus.

We notice the names of the following business men for the first time :

Merchants—D. Hungerford, Boon & Walker, Ransom Godwin, and Aaron Odom, Geo. W. Way, James H. Reynolds, P. Meidzielski, Jacob Fogle, W. Wade & Co., Hamilton, Hurd & Co., McKee & Prickett, E. C. Roberts, Conzelman & Anderson, Neill McNair, James Affleck, Yonge & Ellis, J. S. Smith & Co., Alfred & Porter, Wm. R. Jones, G. B. Terry.

Auctioneers—Thos Pullum and R. S. Moore; *Bakers*—Jones and Crichton ; *Doctors*—Edward Delony, E. T. Taylor, B. Walker ; *Hotel-Keepers*—D. Sullivan, Thomas James, Howard & Lloyd ; *Dentists*—J. B. Hoffman, R. E. Martin ; *Warehouse and Commission*—Wm. P. Yonge ; *Teachers*—Mrs. Seaman, Miss Anderson.

MARRIAGES.

April 3.—Rev Wm. D. Carnes, Rector of Trinity Church, and Lucy Elizabeth Dillingham.

April 19—In Montgomery, Ala., John E. Davis, of Columbus, and Sarah C. Cropp.

May 15—Col. Hines Holt and Sarah A. C. Perry.

May 23—David Walling and Susannah Beall.

June 3—Joseph E. Webster and Caroline E. Ward.

July 9—Launcelot Gambrill and Ann America Pierce.

July 25—At Brattleboro" Vt., I. C. Plant, of Columbus, and Charlotte Walker.

Aug. 28—In Lincoln county, Ky., Thomas P. Grimes, of Columbus, and Martha D. Lucky.

Oct. 23—At McDonough, Robert L. Moore, of Columbus, and Anna J. Askew.

Nov. 1—Wm. L. Lee and Mary Ann Jeter.

Nov. 19—Edward Barnard and Lucy T. Barrow.

Nov. 20—George H. Wynn and Clarissa T. Ormsby.

Dec. 3—Homer Hurd and Miss Angelika L. V. Ruse.

Dec. —In Hamilton, W. A. Bedell and Sarah Switzer.

Dec. 30—Hezekiah Noble and Frances W. Mulloy; Moses M. Simmons and Eliz. Westmoreland

Oct. 29—Isaac Prall and Jane McKee.

Nov. 1—Geo. Howard and Mary Bagley.

Oct. 21—Lewis Williams and Sophia Taylor.

Oct. 23—Thos. Copeland and Barbary Cooksey.

Dec. 9—Francis Clark and Amanda M. Rodgers.

Dec. 5—Thos. Eubanks and Edna Willis.

Nov. 29—Jos. D. Bethune and Jeanett H. McNair.

Nov. 13—Daniel Rowe and Mary McCall.

Nov. 22—Henry G. Robison and Mary Massey.

Dec. 28—John Fox and Jane Harvell

Sept. 9—Hezekiah Taylor and Mary C. Smith.

Dec. 19—John Sauls and Jane Padgett.

March 18—M. D. Sledge and Deborah McGinty,

Dec. 18—David A. Patrick and Mary Brooks.

Oct. 31—James A. Slaton and Mary A. Watson.

Jan. 7—Wash Blackburn and Sellina Ryalls.

Dec. 25—Alex. McDougald and Frances L. Mitchell.

Oct. 14—Felix Blankenship and Sarah J. Mays.

May 20—Thomas Brady and Sarah McDonald.

Dec. 2—Wm. Painter and Nancy Averett.

Dec. 30—Allen Davenport and Martha A. Hawthorn.

Dec. 27—Alfred T. Mann and E. L. Pierce.

Dec. 12—C. Wiley and Mary Baker.
Dec. 11—James H. Berry and Martha Alldridge.
Oct. 16—Wm. A. Brown and Martha E. Low.
Oct. 11—Claiborn Howard and Eliza Terry.
Oct. 16—John J. B. Hoxey and Sarah Terry.
Nov. 11—James Lochala and Elizabeth Laughflin.
Nov. 21 - J. J. Myers and Susan Wild.

DEATHS.

May 7.—Mrs. Sarah McGehee.
June 15.—Mrs. Matilda Brooks.
July 10.—At Auburn, Ala., W. H. Harper, Esq., formerly of Columbus.

1839.

A Year of Health—Faith in Railroads Weakening.

This was not a year of remarkable events in the history of Columbus. Business appears to have been rather dull, but by no means stagnant. The expectations entertained of the success of the railroad connection with the North—in aid of which the city had so liberally done her part by subscription and the authorized issue of bonds to the amount of $750,000—grew faint almost to despondency as the year rolled on. The failure of a scheme of railroad connection with Florida, and of the banking institution connected with it, also had a depressing effect. But it was a year. remarkable for its health, and its freedom from violent personal collisions and local excitements, such as have been so often noticed in the preceding pages.

The city government of this year, elected on the first Saturday in January, was composed of the following gentlemen:

Mayor—Gen. D. McDougald.

ALDERMEN.—1st. Ward—J. C. Holland, C. L. Bass. 2d Ward—John E. Bacon, Neill NcNair. 3d Ward—Jacob I. Moses, J. L. Lewis. 4th Ward—T. M. Sanders, J. W. Watson. 5th Ward—Lewis C. Allen, James Kirvin. 6th Ward—Jos. Sturgis, Martin Brooks.

At a meeting of the Board the following officers were elected:

Treasurer—John Bethune. Marshal—E. C. Bandy. Clerk—Calvin Stratton. Attorney—J. M. Guerry.

At the county election on Monday the following officers were elected :

Tax Receiver—G. W. Short. Collector—James Moss.

School Committee—John Bethune, W. S. Chipley, O. Eley, John Patterson, Joshua R. McCook.

The several wards of the City were designated by the names of streets bounding or running through them, as well as by numbers. They were known as Franklin, Randolph, St. Clair, Thomas, Few and South Wards.

The Council re-ordained the salary of $1,000 for the Mayor, by fixing the salaries of all City officers the same as last year, except that of Treasurer, which was increased to $800.

The office of Deputy Marshal was re-established, with a salary of $800, and Wm. McGehee elected.

There were three papers published in Columbus this year, the *Enquirer, Sentinel and Herald,* and *Georgia Argus.* Council paid each of them $100 for publishing its proceedings.

Council made special contracts with citizens of Georgia and Alabama for crossing the Bridge, the charge for individuals ranging from $5 to $100. The Mail and Telegraph Line of Stages was required to pay $1000 for the privilege.

On the 14th of January a committee appointed to examine the city improvements reported in favor of the immediate filling up of the upper sewer, and stated facts going to show that it was a badly managed enterprise for the city. We copy from their report:

" The expense for the brick and the building of the sewer with the same, without the labor performed by the City Council, cost not less than ten thousand dollars. The original contract for that sewer imposed upon the Council the obligation to excavate and fill up the ditch in which the bricks were laid. This part of our duty has been performed only to a partial extent, as a large portion of the ditch is still unfilled and exposes the whole work to a total loss. We cannot, under such circumstances, hesitate to urge upon the Council the employment of such a number of hands as will enable the Marshal to have the sewer filled up without delay."

The committee also reported against a proposition to divide the commons into suitable lots and rent it out for agricultural purposes, on the ground that the commons was designed for the common benefit of all the people of the city, and its contribution to the beauty and health of the city and the convenience of its people would be impaired by converting it into corn fields.

The report and recommendations of the committee were adopted.

In accordance with authority conferred by Act of the Legislature, Council this year assumed the full patrol service within the limits of the City, enrolled for this duty all citizens liable to State patrol service, and elected John Bethune Regulator of the Patrol, with a salary of $250. He resigned in July, and Calvin Stratton was then elected.

The Sexton reported on the 4th of May, that there had been but one interment in the Cemetery during the month of April, and that one was a child.

At its meeting on the 11th of May, Council appointed a committee to call on the officers of the Chattahoochee Railroad and Banking Company and inquire what were the condition and prospects of the company.

John M. Bethune was elected, on the 31st of August, an Alderman from the 1st or Franklin Ward in the place of James C. Holland, resigned.

On the 23d of September, Council appropriated $1,000 to be expended in the improvement of the channel of the river at Woolfolk's Bar and Uchee Shoals.

Six fisheries on the Georgia side of the river were rented, on the 6th of September, for $973 ; and on the 26th of the same month, three on the Alabama side were rented for $147 —all for the term of three years.

Alderman Allen, of Few Ward, resigned on the 21st of September, and Michael McQuaid was elected in his stead.

On the 19th of October, a committee of Council, appointed
at the request of citizens to report some mode of securing
better protection against fire, reported that the city was
"totally wanting in the means of resistance" in the event of
fire, and that the best means of defence would be water-
works and two or more fire engines; but that the appropriation for the purpose would have to be larger than the City could
make at that time, and therefore it was desirable that the citizens should act, either by private subscriptions or by obtaining
from the Legislature authority to levy a special tax for the
purpose.   The committee also reported an ordinance providing for the establishment of a Board of Fire Wardens, to
consist of the Mayor and Aldermen and one other member
from each Ward, and prescribing their duties and other regulations to guard against fire.   Council adopted this ordinance
on the 2d of November.

The Sexton, at the last meeting in December, reported the
number of interments during the year 44, of which 21 were
children under ten years of age.

The military companies existing at this time were the Columbus Guards, Columbus Blues, and Muscogee Hussars.

The Columbus Lyceum was organized in March—Thos.
Hoxey, President.   Several very interesting lectures were
delivered by members during the year, and it proved to be
one of the most valuable societies the City ever had, by furnishing entertainment and instruction to the people.

INCIDENTS.

On the first Monday, in March, in Girard, Jonathan Edwards was killed by Franklin Word, in an affray.

Jacob Cunningham was arrested in January as the suspected incendiary who burnt the court-house and clerk's office in
October last, and Council loaned L. B. Harris $150 in consid-
eration of his services in arresting Cunningham.

The Chattahoochee Bank was organized in April—George
R. Clayton, President, Edward Carey, Treasurer.

On the first Monday in May three boys were drowned in

the river while bathing. They were sons of George Reese, Mrs. Reese, and Mr. Norris; and later in the month a little son of Mr. Round was drowned in the falls.

Hamilton Duke, a citizen of Talbot county, was fatally stabbed on the 17th of June, in Girard, by Monroe Lynch.

The Fourth of July was celebrated by the reading of the Declaration by Capt. John Peabody, and an address by S. T. Chapman.

The first bale of new cotton was brought in on the 16th of August, by Dr. Thos. Hoxey, and sold to Terry & Moody for 12 cents.

The first steamboat arrival in the fall was that of the Osceola, on the 26th of November.

Harrison, eldest son of Wm. P. Yonge, was killed on the 18th December, by the falling of a piece of timber.

PERSONAL.

The following were teachers of the Female Academy: W. D. Cairns, Principal, Mrs. H. C. Tichnor, Miss M. J. Coolridge, A. Joerson.

At the October election in the county, the "State Rights" ticket was beaten for the first time. John L. Lewis was elected Senator, and Messrs. Watson, McDougald, Livingston, and Guerry, Representatives. But Columbus gave a majority for the "State Rights" ticket, which was composed of Hampton L. Smith for Senator, and Messrs. W. H. Mitchell, Wiley Williams, S. W. Flournoy, and H. C. Sapp, for Representatives.

MARRIAGES.

Jan. 6—James E. Roper and Savannah G. Tilley.

Jan. 20—James Rankin and Agnes Affleck; Peter Crichton and Ann Grieves.

Jan. 27—Wm. Terry and Martha Jones.

May 16—John Dozier and Emily Huff.

June 30—David Ridgeway of New Orleans, and Martha Kimbrough.

Sept. 5—Benj. Walker and Mary J. Howard; Julius R. Clapp and Eleanor H. Howard.

Aug. 29—In Rahway, N. J., Joseph S. Smith, of Columbus, and Margaret H. Jacobs.

Sept. 8—Elisha Reid and Elmira A. Owens.

Sept. 18—Henry L. Benning and Mary Howard, daughter of Col. Seaborn Jones.

Sept. 27—David Moore and Mary A. J. Perryman.

Nov. 27—Elliott H. Muse and Adeline S. Howard.

Dec. 12—Jeremiah Terry and Sarah Ann Frederick.

June 27—Phineas L. Martin and Sarah D. Studstill.

Oct. 3—Lewis M. Durr and Eliza W. Ragland.

March 6—T. V. Rutherford and Frances E. Mitchell.

Dec. 2—Stanmon D. Pitts and Adaline Brown.

June 18—Thos. D. Hays and Louisa Weaver.

Nov. 25—Isaac Williams and Martha A. Godwin.

July 31—E. Rowland and Eliza Harrison.

June 6—E. Morrell and Mary Dishroom.

Dec. 31—Stephen Shaw and S. A. Hammond.

Oct. 20—William Snow and Mary E. Mahone.

Feb. 28—Geo. W. Douglass and Mallissa A. Biggers.

Sept. 30—Wm. Roberts and Nancy Dillard.

Nov. 24—Wm. A. Douglass and Harriet Tarver.

Sept. 25—John A. Huff and E. H. Stallings.

Oct. 1—Robert Motley and S. J. Spears.

Oct. 31—Wm. Myhand and Elizabeth Culver.

June 24—A. L. McDaniel and Nancy Harrison.

Nov. 14—Absalom Lochla and Sarah Williams,

Dec. 8—Ephraim Brown and Susannah Cobb.

Dec. 4—Wm. Thompson and Elizabeth Hearn.

Feb. 28—P. H. Brittain and Orra Williams.

Jan. 31—Alfred Meazles and Martha Height.

Oct. 25—Hezekiah Williams and Sarah C. Seins.

June 20—Nathan Height and Eliza Horton.

July 23—Elbert B. Ramsey and Sarah A. Davis.

Dec. 26—James H. Reed and Elizabeth Gordy.

Oct. 22—Frank E. Baker and E. A. Chapman.

April 23—Peter W. G. Kent and Nancy A. Owens.

Aug. 1—Cornelius Flowers and E. Sizemore.

July 20—Henry Roberts and Margaret Smith.

June 15—James Foran and Margaret Brady.

Oct. 15—John L. Walton and Adelia L. Tharp.

May 15—John Thornton and Mary A. Ellis.

May 12—James Orrington and Nancy Thomas.

Aug. 28—O. L. Olmstead and Mary J. Fuller.

June 6—Levi Coleman and Margaret Brooks.

Sept. 5—Benoni Rhodes and Susan Hyatt.

Nov. 14—Alex. Calhoun and Mary Hobbs.

June 7—James Glenn and Emily Skelton.

May 2—Hardy Benton and Mary Hamnerr.

April 18—Chas. D. Bize and C. Faulkenbury.

Nov. 29—Simeon Mote and Rebecca Roberts.

Oct. 21—W. D. Fontaine and Nancy Bates.

Aug. 11—J. J. Parnell and E. K. Moorfield.

Nov. 3—Aquilla Cobb and Sarah Bagley.

July 3—J. J. Langham and Martha Hollinan.

Aug. 27—Horace Hearn and Martha Williams.

June 16—B. L. Hargrove and Cretia Womble.

June 13—Thos. L. Kilpatrick and E. L. Brunson.

May 30—Thomas Bush and Epsy A. Watkins.

Sept. 11—R. R. Goetchius and Mary A. Bennett.

Dec. 29—R. E. Snowdon and Rebecca J. Smith.

Aug. 21—Andrew J. Spiller and C. Baker.

Aug. 8—James Nilson and Mary A. Simms.

July 23—Agnes J. Brown and Martha S. Wood.

Nov. 18—S. T. Scott and Elizabeth Harrell.

Jan. 31—H. Y. Smith and Lucy A. Willingham.

Feb. 17—Benj. Phillips and Lucretia Self.

March 3—John Weaver and Francis A. Wilson.

March 27—F. M. Myers and Caroline Kirvin.

Jan. 14—Samuel Baker and Arcada Varnadore.

Aug. 6—J. H. Andrews and Elizabeth J. Ashly.

July 4—David J. Barber and Mary L. Bostick.

Jan. 24—Hiram Green and Elizabeth Greer.

Feb. 17—Wm. Ragg and Harriet Harrill.

Sept. 7—John Massey and Georgia A. Russell.

July 9—Wm. Boren and Louisa Haws.

May 30—John L. Ridgeway and Martha A. Kimbrough.

Dec. 10—Jesse J. Kimbrough and Frances A. Watt.

DEATHS.

May 28—In Girard, Malcom Cameron, a native of Virginia.

June 21—Hon. Augustine Clayton, a distinguished lawyer, who had represented the State in Congress and filled other high public positions.

Aug. 21—Mrs. Elizabeth J. Jones.

Sept. ——Miss Sarah Amanda Benning.

1840.

Increasing Business—Large Cotton Receipts—Political Excitement, &c.

The extensive settlement of East Alabama, as a sequence of the removal of the Indians from that section, now began to show its effects in a considerable increase of the trade of Columbus. The cotton receipts were largely augmented, and trade improved in a corresponding ratio. Altogether, the situation seems to have been as favorable as could reasonably have been expected, considering the unsettled condition of business and finances throughout the country.

This was the year of the noted Presidential contest between the political parties supporting Harrison and Van Buren, respectively, and Columbus shared largely in the excitement and enthusiasm of the contest—the majority of the citizens siding with the party that elected Harrison.

At the Presidential election in November, the City gave the Harrison Electoral ticket 824 votes, and the Van Buren ticket 503. In the whole county the vote stood—Harrison 1,044, Van Buren 811.

At the October election of this year J. S. Calhoun was elected Senator, and Messrs. Flournoy, Chipley, Alexander and Sapp (Harrison men) Representatives.

At the municipal election, held on the first Saturday in January, the following gentlemen were chosen Mayor and Aldermen : Mayor, W. H. Harper ; Aldermen, 1st Ward, John W. Campbell, J. C. Austin; 2nd Ward, J. B. Wood, G. W. Martin; 3d Ward, Wiley Williams, J. C. Ruse ; 4th Ward, Homer Hurd, Thomas C. Watson; 5th Ward, John D. Howell, J. L. Morton; 6th Ward, Joseph Sturgis, Hiram Brooks.

In the election by Council at their first meeting the following City officers were chosen: Treasurer, John Bethune, Esq.; Marshal, A. K. Ayer; Clerk, Calvin Stratton; City Attorney, D. Golightly; City Physician, A. Pond.

Mr. Golightly declined the office of City Attorney, and Philip T. Schulz was elected in his stead.

This was an entire change of city officers elected by the people, except the Aldermen of the 6th Ward.

A strong support was given to motions to reduce salaries and one or two reductions were carried on the first vote, but this was subsequently reconsidered, and the salaries as finally agreed upon differed but little from those of the year preceding.

One of the first acts of the new Council was to repeal the ordinance requiring the enrollment of all the citizens for patrol duty. In lieu thereof, each citizen, heretofore liable, was taxed three dollars for exemption, and those refusing to pay this tax were held to be still liable to patrol duty, and ordered to be organized therefor.

Council elected the following health officers for the year 1840: 1st Ward, Dr. A. I. Robison, Dr. S. Boykin, Dr. A. Hunt; 2nd Ward, Dr. John E. Bacon, Dr. W. K. Schley, Thos. W. Berry; 3d Ward, Dr. R. Sankey, Dr. J. J. Boswell, Elisha Reid; 4th Ward, Dr. L. Holt, Thomas Sanders, James Kivlin; 5th Ward, L. C. Allen, Alexander McDonald, E. Wells; 6th Ward, Dr. J. W. Turner, Wm. Blair, B. F. Coleman.

The office of Deputy Marshal was created in January, and Wm. H. Alston elected.

The contract system for crossing the bridge was at first abandoned by this Council, and in lieu thereof a reduction of 33⅓ per cent. was made from the regular rates of toll in favor of citizens of Muscogee and Russell counties. Wood haulers were allowed to cross free with their loads, and lumber haulers at half rates; preachers free. But this resolution was soon reconsidered and the contract system again adopted, with the above named exceptions.

The Treasurer was instructed to issue $20,000 City money, in small notes, to furnish change, and afterwards $525 was paid for the engraving of the notes.

Among other measures of retrenchment proposed was one to dispense with the use of lamps for the year, which only failed by the casting vote of the Mayor, at the meeting on the the 8th of February, was adopted at the meeting on the 19th of the same month, and again reconsidered on the 22d.

The Committee on City Improvements reported that they had not the means of ascertaining the practicability of introducing water into the City, and the finances of the City would not then allow it, though desirable. Adopted.

The county authorities of Russell county, Ala., had assessed the one acre lot in Girard, on which the western abutment of the bridge rested, at $10,000, and taxed it accordingly. A committee of Council, in March, reported that Russell county had a right to make this assessment, but the courts had a right to revise it, and recommended an appeal to the courts. Adopted.

Cotton opened in January at 7 to 7¼ cents, with large receipts, and freights to Apalachicola $2.50 per bale. The price declined during the spring and summer, but advanced again in the fall, when it became apparent that the crop would be smaller than was anticipated. We find it quoted in November at from 8 to 9 cents, and the last quotation in December is from 7 to 9c. The *Enquirer*, on the 28th of April, estimated the receipts of Columbus up to that time, since the 1st of September, 1839, at 50,000 bales, but it had no actual returns. This was fully double the amount that had been received the preceding year to same date.

The first notice of the appearance of the cotton caterpillar, which we have found in our examination of the Columbus papers, is during this year. The destruction by them was very great. Their appearance was first reported on the 26th of August.

The first bale of new cotton was received on the 24th of August. It was grown by Newton Freeman, of Russell county, Ala., and sold at 8¾c.

The Sexton reported interments in the city cemetery from the 1st of January to the 1st of April, 3; from 1st June to 1st July, 7.

On the 12th September A. B. Ragan was elected an Alderman for the Franklin ward, to fill the vacancy occasioned by the resignation of John C. Austin.

On the 10th of October, the committee appointed for that purpose by the Council, reported that they had, in co-operation with a similar committee appointed by the county authorities, examined the new Court-house built by Messrs. John and Wells Godwin, contractors, and had approved and accepted the same. Subsequently the claim of Messrs. Godwin for extra pay for work not included in the contract was submitted to arbitration, and the sum of $6,000 awarded to them for such extra work.

INCIDENTS.

A man named Goodwin was killed in Columbus, on the 7th of April, by one Caldwell, of Girard. He shot Goodwin while the latter was attempting to escape arrest by an officer.

A man named Moody, who had been in the City but a short time and of whom but little was known, committed suicide near the cemetery in April.

On the 27th of June, William Alexander, eldest son of Dr. A. H. Flewellen, was drowned in the Chattahoochee.

Girard, this year, had a postoffice and a newspaper. W. B. Harris, Esq., was Postmaster. The paper was called the *Alabama State Register*, and was edited by Benj. Gardner.

At the 4th of July celebration, Dr. L. Pierce offered prayer, Dr. J. B. Hoxey read the Declaration, and N. L. Howard, Esq., delivered the oration. Col. A. K. Ayer was Marshal of the day.

John Schley, Esq., was appointed Postmaster of the City in July, succeeding Mr. Van Ness, who did not seek a re-appointment, and who had been the Postmaster since 1828.

The steamboat LeRoy, Washington Smith master, exploded her boilers opposite Blount town, on the Chattahoochee river, September 24th, by which six persons were killed and several wounded. Mr. Willis Alston was the only passenger hurt. The boat was owned by mail contractors Hopkins & Stockton.

All the Banks of the State were required to make periodic reports of their condition for publication. It used to be said (perhaps maliciously) that the wheelbarrow acted an important part in these showings, in cities which had more than one bank; that after the specie had been counted in one bank it would be wheeled over to another to be reported in its assets ,also, and thus gave to the whole of them a fictitious strength. This year the Columbus Bank had $377,218 of bills issued, and $163,291 58 of deposits, and due other banks $74,289—$614,798 63. Due by other banks and agents $220,000 82; specie, notes of other banks, &c., $217,297 26—$437,228 68. The St. Mary's Bank reported $29,915 of notes in circulation, and $14,555 52 in specie; the Chattahoochee Railroad and Banking Company had $109,420 notes in circulation and $62,110 87 in specie. The Insurance Bank of Columbus had $5,289 in circulation and $25,790 in specie. All these Columbus banks afterwards broke, but they were paying specie this year, and very few banks in the State were doing so.

The following were ruling prices on Dec. 9th, quoted by J. E. Davis, exchange broker, and F. McMurray, grocer: Sight bills on New York 7 to 7½ per cent. premium; Charleston, 6 per cent; Savannah, 3½ to 4; New Orleans, 4 to 4½; specie, 4 per cent.; bagging, 25 to 35 (the latter India;) rope, 12½; hams, 15; sides and shoulders, 9; butter, 25 to 37; candles, 18 (tallow) to 62½ (sperm;) coffee, 15 to 16; corn, 40; wheat, 75; oats, 37½; brandy, $1 75 to $2; whisky (Irish,) $4;

Monongahela, 87½ to $1; Sugar (N. O.,) 10 to 12; loaf, 18 to 25.

The county officers elected on the 1st Monday in January, were: Sheriff, S. R. Bonner; Clerk Superior Court, A. Levison; Clerk Inferior Court, N. McLester; Tax Collector, T. A. Brannon; Tax Receiver, John C. W. Rogers; Coroner, Bartlett Weeks; Surveyor, John E. Lamar.

At the Spring term of Muscogee Superior Court for 1840, the following gentlemen served as Grand Jurors: John Woolfolk, Bird F. Robinson, John H. Ware, C. D. Stewart, F. D. Toby, David Wright, Elijah Corley, A. L. Watkins, E. C. Bandy, J. Barrow, Peter V. Guerry, Thomas M. Sanders, Josiah Grimes, A. M. Walker, G. W. Ross, A. I. Robison, Elisha Tarver, T. A. Thornton, Asa Bates, Wm. P. Malone.

Dr. Goulding opened a select school in January; and Mr. Wayland, "graduate of an English University," opened a high shool in February.

A meeting of mechanics of the City, opposed to Mr. Van Buren, was held in October, and as we obtain from the list of signers the names of a large number (probably a considerable majority) of the mechanics in Columbus at that time, we copy the list:

F. Toby, carpenter; M. D. Jones, blacksmith; J. S. Norman, saddler; D. W. Upton, carpenter; F. A. Jepson, brickmaker; J. M. Williams and N. McC. Robinson, (afterwards Marshal of city), bricklayers; O. P. McLane, silversmith; Daniel Robinson and Wm. Robinson, engineers; Daniel Roe, tailor; J. Terry, carpenter (afterwards sexton and merchant); Joseph Pranglen, plasterer; Richard Owens, carpenter; WilliamR. Bell, shipcarpenter; John B. Peabody, silversmith; Peter Crichton, baker; W. I. Rylander, blacksmith; William Jepson, Simeon Guthrie, carpenters; J. A. Moore, Sterling Terry, bootmakers: Elisha Reid, silversmith; Homer Hurd, tailor; Oliver Jeter, printer; Moses Simmons, bricklayer; J. D. Hughes, wheelwright; Charles H. Heite, blacksmith; John L. Mustian, R. N. R. Bardwell, John A. Sears, Thomas Nix (afterwards sexton), carpenters; Jos. Johnson, engineer; George Betz, tailor; William Gilbert, saddler; H. C. McKee, J. L. Prickett, carriage makers; J

7

Freeman, William Morman, carpenters.; Nathan Gray, bookbinder;
V. S. Townsley, blacksmith; Jas. Terry, F. A. Bosworth, carpenters;'John F. Bosworth, printer; James Sullivan, Silas McMichael,
carpenters; J. Haller, carriage maker; B. Pricket, do.; J. M. Mc-
Duffie, painter; Randal McNeil, do.; J. M. McClesky, cabinet maker; Jno. N. Harris, carpenter; J. M. Hogan, carpenter; Larkin Farr,
cooper; Wm. Reid, carriage maker; R. T. Marks, painter; E. H.
Day, printer; Chas. Rule, plasterer; Moses Garrett, painter; Jos.
Jepson, carpenter; J. J. Ballinger, carriage trimmer; Wm. A. Piggatt, carpenter; G. A. Dill, do.; J. R. Young, do.; T. R. Herrin-
dine, do.; Francis Terry, do.; T. P. Noblett, do.; Hervey Crews,
do.; Jno. Partridge, do.; Benj. Buell, painter; N. G. Smith, wagon
maker; Jas. Rosseau, do.; Wm. Pride, bricklayer; Benj. Jepson,
brickmaker; J. B. Strupper, candy maker; T. Reid, gun maker (best
gun maker in the United States); J. L. Holmes, carpenter; J. S.
Williams, engineer; W. C. Clapp, tinner; J. C. Alston, Horace
Clapp, R. McNeil, P. K. Edgar, S. R. Andrews, J. S. Walton, A. L.
Alfred, James Reid, carpenters; W. B. Robinson, bricklayer; Jno.
Griffin Thweatt, L. Denigin, printers; George Smith, plasterer; B.
G. Kenneth, carpenter.

The resolutions were subsequently signed by the following:
Wagonmakers—George C., and R. and Richard Yarbrough, William
M. Martin, William Holt, Randal Moore, Enoch Dudley; engineer—
Robert Kelly; brickmakers—Aaron Ferguson, Burnet Ingram, Stephen
Lewis, Wm Salisbury, John Rounds; tailors—Blake Robinson, Henry
Mathews; upholsterer—Wm. Green; carpenters—D. W. Broom, Thos.
Miles, L. Jepson, Jos. Moorefield, Dan'l Sauls, Hiram Howard, Hugh
McCall, W. S. Holstead, Edward Acee, N. Terry, Wiley Adams, J. D.
Harley, D. J. Rees, Thos. Jepson, R. C. Patterson, W. B. Holtzclaw,
T. W. Bowen, G. B. C. Terry, Richard Burt; blacksmith—J. Roberts;
shoemaker—Jno. Mott, Jas. Shaw; cabinet makers—J. M. Morgan,
John May; silversmith—Jacob Fogle; millright—J. J. Purnell; sad-
dler—H. Middlebrook; printer—T. C. Connoly.

So at that time Columbus had 73 white carpenters, 15
blacksmiths, 19 brickmakers and layers, 8 engineers, 14
tailors, &c.—all of the Harrison party.

Hon. M. J. Wellborn was Judge of the Superior Court, and
John H. Watson Solicitor.

The grand jurors on October 17th were: Thomas Berry
(foreman,) James M. Chambers, William Clark, James C.
Cook, Alfred O. Blackmar, John Johnson, David Hudson,
Anderson Hunt, John G. Hitchcock, Micajah W. Thweatt,

William H. Kimbrough, Robert A. Ware, William Y. Barden, Eldridge S. Greenwood, Thos. J. Shivers, Walter H. Weems, George W. Turrentine, John Peabody.

MARRIAGES.

FROM THE NEWSPAPERS.

March 26—James McDuffie and Susan Kent, of Girard.
April 15—In Barnwell, S. C., S. T. Chapman, of Columbus, and Cornelia Isabella Dick.
June 7—George E. Sherwood and Martha W. Spencer.
June 16—James L. Stockton, of Tennessee, and Eliza J. Wimberly.
June 30—John A. Norton and Mary A. E. Sturgis.
Sept. 10—Chester G. Holmes, of Apalachicola, and Eugenia, daughter of Col. W. H. Harper.

We find on the Record of 1839 and on, some marriages recorded which took place before the Records were destroyed in the burning of the Court House in October, 1838. They are inserted here as matters of interest, not having been discovered till the previous years had passed through the press.

FROM THE RECORD.
1835.
March 1—James S. Moore and Martha M. Tarver.
April 23—Ephraim C. Baudy and Mariah E. Burnes; Richard Hooper and Louisa P. Shivers.
May 10—Larkin Farr and Martha Wilks. May 14, John S. Bell and Charlotte Craige.
Nov. 19—Benjamin Wells and Louisa Curtis.
1837.
March 10—James L. DeLaney and Margaret J. Brewer.
Aug. 2—John Johnson and Hannah Briggs.
Oct. 25—James D. Johnson and Eliza Daily.
1838.
Jan. 16—James M. Watt and Treacy McCrary.
March 15—Frances Fayerwether and Mary J. Moore.
June 7—Hero Tapper and Clarissa Evans.
Sept. 29—John Fagen and Eliza Anderson.
May 16—John B. Dozier and Emily E. Huff.
Nov. 28—Wm. M. Clemmons and Elizabeth Phillips.
1840.
Jan. 2—Wm. Lain and Mary A. M. Morris; Andrew J. Baggett and Elizabeth Cook; Wiley Weaver and Eliza Fontaine. Jan. 9, W. H. Howard and Harriet Howard; William Powers and Margaret

Hearn. Jan. 12, Jas. W. Thompson and M. A. Orderly. Jan. 6, Ambrose Davie and Anna Philip. Jan. 23, Elbert Duke and Margaret Lowry. Jan. 21, Neil Culpepper and Eliza Channel. Jan. 27, William Roland and Rebecca Harrison. Jan. 30, Jesse M. Read and Elizabeth R. Ligon.

Feb. 4—Simon W. Driver and Eleanor W. Fleming. Feb.10, Frederick W. Dixon and Mary A. Roland. Feb. 16, Robert C. Patterson and Sarah A. Hickey. Feb. 19, Zena Roland and Malinda Wilson. Feb. 20, H. Vanhorn and Emily Christian. Feb. 23, Samuel Beck and Sarah Rodney; Franklin Greer and Elizabeth Chordre; Alfred T. Slaughter and Martha Williams.

March 2—Thomas Roland and Martha Knotts. March 27, James Abercrombie and Sarah A. Abercrombie.

April 2—Rufus K. Mills, of Alabama, and Sarah A. Porter. April 12, James H. Patrick and Nancy Johnson. April 22, Reuben R. Hudgins and Olive Wells. April 23, Thomas W. Watson and Fredonia C. Holmes. April 30, James Howell and Malinda Shoftner.

May 10—William Barrow and Mary A. Walker,

June 18—John F. Boon and Mary H. John. June 26, John A. Brown and Tamar Blackmar. June 30, Daniel Strough and Mary Cox.

July 2—Thomas Wayland and Jane Leigh. July 8, Edward E. Wade and Lucy Blake. July 15, Dr. Leroy Holt and Mary Ann Sankey. July 29, John A. Walker and Frances M. Coleman.

Aug. 6—Henry J. Eilbeck and Sarah A. H. Cook; William Short and Mary V. P. Lambs. Aug. 5, William J. Duke and Delia Duke. Aug. 10, J. J. Claxton and Susannah Doringer. Aug. 13, James McGrath and Eliza Dobbs. Aug. 20, Matthew Beck and Mary Sanders. Aug. 26, Isham Hicks and C. A. Goss. Aug. 27, James McGowan and Mary Nobles.

Sept. 10—Daniel R. Fox and Catharine McGinty. Sept. 25, Asa Henry and Elizabeth Hortan.

Oct. 22—Robert L. Moore and Mary Askew. Oct. 29, Harvey W. Nance and Elizabeth Blackman.

Nov. 5—John Hatten and Sarah A. E. King. Nov. 12, Sterling J. Terry and Elizabeth A. Chapman; Seaborn Sneed and Ataline Slaughter. Nov. 17, Wm. C. Prather and Emily C. Grimes. Nov. 19, Randall McNeill and Sarah Fisher. Nov. 23, Samuel Webster and Elizabeth Mackey. Nov. 24, Thos. D. Fortson and Eliza. A. Pruett. Nov. 25, Charles Rule and Eveline Giddings. Nov. 26, Wm. Price and Caroline M. Tillman.

Dec. 10—Walter T. Colquitt and Aphia B. Fauntleroy; Henry Reese and Sarah Ann Styles. Dec. 11, Edward Acre and Elizabeth Armstrong. Dec. 17, John I. Grant and Martha Shippey; Robert Newsome and Mary A. Smith. Dec. 27, F. M. Doles and Mary L. Seger. Dec. 30, Jackson Baxley and Harriet Bachelder.

DEATHS.

Jan. 5—Simon Brazille.

Jan. 25—Col. Weston W. Ford.

March 12—Arthur Shaaf, son of Hon. Alfred Iverson.

April 26—Mrs. Harriet Susan Taylor, wife of Dr. E. T. Taylor.

May 6—Mrs. N. D. Laird, wife of Dr. O. P. Laird.

June 26—In Girard, Benj. Pinron Tarver.

June 30—Ann America, child of A. O. Blackmar.

July 7—Near the City, Robt. F. Cook, a native of Virginia.

July 19—Eliza Ann Fletcher, infant child of Josiah Roberts.

August 1—Mrs. Agnew Baker, wife of Rev. Joseph S. Baker, pastor of the Baptist Church.

August 20—Mrs. Catharine Long, wife of Col. N. W. Long, of Russell county.

Sept. 9—Rev. Samuel K. Hodges.

Sept. 10—Joseph D. Bethune.

Sept. 15—Miss Antonette Virginia Rutherford.

Sept. 26—Mrs. Mary Ann Moore, wife of Robt. L. Moore.

Sept. 2—In Muscogee, Wm. Scurlock, a Revolutionary soldier, aged 81.

1841.

Disasters—The Bridge Swept Away—Failure of the Chatta-
hoochee Railroad Scheme.

The two most remarkable events in the history of the City for this year were the destruction of the Bridge by the great "Harrison freshet," and the failure of the projected connection with the Western and Atlantic Railroad. The city, however, escaped complication to any great extent in the failure of the Chattahoochee Railroad and Banking Company, by the return of its bonds and of the mortgage which it had given upon the Bridge. We understand that the negotiation of a part at least of the bonds had been delayed by doubts as to the authority of the city, under its charter, to issue them. Whether, if the bonds had been issued and made available, the company would have been able to prosecute the work, or whether the proceeds would have been profitlessly used in the general derangement of the finances of the country, is a question we will not undertake to decide. But certain it is that an enterprise of great sagacity in its conception, and one promising almost incalculable benefits to Columbus, failed with the Chattahoochee Railroad and Banking Company.

At the election held on the first Saturday in January, the following municipal officers were chosen:

Mayor—John L. Lewis.

Aldermen—1st Ward, Thos. Morris and J. B. Green; 2d, Thos. Berry and a tie between Dr. Hoxey and B. B. Morrell (G. W. E. Bedell was subsequently elected—Dr. Hoxey declining;) 3d, Wiley Williams and J. B. Howard; 4th, R. A. Ware and John Quin; 5th, J. D, Howell and J. L. Morton; 6th, Joseph Sturges and A. J. Abbott.

The following city officers were elected by the Council:

Wm. A. Douglass, Clerk; N. M. C. Robinson, Marshal; John Bethune, Treasurer; Richard Gray, Bridge-Keeper; Hugh McDonald. Deputy Marshal; J. J. B. Hoxey, City Physician; V. S. Townsley, Clerk of the Market; Wm. Rabon Shivers, City Attorney; Thomas W. Dutton, Sexton; R. N. R. Bardwell, Neill McNair, Jacob Barrow, George W. Martin and Horatio Smith, Port Wardens.

It would appear that there was a *tie* between the friends of Harrison and Van Buren, respectively, as the result of the regular election—6 to 6—and at its first meeting Council could not elect city officers because of this equal division. The special election in the 2d Ward resulted in the choice of Mr. Bedell, the Harrison candidate, giving his party seven votes in the Board; and at the second meeting of Council, on the 9th of January, the above named officers were elected.

Mrs. Cassy Ann McGehee was Superintendent of the Hospital.

Council adopted a resolution, in January, asking Congress to make Columbus a port of entry.

Dr. Wm. S. Chipley was President, and Dr. E. T. Taylor, Dr. Wm. K. Schley, Dr. J. J. Boswell, Dr. A. J. Pond, Lewis

C. Allen and Lawrence Fields members of the Board of Health.

The Bridge-keeper, this year, was instructed to have tickets prepared for tolls, and to furnish them to persons purchasing $5 worth or more at 25 per cent. discount.

Fire Wardens this year—Byrd F. Robinson, Benj. Coleman, Wm. R. Bell.

In March, the Board of Directors of the Chattahoochee Railroad and Banking Company proposed that the city should withdraw its subscription to the stock of the company; and in May the city accepted this propostion, receiving back its bonds (which had not been negotiated) and its mortgage on the Bridge then destroyed.

LOSS OF THE BRIDGE.

On the 11th of March of this year the city sustained a great pecuniary loss in the destruction of the bridge by what was termed the "Harrison Freshet." The *Enquirer* of the 17th of that month, gives but a short account of this disaster. It says that on Tuesday evening of the week previous, rain commenced descending and continued to fall in torrents for forty-eight hours, with slight intermissions. The city looked like it was built on a lake. On Wednesday the Chattahoochee began to rise rapidly. The falls and rapids disappeared, and the turbid waters swept on their course. Whole trunks of trees with their roots entire were borne on the current. It had already risen within a few feet "of our noble bridge" when a portion of the no less costly bridge at the factory, a few miles above, was seen descending the stream. It was caught, as it swung around in an eddy, by citizens, and anchored to a tree. The weather-boarding was knocked off the city bridge to save it. The river continued to rise Wednesday night and Thursday at daybreak one end of the structure floated off the pier and dropped down the river, and "never was there a more majestic sight than the departure of that noble bridge on its remarkable voyage." Several parties valked across it a short time before it was gone. The river was then flowing over the flooring. The stage had just reached the Girard side—having passed over—when the bridge floated off. Its course, after leaving the piers, was uninterrupted until it reached Woolfolk's plantation, eight miles below, where it took up new moorings in the centre of a large cotton field, on which the river had never before been known to encroach. It was caught and made fast by Col. Woolfolk and his hands.

The destruction of the bridge was announced to Council at a called meeting, held on the 11th of March, and the Board instructed a committee to make a contract at once for the construction of two flats for temporary ferriage.

Council also adopted a resolution thanking a number of gentlemen for their exertions to save the bridge.

At the meeting of Council on the 27th of March, propositions were submitted for re-building the bridge by the following persons, at the prices named: Joseph Davidson, $15,500; Asa Bates, $15,000; John Bell, $14,800; David Wright, $13,000; P. H. Nolan, $16,000; John Godwin, $15,100. None of these parties proposed to include insurance, except Mr. Godwin, and his bid was accepted, not only on this account, but because he named the earliest time for the completion of the bridge. He was to have it ready for crossing by the 20th July.

In March, Philip A. Clayton was elected an Alderman for the 4th Ward, to fill a vacancy occasioned by the removal of Alderman Ware from the ward; and in May Stephen G. Wells was elected an Alderman of the St. Clair Ward, to fill a vacancy caused by the resignation of Ald. Howard.

At its meeting on the 29th of June the Board adopted an ordinance authorizing the lease of some and sale of other alternate water lots on the river to persons who would contract to make available the water power connected with them, by means of a dam and a race or canal, &c.; and Josephus Echols having agreed to the terms of the ordinance, he was allowed until the first of October to complete his agreement, by bond, &c.

The contract for the sale of the water lots, heretofore uniformally agreed upon, was consummated on the 22d of December, 1841, between the Mayor and Aldermen of the one part and John H. Howard and Josephus Echols of the other part. The river front, west of Bay street, from Franklin street on the north to Crawford street on the south, was laid off by John Bethune, surveyor, in 37 water lots, each lot 72 feet wide. Every alternate lot, being the even numbers from 2 to 36 inclusive, were conveyed in fee simple to Messrs. Howard and Echols, in consideration of the sum of one hundred dollars cash, and on the condition that they should construct a dam across the river and a safe and well constructed canal or race, so as to allow a sufficient head at low water along all the lots, and to keep the dam and race forever in good repair—the dam and race to be commenced within one year from the 30th day of June, 1841, (the date of the bond made by Messrs. Howard and Echols,) to be made available for machinery on lot No. 1 within twenty-seven months, and be completed within five years.

A powder magazine, previously contracted for, having been finished by J. R. Yonge, was accepted by Council in June.

At this time a line of stages ran from Columbus, via Tuskegee, to Franklin, on the Montgomery and West Point Railroad. Columbus also had connection with the Georgia Railroad by a line of stages.

Mr. Godwin had the bridge ready for crossing in July, as per contract, and it was so reported to Council on the 21st of that month. An order for the discontinuance of the ferry was then adopted. Council received the bridge on the 23d of November, though it was not entirely completed at that time.

In August, Willis S. Holstead was elected an Alderman of the 2d Ward, in the place of Alderman Bedell, resigned.

The Powder Magazine was completed this year, accepted by Council, and R. Gray appointed keeper.

The controversy between the city authorities and Dr. S. M. Ingersoll, in reference to the dam across the river constructed by Dr. I., commenced this year. A committee was appointed in December to inquire as to the right of Dr. Ingersoll to build the dam, and whether it was not the cause of the river banks washing away. The committee reported that he had no right to build the dam, and that it was in part the cause of the washing of the banks. They reported in favor of the completion of a breakwater on the Columbus side, then being built by Mr. Godwin, also that the Marshal erect a dam across the wash immediately above the bridge. Adopted.

INCIDENTS.

The Banks in Columbus resumed specie payment in February, as required by an act of the Legislature, but the resumption proved to be of short duration; for they suspended again in March, and in June the Chattahoochee Railroad and Banking Company, of Columbus, closed doors, and H. T. Greenwood protested certain bills of the Columbus Bank to the Governor. A committee was afterwards appointed to examine into the condition of the Chattahoochee Railroad and Banking Company. The bank had in circulation $200,000 of bills, and owned 6,000 bales of cotton, well covered by advances. We judge from editorial remarks that the Stockholders drew out their capital stock, $141,000, before the failure. The Directors afterwards appointed, as trustees, John Bethune, Wm. P. Yonge, and Van Leonard. L. Gambrill was Cashier.

The first new bale of cotton of the season was received on August 21st, from Jas. M. Pruitt, of Russell county, Alabama. It was sold at auction by Smith, Beattie & Co., to Lewis Livingston, at twelve cents, in Central Bank bills, and stored at Wm. P. Yonge's warehouse.

The Muscogee Insurance Company was in operation this year—Directors, John Warren, G. E. Thomas, E. S. Greenwood, John Peabody, T. B. Howard, Kennith McKenzie. President, John Banks; Secretary, Matt. R. Evans.

Among the institutions of Columbus this year was the "Hibernian Benevolent Society," of which John Quin was President. Another was the "St. Andrew's Society," John Bethune President, and Chas. Wise Secretary.

PERSONAL.

The Justices of the Inferior Court of Muscogee, elected this year, were Messrs. Wm. H. Mitchell, Jas. M. Chambers, Wiley Williams, S. A. Bailey and H. C. Sapp; Tax Collector, T. A. Brannon; Tax Receiver, J. W. C. Rogers.

At the 4th of July celebration, N. M. C. Robinson was Marshal of the day; prayer by Rev. L. Pierce, reading of the Declaration by Jas. L. Pierce, Esq.; and oration by A. H. Cooper, Esq.

G. W. E. Bedell was Postmaster of Columbus.

In October, Col. A. McDougald was elected Senator, and Van Leonard, John H. Howard, W. T. Colquitt and J. H. Watson Representatives of Muscogee.

Messrs. Bull, Goulding & Co., were proprietors of the *Enquirer.*

We find these advertisers hitherto unmentioned: John Lloyd, book-keeping teacher; Moses Garrett, window blind and sash factory; James Rousseau, groceries; James T. Eppinger & Co., hats and caps; Wm. R. Shivers, W. P. Sanford & Dowdell, lawyers; W. S. Billing, druggist and physician; Drs. Boswell and Billing, physicians; F. A. Halleter, teacher; W. J. Ellis, school teacher; J. B. Landrum & M. Matthewson, auction and commission business; Hampton S. Smith & Aug. Hayward, warehousemen; Andrew Low & Co., grocers; R. W. B. Munro, principal of the Wynnton Female Academy; G. E. Thomas & L. T. Downing, lawyers; H. W. Nance, grocer; J. A. Dublois, H. T. Hall & F. N. Ruse, warehousemen; Peter McLaren, grocer; G. W. Woodruff & Co., dry goods; J. J. McKendree, J. P.; S. S. Grimes & H. T. Greenwood, grocers.

Rev. W. D. Matthews was Presiding Elder of the Columbus District.

MARRIAGES.

Jan. 3—Wm. Champion and Ann Davis. Jan. 7, Isaac Gallups and Martha Pate. Jan. 15, Augustus G. Smith and Martha McCollister. Jan. 17, Benjamin F. Malone and Susan Ann Burch. Jan. 19, Theophilus Bryan and Lavina Weathers. Jan. 20, Richard Jefferson and Rebecca Hays. Jan. 27, Milton Williams and Mary J. Rutherford. Jan. 31, James Ray and Dicy Bryan.

Feb. 4—John D. Carter and Zoononia Hoxie. Feb. 9, Robert H. Yarborough and Margaret P. Burt. Feb. 13, Paton H. Pinckard and Matilda A. Stone. Feb. 16, Matthew J. Parker and Mary A. Mackey. Feb. 18, Henson S. Estes and Martha J. Gray, Jeptha C. Dean and Isabella King. Feb. 25, Thomas P. Sparks and Matilda Brunson, Benjamin Waller and Matilda Putnam.

March 4—Joseph G. King and Sarah N. McNaughton. March 10, Charles P. Henry and Virginia R. Durrum.

April 13—Algernon S. Ealy and Martha A. Pain. April 15, William H. Lamar and Sarah Sanders, John Johnson and Epsey George. April 17, Francis McMurray and Charlotte L. Goulding. April 27, Joseph S. Pruden and Ann J. S. Orr.

May 2—Irvin Watkins and Elizabeth Johnson. May 5, Francis Victury and Jane Rodgers. May 11, James Barnes and Mary Cooper. May 16, John Dimond and Sarah L. Hollenbeck, John Mitchell and Sarah Lunsford. May 18, Calvin Stratton and Henrietta White· May 20, Thomas O'Brian and Jane Evans.

June 1—William Perry and Sarah C. Jones. June 8, Josiah M. Kent and Rosella Jemison. June 15, Daniel Johnson and Rebecca McGibbony. June 27, Bartlett T. Dean and Nancy Smith.

July 1—Simeon Bennett and Nancy Perry. July 8, Solomon Bickley and Rebecca J. Culver. July 15, Paton Vincent and Malinda Tharp. July 22, Ansalum L. Lawson and Elizabeth Huguely. July 26, Israel W. Roberts and Hester Willers.

Aug. 1—Bradford Wall and Rachel Posey. Aug. 3, John Simpson and Malinda Phillips. Aug. 19, Turner Peck and Tempa A. Laws.

Sept. 2—Nelson McLester and Phebe B. Kirkland : Sampson Cox and Mary A. Clark. Sept. 9, Duncan Cooksey and Gilly A. Tucker. Sept. 23, Anderson McNeal and Elizabeth Thomas. Sept. 26, James J. Chaffin and Nier Marcrum. Sept. 30, Miller H. White and Sarah T. Bennett.

Oct. 4—Hilliard S. Newby and Mary Gray. Oct. 14, Abner G. Coates and Cynthia Huguley. Oct. 17, F. Mc. M. Marks and Adaline A. E. Reed. Oct. 19, Joel C. Wiggins and Martha M. Russell. Oct. 27, Wm. S. Culver and Mary K. Archer.

Nov. 10—James H. Wilson and Charlotte Kelley. Nov. 16, Christopher Chambliss and Amanda M. Edwards, Alexander Dent and Martha Weddington. Nov. 18, James M. Harris and Martha Ray, B. P. Rogers and Sarah A. Underwood. Nov. 23, Bennett M. Raiford and Mary Jane Kent. Nov. 25, Tillman D. West and Caroline Pickard.

Dec. 7—William Iverson and Haney Ann Dawkins, Lewis T. Wimberly and Hannah Pitts, John C. Brassill and Elizabeth Minyard. Dec. 14, Franklin A. Nisbet and Arabella Alexander. Dec. 21, Chas. B. Smith and Martha A. Adams. Dec. 23, John Tillery and Rebecca Powers. Dec. 24, Archibald Armstrong and Louisa Prosser. Dec. 28, Abraham W. Mann and Sarah A. Wilkes. Dec. 29, James Cummings and Jemimah Hays. Dec. 30, William B. Wilkes and Permelia Johnson.

DEATHS.

March 24—David Golightly, Esq.

May 15—Thomas, Son of William and Lucinda Salisbury.

May 27—Mrs. Mary Matilda, wife of W. W. Garrard.

July 10—Benjamin B. Morrell.

July 14—Maria, daughter of Samuel K. Hodges.

July 16—In Greensboro', Mrs. Anna V., wife of James S. Calhoun, Esq., of Columbus.

Aug. 6—Mrs. Caroline McGehee, wife of Samuel W. McGehee, of Barbour County, Ala.

Sept. 5—Mrs. Winnifred Bivins, wife of M. L. Bivins.

Oct. 4—William Gilbert.

Oct. 31—George Smith, a native of Scotland.

There were 53 deaths of white persons in the City this year, of whom 28 were adults, and 25 children. But the above are all the names we can find in the records before us.

1842.

The First Great Fire—Council refuses to have Fire Engines—
Hard up for Cash—Sale of Water Lots, and Stipulations
for Cotton Factories.

At the municipal election held on the first Saturday in
January, there was a tie between John L. Lewis and Dr. W.
S. Chipley, candidates for Mayor, and the following gentlemen
were elected Aldermen:

1st Ward—Thomas Berry, Francis N. Ruse; 2d, Thos. Morris,
Edward Barnard; 3d, N. L. Howard, S. G. Wells; 4th, John
Quin, Thomas Everett; 5th, John D. Howell, Joseph L. Morton;
6th, Joseph Sturgis, A. J. Abbott.

At a special election held on the 15th of January, John L.
Lewis was elected Mayor, by a majority of 30 votes over his
opponent Dr. Chipley.

The following city officers were elected by the Council:

Michael N. Clarke, Clerk, salary $600; Nat. M. C. Robinson,
Marshal, salary $1,000; James M. Hughes, Deputy Marshal, sal-
ary $600; John Bethune, Treasurer, salary $800; Richard Gray,
Bridge-Keeper, salary $600; John J. B. Hoxey, City Physician, sal-
ary $200; Victor N. Townsley, Clerk of the Market, salary $250;
Daniel G. Sauls, Sexton; John Magner, Hospital Keeper.

The City Guard, consisting of 12, was chosen, as follows:
James D. Wilkenson, Augustus A. Dill, Francis Madden,
Benj. F. Coleman, John Sullivan, William H. Thompson,
Simeon Guthrie, William R. Bradford, David J. Barber,
William N. Jackson, Hugh McDonald and John G. Bunnell.

Dr. Wm. S. Chipley was elected President of the Board of
Health, and the following gentlemen chosen members of the
Board: Dr. Anderson Hunt, Dr. A. I. Robison, Dr. Wm. K.
Schley, Richard Sammis, Alex McDougald, Ephraim C.
Bandy.

THE BIG FIRE OF 1842.

Port Wardens elected—Seymour R. Bonner, Jacob Barrow, Frederick Toby, R. N. R. Bardwell and H. T. Hall.

John M. Bethune was elected City Attorney.

The principal city taxes levied this year, in accordance with an act passed by the Legislature on the 10th of December, 1841, were the following: On all white males between 21 and 60 years, in commutation of patrol duty, $1; on all free persons of color between same ages, $6; on every $100 worth of town property, or stock in trade, or capital employed by brokers, exchange merchants, banks, insurance or trust companies, or due by note, or of any other property not otherwise taxed, 25cts.; lawyers, physicians, factors or brokers, $4.

The city and county authorities agreed, in February, upon a plan for improving the public square, by planting ornamental trees, &c., the city and county to share the expense equally.

In March, Willis S. Holstead was elected an alderman of the 2d ward, to fill a vacancy caused by the resignation of Edward Barnard.

Several citizens of the 4th ward petitioned council, in March, for the abatement of "a nuisance," viz: an iron foundry erected in that ward. This petition was referred to a committee of council, who reported against the abatement of the foundry as a nuisance.

On Tuesday night, March 15th, Columbus had a big fire. It originated in a frame building, west side of Broad street, occupied by Rosseau & Choate, as a grocery and dry goods store. That was destroyed; Wm. Amos' two-story wooden building, occupied below by Mr. Abbott, as a grocery store, and Mr. Amos above; Peter Crichton's confectionary and bakery; Wells & Hudgin's dry goods and grocery store; Col. S. Jones' two-story brick building on the corner occupied by Estes & Illges, grocery, Moore & Hodges, and McGough & Crews, dry goods (this was blown up); Mr. Hargrave's brick building, occupied by Boswell & Billing, druggists (this was blown up); Mr. Hargrave's two-story brick building, occupied by Mulford & Adams, dry goods. The clothing store of Geo. C. Sherwood was also blown up. The market house and range below were saved by blowing up houses. Two small buildings and the residence of A. K.' Ayer, on Front street, were blown up. The fire was on the west side of Broad between Randolph and St. Clair streets. The city had not a single fire engine. The following losses are reported: Col. S. Jones' building, $7,000; Ayer's $2,000; Geo. Hargrave's (two houses), $8,000; Lock's $2,000; Crichton and Locks, $3,000 each; Geo. C. Sherwood, $2,000; Wells & Hudgins, and Rosseau & Choate, $10,000 each; McGough & Crews, and Mulford & Adams, $8,000 each; Moore & Hodges, $2,000; Estes & Illges, $5,000; Abbott, $5,000; Boswell & Billing $6,000. Total loss $100,000—little insurance. G. R. Hurlburt, Professor of music, was injured badly by an explosion, and died from the effects.

The origin of this fire was a mystery. Some persons entertained the suspicion that Messrs. Rosseau & Choate fired their own store for the purpose of obtaining the insurance, which was large. But a committee of Council, appointed to investigate the matter, made a report fully exculpating them, and stating facts which showed the suspicion to be unreasonable and unjust. The committee also reported that the house was undoubtedly set on fire intentionally, and Council offered a reward of $500 for the detection and apprehension of the incendiary. This fire also aroused the citizens to the necessity of better safeguards against such disasters, and caused a rigid investigation for the detection of merchants who were keeping more gunpowder in their stores than the city ordinance allowed. Several of them were reported as having violated the ordinance, and they were fined $50 each. Council ordered the powder taken from their stores to be sent to the magazine.

The committee appointed by Council to confer with the citizens on the subject of procuring fire engines, reported on the 15th of April. A majority of the committee, consisting of Messrs. Morton and Howell, reported against the purchase of fire engines at that time, insisting that it would require four engines at a cost of $8,000; that the city was so crowded with wooden buildings that the engines could not be worked with much efficiency; that there was not a sufficient supply of water; and that the city could not now afford the expense. Mr. Quin, the other member of the committee, reported in favor of purchasing the engines, in conjunction with the citizens, who, he said, would make private contributions. He took issue with the majority of the committee upon the points stated above, and contended that experience in other cities had fully established the efficiency of fire engines. The report of the majority of the committee was adopted by Council, by a vote of 6 to 3.

The office of City Physician having become vacant by the removal of Dr. Hoxey from the city, Dr. S. A. Billing was elected in his stead.

John Morgan, elected an Alderman of the 2d ward in place of Ald. Holstead removed from the ward, took his seat in May.

In June, in accordance with resolutions adopted by the citizens in public meeting, Council instructed a special committee to contract with some person for the construction of a dam or breakwater to arrest the encroachment of the river at the upper end of Broad street, then represented to be increasing and alarming. At a subsequent meeting, Council adopted a plan submitted by Ald. Quin, which was for the Marshal, with the city hands and other help to be employed, to fill up the break made by the river, with pine bushes cut from the east commons, and weighted down with rock.

Funds in the city treasury being low and partly in uncurrent money, Council in October authorized the Mayor to negotiate a loan of $20,000, and to mortgage any property belonging to the city as security for its repayment.

At a called meeting on the 18th of November, Council re-

8

solved to offer for sale the remaining water lots belonging to the city, by opening books of subscription until the 1st of December, estimating the property at $20,000 and dividing the interest in shares of $20 each. At the same meeting Council agreed to sell to Dr. J. J. Boswell & Co., for the sum of $150, water lot No. 21, on condition that they put in successful operation thereon a cotton factory before the 1st of August 1844.

Subsequently Council agreed to exchange with Messrs. Howard and Echols, lot No. 1 for lot No. 4.

INCIDENTS.

Henry W. Arnett, a citizen of Harris county, was murdered in Columbus on the night of the 4th of January. —— Green was afterwards hung for the murder.

There was a strong feeling in favor of Texas in her still unsettled relations with Mexico. In March the citizens of Columbus held a large meeting, of which the Mayor was chairman, at which strong resolutions favoring Texas were passed. Large subscriptions were obtained for Texas. B. F. Malone, D. P. Ellis and Dr. Chipley were of the committee of thirty-one to procure additional amounts. Santa Anna then ruled Mexico. Gen. Houston was President of Texas.

Thirty-eight men, styled "Coon Hunters," left Columbus for the Texas army, via Apalachicola. Major J. B. Hoxey commanded.

Jones & Moore's merchant mill, in the upper part of the city, during the spring had floated into the middle of the river. Mr. Bridges, with four men, succeeded in floating it ashore, where it was as good as ever.

We find a notice of the participation of two Columbus volunteer companies in a general muster on the 21st of June. They were the Muscogee Blues, Capt. Schley, and Columbus Guards.

The Sabbath schools of the city celebrated July 4th with speeches, &c. The Wynnton, Methodist Factory, Baptist,

Girard and Presbyterian Sabbath schools are named. Revs. Drs. Baker and Goulding participated.

Gen. Mirabeau B. Lamar, ex-President of Texas, arrived in Columbus on the 12th, and took lodgings at the Oglethorpe House. He was tendered a public dinner.

The first bale of cotton was brought in by Mr. John Odom, of Russell county, on August 15th, and was sold in specie funds to Mr. LeGrand Wright for ten cents.

In September, John Hunter, L. J. Davies, Hall & Moses, D. & J. Kyle, Hill, Dawson & Co., Ruse & Barnard and L. B. Moody were appointed a Board of Trade to report a weekly exchange table. They reported, among other things, Columbus and Planters' & Mechanics' Banks "broke;" City Council's, 10, 20 and 25 per cent. discount; Insurance and Phenix Banks of Columbus, par; sight checks on New York, 2 per cent. premium.

The grand jury at the fall term, reported that Muscogee county owed a debt of $19,683.

Cotton in November $4\frac{1}{4}$ to 6c. in specie funds, and in December $3\frac{1}{4}$ to 6c.

The new and splendid steamer "Columbus," Capt. Allen, arrived in December.

The receipts of cotton from the 1st Sept. 1841 to the 7th May, 1842, (the latest statement we can find) were 40,424 bales.

PERSONAL.

At the county election on the 1st of January, John Mangham was elected Sheriff over M. Dancer; W. Y. Barden, Clerk the Superior Court, over Guerry; Nelson McLester, Clerk of Inferior Court, over A. G. Beckham; McNorton, Tax Receiver, over Lamar; Wilkes, Tax Collector, over Calhoun; [T. A. Brannon was elected Tax Collector in April, to fill a vacancy.] Coleman, Coroner, over Kenney.

W. D. Matthews was Presiding Elder of the Columbus Circuit, and James B. Payne stationed at Columbus.

The April grand jurors were: S. Boykin, J. B. Green, A.

F. Brannon, A. G. Bass, R. A. Ware, W. H. Maynor, John
Logan, B. A. Sorsby, R. H. Greene, E. Tarver, R. N. R. Bardwell, J. J. Boswell, J. J. McKendree, A. Hunt, Thomas Morris, H. S. Smith, H. King, R. A. Greene, T. H. Smith.

William Y. Barden was Clerk of Court.

S. W. Flournoy was announced as editor of the *Enquirer*
in May.

The October election resulted in the choice of McDougald,
Senator, over Flournoy; Baker, Guerry, Pool and Alexander,
for the House, over Leonard, Green, Wynn and Jones—all
the elect Democrats but Leonard.

The grand jury for the fall term was composed of A. H.
Flewellen, John Woolfolk, Van Leonard, A. I. Robison, Sam'l
Koockogey, Jacob Fogle, Aaron Odom, A. L. Grant, Owen
Thomas, M. W. Thweatt, Mansfield Torrance, J. R. Jones,
W. E. Jones, S. C. Lindsey, M. D. Jones, Josiah Beall, Jas.
McGuire, George C. Sherwood.

John L. Lewis was Solicitor, and M. J. Wellborn Judge of
the Circuit.

It was announced on the 3d of October that the *Enquirer*
had been bought by R. T. Marks and Thomas Ragland.

We find mention made, in their advertisements and otherwise, of the following business men not heretofore noticed:

Merchants—D. & J. Kyle, Kyle & Barnett, Mulford & Adams,
B. Wells, J. Ennis, T. M. Hogan, George A. Norris, Wade & Mid-
dlebrook, R. W. Jaques, Greenwood & Grimes, Hamilton, Peyton
& Co., A. M. Cox, Hall, Ruse & Co., J. T. Eppinger & Co., Fos-
ter & Ward, Ayer & Starr, Thomas Bumstead, H. W. Nance, S.
A. Billing, Ware & Pond, J. B. Strupper; J. D. Howell, G. C.
Sherwood, J. & J. Brooks, Ives & Brother, G. W. Woodruff &
Co., Wm. H. Hurd & Co.

Hotel-Keepers—E. & R. L. Bass, the City Hotel; Wm. B.
Phillips, of the Oglethorpe House, afterwards Wm. P. McKeen.

Teachers—Thos. B. Slade, J. M. Hampton, Mrs. Dozier, R. W.
Munro (Wynnton,) J. N. Goodale (Wynnton.)

Auctioneers—John Johnson and Calvin Stratton, Horatio
Smith, Landrum & Co.

Lawyers—Foster, Howard and Pierce, W. W. Murray, Williams & Shivers, Bailey & Cooper, Thomas & Downing, McDougald & Watson, Iverson, Forsyth & Meigs.

Brokers—Davis & Plume; *Dentists*—Charles T. Cushman, Chas. P. Hervey; *Watches and Jewelry*—G. B. Phole, L. A. Le-Gay; *Blind and Sash Factory*—Moses Garrett; *Comb Making, &c.*—D. L. Booher.

Warehouse and Commission—Smith & Hayward, Hall, Ruse & Co., Yonge & Spencer, B. A. Sorsby, Jacob M. Johnson & G. W. Turrentine.

MARRIAGES.

Jan. 6—Reecy Gunn and Emily M. Bugg, Charles West and Clarrissa A. Luckie. Jan. 9, Thomas J. Barbaree and Mary A. Shaw, Samuel G. Prey and Martha J. Monkus, John Culpepper and Celia Pickern. Jan. 13, Richard Pool and Jeanette Oliver. Jan. 23, John W. Parsons and Mary Cordery, John P. Rockmore and Martha C. Needham, James A. Perdue and Nancy Christian. Jan. 25. Robert Boyd and Mary A. McMurray, William J. Bush and Eliza Ann Pate.

Feb. 3—Andrew Boland and Luticia W. Barrington. Feb. 6, Joshua Canter and Eliza Williams. Feb. 8, Jesse Boland and Mary A. Cole. Feb. 16, John Hunley and Mary Christy. Feb. 17, John R. Young and Sophia Morton. Feb. 20, Martin Mimms and Mary J. Padget. Feb. 23, Abner Wilkinson and Matilda Taylor. Feb. 24, Wm. D. Vickery and Mary E. Walding, Newton M. King and Nancy C. Lisle. Feb. 25, Henry Stringfellow and Zilphia Bush. Feb. 27, Garrett B. Clayton and Caroline Duke. Feb. 28, Francis N. Reese and Mary F. Hunt.

March 1—John May and Mary Emmett, Jonathan Hunt, Jr., and Frances Hitt. March 3, Hillery H. Nash and Clarkey Scott. March 4, Philander Thompson and Sarah A. Lester. March 6, James Hyatt and Mary Clark. March 10, John P. Lunsford and Nancy Scott. March 15, Philip G. Heigdon and Jane Gardner. March 17, John Hamell and Emily H. Bosworth. March 20, Dan'l Brewer and Mariah Owens. March 24, Jackson Fontaine and Martha Potts, James Johnson and Martha Smith. March 27, Jackson Williams and Nancy Clyatt. March 29, Daniel J. Smith and Mary Ann Pearson.   March 31, James M. Champion and Elizabeth Willis.

April 2—Jasper S. Smith and Ann Stanley.   April 5, Benjamin W. Walker and Mary Watson.   April 7, Humphrey Posey and Mary Windham, Pleasant Hutchins and Emeline Cole.   April 21, James M. Brooks and Eliza Gray.   April 26, Samuel Lewis and Nicy Ann Brooks.

May 15—Wm. Ritch and Eliza Williams.   May 24, Wm. B. Langdon and Frances B. Peters.   May 29, William Taylor and Elizabeth Parnell.   May 31, Absalom H. Chappell and Loretta Rebecca Lamar.

June 8—Robert B. Murdoch and Lydia Spencer.   June 9, Wilson Wright and Elizabeth Davis.   June 23, Thos. G. Richardson and Lucinda Martin.   June 30, Drury A. Ridgeway and Frances S. Reese.

July 7—Peterson Sanders and Elizabeth Leonard.   July 8, Thos. Morris and Mariah McDaniel.   July 10, Wm. P. Coleman and Sarah C. Livingston.   July 24, Johnathan McClung and Lusina Askew.   July 26, William Dubose and Elizabeth T. Alston.

Aug. 3—John N. Underwood and Zelia A. S. Huckaby. Aug. 24, Andrew Henry and Jane A. Jenkins. Aug. 25, Geo. Allston and Elizabeth Sanders.

Sept. 6—John C. Tozier and Julia A. Sims.   Sept. 8, Richard G. Parkman and Narcissa A. Moore.   Sept. 13, Linson Pickard and Nancy C. Coleman.   Sept. 15, Benjamin Cooper and Eliza Davidson.   Sept. 18, Silas R. Shirey and Piety Drake, Alvin Pruett and Frances Ann E. Mealing.

October 5—Archibald Calhoun and Sarah Jane McMurray. Oct. 6, Elisha Davis and Luticia McCloud.   Oct. 11, Robert P. Colwell and Elizabeth Christian.   Oct. 18, Richard H. Harris and Mary J. Hudson. Oct. 25, James Wall and Elizabeth Cowart· Oct. 27, Gilford Strickland and Rhoda Davis, George G. Henry and Eliza P. Cary.   Oct. 30, Rolin W. Smith and Caroline M. E. Russell.   Oct. 31, Francis M. Brooks and Clementine Beauchamp.

Nov. 14—Richard H. W. Hinton and Mary J. Elder.   Nov. 16, Thomas Hawkins and Mary H. McCoy.   Nov. 17, John H. Hood and Eliza E. Beauchamp. Nov. 20, Benjamin Adams and Jane Hutchins. Nov. 30, Shadrack Wall and Mahala Patrick.

Dec. 6—Solomon Glass and Jane Williams. Dec. 7, William Blount and Sarah Turrentine. Dec. 15, Henry P. Shofner and Margaret Rogers. Dec. 18, William Jones and Martha Ann Walls, Hamilton Good and Eliza Ann Hickey. Dec. 20, Samuel D. Johnson and Kezziah Motley, Geo. S. Hawkins and Josephine O. Sullivan. Dec. 22, Anders Anderson and Petrar Larsen, Edward Baugh and Mary A. King, Wm. Morgan and Nancy Coffer. Dec. 26, John W. Kelly and Sarah C. Martin. Dec. 27, Edward Culpepper and Elizabeth Williams.

DEATHS.

Jan. 20—Robert E. Broadnax.

Jan. 26—Mrs. Martha Wells, wife of S. G. Wells.

Feb. 1—Mrs. Sarah Jane Persons, wife of Dr. J. T. Persons.

April 2—George R. Hurlburt.

June 27—John Thomas, son of J. B. Strupper.

July 5—Robert Walter, son of Mrs. M. F. Beall.

July 10—Peterson Thweatt, Sen.

July 12—Mrs. Martha Howard, wife of Augustus Howard.

Sept. 16—Elizabeth B., daughter of Hockley C. McKee.

The total number of deaths in the city during the year was 63 whites, of whom 33 were adults and 30 children.

1843.

The Remaining Water Lots Sold—Another Startling Tragedy—A Bold Bank Robbery, &c.

The municipal election on the first Saturday in January resulted as follows: Jacob I. Moses was elected Mayor, and the following gentlemen Aldermen: 1st Ward, J. J. McKendree, Willis S. Holstead; 2d Ward, Josiah A. Beall, B. F.

Malone; 3d Ward, Wiley Williams, N. L. Howard; 4th Ward, John Quin, Frederick Wilhelm; 5th Ward, Wm. R. Jones, Joseph L. Morton; 6th Ward, J. A. L. Lee, and a tie.

This Council commenced its work by a material reduction of the salaries of city officers. The following were the salaries agreed upon: Marshal $500, Treasurer $500, Bridge-Keeper $350 and a house free of rent, Clerk of the Market $150, City Physician $200, Attorney no salary.

At a special election held on the 14th of January, Edwin L. Burns was chosen an Alderman of the 6th Ward, to fill the vacancy. The city officers elected by Council were—City Clerk, Calvin Stratton; Marshal, Wm. H. Alston; Treasurer, John Bethune; Bridge Keeper, Wm. W. Martin; Clerk of the Market, V. S. Townsley; Sexton, Jeremiah Terry; City Physician, Dr. Wm. S. Chipley; City Attorney, Hines Holt; President of the Board of Health, Dr. Thomas Hoxey.

Jeremiah Terry having resigned the office of City Sexton, Green D. Sauls was in January elected in his place.

The plan of making private contracts with individuals for crossing the bridge was again adopted this year, the minimum price required being $10 for the year.

A tragedy which startled the city and surrounding country was the killing of Col. Burton Hepburn, on the 5th of January, by Gen. Daniel McDougald. It occurred in the Directors' room of the Insurance Bank, of which Gen. McDougald was President. Col. Hepburn had been connected with Gen. McDougald in business, and the difficulty between them was about their business affairs. It was understood that Hepburn had made threats against McDougald. On the morning of the killing Hepburn entered the office of Gen. McDougald in a threatening manner, or at least McDougald thought his visit was a hostile one, and it was then and there that he shot Hepburn. The killing, on investigation, was found to be an act of justifiable homicide.

By an ordinance adopted on the 4th of February, all persons in the city subject to patrol duty under the laws of the

State were required to perform guard duty in Columbus, under organization and direction by a Regulator of Patrol, whose compensation was to be one-half of the fines and forfeitures collected. Dr. C. P. Hervey was elected Regulator, and in March his salary was fixed at $500 per annum.

The following were the Banks and Agencies located in the city this year, which appears from an order for the commencement of suit against them for taxes that they refused to pay: Bank of Columbus, Planters and Mechanics' Bank, Chattahoochee Railroad and Banking Company, Western Bank of Rome. In March the Bank of St. Marys was removed to Columbus.

The South Commons was this year divided as nearly as practicable into 20 acre lots, and leased for six years, at prices ranging from $1 75 to $2 25 per acre. The committee attending to this matter reported that they found many trespassers upon the Commons, "among them nearly an entire brickyard," and Council ordered the immediate removal of these trespassers. A forty acre lot east of the race course was rented for the same term at $1 50 per acre. The renters were John T. Walker, N. M. C. Robinson and G. W. E. Bedell.

Alderman Burns having resigned, A. J. Abbot was in February elected an Alderman of the 6th ward.

The only fire company of the city this year was the "Columbus Hook and Ladder Company," of which the following were the officers and members:

*Wm. S. Chipley, President; Henry T. Hall, Foreman; *George Peabody, Assistant; R. T. Brice, Secretary; *James Kivlin, Treasurer.

Members: Henry T. Hall, N. M. C. Robinson, F. A. Wright, R. H. Green, John Everett, *B. F. Coleman, *Wm. S. Chipley, A. O. Blackmar, *P. A. Clayton, Jas. S. Norman, J. R. Turnbull, Wm. S. Morton, *Chas. T. Insley, *W. J. McAlister, David Wright, *Jas. A. Bradford, *J. E. Webster, *James Kivlin, John Condon, Benj. Dodge, Josiah Pranglin, Thos. S. Carr, *Wm. Snow, J. S. Arnold, *F. A. Cairnes, J. A. Norton, †J. W. Morgan, J. H. Bishop, Jno. B. Strupper, George Chalmers, John S. Allen, Hiram Young, John C. Young,

Hugh McDonald, R. T. Brice, *A. J. Moses, †J. R. Young, M. Simmons, *G. H. Peabody, Thos. Flemming, A. Anderson, Jos. C. Niles, *I. G. Strupper, N. P. Foster.

On Friday, April 14th, the city was excited by the announcement that the Western Insurance and Trust Company had been robbed of from $50,000 to $100,000. The office was located in the two-story brick building next the Enquirer office, corner Oglethorpe and Randolph streets. It was afterwards occupied as a post-office, and burned many years ago. The families above heard a noise early in the morning. They found the teller, Allen G. Bass, and cashier, R. B. Murdoch, locked in there. According to their statement, as they were putting up money after supper, three armed and masked men rushed forward, blew out the candle and threatened to blow out their brains if they muttered. After the vault had been robbed, they were locked in. The citizens were greatly incensed, and the military companies, police and citizens, were so posted as to prevent all egress from the town. No clue being obtained, on Saturday the Mayor searched the town. Mr. Thomas McKeen had a room in the row of low wooden buildings on Randolph street, between Oglethorpe and Jackson streets. In his room, under the earth in a japonica jar which was freshly watered, a sock was found containing $4,300 of the stolen bills. McKeen was arrested. In the afternoon he was taken by Messrs. A. K. Ayer and N. M. C. Robinson, who had him in charge, in a carriage outside the city. A report became general that McKeen had been allowed to escape by the officers through an understanding with the officers of the Trust Company, in order to get their money back. Pursuit was made and Ayer brought back. He made a speech from the bank porch, and, in conclusion, desired to know what the people wanted. They wanted McKeen back. At 11 at night McKeen was brought

---

*The members whose names are marked by asterisks are all who are now known to be living. The others are all dead, except perhaps the two with a † mark, of whom no information can now be obtained.

back, carried before Judge Sturgis, and, in default of $6,000 bail, sent to jail Sunday morning. During this investigation, it was ascertained that Col. John L. Lewis, Solicitor General, had received from McKeen information where the bulk of money was. Judge Sturgis required him to give $1,000 bail. as a receiver of stolen money. Lewis claimed that in his (Lewis') exertions to secure the money, McKeen, in order to procure his escape, had told him where the bag containing $54,000 was. All the money save $6,000 was recovered. Mr. Allen G. Bass, the teller *pro tem.*, and Mr. Wm. N. Jackson, were also arrested as implicated. The investigators named were Colonel J. H. Howard, R. B. Alexander, Hon. J. S. Calhoun, General James N. Bethune, Judge W. H. Mitchell, General S. A. Bailey, Dr. W. S. Chipley, Wm. F. Luckie, Wm. S. Morton, J. R. Jones.

Wm. N. Jackson afterwards made a confession which was published in pamphlet form, but not in the papers. Lewis' trial occupied a week. Seven panels of 48 each were exhausted before a jury of 12 could be obtained. Judge Cone presided. John Watson, Alex. McDougald, M. J. Wellborn, Seaborn Jones and W. T. Colquitt defended, and Solicitor Gardner, James Johnson, Hines Holt, J. C. Allford and R. Toombs prosecuted. The trial resulted in an acquittal. During the trial one Dr. Smith committed suicide in the court-room by swallowing poison—prussic acid. He had been arrested that morning for stealing corn. About the same time Simples was drowned while trying to swim the river. Officers were trying to arrest him for selling liquor in Alabama without license.

Lewis did not then resign his solicitorship. He and the Democrats charged on the Whigs it was a party fight and prosecution.

The trial of the other parties was continued.

Wm. R. Jones, an Alderman of the 5th ward, having resigned, James H. Wilson was elected on the 1st of April.

Ald. Wilson, of the 5th ward, resigned in May, and States Lewis was elected to fill the vacancy.

At its meeting on the 13th of May, Council passed a resolution accepting an offer of $5,000 made by Major John H. Howard for the remaining water lots belonging to the city. But on the 27th of May this vote was re-considered. This question was one of much perplexity and stirred up some personal feeling. The re-considered resolution having again been called up at the meeting on the 8th of July, and a determination to push it to a decision at that meeting having been announced, Mayor Moses resigned his office on this account, and Council thereupon agreed to postpone further action on the subject until the election of a new Mayor. The election was held on the 22d of July, and Henry T. Hall was returned as elected by a majority of one vote over L. B. Moody; but Mr. Moody contested the election. Council ordered a special meeting for the purpose of considering this contest, and when it met for that purpose on the 25th of July, Mr. Hall, claiming to be Mayor, resigned. Council seems to have regarded his communication as irregular or disrespectful. After some consideration as to the form of proceeding, it agreed to accept the resignation, but ordered that no part of Mr. Hall's communication should be entered on the journal. Another special election for Mayor and for an Alderman in the 4th ward in the place of Ald. Wilhelm, resigned, was ordered to be held on the 5th of August. On that day L. B. Moody was elected Mayor, and Joseph E. Webster Alderman. On the 12th of August Council settled the vexed question by accepting the proposition of Major Howard, binding him to improve the lots by the erection of machinery to be propelled by water within four years, restraining him from erecting any bridge across the river, reserving the city's right to tax the property, and reserving to the citizens the right to fish at any place on the river banks included in the lots sold, with hook, seine or net; also reserving the city's right to use the gravel and sand in the river.

Ald. Lee, of the 6th ward, having resigned, Jacob M. Guerry was elected an Alderman of that ward in June.

The Committee of Ways and Means, in June, reported the city's indebtedness as follows: Amount of city bills then in circulation, $29,221 33; certificates given for city bills on deposit, $15,960; amount due the State, $20,000; amount due prior to 1st June, $2,000—total $67,181 33. The Committee reported that the city revenues were inadequate- to pay this indebtedness within any short time, and recommended the strictest economy and the rendering available of every source of revenue. They also offered an ordinance providing for bonding the city debts, in bonds bearing 8 per cent. interest and payable in eight years. This ordinance was adopted on the 19th of August.

On the 26th of August the select committee appointed for the purpose reported that they had negotiated with John G. Winter a loan of $30,0J0, for which the bonds of the city, bearing 8 per cent. interest, and secured by a mortgage of the bridge, were to be given; the bonds to be redeemable in yearly installments of $8,000, commencing the 1st of January, 1848. This negotiation was ratified by Council.

The President of the Board of Health reported the whole number of deaths in the city from January, 1843, to January, 1844, 72.

We find the names of the following steamers and boxes whose arrivals and departures during this year are announced: Florence, Stapler Captain; Lowell, Niles; General Sumpter, Thompson; Oconee, Greer; box No. 2, Evelyn, Bilbro; Oriole, Woodruff; Agnes, Jenkins; Columbus, Allen; Charleston, Freeman; General Harrison, Van Vechten; boxes Nos. 3 and 4, Kings; Nos. 5 and 6, John Godwin and Asa Bates; Tallahassee, Rynear; Augusta, Hall; Boston, Roland; Louisa, Brown; Siren, Sharples; Apalachicola, Sutton; Augusta, Cadwalader; Robert Fulton.

Cotton took a wide range this year. It opened in January at $2\frac{1}{2}$ to $4\frac{3}{4}$c.; stood at about the same figures in June; the first bale brought 6⅝ in August; the price rose to 7½ to 8⅞ in October, and closed in December at 6 to 9c. With such a year now, dealings in "futures" would make more millionaires and bankrupts than any other speculation in these times of commercial gambling.

A bill to authorize the election of Mayor and Aldermen for Columbus by general ticket, had failed in the Senate by one vote, after passing the House, in December, 1843. So the election of Aldermen continued to be held by wards.

INCIDENTS.

The shock of an earthquake was felt in Columbus on Wednesday night, January 4th, about nine o'clock. The vibrations succeeding the first sensitive shock continued perhaps half a minute. People were badly frightened. The same phenomenon was experienced at Augusta, Madison and Washington, Ga., and Columbia and Hamburg, S. C.

Several fires, believed to have been started by incendiaries, occurred in January and February. The stables of Dr. Bill ing and T. A. Brannon were burned, and an attempt was made to burn W. C. Clapp's tin store.

Washington's birthday was celebrated by the volunteer companies and various societies. In the Baptist church, Mr. John A. Jones read Washington's "Farewell Address," and Mr. James Kellogg delivered an address.

. The *Enquirer* of March 29th says that on Monday of last week Mr. Thomas Fleming was stabbed by Patrick McCarty. He died the next Wednesday. He was followed to the grave by the Hibernian Society and Hook and Ladder Company.

July 4th was celebrated by the two military companies. Procession marched to the Methodist Church, where James T. Eppinger read the Declaration of Independence, and Jas. L. Pierce, Esq., delivered a speech. Captain Bailey then commanded the Columbus Guards, and Capt. Schley the Muscogee Blues The Baptist Sunday School was addressed by Rev. T. B. Slade; the Presbyterian by Rev. Dr. Goulding; and the Wynnton School was entertained at the residence of

Col. Wm. L. Wynn (now the Holt place.) There were the usual barbecues, &c.

The Western Insurance Company of Columbus wound up business in the spring of this year.

First bale of cotton was sent in August 25th, by John Odom, of Russell county, and sold at auction by Greenwood & Ellis to Wm. A. Redd & Co. for 6⅜c.

Mr. James Johnson, of Russell county, was killed by lightning while crossing the bridge over the river, on September 4th. The structure was somewhat damaged.

PERSONAL.

Hon. Joseph Sturgis was Judge of the Superior Court of the Circuit, and J. L. Lewis, Esq., Solicitor. In December the Legislature elected Milton Williams, of Columbus, Solicitor, vice Lewis.

On July 19th is found the announcement of R. T. Marks that he has sold his interest in the *Enquirer* to Flournoy, Ragland & Ector. S. W. Flournoy, Esq., became chief editor.

In October, A. Iverson was elected Senator, over J. S. Calhoun; and Messrs. John H. Howard, J. R. Jones, Willis P. Baker and R. B. Alexander, Representatives. All of these gentlemen, except Mr. Alexander, were Democrats.

Rev. Albert Williams was pastor of the Baptist Church in Columbus.

W. D. Matthews was this year Presiding Elder of the Columbus District of the M. E. Conference, and J. B. Payne minister at Columbus.

The annual meeting and banquet of the St. Andrew's Society was held on December 25th. M. Chisholm was elected President; Vice Presidents—W. S. Morton and John Bethune; Secretary and Treasurer—Charles Wise; Stewards—J. M. Bethune, Duncan McKenzie, and A. C. Morton.

The Board of Health reported the whole number of deaths (whites) in the city during the year, 72—the largest number of which (10) were from diarrhœa. Nine children died of scarlet fever, and 6 of cholera infantum.

MARRIAGES.

January 1—Wm. H. Clem and Louisa R. A. Hanks. Jan. 2, John A. Debloise and Emily Jane Ruse. Jan. 3, Wm. A. Livingston and Emeline Pickard, Alex Jemison and Lucy Ann Brown. Jan. 4, Jas. Lee Sauls and Sarah A. Nix, Alexander Thompson and Elizabeth Reynolds. Jan. 5, John C. Ruse and Musidora A Porter. Jan. 11, Absalom Adams and Loduska E. A. Adams. Jan. 12, Thomas Ginn and Dorcas Newberry. Jan. 12, Thadeus S. Sturges and Margaret A. McCluskey. Jan. 15 John J. B. Hoxey and Caroline C. Cotton. Jan. 18, Wm. McCauley and Martha A. Allen. Jan. 19, Elbridge G. Webb and Martha A. M. J. Pollard, Stephen Johnson and Caroline Tate. Jan 20, Wm. Johnson and Nancy Williams. Jan. 23, Nathan H. Beall and Martha F. Beall. Jan. 30, Samuel McGee and Elizabeth Floyd.

February 8—Robert Brown and Mary Fleming, Robert H. Henry and Susan Houghton. Feb. 9, Micajah C. Wordlaw and Mary J. McBride. Feb. 15, Jesse M. Reid and Ruth E. Prosser. Feb. 19, Wm. McBride and Sarah Brady, Farre Posey and Selethea Ginn. Feb. 22, Reese H. Moss and Nancy Barlow. Feb. 26, Thos. Harrill and Nancy Palmer.

March 2—Amos Ivey and Emily Ray, Thos. R. Robinson and Mary A. Brigman, Mark J. Westmoreland and Jane Brittain. March 9, John H. Brittain and Jane Westmoreland. March 13, James A. Gammell and Missoura A. Williams. March 26, Elkanah Delaney and Elizabeth Glass. March 29, Franklin C. Johnson and Rebecca R. Foote.

April 2—Wm. Terry and Sarah A. Whittington. April 7, John Morgan and Elizabeth Hudson. April 9, Kinyon Adams and Elizabeth Buckner. April 10, Jesse Ostern and Frances Harrison. April 13, Elijah B. Morgan and Isabel Davis. April 19, George Hargraves Jr., and Virginia Forsyth, Jeptha Warden and Frances H. Nickolson. April 20, Dread Bagley and Elizabeth Jones. April 25, John Gallops and Mary Cooksey. April 27, Wm. Moss and Harriet S. Ward.

May 1—John M. Hampton and Ariadna Pruett. May 6, Hartwell Elder and Mary Dimon. May 14, Benj. W. Hastings and

Julina M. Jones, Calvin T. Colson and Sarah Ann Evans. May 23, Henry M. Tompkins and Henrietta M. Bethune.

June 4—George Evans and Ara Paradice. June 6, Robt. M. Gamble and Martha R. Hasson. June 11, James Dunaway and Irena Swift. June 13, Ligrand S. Wright and Sarah L. Kimbrough. June 15, Lovick P. Zuver and Elizabeth J. Westwood. June 20, Lemuel T. Downing and Mary E. Thomas. June 24, James Bustran and Rosa Shoots. June 28, Randolph Wood and Ann Owens.

July 13—John W. Nash and Frances Mahorn. July 19. Benj. F. Marshall and Caroline A. Howard. July 20, Thos. McGinty and Jane Davis, Franklin Lewis and Louisa A. Allums. July 30 Leonard Lock and Mary Laton.

August 1—Robert S. Stockton and Eugenia Broadnax. Aug. 6, Joshua L. O. Davis and Sarah Jane Adams. Aug. 13, Enoch H. Wilson and Hestor Ann R. Parker. Aug. 15, John B. Auchinleck and Emeline Auchinleck. Aug. 17, Howell Davil and Elizabeth Champion. Aug. 24, Henry T. Smith and Elizabeth Graham, Perry D. Raany and Ann Culifer, Chas. Cleghorn and Elizabeth Ross.

September 5—Wm. Nix and Margaret McKinzey. Sept. 13, John West and Eliza Hudson. Sept. 14, John T. Langford and Jane Champion. Sept. 17, John C. Edwards and Matilda A. Gilmore. Sept. 26, John L. Cheatum and Ascenoth A. Patterson.

October 5—Levi L. Peacock and Mary V. P. Short, John A. Jones and Mary L. Leonard, Robert F. Jemison and Martha C, Pitts. Oct. 8, Job B. Parker and Martha Ann Bears. Oct. 12, Jas. W. H. Ramsey and Margaret Lawson. Oct. 17, Wm. S. Adams and Julia A. Minter. Oct. 26, Wm. Brewer and Louisa Williams, John Story and Mary Ann Jordan, Wm. E. Love and Caroline Louisa Calhoun. Oct. 29, Silas McMichael and Caroline Owens.

November 11—James E. Browning and Mary Johnson. Nov. 14, Wm. J. Watt and Sarah A. Garrett. Nov. 23, Henry H. Bradford and Martha Milford, James W. Norman and Elizabeth Majors, John C. Duck and Sarah Dunn.

December 3—Asa McNeil and Emily Underwood, Albert Henry

and Milly Perry.   Dec. 12, Thomas Dann and Augusta Dozier, Wm. P. McKeen and Martha W. McCluskey.   Dec. 15, Benjamin D. Watson and Frances Bartlette.   Dec. 17, Robt. Johnson and Martha A. Jones, John Smith and America Ann Scroggins, Marian Bethune and Frances Jane Phelps, Thos. J. Powers and Jane Williams.   Dec. 25, Alfred Johnson and Sarah Roberts. Dec. 26, Nathaniel D. Massey and Ruthy Smith, William F. Mullins and Margaret Ann Dent.   Dec. 28, James H. Gilmore and Mary Jane Orr.

DEATHS.

Feb. 9—Philip, infant son of Lewis Livingston.

Feb. 14—Wm. C. Bissell, a native of Norwich, Vermont.

Feb. 25—In Wynnton, Bird B. Mitchell, in the 65th year of his age.

March 23—Howard Chandler, infant son of Julius R. Clapp.

March 31—In Girard, Lewis Townsend, aged about 40 years.

April 14—At Mt. Meigs, Ala., Gen. James C. Watson—long a prominent citizen of Columbus.   His age was 56 years.

May 13—Mrs. Ann Jones, wife of Andrew P. Jones.

May 24—Leopold, infant son of John B. Green.

June 11—Margaret P., daughter of Dr. E. L. DeGraffenried.

June 27—In Wynnton, Jacinta Marks, infant daughter of R. W. B. Munro.

July 5—Thomas Scott, infant son of Dr. E. L. DeGraffenried.

July 3—Ann Elvira, daughter of Wm. H. Mitchell.

July 23—Sarah Ann, infant daughter of William C. Perry.

July 29—In Macon, Miss Rebecca Ann Lamar, daughter of Gen. Mirabeau B. Lamar—formerly of Columbus.

Aug. 9—Raunald McNeil, aged 36.

Sept. 10—Richard W., infant son of Robt. H. Green.

Sept. 13—Francis Deblois, infant son of F. N. Ruse.

Sept. 23—Near Columbus, Capt. Francis M. Marks, aged 40 years.

Sept. 18—In Cherokee county, John G., eldest son of T. B. Howard, of Columbus.

Sept. 19—Hugh McDonald, aged about 35 years.

Oct. 7—Mrs. Mary Irving Williams, wife of Rev. Albert Williams.

Oct. 9—In Florence, Ga., Major Jesse L. Bull, formerly of Columbus.

Oct. 24—Mrs. M. L. Reed, wife of Murray Reed.

Nov. 7—William J. Vincent, of Charleston S. C.

Nov. 7—David Henry, infant son of Gen. S. A. Bailey.

Nov. 23—In Boston, Thomas Burnstead, formerly of Columbus.

NOTE—Scarlet fever prevailed in Columbus this year, and most of the children named above died of that disease.

1844.

A Fair Commercial Year—Valuation of City Property—The First Fire Engine—Political Excitement High, &c.

This was a year of heavy cotton receipts, and apparently of a commercial business correspondingly large. The receipts of cotton were 74,721 bales up to the 17th of April, which is the latest statement we can find. This was about seven thousand bales more than had been received to the corresponding date in 1843. Prices were pretty good in the winter and spring, being 9 to $9\frac{1}{2}$c. in January and February, $5\frac{1}{2}$ to 9 in March, and $4\frac{1}{2}$ to 7c. in April. But they continued to decline, until in October the quotations were $3\frac{1}{2}$ to 5 cents, in November $4\frac{1}{4}$ to $4\frac{3}{4}$c., and in December 3 to $4\frac{5}{8}$c. The receipts from the 1st of September to the 25th of December this year were 40,024 bales.

The municipal government for this year, elected on the first Saturday in January, was composed as follows: Mayor, L. B. Moody. Aldermen—First Ward—J. J. McKendree and W. S. Holstead; Second—J. A. Beall and B. F. Malone; Third—N. L. Howard and R. N. R. Bardwell; Fourth—John Quin and John Everett; Fifth—J. L. Morton and States Lewis; Sixth—Jacob M. Guerry and John A. Norton.

This was the year of the memorable contest for the Presidency, in which Clay and Polk were opposing nominees, and political feeling ran so high even in January, that we find in the papers the politics of each man elected or appointed to a city office. The Mayor elect is put down as a Whig, the Aldermen from the 1st, 2d and 3d Wards as Whigs, and those from the 4th, 5th and 6th as Democrats.

The following city officers were elected by Council at its meeting on the 8th of January: Clerk, Calvin Stratton; Treasurer, John Johnson; Marshal, E. C. Bandy; Deputy Marshal, J. M. Hughes; Bridge Keeper, W. W. Martin; Attorney, Wiley Williams; Physician, John B. Hoxey; Clerk of Market, William W. Tilley; Keeper of Hospital, B. Ingram; Sexton, Jerry Terry; Port Wardens—L. Livingston, J. R. Young, H. Young, F. Wilhelm and John Kyle.

All Whigs, except Messrs. Williams, Bandy, Hughes and Wilhelm.

Salaries for the year were fixed as follows: Clerk of Council, $350; Marshal $500; Deputy Marshal, $500; Treasurer, $500; Bridge Keeper, $400; City Physician, $200; Clerk of Market, $150.

Health officers elected by Council: Dr, Thos. Hoxey, President; Alex. McDougald, John Rounds, Dr. S. A. Billing, Dr. M. Woodruff, Joseph Kyle, James Barron, Thomas Sanders, James Kivlin, W. W. Torry, Charles Wise. Mr. Torry resigned in March, and Wm. Allen was appointed.

Fire Wardens—R. H. Green, N. M. C. Robinson, H. T. Hall, F. A. Wright, J. S. Norman, B. F. Coleman.

Contracts for crossing the bridge were made this year again.

An ordinance was passed in January, requiring the owners of all houses on Broad street, from Franklin to Thomas street, to number them.

The first fire company of Columbus was the one organized in 1843, as a Hook and Ladder Company. Its roster is given in the preceding chapter. In 1844, in accordance with an act of the Legislature, it resolved itself into an engine fire company, receiving its engine by steamer on the 20th of January. The funds for its purchase had been furnished by the citizens. The company, numbering about 75 members, turned out to receive it and convey it to the engine house. They were in uniform and made a fine appearance. The organization of the Hook and Ladder company was retained.

This engine is still in Columbus, and up to quite a recent period was in active service. It is now laid up because the company last using it have obtained a newer engine.

At the first fire which occurred after the arrival of the engine, the company turned out promptly, but the scarcity of water prevented the efficient working of the engine.

The following were the principal city taxes levied this year : On every $100 worth of town property, stock in trade, capital employed by brokers or exchange merchants, stock in bank, insurance or trust company, or money loaned, 25 cents ; on each negro slave, 25c.; free persons of color $6 ; practitioners of law, physic, factors or brokers, $4 each ; retail liquor license, $25.

In February, Council appointed Messrs. Thomas Morris, Theobold Howard and B. F. Coleman, Appraisers, to assess the value of the real estate of the city. These gentlemen reported the total valuation $1,266,055, which is the first report of the kind we have been able to find.

States Lewis, Alderman of the 5th Ward, resigned in February; and B. F. Malone, Aldermen of the 2d Ward, in March. W. W. Torry was elected in the place of Mr. Lewis, and N. M. C. Robinson in place of Mr. Malone.

Messrs. Howard and Echols made application for an extension of the time within which they were required to complete the dam across the river, and it was extended to the first of November of this year.

On the 10th day of April a contract between the Mayor and Aldermen on the one part, and Col. John H. Watson on the other part, was signed, by which Col. Watson was authorized to bring water into the city by means of aqueducts—the privilege to continue for forty years, but not to the prevention of similar works by the city authorities or other persons. No money consideration is expressed in the agreement, but it is plain that Col. Watson was to find reimbursement in tolls for water supplied to the citizens.

A committee of Council made a report, on the 15th of June, upon the petition of Mrs. Seaborn Jones, President of the Methodist Female Benevolent and Educational Society, asking a deed to certain lots in the northeastern portion of the city, for the purpose of erecting an asylum thereon. The committee reported that those lots had never been sold, and the title appeared to be still in the State, and recommend that Council approve the grant of the lots by the State and confirm it by the grant of any interest which the city might have in them. The report was accepted.

On the same day Council deeded to Jonathan Bridges a lot next on the north side to water lot No. 1, and west of Bay street, in consideration of Bridges' completing the sewer crossing the lot and keeping it in perpetual repair.

In December, Council made a contract with Patrick Adams for the completion of the sewer at the foot of St. Clair street, and the one between the bridge and the wharf, by their extension to the river and the construction of wells or reservoirs above their mouths—the work to be completed in one year, and the price to be paid $1,600.

On the 25th of December, the *Times*, after alluding to the business activity and bustle then apparent on the streets, recapitulated the business and industrial establishments of the city as follows:

"There are in the city 209 establishments where a regular business is carried on. They are as follows:

"Dry good stores 26, grocery stores 57, provision stores 24, silver smiths 5, clothing stores 5, hat store 1, hardware stores 2, book and stationery stores 2, saddle and harness 3, tobacconist store 1, shoe stores 7, bar rooms 17, auction stores 2, drug stores 5, crockery store 1, confectioner 1, tin ware 2, cabinet warehouses 4, bakeries 3, cotton warehouses 5, livery stables 4, hotels 4, book binderies 2, iron foundry 1, printing offices 3, bank and bank agencies 4, blacksmiths 10, carriage warehouses 2, cotton gin maker 1, wheelrights 3.—Total 209.

"There are besides, about 35 lawyers and 25 physicians, 5 churches, with regular pastors, to-wit: The Presbyterian, Baptist, Episcopal, Methodist, and Roman Catholic.

"There is a large cotton factory on the river nearly completed, which we hope to see followed by many more, which will doubtless be the case, as the falls in the river at the city afford the finest water power in the world.

"Columbus is beautifully situated on a broad and noble plain, around which the Chattahoochee sweeps, and is hemmed in by high hills, on both the Georgia and Alabama side. Level as the plain is, it is perfectly drained by the well-timed enterprise of former city authorities. The health of the place is unrivaled, as the statistics of the county show, that nowhere, not only in this latitude, nor in any other latitude in the United States, has the mortality been less in proportion to population.

"The annual income of the city, is in round numbers, $20,000; its municipal expenses about $5,000 or $6,000. The debt of the Corporation is something the rise of $40,000, about three-fourths of which is held by John G. Winter, and the balance is due to the State of Georgia. Nothing but judicious management is necessary to give a proper direction to the natural resources of Columbus, to develope its business energies, and to double its wealth, trade and population, in a few years."

INCIDENTS.

There was a great deal of rain in January, and the river rose higher than at any time since the white settlement of Columbus, except on the occasion of the "Harrison Freshet" in 1841, and it was very near as high as then. The stages then running from Columbus east to Madison, and west to Franklin on the Montgomery and West Point Railroad, were stopped for a week by high water.

On Monday, March 11th, Henry Clay, the Whig candidate for President of the United States, visited Columbus. He came in a stage-coach from Montgomery. When near here he was welcomed by Major W. B. Harris, and the Russell County Clay Club escorted him to the city bridge. Major James Holland was Marshal. An immense multitude, with Col. A. K. Ayer, met him. Mr. Clay was put in a carriage drawn by six cream horses, and amid shouts of welcome was carried to the old Oglethorpe Hotel. He was escorted to a platform in front, where he was welcomed in a long speech by Col. Hines Holt, to which he eloquently replied. Thousands present. In the afternoon Mr. Clay received his friends. A daughter of the late Dr. A. L. Acee, of Talbot County, then not thirteen years of age, presented him with a beautiful and highly finished lance. Mr. Clay remained in Columbus two days and then went on his way to Washington.

On Friday night, March 22d, the $4,000 residence of P. A. Clayton was burned, and his family barely escaped with their lives. The lottery office narrowly missed being destroyed that day.

The Methodist Conference was held in Columbus in January, Bishop Soule presiding. The ministers attending were most hospitably entertained by the citizens, and passed resolutions of thanks for their generous reception.

The Phœnix Bank, of Columbus, closed doors in March. The President, F. Martine, was arrested in New York and brought back to Columbus, and committed to answer the charge of fraud. The outstanding circulation of this bank did not exceed $35,000, and it was said that the citizens of Columbus did not lose more than $10,000 by it. It was an institution established here by foreigners and New Yorkers, and appears to have been run for their private purposes, though a few good citizens had some stock in it. Its chief stockholders were G. Kostar, F. Martine, A. Mayor, and Lentilton & Co., all them of or recently from New York, and formerly from Europe. Nathan McGehee was also a large stockholder. It was charged that Kostar had drawn out the specie and fled to Europe. The bank was a resuscitated "wild cat" upon the ruins of the Farmers' Bank of Chattahoochee. Martine was in May released on *habeas corpus*.

On the 26th of April, Columbus Lodge of the I. O. O. F. celebrated the introduction of the Order in the United States. Alex. H. Cooper delivered the address. A. K. Ayer, J. S.

Norman, M. Woodruff, T. K. Wynne, and L. B. Lemmon, constituted the committee of arrangements.

On the 5th of June the fine residence of Mr. Wiley E. Jones, in the suburbs of Columbus, was burned by an incendiary, afterwards discovered to be a mulatto girl belonging to the family, who was arrested, confessed, and was whipped and imprisoned. She said she burned the house because she was not permitted to see a young man as often as she wished.

July 4th was celebrated by the Columbus Guards. At the Methodist church the Declaration of Independence was read by L. T. Downing and an address delivered by A. J. R. Bowdre. The Sunday schools celebrated it in the Baptist church where Rev. Mr. Curry delivered an address, and Revs. Dr. Goulding and Mr. Slade assisted.

The Methodist church in Columbus passed strong resolutions condemning the action of the General Conference regarding Bishop Andrew, and favoring a division of the church. The committeemen were Dr. A. H. Flewellen, J. M. Chambers, Seaborn Jones, Van Leonard and Geo. F. Foster. Dr. L. Pierce was present and favored the action. Daniel Curry, the pastor, and an opponent of slavery, left in consequence.

The election of Polk and Dallas was celebrated with an illumination of the houses of Democrats in Columbus and other demonstrations of delight.

PERSONAL.

On January 1st T. A. Brannon was elected Sheriff; Buckner Beasly, Clerk of the Superior Court; Nelson McLester, Clerk of the Inferior Court; F. A. Jepson, Tax Collector; P. M. Thomas, Tax Receiver; John Bunnell, Coroner; Thos. J. Hand, Surveyor.

Mrs. James N. Bethune, assisted by Mrs. Janette Bethune, had charge of the Muscogee Female Seminary this year; Rev. T. B. Slade continued his High School; H. H. McQueen had an English and Classical School; Dr. Andrews had a High School for boys; James H. Hampton continued his

Superintendence of the Columbus Female Seminary; W. B.
Leary had a Classical and Mathematical School; J. H. Goodale was principal of the Wynnton Male Academy, and R. W.
B. Munro of the Wynnton Female Academy. Mr. O'Hara,
aided by his daughters, was also engaged in teaching. It
appears that Columbus and its vicinity were well provided
with schools and accomplished teachers.

Thos. Samford was P. E. and Daniel Curry stationed M. E.
minister at Columbus this year.

On the 10th of April, Mr James Van Ness retired from the
joint proprietorship of the *Columbus Times*, and John Forsyth became associated with Wm. L. Jeter in its management.

A most lamentable occurrence, on the 22d of October, was
the death of Mr. James C. Cook, Sr., one of the oldest citizens
of Columbus, who was killed by a runaway horse. He was
thrown from his buggy against a tree at his own door.

On the 9th of November, as two little boys about ten years
of age, were firing a toy cannon, one of them, a son of Hon.
Joseph Sturgis, stooped before the gun and received the
charge in his neck, killing him in a few minutes.

MARRIAGES.

January 2—John Hazelton and Adaline Ramsey. Jan. 4, Jas.
W. Johnson and Elizabeth Hastings. Jan. 15, Thompson Cream-
er and Caroline R. Piggott. Jan. 18, Elisha C. Bowen and Elvira
C. Bevill. Jan. 22, William Wadsworth and Mary Watley.

February 1—Jonathan Weaver and Emily Moye. Feb. 2,
David Snell and Cornelia L. Snellgrove. Feb. 5, Jacob Dorff
and Nancy Hopkins. Feb. 8, Edmond Pass and Amelia A. Hill,
James Thompson and Nancy Williams. Feb. 13, Lewis P. Mosely
and Mary Ann McCouney. Feb. 15, Joseph Carswell and Priscilla G. Baker. Feb. 17, Oscar P. Jones and Eliza Mooney. Feb.
21, Gottlieb Conzelman and Jorgine Gronbeck. Feb. 22, Geo. R.
Dingle and Nancy Sealy. Feb. 25, Wm. G. Booth and Sarah E.
Parker.

March 1—David H. Funderburke and Martha Ann Pope.
March 7, John Fussell and Sarah Powell. March 21, Richard

Patten and Martha A. B. Hodges, Robt. G. Mitchell and Jane Ann Cook. March 24, Daniel D. Ridenhour and Mary A. Patillo. March 25, Owen Duffee and Sarah Lowther. March 26, Robert T. Simons and Sarah A. L. Patrick. March 28, Benjamin Alford and Frances Wilson. March 31, Rheddock Smith and Mary Wade.

April 6—Arthur McGill and Catharine Sanders. April 30, Andrew J. Risher and Minerva McMichael.

May 6—Allen A. Goldsmith and Mary Jeter. May 22, Jas. W. Hewitt and Caroline Rowell. May 23, Wm. H. Pickard and Rosetta Culpepper, Geo. W. Robinson and Caroline A. Sanders· May 26, Simeon Dean and Ann Willingham, Daniel W. Brown and Sabina A. Bailey.

June 6—Thos. J. Abbott and Eliza Pernoy. June 12, Thos. M. Baldwin and Sophia Dobbs. June 20, Geo. H. Betz and Mary Jane Miller. June 25, Williamson Rodgers and Elizabeth J. Colson.

July 17—Hyman Allbritton and Louisa Farmer. July 20, Jos. C. Payne and Amanda J. Reed. July 27, Hansford C. Patterson and Sarah E. Bell.

August 2—John Collins and Matilda Scoggins. August 10, Edward M. Dozier and Behethala Brunson. August 11, Eli Gray and Eliza Gray. August 13, D. C. Miller and Mildred R. Alston. August 18, Osborn Eley and Jane Russell. August 20, Stephen D. Pepper and Sarah Falkenbury. August 26, William Howell and Angeline Hearn. August 29, Edward E. Sizemore and Jane E. E. Worsham.

September 4—Jesse Wood and Margaret Ivey, Daniel Collins and Bethire R. Stuart. Sept. 5, Peter J. Gillstrap and Sarah Q. A. Parker, Christopher Culpepper and Mary Boland. Sept. 8, John Calvin and Elizabeth Whatley. Sept. 11, Joseph Brown and Elizabeth Kelley. Sept. 19, Henry Morris and Adaline Pike. Sept. 22, Wm. A. Lowe and Ann Thurman.

October 2—James Chordry and Martha Phillips. Oct. 7, Pinkney Hazzelton and Clarrissa Doles. Oct. 10, Joseph Morris and Almenia R. Craigg, Alexander H. Cooper and Ann E. Billups. Oct. 13, Jas. A. Booth and Mary Ann Pope, Major J. Harris and Martha Hearn. Oct. 24, Wm. S. Green and Virginia E. Rogers. Oct. 29, Jas. M. Cobb and Elizabeth McNorton.

November 3—Jonas B. Russell and Susan Morris. Oct. 5, James J. Brown and Elizabeth Mott. Oct. 6, Jacob Johnson and Mary C. Higdon. Oct. 7, Jas. C. Cook and Mary Louisa Redd, Washington Purnell and Phebe Mahon, Randal Jones and Frances Cannon. Oct. 14, Augustus Howard and Ann J. Lindsay. Oct. 17, David B. Edwards and Elizabeth Johnson. Oct. 28, Jos. W. Woolfolk and Lucinda M. Winter, John Etheridge and Nancy Castleberry.

December 5—Jas. D. Williford and Almira V. Brooks. Dec. 12, Thos. Jordan and Emily Wiggins, George W. Tomberlin and Jane Rogers. Dec. 18, Samuel Cowles and Nancy S. Rockmore. Dec. 19, Jas W. Gibson and Mary Gray, Josiah Morris and Sarah E. Harvey. Dec. 22, John Odom and Mary Ealy. Dec. 27, Thos. Lowry and Mary L. Stallings. Dec. 31, Geo. W. Christian and Mary Smith.

DEATHS.

Jan. 12—Mrs. Elizabeth Johnson, wife of Jacob M. Johnson.

Feb. 10—Pearce A. Phillips, "the last of his father's house", in the 19th year of his age.

March 9—Capt Wm. R. Bell, a native of Beaufort, N. C.

May 18—Mrs. Mary F. Cleveland, widow of Hon. Jesse F. Cleveland.

July 7—Milton Williams, Esq., Solicitor of the Chattahoochee Circuit.

August 8—Mrs. Mary Ann Terry, wife of G. B. Terry.

August 22—Adaline Blackmar, infant daughter of James D. and Eliza A. Johnson.

August 24—Edward W. Williams, formerly of Savannah.

August 28—Camillus T. Moise, aged 27 years.

August 31—James Hugh, son of G. B. Terry.

Nov. 9—Joseph A., son of Hon. J. S. Sturgis.

The Board of Health reported the total number of deaths during the year 1844, 75, of whom 21 were men, 16 boys, 14 women, 11 girls, 13 children, and 6 unknown. The diseases most fatal were fevers, of which 11 died, of consumption 10, and of bowel complaints 10. All these deaths were those of white persons.

1845.

Manufacturing Enterprise Increasing—Contemplated Railroad Connections—Trouble About the Bridge—The Cemetery Enlarged, &c.

The municipal election on the first Saturday in January, for Mayor and Aldermen, resulted as follows:

Mayor, John G. Winter; Aldermen, First Ward—W. S. Holstead, J. J. McKendree; Second Ward—Dr. M. Woodruff and B. F. Malone; Third Ward—R. N. R. Bradwell, H. C. Anderson; Fourth Ward—A. K. Ayer, Jas. Everett; Fifth Ward—Wm. B. Robinson, J. L. Morton; Sixth Ward—A. G. Marshall and Jas. Green. Dr. Hoxey ran against Winter. The election was by wards.

Council met on Monday, the 6th of January, and chose the following city officers, with the salaries annexed: William Brooks, Marshal, salary $500; Neil G. Smith, Deputy Marshal, salary $500; George W. Turrentine, Treasurer, $500; Calvin Stratton, Clerk of Council, $350; W. W. Martin, Bridge Keeper, $400; J. B. Hoxey, City Physician, $200; W. W. Tilly, Clerk of the Market, $150; Wiley Williams, City Attorney; B. Ingram, Keeper of the Hospital; Jeremiah Terry, Sexton; Dr. Thos. Hoxey, President of the Board of Health.

The following gentlemen were elected Health officers, two for each ward: Wm. Y. Barden, Robert H. Green; John Kyle, Dr. S. A. Billing; Dr. E. L. DeGraffenried, N. L. Howard; N. M. C. Robinson, P. A. Clayton; W. W. Torry, William Alley; Joseph Wiggins, John A. Norton. Afterwards J. M. Wesson was elected in the place of Wm. Y. Barden, resigned.

Five Port Wardens were elected, as follows: T. M. Hogan, Wm. Barrow, F. G. Davis, John R. Young, and George W. Martin.

The following gentlemen were elected Fire Wardens: J. C. Ruse, John Condon, James S. Norman, George A. Peabody, Lewis Livingston, B. F. Coleman.

The tax ordinance of this year imposed about the same general rates of taxation as that of 1844.

The contract system for crossing the bridge by the year was again adopted—no contract for less than $10.

In January, Council appointed Messrs. E. W. B. Spivey, John T. Walker, and Wm. H. Alston, Appraisers, to assess the value of the real estate of the city. They reported, on the 4th of February, the whole valuation $1,192,295, being somewhat less than the previous year's assessment.

The Committee on Police appointed the following City Guard for the year, to be paid each $15 per month: T. A. Bosworth, Silas McMichael, T. W. Dickson.

The Committee on Finance reported in January that the city would have to pay during the year $3,600 to John G. Winter, $9,000 to the State, and $333 to Patrick Adams, besides about $1,000 of accounts for last year and the current expenses of the city for the present year. By arrangement, Messrs. Mustian and Mott had agreed, in consideration of the passage of the bridge by their line of stages, to hold over until the end of the year, without interest, $3,200 of the city's certificates of deposit held by them.

The above report was referred to the Committee on Ways and Means, and this Committee reported the entire indebtedness of the city about $63,750, of which amount $4,791 was then due, and $10,171 23 would fall due during the year—making in all $14,961 90 for the year to be provided for, besides $7,500 estimated current expenses. They estimated the income at $17,637 90—leaving $4,824 to be provided for, besides a small amount of city bonds, certificates, &c., that might have to be redeemed.

Besides a considerable amount of the city's bills still in circulation, a large quantity of "shinplasters" issued by other corporations and by individuals were afloat. We copy from the *Enquirer* the following quotations for March of this irredeemable currency:

Bank of Columbus bills 70 per cent. discount; Phœnix Bank, of Columbus, no sale; Irwinton Bridge, 25 per cent. discount; Insurance Bank, of Columbus, no circulation; Chattahoochee Railroad and Banking Company, broke; City Council of Columbus, 10 per cent. discount; Scott & Carhart's shinplasters, at par; E. & R. Graves' shinplasters, 10 per cent. discount; Sight Checks on New York and Boston, ½ per cent. premium.

Columbus had the following fire-proof warehouses: H. S. Smith & Co.'s, capacity 14,000 bales; J. C. & F. N. Ruse's, 15,000; Yonge, Garrard & Hooper's, 15,000. E. S. Greenwood & Co. were building a fire-proof warehouse with slate roof—capacity, 10,000 bales. Each warehouse opened west on a street that extended to the river.

A committee of Council reported in favor of the enlargement of the cemetery by the addition of 602 feet in length and 320 feet in width, and the enclosure of the whole under one new fence; also a sale of burying lots to defray the expense of this improvement. Whereupon Council appointed another committee to have a survey of the grounds made, and to carry out the plan and recommendations of the first committee, if it could be done without expense to the city.

In March, Alderman Everett, of the 4th Ward, resigned, and P. A. Clayton was elected in his stead.

Permission was given to the "Columbus Engine Company" to erect a fire engine house on the west side of Front street, at its junction with St. Clair street—where the engine house now stands. On the 19th of April Council appropriated $200 towards building the house.

We learn from a memorial presented to Council by Messrs. John H. Howard and Josephus Echols, that their companys' cotton factory had in operation this year about 1,100 spindles and 20 looms. They also reported that their upper canal, when completed, would supply water enough to propel 200,000 spindles. They asked a release from their obligation to construct the lower canal within a specified time, and for absolute deeds to the water lots, which would enable them to effect sales of a portion of them and thus extend the manufacturing business of the city. Council adopted a resolution agreeing to the requests contained in the memorial.

This action of Council appears to have met with opposition from the citizens. At a called meeting of Council on the 21st April, the clerk was directed to publish a hand bill calling a meeting of citizens to consider the memorial of Messrs. Howard and Echols, on the following Friday evening; and at its regular meeting on the 26th of April, Council passed a resolution declaring that its former action was not intended to release Messrs. Howard and Echols from or modify any of the conditions respecting the dam and upper race, or any of the reservations of the city in the original contract, in regard to the fisheries, the right to take gravel, and the keeping of the dam and upper race in good repair forever.

In this connection the *Enquirer* states: "Col. Farrish Carter, of Scottsboro', and Dr. Baird, of Alabama, have purchased large interests in factories here. They now have 1,200 spindles at work; very soon they will have 3,500. They will proceed to erect additional buildings, and in twelve months will have from 10,000 to 15,000 spindles in operation.

By resolution, adopted on the 9th of June, the Marshal was instructed to have a ditch cut so as to turn the branch running through Randolph and Forsyth streets into the ditch back of the city.

Under the head of "What Next," the *Times* of April 16th, refers to the project of Telegraphic connection with New York, via New Orleans and Mobile, as follows, the Telegraph having only been brought into practical use the year before (May 27,) by a line between Baltimore and Washington:

"A new and grand project is on foot, which, if successful, will produce the astounding result of getting one's news in Columbus from New York, by the way of Mobile and New Orleans. Is not the world going ahead too fast ? Space is annihilated as to the transition of mind, and almost to matter, by the Telegraph and Steam."

The *Times* this year urgently advocated an effort on the part of the city to have the Montgomery and West Point Railroad brought to Columbus. It was then only completed to Auburn, 35 miles from Columbus.

On the 18th of August a committee of mechanics, appointed by Council, reported the bridge to be in a condition needing repairs—the floor sunk in some places, some of the supporting timbers out of perpendicular line, and parts of the structure swayed down stream. Council passed a resolution calling upon Mr. Godwin, the builder, to observe his contract, which required him to keep the bridge in good repair for the space of five years.

At its meeting on the 15th September, Council adopted the following preamble and resolutions:

"Whereas, on the first of January, the City Council in assessing the taxes for the year 1845, and regulating tolls across the bridge for said year, relieved several articles from any liability to pay the tolls that should come across the bridge from Alabama for the mutual benefit of Columbus and Girard; and whereas, it is known to this Council that the authorities of Russell county, Ala., have imposed a tax or toll upon all wagons, carriages, men and horses and foot passengers, thereby militating materially against the interests of this city, and not extending to Columbus that leniency that the authorities of the city have to Alabama, which the principles of justice would dictate,

"*Be it Resolved*, That for the purpose of removing that obstruction (the toll across said bridge in Girard, Ala.) which materially involves the interest of Columbus as well as Girard and the county of Russell, a committee of three be appointed by the Chair, whose duty it shall be to confer with the authorities of Russell in relation to the propriety of enforcing and collecting such toll, and in the event that said committee should not be able, after a consultation had, to effect or dispense with said toll, the bridge-keeper be instructed forthwith to make all persons residing in Russell county alone to pay all tolls across the bridge at Columbus that they have been released from heretofore, also to collect toll from foot passengers who reside in Russell county, but none others."

The committee appointed were Aldermen Marshall, Mc-Kendree and Robinson.

On the 8th of October, Council passed a resolution instructing the bridge-keeper to collect tolls from all foot passengers across the bridge except from citizens of Muscogee county; also a resolution appointing a committee of three to make inquiries in regard to the lawfulness of constructing a bridge across the creek in Girard, and to confer with Col. Banks about building it on his land.

It appears in the proceedings of Council that the bridge over the creek in Girard was released from toll before the close of the year, and that Benj. H. Baker, of Russell county, Ala., was largely instrumental in effecting this adjustment.

On the 25th of October Council substantially reconsidered the above action.

A resolution was adopted in October, fixing the price of lots in the new burying ground at $5, that being the highest price bid.

Council adopted resolutions in October, appointing a committee of citizens to attend a convention in Macon of the stockholders of the Central Railroad, to see what could be done towards procuring an extension of that road from Macon to Columbus, or connecting with it at Barnesville.

The committee went to Macon, and had a conference with the Central Railroad officers. Columbus wanted connection with Macon via Barnesville (the Macon and Western Railroad, then called the Monroe Railroad, was being extended to Atlanta.) The Central road, however, wanted a direct line to Columbus. L. O. Reynolds, surveyor of the Central, reported the distance between Barnesville and Columbus seventy-two miles, and between Macon and Columbus little less than one hundred. The cost of both would be about the same—$1,000,000. The result was that President R. R. Cuyler and the Board advocated the lower line, and looked to a connection with the Montgomery road at Auburn, to which point it had been extended. The Board recommended to the stockholders of the Central Railroad: To ask an amendment of the charter to extend the road to Columbus; to authorize a new subscription of $1,000,000 (one-fourth to be paid on subscribing) for that purpose. If that be not adopted, to incorporate a new company to build a road from the Central Railroad to Columbus by the lower route. If application be made by others for a charter from Barnesville to Columbus, no opposition or unfriendly feeling to be exhibited against it. If both charters be granted, an understanding may be had by which one of the two projects may be carried on and the other abandoned. Subsequently the Legislature incorporated the Muscogee Railroad Company; also, to change the name of the Munroe Railroad to Macon and Western, with power to extend a branch to Columbus.

There was some excitement on the subject of small-pox in October and November. A Dr. McGoulrich, of Macon, had sent to Columbus, in the stage, a small-pox patient, stating that he knew his disease was only chicken-pox, but there was evidence to show that he had admitted that he knew it to be a case of small-pox, and had sent off the patient to get rid of him. Council transmitted the evidence in the case to the authorities of Macon.

A building had been selected in the Sixth Ward for the temporary reception of persons who had been exposed to small-pox, and this building was torn down by residents of the ward. Council instructed the Marshal to commence prosecution against the parties who destroyed the building.

It does not appear that the disease obtained much foothold, but it occasioned much alarm, and led to the adoption of vigorous measures to prevent its spread. A circus company in the city was prohibited from performing because one of its members had the disease; measures were taken, in co-operation with the county authorities, to quarantine or remove all cases to the hospital, and provision was made for general vaccination.

The county census takers reported in December that they had taken the census of the city of Columbus separately, and made the following return:

773d District—Free white persons, 1,963; slaves, 1,230; free persons of color, 25. Total, 3,218.

668th District—Free white persons, 1,096; slaves, 521; free persons of color, 31. Total, 1,648.

Aggregate population, 4,886; aggregate number of families, 597.

The total population of Muscogee county was 16,343.

We find mention of the following hotels in Columbus this year: Oglethorpe House, on the corner of Oglethorpe and Randolph streets, Commodore Hurd, landlord; Mansion House, on Broad street, above Bryan, Captain Barrow, landlord; City Hotel, corner of Broad and St. Clair streets, the Messrs. Bass, landlords; Kentucky House, on Oglethorpe street, above the Oglethorpe House, Wm. Perry, landlord; Central Hotel, corner of Broad and Randolph streets, G. W. Dillard, landlord.

The *Enquirer* of December reported, "the manufacturing excitement is largely on the increase. Messrs. Howard, Bridges, Carter, Baird and Jeter are pushing their improvements ahead. Messrs. Van Leonard and others, are also erecting a factory a mile or two above our city. Messrs. Clapp, Chandler and Stewart are successfully and most profitably employed in manufacturing several descriptions of cotton goods. We have heard of other companies formed or to be formed."

On Friday, 19th of December, about midnight, a fire broke out in Mitchell & Baugh's store on Broad street, one door below Banks' corner and opposite Lyceum Hall, and in a few hours the entire square, bounded by Broad, Randolph, Oglethorpe and Bryan streets (except that small portion above Mr. Well's refectory on Oglethorpe) was converted into a heap of ruins. Loss $150,000. The Oglethorpe and other houses were on fire, but were put out. Water was scarce. The Columbus Guards guarded the property. The origin of the fire was unknown. The Columbus *Times* office was burned, but enough material saved to go on. The *Enquirer* building, opposite the square, was threatened and office moved. What was known as the "granite block," valued at $18,000, on Oglethorpe street, belonging to D. McDougald, was burned. Most of the houses on the block were of brick. Banks and Winter lost heavily. The block was then one of the busiest in the city. Dr. R. A. Ware's residence was saved.

Mr. Josiah Pranglin, an active and valuable member of the Fire Company, had a wall to fall on him and break both his thighs and otherwise injure him. He got well.

Among the boats running this winter were the Columbus, Notion, Lotus, Boston, Apalachicola, Augusta, Peytona and Emily.

The *Times* of the 8th January publishes a letter from President Polk regretting he cannot take Columbus in his route to Washington City, and receive the hospitalities of the Democracy tendered him through a committee of the party, consisting of Messrs. Jacob M. Guerry, Walter T. Colquitt, and Seaborn Jones.

Columbus seems this year to have had much trouble with the money currency then used, and the *Times* has a strong editorial on the "Uselessness and viciousness" of the "Shinplaster System," and asks the question, "When are we to be delivered from a shinplaster currency?" Some of the merchants were refusing to take the "shinplasters."

Montgomery was now pushing her railroad towards West Point. The following report of altitudes, &c., made by M. A. A. Dexter, chief engineer, may be of interest now: "You will perceive that Montgomery and Columbus are on the same level. West Point is 400 feet above either point. The Montgomery Railroad has 1,000 feet absolute elevation each way to the summit. A road to Columbus would have but some 600, and possibly less. This saving of 400 feet or more in elevation would effect an enormous aggregate in favor of the Columbus branch in a year's running."

Cotton took a wide range in prices this year. It opened in January at 2 to 4½c., principal sales at 3 to 3½c. The first bale of the new crop was brought in on the 5th of August, by Thos. Gilbert, of Stewart county, and sold to Mr. LeGrand Wright at 8¼c. The market for the new commercial year opened in September at 6½ to 7c., and drooped to 5½ to 6½c in November. The closing quotations, December 16th, were 5½ to 6½c. The receipts of the year ending August 31st were *about* 85,000 bales, an *estimated* falling off of about 30,-000 from the preceding year's receipts.

INCIDENTS.

A new Presbyterian Church—the building now used for the Male Public School—was dedicated on the 25th of January. Rev. Dr. Goulding officiated.

John C. Tozier, of Columbus, on March 18th, was killed by falling out of the stage from Macon. Both wheels passed over him.

A Board of Trade was organized in Columbus on the 3d of July, with Henry King, chairman, and C. E. Mims, secretary.

Rev. Thomas Jepson, of the M. E. Church, was thrown from his horse on August 12th, nine miles north of Columbus, and died four hours after. His age was 40 years·

The mail and travel connections of Columbus, as late as this year, were all made by stages and boats. Messrs. Mustian & Mott ran a line of stages connecting the Central with the Montgomery·and West Point Railroad. The point of connection on the last named road was Chehaw at this time. The Northern mail for Columbus came by stage from La Grange.

The steamer Siren, Captain Sharpless, plying between Chattahoochee and Apalachicola Bay, burst one of her boilers, Feb. 26th, as the boat was rounding out from Toney's Landing, and killed six whites and four blacks, among the former a son of Mrs. Tilley, of Columbus. The killed, with the exception of one of the blacks, were a part of the crew.

The steamboat Lowell, Captain Moore, was snagged and

sunk on March 4th, a few miles below Fort Gains, on the Chattahoochee river, at a place called "the Cowpen." The principal part of her cargo and machinery was saved. The boat was represented as not worth raising if it were practicable.

The steamer Viola, Captain Van Vechten, was snagged and sunk in the Flint river, a few miles below Albany, about the same time. She was represented as a total wreck and about one-half of her cargo—1,030 bales of cotton—a total loss. Captain V. owned half of the "Siren," which had blown up a few weeks before.

The steamer Charleston, Captain Freeman, collapsed one of her boilers, while crossing Uchee Shoals, sixteen miles below Columbus, on the 3d of May. Fortunately only one person, a negro man, was injured, and he only slightly scalded.

On Saturday, June 21st, the Columbus Guards started on a visit to LaGrange. The brass band numbered sixteen pieces, taught by Sergt. Berneriter, leader of the United States band at Fort Moultrie. They returned via the White Sulphur Springs, where they were given a ball. The company numbered sixty men. Officers—P. T. Schley, Captain; Jno. E. Davis, 1st Lieutenant; E. R. Goulding, 2d Lieutenant; John Forsyth, 3d Lieutenant. They paraded in Columbus July 4th. Hon. M. J. Wellborn, an honorary member, delivered an oration, and D. Chandler Holt, a member, read the Declaration of Independence.

PERSONAL.

The following county officers were elected on the 6th of January: Justices of the Inferior Court, Kenneth McKenzie, John M. Bethune, N. L. Howard, G. W. Ross, and Josephus Echols; Tax Collector, Jacob W. Frost; Tax Receiver, J. C. W. Rogers.

Of the Columbus Methodist Episcopal District, Rev. T. Samford was appointed presiding elder, and Rev. J. E. Evans to be pastor at Columbus

Sam'l W. Flournoy retired from the editorial chair of the *Enquirer*, and was succeeded by Col. J. S. Calhoun.

Mr. Wm. L. Jeter, who had been connected with the *Times* sold his interest in that paper to Mr. Marcus Johnston, formerly editor of the Macon *Democrat*. It is announced in the issue of April 23d.

The *Enquirer* of May 21st is in mourning for the death of Dr. W. B. Ector, late proprietor and editor of the paper.

The Superior Court, Judge Sturgis presiding, met in Columbus. Grand Jurors were: W. P. Yonge, foreman; W. E. Jones, Geo. W. Jones, S. F. Grimes, Wm. Amos, John Hunter, G. Harris, J. J. McKendree, P. Hazzleton, E. Barnard, H. Crew, P. D. Redding, W. J. Rylander, W. A. Bedell, W. H. Kimbrough, J. B. Hill, John Smith, W. A. Douglas, W. B. Roquemore, E. C. Bandy, D. McDougald, W. P. Malone, R. H. Greene. Lawyers present were Hon. Seaborn Jones, H. L. Benning, Hines Holt, R. B. Alexander, James Johnson, Wiley Williams, Judge Cone, A. Cooper, Thad. Sturgis, N. L. Howard, Alex. McDougald, Gen. Bethune, John Schley, Gen. Bailey, J. M. Guerry, A. J. R. Boudre, E. Goulding, C. J. Williams, A. Iverson, Porter Ingram, T. F. Foster, John Forsyth, W. C. Holt, J. Echols, A. S. Foster, J. L. Stephens, C. S. Rockwell.

John Forsyth was appointed Postmaster of Columbus vice G. W. E. Bedell, and took the office in July.

The following were graduates of the Slade Female Institute. They read compositions on Thursday, July 10th, in the Baptist Church : Miss Lucy A. Pitts, subject—Benevolence ; Miss Catharine L. Turrentine—Turn Over a New Leaf ; Miss Sophia H. Shorter—Wisdom and Knowledge ; Miss Cornelia M. Phelps—Contemplation ; Miss Amanda C. Jernigan—Difficulty of Originating a Thing ; Miss Mary E. Rose—He Labors in Vain Who Strives to Please All; Miss Lucy A. Barnett—When I Leave School; Miss Mary E. Key—death of her mother prevented her attendance. Col. Weeden was musical instructor. L. T. Downing, Esq., delivered the address.

Capt. S. A. Bailey, having resigned the Captaincy of the

Columbus Guards, Captain P. T. Schley, was elected in his stead early in February.

In October, James S. Calhoun was elected Senator, and John L. Mustian and N. L. Howard, Representatives of Muscogee county—all Whigs.

Allen Lawhon, Intendant of the town of Columbus in 1832 and 1833, was a native of North Carolina. He removed from that State first to one of the eastern counties of Georgia, and thence to Columbus in 1830. He was a lawyer by profession, and was a man of energy and public spirit, making many friends by his intelligent interest in all matters of local improvement. He removed from Columbus to Cherokee Georgia in 1840, and there engaged in prospecting and mining for gold. He died about the year 1858.

John Fontaine, first Mayor of the city of Columbus, was one of its earliest settlers. He was one of its best and most extensive business men—a man of large mercantile and planting interests, also prominently connected with its manufacturing enterprises. He was noted for conscientiousness and uprightness in all his dealings. During the late civil war he was distinguished for his charities and his efforts to keep down the rise of prices that so seriously injured the cause of the Confederacy. He died on the 4th of November, 1866, in the 76th year of his age.

Gen. Daniel McDougald was a native of North Carolina. He removed to Washington county, Ga., when only eighteen years of age, and thence to Western Georgia. Before settling in Columbus he represented Harris county in the Senate of Georgia. He was for many years a Major General of the militia of Georgia. Removing to Columbus, his fine abilities and popular manners made him at once a favorite of the people. He was, as is shown in preceding pages, several times elected to represent Muscogee county in the Legislature, of which body he was one of the shrewdest and most influential members. He was a man of generous and impulsive disposition, of enlarged charity and patriotic public spirit. Few men had warmer or more devoted friends, though he had also some enemies, chiefly because of his activity and zeal as a politician. He was an excellent judge of human character, and seldom made mistakes in his estimates of men. He died on the 8th of September, 1849, in the 51st year of his age.

MARRIAGES.

January 2—Reuben N. Powell and Mary Ann Hall. Jan. 3, William Morris and Lydia Fuller. Jan. 9, Geo. Washington and Mary A. McCain, Richard Holmes and Elizabeth Cochran. Jan. 16, Jeremiah A. Thompson and Catharine E. Thompson. Jan. 19, Henry R. Clem and Martha A. H. McMurrain. Jan. 24, Geo. W. Hallman and Eliza E. Green. Jan. 26, John Ellis and Harriet Miller. Jan. 28, James M. Waddell and Rachel A. Jemison. Jan. 30, Alfred Sweet and Susan McMichael.

February 5—John R. Billups and Clara Boykin. Feb. 6, James Patillo and Susan Holmes. Feb. 10, Henry C. Bradley and Mary Jane Turner. Feb. 13, William M. Lyle and Mary A. E. F. Rogers. Feb. 16, Archibald C. Tritt and Frances H. Faulkenbury. Feb. 22, Gideon Saul and Elizabeth Sharp.

March 6—Robert H. Rogers and Elizabeth Ann Thomas. March 13, James Witt and Mary Ann McDaniel. March 16, Bradford Peddy and Mary Pace.

April 15—Henry Jones and Elizabeth Bagley. April 16, Wm. H. Mann and Eliza Perry. April 17, Wm. R. Albritton and Zilphia Ann King, Lunsford R. Dean and Mary Austin.

May 13—Absalom Eiland and Elizabeth Pace. May 15, Samuel B. Harvel and Martha Ann S. Nix. May 17, Franklin Truster and Louisa Magner. May 28, John M. McMurren and Mary Ann Motley. June 29, Forbes Bradley and Theresa A. M. Clark.

June 1—Elijah Simpson and Martha Hearn. June 10, William Allen and Mary Cooper. June 12, Rufus Sharp and Malissa Cannon. June 15, Martin Mooney and Rachel Cauley. June 19, Sandford Wamack and Frances M. Hanks. June 30, Stephen G. Wells and Ann Perryman.

July 23—Marcus De LaFayette Sanders and Frances Ann Spigers. July 24, Frederick Shaefer and Massino Groinbeck. July 29, Wm. Walling and Isabella Rogers. July 30, George W. Martin, Jr., and Savannah Jane Forsyth, Reuben Bailey and Eliza Blann.

August 2—Hillery H. Nash and Rhoda Wilson. August 7, John Thornton and Lucinda Ellis. August 14, Randolph B. Moore and Martha L. Forsyth, John W. Barrow and Lucy Ann Jones. August 19, Ab. Dean and Sarah M. Glenn.

September 2—James L. Parks and Sophia Parks. Sept. 11, James

Meeler and Catharine M. Williams. Sept. 14, Joseph M. K. Hearn and Elizabeth Ann Stanford. Sept. 18, Jno. N. Barnett and Lucy A. Pitts, Robert Greer and Lucinda M. Booth. Sept. 23, Jesse Moore and Martha Alford. Sept. 28, Elijah G. Raiford and Elizabeth D. Munroe. Sept. 29, James Simmons and Frances J. Taylor.

October 2—James M. Parkman and Bethany C. Bryan. Oct. 3, Calvin Bland and Lucinda Morgan. Oct. 5, Jos. Robinson and Martha Brown. Oct. 11, James L. Weaver and Elizabeth Jane Mann. Oct. 14, James Morgan and Susan Cartledge. Oct. 16, Leonard K. Rowe and Mary Ann Champion. Oct. 23, James M. Smith and Sarah Cannon. Oct. 25, Willis M. Reeves and Elizabeth A. Bussey.

November 2—Sidney A. Smith and Rebecca Flinn. Nov. 6, Hiram L. Cautran and Susan Berrien Moss. Nov. 20, Felix Hity and Jane Sauls, Geo T. Allen and Eliza C. Fergerson. Nov. 21, David Boswell and Milly A. Bustin. Nov. 23, Morgan McGowen and Emily Darden. Nov. 27, Jeremiah Peddy, Jr., and Mary Ann Frasier, Wm. W. Glenn and Nancy Boyd.

December 2—Edward H. Ranse and Amanda Williams, Benjamin Aycock and Eliza Ann Witt. Dec. 4, L. T. Prince and Mary P. NcGill. Dec. 7, John A. Macon and Elizabeth J. Morris. Dec. 14, Reuben Millsaps and Mary McGovern, John McGovern and Mary Ann Delk. Dec. 17, Jacob W. Frost and Martha Ann Logan. Dec. 25, John G. Smith and Charlotte Evans, Edmund Roland and Alcy Williams. Dec. 28, Charles B. Frederick and Sarah Ann Terry, Asa T. Berry and Martha Ann Morgan. Dec. 31, James P. Durr and Martha Mizell, Williamson Rogers and Murial Caroline Adams.

DEATHS.

February 27—Mary Frances, infant daughter of F. N. Ruse.
March 2—Mrs. Martha Angelina, wife of Dr. A. M. Walker.
April 5—Miss Amelia, daughter of Dr. James B. Slade, of New Orleans. She died in Columbus.
April 5—In Girard, Pleasant G. Clay.
April 17—Mrs. Ann Elizabeth, wife of Alex. H. Cooper, Esq.
May 16—Dr. Wiley B. Ector.
May 22—Mrs. Mary A. Thomas, wife of Grigsby E. Thomas Esq.
June 8—Miss Antoinette Rosseau.
June 27—In Girard, James Allen, infant son of Wm. B. Martin.
July 27—Near Columbus, Dr. E. N. C. Leonard.
July 21—Samuel Albert, infant son of Dr. S. A. Billing.
Sept. 9—Mary Harriet, infant daughter of Col. Hines Holt.
Sept. 18—Mrs. S. H., wife of Dr. H. C. Phelps, of Columbus.
Sept. 28—Mary Claudia, infant daughter of J. E. and C. E. Webster.
Nov. 4—John Thomas, infant son of H. F. Williams.

INDEX.

1827.

A Trading Town, 5; Commissioners appointed to lay it out, 6; The appearance of the proposed site, 6; Location of houses prior to sale of lots, 6; Springs and scenery along the river banks, 7; Appearance of the river, 7; Indians fishing, 7; Indian territory, 8; An old writer's description of the locality, 8; Natural advantages, 8; Extent of the wagon and river trade, 8; The future prospects of Columbus, 9.

1828.

Interest abroad in reference to Columbus, 9; Complaint against tardy action of Commissioners, 10; Population early in the year, 10; Indians, 10; The *Enquirer* established, 10; Advantages of the place for new comers, 11; River improvement and State Engineer's report, 11; First sale of lots, 12; Improvements, 12; Population at the close of year, 13; First person buried in Cemetery, 13; Fourth July celebration, 13; First manufacturing establishment, 13; First steamboat, 14; Hotels, 15; Presidential vote, 15; The first bale cotton sold, 15; Court and county officers and grand jurors, 15; County senator and representative, 15; M. B. Lamar, 16; Walter T. Colquit, 16; Marriages and deaths, 16; Business and professional men, 16, 17; Quotations of merchandise, 17.

1829.

Town incorporated and election of town officials, 17; Election of county officers, 17; Town fisheries, 18; First ordinance of the municipal government, 18; Northern and southern mail, 18; Remaining town lots sold, 18; Certain named streets to be cleared, 18; Improvements of Columbus, 18, 19; Apprehension of Indian troubles, 19; Road laid out from Decatur to Columbus, 19; First bank organized, 19; Steamboat arrivals during year, 19; Mr. E. Avery drowned, 19; Great rise of the Chattahoochee, 20; W. A. Spalding drowned, 20; Temperance society organized, 20; County senator and representative elected, 20; First load of new cotton, 20; Jurisdiction of Superior Court, 20; Town tax, 21; Military companies, 21; Fourth July celebration, 21; Marriages and deaths, 21; Names of business and professional men, 21.

1830.

Continued improvement, 22 ; Population, 22 ; Early difficulties of steamboat navigation, 22, 23 ; Removal of Indians agitated, 23 ; The first fire, 23 ; Debating society, 23 ; Municipal election, 23 ; New paper, 23 ; Controversy with U. S. army officer, 23 ; Discovery of gold, 23 ; Fourth July and Masonic celebrations, 24 ; County senator and representative, 24 ; First steamboat arrival of the winter, 24 ; County officers and grand jurors, 25 ; Julius C. Alford, 25 ; Ulysses Lewis, 25 ; Marriages, deaths, merchants and professional men, 26 ; Quotations of cotton and merchandise, 26.

1831.

Increasing business, 26 ; Municipal election, 27 ; Farmers' Bank of Chattahoochee organized, 27 ; Fire company formed, 27 ; A large dwelling burned, 27 ; Indians suffering from small-pox and want of food, 28 ; Presbyterian church dedicated, 28 ; Local causes of sickness, 28 ; Mail routes, 28, 29 ; Names of steamboats, &c., 29 ; Muscogee Bible Society, 29 ; Fourth July celebration, 29 ; Columbus Volunteers organized, 29 ; Cotton, 30 ; County senator and representative, 30 ; Personals, 30 ; Quotations, 30 ; Merchants, &c., 30, 31 ; Marriages and deaths, 31.

1832.

First bridge across Chattahoochee, 32 ; Municipal officers, 32 ; Duel between Gen. S. Woolfolk and Maj. J. T. Camp, 32, 33 ; 100th anniversary of Washington's birth-day, 33 ; Congress donates land for bridge abutment in Alabama, 33 ; Purchase of Marshallville (Girard), 34 ; Export trade, 34 ; Financial condition of banks, 35 ; General prosperity, 35 ; Legislative enactment for Mayor's Court, 35 ; Gin factory started, 35 ; Indian treaty and proposed removal of Indians, 35, 36 ; Bank of Columbus, 36 ; Fourth July celebration, 36 ; Female Academy and other schools, 36 ; Cholera alarm, 36 ; Presidential election, 36 ; Cotton, 36, 37 ; Personals, 37 ; Spring and fall grand jurors, 37 ; County officers, 37 ; Marriages and deaths, 38 ; Business and professional men, 38.

1833.

Steady business year, 39 ; High political excitement, 39 ; Municipal officers, 39 ; Inferior Court judges, 39 ; Dread of cholera, 39, 40 ; Maj. Camp killed by Col. Milton, 40, 41 ; Indian territory, 41 ; Russell county formed, 41 ; Market house burned, 41 ; Steamboat Georgia sunk, 42 ; Cotton and other quotations, 42 ; Sam'l R. Andrews, 42 ; Dr. S. M. Ingersoll, 42 ; Seaborn Jones, 42, 43 ; John Godwin, 43 ; Sol Smith, 44 ; Personal notices, 44, 45 ; Marriages and deaths, 45.

1834.

Town of Girard (Marshall's Reserve) laid out, 45, 46 ; The bridge question, 46, 47 ; Number of steamboats, 47 ; Bank of Chattahoochee suspends, 47 ; Episcopal association formed, 47 ; Business lively, 48 ; Steamer Columbus,

1838.

1839.

1840.

1841.

Full Name Index
to
"Columbus, Georgia 1827—1865"

PART I

ABBOT
J. J., 135

ABBOTT, 125, 126

ABBOTT
A. J., 116, 124
Thomas J., 153

ABERCROMBIE
James, 114
Miss Martha E., 31
Miss Sarah A., 114

ACRE
Edward, 114

ADAMS, 15

ADAMS
Absalom, 142
Benjamin, 133
Kinyon, 142
Loduska E. A., 142
Martha A., 123
Murial Caroline, 169
Patrick, 148, 156
Sarah Jane, 143
Wiley, 112
Wm. S., 143

ADAMS & MULFORD, 126,
130

AFFLECK
James, 97
Miss Agnes, 103

ALBRITTON
Wm. R., 168

ALCEE
Dr. A. L., 150

ALEXANDER, 71, 106, 130

ALEXANDER
Arabella, 123
R. B., 137, 141, 166

ALFORD
Benj., 153
E. C., 25
Julius C., 16, 25
Maj., 73, 75
Martha, 169
Mrs. Catharine, 45

ALFORD & WINSTON, 17

ALFRED
A. L., 112

ALFRED & PORTER, 97

ALLBRITTON
Hyman, 153

ALLDRIDGE
Miss Martha, 99

ALLEN, 101, 139

ALLEN
Capt., 129
Geo. T., 169
James M., 71
John S., 54, 79, 135
Lewis C., 26, 36, 51, 99,
117
L. C., 27, 37, 89, 107
Martha A., 142
William, 168
Wm., 146

ALLEN L. C., 30

ALLEN & HILL, 57

ALLEN & POWERS, 21

ALLEN & YOUNG, 87

ALLEY
William, 155

ALLFORD
J. C., 137

ALLSTON
Geo., 132

ALLUMS
Louisa A., 143

ALSTON
Col. P. H., 16
Elizabeth T., 132
J. C., 112
Mildred R., 153
Miss Clementina, 88
Philip H., 6
Willis, 110
Wm. H., 107, 134, 156
W. H., 30

AMOS
Wm., 125, 166

ANDERSON

Anders, 133
A., 136
Capt., 65
H. C., 54, 155
Miss, 97
Miss Eliza, 113

ANDERSON &
CONZELMAN, 97

ANDREW
Bishop, 151

ANDREWS
Dr., 151
J. H., 105
Samuel R., 18, 42
S. R., 25, 37, 39, 44, 81,
89, 112

ARCHER
Mary K., 122

ARMSTRONG
Archibald, 123
Elizabeth, 114

ARNETT
Henry W., 128

ARNOLD
J. S., 135

ASHLY
Miss Elizabeth J., 105

ASKEW
Lusina, 132
Mary, 114
Miss Anna, 98

ATWOOD
T. G., 79

AUCHINLECK
Emeline, 143
John B., 143

AUSTIN
John C., 109
J. C., 106
Mary, 168

AVERETT
Miss Nancy, 98

AVERRETT, 157

AVERY
Elisha, 16, 19

AYCOCK
Benjamin, 169

AYER
A. K., 50, 79, 107, 126, 136, 149, 150, 155
Col. A. K., 109

AYER & HAYWARD, 80

AYER & SMITH, 45

AYER & STARR, 130

BACHELDER
Harriet, 114

BACON
Dr. John E., 88, 107
John E., 99
JOHN E. & CO., 87

BAGGETT
Andrew J., 113

BAGLEY
Dread, 142
Elizabeth, 168
Miss Mary, 98
Miss Sarah, 105

BAILEY
Captain, 140
Capt. S. A., 166
David Henry, 145
General S. A., 137
Gen., 166
Gen. S. A., 145
Reuben, 168
Sabina A., 153
Samuel T., 16
S. A., 79, 121

BAILEY & COOPER, 131

BAILEY & GORDON, 30

BAIRD, 162

BAIRD
Dr., 158

BAKER, 130

BAKER
A. B., 79
Benj. H., 160
Frank E., 104

Miss C., 105
Miss Mary, 99
Mrs. Agnew, 115
Priscilla G., 152
Rev. Dr., 129
Rev. John, 36, 37, 49
Rev. Joseph S., 115
Samuel, 105
Willis P., 30, 45, 141
W. P., 18

BALDWIN
Thos. M., 153

BALL
Tuscan H., 26
T. H., 21

BALLINGER
J. J., 112

BALSAN
Dr. H., 57

BANDY
Ephraim C., 113, 124
E. C., 100, 111, 146, 166

BANKS, 163

BANKS
Col, 160
John, 89, 121

BARBAREE
Thomas J., 131

BARBER
David J., 105, 124

BARDEN
William Y., 113, 130
Wm. Y., 155
W. Y., 129

BARDWELL
R. N. R., 111, 116, 125, 130, 145

BARLOW
Nancy, 142

BARNARD
Edward, 98, 124, 125
E., 166

BARNARD & RUSE, 129

BARNES
James, 122

BARNETT
Jno. N., 169
Miss Lucy A., 166

BARNETT & KYLE, 130

BARNEY
Capt., 65

BARRINGTON
Luticia W., 131

BARRON
James, 146

BARROW
Capt., 162
Jacob, 116, 125
John W., 168
J., 111
Miss Lucy T., 98
William, 114
Wm., 156

BARTLETT
Cosam Emir, 40
C. E., 37, 55

BARTLETTE
Frances, 144

BASCOMB
John, 56

BASS, 162

BASS
Allen G., 54, 136, 137
A. G., 85, 130
Charles L., 37, 54, 88
Chas, 78
C. L., 50, 99
E., 130
Miss Elizabeth R., 88
R. L., 130

BASS & CALHOUN, 88

BATES
Asa, 21, 25, 27, 49, 51, 54, 81, 87, 111, 118, 139
Col., 69
Col. Asa, 91
Miss Nancy, 105

BAUGH
Edward, 133

BAUGH & MITCHELL, 162

BAXLEY
Jackson, 114

BAXTER WILEY & FORT, 21

BEALL
Col. Thomas, 74, 76
Elias, 6
Josiah, 130
Josiah A., 133
J. A., 145
Martha F., 142
Miss Susannah, 98
Mrs. M. G., 133
Nathan H., 142
Robert Walker, 133

BEARD
Thomas, 38

BEARDSLEY
Wm. & Co., 45

BEARDSLEY & WADE, 87

BEARS
Martha Ann, 143

BEASLEY
Buckner, 151

BEATTIE-SMITH & CO., 120

BEAUCHAMP
Clementine, 132
Eliza E., 133

BECK
Matthew, 114
Samuel, 114

BECKHAM
Albert G., 79
A. G., 129

BEDELL, 119

BEDELL
G. W. E., 54, 87, 116,
121, 135, 166
Mary, 26
W. A., 98, 166

BEDELL & WALKER, 57

BEDELL & WALKER'S CITY HALL, 49

BELL
Capt., 65
Capt. Wm. R., 154
John, 118
John S., 113
Sarah E., 153
William R., 111
Wm. R., 117

BENDER
Joseph, 79
Jos., 54

BENNETT
J., 38
Miss Amelia, 31
Miss Mary A., 105
Sarah T., 122

BENNING
Henry L., 104
H. L., 86, 166
Sarah Amanda, 105

BENTON
Hardy, 105

BERNERITER
Sergt., 165

BERRY
Asa T., 169
Capt., 65
James H., 99
Mrs., 78
Thomas, 89, 124
Thomas W., 107
Thos., 116

BERTHELOT
James A., 30, 36

BETHUNE
General James N., 137
Gen., 166
Gen. James N., 4, 38
Henrietta M., 143
James, 88, 97
James N., 24, 44
John, 76, 81, 88, 89, 100,
101, 107, 116, 119, 120,
121, 124, 134, –

141
John M., 101, 125, 165
Joseph D., 115
Jos. D., 98
J. M., 141
J. N., 50
Marian, 144

Mrs. James N., 151
Mrs. Janette, 151

BETHUNE & CLINE, 38

BETHUNE & HOLLAND, 80

BETZ
George, 111
Geo. H., 153

BEVILL
Elvira C., 152

BICKLEY
Solomon, 122

BIGGERS
Miss Mallissa A., 104

BILBRO, 139

BILBRO
John A., 88
Miss Martha, 31

BILLING
Dr., 50, 140
Dr. S. A., 127, 146, 155,
169
Samuel, 50
Samuel Albert, 169
S. A., 130
W. S., 121

BILLING & BOSWELL, 125, 126

BILLUPS
Ann E., 153
John R., 168
Robert, 71

BIRD
Fitzgerald, 16, 17, 27
O. W., 38
Ransom, 54

BIRD & BUCKHAM, 38

BIRD & SULLIVAN, 21

BIRDE
Girard, 30

BISHOP
J. H., 135

BISSEL
E. E., 17

BISSELL
Edwin E., 15
E. E., 15, 26, 27
Wm. C., 144

BIVINS
M. L., 123
Winnifred, 123

BIZE
Charles, 82
Chas. D., 105

BIZE & WICKS, 80

BLACKBURN
Wash, 98

BLACKMAN
Elizabeth, 114

BLACKMAR
Alfred O., 112
Ann America, 115
A. O., 115, 135
Miss Tamar, 114

BLAIR
Wm., 107

BLAKE
Miss Lucy, 114

BLALOCK
Mr., 55

BLANCE
John C., 24

BLAND
Calvin, 169
E., 45

BLANKENSHIP
Felix, 98

BLANN
Eliza, 168

BLOME
Mrs. H., 45

BLOODWORTH
James, 76

BLOUNT
William, 133

BOHANNON

Mary Ann, 26

BOLAND
Andrew, 131
Jesse, 131
Mary, 153

BOND
Nathaniel P., 21, 38
N. B., 29

BOND & WARE, 130

BONNER
Rep., 56
Seymour R., 73, 125
S. R., 51, 80, 81, 111

BONNER & PHELPS, 16

BONNEY
Benj., 51, 57

BOOHER
D. L., 131

BOON
John F., 114

BOON & WALKER, 97

BOOTH
Capt., 65, 67
Jas. A., 153
Lucinda M., 169
William G., 152

BOREN
Wm., 105

BORING
Rev. Jesse, 44
Rev. J., 30

BOSTICK
A. C., 50
Miss Mary L., 105

BOSWELL
David, 169
Dr., 77, 121
Dr. J. J., 107, 116
Dr. J. J. & CO., 128
J. J., 57, 130

BOSWELL & BILLING, 125, 126

BOSWORTH
Emily H., 131

Francis, 76
F. A., 112
James, 38
John F., 112
T. A., 156

BOUDRE
A. J. R., 166

BOWDRE
A. J. R., 151

BOWEN
Elisha C., 152
T. W., 112

BOYD
Nancy, 169
Robert, 131

BOYKIN
Clara, 168
Dr. S., 107
S., 129

BRADFORD
Henry H., 143
Jas. A., 135
William R., 124

BRADLEY
Forbes, 168
Henry C., 168

BRADWELL
R. N. R., 155

BRADY
Miss Margaret, 104
Sarah, 142
Thomas, 98

BRANHAM
Joel, 27

BRANNON
A. F., 130
T. A., 111, 121, 129, 140, 151

BRASSILL
John C., 123

BRAZILLE
Simon, 115

BREWER
Dan'l, 131
Miss Margaret J., 113
Mrs., 69

Wm., 143

BRICE
R. T., 135, 136

BRIDGES, 128, 162

BRIDGES
Jonathan, 148

BRIGGS
Miss Hannah, 113
Mrs., 51

BRIGMAN
Mary A., 142

BRITT
Col. D. J., 55

BRITTAIN
Jane, 142
John H., 142
P. H., 104

BROADNAX
Dr., 31, 37
Eugenia, 143
Robert E., 133

BROCKWAY
Capt., 60

BRODEE
F. R., 45

BROOKS
Almira V., 154
Francis M., 132
Hiram, 106
James M., 132
J. & J., 130
Martin, 99
Matilda, 99
Miss Margaret, 104
Miss Mary, 98
M., 89
Nicy Ann, 132
Terrill, 26
William, 155

BROOM
D. W., 112

BROWN, 139

BROWN
Agnes J., 105
Daniel W., 153
Ephraim, 35, 104

James, 16
James J., 154
John A., 114
Joseph, 153
Lucy Ann, 142
Martha, 169
Miss Adaline, 104
Morgan, 76
Robert, 142
Robert Henry, 31
Wm. A., 99

BROWNING
James E., 143

BRUNSON
Behethala, 153
Matilda, 122
Miss E. L., 105

BRYAN
Bethany C., 169
Dicy, 122
Theophilus, 122
Thos. P., 45

BRYANT
James D., 76

BRYANT'S FERRY, 58

BUCKHAM & BIRD, 38

BUCKLER
Samuel E., 15, 16

BUCKLEY
G. W. & CO., 87

BUCKNER
Elizabeth, 142

BUELL
Benj., 112

BUGG
Edmund, 27, 31
Emily M., 131
Thomas J., 88

BULL
Major Jesse L., 145

BULL-GOULDING & CO.,
121

BUMSTEAD
Thomas, 130

BUNDY

Ephraim, 27

BUNNELL
John, 151
John G., 124

BURCH
Gerard, 56, 97
Susan Ann, 122

BURNES
Miss Mariah E., 113

BURNS
Alderman, 135
Edwin L., 134

BURNSTEAD
Thomas, 145

BURT
Margaret P., 122
Richard, 112

BUSH
Thomas, 105
William J., 131
Zilphia, 131

BUSSEY
Elizabeth A., 169

BUSTIN
Milly A., 169

BUSTRAN
James, 143

BUTLER
Samuel, 66

BUTT
Miss Mary Ann, 38
Moses, 23
M., 27
M. M., 21

BUTTS
James R., 80
William, 54

CADWALADER, 139

CADY
S. C., 45

CAIRNES
F. A., 135

CAIRNS
W. D., 103

CALHOUN, 129

CALHOUN
Alex, 76
Alex., 104
Anna V., 123
Archibald, 132
A., 80
Caroline Louisa, 143
Col. J. S., 165
Hon. J. S., 137
James, 76
James S., 123, 167
Jas. S., 89
Judge, 78
J. S., 49, 50, 55, 78, 81,
  85, 90, 97, 106, 141
Mayor, 95
Rep., 56

CALHOUN & BASS, 88

CALVIN
John, 153

CAMERON
Malcom, 105

CAMP
Harriet, 51
Joseph T., 21, 27
Major Joseph T., 32, 33
Maj. Joseph T., 40, 41,
  51

CAMPBELL
John W., 106
J. H. P., 59, 96
J. P. H., 51, 53, 54
J. W., 85, 87

CANNON
Frances, 154
Malissa, 168
Sarah, 169

CANTOR
Joshua, 131

CAR
Tom, 69

CARESE
R. W., 96

CAREY
Edward, 27, 45, 102

CARNES, 87

CARNES
Rev. Wm. D., 98
Robert W., 48
R. W., 45, 50

CARR
Paddy, 62, 75
Thos. S., 135

CARROLL, 40

CARSWELL
Joseph, 152

CARTER, 162

CARTER
Col. Farrish, 158
John D., 122

CARTLEDGE
Susan, 169

CARY
Eliza P., 132

CARY & DAY, 87

CASHION
S. R., 54

CASTLEBERRY
Nancy, 154

CAULEY
Rachel, 168

CAUTRAN
Hiram L., 169

CHAFFIN
James J., 122

CHALMERS
George, 135

CHAMBERS
Jas. M., 121
J. M., 151

CHAMBLESS
John D., 20

CHAMBLISS
Christopher, 123

CHAMPION

Elizabeth, 143
James M., 132
John, 143
Mary Ann, 169
Wm., 122

CHANDLER, 162

CHANNEL
Miss Eliza, 114

CHAPMAN
Elizabeth A., 114
Miss E. A., 104
S. T., 103, 113

CHAPMAN & FLOURNOY-
  MARKS, 96

CHAPPELL
Absalom H., 132
George A., 79

CHEATUM
John L., 143

CHIEF JIM BOY, 71

CHIEF NEAH-EMARTHLA,
  72

CHIEF TUCKABATCHEE
  HARJO, 71

CHILANCHA, 78

CHILDERS
Dr., 37
James, 36

CHILDERS & WILSON, 38

CHIPLEY, 106

CHIPLEY
Dr., 128
Dr. Wm. S., 116, 134
Dr. W. S., 124, 137
Wm. S., 135
W. S., 89, 100

CHIPLEY & MILLS, 38

CHISHOLM
M., 141

CHOATE & ROSSEAU, 125,
  126

CHORDRE

-6-

Miss Elizabeth, 114

CHORDRY
James, 153

CHRISTIAN
Elizabeth, 132
Geo. W., 154
Miss Emily, 114
Nancy, 131

CHRISTY
Mary, 131

CLAPP, 162

CLAPP
Horace, 112
Howard Chandler, 144
Julius R., 103
W. C., 112, 140

CLARK, 40

CLARK
Francis, 98
James, 82
Lieut., 23
Mary, 131
Mary A., 122
Michael N., 38, 76
Mr., 83
M. N., 44, 77, 81
Theresa A. M., 168
Wm., 37

CLARK & NOURSE, 30

CLARKE
Michael N., 124

CLARK-TARVER & CO., 80

CLAXTON
J. J., 114

CLAY
Gov., 67
Henry, 149
Mr., 150
Pleasant G., 169

CLAYTON
Augustine, 105
Garrett B., 131
George R., 102
Philip A., 118
P. A., 54, 135, 150, 155, 157

CLEGHORN
Chas., 143

CLEM
Henry R., 168
Wm. H., 142

CLEMMONS
Wm. M., 113

CLEVELAND
Jesse F., 154
John A., 31
Mrs. Mary F., 154

CLIFTON
A. S., 26, 37, 39, 50, 51
Dr., 37

CLIFTON & KENNEDY, 30

CLINE, 44

CLINE & BETHUNE, 38

CLYATT
Nancy, 131

COAKER
Arian, 17

COATES
Abner G., 122

COBB
Aquilla, 105
James M., 153
Miss Susannah, 104

COCHRAN
Elizabeth, 168

CODE
John, 79

CODE & MATHEWS, 51

CODE & MATTHEWS, 57

COFFER
Nancy, 133

COGBILL, 44

COKER
Miss Dorothy, 21

COLE
Emeline, 132
Mary A., 131

COLEMAN, 129

COLEMAN
Benj., 117
Benj. F., 124
B. F., 107, 135, 146, 147, 156
Capt., 65
Jas., 37
John, 37
Levi, 104
Miss Frances M., 114
Nancy C., 132
Wm. P., 132

COLLINS
Daniel, 153
Dr. Robert, 34
John, 153
Robert, 46

COLQUITT
Judge W. T., 49
Walter T., 15, 16, 50, 79, 114, 163
W. T., 50, 86, 87, 121, 137

COLQUITT RAGAN & GRANT, 87

COLQUITT- HOLT & ECHOLS, 88

COLSON
Calvin T., 143
Elizabeth J., 153
Miss Frances, 88

COLUMBUS COTTON FACTORY, 96

COLUMBUS ICE CO., 48

COLUMBUS MERCHANT MILLS, 49

COLWELL
Robert P., 132

CONDON
John, 135, 156

CONE
Judge, 137, 166

CONNOLY
T. C., 112

CONZELMAN
Gottlieb, 152

CONZELMAN &
ANDERSON, 97

COOK
F. S., 27
Henry C., 4
James C., 50, 92, 112
James C. (Sr.), 152
Jane Ann, 153
Jas. C., 154
Miss Elizabeth, 113
Robt. F., 115
Sarah A. H., 114

COOKSEY
Duncan, 122
Mary, 142
Miss Barbary, 98

COOLEY
S. J., 15

COOLRIDGE
Miss M. J., 103

COOPER
Alex, H., 150
Alexander H., 153
Alex. H., 169
A., 166
A. H., 121
Benjamin, 132
David, 38
Mary, 122, 168
Mrs. Ann Elizabeth, 169

COOPER & BAILEY, 131

COPELAND
John N., 80
Thos., 98

CORDERY
Mary, 131

CORLEY
Elijah, 111

COTTON
Caroline C., 142

COWART
Elizabeth, 132
J. W., 86

COWLES
Samuel, 154

COX
A. M., 130
Darius, 45
Miss Mary, 114
Sampson, 122
Thomas, 15
Thos. W., 20

CRAIGE
Miss Charlotte, 113

CRAIGG
Almenia R., 153

CRANDALL SMALLEY &
CO., 87

CRATE
Capt., 65

CRAWFORD
James B., 16
Wm. H., 43

CREAMER
Thompson, 152

CRENSHAW
Miss Susan M., 88

CREW
H., 166

CREWS
Hervey, 112

CREWS & McGOUGH, 125,
126

CRICHTON
Peter, 103, 111, 125

CRICHTON & JONES, 97

CRICHTON & LOCK, 126

CROPP
Miss Sarah C., 98

CROWELL
Col., 56, 59

CULIFER
Ann, 143

CULPEPPER
Christopher, 153
Edward, 133
John, 131

Neil, 114
Rosetta, 153

CULVER
Miss Elizabeth, 104
Rebecca J., 122
Wm. S., 122

CUMMINGS
James, 123

CUNNINGHAM
Jacob, 102
J. L., 37
Thos., 82

CURRY
Daniel, 151, 152
Rev. Mr., 151

CURTIS
Miss Louisa, 113

CUSHMAN
Charles T., 131

CUYLER
R. R., 160

DANCER
M., 129

DANIEL
James, 27
Jas., 44
Robert, 15

DANN
Thomas, 144

DARDEN
Emily, 169

DAVENPORT
Allen, 98

DAVIDSON
Eliza, 132
Joseph, 118

DAVIE
Ambrose, 114
Thomas, 37

DAVIES
L. J., 21, 37, 45, 129

DAVIL
Howell, 143

DAVIS, 23, 63

DAVIS
A .B., 37
Ann, 122
A. B., 89
Elisha, 132
Elizabeth, 132
F. G., 156
Isabel, 142
Jane, 143
Jno. E., 165
John E., 54, 85, 98
Joshua L. O., 143
J. E., 110
Miss Sarah A., 104
Mrs., 16
Rev. Mr., 52
Rhoda, 132
Thomas, 25

DAVIS & PLUME, 131

DAWKINS
Haney Ann, 123

DAWSON
Capt., 65
Henry C., 14, 17
H. C., 30
Miss Jacintha E., 21

DAWSON-HILL & CO., 129

DAY
E. H., 112

DAY & CARY, 87

DEAN
Ab., 168
Bartlett T., 122
David, 25
Jeptha C., 122
Lunsford R., 168
Simeon, 153

DEAN & SHAW, 21

DEBLOISE
John A., 142

DeGILSE & GORMAN, 87

DeGRAFFENRIED
Dr., 22, 28
Dr. E. L., 44, 47, 144, 155
E. L., 6, 16, 20
Margaret P., 144

Thomas Scott, 144

DELANEY
Elkanah, 142
James L., 113

DELAUNEY
Alphonso, 54

DELGADO
Isaac, 2

DELK
David, 71
Mary Ann, 169

DELONY
Edward, 97

DENIGIN
L., 112

DENNARD
Capt., 65

DENNIS
Thos. M., 37

DENT
Alexander, 123
Capt., 65
Margaret Ann, 144

DEXTER
M. A. A., 163

DIBBLE
Mr., 27

DICK
Miss Cornelia Isabella, 113

DICKSON
T. W., 156

DILL
Augustus A., 124
G. A., 112

DILLARD
George W., 17, 30, 51, 76
G. W., 15, 30, 162
Louisa, 26
Miss Nancy, 104

DILLINGHAM
Geo. W., 38, 50
G. W., 27, 32, 37, 38

John, 79
Lucy Elizabeth, 98

DILLINGHAM & TARVER, 30

DIMMICK
B. C., 56

DIMON
Mary, 142

DIMOND
John, 122

DINGLE
George R., 152

DISHROOM
Miss Mary, 104

DIXON
Frederick, 114

DOBBS
Eliza, 114
Miss Lydia, 21
Sophia, 153

DOBSON
Capt., 65

DODGE
A., 51
Benj., 135

DOLES
Clarrissa, 153
F. M., 114

DORFF
Jacob, 152

DORINGER
Susannah, 114

DOUGLAS
W. A., 166

DOUGLASS
Geo. W., 104
Wm. A., 104, 116

DOWDELL & SANFORD, 121

DOWNING
Lemuel T., 143
L. T., 121, 151, 166

DOWNING & THOMAS, 131

DOZIER
Augusta, 144
Edward M., 153
John, 103
John B., 113
Mrs., 130

DRAKE
I. S., 45
Piety, 132
R. S., 38

DRIGGEERS
Daniel T., 88

DRIVER
Simon W., 114

DUBLOIS
J. A., 121

DUBOSE
William, 132

DUCK
John C., 143

DUDLEY
Enoch, 112
Peter, 12, 15, 17

DUFFEE
Owen, 153

DUKE
Caroline, 131
Delia, 114
Elbert, 114
Hamilton, 103
Wm. J., 114

DUKES
Miss Ann, 16

DUNAWAY
James, 143

DUNN
Sarah, 143

DURR
James P., 169
Lewis M., 104

DURRUM
Virginia R., 122

DUTTON

Thomas W., 116
Thos. W., 45

DUTTON & STANLEY, 31

EALY
Algernon S., 122
Mary, 154

EARLY
J. M., 51

ECHOLS, 128, 147, 158

ECHOLS
Josephus, 51, 118, 119,
157, 165
Philip H., 57

ECHOLS COLQUITT &
HOLT, 88

ECTOR
Dr. Wiley B., 169
Dr. W. W., 166
W. B., 89

ECTOR-FLOURNOY &
RAGLAND, 141

EDGAR
P. K., 112

EDWARDS
Amanda M., 123
David B., 154
John C., 143
Jonathan, 102

EFIEMATTA, 36

EILAND
Absalom, 168

EILBECK
Henry J., 114

ELDER
Hartwell, 142
Mary J., 132

ELEY
Osborn, 153
O., 100

ELLIOTT
George W., 30, 44

ELLIS

D. P., 128
John, 168
J., 88
Lucinda, 168
Miss Mary A., 104
W. J., 121

ELLIS & GREENWOOD, 141

ELLIS & YONGE, 97

ELLISON
Miss Margaret C., 31

ELVIRA
Miss, 50

EMMETT
Mary, 131

EMOTT
Eliabeth, 154

ENNIS
J., 130

EPPINGER
E. T. & CO., 130
James T., 140
James T. & CO., 121

ESTES
Henson S., 122

ESTES & ILLGES, 125, 126

ETHERIDGE
John, 154

EUBANKS
Thos., 98

EVANS
Capt., 65, 68
Capt. T. C., 59
Charlotte, 169
George, 143
Jane, 122
Matt. R., 37, 121
Miss Clarissa, 113
M. R., 53, 54, 79
M. R. & CO., 26
Rev. J. E., 165
Sarah A., 143
Thomas C., 50, 97
Thos. C., 76
T. C., 81

EVANS & MORRIS, 38

EVERETT
Jas., 155
John, 135, 145
Thomas, 124

EZEKIEL
Emanuel, 82

FAGEN
John, 113

FAIRCHILD
F. A., 51

FALKENBURY
Sarah, 153

FANNIN, 78

FANNIN
James W., 20
James W. (Jr.), 16
J. W., 25
J. W. (Jr.), 37

FARLAN
C. M., 37

FARLIN & NAFEW, 16

FARMER
Louisa, 153

FARR
Larkin, 112, 113

FARRINGTON
Maj. Rufus M., 16

FAULKENBURY
Frances H., 168
Miss C., 105

FAUNTLEROY
Aphia B., 114

FAYERWETHER
Frances, 113

FEATHERSTON
Edward, 79
E., 38
Gen. Edward, 49

FEATHERTON
E., 30

FELTON & HUDSON, 38

FERGERSON
Eliza C., 169

FERGUSON
Aaron, 112
B., 80

FEW
Ignatius, 6
I.A, 37
Rev., 36
Rev. Ignatius A., 44
Rev. Mr., 33, 60

FIELD
Miss Sarah Ann, 56

FIELDS
Lawrence, 117
Wm. H., 80

FISHER
Gabriel S., 45
Sarah, 114

FLEMING
Mary, 142
Miss Eleanor, 114
Thomas, 140

FLEMMING
Thos., 136

FLETCHER
Eliza Ann, 115
Geo. W. & Co., 45

FLEWELLEN
A. H., 130
Capt., 65
Dr. A. H., 109, 151
William Alexander, 109

FLINN
Rebecca, 169

FLOURNOY, 79, 106

FLOURNOY
Major Wm. B., 59
Robt. S., 54
Samuel W., 42, 45, 50
Sam'l W., 165
S. L., 44
S. W., 49, 103, 130
Wm., 63

FLOURNOY-MARKS &
CHAPMAN, 96

FLOURNOY-RAGLAND &
ECTOR, 141

FLOWERS
Cornelius, 104

FLOYD
Capt., 65
Elizabeth, 142

FLUKER
Miss Rebecca M., 88

FLYNN
Patrick W., 27
P. W., 39

FOGLE
Jacob, 97, 112, 130

FOGLE & FOSTER, 57, 87

FONTAINE, 38

FONTAINE
Jackson, 131
John, 4, 21, 44, 76, 167
J., 15
Miss Eliza, 113
Mr., 55
W. D., 105

FONTAINE J. MAHARREY
LOVE & CO., 15

FONTAINE & SPALDING,
20

FONTAINE & STEWART,
24, 38

FOOTE
Rebecca R., 142

FORAN
James, 104

FORD
Col. Weston W., 115

FORSYTH
Gov., 6, 11, 44
Hon. John, 31
John, 152, 165, 166
John (Jr.), 55
Martha L., 168
Miss Julia Frances, 31
Savannah Jane, 168
Virginia, 142

FORSYTH-IVERSON-
MEIGS, 131

FORT & WILEY BAXTER,
21

FORTSON
Thos. D., 114

FOSTER, 131

FOSTER
A. S., 166
Geo. F., 151
N. P., 136

FOSTER & FOGLE, 57, 87

FOSTER & WARD, 130

FOX
Daniel R., 114
John, 98
Mr., 95

FRASIER
Mary Ann, 169

FREDERICK
Charles B., 169
Miss Sarah Ann, 104

FREEMAN, 139

FREEMAN
Capt., 165
J., 112
Newton, 109

FROST
Jacob W., 165, 169

FULLER
Lydia, 168
Miss Mary J., 104

FUNDERBURKE
David H., 152

FUSSELL
John, 152

GAITHER
Capt., 65

GALLOPS
John, 142

GALLUPS

Isaac, 122

GAMBLE
Robt. M., 143

GAMBRILL
Launcelot, 98
L., 120

GAMMAGE
T. T., 17, 26

GAMMELL
James A., 142

GARDNER
Benj., 109
Jane, 131
Solicitor, 137

GARLAND
David H., 51

GARMANY
Capt., 65, 70, 71

GARRARD
Mary Matilda, 123
W. W., 123
YONGE & HOOPER, 157

GARRETT
Moses, 112, 121, 131
Sarah A., 143

GARRISON
Henry P, 51

GARTRELL
Miss Mary Ann, 21

GEHEE
Wm., 89

GEORGE
Epse, 122

GETTINGER
Philip, 82

GIBSON
Jas. W., 154

GIDDINGS
Eveline, 114

GILBERT
Thomas, 1
Thos., 164
William, 111, 123

Wm., 81
W., 89

GILLSTRAP
Peter J., 153

GILMORE
James H., 144
Matilda A., 143

GINN
Selethea, 142
Thomas, 142

GLASS
Elizabeth, 142
Solomon, 133

GLENN
James, 104
Sarah M., 168
Wm. W., 169

GODFREY
James G., 38
James Y., 77

GODWIN, 119, 120, 159

GODWIN
John, 32, 43, 109, 118,
139
J., 91
Miss Martha A., 104
Ransom, 97
Wells, 109
W., 91

GOETCHIUS
R. R., 105

GOLD
T. R., 87

GOLDSMITH
Allen A., 153

GOLIGHTLY
David, 123
D., 107

GOOD
Hamilton, 133

GOODALE
J. G., 152
J. N., 130

GOODALL
Mrs., 45

Samuel, 45

GOODWIN
Mr., 109

GORDON
Thomas G., 16, 17, 54, 76
T. G., 81

GORDY
Miss Elizabeth, 104

GORMAN & DeGILSE, 87

GOSS
C. A., 114

GOULDING
Charlotte L., 122
Dr., 111
E., 166
E. R., 165
Rev., 151
Rev. Dr., 129, 140, 164
Thomas B., 54

GOULDING-BULL & CO., 121

GRAHAM
Elizabeth, 143

GRANT
A. L., 54, 130
John I., 114

GRANT COLQUITT & RAGAN, 87

GRANT & WHITTICH, 45

GRAY
Eli, 153
Eliza, 132, 153
John C., 88
Martha J., 122
Mary, 122, 154
Nathan, 112
Richard, 76, 116, 124
R., 120

GREEN, 128, 130

GREEN
Eliza. E., 168
Hiram, 105
Jas., 155
J. B., 51, 116, 129
J. B. & CO., 87

Leopold, 144
Miss Martha, 45
Mr., 61
Richard W., 144
Robert H., 155
Robt. H., 144
R. H., 135, 146
William S., 153
Wm., 112

GREENE
Jos. B., 54
R. A., 130
R. H., 130, 166

GREENWOOD
Eldridge S., 113
E. S., 54, 79, 120
E. S. & CO., 87
H. T., 120, 121
J. D., 54

GREENWOOD & CO., 57

GREENWOOD & ELLIS, 141

GREENWOOD & GRIMES, 130

GREER, 139

GREER
Franklin, 114
Miss Elizabeth, 105
Robert, 169

GREGORY
A. M., 86

GRESHAM
A. Y., 24, 26
Captain A. Y., 21

GRIEVE
George, 79, 80

GRIEVES
Geo., 38
Miss Ann, 103

GRIFFIN
Andrew B., 15
Andrew B.(Esq.), 26
A. B., 25, 31
A.B., 37
Mary M., 31

GRIGG
Miss, 36

GRIGGS
David C., 88

GRIMES
Emily C., 114
Josiah, 45, 111
S. F., 166
S. S., 121
Thomas P., 54, 98

GRIMES & GREENWOOD, 130

GRIMES & SMITH, 87

GRINAGE
Miss Josephine, 31

GROINBECK
Massino, 168

GRONBECK
Jorgine, 152

GUAYARD
R. P., 30

GUERRY, 103, 129, 130

GUERRY
Jacob M., 139, 145
J. M., 100, 166
Peter V., 111

GUNBY
Miss, 36
Miss Frances, 31, 38

GUNN
Reecy, 131

GUTHRIE
Simeon, 111, 124

GUYARD
Captain, 47

GUYARD & JORDAN, 87

GUYON
Mrs., 45

HALE
Miss Pamela, 38

HALL, 139

HALL
Harvey, 30, 38, 50

Henry T., 135, 138
H. T., 121, 125, 146
Jas. C., 29
Mary Ann, 168
Sampson, 45

HALL & MOSES, 87, 129

HALLAM
James, 6

HALLENBECK
Garret, 50
Garrett, 26, 29, 31

HALLER
J., 112

HALLETER
F. A., 121

HALLMAN
Geo. W., 168

HALL-RUSE & CO., 130, 131

HAMELL
John, 131

HAMILL
A., 37
Rev. Andrew, 45
Rev. A., 30

HAMILTON, 130

HAMILTON-HURD & CO., 97

HAMMILL
Rev. Mr., 21

HAMMOND
Miss S. A., 104
Mr., 63

HAMNER & JAMES, 77

HAMNERR
Miss Mary, 105

HAMPTON
Col., 56
James H., 151
John M., 142
J. M., 130

HAND
Thos. J., 151

HANKS
Frances M., 168
Louisa R. A., 142

HANSILL'S SPRING, 35

HARALSON & LEWIS, 88

HARDAWAY
R. S., 79
Sam, 62
Samuel G., 61

HARDAWAY'S FERRY, 60

HARDEMAN
Capt., 65

HARDEN
Clara Cornelia, 88

HARDIN
Capt., 65

HARDY
Charles, 56

HARGRAVE, 125, 126

HARGRAVE
Geo., 126

HARGRAVES
George(Jr), 142

HARGROVE
B. L., 105
Wm. D., 27, 37, 50
W. D., 39

HARGROVES
Wm. D., 50

HARLEY
J. D., 112

HARPER
Col. W. H., 113
Miss Eugenia, 113
Miss Harriet, 38
Wm., 54
Wm. H., 30
W. H., 38, 99, 106

HARPER THORNTON & LIVINGSTON, 87

HARPER & JONES, 30

HARRELL
Miss Elizabeth, 105

HARRILL
Miss Harriet, 105
Thos., 142

HARRIS
G., 166
James M., 123
Jno. N., 112
L. B., 102
Major J., 153
Major W. B., 149
Rev. Mr., 52
Richard H., 132
W. B., 109

HARRIS & MANLEY, 30

HARRISON
Frances, 142
J. J., 56
Miss Eliza, 104
Miss Nancy, 104
Miss Rebecca, 114

HARVEL
Samuel B., 168

HARVELL
Miss Jane, 98

HARVEY
Sarah E., 154

HARVILL
Andrew, 20

HARWELL
H. J., 45
Western, 80

H. J., 50

HASSON
Martha R., 143

HASTINGS
Benj. W., 142
Eliza., 152

HATTON
John, 114

HAWKINS
Geo. S., 133
Thomas, 132

HAWS

Miss Louisa, 105

HAWTHORN
Miss Martha A., 98

HAYES
William, 26

HAYS
Jemimah, 123
Rebecca, 122
Thos. D., 104

HAYWARD
Aug., 121

HAYWARD & AYER, 80

HAYWARD & SMITH, 131

HAYWOOD
Augustus, 88

HAZELTON
John, 152

HAZZELTON
Pinkney, 153
P., 166

HEAD
Samuel B., 15, 17

HEARN
Angeline, 153
Horace, 105
Joseph M. K., 169
Martha, 153, 168
Miss Elizabeth, 104
Miss Margaret, 113

HEIGDON
Philip G., 131

HEIGHT
Miss Martha, 104
Nathan, 104

HEITE
Charles H., 111

HENDRICKS
Capt., 65

HENRY
Albert, 143
Andrew, 132
Asa, 114
Charles P., 122
George G., 132

Jim, 67, 68, 69, 72, 73,
  78, 87
Robert H., 142
Robt., 15

HEPBURN
Burton, 36, 46, 54
Col. Burton, 134
H., 55
Senator, 56

HERRING
James, 87

HERRINGDINE
T. R., 112

HERRON
S. J., 80, 88

HERVEY
Dr. C. P., 135

HERVEY. Chas. P., 131

HEWETT
James W., 153

HEYWARD
Augustus, 51

HICKEY
Eliza Ann, 133
Miss Sarah A., 114

HICKS
Isham, 114

HIGDON
Mary C., 154

HIGHTOWER
C., 76
Jona., 76

HILL
Amelia A., 152
A. C., 80
Capt., 65
H. K., 37
H. W., 88
James, 78
Jas. L., 54
J. B., 166

HILL & ALLEN, 57

HILLIARD
Henry W., 24, 26
H. W., 29

HILL-DAWSON & CO., 129

HINCH
M. M., 30

HINTON
Miss Catharine D., 38
Richard H. W., 132

HITCHCOCK, 87

HITCHCOCK
Col. Jas., 38
James, 26, 27, 39, 96
James M., 31
Jas., 17
John G., 112
J., 30
J. P., 54
Wm. A., 38

HITT
Frances, 131

HITY
Felix, 169

HOBBS, 63

HOBBS
Miss Mary, 104

HODGES
Capt., 65
George C., 89
Henry, 54
Maria, 123
Martha A. B., 153
Rev. Samuel K., 97, 115
Rev. S. K., 49
Samuel K., 123
S. K., 30, 80

**HODGES & MOORE, 125,
126**

**HODGES-MOORE & CO.,
24, 26**

**HODGES-MOORE &
JONES, 21**

HOFFMAN
J. B., 97

HOGAN
J. M., 112
T. M., 130, 156

HOLCOMB WILLIAMS &
ROBINSON, 87

HOLLAND, 79

HOLLAND
Almina, 26
James, 149
James C., 15, 39, 101
James H., 71
Jas. C., 56
J. C., 49, 97, 99
Robert, 71
William, 31
Wm., 25, 37, 56

HOLLAND & BETHUNE,
80

HOLLENBECK
Sarah L., 122

HOLLINAN
Miss Martha, 105

HOLMES
Chester G., 113
J. L., 112
Miss Fredonia C., 114
Richard, 168
Susan, 168

HOLSTEAD, 127

HOLSTEAD
Willis S., 119, 125, 133
W. S., 80, 112, 145, 155

HOLT, 141

HOLT
Col. Hines, 98, 150, 169
Dr. Leroy, 114
Dr. L., 107
D. Chandler, 165
Hines, 54, 134, 137, 166
Lieut. Hine, 86
Mary Harriet, 169
William, 112

HOLT COLQUITT &
ECHOLS, 88

HOLT & PERSONS, 88

HOLTZCLAW
W. B., 112

HOOD
John H., 132

HOOPER
GARRARD & YONGE, 157
Richard, 113
R., 80, 88, 89

HOOPER THORNTON &
LIVINGSTON, 86

HOPKINS
Nancy, 152

HOPKINS & STOCKTON,
110

HORTAN
Elizabeth, 114

HORTON
Miss Eliza, 104

HOUGHTON
Jas. R., 54
Susan, 142
Theobald, 54

HOUSTON
Gen., 128
Gen. Sam, 62

HOWARD, 128, 131, 147,
158, 162

HOWARD
Augustus, 133, 154
Caroline A., 143
Claiborn, 99
Colonel J. H., 137
Gen., 41
Gen. N., 37
George, 98
Hiram, 112
James W., 77
John G., 144
John H., 119, 121, 141,
157
Julia Ann, 21
J. B., 116
J. H., 97
Major, 69
Major John A., 74
Maj. John H., 138
Martha, 133
Miss Adeline S., 104
Miss Eleanor H., 103
Miss Harriet, 113
Miss Mary, 104
Miss Mary J., 103
Nicholas, 12, 15, 17, 37,
56

N., 50, 85
N. L., 96, 109, 124, 134,
145, 155, 165, 166,
167
Theobold, 147
T. B., 77, 121, 144
W. H., 113

HOWARD & LLOYD, 97

HOWARD & WITTICH, 87

HOWARD'S HOTEL, 21, 24

HOWELL, 127

HOWELL
James, 114
John D., 106, 124
J. D., 116, 130
William, 153

HOWELL & LAWHON, 30,
38

HOXEY
Captain, 59
Capt., 65
Dr., 49, 116, 127, 155
Dr. J. B., 109
Dr. Thomas, 134
Dr. Thos., 103, 146, 155
John B., 146
John J. B., 99, 124, 142
J. B., 155
J. J. B., 116
Major J. B., 128
Major Thomas, 68
Thos., 45, 102

HOXIE
Zoononia, 122

HUCKABY
Zelia A. S., 132

HUDGIN & WELLS, 125

HUDGINS
Reuben R., 114

HUDGINS & WELLS, 126

HUDSON
David, 54, 112
D., 90
Eliza, 143
Elizabeth, 142
Jonathan A., 25, 50
Jona. A., 15, 16, 36

J. A., 31
Mary J., 132
Mrs. Martha, 50

HUDSON & FELTON, 38

HUDSON & THORNTON, 26

HUFF
John A., 104
Miss Emily, 103
Miss Emily E., 113

HUGHES
James M., 124
J. D., 111
J. M., 146

HUGUELY
Elizabeth, 122

HUGULEY
Cynthia, 122

HUNGERFORD
A., 21
D., 21, 97

HUNLEY
John, 131

HUNT, 71

HUNT
Anderson, 112
A., 130
Dr. Anderson, 124
Dr. A., 107
Jonathan (Jr), 131
Mary F., 131

HUNTER, 71

HUNTER
John, 129, 166

HURD
Commodore, 162
Homer, 98, 106, 111
Wm. H. & Co., 130

HURD-HAMILTON & CO., 97

HURLBURT
George R., 133
G. R., 126

HUTCHINS
Jane, 133

Pleasant, 132

HYATT
James, 131
Miss Susan, 104

ILLGES & ESTES, 125, 126

INDIAN BOY, 16

INGERSOLL
Dr., 60
Dr. Stephen M., 42
Dr. S. M., 95, 120
S. M., 29, 30

INGRAM
Burnet, 112
B., 146, 155
Porter, 166

INSLEY
Chas. T., 135

IRWIN, 71

IVERSON
A, 141
Alfred, 30, 31, 45, 115
A., 27, 54, 87, 166
B. V., 45
William, 123

IVERSON-FORSYTH-MEIGS, 131

IVES
Miss Jane C., 50

IVES & BROTHER, 130

IVEY
Amos, 142
Giles, 76
Margaret, 153
McGirt, 45
Mrs. Mary, 45

JACKSON, 15

JACKSON
Jona. P., 38
J. P., 25, 30, 37, 38
Samuel M., 54
S. M., 88
Thomas L., 47
William N., 124
Wm. N., 137

JACKSON HOTEL, 30

JACOBS
Miss Margaret H., 103

JAMES
Mr., 82
Thomas, 97

JAMES & HAMNER, 77

JAQUES
R. W., 130

JEFFERSON
Joseph, 80
Richard, 122

JEMISON
Alex, 142
Rachel A., 168
Robert F., 143
Rosella, 122

JENKINS, 139

JENKINS
Jane A., 132

JEPSON
Benjamin Sr., 21
Benj., 112
F. A., 111, 151
Jos., 112
Lem., 76
L., 112
Rev. Thomas, 164
Thos., 112
William, 111

JERNIGAN
Col., 70
Miss Amanda C., 166

JESSUP
Gen., 64, 71, 72, 73

JETER, 162

JETER
Garland, 31
Mary, 153
Miss Mary Ann, 98
Mrs. Margaret, 38
Oliver, 21, 31, 37, 111
Wm. L., 45, 54, 152, 166
W. L., 48

JEWETT

E., 25
Mrs., 21

JIM BOY, 72

JOERSON
A., 103

JOHN
Miss Mary H., 114

JOHNSON
Adaline Blackmar, 154
Alfred, 144
Capt. James, 21
Daniel, 122
Eleanor, 31
Eliza A., 154
Elizabeth, 122, 154
Franklin C., 142
Henry, 26
Jacob, 154
Jacob M., 45, 54, 131, 154
James, 17, 131, 137
James D., 113, 154
Jas. D., 54
Jas. W., 152
John, 80, 112, 113, 122, 130, 141, 146
Josiah, 58
Jos., 111
Mary, 143
Miss Nancy, 114
Permelia, 123
Robert G., 31
Robt., 144
Samuel D., 133
Stephen, 142
Wm., 142

Mrs. Elizabeth, 154

JOHNSON NUCKOLLS & CO., 87

JOHNSON & WAY, 79

JOHNSTON
John, 37
Marcus, 166

JONES, 130

JONES
Andrew P., 54
Ann, 144
A. P., 80
Col., 85
Col. Seaborn, 104

Col. S., 125, 126
Elizabeth, 142
Elizabeth J., 105
Geo. W., 54, 166
Henry, 168
James R., 85
Jas. H., 54
John, 54
John A., 140, 143
Julina M., 143
J. R., 130, 137, 141
Lucy Ann, 168
Martha A., 144
Miss Martha, 103
Moses, 50
Mrs. Martha Ann, 50
Mrs. Seaborn, 148
Mr. Wiley E., 151
M. D., 111, 130
Oscar P., 152
Randal, 154
Robert, 27
Robt. A., 88
Rob't, 20
Sarah C., 122
Seaborn, 29, 30, 42, 79, 137, 151, 163, 166
William, 133
Wm. R., 97, 134, 137
Wm. & CO., 38
W. E., 130

JONES & CRICHTON, 97

JONES & HARPER, 30

JONES & MOORE, 128

JONES & MOORE-HODGES, 21

JORDAN
John D., 54
Mary Ann, 143
Thos., 154
Thos. G., 82

JORDAN & GUYARD, 87

J. S. SMITH & CO., 97

KEAGY
A. L., 38

KELLEY
Charlotte, 123
Elizabeth, 153

KELLOGG

James, 140

KELLY
John W., 133
Robert, 112

KENDRICK
Capt., 65

KENNEDY
J. B., 30

KENNEDY & CLIFTON, 30

KENNEDY & SCOTT, 26, 30

KENNETH
B. G., 112

KENNEY, 129

KENNEY
B. G., 97

KENNON
Miss Martha H., 56

KENT
Josiah M., 122
Mary Jane, 123
Miss Susan, 113
Peter W. G., 104

KERNIN, 96

KEY
Miss Mary E., 166

KILGORE
Francis B., 76
Jordan, 76
Joseph T., 39
Jos. T., 50
J. T., 30, 45

KILLGORE
Joseph T., 56

KILPATRICK
Thos. L., 105

KIMBROUGH
Jesse J., 105
Miss Martha, 103
Miss Martha A., 105
Sarah L., 143
William H., 113
Wm. H., 38
W. H., 30, 166

KING
Henry, 87, 164
H., 130
Isabella, 122
Joseph G., 122
Mary A., 133
Newton M., 131
Sarah A. E., 114
Zilphia Ann, 168

KINGS, 139

KINGSBERRY, 26

KIRK
Wm., 37

KIRKLAND
Miss Harriet, 50
Phebe B., 122

KIRVIN
James, 99
Miss Caroline, 105
Stephen, 37

KIVLIN
James, 21, 26, 30, 37,
48, 80, 107, 135, 146

KNOTTS
Miss Martha, 114

KOOCKOGEY
Sam'l, 130

KOOCKOGY
Samuel, 15

KOSTAR
G., 150

KYLE
D, 130
D., 129
John, 146, 155
Joseph, 146
J., 129, 130

KYLE & BARNETT, 130

LACEY
Isaac, 71

LaHATT
Charles H., 88

LAIN

Wm., 113

LAIRD
Dr. O. P., 115
Mrs. N. D., 115

LAMAR, 24, 129

LAMAR
Gen. Mirabeau, 129
Gen. Mirabeau B., 144
Gen. M. B., 86
John E., 111
J. E., 97
Loretta Rebecca, 132
Mirabeau B., 10, 16
Mrs. M. B., 26
M. B., 17, 20, 43, 48, 50
M. B. (Esq.), 24
Rebecca Ann, 144
William H., 122

LAMBS
Mary V. P., 114

LAMKIN
John T., 51, 52

LANDRUM
J. B., 121

LANDRUM & CO., 130

LANE
Capt., 65

LANG
Thomas, 15, 16, 38

LANGDON
Wm. B., 132

LANGFORD
Geo. N., 37
John T., 143

LANGHAM
J. J., 105

LANGSTON
S. W., 45

LARSEN
Petrar, 133

LATHROP
Henry P., 54

LATON
Mary, 143

LAUGHFLIN
Miss Elizabeth, 99

LAWHON, 79

LAWHON
Allen, 30, 39, 50, 55, 167
A., 56, 89
Gen. Allen, 47
Q. A., 54
Samuel, 32

**LAWHON & HOWELL, 30,
38**

LAWHON & MILTON, 38

LAWRENCE
Augustus, 88

LAWS
Tempa A., 122

LAWSON
Ansalum L., 122
Margaret, 143

LEACOCK
Levi L., 143

LEARY
W. B., 152

LEDYARD
E. D., 51, 57

LEE, 139

LEE
Henry, 44
J. A. L., 134
Wm. L., 98

LeGAY
L. A., 131

LEIGH
Miss Jane, 114
Mrs., 88

LEMMON
L. B., 151

LENTILTON & CO., 150

LEON
Lewis, 30

LEONARD, 130

LEONARD
  Dr. E. N. C., 169
  Elizabeth, 132
  Mary L., 143
  Van, 120, 121, 130, 151,
    162

LESTER
  Sarah A., 131

LEVISON
  A., 87, 111

LEWIS
  Colonel Ulysses, 13
  Col., 19
  Col. John L., 137
  Col. Ulysses, 24
  Felix, 38
  Franklin, 143
  John L., 103, 124, 130
  John L.., 116
  J. L., 85, 89, 99
  Samuel, 132
  States, 138, 145, 147
  Stephen, 112
  Ulysses, 16, 17, 25, 43
  U., 50

  J. L., 141

LEWIS & HARALSON, 88

LIGON
  Alex., 37
  Capt., 65
  Miss Elizabeth, 114

LINDSAY
  Ann J., 154

LINDSEY
  S. C., 130

LISLE
  Nancy C., 131

LIVINGSTON, 103

LIVINGSTON
  Lewis, 54, 88, 120, 144,
    156
  L., 146
  Philip, 144
  Sarah C., 132
  Wm. A., 142

LIVINGSTON THORNTON &
  HARPER, 87

LIVINGSTON THORNTON &
  HOOPER, 86

LLOYD
  John, 121

LLOYD & HOWARD, 97

LOCHALA
  James, 99

LOCHLA
  Absalom, 104

LOCK, 126

LOCK
  Leonard, 143

LOCK & CRICHTON, 126

LOGAN
  John, 80, 130
  Martha Ann, 169

LONG
  Catharine, 115
  Col. N. W., 115

LOPEZ
  David, 38

LOVE
  Capt., 65
  Frances, 30
  John, 30, 38
  John H., 42, 54
  Pole boat owner, 15
  Wm. E., 143

LOW
  ANDREW & CO, 121
  Miss Martha E., 99

LOWE
  Wm. A., 153

LOWRY
  Miss Margaret, 114
  Thos., 154

LOWTHER
  Sarah, 153

LOYD
  Capt., 65

LUCAS
  Adelia Maria, 31

  B. A. G., 49
  B. G., 25
  B. G. G. A., 30
  Caroline Eliza, 31
  Delia, 31
  E. B., 15
  E. I., 25
  Georgia Adaline, 31
  James D., 39
  Martha, 31
  Mary H., 31
  Rev. Silas Emmett (Jr.), ?
  Robert, 31
  William D., 17, 32
  Wm. D., 31
  W. D., 15, 20, 25, 30, 37

LUCKIE
  Clarissa A., 131
  Wm. F., 137

LUCKY
  Miss Martha D., 98

LUNSFORD
  John P., 131
  Sarah, 122

LYLE
  William M., 168

LYNCH
  Capt., 65
  Monroe, 103

LYONS
  J. R., 25

LYTLE
  Samuel, 80

MACALL
  Miss Henrietta C., 50

MACKEY
  Dr. George B., 88
  Elizabeth, 114
  Mary A., 122

MACON
  E. H., 38
  John A., 169

MADDEN
  Francis, 124

MAFFITT
  Rev. John Newland, 16

MAGNER
John, 124
Louisa, 168

MAHARREY
Robert, 15

MAHARREY LOVE & CO.,
15

MAHON
Phobe, 154

MAHONE
Miss Mary E., 104

MAHORN
Frances, 143

MAJORS
Elizabeth, 143

MALONE, 147

MALONE
Ben F., 54
Benjamin F., 122
B. F., 128, 134, 145, 147,
    155
J. W., 26
Margaret M. L. W., 26
Mrs. Catharine, 45
Wm. P., 38, 45, 50, 111
W. P., 166

MANGHAM
John, 129
John C., 80

MANLEY
A. P., 38

MANLEY & HARRIS, 30

MANLEY & RICHARDS, 26

MANN
Abraham W., 123
Alfred T., 97, 98
Elizabeth Jane, 169
Rev. A. T., 96
Wm. H., 168

MANNING
Simon, 20

MARCRUM
Nier, 122

MARKS, 24

MARKS
Capt. Francis M., 144
F. Mc. M., 122
Mrs. Jane L., 21
Orderly Sergeant, 21
Richard T., 20, 21
R. T., 18, 23, 42, 48, 54,
    112, 130, 141

MARKS-CHAPMAN &
FLOURNOY, 96

MARSHALL, 160

MARSHALL
A. G., 155
Ben, 31, 60, 64
Benjamin, 34, 36
Benj. F., 143

MARTIN
B., 52
George W., 54, 116, 156
George W.(Jr.), 168
G. W., 106
James Allen, 169
James C., 71
John H., 1
Lucinda, 132
Phineas L., 104
Rev. Barkley, 24
R. B., 51
R. E., 97
Sarah C., 133
Thos. S., 38
William M., 112
Wm., 21
Wm. B., 169
Wm. W., 134
W. W., 146, 155

MARTINE
F., 150

MASSEY
B., 45
John, 105
Miss Mary, 98
Nathaniel D., 144

MATHEWS
Henry, 87, 112

MATHEWS & CODE, 51,
57

MATTHEWS
Henry, 54
Rev. W. D., 122

W. D., 141

MATTHEWSON
B., 55
M., 121

MATTHEWS. W. D., 129

MAY
John, 112, 131

MAYNOR
W. H., 130

MAYOR
A., 150

MAYS
Miss Sarah J., 98

McALISTER
W. J., 135

McARN
A., 87

McBRIDE
Mary J., 142
Mr., 58
Wm., 142

McCAIN
Mary A., 168

McCALL
Capt., 65
Hugh, 112
Miss Caroline, 45
Miss Elenora, 88
Miss Eleonora, 38
Miss Mary, 98

McCANTZ
Thos., 80

McCAREY
Richard, 76

McCARTY
Patrick, 140

McCAULEY
Wm., 142

McCLESKY
G. J., 36
Harris, 31
John, 31
J. M., 112

McCLINTOCK
H. R., 51

McCLOUD
Luticia, 132

McCLUNG
Johnathan, 132

McCLUSKEY
Margaret A., 142
Martha W., 144

McCLUSKY
John, 30

McCOLLISTER
Martha, 122

McCOOK
Joshua R., 100

McCOUNEY
Mary Ann, 152

McCOY
Mary H., 132

McCRARY
Miss Treacy, 113

McDANIEL
A. L., 104
B. F., 87
Hugh, 76
Mariah, 132
Mary Ann, 168

McDANIEL & WILHELM, 88

McDONALD
Alexander, 107
Hugh, 116, 124, 136, 144
Miss Sarah, 98

McDOUGALD, 103, 130

McDOUGALD
Alex, 124
Alexander, 59
Alex., 98, 137, 146, 166
Col. A., 121
Col. Daniel, 34
Daniel, 36, 46
D., 163, 166
Gen., 67, 68
Gen. Daniel, 54, 134, 167
Gen. D., 52, 89, 99

McDOUGALD & WATSON,

131

McDUFFIE
James, 113
J. M., 112

McFARLAND
J. B., 80

McGEE
Samuel, 142

McGEHEE
Caroline, 123
Cassy Ann, 116
Isaac, 56
John, 76
Mr., 24
Nathan, 150
Samuel W., 123
Sarah, 99
Wm., 76, 100

McGIBBONY
Rebecca, 122

McGILL
Arthur, 153

McGILLIVRAY
William, 36

McGINTY
Miss Deborah, 98
Sarah, 114
Thos., 143

McGOUGH & CREWS, 125,
126

McGOULRICH
Dr., 161

McGOVERN
John, 169
Mary, 169

McGOWAN
James, 114

McGOWEN
Morgan, 169

McGRATH
James, 114

McGUIRE
Jas., 130

McINTOSH

Gen. Wm., 16
Miss Sarah, 16

McINTOSH HALL, 30

McINTOSH HOUSE, 14

McKAY
Mr., 61

McKEE
Elizabeth B., 133
Hockley C., 133
H. C., 111
Miss Jane, 98

McKEE & PRICKETT, 97

McKEEN
Elizabeth S., 88
Mr., 137
Thomas, 136
Thomas C., 51
Thos. C, 88
Wm. P., 82, 88, 130, 144

McKENDREE, 160

McKENDREE
J. J., 121, 130, 133, 145,
155, 166

McKENZIE
Duncan, 141
Kenneth, 121, 165

McKINZEY
Margaret, 143

McKISSACK
Mrs., 63
Mr., 63

McLANE
O. P., 111

McLAREN
Peter, 121

McLESTER
Jos. D., 97
Nelson, 122, 129, 151
N., 111

McMICHAEL
Minerva, 153
Silas, 112, 156
Susan, 168

McMICHAELS

Silas, 143

McMURRAIN
Martha A. H., 168

McMURRAY
Francis, 122
F., 110
Mary A., 131
Sarah Jane, 132

McMURREN
John M., 168

McNAIR
Miss Jeanett H., 98
Neill, 97, 99, 116

McNAIR & NEIL, 87

McNAUGHTON
Sarah N., 122

McNEAL
Anderson, 122

McNEIL
Asa, 143
Randal, 112
Raunald, 144
R., 112

McNEILL
Randall, 114

McNORTON, 129

McNORTON
Elizabeth, 153
Neill, 25

McQUAID
Michael, 101

McQUEEN
H. H., 151
Thos., 87

MEALING
Frances Ann, 132

MEAZLES
Alfred, 104

MEELER
James, 169

MEIDZIELSKI
P., 97

MEIGS-IVERSON-FORSYTH, 131

MERRELL
Lemuel, 30

MERSHON
A. R., 21, 25, 30

MICCO
Neah, 69, 72

MIDDLEBROOK
H., 112

MIDDLEBROOK & WADE, 130

MIDDLETON
Wm., 21

MIEDZIELSKI
P., 86

MIIMS
C. E., 164

MILES
Thos., 112

MILFORD
Martha, 143

MILLEN
I. B., 80

MILLER
Capt., 65
D. C., 153
Harriet, 168
Mary Jane, 153

MILLIKEN
Henry B., 54
H. B., 45
M. B., 51

MILLS
Rufus K., 114

MILLS & CHIPLEY, 38

MILLS & UNDERWOOD, 26

MILLSAPS
Reuben, 169

MILTON
Col. John, 40, 41, 48
John, 30, 43, 50

MILTON & LAWHON, 38

MIMMS
Martin, 131

MIMS
Allen, 55
Allen J., 79
Charles E., 79
C. E., 27
Drury, 37

MIMS & RIDENHOUR, 80

MINTER
Julia A., 143

MINYARD
Elizabeth, 123

MITCHELL
Ann Elvira, 144
Bird B., 144
Isaac, 57
John, 122
Judge W. H., 137
Miss Frances E., 104
Miss Frances L., 98
Monroe, 55
Robt. G., 153
Wm., 55
Wm. H., 121, 144
W. B., 61
W. H., 85, 103

MITCHELL & BAUGH, 162

MIZELL
Martha, 169

MOISE
Camillus T., 154

MONGHON
Wm., 76

MONKUS
Martha J., 131

MONTAGUE
George, 50

MONTAGUE & POMROY, 38

MONTGOMERY
James, 79

MOODY

-23-

L. B., 129, 138, 145
Mr., 109

MOODY & TERRY, 103

MOONEY
Eliza, 152
Martin, 168

MOORE
Abraham F., 27
A. F., 24, 30
Capt., 164
David, 76, 104
James S., 113
Jas. S., 55
Jesse, 169
J. A., 111
Mary Ann, 115
Miss Mary J., 113
Narcissa A., 132
Randal, 112
Randolph B., 168
Rev., 24
Robert L., 98, 114
Robt. L., 115
R. S., 97

MOORE & HODGES, 125, 126

MOORE & JONES, 128

MOOREFIELD
Jos., 112

MOORE-HODGES & CO., 24, 26

MOORE-HODGES & JONES, 21

MOORFIELD
Miss E. K., 105

MORGAN
Elijah B., 142
James, 169
John, 127, 142
J. M., 112
J. W., 135
Lucinda, 169
Martha Ann, 169
Wm., 133

MORGAN & PERRY, 38

MORGAN & SMITH, 30, 38, 87

MORMAN
William, 112

MORRELL
Benjamin B., 123
B. B., 116
E., 104

MORRIS
Elizabeth J., 169
Henry, 153
Joseph, 153
Josiah, 55, 154
Miss Mary A. M., 113
Richard W., 55
Susan, 154
Thomas, 130, 147
Thos., 116, 124, 132
Wm., 168

MORRIS TURNER & CO., 87

MORRIS & EVANS, 38

MORTON, 127

MORTON
A. C., 141
Joseph L., 124, 134
J. L., 106, 116, 145, 155
Sophia, 131
Wm S., 135
Wm. S., 137
W. S., 141

MOSELY
Lewis P., 152

MOSES, 138

MOSES
A. J., 136
Jacob I., 38, 55, 99, 133
James I., 16

MOSES & HALL, 87, 129

MOSS
James, 100
Reese H., 142
Susan Berrien, 169
Wm., 142

MOTE
Simeon, 105

MOTLEY
Kezziah, 133
Mary Ann, 168

Robert, 104

MOTT, 156

MOTT
Jno., 112

MOTT & MUSTIAN, 164

MOYE
Emily, 152

MULFORD & ADAMS, 126, 130

MULLALLY
William, 25

MULLINS
William F., 144

MULLOY
Miss Frances W., 98

MUNK
Capt. Sol. W., 88

MUNRO
Jacinta M., 144
R. W., 130
R. W. B., 121, 144, 152

MUNROE
Elizabeth D., 169

MURDOCH
Robert B., 132
R. B., 136

MURRAY
Joseph F., 50
Rhoderic, 17
W. W., 131

MUSE
Elliott H., 104

MUSTIAN, 156

MUSTIAN
John L., 111, 167

MUSTIAN & MOTT, 164

MYERS
F. M., 105
J. J., 99

MYRICK & WELCH, 80

NAFEW
D. B., 37

NAFEW & FARLIN, 16

NANCE
Harvey W., 114
H. W., 121, 130

NASH
Hillery H., 131, 168
John W., 143

NEAH-AH-MATHLA, 69, 70

NEA-MICCO
Chief, 64

NEEDHAM
Martha C., 131

NeGill
Mary P., 169

NEIL & McNAIR, 87

NELMS
William, 80

NELMS & PRESTON, 87

NEWBERRY
Dorcas, 142

NEWBY
Hilliard S., 122

NEWSOME
Robert, 114

NICHOLAS, 97

NICHOLS
E. D., 80
Wm., 56

NICKOLSON
Frances H., 142

NILES, 139

NILES
Jos. C., 136
J. T., 80
J. T. & CO., 87

NILES & RICHARDS, 57

NILSON

James, 105

NISBET
Franklin A., 123

NIX
Martha Ann S., 168
Sarah A., 142
Thomas, 111
Wm., 143

NOBLE
Hezekiah, 98

NOBLES
Mary, 114

NOBLETT
T. P., 112

NOLAN
P. H., 118

NORMAN
C., 80
James, 37
James S., 156
James W., 143
Jas. S., 21, 135
J. S., 28, 111, 146
J.S., 151

NORRIS, 103

NORRIS
George A., 130

NORTON
E. Sigourney, 55, 76, 96
E. S., 30, 37, 38, 81
John A., 113, 145
J. A., 135

NOURSE
Hiram, 32, 37

NOURSE & CLARK, 30

NUCKOLLS
Nathaniel, 55

NUCKOLLS JOHNSON &
CO., 87

ODOM
Aaron, 130
John, 50, 129, 141, 154
Mrs. Jane, 50

ODUM
Aaron, 87, 97

OGLETHORPE HOUSE, 62

OLIVER
Jeanette, 131

OLMSTEAD
O. L., 104

OPOTHEOHOLO
TUCKABATCHEE HADJO,
36

OPOTHLAYOHOLO, 72

ORDERLY
Miss M. A., 114

ORMSBY
Miss Clarissa T., 98

ORR
Ann J. S., 122
Mary Jane, 144

ORRINGTON
James, 104

OSTERN
Jesse, 142

OWENS
Ann, 143
Augustus, 95
Benj., 66
Caroline, 143
Col. Hardeman, 44
Hardeman, 37
Mariah, 131
Miss Elmira A., 104
Miss Nancy A., 104
Richard, 45, 111
Samuel, 80
W. H., 88

O'BRIAN
Thomas, 122

O'HARA
Mr., 152

PACE
Elizabeth, 168
Mary, 168

PADGET
Mary J., 131

PADGETT
Miss Jane, 98

PAGE
John R., 15, 17, 23

PAIN
Martha A., 122

PAINTER
Wm., 98

PALMER
Nancy, 142

PALMER'S THEATRE, 44

PARADICE
Ara, 143

PARHAM & PURVES, 38

PARKER
Ann R., 143
Job. B., 143
Matthew J., 122
Sarah E., 152
Sarah Q. A., 153

PARKMAN
James M., 169
Richard G., 132

PARKS, 87

PARKS
James L., 168
Miss Sarah D., 16
Sophia, 168

PARNELL
Elizabeth, 132
J. J., 105

PARR
D. W., 30

PARSONS
John W., 131
Miss Mary Angeline, 50

PARTRIDGE
Jno., 112

PASS
Edmond, 152

PATE
Eliza Ann, 131

Martha, 122

PATILLO
James, 168
Mary A., 153
Simeon, 50

PATRICK
David A., 98
James H., 114
Mahala, 133
Sarah A. L., 153

PATTEN
Richard, 153

PATTERSON
Ascenoth A., 143
Hansford C., 153
John, 100
Robert C., 114
Robt., 76
R. C., 112

PAXTON
Samuel, 76

PAYNE
James B., 129
Jos. C., 153
J. B., 141

PEABODY
Capt. John, 103
C. A., 45
George, 135
George A., 156
Geo. H., 45
G. H., 136
John, 113, 121
John B., 111
J. B., 87
Mrs., 45

PEARSON
Capt., 65
Mary Ann, 132

PECK
Turner, 122

PEDDY
Bradford, 168
Jeremiah (Jr.), 169

PEDEN
Henry W., 71

PEPPER
Stephen D., 153

PERDUE
James A., 131

PERNOY
Eliza, 153

PERRY
Eliza, 168
Mary, 26
Milly, 144
Miss Sarah A. C., 98
M. W., 38, 89
William, 122
William C., 144
Wm., 162

PERRYMAN
Ann, 168
Miss Mary A. J., 104

PERSONS
Dr. J. T., 133
Sarah Jane, 133

PERSONS & HOLT, 88

PETERS
Frances B., 132

PEYTON & CO., 130

PHELPS
Dr. H. C., 169
Frances Jane, 144
Henry C., 17, 35, 39, 76
H. C., 16, 25, 30, 32, 87
Miss Cornelia M., 166
Mrs. S. H., 169

PHELPS & BONNER, 16

PHILIP
Miss Anna, 114

PHILLIPS
Benj., 105
Malinda, 122
Martha, 153
Miss Elizabeth, 113
Pearce A., 154
Wm. B., 130

PHOLE
G. B., 88, 131

PICKARD
Caroline, 123
Emeline, 142
Linson, 132

Wm. H., 153

PICKERN
Celia, 131

PIERCE, 131

PIERCE
Dr. L., 109, 151
Jas. L., 121, 140
Lovick, 79
L., 79
Miss Ann America, 98
Miss E. L., 98
Rev. Dr., 86
Rev. L., 121

PIGGATT
Wm. A., 112

PIGGOT
Caroline R., 152

PIKE
Adeline, 153

PINCKARD
Paton H., 122

PINHORN
Geo. W., 77

PITKIN
T., 80

PITTS
Hannah, 123
Lucy A., 169
Martha C., 143
Miss Lucy A., 166
Stanmon D., 104

PLANT
I. C., 98
J. C., 87

PLUME & DAVIS, 131

POLLARD
Martha A. M. J., 142

POMEROY
Chancey, 45

POMROY & MONTAGUE, 38

POND
A., 107
Dr. A. J., 116

POOL, 130

POOL
Richard, 131

POPE
Martha Ann, 152
Mary Ann, 153

PORTER
Capt., 65
Jacob C., 76
Miss Sarah A., 114
Musidora A., 142

PORTER & ALFRED, 97

POSEY
Farre, 142
Humphrey, 132
Rachel, 122

POSHMATAHA
Chief, 4

POTTS
Martha, 131

POWELL
Reuben N., 168
Sarah, 152

POWERS
E. E., 51
Rebecca, 123
Thos. J., 144
William, 113

POWERS & ALLEN, 21

PRALL
Isaac, 98

PRANGLEN
Joseph, 111

PRANGLIN
Josiah, 135, 163

PRATHER
Wm. C., 114

PRATT
Daniel, 32

PRESTON & NELMS, 87

PREY
Samuel G., 131

PRICE
Wm., 114

PRICKETT
B., 112
J. L., 111

PRICKETT & McKEE, 97

PRIDE
Miss Laura M., 38
Miss Sarah, 31
Wm., 45, 112

PRINCE
John G., 30
L. T., 169

PROSSER
Louisa, 123
Ruth E., 142

PRUDEN
Joseph S., 122

PRUETT
Alvin, 132
Ariadna, 142
Eliza. A., 114

PRUITT
Jas. M., 120

PRYOR
C. S., 55

PULLUM
Thos., 97

PURNELL
J. J., 112
Washington, 154

PURSON
Miss Alsey, 88

PURVES & PARHAM, 38

PUTNAM
Matilda, 122

QUARLES, 69, 73

QUIN, 127

QUIN
John, 51, 116, 121, 124, 134, 145

RAANY
Perry D., 143

RADCLIFF
J. W., 17

RADCLIFF & ROBERSON, 21

RAGAN
A. B., 109

RAGAN COLQUITT & GRANT, 87

RAGEN
A. B., 4

RAGG
Wm., 105

RAGLAND
Miss Eliza W., 104
Thomas, 130

RAGLAND-FLOURNOY & ECTOR, 141

RAIFORD
Bennett M., 123
Elijah G., 169

RAMSEY
Adeline, 152
Elbert B., 104
Jas. W. H., 143

RANDALL
Henry H., 55

RANKIN
James, 103

RANSE
Edward H., 169

RARL
Daniel C., 80

RAY
Emily, 142
James, 122
Martha, 123

READ
Capt., 65
Hiram, 89
Jesse M., 114

READ & TALBOT, 87

REDD
Mary Louisa, 154
Wm. A. & Co., 141

REDDING
P. D., 166

REDMON
Srah Jane, 88

REED
Adaline A. E., 122
Amanda J., 153
James H., 104
Mrs. M. L., 145
Murray, 145

REES
D. J., 112

REESE
Daniel J., 80
Frances S., 132
Francis N., 131
George, 103
Henry, 114

REEVES
Willis M., 169

REID
Elisha, 79, 104, 107, 111
James, 112
Jesse M., 142
Miss Sarah, 88
T., 112
Wm., 112

REYNOLDS
Elizabeth, 142
James H., 97
Jas. H., 55
J. H., 87
L. O., 160

RHODES
Benoni, 104

RIBA
F., 80

RICHARDS & MANLEY, 26

RICHARDS & NILES, 57

RICHARDSON
Henry L., 88

Thos. G., 132

RIDENHOUR
Daniel D., 31, 153

RIDENHOUR & MIMS, 80

RIDGEWAY
David, 103
Drury A., 132
John L., 105

RILEY
James, 45

RISHER
Andrew J., 153

RITCH
Wm., 132

ROBERSON & RADCLIFF, 21

ROBERTS
E. C., 97
Henry, 104
Israel W., 122
Josiah, 115
J., 112
J. L., 89
Miss Rebecca, 105
Sarah, 144
Wm., 104

ROBERTSON
Mathew, 79
M., 89
P., 15

ROBINSON, 160

ROBINSON
Bird F., 111
Blake, 16, 112
Byrd F., 117
Daniel, 111
Elizabeth, 16
George W., 153
Jos., 169
Lucy, 16
M. C., 81
Nath. M. C., 76
Nat. M. C., 124
N. M., 111
N. M. C., 89, 116, 121, 135, 136, 146, 147, 155
Pleasant, 21
Thos. R., 142

Wm., 111
Wm. B., 84, 155
W. B., 112
Zoroaster, 17

ROBINSON WILLIAMS & HOLCOMB, 87

ROBISON
A. I., 111, 130
Dr. A. I., 107, 124
Henry G., 98
Monoah D., 96

ROCKMORE
John P., 131
Nancy S., 154

ROCKWELL
Clarissa, 31
C. S., 166
Stoddard, 31

RODGERS
Jane, 122
Miss Amanda M., 98
Williamson, 153

RODNEY
Miss Sarah, 114

ROE
Capt., 65
Daniel, 111

ROGERS
B. P., 123
Isabella, 168
Jane, 154
Job, 39
John C. W., 111
J. C. W., 165
J. W. C., 121
Margaret, 133
Mary A. E. F., 168
Robert H., 168
Thomas, 15
Virginia E., 153
William, 45
Williamson, 169
Wm., 37

ROLAND, 139

ROLAND
Edmund, 169
Miss Mary A., 114
Miss Zena, 114
Thomas, 114
William, 114

ROOT
Mr., 19
Wm., 37

ROPER
James E., 103

ROQUEMORE
W. B., 166

ROSE
Miss Mary E., 166

ROSS
Elizabeth, 143
Geo. W., 79
G. W., 111, 165
G. W. & CO., 88

ROSSEAU
Jas., 112
Miss Antoinette, 169

ROSSEAU & CHOATE, 125, 126

ROSSON
Elijah, 79

ROUND, 103

ROUNDS
John, 112, 146

ROUSSEAU
James, 121
J. & Co., 80

ROWE
Daniel, 98
Leonard K., 169

ROWELL
Caroline, 153

ROWLAND
E., 104

ROZAN
A. B., 4, 89

RULE
Charles, 114
Chas., 112

RUSE
Emily Jane, 142
Francis, 55
Francis Deblois, 144

Francis N., 124
F. N., 121, 144, 157, 169
John C., 142
J. C., 106, 156, 157
Mary Frances, 169
Miss Angelika L. V., 98
Peter, 51

RUSE & BARNARD, 129

RUSE & STARR, 87

RUSE-HALL & CO., 130, 131

RUSH
Capt., 65

RUSSELL
Capt., 65
Caroline M. E., 132
Jane, 153
Jonas B., 154
Martha M., 122
Miss Georgia A., 105
Stoddard, 15
William, 26
Wm., 31

RUTHERFORD
A. S., 30
Capt. A. S., 29
Mary J., 122
Miss Antonette Virginia, 115
Thacker V., 55
T. V., 104

RUTHERFORD & TONEY, 80

RUTLEDGE
Miss Ann L., 88

RYALLS
Miss Sellina, 98

RYLANDER
W. I., 111
W. J., 166

RYNEAR, 139

SALISBURY
Lucinda, 123
Thomas, 123
William, 123
Wm., 55, 112

SAMFORD
    Rev. Thomas, 97
    Rev. T., 165
    Thomas, 56, 152

SAMMIS
    Richard, 124

SANDERS
    Carolina A., 153
    Catharine, 153
    Elizabeth, 132
    Marcus De LaFayette, 168
    Mary, 114
    Miss Helen, 45
    Peterson, 132
    Sarah, 122
    Thomas, 107, 146
    Thomas M., 111
    T. M., 99

SANFORD
    Capt., 65
    Gen., 67, 69
    Maj. Gen., 72

SANFORD & DOWDELL,
    121

SANKEY
    Dr. R., 107
    Miss Mary Ann, 114

SANTA ANNA, 128

SAPP, 106

SAPP
    H. C., 97, 103, 121
    Theo., 45

SAUL
    Gideon, 168

SAULS
    Daniel G., 124
    Dan'l, 112
    Green D., 134
    Jane, 169
    Jas. Lee, 142
    John, 98

SCHLEY
    Captain P. T., 167
    Capt., 128, 140
    Capt. P. T., 59
    Dr. Wm. K., 116, 124
    Dr. W. K., 107
    Gov., 67, 73
    John, 38, 110, 166

Philip T., 4, 79
P. T., 165
W. K., 89

SCHULZ
    Philip T., 4, 107

SCIPIO, 69

SCOGGINS
    Matilda, 153

SCOTT
    Alexander, 39
    Clarkey, 131
    Gen., 64, 71, 72, 73
    Ira, 17
    I., 16
    I. T., 16
    Joel B., 15, 16
    Maj. Gen. Winfield, 76
    Nancy, 131
    S. T., 105

SCOTT & KENNEDY, 26,
    30

SCROGGINS
    America Ann, 144

SCURLOCK
    Wm., 115

SEALY
    Nancy, 152

SEAMAN
    Mrs., 97

SEARS
    John S., 111

SEGER
    Mary L., 114

SEINS
    Miss Sarah C., 104

SELF
    Miss Lucretia, 105

SEWELL
    Boon, 88

SHAAF
    Arthur, 115

SHAEFER
    Frederick, 168

SHARP
    Elizabeth, 168
    Rufus, 168

SHARPLES, 139

SHARPLESS
    Capt., 164

SHAW
    Jas., 112
    Mary A., 131
    Stephen, 104

SHAW & DEAN, 21

SHEPHERD, 70

SHERWOOD
    George C., 130
    George E., 113
    Geo. C., 126
    G. C., 130

SHIPPEY
    Martha, 114

SHIREY
    Silas R., 132

SHIVERS
    George S., 50
    James & Co., 49
    Miss Louisa P., 113
    Thomas J., 55
    Thos. J., 113
    Wm. Rabon, 116
    Wm. R., 121

SHIVERS & WILLIAMS, 131

SHOFNER
    Henry P., 133

SHOFTNER
    Miss Malinda, 114

SHOOTS
    ROSA, 143

SHORT
    G. W., 87, 100
    Mary V. P., 143
    Wm., 114

SHORTER
    Eli S., 39, 52
    E. S., 27, 38, 49, 50, 53,
    54
    James H., 30

Jas. H., 38
Judge Eli S., 79
Miss Mary Jane, 88
Miss Sophia H., 166

SIMMONS
James, 169
Moses, 111
Moses M., 98
M., 136

SIMMS
Miss Mary A., 105
Wm., 71

SIMONS
Robt. T., 153

SIMPLES, 137

SIMPSON
Elijah, 168
John, 122

SIMS
Julia A., 132

SIZEMORE
Edward E., 153
Miss E., 104

SKELTON
Miss Emily, 104

SLACK
Thos., 21

SLADE
Dr. James B., 169
Miss Amelia, 169
Rev., 151
Rev. T. B., 140, 151
Thos. B., 130

SLATON
James A., 98

SLAUGHTER
Alfred T., 114
Ataline, 114

SLEDGE
Charles M., 38
Mrs., 31, 38
M. D., 98

SLOAN
Capt., 65

SLUCK

Thomas, 15

**SMALLEY CRANDALL &
CO., 87**

SMITH
Alfred, 88
Augustus G., 122
Capt., 65
Chas. B., 123
Daniel J., 131
Dr., 137
E. J., 36
George, 27, 112, 123
Hampton L., 103
Hampton S., 39, 76, 121
Henry T., 143
Horatio, 116, 130
H. S., 37, 84, 89, 130
H. S. & CO., 26, 157
H. Y., 105
Isaac A., 50
James M., 169
Jasper S., 132
John, 144, 166
John G., 169
Joseph S., 103
J. S. & CO., 38
Martha, 131
Mary, 154
Mary A., 114
Miss Margaret, 104
Miss Mary C., 98
Miss Rebecca J., 105
Mrs. E. J., 45
Nancy, 122
Neil G., 155
N. G., 112
Rheddock, 153
Rolin W., 132
Ruthy, 144
Sidney A., 169
Simon L., 17
Sol, 44
Sol., 37
T. H., 130
Washington, 110

SMITH & AYER, 45

SMITH & GRIMES, 87

SMITH & HAYWARD, 131

**SMITH & MORGAN, 30,
38, 87**

SMITH-BEATTIE & CO., 120

SNEED

Seaborn, 114

SNELGROVE
Capt., 66

SNELL
David, 152

SNELLGROVE
Cornelia L., 152

SNOW
William, 104
Wm., 135

SNOWDON
R. E., 105

SORSBY
Battle A., 50
B. A., 17, 18, 21, 87, 130,
131

SOULE
Bishop, 150

SOUTHERN
John, 79

SOUTHMAYD
Andrew, 80

SPALDING
W. A., 20

**SPALDING & FONTAINE,
20**

SPARKS
Thomas P., 122

SPEARMAN
John, 38

SPEER
Anderson, 39

SPENCER
Lydia, 132
Miss Martha W., 113
R. P., 79

SPENCER & YONGE, 131

SPIGERS
Frances Ann, 168

SPILLER
Andrew J., 105

SPIVEY
E. B. W., 29
E. W. B., 37, 45, 156

SPRINGER
Miss Mary, 38

SPRINGER'S OPERA
HOUSE, 13

SQUIRE
Harvey H., 38

SQUIRE & TARVER, 38

STALLINGS
Mary L., 154
Miss E. H., 104

STANFORD
Elizabeth Ann, 169

STANLEY
Ann, 132

STANLEY & DUTTON, 31

STAPLER, 139

STAPLER
John W., 50

STARR
E. W., 79

STARR & AYER, 130

STARR & RUSE, 87

STEP, 71

STEPHENS
J. L., 166

STEWART, 162

STEWART
Capt., 65
Charles D., 32, 39
Chas. H., 55
C. D., 111
Mr., 27, 55

STEWART & FONTAINE,
24, 38

STINSON
Capt., 65

STOCKTON

James L., 113
Robert S., 143

STOCKTON & HOPKINS,
110

STONE
Matilda A., 122

STORY
John, 143

STRATTON
Calvin, 38, 100, 101, 107,
122, 130, 134, 146,
155

STRICKLAND
Gilford, 132

STRINGFELLOW
Henry, 131

STROUGH
Daniel, 114

STRUPPER
I. G., 136
Jno. B., 135
John Thomas, 133
J. B., 112, 130, 133

STUART
Bethire R., 153

STUDSTILL
Miss Sarah, 104

STURGES
Joseph, 116
Jos. L., 87
Thadeus S., 142

STURGIS, 166

STURGIS
Hon. Jos., 152
Joseph, 106, 124, 141
Joseph A., 154
Jos., 99
Judge, 137
Miss Mary A. E., 113
Thad., 166

STYLES
Sarah Ann, 114

St. JOHN
John, 55

SULLIVAN
Dr. J. C., 31
D., 97
James, 112
John, 124
Josephine O., 133

SULLIVAN & BIRD, 21

SULLY
Chester, 2
Samuel, 2, 50
Thomas, 2

SUTTON, 139

SWEET
Alfred, 168

SWIFT
Irena, 143

SWITZER
Miss Sarah, 98

TAGGERT
Thomas E., 55

TALBOT & READ, 87

TALLY
Mrs., 88

TAPPER
Hero, 113

TARVER
Benjamin, 15
Benj. Pinron, 115
B., 25
B. & CO, 26
B.P., 38
Elisha, 32, 38, 82, 111
E., 130
Miss Harriet, 104
Miss Martha M., 113
Miss Mary Ann, 50
Rev. Elijah, 50

TARVER & DILLINGHAM,
30

TARVER & SQUIRE, 38

TARVER-CLARK & CO., 80

TATE
Caroline, 142
J. V., 71

TATOM
Caroline, 26

TAXLEY
Wiliam, 21

TAYLOR
Dr. E. T., 115, 116
E. T., 97
Frances J., 169
Harriet Susan, 115
Hezekiah, 98
H. R., 24, 25
John, 21, 26, 30
Matilda, 131
Miss Sophia, 98
Wm., 132

TERRY
Francis, 112
G. B., 51, 80, 97, 154
G. B. C., 112
James Hugh, 154
Jas., 112
Jeremiah, 104, 134, 155
Jerry, 146
J., 111
Miss Eliza, 99
Miss Sarah, 99
Mrs. Mary Ann, 154
N., 112
Sarah Ann, 169
Sterling, 111
Sterling J., 114
Wm., 76, 103, 142

TERRY & MOODY, 103

THARP
Matilda, 122
Miss Adelia L., 104

THOMAS
Edward Lloyd, 10, 13
Elizabeth, 122
Elizabeth Ann, 168
Grigsby E., 26, 30, 52
G. E., 27, 32, 37, 50, 84,
    120, 121
Judge, 41
Mary E., 143
Miss Nancy, 104
Miss Sophia W., 21
Mrs. Mary A., 169
Owen, 130
P. M., 151
Samuel B., 79
Thomas (son of E. L.), 13

THOMAS & DOWNING, 131

THOMPSON, 139

THOMPSON
Alexander, 142
Catherine E., 168
James, 152
Jas. W., 114
Jeremiah A., 168
John, 54
Philander, 131
William H., 124
Wm., 104

THORNTON
A. J., 37
Dr., 37
Dr. Hudson A., 21
Dr. H. A., 88
Elizabeth R., 88
H. A., 50
John, 104, 168
J., 37
Mrs. Judith W., 21
T. A., 111

**THORNTON HOOPER &
    LIVINGSTON, 86**

**THORNTON LIVINGSTON &
    HARPER, 87**

THORNTON & HUDSON, 26

THURMAN
Ann, 153

THWEAT
W., 112

THWEATT
James, 31
Jno. Griffin, 112
Miss, 21
M. W., 30, 77, 130
Senator Peterson, 133

THWEATTE
M. W., 27

TICHNOR
Mrs. H. C., 103

TICKNOR
Miss Lucy E., 38

TILLER
Paul H., 80

TILLERY
John, 123

TILLEY
Miss Savannah G., 103
Mrs., 164
William W., 146

TILLMAN
Caroline M., 114

TILLY
W. W., 155

TINSLEY
W. B., 48, 50

TOBY
Frederick, 125
F., 111
F. D., 111

TOMBERLIN
George W., 154

TOMLIN
Miss Sophia, 16

TOMPKINS
Henry M., 143

TONEY
Washington, 55
Wm., 87
W., 87

**TONEY & RUTHERFORD,
    80**

TOOMBS
Capt., 65
R., 137

TORRANCE
Mansfield, 130

TORRENCE, 87

TORRENCE
Ebenezer, 39, 49
Miss Maria A., 45
M., 50

**TORRENCE UNDERWOOD
    & CO., 87**

TORRY
W. W., 146, 147, 155

TOWN

Ithiel, 32

TOWNSEND
John, 15, 25, 37, 39, 55,
56, 77
Lewis, 144

TOWNSLEY
Victor N., 124
V. S., 112, 116, 134

TOZIER
J C., 164
John C., 132

TRIPLETT
Hillery, 15, 44

TRITT
Archibald C., 168

TROTTER
Nathaniel, 80

TROUP, 40

TROUP
Capt., 65

TRUSTER
Franklin, 168

TUCKER
Gilly A., 122

TURNBULL
J. R., 135

TURNER
Dr. J. W., 107
J. A. S. & CO., 45
Mary Jane, 168

TURNER MORRIS & CO.,
87

TURRENTINE
George W., 113, 155
G. W., 131
Miss Catharine L., 166
Sarah, 133

TUSCOONA FIXICO, 78

UNDERWOOD
Dr. Wiley J., 26
Emily, 143
John N., 132
Sarah A., 123

UNDERWOOD TORRENCE
& CO., 87

UNDERWOOD & MILLS, 26

UPTON
David W., 25
D. W., 111

URQUHART
Captain J. A., 59
Capt., 65
Capt. John A., 73
Dr. John A., 88
John A., 45
J. A., 50, 54

VAN BUREN
Mr., 111

VAN NESS, 38, 44

VAN NESS
James, 13, 15, 16, 17,
20, 23, 24, 33, 52, 96,
152
Mr., 110

VAN VECHTEN, 139

VAN VECHTEN
Capt., 165

VANCE
Miles M., 76

VANHORN
H., 114

VARDEMAN
Capt., 65

VARNADORE
Miss Arcada, 105

VASON
Miss Emily R., 88

VICKERY

Wm. D., 131

VICTORY
John, 68

VICTURY
Francis, 122

VINCENT
Paton, 122
William J., 145

VINSON
Mary, 51
Peyton, 51

WADDELL
James M., 168

WADE
Edward E., 114
Mary, 153
W. & CO., 97

WADE & BEARDSLEY, 87

WADE & CO., 87

WADE & MIDDLEBROOK,
130

WADSWORTH
James, 36
Wm., 152

WALDING
Mary E., 131

WALKER
A. M., 51, 111
Benjamin w., 132
Benj., 103
B., 97
David E., 55
Dr. A. M., 169
Ellen Emeline, 88
John A., 114
John T., 55, 79, 135, 156
Miss Charlotte, 98
Miss Mary A., 114
Mrs. Martha Angelina, 169
Wm. (Sr.), 31

WALKER & BEDELL, 57

WALKER & BOON, 97

WALL
Bradford, 122
James, 132
Shadrack, 133

WALLER
Benjamin, 122

WALLING
Daniel, 87

David, 98
D., 77
Wm., 80, 168

WALLS
Martha Ann, 133

WALTON
John L., 104
J. S., 112

WAMACK
Sandford, 168

WARD
Harriet S., 142
Miss Caroline E., 98

WARD & FOSTER, 130

WARDEN
Jeptha, 142

WARE
Dr. Robert A., 31
Dr. R. A., 163
John H., 111
J. H., 80
Robert A., 113
Robt. A., 54
R. A., 85, 89, 116, 130

WARE & BOND, 130

WARREN
John, 31, 84, 120
Martha Caroline, 31
Sophia, 31

WASHINGTON, 33, 42

WASHINGTON
Geo., 168

WATKINS
A. L., 25, 111
Irvin, 122
Miss Epsy A., 105

WATLEY
Mary, 152

WATSON, 103

WATSON
Benjamin D., 144
Col., 148
Col. John H., 147
Col. J. H., 58
Elizabeth, 51

Gen. James, 36
Gen. James C., 51, 144
James C., 36, 46
John, 58, 137
John H., 112
J. C., 85, 87
J. H., 121
J. W., 99
Mary, 132
Miss Mary A., 98
Thomas C., 106
Thomas W., 114

WATSON & McDOUGALD, 131

WATT
Wm. J., 143

WAY
Geo. W., 97

WAY & JOHNSON, 79

WAYLAND
Mr., 111
Thomas, 114

WEATHERS
Lavina, 122

WEAVER
James L., 169
John, 105
Jonathan, 152
Miss Louisa, 104
Wiley, 113

WEBB
Elbridge G., 142
Isaac W., 37

WEBSTER
C. E., 169
Joseph E., 98, 138
J. E., 135, 169
Mary Claudia, 169
Samuel, 114

WEDDINGTON
Martha, 123

WEEDEN
Col., 166

WEEKS
Ashley, 81
Bartlett, 111
Bartley, 81

WEEMS
Walter H., 113

WELBORN
Dr., 63

WELCH & MYRICK, 80

WELL, 162

WELLBORN
Marshall J., 57, 97
M. J., 86, 112, 130, 137, 165
William J. W., 16

WELLS
Benjamin, 113
B., 130
E., 107
E. & CO., 30
Martha, 133
Matthew, 21
Miss Olive, 114
Stephen G., 118, 168
S. G., 124, 133

WELLS & HUDGIN, 125

WELLS & HUDGINS, 126

WERE
R. A., 80

WEST
Charles, 131
John, 143
Robert K., 31
Tillman, D., 123

WESTMORELAND
James H., 38
Jane, 142
Mark J., 142
Miss Eliz., 98

WESTWOOD
Elizabeth J., 143

WHATLEY
Elizabeth, 153

WHEELOCK & WILLARD, 57

WHITE
Henrietta, 122
Joseph, 15
J. S. W., 45
Miller H., 122

Miss Margaret, 88

WHITESIDES
John, 80

WHITTICH & GRANT, 45

WHITTINGTON
Sarah, 142

WICKS & BIZE, 80

WIGGINS
Emily, 154
Joel C., 122

WILD
Miss Susan, 99

WILEY
C., 99

WILEY BAXTER & FORT, 21

WILHELM, 138

WILHELM
Frederick, 134
F., 146

WILHELM & McDANIEL, 88

WILKENSON
James D., 124

WILKES, 129

WILKES
Sarah A., 123
William B., 123

WILKINSON
Abner, 131

WILKS
Miss Martha, 113

WILLARD & WHEELOCK, 57

WILLERS
Hester, 122

WILLIAMS
Alcy, 169
Amanda, 169
Catharine M., 169
C. J., 166
Edward W., 154

Eliza, 131, 132
Elizabeth, 133
Hezekiah, 104
H. F., 169
Isaac, 104
Jackson, 131
Jacob, 80
Jane, 133, 144
John, 76
John Thomas, 169
J. M., 111
J. S., 112
Lewis, 98
Louisa, 143
Mary Irving, 144
Milton, 122, 141, 154
Miss Martha, 105, 114
Miss Orra, 104
Miss Sarah, 104
Missoura A., 142
Nancy, 142, 152
Rev. Albert, 141, 144
Turner, 80
Wiley, 85, 88, 89, 103, 106, 116, 121, 134, 146, 155, 166
Wiley & Brother, 87

WILLIAMS HOLCOMB & ROBINSON, 87

WILLIAMS & SHIVERS, 131

WILLIAMSON
Wm., 37, 77
W. C., 55

WILLIFORD
Jas. D., 154

WILLINGHAM
Ann, 153
Miss Lucy A., 105

WILLIS
Elizabeth, 132
Miss Edna, 98

WILSON, 138

WILSON
Dr. John J., 33
Dr. J. J., 37
Enoch H., 143
Frances, 153
Irishman, 16
James H., 123, 137
Miss Francis A., 105
Miss Malinda, 114
Rhoda, 168

WILSON & CHILDERS, 38

WIMBERLY
H. F., 88
H. S., 54
Lewis T., 123
Miss Eliza J., 113

WINDHAM
Mary, 132

WINNIFRED
Mrs., 88

WINSTON & ALFORD, 17

WINTER, 163

WINTER
John G., 139, 149, 155, 156
Lucinda M., 154

WISE
Charles, 141, 146
Chas., 121

WITT
Eliza Ann, 169
James, 168

WITTICH, 57

WITTICH
Earnest L., 76
E. L., 50, 52, 53, 54, 79

WITTICH & HOWARD, 87

WODSWORTH
James, 37

WOMBLE
Miss Cretia, 105

WOOD
Jesse, 153
J. B., 106
Miss Anna C., 88
Miss Martha S., 105
Randolph, 143

WOODLIFF
William, 17

WOODRUFF, 139

WOODRUFF
Dr. M., 146, 155

G. W. & CO., 121, 130
M., 151
Philo D., 26
Phil. B., 37
R., 51, 57

WOODWARD
Gen., 71
Gen. Thomas S., 62

WOOLFOLK
Col., 118
Gen. Sowell, 32, 33
John, 50, 96, 111, 130
Jos. W., 154
Mrs., 50
R. T., 21
Samuel, 50
Sowell, 15, 16, 21, 24, 27, 30
S. & R. T., 20

WOOLFOLK'S BAR, 12

WOOLFOLK'S BEND, 60

WOOLFOLK'S MOUND, 14

WOOLFOLK'S Sand Bar, 91

WORD
Franklin, 102

WORDLAW
Micajah C., 142

WORSHAM
Jane E. E., 153

WRIGHT
David, 111, 118, 135
F. A., 135, 146
LeGrand, 129, 164
Ligrand S., 143
Wilson, 132

WYATT
James M., 113
Miss Frances A., 105

WYCHE
R. D., 37

WYEKS
Bartlett, 44

WYNN, 130

WYNN

Col. Wm. L., 141
George H., 98
Mrs. Ann Elizabeth, 50
Wm. L., 50, 77

WYNNE
T. K., 151

YARBOROUGH
Robert H., 122

YARBROUGH
George C., 112
Moses, 38
Richard, 112
R., 112

YEAMAN'S CIRCUS, 44

YONGE
GARRARD & HOOPER, 157
Harrison, 103
J. R., 119
Wm. P., 79, 97, 103, 120
W. P., 166

YONGE & ELLIS, 97

YONGE & SPENCER, 131

YOUNG
Hiram, 135
H., 146
John C., 135
John R., 131, 156
J. R., 112, 136, 146

YOUNG & ALLEN, 87

ZUVER
Lovick P., 143
Col. Wm. L., 141
George H., 98
Mrs. Ann Elizabeth, 50
Wm. L., 50, 77

Columbus, Geo.,

Selection as a "Trading Town"

IN

1827,

TO ITS

Partial Destruction by Wilson's Raid,

IN

1865.

HISTORY—INCIDENT—PERSONALITY.

PART II—1846 TO 1865.

COMPILED BY JOHN H. MARTIN.

COLUMBUS, GA.
PUBLISHED BY THOS. GILBERT, PRINTER AND BOOK-BINDER.
1875.

INDEX.

COLUMBUS, GA.

1846.

The Bridge Troubles—Military—Organization of Regiment
for Mexican War—"The Great Fire."

The dispute between the city authorities and the people of
Russell county about the crossing of the bridge was renewed
this year. Some citizens of Alabama erected a toll gate and
demanded toll at the western abutment of the bridge. The
City Council, on the 18th of March, passed an ordinance
requiring of every foot passenger in Russell county $6\frac{1}{4}$ cents
for passing over the city bridge; also, to charge citizens of
said county for wood, lumber, or anything previously passed
free; also requiring the said ordinance to remain in effect so
long as tolls are demanded at the toll-gate erected at the abutment of the bridge in the town of Girard, and that proper
counsel be employed to use legal measures to have such toll-
gate removed.

On the 10th of July Council appointed a committee, composed of John Banks, John R. Dawson and Kenneth McKenzie, to confer with a committee appointed by the Court of
Roads and Revenue of Russell county, Alabama, in relation
to the adjustment of the existing difficulties in regard to the
bridge.

In September the Commissioners' Court of Russell county
rescinded the order for establishing a toll-gate near the west-

ern end of the bridge, in Girard. Whereupon the City Council adopted a resolution authorizing the crossing of agricultural produce, wood, &c., free of toll.

The Orphan Asylum (an institution undertaken by some of the ladies in 1844) was this year open for the reception of the orphan poor.

The City Light Guards were organized June 28th. The officers were, A. H. Cooper, Captain; D. P. Ellis, First Lieut.; A. G. Redd, Second; S. K. Hodges, Third; Wm. H. Pruden, First Sergeant; F. C. Johnson, Second; J. M. Hughes, Third; R. B. Kyle, Fourth; A. C. Brown, First Corporal; R. R. Hudgins, Second; John Wilmer, Third; J. A. L. Lee, Fourth.

This was the first year of the war with Mexico, and Columbus shared largely in the excitement which it occasioned. The Governor of Georgia in response to a call by the President of the United States, invited the enrollment of volunteers, and Columbus was selected as the place of rendezvous of a regiment of infantry. The volunteers arrived about the middle of June, and were reviewed by Gov. Crawford. The officers of the regiment were H. R. Jackson, of Savannah, Colonel; Thos. Y. Redd, of Columbus, Lieut. Colonel; Chas. J. Williams, of Columbus, Major; John Forsyth, of Columbus, Adjutant; Jas. Kellogg, Colonel's Private Secretary; S. M. McConnel, of Cherokee, Sergeant Major; B. F. McDonald, of Marietta, Q. M. Sergeant; Drs. J. J. B. Hoxey and W. E. Beall, of Columbus, Surgeon and Assistant; Rev. Mr. Cairnes, Chaplain.

Principal Musicians, Geo. Gatehouse and Dennis Holland, of Savannah.

The following ten companies composed the regiment: We give the Captain of each and the officers in full of the three Columbus companies: Columbus Guards, Columbus—John E. Davis, Captain; John Forsyth, First Lieutenant; C. P. Hervey, Second; Roswell Ellis, First Sergeant; Jos. King, Second; W. C. Holt, Third; W. C. Hodges, Fourth; W. G.

Andrews, First Corporal; V. D. Tharpe, Second; Jas. Hamilton, Third; R. A. McGibony, Fourth.

Crawford Guards, Columbus—John Jones, Captain; R. G. Mitchell, First Lieutenant; J. S. Dismukes, Second; T. Shoemaker, First Sergeant; H. S. Teasdale, Second; A. M. Sauls, Third; D. A. Winn, Fourth; John May, First Corporal; John Lochaby, Second; James B. Wells, Third; N. J. Peabody, Fourth.

Georgia Light Infantry, Columbus—J. S. Calhoun, Captain; E. R. Goulding, First Lieutenant; H. C. Anderson, Second; W. B. Philips, First Sergeant; A. B. Hoxey, Second; W. T. Smith, Third; M. H. Blandford, Fourth; R. H. Howard, First Corporal; A. Scott, Second; Thos. Reynolds, Third; Geo. Lindsay, Fourth.

The other companies were Canton Volunteers, Cherokee county; Richmond Blues, Augusta; Macon Guards, Macon; Fannin Avengers, Pike County; Kennesaw Rangers, Cobb county; Sumter County Volunteers; Jasper Greens, Savannah. Regiment numbered 893 men.

The regiment was presented with a United States Flag by Miss Mary Ann Howard (the late Mrs. Chas. J. Williams) which was received by Col. Jackson. The regiment left on Sunday, June 28th, crossed on the lower bridge, crowds of people looking on, and marched to Chehaw, and railroaded to Montgomery and were carried thence to Mexico, where they remained twelve months, but had no part in the many battles, but were engaged in several skirmishes. City Council gave $300 to Columbus Guards.

The city election, on the first Saturday in January, resulted in the choice of John G. Winter as Mayor, without opposition, and the following gentlemen as Aldermen: 1st Ward, W. S. Holstead, J. C. Ruse; 2d Ward, Dr. M. Woodruff, Dr. S. A. Billing; 3rd Ward, R. N. R. Bardwell; 4th Ward, John Quin; 5th Ward, N. M. C. Robinson, J. L. Morton; 6th Ward, B. F. Coleman, Jos. Wiggins. Dr. Stewart in the 3rd and J. H. Shorter in the 4th, were the next highest candidates in their respective Wards, but as the law required a clear majority · to elect, and the votes were divided among several candidates in each of these Wards, only one was chosen in each. Col. Winter received 498 votes, and no candidate receiving less than 400 was elected an Alderman. We compute the whole number of votes cast at about 620.

At a subsequent special election for Aldermen of the 3rd and 4th Wards, Dr. Stewart was elected for the 3rd, and J. H. Shorter for the 4th.

The following officers were elected by the City Council: Wm. Brooks, Marshal; J. M. Hughes, Deputy Marshal; C. Stratton, Clerk; G. W. Turrentine, Treasurer; Richard Burt, Bridge Keeper; W. Tilly, Clerk of the Market; Mrs. McGehee, Hospital Keeper.

From the Treasurer's report we learn that the receipts of the city for the year 1845 were $24,696, including cash on hand at the beginning of the year $1,956. The expenditures were $24,696, including $24 cash on hand. The revenue from the bridge was $9,717. The city debt at that time was $56,655, of which $30,000 was due to John G. Winter on account of a loan.

The *Enquirer* of the 24th of January congratulated the city on the prospect of the construction of the Southwestern Railroad at an early day. It announced the opening of books of subscription at Macon, Columbus, and intermediate places.

Messrs. B. Beasly, F. Toby and M. N. Clark, who had been appointed to assess the cash valuation of the real estate in the city, reported in March that they made the total valuation $1,233,245, being $40,950 more than that of the previous year.

The city authorities this year manifested much concern for the proper care of the poor within its limits. Alderman Woodruff was active and zealous in this behalf. Council requested the Superior Court of Muscogee county to levy 10 per cent. upon the State tax upon persons and property in the city for the support of the poor. In April an ordinance was adopted providing for the election annually of a Board of Commissioners of the Poor, whose duty it should be to ascertain the necessities of the poor and distribute the fund raised for their relief. Asa Pond, Wm. Amos, Lewis C. Allen, Theobold Howard and M. Woodruff were elected Commissioners.

The first Mayor's Court of the city was organized this year, under authority of an act of the Legislature, and a code of ordinances defining the offences coming within the jurisdiction of the Court was adopted.

The bridge tolls this year were appropriated exclusively to the payment of the debt due to the State of Georgia.

The most disastrous fire the city ever sustained occurred on the morning of October 9th, this year. The fire originated in the wood and blacksmith shops of Marcus D. Jones, on Oglethorpe street, northwest of the court-house, and burnt the two blocks between St. Clair and Crawford and Oglethorpe and Front streets except the Fontaine House, most of the two blocks south of these, and the flames thence went westward to the river. The fire was arrested one-half square below the bridge, and one square above the boat landing. The loss in houses, goods, furniture, &c., was estimated at $250,000. The number of sufferers about 700—400 of whom were greatly injured. No loss of life. Mr. Mariner received a lick and fell from the second story of the City Hotel. The fire swept down the most of five squares, and a few houses of the sixth square. It consumed the livery stable of James Bradford & Co., and all the houses between that and Janny's foundry (the latter was saved). The shop on the corner north (where Muscogee Home now is) occupied by T. and E. Reid, gin makers, was consumed, also the large wooden building known as City Hotel, owned by D. McDougald (Georgia Home Bank building is now on the site). The wind

blew briskly southwest. The market-house, then at the intersection of Broad and St. Clair streets, caught and was
consumed, and then the flames took down southward on
both sides of Broad street. On the east side were consumed
the goods of Reuben Shorter; James Ligon, groceries and
provisions; Lesterget's do.; Charles Kendall's do.; T.
Sanders' cabinet shop; Dr. Thos. Hoxey's shop and medi-
cines; I. B. Hoxey's grocery; I. G. & J. B. Strupper's goods
and residence; Hamilton & Co's clothing and $300 in cash;
J. Kivlin's Sans Souci and residence, worth $15,000, insur-
ance $5,000; John Ligon & Tilley's grocery; Shaeffer's gun
shop; Thomas Treadwell's residence; Turean's grocery; J.
S. Norman's saddle shop and one story house; Dr. Young's
office; Chas. Fuch's bakery; Phil. Reynolds and J. Rowe's
bar-room; McIntosh Row, occupied by Theobold Howard
and others, as residences; Dillingham's corner, owned by
Wells & Toby; Henry Matthew's residence; Rev. W. D.
Cairnes' building; W. P. Baker's and Mrs. Tichnor's residences and Miss Edmundson's school room. Here the fire on
the east side of Broad was stopped. It had swept two
squares south, consuming every house on the first from St.
Clair street, except Janny's foundry, the old theatre, a small
grocery, and on the square south of Crawford everything
except a few houses on the side west of the court-house.

At the same time, the west side of Broad, south of St.
Clair, was fired, and every house was consumed save the
Fontaine residence. Wm. P. Yonge's residence, west of this,
was saved, owing to the direction of the wind. The fire
passed Rankin's corner, (Broad and Crawford streets,) burnt
the Democratic Liberty-Pole, consumed all of Battle Row,
crossed over to the west side of Front street, and destroyed
the residence of Mr. Rankin; Yonge, Garrard & Hooper's
warehouse being saved after a hard fight; burned John
Whitesides' stables near the river, but his tavern was saved.
All that part of the square from Broad and Crawford, south
to the bridge, was consumed, including several houses blown

up. The fire was arrested just one-half square below the bridge, and one square from the steamboat landing.

The principal sufferers on the west side of Broad street were: Hill, Dawson & Co. (saved goods,) building $5,000; D. W. Orr & Co., clothing; Mrs. A. B. Davis, store-house, bank building and residence; J. S. Smith & Co., clothing; A. M. Cox, grocer; George Hargraves, building, $3,000; Luke Reid, shoe and saddle store; Messrs. Peabody; A. Calhoun, grocer; S. & F. W. Sartwell, dry goods and groceries $10,000; J. N. Harris & Co., $5,000; E. Wells & Co., shoe store; John Code, tailor, $800; James Sullivan, grocer, $11,000; L. J. Davies, dry goods; Patillo's boarding house; Mrs. Davies, milliner, heavy loss; William Rankin, store and goods, and residence on Broad street, $15,000; B. Wells, several stores; William Tarbutton, owner of old Columbus Hotel, (Jake Burrus' old corner;) William Tarbutton, $1,000; Wiley Adams; Dr. Thornton, two tenements; Gunn, provisions; Mrs. E. Webster, two stores, $800; J. W. Campbell, workshop; S. Hoffman, grocery and residence blown up, $800. On Bridge street—J. Code, residence; Dr. Rogan's house; N. L. Howard, two houses; John Quin and Joseph Walton, stores.

On Front—Residences of Mrs. L. J. Davies, Mrs. James A. Shorter; William Owens, Colonel Jones' building, and all others down to a half square below the bridge on the west side of Front street. On Battle Row, or Crawford street— J. Boulter, Thomas McCarty, B. Weeks, P. Sullivan.

The heat was so intense on Broad street, that goods took fire after being removed from the stores. Fabulous sums were offered for drays to haul off goods. The only fire engine (No. 1) came near being burned.

Girard narrowly escaped from cinders.

Council appealed to the public for aid in behalf of the sufferers, and John Quin, acting Mayor, issued a proclamation in accordance. A committee was appointed to solicit aid.

Committee, on October 12th, reported 80 persons had been supplied with food.

Savannah contributed $1,400; Macon, $505; Montgomery, $493 40; Columbus, in money and goods, $1,603 75. The Governor gave delay in the collection of taxes; Astor House, New York, $50.

Relief was offered on this plan—entire losses not exceeding $100—75 cents on the dollar; not exceeding $200—50 per cent., and the balance of the fund equally divided among sufferers.

To replace the burned apparatus of Fire Company No. 1, $135 were appropriated.

INCIDENTS.

The initiatory steps towards the building of the Mobile and Girard Railroad were taken this year. The Alabama Legislature chartered a company styled "the Girard Railroad Company," with James and Anderson Abercombie, Wm. Davis, S. M. Ingersoll, J. Godwin, W. B. Harris, J. Drummond, W. Burnett, R. S. Hardaway, B. Baker, E. Morfell, J. Allen, W. Luther, T. Kemp, B. S. Mangham, —— Floyd and N. W. Long, as Commissioners. Capital not to exceed $5,000,000, in shares of $100 each. The road to extend from Girard to intersect or connect with the navigable waters of Mobile Bay, or with the railroad leading from Montgomery to West Point, at the nearest and most suitable point of said road.

Other railroad enterprises in which Columbus was then concerned, were the building of a projected road to Macon or Barnesville, to intersect the Central or Macon and Western, and the construction of a road to Atlanta. John G. Winter was President of the company having the last named project in charge.

On the 4th of April F. S. Wingate shot and killed John Conley with a pistol. Wingate crossed the river and made his escape.

The Muscogee Riflemen were organized on the 4th of July, with M. N. Clarke, Captain; Wm. R. Jones 1st Lieutenant; M. Reid, 2d; John B. Wells, Ensign; N. P. Foster, 1st Sergeant; Chas. Torrean, 2d; J. W. Frost, 3rd; J. B. Hicks, 4th; Levi Duck, 1st Corporal; I. Trawick, 2d; E. L. Hall, 3rd; Peter McGar, 4th.

The first new bale of cotton of the season was brought in from the plantation of James Chapman, in Russell County, Alabama, and brought 10c., A. G. Lawrence being the purchaser.

On October 14th cotton was quoted at 7 to 8½c.; on the 21st, 8½ to 8⅜c., from wagons; on November 3rd, 8 to 8⅜c.

PERSONAL.

The following were the county officers of Muscogee, elected in January: Sheriff—John M. Bethune over J. A. L. Lee; Clerk Superior Court—Thad S. Sturgis over B. Beasley; Clerk Inferior Court—R. G. Mitchell over John Johnson; Tax Collector—F. A. Jepson over T. H. Kendall; Tax Receiver—A. Stephens over D. Parkman; County Surveyor—P. Lamar over T. J. Hand; Coroner—T. O'Brien over G. B. Terry.

The Grand Jury for the January term consisted of J. S. Calhoun, foreman; A. Levison, M. N. Clarke, K. McKenzie, S. G. Wells, James Shaw, L. Cherry, B. F. Malone, H. Livingstone, H. C. Dawson, O. P. Tillinghast, W. L. Wynn, Thos. J. Shivers, E. S. Greenwood, J. C. Cook, Davis Mulford, S. C. Lindsay, E. Dudley, P. McLaren, M. Woodruff, D. Adams. They presented as a nuisance so many change bills; also the trading and trafficing with negroes, and allowing negroes to keep bar-rooms. Judge Sturgis presided over the Court. Hon. R. B. Alexander was appointed Judge of the Circuit soon afterwards.

Rev. James A. Wiggins was presiding Elder of the Columbus M. E. District, and Rev. J. E. Evans stationed at Columbus.

R. Burt resigned the position of bridge-keeper in June, on account of the difficulty of enforcing the regulations, and Wm. W. Martin was elected in his stead.

The Grand Jury for the April term consisted of S. W. Flournoy, foreman; E. C. Bandy, Wm. Amos, L. C. Allen, G. B. Terry, Jas. Sullivan, Calvin Stratton, S. Weems, M. Chisholm, R. W. Fox, A. Peabody, T. Howard, Wm. Rankin, James Kivlin, Van Leonard, G. S. McGehee, T. A. Brannon, T. J. Terry, and Leroy Holt.

James Kivlin was elected, in July, an Alderman of the 4th Ward, in the place of James H. Shorter, deceased.

Alderman Robinson having removed from the 5th Ward, S. R. Andrews was in September elected an Alderman for said Ward.

Council, in December, adopted a resolution that Messrs. Echols & Howard had faithfully performed their contract for the improvement of the water lots.

The following boats arrived and departed during the winter of this year: Lotus, Allen master; Champion, Cadwallader master; Peytona, Greer master; Viola, Van Vechten master; Mary Ann Moore, Moore master; Nation, McAlister master; Boston, Morton master; Emily, Hall master; Columbus, Stapler master; Eufaula, Thompson master; Albany, ——— master.

The following list includes the names of all the business and professional men advertising in the *Enquirer* this year:

Merchants.—E. & M. Meidner, J. Ennis & Co., George Durham, R. A. Ware, Greenwood & Ellis, J. M. Tarbot & Co., E. Barnard & Co., Hall & Moses, Pond & Willcox, Moody & Durr, A. H. McNeil, Bruno & Virgins, P. McLaren, Wesson & Booher, S. B. Hamilton, J. I. Ridgway, S. B. Purple, Ridgway & Barden, L. L. Cowdery, Winter & Epping, L. J. Davies, B. Wells & Co., Strong & Wood, H. H. Woodruff, Brokaw & Clemons, D. & J. Kyle, J. S. Smith & Co., Jas. F. Watson, Jas. Dwight, B. B. deGraffenried, J. & I. G. Strupper, Wynn & Chandler, Jos. B. Green, J. W. Pease, M. Pecare & Co., Wm. A. Redd & Co., G. B. Terry, G. W. Woodruff, Sammis & Rooney, Johnson & Frost, Mygatt & Hodges, Q. C. Terry, Hill, Dawson & Co., D. W. Orr & Co., Ives & Bro., Wade & Middlebrook, Aug. L. Grant, Birdsong & Sledge, A. J. Robison, J. H. Merry, Stanford & Ellis, A. A. Denslow, Hogan & Cooper, Robert Carter.

Teachers.—R. W. B. Munro, Miss O'Hara and Sister, Mr. O'Hara, Miss A.

B. Alexander and Miss D. Pease, Mr. Boyden, J. H. Goodale, Thos. B. Slade, Mrs. Bethune, John G. Baker, Thos. G. Pond.

Restaurants.—Wm. B. Ferrell, E. A. White.

Cabinet Wareroom—Henry Willers.

Dentists—J. Fogle, O. P. Laird, C. T. Cushman.

Auction and Commission—N. McRobinson, A. K. Ayer.

Lawyers—John M. Bethune, C. S. Rockwell, A. G. Foster, Hines Holt, Wm. Dougherty, M. Johnston, L. T. Downing.

Book-Binder—R. Tanner.

Cotton Brokers—Hanserd & Morris.

Warehouses—Ruse, Patten & Co., Yonge, Garrard & Hooper, Greenwood & Co., Hooper & Ridgway, Ed. J. Hardin.

Doctors—E. M. deGraffenried, Boswell & Billing, Holt & Butt, Wildman & Craig, Thos. Hoxey, Dr. Goulding.

Iron Foundries—Israel H. Janney, Joseph Colwell & Co.

Carriage Repositories—H. C. McKee, J. B. Jaques.

Hotels—Oglethorpe House, by R. L. Bass; City Hotel, by Murry Reed and Isaac Mitchell; Kentucky House, by W. Perry

Ice Dealer—John Byrne.

Gin Makers—Templeton Reid, E. Y. Taylor & Co., (in Girard.)

Livery Stable—Jas. A. Bradford.

Boarding House—Mrs. Teasdale.

Millinery—Miss C. W. Alexander, Mrs. Dessau.

Gunsmith—F. Shaefer.

Deguerreotype Gallery—Mr. Lovering.

MARRIAGES.

January 4—Greene S. Duke and Pyrene C. Webb. January 6, George W. Howard and Caroline E. Smith. Jan. 8, Jeremiah Massey and Frances Broadnax, John Jones and Elizabeth Emily Tilly. Jan. 11, David Magouirk and Margaret Duke. Jan. 14, George Thornton and Rebecca Thornton. Jan. 26, John Mosey and Martha Byus. Jan. 27, Simon P. Bickley and Martha A. Culver.

February 5—Peter Diffley and Jane Wade, Richard Ector and Eleanor M. S. Ector. Feb. 11, Wm. A. Shofner and Mary Ann Turnage. Feb. 12, Henry H. Epping and Barbary C. Cubbage. Feb. 13, John Houston and Martha J. McClure. Feb. 15, Morton Kelsey and Georgian V. Marcrum. Feb. 18, Lambert Spencer and Venona Mitchell. Feb. 22, Alexander C. Green and Mary Burns.

March 1—Shadrack Walls and Nancy Cordry. March 2, Salathal N. Cropman and Caroline Crandall, Gregory Ortagus and Mrs. Stacy Ann Lee, Martin Castello and Permelia Gouter. Feb. 4, James W. Johnson and Sarah Garrison. March 5, Alanson M. Cox and Georgiana M. Affleck. March 10, Lester L. Cowdery and Eveline Rule. March 18, Thos. M. Clowers and Louisa Warren. March 23, William C. Swann and Delila E. Brown. March 24, Hiram Hooker and Mary Bell. March 25, Stephen Z. Harnesberger and Susan Norris. March 26, George C. Benton and Frances M. Stallings, Wm. L. O'Stein and Harriet S. Adams.

April 2—Jonathan Cordry and Elizabeth Tomlinson. April 12, James M. Baggett and Mary Ann Pike. April 26, Thomas Cransby and Mary Simpson. April 30, Doctor H. Sanders and Martha Walters.

May 12—Nelson McLester, Esq., and Mary C. Redd. May 17, Jno. M. Jones and Elizabeth J. Rogers, Charles King and Caroline Ligon. May 23, Ichabod B. Hoxie and Euphemia Allen.

June 2—Josiah Pranglin and Jane Ann Giddings. June 3, Jas. H. Edmundson and Susan Ramsay. June 4, James P. Duck and Caroline E. Dimon, Jas. Francis and Louisa F. Perryman. June 11, James Slaughter and Eleanor Williams. June 16, Cary C. Willis and Mary F. Huff. June 21, Wiley Sizemore and Mary Askew.

July 5—Jesse Clay and Nancy Caroline Bryan. July 7, Edward W. Nix and Ann Harvell. July 9, Brady F. Warner and Matilda M. Brown. July 23, David Culpepper and Caroline Hays. July 29, Edward S. Ott and Ann A. Alston, Richard L. Butt and Elizabeth C. Leonard.

August 2—John Kingsbury and Missouri Ann Grey, Thomas W. Ballard and Jane Hawthorn. Aug. 10, James Johnson and Nancy Amanda Roach. Aug. 12, John F. Bosworth and Augusta F. Reeves.

September 6—William A. Livingston and Mary A. Cooper. Sept. 10, Matthew Knight and Martha Ann Bryley. Sept. 18, Jacob Williams and Eliza Adams. Sept. 22, Edwin N. Hyatt and Mary Jane Lee. Sept. 24, Caleb Gallops and Sarah Palmer. Sept. 27, George W. Smith and Sarah Mann.

October 1—Wm. A. Beach and Caroline L. Neuffer. Oct. 5, John Crosby and Sarah Rawl. Oct. 6, Wiley L. Day and Sarah Ann Elizabeth Andrews, William H. Smith and Nancy Ann Edwards. Oct. 7, Jas. Hall and Frances Ballard. Oct. 8, Jesse D. Hadley and Malinda R. Teel. Oct. 15, Benjamin W. Moon and Arabella T. Eldred. Oct. 18, Zachariah Gammel and Elizabeth Osborn. Oct. 22, Edward Christian and Rachel Witt. Oct. 28, Francis M. Gray and Mentoria E. Mead.

November 3—William Walker and Harriet E. Shay, Luke Crandall and Martha E. Rawson. Nov. 4, Wesley Gray and Emeline Jones. Nov. 12, Jas. W. McCullers and Lucinda Scroggins, Abraham Miller and Martha Morgan, Henry Hall and Mary A. Nisbett. Nov. 13, Wm. McConnell and Tabitha Olive Kent. Nov. 24, Jordan L. Howell and Elizabeth S. Johnson. Nov. 25, James H. Carter and Henrietta M. Harden. Nov. 26, James A. Redding and Caroline P. Davis, Vincent H. Harrison and Martha Roland, James Twilley and Catharine Davis. Nov. 29, Elijah Padgett and Axupershanee Johnson.

December 3—Q. Carlyle Terry and Elizabeth G. Goulding. Dec. 10, Thos. J. Tipper and Emily Vickers, Abner Buchanan and Ninetta L. Chisolm. Dec. 11, Jno. E. Renfroe and Martha Ann Daniel. Dec. 13, Anda McNeel and Martha Weathers. Dec. 16, William J. McBride and Mary Ann Wall.

Dec. 17, Charnel Hightower and Amanda Henry. Dec. 20, Jasper Harris and Judith Ann Buckner. Dec. 21, William C. Owens and Catharine Simpson. Dec. 22, Wade H. T. Powell and Mary E. Dade, Jno J. Rockmore and Sarah Jane Edwards. Dec. 24, Sampson D. Helms and Missouri Parker, Simeon Perry and Emily Kilpatrick. Dec. 30, William H. Spurgers and Ann Prickett. Dec. 31, Israel H. Jamsey and Mary Jane O'Hara, Jourdan Hightower and Jane Henry, Slakely Lamberth and Mary Ann Fincher.

DEATHS.

January 23—Arthur B. Davis. Jan. 28—Dr. A. S. Clifton. Jan. 29, Jeremiah Mullens.

March 5—Francis N. Ruse. March 7, Mrs. Martha T. Redd.

April 4—Mrs. Harriet A. Wildman.

June 7—Mrs. Caroline Crossman. June 11, John Logan. June 29, Mrs. Martha W. Harris.

July 3—Eugene, infant child of John A. Jones. July 10, Wm. B. Chandler, of Sumter county.

August 11—Mrs. Mary Emma Bronson. Aug. 16, Mrs. Frances Eliza Rutherford. Aug. 18, Mrs. Mary Hodges. Aug. 27, Anna Lewis, infant daughter of L. D. Minter.

September — Stephen D. Pepper. Sept. 7, Mrs. Barbara Catherine Epping. Sept. 14, Jared Irwin, infant son of Elisha F. Kirksey.

October 16—Jonathan Niles, of Providence, R. I.

1847.

Two Destructive Fires—Land Donated and City Subscription to Muscogee Railroad Company.

The following was the result of the election held on the first Saturday in January for Mayor and Aldermen: Mayor, Wiley Williams; Aldermen—1st Ward, J. J. McKendree, Willis T. Holstead; 2d Ward, no election; 3d Ward, R. N. R. Bardwell, George Pitts; 4th Ward, H. J. Smith, and no choice for one; 5th Ward, James Kivlin, J. L. Morton; 6th Ward, Benj. F. Coleman, J. R. Green.

Subsequently, John G. Winter and Davenport Ellis were elected Aldermen of the 2d Ward, and John Quin of the 4th Ward.

Calvin Stratton was re-elected Clerk; George W. Turrentine, Treasurer; William Brooks, Marshal; Jas. M. Hughes, Deputy Marshal; Wm. W. Martin, Bridge-keeper; M. Woodruff, City Physician; James Johnson, City Attorney; Chas. Kendall, Clerk of the Market; R. T. Simons, Sexton; C. A. McGehee, Hospital Keeper.

The first omnibus appears to have been licensed this year. H. W. Van Veighten and others were authorized to run an omnibus from the post-office to the wharf and other points in the city, for the purpose of conveying passengers.

The Fire Wardens elected in January were John C. Ruse, Henry T. Hall, John Strupper, R. R. Goetchius, L. W. Wells, Peter Crichton.

Board of Health—Dr. Thos. Hoxey, J. B. Hoxey, S. A. Billing, John S. Allen, Mansfield Torrence, Joseph Kyle, E. Birdsong, Benj. Wells, Joseph Wiggins, R. S. Stockton.

Port Wardens—Lewis C. Allen, Frederick Toby, T. M. Hogan, Wm. H. Praden, V. S. Cady.

Commissioners of the Poor—John Johnson, M. Woodruff, William Amos, Theo. Howard, Lewis C. Allen.

Messrs. John Bethune, Frederick Toby and Joseph E. Webster, assessors, reported the aggregate value of real estate in the city $1,333,825.

The newspapers of Columbus, this year, were the *Enquirer*, *Times*, and *Democrat*.

On Wednesday, at 7 o'clock P. M., March 1st, a fire broke out in J. M. Tarbox's book-store, located on the east side of Broad street, midway between Randolph and St. Clair streets. Fronting Broad street were destroyed Tarbox's book-store, Wade & Middlebrook's saddlery-store, Hall & Moses, hardware; E. & M. Meidner, dry goods; Sammis & Rooney, furniture; Meinhem & Co., dry goods; A. H. McNeil, shoes; Holden's oyster house and confectionery; Geo. H. Betz, tailor;

Fogle & Cushman, dentist rooms; the clothing and millinery store of Mr. and Mrs. Dessau. The fire passed thence to Oglethorpe street, destroying Hatcher & Pitts' livery stable The Episcopal church building was several times on fire. Several wooden houses on Oglethorpe were cut down, and the building occupied by the *Enquirer* as a press room was blown up. The fire engine did all it could. Mr. George H. Peabody was seriously injured by a fall from the vestry of the Episcopal Church. The heaviest losers were Sammis & Rooney, Kyle & Barnett, G. W. Woodruff, Wade & Middlebrook (fully insured,) A. K. Ayer, Hall & Moses ($13,000 above insurance,) P. A. Clayton, and others. Total loss about $80,000; insurance $40,000.

On March 20th, at 5 A. M., Harden's large wooden warehouse, occupied by Hall & DeBlois, agents for the Lowell factory companies, and owned by the Milledgeville Bank, was burned with 1,281 bales of cotton, owned by various parties; and 900 sacks salt, 125 barrels of molasses and 75 of whiskey, owned by Barnard & Schley (insured.) The rear building of Redd & Co.'s store, with 200 sacks of salt, bacon, etc., was also burned. Loss $60,000. The warehouse was located where the Planters' Warehouse now is. This fire was believed to have been the work of an incendiary.

On the 23d of March, Council held a special meeting to take action in regard to the supposed incendiary origin of the late fires. A resolution was adopted authorizing the Mayor to offer a reward of $1,000 for the apprehension and conviction of any such incendiary.

On the 25th of March, Wm. Brooks resigned the office of Marshal, and James M. Hughes, Deputy, was elected Marshal. George Gullen was elected Deputy Marshal.

We find the names of the following boats that were plying the river in the early part of this year: Lotus, Champion, Peytona, Viola, Mary Ann Moore, Nation, Boston, Eufaula, Emily, Charleston, Albany, Apalachicola, Cadwallader.

Notwithstanding heavy losses by three destructive fires

within a few months, the citizens of Columbus contributed $789 40 for the relief of the people of Ireland, then suffering from famine.

A new Market House, near the intersection of Oglethorpe and Crawford streets, having been completed by Messrs. P. Adams and J. L. Morton, the stalls were rented in May. We find that some of the stalls were rented by Richard Roberson, Barshall & Gittenger, Charles G. Bize, Amos & Jones.

J. J. McKendree having resigned as Alderman of the 1st Ward, A. B. Ragan was elected in his stead.

The following decree of Chancellor Ligon of Alabama, in the case of the Mayor and Council of Columbus vs. Lewis Davis and others, was laid before Council on the 17th of June, and spread upon its minutes : "It is ordered, adjudged and decreed, that the injunction heretofore awarded in this case be made perpetual, and that the said defendants and each and every of them and their successors in office of those of them which constituted the Court of Commissioners of Revenue and Roads for the county of Russell, be forever enjoined from obstructing in any way the streets and highways in the bill mentioned to the injury of the franchise of complainant."

On the 30th of June a special meeting of Council was held to consider a proposition of the Muscogee Railroad Company in regard to obtaining a lot of ground on the east commons for the purpose of locating a depot. The following resolution was adopted :

Resolved, That this body authorize the Muscogee Railroad Company to locate their depot on the east common, between Randolph and Bryan streets, and to occupy a space of ground for said depot, and for no other than railroad purposes, not exceeding the breadth between the two streets, and not over 1200 feet long, leaving a street on the east and another on the west end of said depot—which said streets shall be as much as 200 feet wide; and with the amendment that the title shall revert to the city when the road shall cross the river at any point above St. Clair street.

In August, P. A. Clayton was elected Alderman of the 4th Ward, vice H. J. Smith, resigned.

Council appropriated $300 to aid in buying a new engine.

On the 16th of September the Telegraph Company petitioned for permission to erect poles and extend their line through the city, and on the 7th of October Council granted the company the right to cross the commons, the streets, and the river, by attaching the wires to the bridge.

There was considerable feeling in Council and among the citizens, in October, on the subject of renting a portion of the commons for a race track. Council at first resolved to rent it for that purpose for a term of years, but afterwards reconsidered the resolution, and on the 28th of October, after receiving a numerously signed protest by citizens against any such appropriation of the commons, the whole subject was laid on the table.

Col. J. L. Mustian having made a proposition to Council to complete twenty miles of the Muscogee Railroad, commencing at Columbus, if the city would give him a bonus of $20,000, and it being represented that a project was on foot to build a road from the Georgia Western Railroad to West Point, which would materially interfere with the trade of Columbus, Council called a meeting of citizens on the 29th of October, to consider the question. This meeting adopted a resolution requesting the Council to subscribe for 1500 shares of the Muscogee Railroad, payable in bonds. At its meeting on the 2d of November, Council adopted an ordinance "to authorize and require the Mayor of the city of Columbus to subscribe in the name and for the benefit of the Mayor and Council of the city of Columbus for fifteen hundred shares in the stock of the Muscogee Railroad Company, to authorize the issue of city bonds for $150,000 in payment of the same, and to provide for the representation of said stock in all meetings and elections which may be held by the stockholders of said company." The ordinance provided that $15,000 of said bonds should become due and payable each year, commencing on the 1st day of January, 1853, until the whole should be paid by the 1st of January, 1863. At a meeting

3

on the 11th of November, Council adopted an amendment to this ordinance, asking the Legislature to grant authority to levy an additional tax sufficient to pay the annual interest on these bonds.

Subsequently, on motion of Alderman Morton, Council adopted a resolution appointing a committee to ascertain and report what arrangements could be made, by means of a county subscription, to expedite the building of a railroad connecting the Muscogee Railroad with a railroad at Barnesville.

The Finance Committee reported in December that the income of the city Treasury for the year, ordinary and extraordinary, had been $24,280 69, against $21,400 the previous year, and the amount of city debt paid off during the year a little less than $10,000, besides $3,000 of extraordinary expenses, leaving the current expenses of the city about $10,500. The debt of the city at that time was $42,466.

The city sexton reported 12 interments, of both whites and blacks, for the first quarter of this year, and 22 for the second quarter. We have been unable to find any report for the last two quarters.

INCIDENTS

Mary Ann Coursey, a white girl, aged 13 years, was fatally shot in the head with a pistol, by Jones Butler, on March 1st. He was arrested in Girard, and lodged in the Columbus jail.

The Howard Manufacturing Company was organized for the purpose of building a cotton factory—building to be 125x48 feet, five stories high, and run 5,000 spindles. Directors—Van Leonard, J. C. Cook, E. T. Taylor, Harvey Hall and J. I. Ridgway. President, Van Leonard; Superintendent, Jonathan Bridges. The corner stone was laid on Aug. 28th. There were two factories in active operation in Columbus at that time—the Coweta and the Columbus.

The war with Mexico was progressing this year, and Columbus took a lively interest in the contest. A battalion of six companies of mounted volunteers, of which J. S. Calhoun had been appointed Lieutenant-Colonel, left Columbus early in September. Dr. J. F. Bozeman was surgeon. The companies were commanded by Captains E. R. Goulding, H. Kendall, C. H. Nelson, C. A. Hamilton and W. T. Wofford. Colonel Calhoun was given a horse by General McDougald and received another from Daniel Griffin.

On the 26th November, Mr. Randal Jones, an aged citizen of Muscogee, was thrown from his horse, near the residence of Judge Thomas, on the Hamilton road, and killed.

The steamboat H. S. Smith, built in Columbus, was launched at the boat yard on the 27th of November.

A. G. Smith, of Columbus, was killed near Matamoras by Mexicans, while, with a Mexican, he was hunting mules.

PERSONAL.

The officers of Columbus Fire Company No. 1 for this year, were R. A. Ware, President; H. T. Hall, Foreman; Wm. Snow, Assistant Foreman; J. B. Strupper, Treasurer; V. H. Cady, Secretary.

The Georgia M. E. Conference appointed Rev. A. J. Wiggins, Presiding Elder of the Columbus District, and Rev. Jesse Boring as pastor at Columbus.

On Tuesday, August 17th, the Columbus Guards reorganized and elected S. A. Bailey, Captain; John E. Davis, 1st Lieutenant; R. Ellis, 2d Lieutenant; Joseph King, 3d Lieutenant; W. C. Hodges, 4th Lieutenant; Sergeants—W. G. Andrews 1st, Erastus Reed 2d, F. J. Abbott 3rd, J. M. Hughes 4th; Corporals—J. R. Ivey 1st, A. Ellis 2d, P. Alston 3rd, John King 4th; James Hamilton, Secretary and Treasurer; T. Schoonmaker, Quartermaster. John E. Davis, on account of business, declined the captaincy and also the position of 1st Lieutenant. John Forsyth was then elected 1st Lieutenant.

In October, R. T. Marks was elected Senator, and John Bethune and N. L. Howard, Representatives of Muscogee.

They were the Whig candidates. The following county officers were elected : Sheriff, Col. A. S. Rutherford ; Clerk Superior Court, Major E. J. Hardin ; Clerk Inferior Court, Robt. Mitchell ; Tax Collector, J. W. Edwards ; Receiver, D. J. Rees ; Coroner, G. B. C. Terry.

The Columbus *Enquirer*, Columbus *Times*, and Muscogee *Democrat* were the papers published in Columbus.

MARRIAGES.

January 3—Benjamin A. Berry and Mahala A. O'Neal. Jan. 7, Stephen A. Doles and Mary Ann E. Hazelton, Anderson Williams and Mary Ann Smith. Jan. 11, Madison T. Key and Samantha Maddux, Barney Mullany and Ann Putnam. Jan. 21, George W. Cowdery and Rosa E. Purple. Jan. 28, Patrick Holehan and Samantie Boraw.

February 9—Carter Newson and Lucy Ann Smith. Feb. 13, Jno. W. Harned and Josephine Robinson. Feb. 21, Wm. H. Griswold and Mary E. Andrews.

March 8—Jno. R. Garrett and Martha Ann Garrett. March 11, Simon Sartwell and Mary Ann Moore. March 18, Thos. C. Hill and Sarah T. Pool. March 23, Robert H. Boon and Sarah Ann Brown. March 26, Mandley W. Ellison and Sarah Gilbert. March 28, Harvey Matthews and Eleanor Carr.

April 1—Jeremiah Cox and Rebecca Knowles, William W. Townsend and Lucinda A. Richardson, Thos. J. Pool and Martha E. Shippey. April 8, William Marler and Sileta Maddox, William J. Bradley and Susan Dillard, Edmond McGlawn and Martha Irvin Tullis. April 15, James Barlow and Frances Tomblin. April 18, Lawrence Lincs and Ellen Octavia Bugbee. April 27, David Fountain and Eliza McCardel. April 29, Uriah Helms and Martha Foster, John C. Wellborn and Mary A. Pease.

May 5—Hardy B. Carraway and Virginia C. Burton. May 6, Bartley M. Cox and Lucy H. Watt. May 9, Franklin Newberry and Polley Ann Williams. May 10, John T. Copeland and Mary F. Cox. May 11, William Whatsey and Elizabeth Renfroe. May 16, James Brunette and Louisa Matilda Gilley. May 19, Wm. Henry Chambers and Ann Lane Flewellen. May 20, John Young and Salina Cowart. May 23, John Mack and Martha Bagley. May 27, Henry Turnage and Jane Elizabeth Armstrong. May 30, Jno. W. Boland and Elizabeth Darden, Liomel H. Turner and Louisa M. Bryan.

June 3—Jeremiah E. Langford and Mary Jane Jackson. June 8, Lerry C. Mims and Salitha Ann Killian, Littleberry B. Phillips and Mrs. Mary A. Pruett, Andrew Jackson Welch and Margaret Elizabeth Rogers. June 13, Geo. H. Sims and Sandal Webb, Robt. D. Greene and Elizabeth L. Coleman. June 15, Silas R. Brown and Sarah A. E. Jones. June 22, Wesley Boyd and Elizabeth Hall. June 27, William Thomas and Amanda Foster. June 29, William McElrath and Nancy Artimus Mass.

July 1—George W. Welch and Nancy B. McNeil. July 2, James M. Halley and Margaret Dunn. July 11, Samuel J. Crow and Frances Elizabeth Owens. July 13, John T. Decker and Lurany C. Chapman.

August 1—Patrick Gillespia and Fredericka N. Albricht. Aug. 3, Samuel Watkins and Betsy B. McCall. Aug. 15, Jepthah H. Clements and Elizabeth A. McDonald. Aug. 19, Uriah Williams and Nancy Johnson, Jas. E. Broadnax and Martha Watkins. Aug. 26, John W. Perry and Lovey L. John. Aug. 29, Major LeGrand Guerry and Rhoda Amelia Cook. Aug. 31, Seaton Ira Clark and Mary Jane Burt.

September 8—Thomas W. Christian and Mary Jane Greer. Sept. 12, Charles Beck and Emily Wilson. Sept. 16, Michael W. Whitman and Mary Adams, William P. May and Nancy A. F. Pace. Sept. 23, Thomas Wilson Blackburn and Elizabeth Susan Kirkpatrick. Sept. 26, Reuben Leggit and Persilla Lunsford, Amos Hicks and Martha Colyer. Sept. 30, William Maxey and Mary Field.

October 7—Joseph West and Elizabeth A. Parkman. Oct. 12, Woody A. Moor and Mary E. Paramore. Oct. 14, George W. Hunter and Margaret Elder. Oct. 17, Augustus L. Edwards and Susan E. Rockmore. Oct. 21, Robert Garven and Louisa Gass. Oct. 31, Jacob Parker and Nancy Davie.

November 7—Allen Whatley and Eliza Jane Blackman. Nov. 11, Francis Kromer and Mary O'Conner. Nov. 18, Joshua Wilson and Mary Ann Murry. Nov. 25, Barnabas Cook and Dorcas Hicks. Nov. 30, John Henry Mealing and Martha Burt.

December 2—Alsey Dean and Eliza Weaver, Harvey King and Sarah A. Butt. Dec. 5, Jno. W. Wood and Repsey Ann Hall. Dec. 7, Hezekiah W. Edwards and Ann H. Harrison. Dec. 14, Isaac W. Orr and Eliza Santhall. Dec. 16, John Key and Susan Parkman. Dec. 21, Peter K. Edgar and Harriet E. Brenizer. Dec. 22, John Johnson and Sarah Motley. Dec. 23, David R. Snell and Parmilla Ann Mullin, Allen W. Sanders and Elizabeth Perry. Dec. 25, William Helms and Nancy Stearns. Dec. 26, Enoch Willett and Martha Ann P. Williams. Dec. 28, Richard A. Warner and Amanda D. Terry. Dec. 30, Laban C. Pool, and Mrs. Jane Needham, John H. Massey and Caroline Johnson, Calvin Hilliard and Julia Ann Bell.

DEATHS.

Jan. 5—Mrs. Thomas Morris, daughter of William Ragland.
Dec. 27, 1846—Littleton Atkinson, aged 29 years.
February—Ebenezer C. Chandler. Feb. 29—Mrs. John Hazleton, aged 21 years. Feb. 22—John Dicken, aged 40 years.
March 23—Mrs Milly Bryant.
April 18—At Col. Banks' Wynnton residence, Mrs. Josephine, wife of Judge Hawkins, aged 33 years.
May 1—Mrs. Mary Eugenia Downing. May 13—Mrs. A. P. Reynolds, aged 43 years. May 23—J. C. McGibony, aged 51 years.
June 26—Nathan Seymour, of Apalachicola, aged 55 years. June—R. B. Lee, late member Georgia Light Infantry in Mexico.

July 10—Mr. Thomas Kimbrough, aged 60, and Mrs. B., wife of A. M. Kimbrough, of Muscogee county.

Aug. 2—Wm. Henry, son of J. N. and Lucy A. Barnett, aged one year and seven days. Aug. 6—Henry Matthews, a native of England, but many years a citizen of this State, aged 46 years.

Sept. 5—Joseph A., infant son of S. C. Lindsay, aged 11 years. Sept. 7— Mrs. Cynthia Ragan, aged 60 years. Sept. 15—Mrs. Lemuel Cherry, aged 32 years. Sept. 27—Joseph Grimes, aged 56 years.

1848.

New Fire Company—Muscogee Rail Road Subscription Ratified—Trades, Professions, &c.

Under an amendment of the charter, the citizens this year, for the first time, elected the Marshal, Deputy Marshal, Treasurer and Clerk. The election was held on the first of January, and resulted as follows: Mayor, S. W. Flournoy; Aldermen—1st Ward, W. Y. Barden, W. S. Holstead; 2d Ward, Harvy Hall; 3d Ward, Jno. Johnson, Joseph Brooks; 5th Ward, S. R. Andrews, Lewis C. Allen; 6th Ward, B. F. Coleman; Marshal, J. M. Hughes; Deputy Marshal, George Gullen; Treasurer, R. H. Green; Clerk, Calvin Stratton. No choice was made at this election for one Alderman each in the 2d and 6th Wards, and two in the 4th. Subsequently, J. A. L. Lee was elected to the vacancy in the 2d Ward; P. A. Clayton of the 4th, and Wm. R. Jones of the 6th, Col. Wm. M. Lee of the 4th.

Council elected A. G. Foster, City Attorney; Dr. Thos. Hoxey, City Physician; Wm. W. Martin, Bridge Keeper; Jerry Terry, Sexton; B. Weeks, Clerk of Market; B. Ingram, Hospital Keeper. Board of Health—Dr. T. W. Grimes, President; Joseph King and G. W. Turrentine, of First Ward; S. A. Billing and John Kyle, of Second; Joseph Kyle and Mansfield Torrence, of Third; D. McArthur and J. W. Frost, of Fourth; J. Kivlin and J. L. Morton, of Fifth;

Joseph Wiggins and J. R. Greene, of Sixth. Port Wardens—
LeGrande S. Wright, C. E. Mims, B. F. Malone, T. M. Hogan, H. T. Greenwood.

Clerk of Council was paid $400; Marshals $500 each;
Treasurer $600; Clerk of Market $150; Bridge Keeper
$600; City Physician $260.

Vigilant Fire Company No. 2 was organized this year, and
the Fire Department of Columbus was organized by the
election of H. T. Hall as Chief Engineer, and B. J. Matthews
Assistant. The following were the officers of the two com-
panies constituting the Department: Of Columbus No. 1, R.
A. Ware was President; W. Foster, Foreman; I. G. Strup-
per, Assistant; J. D. Johnson, Secretary; R. H. Greene,
Treasurer. No. 2, R. H. Taylor, President; L. T. Woodruff,
Foreman; R. T. Brice, Assistant; John H. Davis, Secretary;
R. Patten, Treasurer.

The corner stone of Odd Fellows' Hall, near the corner of
Oglethorpe and St. Clair streets, was laid on the 29th of
January,

On the 2d of February, Council, in accordance with an
agreement entered into with the officers of the Muscogee
Railroad Company (John G. Winter, President,) subscribed
for 1,500 shares in the stock of said company, with the following conditions: Council agreeing to pay quarterly to the
Company $7,500. If the Directors call in stock faster than
quarterly the city will issue 7 per cent. bonds to said Company, to be taken at par by it; provided, said Railroad Company put the whole line, from Columbus to Barnesville, on the
M. & W. R.R., under contract as soon as practicable, and ex-
pend the city money on the west half of said railroad; provided, also, said company receive from citizens, for freight
and passage, all the scrip issued by City Council—provided
the same shall not exceed $20. Council shall not subdivide
the annual tax.

Subsequently the citizens, by a vote of 339 to 27, approved

a special railroad tax for the term of two years to meet this subscription, viz: 2 per cent. on real estate and ¼ of one per cent. on sales of merchandise and banking business.

J. L. Morton, John T. Walker, and Frederick Toby, were elected city assessors. They made a return of the census of the city as follows: White males, 1,701, white females 1,543, slaves owned by residents 1,522, by non-residents 266, free persons of color 42—total 5,074. They reported that this did not include a large number of persons who did business in the city but resided in the suburbs.

There were 125 persons with no trade or profession, 8 clergymen, 25 lawyers, 18 physicians, 6 dentists, 12 printers and publishers, 303 merchants and clerks, 29 brokers and factors, 3 auction and commission merchants, 75 shopkeepers, 7 silversmiths, 2 book-binders, 4 music professors, 10 bankers and clerks, 12 manufacturers, 6 machinists, 72 carpenters, 5 blacksmiths, 17 wheel and carriage makers, 5 brass and iron founders, 46 steamboat men, 13 cabinet makers, 12 sign and house painters, 4 saddle and harness makers, 7 tinners, 16 tailors, 2 gunsmiths, 16 brickmakers and plasterers, 3 bakers, 2 coopers, 1 dyer and scourer, 1 hatter, 1 marble-cutter, 4 artists.

The Finance Committee reported in March that the debts of the city which should be paid during the year, amounted to $9,920, and the total necessary expenses were estimated at $26,100. The resources, including $9,000 from the bridge and $9,800 from taxes, were estimated at $21,175, showing a deficit of $4,925.

Council levied the following taxes for the year: On white males between 12 and 60 $1 00; free males of color $6 00; on every $100 of negro slaves 25 cents; owned outside and working in city 75 cents; lawyers and physicians $4 00; on every $100 of money loaned 25 cents; merchandise 25 cents —excepting sugar, coffee, molasses, iron, bagging, rope or salt 12½ cents; each negro offered for sale by trader $1 00;

every $100 invested in banks 25 cents; real estate 25 cents on every $100 of value, &c.; and an extra railroad tax of 2 per cent. upon real estate, for railroad purposes.

Council elected as Fire Wardens, J. C. Ruse, 1st Ward; George Strupper, 2d; Wm. K. Schley, 3rd; John B. Strupper, 4th; L. W. Wells, 5th; J. M. Tarbox, 6th.

On the night of June 21st, at 3 A. M., the livery stables of Hatcher, Leary & Co. were burned, with the adjacent carriage houses, &c., together with a large quantity of corn, fodder and other provender, and fifty valuable horses. The large building on the corner known as Shylock's Bank, as also the Episcopalian Church, were on fire several times but were put out by the fire companies, aided by citizens. Among the number who distinguished themselves were Mr. Hanserd and Capt. Van Veichton, of Apalachicola. The *Enquirer* narrowly escaped. Mr. Anderson lost his building and a large lot of meat, lumber and salt. Loss about $12,000. Hatcher & Pitts rebuilt the stables, and on the night of September 7th they were again burnt out, losing that time twenty-one horses—making a loss of seventy-one horses burned in two months.

The Telegraph lines reached Columbus in July of this year.

Council this year adopted and had printed a new code of ordinances drawn up and compiled by the City Attorney and passed upon separately.

On the 29th of July, Whitby Foster was elected an Alderman of the 5th Ward, in place of Alderman Andrews who had removed from that Ward; and William Amos was in September elected an Alderman of the 5th Ward, to fill the vacancy occasioned by the resignation of Whitby Foster.

This appears to have been a sickly summer for the city. We learn from the sexton's report that there were 23 interments in July, and that diarrhea, measles, scarlet and other fevers had their victims. But the report does not give the names of the persons buried. In August there were 24 interments, the same disease prevailing. In September 19—diarrhea, scarlet fever and worms being most fatal.

The Treasurer reported the receipts of the City Treasury this year $25,086 39, and the disbursements $25,079 30. The Treasurer also reported the payment during the year of $8,-963 90 of the indebtedness of the city, and that the debt at the close of the year was about $35,000.

The receipts of cotton up to the 27th of May amounted to 56,759 bales. We cannot find any report for the balance of the commercial year. The quotation at that time was 4¼. to 5¼ c.

There was much excitement on account of the frequency of fires, believed to be incendiary, this year. Council offered a reward of $500 for the arrest of the incendiaries, with proof to convict.

The following were quotations of produce and merchandise in December: Cotton 4¼ to 5¼c., bagging 22 to 25c. per yard, candles—sperm 35c. per pound, tallow 18 to 20c., coffee—Rio 8 to 9c., Java 12¼c., molasses 28 to 30c., corn 35 to 40c., lard 7 to 8c., fodder 50 to 60c., wheat 80c. to $1, whiskey 27 to 30c., American brandy 45 to 50c., cogniac $3 to $4, salt $2 per sack, brown sugar 7 to 10c., loaf 12½c., nails 5 to 6c., meal 45c., bacon sides and shoulders 5 to 6c., hams 8 to 10 cents.

INCIDENTS.

Council rented the Columbus fisheries to M. N. Clark for the years 1849, 1850 and 1851, and by him they were let to N. P. Foster.

An intelligent Mexican youth who accompanied Col. J. S. Calhoun on his return from the war, was drowned while bathing in the river on Sunday, August 27th. His body was recovered.

During October, Dr. T. W. Grimes, President of the Board of Health, reported the death of 13 whites and 5 blacks.

The Odd Fellow's new Hall was dedicated on Friday, Nov.

17th. Col. S. R. Blake, of Macon, delivered the address. A supper was given at night by the ladies for the benefit of the Odd Fellow's Institute. Admission $1 50.

On December 26th, the wooden building owned by Mrs. Shorter, and adjoining her residence on Broad street, was burned.

PERSONAL.

Amos & Jones, Richard Roberson, James Schuyler, Joln D. Arnold, Gittinger & Barschall, had stalls in the market.

Grigsby E. Thomas, Marshall J. Wellborn, Kennith Mc-Kenzie, A. H. Flewellen and Wm. Amos were Trustees of the Muscogee Asylum for the Poor.

Wm. F. Serrell was elected surveyor of Columbus by Council.

R. Sims, Wiley Williams, Hon. W. T. Colquitt, R. H. Clark, Willis A. Hawkins, Hon. M. J. Wellborn, Benj. W. Clark, J. C. Mounger and Thos. C. Speer were admitted to practice law in the Supreme Court in July.

Charles J. Williams was Solicitor General; E. J. Hardin, Clerk of the Court; R. B. Alexander, Judge.

The Grand Jury for the fall term consisted of Lock Weems, Foreman, B. A. Sorsby, J. H. Butt, Robert Boyd, Jacob Parker, Amos Schumpert, James B. Hicks, John Quin, V. R. Tommey, J. M. Read, J. M. Cook, W. A. Chisolm, Robert Carter, Dozier Thornton, J. B. Baird, H. J. Eelbeck, Jonathan Bridges, W. M. Jepson, J. J. Jackson and George W. Jones.

The stockholders of the Muscogee Railroad elected as Directors, J. H. Howard, R. S. Hardaway, R. A. Ware, R. B. Alexander, S. A. Bailey, Harvey Hall, Jas. Wimberly. The Board elected J. H. Howard President.

MARRIAGES.

January 7—Wm. H. Edwards and Sarah Cureton. Jan. 9, Robert W. Windham and Tabitha Smith. Jan. 11, Josiah J. Howell and Frances Jane Harris, John W. Pease and Jane Ann Norman. Jan. 13, Leonard P. Nelson and Catharine Welch, Anderson B. Nelson and Sarah Welch. Jan. 20, Rev.

Oliver R. Blue and Ann E. Howard. Jan. 21, Granville L. Robinette and Cinthia J. Rees. Jan. 27, Chas. S. Harrison and Lucy E. Sturgis. Jan. 30, William W. Barbaree and Sealy Dillard.

February 2—Oscar V. Brown and Martha W. Kimbrough. Feb. 5, Henry Jones and Martha Bradford. Feb. 11, Wm. Freeman and Adaline Dunning. Feb. 17, William H. Alford and Eliza Webb, Abraham Staton and Julia A. Taylor. Feb. 19, Greene Taylor and Mary Ann Tellis. Feb. 27, William Miles and Martha Lindsey, John Barbarra and Christian Hereubee.

. March 1—Jabez Hamlin Whittelsey and Emily Ann Schley. March 2, John B. Vickery and Priscilla Johnson. March 5, Howell Heti and Lucinda Pitch. March 7, John Martin and Susan Kite, Joseph Brunson and Ann E. Carthidge. March 9, Christian N. Pike and Maranda A. Webb. March 14, Wm. Allen and Nancy Haster. March 16, Nathan Miller and Narcissa Burren. March 19, Richard Williams and Mary Ann McGuist. March 26, James J. Ritch and Jane Fountain. March 22, Francis D. Oliver and Mary Hand. March 23, Richard R. Davis and Mary E. Twilley. March 30, Sam'l C. Dodson and Elizabeth C. Duncan.

April 10—James Griffin and Martha Rogers. April 18, Joseph S. Vickery and Sarah M. Johnson. April 29, Mathew Knight and Epsy Phillips.

May 4—William Hill and Eliza Bryley. May 8, Alonza Balsh and Eliza Caroline McClain.

June 1—Samuel Weaver and Nancy Roberts. June 7, Stephen S. Brooks and Nancy A. Hunley. June 15, James Morgan and Rebecca E. Coffee. June 22, Elijah T. Willis and Mary Ann Dillman. June 28, James S. Collins and Mary Jane Hamil. June 29, Jasper Jones and Mary Bush.

July 1—Samuel Aenchbacker and Rebecca Owens. July 2, Daniel A. Woolbright and Martha E. Woolbright. July 9, Benjamin Bryant and Catharine Wilson. July 11, Alexander H. Cooper and Eliza C. Harris. July 25, Robert D. Cox and Eliza A. Cox.

August 10—Harrison Gresham and Nancy Wooton, Benjamin Harvey and Mary E. Cox. August 22, Dr. Alexander L. Martin and Mrs. Elizabeth M. Dart. August 24, Young E. Walters and Susannah Smith, Michael S. Walters and Winnifred Majors.

September 3—Wm. E. Cox and Sarah Ann Margaret Reighley. September 4, William Williams and Elizabeth Wiley. Sept. 6, John Hamilton and Ann M. Jefferson, Samuel Caldwell and Eliza Brown, David W. Hooks and Matilda Catharine Walters. Sept. 7, Elza C. Grant and Nancy Hayes. Sept. 13, David K. Tant and Martha Ann Rounds. Sept. 14, Roswell Ellis and Frances A. Mangham, John H. Davis and Martha Ann Calhoun, John S. Vanpitt and Sarah A. Burnett, John R. Presley and Matilda Driscoll.

October 3—William Ryall and Louisa Baggett. Oct. 15, Nathan H. Short and Malinda Weaver. Oct. 17, James B. Ayres and Eliza Ann Lamb. Oct. 22, William B. Stephens and Sarah M. McMichael. Oct. 29, Claudius S. Lawhon and Ann Jane Bonnell.

November 2—John King and Mary Ann Conner.   Nov. 3, David Averett and Mary A. Thompson.   Nov. 4, William Miller and Caroline Greene.   Nov. 6, John Hurst and Augusta Ann Whipple.   Nov. 12, William Champion and Bethany Austin.   Nov. 18, George W. Robinson and Ann E. Wood.   Nov. 21, Enoch J. Wall and Elizabeth Stringer.   Nov. 22, Edward W. Suvell and Maria S. Chapman.   Nov. 23, Joel Williams and Eliza Wiley.

December 3—Wiley M. Reeves and Elizabeth Kent.   Dec. 6, Whitman C. Alford and Phebe Jane Sammis, James W. Smith and Mary A. Hines, Allen Cowart and Frances A. E. Comer.   Dec. 7, Gillum Carpenter and Martha Ann Chase.   Dec. 8, Wiley Wamach and Jane Pike.   Dec. 13, Eaton P. Miller and Cinthia McVay.   Dec. 14, Francis Marion Christopher and Sarah Salina Boyd.   Dec. 20, James Howard and Eveline White.   Dec. 21, Richard M. Gray and Mary J. W. Hayes.   Dec. 26, William T. Shippey and Elizabeth A. Pool.

DEATHS.

February 25—Mrs. Ebenade Adams.

March 8—Captain Moses Butt.   March 10—Mrs. Elizabeth Griswold. March 16—Dr. Iddo Ellis.

April 3—Mrs. Caroline Dunn.   April 13—Thomas M., infant son of Thos. M. Hogan.   April 29—Fanny Blount, infant daughter of Rev. Thos. B. Slade. April 30—Horace, infant son of W. H. Griswold.

May 19—Mrs. Mary Ann, wife of Michael Kelly.

June 1—Ann Elizabeth, infant daughter of William Perry.   June 2—Thos. Hoxie, Jr.   June 10—Evans Wimberly (of Florida.)   June 11—Charles Augustus, infant son of George W. Hardwick.   June 21—Rev. Thomas Goulding, Pastor of the Presbyterian Church.   June 23—Miss Eliza J. Redd.

July 2—Alexander J., son of John Hunley.   July 17—Mary Dillard, infant daughter of James Kivlin.   July 20—George Pendleton, infant son of Richard Hooper; Mrs. Eliza J. Barden, wife of Wm. Y. Barden.   July 25— Mary Jane, daughter of Neil G. Smith.

Sept. 7—Henry C. McKendree; and on the 9th, Caroline Eliza McKendree —children of John J. McKendree.   Sept. 15—Washington Irving, infant son of Joseph E. Webster.   Sept. 19—William Frederick, son of G. E. Thomas. Sept. 24—Col. Thomas F. Foster.

Oct. 3—James Franklin Rees.   Oct. 23—Miss Mary Jane, daughter of John Lloyd.

Nov. 8—Joseph Alexander (of Pennsylvania.) Nov. 27, Jeremiah Thornton.

1849.

A Year of Manufacturing and Rail Road Enterprises.

The *Enquirer* of the 2d of January opened the new year with the expression of sanguine hopes for the future of Columbus, and a brief reference to some improvements then in progress. We copy the article, mainly to show the condition at that time of enterprises since completed, as we are still far from the realization of the anticipations of the paper:

OUR CITY—ITS PROSPECTS—RAILROAD—CAPITAL—MANUFACTURES, &c.— At the commencement of the new year we look at home and around us with lively hopes and expectations of the future.

The Muscogee Railroad is now fairly on the progress of construction, not upon paper, but *over ground.* Suffice it to say, that the capital and energy now brought to this work can accomplish *anything.*

Our Factory improvements are going up beyond our most sanguine expectations, and their success is equaling the most sanguine anticipations of those engaged in them. All that is wanting to make our city not only the Lowell of the South, but of the United States, is capital, and that is rapidly tending towards it.

Col. Farish Carter, long and favorably known to the people of Georgia, not only as a large capitalist, but as a man of great caution and prudence, has now near completion one of the largest class of Factory buildings, and it is said intends immediately to erect another. In these it is his purpose to employ slave labor, thus diverting a portion of this from the production to the manufacture of our great staple. [Slaves were not employed in this Factory.]

We learn with much pleasure that this is now his place of residence. A few more citizens of the same sort, and of similar means and confidence in the value of investments here, and we mean what we say, that more cotton can and will be manufactured at and near Columbus than at any other point in the Union.

The municipal election in January resulted in the choice of Samuel W. Flournoy as Mayor, and the following Aldermen: W. Y. Barden and W. S. Holstead, 1st Ward; Harvey Hall and J. A. Lee, 2d; J. B. Brooks and T. K. Wynne, 3d; P. A. Clayton and M. Woodruff, 4th; L. C. Allen and F. A. Jepson, 5th; F. M. Brooks and A. A. Dill, 6th.

R. H. Greene was elected City Treasurer; C. Stratton, Clerk; J. M. Hughes, Marshal; George Gullen, Deputy Marshal.

Council, at its first meeting, elected David Gunn, Clerk of the Market; Wm. W. Martin, Bridge keeper; B. Ingram, Hospital keeper; Jere Terry, Sexton; R. D. S. Bell, City Attorney; Joseph King, L. M. Durr, N. M. C. Robison, John

Kyle, Joseph Kyle, Dr. J. J. Boswell, R. R. Goetchius, Wm. Mathewson, J. L. Morton, John Wooten, J. M. Tarbox and A. J. Abbott, Health Officers; Josiah Morris, T. M. Hogan, L. S. Wright, Daniel McArthur and B. F. Malone, Port Wardens.

The contract system for crossing the bridge was continued to regular passers.

At its meeting on the 9th of January, Council elected John C. Ruse, Wm. K. Schley, V. H. Cady, J. B. Strupper, L. W. Wells and B. F. Coleman, Fire Wardens. Dr. Thos. Hoxey was elected City Physician and President of the Board of Health.

An ordinance was passed in January, requiring the Mayor to hold a Mayor's Court on Tuesday of each week, and oftener if necessary, and authorizing him to inflict such fines and penalties upon offenders as he may deem just and proper, not exceeding the limits defined by law. The Mayor's salary to be $500 a year.

In February Council appropriated $1,000 to the Fire Department, for the purchase of a new fire engine, contingent on the raising of an equal amount by the citizens for the same purpose.

The Committee on Finance reported on the 13th of March : The city receipts from January 14th, 1848, to December 30th, were $25,086 39, and expenses $25,079 30, leaving a balance of $7 09. City owed about $35,000 exclusive of interest, the principal items of which are loan account to John G. Winter $16,000; debt to State $3,500, [collection suspended until 1850;] bonds issued for city bills $3,500; city bills outstanding $8,000. Of the $7,500 of railroad tax asked for by the Muscogee Railroad Company only $1,366 53 had been collected.

By a fire on the 17th of February, the large two-story building on the northwest corner of Broad and Randolph streets was burned. The building was occupied by Malone

& Hudson as a wholesale dry goods and grocery store; by Mr. Simons as a provision store, and by Dr. Woodruff as an office.

Another fire occurred on the 3d of April. The stables of Messrs. Mustian & Mott, with a large quantity of feed for their stock, were destroyed. They saved their horses, stages, &c.

Robt. H. Greene having resigned the office of City Treasurer, Hezekiah Noble was in May elected to that position.

Council, on the 14th and 26th of May, adopted an ordinance authorizing the issue of bonds to the amount of $150,000, in discharge of the subscription of stock to the Muscogee Railroad Company.

Wiley Williams was in June elected an Alderman of the 5th Ward, vice Lewis C. Allen, resigned.

The "Columbus Factory" Company was incorporated this year, the location of the Factory to be three or four miles above Columbus, on the river. The leading corporators were Charles D. Stewart, J. Fontaine, J. R. Clapp, Henry D. Meigs and George Stewart.

Col. Winter's flouring mills were completed and commenced grinding this year, and a contract was made for the building of Temperance Hall. The corner stone of the latter was laid on the 22d of December. The Masons, Odd Fellows, Sons of Temperance and Cadets took part. Prayer was offered by Rev. J. E. Dawson, of the Baptist Church. Judge G. E. Thomas delivered the address, and Rev. Dr. Carns, of the Episcopal Church, made the closing prayer. James Kivlin was chief marshal of the day. Capt. P. T. Schley conducted the laying of the stone according to the rites and customs of the Masonic fraternity.

The Rock Island Mill, a short distance above the city, on the river, commenced making paper this year.

Authority was given by Council this year, to the Trustees of the Methodist Episcopal Church of Columbus, to build a church for the negroes of that denomination on the east common. Opposition was made in Council, and an application by a property holder in that vicinity for an injunction to restrain it as a nuisance, was refused by the Superior Court. The location selected was opposite the south corner of St. Clair and Mercer streets.

In September, after the failure of a proposition that the city should do the work, authority was given to Messrs. Greenwood, Ruse, Patten & Brice, H. S. Smith & Co., and R. M. Gunby, to build a plank road from the warehouse of H. S. Smith & Co., to the city wharf, for the hauling of cotton, &c.

We cannot find a full report of the deaths in the city for the whole year. The Sexton's reports for the months named show the following interments: May, eight whites and three blacks; June and July, thirteen whites and nine blacks; August, ten whites and ten blacks; September, nine whites and three blacks; October, nine whites and two blacks.

The receipts of cotton to the 7th of May amounted to 66,738 bales. We cannot find any report for the balance of the season. Prices opened in January at $4\frac{1}{2}$ to 6 cents, which quotations were but little varied during the spring. In September the quotations were $8\frac{1}{2}$ to $9\frac{1}{4}$ cents, and in December 9 to $9\frac{1}{2}$ cents.

INCIDENTS.

The gin factory of E. T. Taylor was removed from Girard to Columbus.

The steamer Viola, Captain Van Vechten, sunk on her downward passage, at the head of Snake shoals, on February 16th. Cargo saved; boat, owned by commander, was a total loss.

February 22d was celebrated by the Columbus and City Light Guards—the first commanded by Captain Forsyth, and the last by Lieutenant Stanford, and the battalion by the senior Captain, A. H. Cooper. Splendid ball at Concert Hall at night.

Ex-President James K. Polk reached Columbus on March

4

15th. A large crowd accompanied him from General Lowe's residence, in Harris county. He was conveyed into the city in a carriage drawn by four horses, preceded by a band of music. His wife and nieces followed in a carriage drawn by four gray horses. At the Court-house he was welcomed by Colonel Seaborn Jones, to which he briefly replied. Afterwards he was escorted to the residence of Judge Colquitt. Colonel Mangham, the proprietor, gave a big dinner at the Oglethorpe House with toasts and speeches. The ladies gave a supper in Council Chamber to Mrs. Polk and her nieces. Rain kept many away.

On Monday, May 28th, the steamboat Emily burst a boiler just as she was about leaving her wharf at Apalachicola—only two or three revolutions of her wheel had taken place. There was a full cargo and thirty-five persons on board. Wm. Magner, the watchman, and two negroes were scalded to death, and a white boy named Clark and two negroes were drowned. Several other persons were injured.

The first bale of new cotton was brought in on the 16th of August by Robert Laney—quality, good middling—brought ten cents; stored with Greenwood & Gray.

Master W. Park, aged 16 years, son of the late Dr. Ezekiel E. Park, of Alabama, was killed September 15th, by the accidental discharge of his gun, near Columbus.

PERSONAL.

Henry T. Hall was Chief Engineer of the Fire Department, and B. J. Matthews Assistant. James D. Johnson was Secretary of Fire Company No. 1, and Richard Patten of Fire Company No. 2.

John Johnson, Lewis C. Allen, Wiley Williams, Asa Pond and Kenneth McKenzie were Trustees of the Asylum for the Poor.

Market stalls were rented this year to Mr. Schuyler, Philip Gittinger, Richard Robison, Wm. R. Jones, and J. D. Arnold, leaving several stalls unrented. The aggregate rents for those rented were $209 a year.

John Forsyth was Postmaster of Columbus the first part of this year, and J. A. L. Lee for the balance of the year.

Wm. F. Serrell was City Surveyor. Miles G. Pope was jailor of the county.

The county elected as Justices of the Inferior Court, A. G. Foster, J. Wimberly, S. R. Andrews, J. M. Renfroe and T. A. Brannon. Tax Receiver, D. J. Reese. Tax Collector, H. J. Smith.

The following Magistrates were chosen : J. E. Webster and Col. John Quinn for the Lower Town District, with Brown and Ligon as Bailiffs, and J. J. McKendree and J. L. Howell for the Upper Town District, with Lloyd and Nix, Bailiffs.

John Forsyth, Esq., retired from the editorial control of the Columbus *Times*, and was succeeded by Gen. James N. Bethune. The former had been editor of the paper for seven years.

The Methodist Conference, at Augusta, assigned Lovick Pierce as Presiding Elder of the Columbus District, and Samuel Anthony to the pastorate of St. Luke Church, and Harry H. McQueen to the colored charge.

The grand jury of the May Term was composed of Kenneth McKenzie, foreman, John Mullins, S. J. Hatcher, John Jockmass, R C. Shorter, LeGrand S. Wright, Peter Farrar, J. P. Illges, A. L. Grant, J. J. McKendree, Michael Woodruff, R. S. Stockton, J. H. Kirvin, G. A. Norris, A. M. Walker, P. A. Clayton, D. F. Willcox, R. P. Spencer. Charles J. Williams was Solicitor General, E. J. Hardin, Clerk, and R. B. Alexander, Judge.

The second panel of the Grand Jury of Muscogee County was composed of J. C. Cook, foreman, J. T. Niles, Ed. Birdsong, Benj. Jefferson, F. Toby, J. A. Urquhart, L. S. Wright, Aaron Fergurson, Van Leonard, Asa Pond, Theobold Howard, E. C. Bowen, W. J. Ridgill, Asa Lynch, Daniel McArthur, W. E. Jones, J. K. Redd, R. P. Spencer.

January 3—Robert L. Dent and Elizabeth Williams. Jan. 11, Hugh Peyton'Robinson and Mary Emeline Garrett, Thomas Berge and Sarah Ray. Jan. 18, James T. Flewellen, Esq., and Henrietta H. Fontaine, William Stephens and Sarah Ann Briley. Jan. 25, Elisha P. Greer and Martha F. Baugh, William H. Long and Mary A. Faulkenbury, Lemuel A. Green and Mary E. Day. Jan. 27, Felix M. Harris and Martha Dunn. Jan. 28, William O. Nickleson and Martha E. Leggett.

February 4—Septamus W. Dalton and Maria N. Odom. Feb. 5, Burton Bartwell and Harriet S. Peacock. Feb. 6, James B. Wells and C. A. M. Adams. Feb. 11, Loveless S. Ginn and Martha Elizabeth Henry. Feb. 18, John Pettiss and Elizabeth Bius. Feb. 28, James Vernoy and Mary E. Lawrence.

March 1—Robert B. Helmes and Louisa J. Parramore. March 11, Henry Kent and Mary Ann Jones. March 29, Hugh G. Ivey and Margaret E. Hinton.

April 4—Geo. W. Richardson and Lucy L. Wood. April 10, Moses Land and Salina Huckaby. April 17, Dr. Jos. Jones and Cornelia C. Bethune.

May 1—Thos. Schley and Eliza E. Greene. May 8, John M. Whigham and Mary Ann S. Majors. May 9, Alexander A. Lowther and Mary C. Shaaf. May 10, John Williams and Nancy J. Glawn. May 16, John W. Solomon and Elizabeth J. Covington. May 20, Jeremiah Culpepper and Elizabeth Rowell. May 23, Rhisa Jones and Lucinda Cobb. May 27, Lemuel Cherry, Esq., and Emeline Gunn. May 29, John J. Hickey and Ann S. Prince. May 30, Francis M. Doles and Mary F. Jones.

June 6—James G. Bourt, Esq., and Lucy Ann Spear. June 10, Daniel Fry and Clara Turner, Stephen Bedsale and Harriet Averett. June 11, Ezekiel Cooper and Matilda Graves. June 15, Jesse W. Allen and Frances Odom. June 16, Wm. H. Griswold and Caroline M. Andrews. June 21, William Taylor and Tabitha McNaughton. June 24, Francis Searls and Malvina Terry.

July 3—William Hally and Ann Wood. July 15, Richard D. Sizemore and Mary M. Revel. July 25, William T. Sparks and Jane Morman. July 28, Phillip Jacobs and Mary Jordan.

August 5—Henry B. Treadwell and Martha Holmes. Aug. 7, Enoch Dudley and Martha D. Harris. Aug. 9, James M. Cobb and Susan I. Cobb. Aug. 13, John A. Sutton and Rebecca Williams. Aug. 22, Perry E. Wimberly and Martha E. Christmas.

Sept. 5—Henry Roan and Ann Worsham. Sept. 31, William E. Adams and Elizabeth A. Everett.

October 9—Samuel H. Wiley and Sarah E. Carnes. Oct. 18, Levi Smith and Mary Ann Spears. Oct. 28, John Dees and Nancy Price.

November 8—George Hungerford and Cornelia F. Pond, Dawson A. McRae and Lucy C. Turrentine, James Boland and Elizabeth Culpepper. Nov. 20, John H. Lee and Sophronia E. Walker, Thomas A. Gammell and Mary Odom. Nov. 22, Thomas S. Hays and Margaret F. Robinson. Nov. 27, Lewis S. Mitchell and Frances J. Daniel. Nov. 28, John A. Johnston and Elizabeth

A. Saul. Nov. 29, Samuel A. Whigham and Sarah A. Lawson,. Charles P. King and Susan Brown.

December 6—Bartlett W. Whitehurst and Nancy A. Ennis, William N. King and Mary A. Covington, Nehemiah Stephens and Eliza McCullers. Dec. 7, Lemuel T. Downing and Caroline L. Urquhart. Dec. 9, James J. Todd and Elizabeth Decker. Dec. 12, John Culbertson and Elizabeth Simmons, Riley F. Ray and Frances P. Beler. Dec. 16. William Shaw and Sarah V. C. Pope, William R. Searls and Sarah Scott. Dec. 17, Daniel Griffin and Rebecca E. Monkey. Dec. 20, Lafayette Harp and Callie King. Dec. 24, David Henry and Sarah Williams. Dec. 25, Hiram Uldrick and Matilda Green. Dec. 26, Jacob Fussell and Mary J. Harrison. Dec. 31, Charles Williams and Amanda Payne.

DEATHS.

February 4—Mrs. Frances E. Farrior, of Montgomery, Alabama.

April 30—Miss Martha Jane Cox, of Troup county.

May 21—Eva, infant daughter of Col. Hines Holt; also, on the same day, Hines, infant son of Col. Holt.

June 16—Mrs. Mary A. E. Norton. June 17, P. T. Schley, son of Dr. Wm. K. Schley of Columbus—killed by the explosion of a can of camphene, in Oxford, Ga.

July 2—Clara Rosalia, daughter of Wm. Perry. July 8, William Salisbury, aged 46 years. July 11, Mrs. Eloise, wife of Thos. B. Goulding. July 14, John James Sullivan. July 23, Anna Rosina, infant daughter of Jacob Fogle. July 24, William P. Malone, in the 48th year of his age.

August 13—Mrs. Clara Meigs, widow of Prof. Josiah Meigs.

October 11—D. B. Prescott, aged 35 years. October 20, Mrs. Elizabeth Brown.

November 1—Gen. Nicholas Howard, in the 63rd year of his age. Nov. 12, George W., son of Charles E. Mims. Nov. 25, Mrs. Elizabeth N. Daniel, wife of Wm. Daniel. Nov. 26, George W. Hardwick, one of the proprietors of the *Enquirer*, in the 31st year of his age.

1850.

Progress of the Mobile and Girard R. R.—A Quiet Year.

The following officers of the municipal government were elected on the 5th of January: Mayor, Willis S. Holstead. Aldermen—1st Ward, S. F. Grimes and J. W. Warren; 2d,

J. A. Urquhart and N. McRobinson; 3d, T. K. Wynne and Theo. Stewart; 4th, R. C. Shorter and S. R. Andrews; 5th, F. M. Brooks and Alex. Lowther; 6th, A. A. Dill and J. M. Traywick. Treasurer, J. L. Howell; Clerk, Calvin Stratton; Marshal, T. M. Hogan; Deputy, George Gullen. Salaries of Mayor and Clerk of Council were made $500 each; Treasurer, $600; Marshal and Deputy Marshal, $560 each; Clerk of Market, $150; City Physician, $350; Bridgekeeper, $600.

City Council elected the following: Clerk of Market, Thos. Nix; Sexton, Jeremiah Terry; Bridge-keeper, Wm. W. Martin; City Physician, J. F. Bozeman; Hospital-keeper, Burnet Ingram; Attorney, A. G. Foster. Health officers: W. Y. Barden and L. Livingston, 1st Ward; R. A. Ware and S. A. Billing, 2d; Joseph Kyle and M. Torrance, 3d; E. Dudley and W. Matthewson, 4th; W. C. Cooper and John Wooten, 5th; T. R. Herrandyne and John Munn, 6th. Port Wardens: I. T. Robinson, J. C. Brewer, J. W. Frost, J. M. Hughes and G. W. Cowdery.

The Finance Committee reported that the total receipts of the city treasury for the year 1849 were $22,675 53, and the total disbursements $22,159 49. They reported the total liabilities of the city $22,724 (of which the larger item, $8,000, was an indebtedness to John G. Winter,) and the total resources, including bridge tolls and taxes to be collected for the year, $22,140.

Some nuisances were not easily abated under the "peculiar and careful" tactics then understood, as appears from the minutes of Council. In January, Alderman Brooks announced that a "house of ill fame" had been opened in the old Theatre building on Crawford street, "under the auspices and management of Mr. Jones," to the great annoyance of families in the neighborhood; and he moved that a committee be appointed to inquire into the facts and report. At a subsequent meeting the committee reported that "after a careful and laborious examination" they had satisfied themselves that "there was something decidedly rotten in Denmark; but from the peculiar and careful manner in which the implicated party conduct themselves, it will be impossible to reach the accused in the manner now pursued;" and the matter appears to have been dropped.

The Assessors appointed to value the city property reported the total valuation $1,390,825, not including about $250,000 not taxed.

City taxes this year—on real estate, one-fourth of one per cent.; on every $100 worth of merchandise sold, 20 cents; poll tax $1, &c. There was also an extra tax of one-fifth of one per cent. on all town property, one-twentieth of one per cent. on sales of merchandise, one-fourth of one per cent. on banks, &c., 25c. on polls, and one-eighth of one per cent. on slaves, to pay interest on railroad bonds.

The work of surveying for the track of the Mobile & Girard Railroad was progressing this year. The *Enquirer* of the 2d of July reported one hundred and sixty miles of the route then surveyed by Engineer Cooper, accompanied by the President, Maj. R. S. Hardaway; also that subscriptions obtained along the route exceeded the most sanguine anticipations. The grading of the road for a distance of 150 miles from Girard had all been taken. [Not completed yet!] The officers of the Company were R. S. Hardaway, President; W. B. Harris, Secretary; Gen. Anderson and James Abercombie of Russell, John Egerton of New Orleans, Wm. A. Hardaway of Mobile, and R. S. Hardaway of Columbus.

John Munn was elected an Alderman of Ward 6, in the place of Ald. Traywick removed from the ward.

A special election was held on the 2d of November for a Marshal and two Aldermen to fill vacancies. N. Mc. Robinson was elected Marshal, J. W. King Alderman for the 3rd Ward, and H. H. Epping Alderman for the 5th Ward. Robt. A. Ware was elected an Alderman of 2d Ward in November, in place of Alderman Robinson elected Marshal.

The receipts of cotton up to the 15th of June amounted to 59,519 bales. Prices 10¾ to 11¼c.

The Rock Island Paper Mills commenced supplying the city press with newspaper about the first of this year.

The *Southern Sentinel* was started in January, by Wm. H. Chambers, Esq., to whom Dr. Andrews had sold the *Democrat*. The *Enquirer* and *Times* were the other city papers.

Cotton was quoted at 11 to 12½c. in January, and declined a little during the spring.

The steamer H. S. Smith, with a cargo of one thousand bales of cotton, was entirely consumed by fire on the night of the 24th of March, at Fontaine's Landing on the Chattahoochee. Gen. Irwin was drowned in jumping overboard, and three negroes were either drowned or burned.

An Agricultural Fair, that attracted much interest, was held in Columbus on the 20th, 21st and 22d of November.

Royal Wright, son of David Wright, Esq., was killed on the 23d of November, in a rencontre with a man named Robinson. Robinson was from Atlanta.

Cotton in December was quoted at 11 to 12½c.

PERSONAL.

W. P. Baker, H. T. Hall, Dr. W. K. Schley, J. B. Strupper, L. W. Wells, and B. F. Coleman were Fire Wardens.

B. J. Mathews was Chief Engineer, and A. Porter, Assistant, of the Fire Department; J. B. Strupper, Foreman of Co. 1, and J. H. Merry, Assistant; H. T. Hall, Foreman of No. 2, and L. T. Woodruff, Assistant; Thos. L. Larus, Foreman of No. 3, and Sam. W. King, Assistant.

On January 7th, the Muscogee Railroad stockholders re-elected as directors, Major J. H. Howard, R. S. Hardaway, Dr. R. A. Ware, Gen. S. A. Bailey, Judge R. B. Alexander, Harvey Hall and Major James Wimberly.

The County election came off January 7th, and resulted as follows; F. A. Jepson, for Sheriff, by 26 majority over F. G. Wilkins; E. J. Hardin, Clerk Superior Court, by 29 over P. A. Clayton; Isaac Mitchell, Clerk of Inferior Court, over Tillery and W. M. Reeves; D. J. Rees, Tax Receiver, over

Fergurson; Noble, Tax Collector, over Edwards; J. B. Hicks, over Terry, for Coroner; Serrell for Surveyor.

On Saturday, February 9th, Alex. C. Morton was elected 2d Lieutenant, I. C. Chandler, 3rd, and R. D. S. Bell, 4th, of the City Light Guards. A. H. Cooper was Captain.

The Annual Georgia M. E. Conference was held at Marietta. S. Anthony was appointed Presiding Elder of the Columbus District, and Lovick Pierce and Joseph S. Key at Columbus.

MARRIAGES.

January 1—Samuel D. Harp and Sarah C. McCook. Jan. 3, Mason A. Bush and Charlotte Bedsole. Jan. 6, Shadrick Smith and Jane Walls. Jan. 8, John W. Patterson and Cornelia A. McMurray. Jan. 9, James Turnage and Elizabeth Hyatt, Nathan M. Brickhouse and Cecilia Bugg. Jan. 10, William T. Lawson and Susan A. Blankenship, John T. W. Coleman and Emily G. Horn. Jan. 17, Samuel Backman and Mary M. Tilley, William T. Whitton and Penelope Elder. Jan. 18, James Butler and Elizabeth Screws. Jan. 23, John Ligon and Mary E. Ridenhour. Jan. 24, Henry P. Fisher and Martha E. Fitner. Jan. 25, James Bailey and Emily Tipton. Jan. 27, John O. Maguirt and Jane Massey. Jan. 30, Alexander M. Wynn and Maria C. Howard.

February 5—James H. Bozeman and Sarah A. E. Stanfield. Feb. 6, Wm. J. Kellett and Emily Norman. Feb. 13, George S. Davis and Mary D. Warren. Feb. 14, David Dean and Nancy A. Glenn. Feb. 18, James A. Farley and Sarah E. Hoxey. Feb. 19, Wm. H. Munro and Louisa Cobb. Feb. 21, Levi Whatly and Mary A. Screws.

March 3—Michael H. Durr and Mary V. McGehee. March 10, John W. C. Baily and Elizabeth Benton. March 11, Wm. Yearty and Sarah Lockhart. March 13, James H. Renfroe and Elizabeth Crouch. March 17, Isaiah Willett and Sarah Maddox. March 20, William F. Fincher and Mary Hyatt. March 24, Jonathan P. Cordery and Mary Rowell.

April 1—Robert Barker and Mary Hackney. April 2, William G. Beckwith and Emma L. Hicks. April 3, George W. Woodruff and Virginia Lindsey. April 7, Asa Newsom and Nancy A. Chapman. April 14, Martin G. West and Sarah A. Morris. April 18, John Jewell and Martha Gulledge. April 24, John L. Terry and Julia A. L. Land. April 26, Charles W. Westmoreland and Sarah E. Burns.

May 1—Timothy Markham and Nancy Ligon. May 3, Enoch Fussell and Mary E. Morgan. May 5, Frank L. Mason and Lucinda Sanders, George W. Clark and Lurana F. Ivey. May 8, Henry J. Lamar and Valina B. Jones. May 11, Newsom Randall and Penelope C. Ratliff. May 12, James Welch and Louisa Maddox. May 16, Hugh R. Rodgers and Tabitha A. Miller. May 28, Oliver Danforth and Emma A. Nagle, Joseph C. Brewer and Ellen

MARRIAGES.

A. Fleming, May 29, Benjamin F. Markrum and Sarah Ann Ennis. May 30, John W. Hewell and Sophronia E. Harp.

June 2—William W. Morgan and Lucinda Williams. June 6, Joseph King and Harriet R. Bell. June 13, Ambrose Nix and Mary J. Edwards. June 19, John Hughes and Ann B. Cox. June 20, Thomas Hunt and Mary Renfroe. June 23, John Jackson and Maria King.

July 3—James Ligon and Sarah A. Tommey, Samuel M. Carter and Emily L. Colquitt. July 7, Andrew J. McKenzie and Catharine Barbaree. July 11, Abraham Odom and Eliza A. English. July 12, John Newberry and Laney Robinson. July 13, Charles L. Geer and Matilda Hatcher. July 16, Lewis S. McCall and Ann Morris, Charles T. Cushman and Jane A. W. Shaw. July 18, Irving Watkins and Lucretia J. Napier. July 23, William Dubois and Elizabeth E. Craig. July 24, Geo. A. Christian and Salina Shofner, Stephen B. Dean and Margaret L. Cunning. July 31, William Wooton and Betsey Stephens. July 4, Thos. I. Patrick and Elsey Waters.

August 13—John M. Traywick and Minerva E. Thompson. Aug. 14, Edward S. Martin and Margaret J. Culpepper. Aug. 15, John R. Merritt and Susan Proctor. Aug. 18, William Tillery and Mary E. Waters, Charles J. Davenport and Martha A. E. Gibson. Aug. 21, Elias Sanders and Sarah A. Bartlett. Aug. 27, Walker P. Jones and Frances McNaughton.

September 1—Lewis Moody and Lucinda Langley, Thomas H. Reynolds and Mary F. Boring. Sept. 4, William M. Allen and Delilah Odom. Sept. 5, Orman Oliver and Nancy Williamson. Sept. 7, Obadiah Whittenton and Mary A. Newsom. Sept. 8, John T. Damill and Lucinda Ougle. Sept. 12, Andrew J. Ousley and Martha A. Jordan, Davie G. W. Davis and Elizabeth P. Moss. Sept. 19, John C. Lewis and Martha Fletcher. Sept. 22, Jesse Wall and Susan Harvell. Sept. 23, Wm. H. Sauls and Sarah J. Brown. Sept. 24, Rufus Carr and Gasoline Griffin. Sept. 26, Joseph J. Painter and Rebecca J. Osborn, John Martin and Eleanor G. Wood.

October 3—William H. Hinson and Elizabeth A. Luker. Oct. 8, John G. Hortman and Frances Rees. Oct. 9, Abner H. Flewellen and Sarah E. Hardaway. Oct. 15, Henry Rees and Pallentine Ivey. Oct. 16, Isaac C. Chandler and Sarah M. Thomas, John Brittenham and Lucinda Dennis. Oct. 17, Richard Williams and Rachel A. Rodgers. Oct. 20, John Flynn and Sarepta Helms. Oct. 23, Richard H. Lockhart and Arabella J. Howard. Oct. 24, Christopher C. Morgan and Adaline Culpepper. Oct. 26, Thomas W. Peddy and Elizabeth Maynor. Oct. 31, John L. Parker and Nancy K. Edwards.

November 5—Mijamon Moon and Sarah A. G. Paul, Thomas M. Towler and Sarah E. Boland. Nov. 7, Joseph McCall and Mary Drenon. Nov. 10, George W. Cobb and Mary Berry. 13, William Welch and Catharine Nelson. 14, John Byard and Sarah Cooper. 23, Walter C. Manning and Rebecca M. Shellman. 27, James W. Warren and Sarah V. Howard, Wiley Adams and Sarah A. E. Tooke.

December 5—Presley Tillery and Lucinda Dukes, S. M. J. Wimberly and Mary A. Pickett. Dec. 11, Daniel B. Bird and Mary V. Butt. Dec. 12, Wm.

B. Willis and Lucinda J. McLendon. Dec. 13, Matthias Barringer and Sarah Pryor. Dec. 15, Samuel J. Flemming and Eliza Culpepper. Dec. 18, Grisham Scroggins and Mary A. E. Daukins, William P. Aubry and Rosa M. Forsyth, David H. Wynn and Mary F. Dennis. Dec. 23, George S. Cary and Margaret S. Thweatt. Dec. 24, Drewery Pate and Martha Ivey. Dec. 29, Jonathan Cordery and Angelina Wall. Dec. 30, Michael L. Walters and Haner A. M. Webb.

SEXTON'S REPORT OF DEATHS.

January 2—Mr. Benson, aged 40 years; 4, child of John Kelly; 4, Frances A. Duffie, aged, 40; 9, Sarah Ann Holt, aged 29; 10, Elizabeth Sanders, aged 62; 12, Wm. H. Ayer, aged 10; 15, Rudolph H. Ayer, 12; 15, child of Mr. Gammel; 20, Patrick Gellen, aged 13; 31, George W. Turrentine; 31, Hon Wm. Griggs. Also 5 negroes in January.

(We find no report for February.)

March 6—Peggy Dodson, aged 50; 9, Ann Murdock, aged 30; 16, John Schaeffer, aged 40. Also 3 negroes in this month.

April 1—John Williams, aged 30 years; 2, child of Mrs. Moore; 6, Richard Tarborough, 43; 8, child of M. Stephens; 9, Wm. Tarbutton, aged 40; 10, child of Mr. Mariner; 19, child of Mr. McElrath, aged 1; 25, Amanda Byard, aged 25; 29, Elizabeth Hall, aged 45. Also 6 negroes in this month.

May 5—Child of C. Wise, aged 5 months; 5, child of Mr. King, aged 1 year; 6, Abraham Clark, aged 5; 6, child of Mrs. Hooper; 8, child of O. Anderson, aged 1; 9, Abram Curry, aged 67; 9, Benj. Sutton, aged 20; 22, Ellen Mobley, aged 20; 26, Susan Kent, aged 49; 30, child of Mrs. Hooper, aged 10. Also 4 negroes in this month.

DEATHS.

(FROM THE NEWSPAPERS.)

May 18—Mrs. M. F. Weems, wife of Locke Weems.

June 5—Mrs. Kimbrough, wife of Wm. H. Kimbrough. June 6, Mrs. E. A. Billups. June 24, Mary Jane, infant daughter of E. H. Musgrove.

July 10—Mrs. Eleanor M. S. Ector. July 11, Mary Elizabeth, infant child of Peter K. Edgar. July 14, Thos. Bostwick, aged 30 years.

August—Wm. B. Christian. August 9, Mrs. Harriet, wife of Peter K. Edgar.

September 7—Patrick Tiervey, aged 24. Sept. 10, John M. S. Brooks, aged 24. Sept. 10, (at Savannah) Nelson McLester, of Columbus. Sept. — David M. Clarke. Sept. 22, Mrs. Sarah A., wife of H. S. Smith. Sept. 23, Willis M. Reeves.

October. 11—Cosam Emir Bartlett, aged 57 years (formerly editor of a Columbus paper.) Oct. 22, Mathew Brannon.

November 12—Miss Julia H. Pledge, in the 15th year of her age. Nov. 27, Mrs. E. A. Redd, wife of Wm. Redd, Sr.

December 13—Philip, infant son of Thos. Schley. Dec. —, John Neuffer, aged 79. Dec. 30, William Holtzclaw.

1851.

Water Works Agitated—Subscription to Mobile & Girard R. R.

The city officers elected on the first Saturday in January were Willis S. Holstead, Mayor; Aldermen—1st Ward, Thomas B. Slade and Lewis M. Durr; 2d, John A. Urquahart and R. A. Ware; 3rd, John H. Madden; 4th, Samuel R. Andrews and John M. Trawick; 5th, A. A. Lowther and Wm. Mahaffey; 6th, A. A. Dill. Subsequently, Wm. Mathewson was elected an Alderman of the 6th Ward, and J. W. King of the 3rd Ward. Calvin Stratton was elected Clerk; Jordan L. Howell, Treasurer; N. Mc. Robinson, Marshal; George Gullen, Deputy Marshal.

Council elected Thos. Nix, Clerk of the Market; Wm. W. Martin, Bridge Keeper; Dr. F. A. Stanford, City Physician; Burnet Ingram, Hospital Keeper; Adam G. Foster, City Attorney; Jere Terry, Sexton. Health officers—John Kyle, J. F. Bozeman, Mansfield Torrence, Thad. Sturgis, M. Woodruff, J. W. Frost, Wm. C. Cooper, J. L. Morton, John Munn, Michael N. Clark. Port Wardens—Thos. M. Hogan, F. G. Wilkins, R. C. Shorter, J. C. Brewer, James McGuire.

A. Porter was Chief Engineer of the Fire Department, and J. L. Morton Assistant; J. B. Strupper, Foreman, and Wm. Snow, Assistant of No. 1; H. T. Hall, Foreman, and J. Barrenger, Assistant of No. 2; T. P. Larus, Foreman, and W. L. Salisbury, Assistant of No. 3. Fire Company No. 1 numbered 61 men; No. 2, 38 men; No. 3, 24 men. Each had an engine.

The Finance Committee in April reported the total liabilities of the city, $25,175, and the probable revenue of the year, $23,475.

Reuben C. Shorter was in April elected an Alderman of the 4th Ward, in the place of Alderman Trawick, removed from the city; and Wm. Brooks elected in May an Alderman of the 6th Ward, vice Alderman Dill, removed.

At its meeting on the 12th of July, Council granted to the manufacturing companies and sundry citizens, petitioners, authority to erect a foot bridge across the river, opposite the Howard Factory, but reconsidered and rejected it at another meeting. This project was never consummated, and in a few years afterwards what is known as the "upper bridge" was built near the locality named.

The population of Columbus, according to the United States census taken this year, was—free 3,684, slave, 2,258— total, 5,942. The whole population of Muscogee county was 18,623, of which 10,447 were whites, and 8,176 slaves. The amount of capital then invested in manufactures was $841,- 517, of which there was invested in the manufacture of cotton and wool, $493,000.

On the 26th of July a committee of Council reported upon the practicability of supplying the city with a sufficiency of pure and wholesome water. They reported that they had, "for reasons deemed sufficient," abandoned all the plans proposed except one, which was the introduction of water from neighboring springs by pipes. They submitted a report from Engineer L. W. Dubois, to the effect that water enough, and of good quality, could be obtained from springs on the Summerville heights, on the Alabama side. But the committee did not recommend this, for the reason that the sources of the supply were in "another jurisdiction." Council appointed a committee to ascertain whether and on what terms the water on the Alabama side could be had for the use of the city.

In October the committee reported other surveys and estimates made by Mr. Dubois—one for bringing the water of the river from Lover's Leap, the other for bringing it from Wynn's Hill. The cost of bringing the water to the city from Lover's Leap was estimated at $28,282 06, from Wynn's Hill $32,668 75; works at the city for the former $25,842 92, for the latter $30,937 35.

Wm. Mahaffey was elected Marshal in October.

At a public meeting held on the 4th of November, the citizens voted authority to the Council to subscribe $150,000 to the stock of the Girard Railroad Co., on the assurance that with this subscription to buy rails, &c., the road would be promptly put into running order as far as Chunnenuggee; and on the 5th of November Council appointed a committee to confer with the Directors of the road and arrange all the details of the subscription. On the 25th of November, the committee reported an agreement with the Directors of the road which Council unanimously ratified. The Council reserved the right to connect with the road by means of a bridge across the river, and to have the trains of the road run across it.

Theopholis Stewart of the 3rd, and John Lloyd of the 5th Ward, were elected Aldermen in November.

Large private subscriptions for plank roads to Greenville and to Lumpkin were made by citizens this fall. But Council, while admitting the importance of these roads, declined to take stock, on account of existing indebtedness.

On the 9th of December, Council resolved to loan the Muscogee Railroad $75,000 of the city's bonds, taking a mortgage on the road as security.

On the 31st of December, trains commenced running over twenty miles of the Muscogee Railroad, then finished, from the Columbus terminus. Connecting stages ran to Oglethorpe and to Barnesville.

INCIDENTS.

Temperance Hall was "dedicated" on the night of the 8th of January, with interesting ceremonies. "Uncle Dabney Jones," the great apostle of Temperance, delivered an address.

Milton Robbins this year established a ropewalk in Girard.

The postoffice was this year removed to the large brick building corner of Randolph and Oglethorpe streets, where it remained until the building was destroyed by fire.

An engine was placed on the Columbus end of the Muscogee Railroad in April, but the road had not then been finished to Fort Valley. The ladies aided, but we have not found to what extent, in raising the money for the purchase of this engine, by a fair held in March.

A great revival of religion was manifested in the city this year. Meetings were continued for a month or six weeks at the Methodist church, and more than two hundred persons professed religion.

An Agricultural Fair held in Temperance Hall in November was pronounced quite a success.

The receipts of cotton to the 21st of June amounted to 55,-659 bales. Prices—in January, 11 to 12½ c.; in April, 7 to 10c.; in October, 6 to 6½c.; in December, 6¼ to 7⅛c.

PERSONAL.

H. Noble was Tax Collector, and James Fergurson Tax Receiver of Muscogee county.

The Georgia M. E. Conference, which met in Savannah, sent Rev. W. M. Crumley to Columbus, and appointed Rev. S. Anthony, Presiding Elder of the Columbus District. Rev. T. Bermingham was the Catholic Priest at Columbus.

The following persons rented stalls in the Market this year: Wm. R. Jones, P. Gittinger, Arnold & Robertson, E. B. W. Spivey, Richard Robertson, Charles Bize, Alex. W. Robertson. The aggregate amount which they rented for was $237 50.

MARRIAGES.

January 1—Leonard R. Cooley and Julia A. Henly. Jan. 2, Wesley P. Williams and Mary A. Chapman, George S. Martin and Elizabeth Gammell. Jan. 3, James P. Russell and Margaret Rowell, William Wilkinson and Mary A. Cordery. Jan. 7, Pleasant Odom and Elizabeth McKenzie. Jan. 8, Jesse H. Wyatt and Emily Rentfroe. Jan. 9, Elisha A. Jackson and Frances E. Morris, John W. Watkins and Eliza A. Massey. Jan. 11, Daniel Wilkinson and Elizabeth Browning, Jesse T. Sutton and Caroline Osteen. Jan. 23, Edward H. Bernhard and Ann E. Hemphill, Wright McCook and Ruhama Harp. Jan. 29, William M. Maxley and Emily M. Beck. Jan. 30, David Jones and Rebecca A. Newberry.

February 6—James F. Bozeman and Evaline A. Chambers. Feb. 11, John W. Payne and Lurany Jones. Feb. 16, Walton Doles and Sarah Buckler. Feb. 18, John Bunnell and Louisiana J. Osteen.

March 6—William J. Wright and Martha Simmons. March 13, Elijah Morgan and Sophy A. F. Lanier. March 20, Amos R. Nelson and Sarah J. Willett, Green J. Mann and Susan Ann Kite, James Bonner and Martha A. Smith. March 25, George W. Lovett, and Sarah Brassill, Clark P. Lanier and Sarah F. Chapman. March 26, Jacob Hydrick and Martha Bugg.

April 1—Gilbert Kent and Sarah Lawrence. April 15, William J. Harrell and Harriet Cordery. April 16, John T. Pry and Epsy A. Bush. April 20, James M. Cobb and Isabella Lee. April 24, Benjamin Brown and Janet Stephens. April 29, Thomas E. Motley and Harriet Moore.

May 4—Jacob H. Faulkenbury and Artamesia A. Stephens. May 6, Lycurgus Madox and Sarah A. Kent. May 8, William Jones and Martha A. Stephens, John H. Glanton and Elizabeth Welch. May 13, Barney Barnes and Sarah E. Mitchell. May 14, Milledge G. McKennie and Louisiana F. Warren. May 22, Elijah Vickers and Ariadna A. Evans. May 25, Milton A. Smith and Henrietta H. Goulding. May 27, Everard H. Abercombie and Pauline Lewis. May 28, Robert H. Sullivan and Mahulda Jordan. May 31, William M. Hale and Harriet Welch.

June 1—John Clark and Mary A. Alford, Edward F. Rogers and Isabella Mann. June 5, George W. Fisher and Frances A. Wimberly. June 11, James Caulfield and Elizabeth Locklier. June 12, Thomas Summergill and Mary McCallister. June 19, Thomas J. Brown and Frances Bowen. June 22, Alexander Hall and Lucinda George. June 25, Lyman B. Townsley and Mary J. Peabody. June 26, James R. McDonald and Mary J. McNeal.

July 1—Jeremiah Gammell and Arabella A. A. Reynolds. July 3, Neil McMillen and Rhoda A. Moon, George Stein and Mary Blankenship, Simeon Weldon and Nancy J. Taylor. July 5, John J. Ingram and Julia A. Perry. July 8, Jacob Neagle and Mary Madden. July 12, Eli Frost and Frances Goen. July 15, Benjamin F. Graves and Sarah H. Sauls. July 21, James H. McMicken and Nancy Copeland. July 22, Edwin G. Thornton and Martha F. B. Jones.

August 6—Henry W. Verstille and Ellen J. Lockhart, Anthony Martin and Frances Allum, Andrew Gaskey and Julia Algood, August 7, John W. King and Mary J. Kimbrough. August 14, John J. Collins and Rebecca Kerbo. August 17, William W. Stewart and Susan J. Roberts. August 21, Isham Turner and Mary J. Jemison. August 24, William M. Taylor and Sarah J. Robinson.

September 7—Seaborn Bryant and Frances Garrett. Sept. 11, Samuel P. Leggett and Martha A. Johnson, Washington Watkins and Mary A. Whitton. Sept. 16, Eugene A. Smith and Frances A. Reese. Sept. 17, H. H. McQueen and Mary E. Rudledge. Sept. 22, James D. Britt and Mary A. Pomeroy. Sept. 25, William H. Harris and Sarah A. King, William C. Daniel and Cornelia M. Phelps. Sept. 30, Joseph J. Jones and Caroline E. Lloyd, Thomas D. Fortson and Georgia E. Mealing.

October 2—James T. Norman and Mary E. Dean. October 8, William R. Brown and Mariah E. Broadnax. Oct. 9, Adolphus D. Metts and Mary Ball.

Oct. 15, George T. Hurt and Nancy J. Flewellen. Oct. 16, James O. A. Tucker and Martha E. Dyer. Oct. 23, Elisha F. Garrett and Elizabeth H. Robinson. Oct. 27, Daniel G. Watson and Evaline Keiner. Oct. 31, John W. Mardis and Susan J. Smith.

November 3—William Boyd and Mahulda McGowen. November 6, Benjamin A. Fussill and Sidney A. F. Osteen. November 9, Green S. Childs and Frances A. Napier, John H. Walsingham and Eliza A. O'Quin. November 16, John W. Whytal and Charlotte A. Kidder. November 25, Isaiah Willett and Sarah Clark. November 27, James N. Fussell and Zilpha L. Hall, Benjamin Ryans and Celia A. Tinnon. Nov. 30, Wentworth S. Marble and Hannah E. Chase.

December 2—Thos. Duffield and Amanda Johnson, James A. Bell and Caroline E. Brown. December 3, Arnold Seals and Eleanor A. Reid. December 4, William J. Chapman and Sarah J. Tinnon, Benjamin F. Wallace and Cynthia A. E. Morrell. December 7, John Ward and Mary S. Cary, William T. Webster and Sarah A. Wiggins. December 11, David Jones and Henrietta Tarver, John B. Jones and Creecy A. Cobb, James Pierce and Eliza Gilbert, Richard E. Jones and Elizabeth Jones. December 14, Francis J. Abbott and Martha G. Garrison. December 18, Sanders E. Echols and Martha E. Perry. December 19, Robert Johnson and Ann M. Sinclair. December 21, William Waters and Margaret A. Hunter. December 23, James J. W. Biggers and Caroline E. Williams, Horace Mathews and Elizabeth Dennis. December 25, Robert Knowles and Martha J. Hammock, Thomas Reynolds and Nancy F. Reynolds.

SEXTON'S REPORT OF DEATHS.

January 3—Jesse King, aged 51 years. Jan. 3, James Welch, 49 years. Jan. 5, Alex. Flewellen, 8 years. Jan. 10, T. Smith's child, 1 year. Jan. 10, H. Hall's child, 1 year. Jan. 13, George Sherwood, 36 years. Jan. 18, Perry Robison, 21 years. Jan. 25, Thomas Lee, 26 years. Jan. 26, Mrs. Adou, 68 years. Jan. 30, Sarah Barringer, 28 years. Also 3 negroes in January.

February 4—Jane L. Marks, aged 64 years. Feb. 10, child of Mr. Harp, aged 1 day. Feb. 12, child of Wm. F. Luckie, aged 8 months. Feb. 13, child of Mr. Newberry, 5 months. Feb. 15, Robert B. Alexander, 40 years. Feb. 21, Eliza Robinson, 31 years. Feb. 22, Wm. E. Robinson, 37 years. Feb. 28, Martha Mims, 74 years.

March 9—Mary Ann Corry, 62 years. March 9, Martin J. Kendrick, 22 years. March 11, Bridget Hudson, 41 years. March 14, Patrick Clark, 48 years. March 15, Wm. Brown, 52 years. March 16, Caroline Stein, 26 years. March 16, James Osborn, 56 years. March 22, Joseph Meredith, 51 years. March 24, Emeline Crews, 18 years. March 24, Thomas McCarty, 53 years.

April 1—Caroline Burton, 38 years; ——Chapman, 9 years; George C. Hooper, 41 years. April 4, Wiley G. Roper, 41 years; Sarah Willett, 17 years. April 5, John Winn, 51 years. April 7, child of Col. Wyley, 2 years. April 8, James Shaw, 52 years; John Brooks, 6 years. April 12, Matilda Packman, 19 years. April 13, Mary Hammock, 19 years. April 18, John C.

Leitner, 39 years; child of Mrs. Packman, aged 7 days. April 22, child of John Brown, 1 year. April 24, child of Mr. King, 7 days. April 25, child of Sterling F. Grimes, 10 days. April 28, child of Thos. Herendine, 2 years; child of Samantha George, 8 years; child of Mr. Bobitt, 1 year. April 29, child of Mr. Willett, 1 year. April 30, Solomon Curlee, 8 years. Also 7 slaves in February, and 4 in March.

May 16—child of George W. Winter, aged 5 months. May 20, Benjamin Napier, 6 years. May 21, child of Henry Teasdale, 1 year. May 25, child of S. B. Harvill, 1 year; child of W. T. Colquitt, 1 year. May 27, Jennette Veaneman, 6 years. May 30, Parmelia Wilkins, 36 years. Also 6 slaves in May.

June 3—Jane Busbee, aged 26 years. June 13, child of R. Hooper, 2 years. June 14, Isabella Holly, 17 years. June 15, —— Hickey, 35 years. June 23, Richard A. Long, 31 years. June 24, child of John Byard, 3 weeks. June 30, James Bishop, 26 years. Also 10 slaves in June.

July 1—Miss Jackson, aged 51 years. July 4, child of Mr. Renfroe, 1 month. July 9, child of Mr. Burbee, 2 years. July 15, Sarah A. Riley, 26 years. July 18, James Bryant, 17 years. July 22, child of A. Backer, 1 year. July 23, Clara Hamill, 15 years. July 26, Stephen Gilpin, 18 years. July 30, Henry Madden, 33 years. Also 6 slaves in July.

August 2—Templeton Reid, aged 65 years. Aug. 5, child of Mr. Robison, 1 year. Aug. 8, H. C. Anderson, 35 years. Aug. 14, Sarah Nolen, 29 years. Aug. 19, child of Mr. Fairchild, 3 years. Aug. 20, Nancy McCarty, 57 years. Aug. 21, child of P. Adams, 3 months. Aug. 22, child of J. E. Webster, 1 year. Aug. 23, Jacob Seismund, 41 years. Aug. 24, Mary Long, 21 years. Aug. 25, P. N. Jernigan, 25 years. Aug. 29, Jere. Collins, 63 years. Aug. 31, child of Mr. Napier, —. Also 7 slaves in August.

September 6—Esau Pike, aged 60 years. Sept. 12, Joseph Frost, 24 years. Sept. 14, John Gunn, 4 years. Sept. 15, Sarah Holly, 52 years. Sept. 20, child of H. Smith, 2 years. Sept. 22, Charles Williams, 12 years; Gilbert Clark, 50 years. Sept. 23. N. McRobinson, 41 years. Sept. 26, James Dennis, —. Sept. 27, Lovick Switzer, 21 years. Sept. 30, Emeline Jordan, 24 years. Also 3 slaves in September.

Here the official record ends, and we can only republish such obituary notices as we find in the newspapers:

Oct. 12—Samuel J. Crow, aged about 37 years.

Nov. 8—Mrs. Martha Ann Davis, wife of John H. Davis.

Nov. 24—Robert M., son of Thomas J. Shivers.

Nov. 27—Theobold Howard, aged 48 years.

Dec. 26—Richard T. Brice, aged 39 years.

1852.

Opelika Branch Railroad—Gas Light Company Formed.

J. L. Morton, Wiley Williams, R. M. Gunby and M. N. Clark were candidates for Mayor at the January election, and the vote stood—Morton 235, Williams 188, Gunby 162, Clark 25. The Aldermen elect were: 1st Ward, Lewis M. Durr and Thos. B. Slade; 2d, Dr. A. I. Robison and Wm. Perry; 3d, Dr. T. Stewart and Thos. M. Hogan; 4th, R. C. Shorter and John Quin; 5th, A. A. Lowther and H. H. Epping; 6th, Wm. Matheson (and Thos. R. Herndine was afterwards elected.) James M. Hughes was elected Marshal; A. M. Robertson, Deputy Marshal; Calvin Stratton, Clerk; and Jordan L. Howell, Treasurer.

Council, at its first meeting, elected Beverly A. Thornton City Attorney; Jere Terry, Sexton; Thos. Nix, Clerk of the Market; Wm. W. Martin, Bridge-keeper; B. Ingram, Hospital keeper. The following gentlemen were elected Health Officers: Dr. Thos. Hoxey, J. L. Barringer, Jos. Kyle, Jas. M. Everett, Wm. Danerly, George Pitts, Charles Wise, Wm. C. Cooper, Isaac Mitchell, Wm. Brooks.

Dr. J. B. Hoxey was elected City Physician; and the following gentlemen Port Wardens: F. G. Wilkins, John C. Calhoun, A. K. Ayer, Edward Birdsong, James McGuire.

The Fire Wardens for this year were—J. A. Deblois, H. T. Hall, John H. Madden, J. B. Strupper, P. Adams, Ezekiel Davis.

Quite a flurry was created in Council, in January, on the subject of repealing the ordinance of 1851 which located and regulated the negro marts of the city. Council refused to lay on the table an ordinance amending the ordinance of 1851; whereupon Aldermen Slade, Durr, Lowther, Stewart and Slaughter tendered their resignations, which Council refused to accept. But these Aldermen retired, and at an election held on the 4th of February, Messrs. Wm. C. Gray, Wm. Y. Barden, Richard P. Spencer, George W. Lively and Wm. Williamson were elected in their places. [The fair presumption is that the amendatory ordinance was passed, but the record does not show it. It allowed the negro traders to bring their slaves into the city for sale in the day-time, but required them to be kept on the South Common at night.]

Wm. Brooks was in February elected an Alderman of the 6th ward, in the place of Ald. Matheson, resigned.

The appraisers appointed by Council reported the valuation of real estate $1,516,970, showing a small but steady increase for several years. The city debt at that time amounted to $3,200, besides some unpaid railroad subscriptions. The receipts from all sources were about $27,500, and the expenses, with Muscogee Railroad interest, about $24,000.

The *Enquirer* of April 20th indulged in fond anticipations of the growth and prosperity of Columbus as soon as the progressing railroads afforded better facilities for commerce. The article stated that almost all the dry goods then consumed in this section were wagoned from Macon at heavy expense; but that when the Muscogee Railroad was finished, such goods could be sold in Columbus as cheap as at Macon or Savannah. It looked also for a great increase of trade from the Girard Railroad, and urged the importance of constructing plank roads or some other improvements to facilitate trade with the counties north and south of Columbus.

Col. John G. Winter's Bank of St. Marys suspended specie payments on the 23d of April. The circulation was stated to be about $350,000.

The cars on the Muscogee Railroad commenced running 25 miles on the 18th of May.

The first substantial movement towards the building of the Opelika Branch Road, of which we find any mention, was a proposition by the city of Savannah, in May of this year, to loan the credit of that city to the amount of $100,000 in aid of the enterprise. Curiously, the *Enquirer* regarded it with suspicion—as a move in opposition to the Girard road. This subject was warmly discussed on both sides through the columns of the city press. Several meetings of citizens were held to consider the policy of a city subscription of $50,000, and finally a poll was opened, when the citizens, on the 12th of June, voted in favor of a conditional subscription. The vote stood—for a subscription, provided other parties subscribe a like amount of $50,000, and that the road cross the river, 192; for subscription unconditionally, 52; no subscription, 85. The *Times* advocated the road and the subscription.

Jos. S. Pruden was in July elected an Alderman of the 4th Ward, vice Alderman Epping, resigned.

The total population of Muscogee county this year was 18,750.

A committee of Council this summer made a contract with Jonathan Bridges for boring an artesian well, but Council did not ratify the contract. The *Times* of November 9th said of the water supply of the city:

We do not know a community that is so poorly supplied with this first necessity for health, comfort and cleanliness (water) as Columbus. There are many families in the city who have no regular and certain source from which to derive their daily supplies of this precious element, and whose servants are actually obliged, at every turn of the water-bucket, to go forth on a foraging expedition in search of it. The water works are as good as used up. No attention is paid to the pipes furnishing the supply, and it is only occasionly that some half a dozen hydrants in very low localities, run. Those in more elevated positions are as dry as the miraculous rock before Moses touched it with his rod.

[This refers to a system of wood pipes and hydrants by which certain parties furnished citizens paying for it with water brought into portions of the city from "Leonard's Spring," about three miles from the city.]

A gas company, at the head of which was Mr. James Hoy, of Trenton, N. J., made a proposition in November to light the city with gas. Council appropriated $10,000 to the capital stock of the company. The company was known as the "Columbus Gas Light Association." John Forsyth was chosen President, Henry T. Hall, Secretary, and Messrs. Daniel Griffin, Henry T. Hall, W. G. Clemons, John Forsyth and J. L. Morton, Directors.

INCIDENTS.

The Histrionics, a dramatic company composed of resident citizens, gave a number of very pleasant and creditable entertainments this spring. On the evening of the 2nd of April they performed a national drama written by the gifted Mrs. Caroline Lee Hentz, then of Columbus, which was pronounced a production of extraordinary merit, and received with much applause. It was entitled "Lamorah, or the Western Wild."

The Baptist State Convention met in Columbus in April—Thomas Stocks, Esq., Moderator.

A "Citizen Merchant," writing in June, claimed that the Eagle Manufacturing Company were then making osnaburgs "superior to any in the world, being heavier and made out of better cotton"; also that the goods of this company were sold quite as low, and in some cases lower, than the same qualities of goods were sold in New York.

The house of J. J. McKendree, Esq., at the upper end of Oglethorpe street, was consumed by fire on the morning of the 21st of June; also a kitchen on the adjoining lot, of Mr. J. B. Wright.

The *Times* reported the discovery of a valuable mineral spring immediately on the river and under the bank, on the east side, four miles above the city. The water was represented as unusually clear and cool, and containing both iron and sulphur. As the *Times* said that the railroad *about to be* constructed to West Point would pass within twenty steps of the spring, perhaps our citizens of the present day will have no difficulty in finding it.

Another very creditable Agricultural and Horticultural Fair was held during the first week in October. Council appropriated $150 to aid it.

A two-story brick building owned by Messrs. Mott and Cleghorn, and occupied by Mr. S. C. Pryor as the "Exchange" bar and billiard room, was burned on the 15th of November.

An extraordinary and disastrous flood in the river occurred on the 25th of November. During hard rains the river rose thirty feet, and "a section of the east wall of the reservoir extending from the Eagle Factory to the Palace Mills and Variety Works, gave way under the pressure of water, and carried with it the flume of the Palace Mills and the bridge which connected the Variety Works with the shore." Fifteen men and a boy were in the Works at the time, and these were cut off from the main land by a current which no boat could cross. The river was still rising at the rate of three feet an hour. After a number of unsuccessful efforts, communication was established by means of a light cord and weight at first and then by ropes passed, connecting the second story of the Variety Works with a pile of rock on shore. A basket was made to slide upon the ropes, drawn by cords, and in this frail conveyance the people in the Variety Works were taken from their perilous position to the land. Mayor J. L. Morton fell from a rock into the river, swam thence to another rock, where he had to remain until communication was in like manner established with him and he was rescued. The damage done to all the factory business was very great. The machinery in the Variety Works, the Palace Mills, and all the Factories except the Coweta, which stood at the dam (now known as the old upper dam) was stopped. Four or five hundred operatives and their families were temporarily thrown out of employment.

The Female Orphan Asylum was destroyed by fire on the night of the 9th of December. But the citizens raised in a few hours a subscription of $1,700 to rebuild it.

The 4th of July was celebrated by the City Light Guards, the Ringgold Artillery, and the Fire Companies, by an excursion on the railroad, some 22 miles from the city. The declaration was read by Private Salisbury, and the oration delivered by Thomas J. Nuckolls, Esq. The Columbus Guards went to Montgomery and had a fine time there.

The first bale of new cotton was received on the 20th of August, from the plantation of Charles Fisher, Esq., of Muscogee county. It was sold at 10 cents.

The third annual Fair of the Georgia and Alabama Agricultural Society was held in Columbus on the 6th and 7th of October.

Five deaths occurred in the city during the first week in December, from cholera morbus caused by eating bad oysters. A report got out in the country that it was Asaitic cholera.

Up to the 15th of May, Columbus received 42,976 bales of cotton. Prices in January, $5\frac{1}{2}$ to 7 cents; in May, $6\frac{1}{4}$ to $8\frac{1}{4}$; in October, $8\frac{1}{2}$ to $9\frac{1}{2}$ cents.

PERSONAL.

The M. E. Church appointments for Columbus were Revs. W. Crumley, J. L. Pierce and T. H. Jordan. Rev. J. E. Evans was Presiding Elder of the District.

A. S. Rutherford was Sheriff; John Sturgis, Clerk of the Superior Court; A. P. Jones, Clerk of the Inferior Court; John Johnson, Ordinary; H. Noble, Tax Collector; Dan. J. Reese, Tax Receiver; J. B. Hicks, Coroner; and Philip Lamar, County Surveyor of Muscogee county.

T. Lomax, Esq., became one of the editors of the *Southern Sentinel* in February.

MARRIAGES.

January 1—William Y. Barden and Eliza D. Jernigan, Francis G. Wilkins and Lucinda King. Jan. 4, Benjamin A. Hearn and Mary Decker. Jan. 5, Willis H. Jones and Cynthia A. Pace. Jan. 11, James Castleberry and Susan J. Cobb. Jan. 15, Nathaniel A. Deblois and Angelica L. Hurd, Hannibal Harrold and Elizabeth R. Howell. Jan. 20, George H. Decker and Sarah Gibbs. Jan. 22, Isham Gallups and Charlotte T. Johnson, John Ramsey and Pauline S. E. Bazemore. Jan. 25, Joshua Hutchins and Sarah A. Joins. Jan. 28, Thomas J. Cobb and Harriet A. Flannigan.

February 1—Eldred A. Chatterton and Rachel Lewis. Feb. 2, William Robinson and Georgia A. Kelly. Feb. 4, James Whipple and Alsey W. Mays. Feb. 5, Joel T. Scott and Navini J. Wood, Hervey M. Cleckley and Frances P. Schley. Feb. 11, Stephen F. McGehee and Adaline Browning. Feb. 15, Henry Smith and Matilda Taylor. Feb. 24. John M. Jones and Cordelia A. Ridgeway.

March 4—Madison T. Key and Amanda C. Jernigan, Anderson H. Holmes and Elizabeth Garrett. March 18, Martin Duke and Felicia A. Phelps. March 19, John W. Suggs and Nancy M. Austin.

April 5—William B. Fansett and Nancy Carlile. April 15, Henry M. Morris and Jane E. Searls. April 21, Davis Owen and Catharine B. Lestergett. April 22, William H. Cochran and Priscilla Crawford. April 29, Joseph A. Hewell and Aquilla A. V. Dean, Henry Mangham and Louisa Sempler.

May 4—Thomas J. Trammell and Permelia E. Gunn, Benjamin F. Ray and Annetta J. Hall. May 5, George M. Lucas and Sarah P. E. Edwards. May 13, Alexander B. Huey and Susan A. Edwards. May 20, Henry Johnson and Irene Stanfield. May 22, John H. Webb and Sarah R. Gordy.

June 6—James W. Rolen and Martha A. Carter, William M. Lewis and Martha A. Mason. May 10, Benjamin F. Newberry and Sarah J. Starke. June 20, John King and Elizabeth Brown. June 24, Lewis Scott and Martha A. Owen. June 30, Madison L. Patterson and Augusta P. Benning.

July 1—William M. Watts and Sarah F. Johnson, Charles Brady and Rosannah Foran. July 4, Hugh Hall and Isabella A. Senn. July 10, Robert F. Pickren and Susan A. Wall. July 13, DeWitt F. Willcox and Julia C. Carnes, Edward W. Brannon and Mary A. Crouch. July 16, Anthony F. Rodgers and Martha A. Rowell. July 21, Lafayette Walker and Elizabeth Stephens.

August 8—Hamilton Boland and Evaline Jones. Aug. 29, Andrew J. Floyd and Sarah V. Shippey. Aug. 31, James H. John and Elizabeth J. McGlaun.

September 1—John G. Brooks and Permelia Castillo. Sept. 9, John Laman and Mary M. Rodgers. Sept. 23, Vincent L. Averett and Rosannah E. Stephens. Sept. 28, Samuel E. Whittaker and Henrietta Leonard.

October 4—Eldridge H. Calhoun and Ellen Blankenship. Oct. 5, Asa W. Chapman and Laura A. Ward. Oct. 13, Abner C. Flewellen and Sarah T. Shepherd. Oct. 14, Henry S. Duffee and Elizabeth M. Rus, Wootson Gooldsby and Epsy Johnson. Oct. 19, Cyrus A. Royston and Mary F. Calloway.

November 3—Jesse Goodwin and Mary C. R. Johnson. Nov. 7, Joseph J. Shippey and Martha A. Hamar. Nov. 9, William E. Bryan and Elvira A. R. Randall, John E. Dennard and America Atkinson, John J. Oliver and Mary C. McGrady. Nov. 10, Simon Stern and Betty Heller. Nov. 11, James Burrays and Martha Putnam. Nov. 14, George W. Cherry and Elizabeth Dean, John N. Bragg and Harriet Watkins. Nov. 18, David Garris and Mary Robinson. Nov. 29, Samuel Klein and Mina Wolff.

December 2—Thomas B. Norris and Rebecca J. Cook. Dec. 5, Jeptha D. Wilkinson and Barbara A. Reed. Dec. 7, Henry W. Wood and Mary E. Patterson. Dec. 10, James Thomas and Elizabeth Harper. Dec. 11, Benjamin F. Nunnelee and Elizabeth Shippey. Dec. 16, Bassill M. Milton and Jane Johnson, Thomas Hamar and Sarah J. Lokey. Dec. 19, James Eyre and Catharine Murphy. Dec. 21, Daniel Y. Morrell and Susannah Wallace, Wherry M. Cannon and Belsy A. Nelson. Dec. 23, Francis A. Yarbrough and Caroline Rodgers, Joseph Dimon and Sarah M. Skinner, Henry L. Martin and Rosannah Stewart. Dec. 29, Benjamin F. Doles and Elizabeth J. Holcomb.

DEATHS.

(FROM THE SEXTON'S REPORTS.)

January 4—Cornelia Brickhouse; 6th, James Ivey; 7th, child of David Hudson; 8, Miss Lewis; 17, Mr. Herne; 18, Elizabeth Calhoun; 22, child of Mr. Eaton; 23, James Simpleman; 25, Mr. Browning; Elizabeth Eaton; 31, George Robison.

February 5—Shadrack Sanders; 6, Mary Wilson; 10, —— Conoway; 11, Thomas Maddox; 13, child of John Clark; 15, Nancy Loving; 25, Mr. Pike; 29, Esther Jepson.

July 1—James Savage; 2, a child of Mr. Lewis; 8, a child of Mr. Holley; 10, a child of Mr. Whittlesey; 14, John Vansant; 17, child of Mrs. Crossman; 20, child of J. Chisholm; 21, James Hammock; child of Mr. Lloyd; 23, child of M. McGowen; child of Mr. Van; Patrick Sullivan; child of Mrs. Tendall; 29, child of Mr. Nix.

August 1—Child of Mr. Norris; 5, Jordan Newby; child of Sarah Sanders; 12, Henry Crumwell; 13, J. F. Chisolm; 15, Mrs. Magner; child of Mrs. Stubblefield; 17, John Lewis.

September 1—Child of Mrs. Pettis; 5, Ann McKenzie; 9, child of Mrs. Hiatt; child of Mrs. Hackrey; 11, Miss Murphy; Martha Faulkenberry; 12, child of Sarah Sanders; 26, Willis S. Cooper; 27, Mrs. Webster; child of Mr. Finchin; 28, child of Mr. Webster; child of Mrs. Stafford; 30, John McCarty; child of Mr. Garbin.

(FROM THE NEWSPAPERS).

January — (At Panama) George Chalmers, of Columbus.

March 4—Mrs. Sarah Vivian, wife of James W. Warren. March — James H. Scott.

April 13—James T. Rives.

May — Mrs. Nancy Baugh.

June — R. A. Owens; 18, Laura Winship, daughter of John R. Sturgis; 19, Mrs. Frances Vivian Schley; 25, Robert Parham, infant son of O. V. Brown.

October — James L. Baugh; 15, Franklin Duncan; Lucien Strawn, infant son of H. H. Barrow; 28, Miss Amanda F. A. Patrick; 29, John R. Dawson.

November 17—(in Alabama) George W. Cowdery, of Columbus.

December 11—Edgar Perry, son of Hines Holt; Dr. John J. B. Hoxey.

1853.

Water Works—Mobile and Girard and Opelika Railroads.

City officers elected on the first Saturday in January : J. L. Morton, Mayor; Aldermen—F. G. Wilkins, Wm. B. Robinson, Wm. Perry, A. I. Robison, O. Danforth, T. M. Hogan, F. Jepson, George Pitts, Wm. Daniel, Wm. Matheson, Wm. Brooks. Clerk, Calvin Stratton ; Treasurer, J. L. Howell; Marshal, James M. Hughes; Deputy Marshal, A. M. Robinson. Council elected Edgar G. Dawson, City Attorney ; Wm. M. Bosworth, Clerk of the Market ; Jere Terry, Sexton ; Dr. T. J. Brooks, City Physician ; Ephraim C. Bandy, Bridge Keeper ; Burnet Ingram, Hospital Keeper ; Joel T. Scott, Magazine Keeper ; E. Birdsong, J. C. Calhoun, J. S. Hill, J. S. Ivey and Lewis Livingston, Port Wardens; Willis Holstead, Wm. Y. Barden, Dr. T. Hoxey, J. K. Redd, J. M. Everett, W. G. Andrews, John Kyle, J. W. Frost, Wm. C. Cooper, Pat Adams, J. Seely and T. R. Herendine, Health Officers ; E. Barnard, H. T. Hall, Wm. Gesner, R. R. Goetchius, George H. Peabody and Thos. W. Kelly, Fire Wardens; Thomas Ragland, City Printer.

Wiley Williams was on the 8th of January elected an Alderman of the 5th Ward.

An ordinance authorizing the issue of bonds to pay the city's subscription of $150,000 to the Girard Railroad, was finally passed on the 26th of January.

Judge Iverson having, in January, proposed to sell to the city the water-works then supplying water from the neighboring springs, a committee of Council made a report on the extent and condition of these works, from which we copy the following:

That the franchise or privilege granted by the Mayor and City Council of Columbus to the original proprietor, was for forty years, and made in 1844 it still has 32 years to run ; that the proprietors have a deed of the present spring or fountain head from Col. Seaborn Jones, which has 25 years to run ;

that easment or parol licences have been obtained from the owners of the lands through which the pipes run; that there is a written license from Col. John Woolfolk, which is on record; that the distance from the spring, which is commonly known as Leonard's Spring, to Broad street in the city is about three miles; that there is a chain of pine logs of $3\frac{1}{4}$ inches calibre from the spring to Broad street, and lateral pipes of smaller dimensions in several other streets, making in all probably four miles. The first two miles, beginning at Leonard's Spring, is considered by your committee in good order; the balance of the pipes are in bad order and require repairing, but to what extent your committee has been unable to ascertain; that the water flows freely through the first two miles, but is obstructed in the latter, and that therefore the supply reaching the city is limited and greatly less than the spring could afford. The spring (according to measurement by B. V. Iverson) discharges at the rate of 150 gallons per minute, making over 200,000 gallons per day—a supply which, if conducted to the city, would be sufficient for a population ten times larger than the present. At the present there is not probably one-fourth of the supply discharged into the pipes at the spring, from the imperfect condition of the works; at, however, the outlay of $100, the whole of the water could be discharged into the pipes at the fountain head; that more than three-quarters of the water that enters the pipes is lost on its way to the city; that the number of hydrants heretofore supplied has varied from 40 to 90 per annum, as the supply warranted; at present the number in actual use is between 40 and 50. There is no doubt that if the supply of the water was constant and abundant, the number of hydrants would in a short time, probably within two years, reach 300 hydrants, at an average of $10 each, which would bring a revenue of $3,000 per annum. There is no doubt that Leonard's Spring, the present fountain head, is not only the best, but the only source in the vicinity of the city from which a supply of good spring water can be obtained.

The Committee proposed the construction of a reservoir about one mile from the city, at some point below Woolfolk's spring, into which the existing wooden pipes would conduct the water from the spring, and a chain of iron pipes from this reservoir into the city—say of 6 inch caliber. They estimated the cost as follows: Purchase from the proprietors, $3,000; reservoirs and conductors at Leonard's, $100; reservoir below Woolfolk's Spring, $75; cost of one mile of iron pipes from last reservoir, $6,000—making in all $9,175. They estimated that a sufficient quantity of water could be brought into the city and 300 hydrants be erected at an expense which would not exceed $10,000. They recommended the acceptance of Judge Iverson's proposition.

On motion of Alderman Williams, Council authorized the Mayor to employ a competent engineer to make a survey of the route and report. It also instructed a committee to ascertain at what price the fee simple title to the springs could be obtained. We do not find any report on these questions by the engineer, but a few weeks afterwards Judge Iverson asked for an extension of the privilege for supplying the city with water, and the City Attorney was instructed to draw up a contract to that effect. The committee reported that the fee simple title to the springs could be bought from Colonel Jones for $2,000. The report was laid on the table.

Charles T. Pollard, President of the Montgomery and West Point Railroad Company, in August, asked a modification of the restrictions imposed by the city in subscribing to the stock of the Opelika Branch. He asked the right of way across the river and over the North Commons to a designated depot lot. A committee of Council reported against any connection of the road with the Muscogee depot, and against granting a lot for a depot at the place asked, but proposed granting a lot on the North Common north of Oglethorpe and Jackson streets. The committee reported a contract to this effect on the 26th of August, which Council adopted. The Railroad company was to pay for the lot or right of way by a certificate for 120 shares of stock in the road. Council subsequently reconsidered this action.

A question of much interest and controversy during the fall and winter of this year was a second subscription of $150,000 to the stock of the Girard Railroad (now called the Mobile & Girard Road.) The question had been submitted to a vote of the people, and decided in favor of the subscription; but its opponents in Council contended that the vote was so small that it could not be regarded as a certain expression of the popular will. They proposed to submit it again to the people at the regular city election in January. The supporters of the subscription insisted that the funds were needed at once to procure iron for about 22 miles of the road bed then about ready, commencing at Girard. A condition of the subscription was that it should be expended on that part of the road between Girard and Union Springs. The ordinance authorizing the subscription was finally adopted in November. The Mayor entered a protest, and many motions to delay or impose conditions were made in Council.

INCIDENTS.

The city assessors reported their valuation of the taxable property in the city $1,597,925.

The cars on the Muscogee Railroad were running this spring to Butler, and the Southwestern Railroad was completed from Macon to Reynolds within ten miles of Butler. This gap was filled up in May, and a continuous railroad communication opened to Savannah.

A great railroad jubilee, to celebrate the completion of the railroad line to Macon, was held in the city on the 20th of of May. Among other interesting incidents, the Mayor produced some water from the Atlantic ocean and mingled it with the water of the Chattahoochee, in typical union.

A fire on the night of the 19th of February consumed the old Theatre building on Crawford street, the livery stable of Dudley & Martin, and the residence of Mrs. A. J. Hall. Messrs. Dudley and Martin lost most of their carriages, buggies, &c.; Mrs. Hall, all of her provisions and kitchen furniture; and other persons lost goods in the houses. The fire originated in the Theatre building, and was believed to have been the work of an incendiary.

The steamboat Retrieve struck a rock in the river, a short distance above the junction of the Flint and Chattahoochee, and sunk on the 18th of February. She was going down, and had 1,000 or 1,200 bales of cotton, much of which was lost A negro man of Columbus was drowned.

A very severe storm swept over the city on the 8th of March, unroofing and otherwise damaging houses, prostrating chimneys, fences, &c. The damage done in the city was estimated at $50,000 or $100,000. No lives were lost. The new Methodist Church in Girard and the bridge across the creek were blown down, and the storm swept a considerable portion of the country with like effects.

William, eldest son of Judge Robt. B. Alexander, deceased, lost his life on the 5th of March, by an accidental punch or stroke with a small piece of wire in the hands of another boy with whom he was playing. The wire entered his forehead just above one eye, and penetrated to his brain.

There were very heavy rains about the middle of March, and the river rose to a great height. The train of cars on the Muscogee Railroad fell from a trestle which gave way, some eight or nine miles from the city, on the 18th, and Mr. Charles D. Schoomaker, the engineer, and a fireman named Gilmore were instantly killed. No passengers were hurt.

Charnot Newberry was killed by Lewis Jernigan, in a difficulty between them at the corner of Oglethorpe and Franklin streets, on the 27th of March. Pistols were used.

Joseph Updegraff was on the 17th of April, run through the body with a sword cane, by Britton McCullers, and died a few days afterwards.

On the 27th of May, the kitchen of F. G. Wilkins on Oglethorpe street, and the same night the dwelling of Mrs. Williams on Forsyth street, were burned.

A woman named Fish fell or threw herself into the river on the 24th of May, and was drowned.

Council in September subscribed $10,000 to the stock of the Gas Company, payable in bonds. The bonds were made payable in 25 years, bearing 7 per cent. interest.

The receipts of cotton up to the 16th of May amounted to 55,893 bales. Prices—$7\frac{1}{2}$ to $9\frac{1}{2}$c. in January, $7\frac{1}{4}$ to $9\frac{1}{4}$ in March, $9\frac{1}{2}$ to $10\frac{1}{8}$ in April, $8\frac{1}{2}$ to 10 in May, 9 to $9\frac{1}{2}$ in October, 8 to 9 in December.

The factories, that had been compelled to suspend after the breaking of the dam in the spring, resumed work in June; also the Palace Mills.

The extensive building used by Messrs. J. & M. Barringer as a sash and blind factory and carpenter's shop, was burned on the 1st of July.

The first bale of new cotton was brought in on the 18th of August, by A. H. Rowell, of Russell county, Alabama, and sold at 11 cents.

The steamboat Franklin, on a trip from Columbus to Apalachicola, with 1,100 bales of cotton, took fire on the 27th of December, and was consumed, cargo and all.

PERSONAL.

Jordan L. Howell and John J. McKendree were in January elected Magistrates of the Upper District, and F. M. Brooks and John Quin of the Lower; James Lloyd, Wm. Nix, John Tilly and E. H. Calhoun, Bailiffs; Bethune, Weems, Ragland, Flewellen and McGuire, Justices of the Inferior Court; Noble, Tax Collector; Rees, Tax Receiver.

Messrs. Gettinger & Barschall, Arnold & Robinson, Patrick Duffie, Thos. S. Hays, Richard Robinson and Charles Bize had stalls in the market this year. Their aggregate rents amounted to $178.

R. C. Forsyth was appointed Postmaster this year.

Edward Birdsong was in June elected Clerk of the Superior Court, vice John Sturgis, deceased.

Robt. T. Simons and John Cleghorn were elected extra Deputy Marshals in February.

Thos. W. Scoonmaker was, on the 1st of March, sworn in as an Alderman in place of O. Danforth, resigned.

E. H. Musgrove was in March elected an Alderman in the place of Ald. Robinson, resigned.

John T. Ector and F. M. Gray were elected Aldermen in October, to fill vacancies.

James J. Slade was in June elected an Alderman, to succeed Ald. Wilkins, resigned.

MARRIAGES.

January 3—William W. Whipple and Mauria Fletcher; 5, William Rynehart and Mary A. E. Hinton; 6, John W. B. Mehaffey and Susan Copeland; James M. Simmons and Letitia B. Marcrum, Thos. Hudson and Eliza Vickers; 8, Richard H. Shirley and Mary Ann Smith; 19, Benjamin Wooton and Elizabeth Read; 22, John Younger and Margaret Thompson; 25, Benjamin S. Cummins and Mary T. Lokey; 27, Edward M. Weems and Teresa E. Sapp.

February 6—Luther T. Vinson and Elizabeth C. Nix; 8, John T. Pruett and Susan R. Mealing; 10, James A. Caffey and Mary A. E. Lanier; 15, Allen Lambertson and Fannie Brown; 16, Thomas L. Morris and Martha E. Wilson, Benjamin Beall and Henrietta S. Hodges; 17, Kinsey Davis and Harriet Piggot, Charles E. Dexter and Clara M. Hodges; 20, William Hawes and Martha Smith; 24, Richard C. Taff and Nancy A. P. I. Hale.

March 10—George T. Bray and Sarah Eady, Thomas J. Watt and Sarah J. Kimbrough, Enoch Bland and Lucy A. Jemison; 27, Miles A. Hearn and Mary Corlee, Joseph P. Whittlesey and Rebecca J. Schley, Cornelius S. Whittlesey and Ann Maria Schley; 31, Aaron Fussell and Elizabeth Wooton.

April 6—Henry H. Sizemore and Cassa A. F. Goss; 10, Jonathan A. B. Williams and America A. Frazier; 14, Elijah Martin and Lucinda Champion; 20, Joseph W. Morris and Elizabeth Jones; 27, Isaac T. Robinson and Mary A. Meacham; 28, David Gunn and Mary A. Nappier.

May 5—William D. Miller and Isabella Browning; John I. Day and Nancy A. Brooks; 8, Gideon Easterwood and Laney Owens; 12, Charles A. Hausler and Scilla A. Roscoe; 13, William D. Brooks and Sarah J. Scott; 15, Sherard Statham and Abigail Pike; 19, James M. C. Luker and Elizabeth Blackmon; 29, Calvin A. Hearn and Epsy J. Hall; 31, Robert Badkins and Judith Updergraff.

June 16—James Lockhart and Amanda Parker; 22, Henry T. Hood and Elizabeth Averett; 30, Bryant Howell and Nancy A. Brooks.

July 5—Lovic P. Faun and Mary J. Haskin; 7, William C. Rice and Sarah E. King; 8, William McCandless and Sarah A. F. Nix; 14, Thomas G. Pond and Mary C. Jones; 17, James H. Jones and Susan Clark; 19, William D. Johnson and Anna L. Twitty; 23, John Butts and Mary Kale; 24, George W. Gunn and Amelia Milam.

August 1—James R. Rodgers and Anna M. Hudson; 2, John L. Truax and Ida Burnes; 3, Daniel M. Patterson and Mary Fudge; 4, Jas. Measels and Mary Monkus, William Davidson and Leah Colee; 7, Thomas J. Stephens and Mary E. Sessions, James C. Hall and Sarah Riley; 11, Joshua G. Cobb and Matilda A. Phillips; 14, Joseph G. Terry and Sarah A. Teat; 16, Casper Lewis and Catharine Roland, Charles Field and Nancy Roland; 18, Thomas J. Skinner and Louisiana Patrick; 25, Thomas Jordan and Levinia C. Arnold; 28, James Smith and Sarah Lipsey.

September 2—William E. Brooks and Martha Allen; 4, William F. Pike and Mary J. Mason, James W. Wilson and Susan Cook; 8, Henry C. Vigal and Helen Wooldridge; 14, Edmund Cartledge and Euphemia G. Thornton; 20, Burrill Bartlett and Amanda M. Thomas; 22, Walker Cartledge and Priscilla Cartledge, John S. Wellborn and Amanda S. Barron; 27, James N. Smith and Elizabeth Lee; 29, Robert Reid and Sarah Joins.

October 2—William Phillips and Abey E. Sanders; 9, Burrill Bartley and Eliza Bartley; 13, Thomas J. Coleman and Mary A. E. Baker, Lewis Robinson and Elafan Northington; 15, David Culpepper, jr., and Elizabeth Butler; 16, Adam P. Jones and Sarah A. Weaver; 18, Charles A. Goosuch and Parshamia L. Cook; 24, William Holley and Elizabeth Kelly; 25, James Bond and Sarah Silas; 28, John W. Rutledge and Martha C. Roland.

November 3—Jacob Heil and Frederika E. Sternberg; 6, Henry J. King and Mary E. McCook; 7, David Richey and Martha Lewis; 17, David Wynn and Susan Wooldridge; 20, William A. Bartlett and Rutha Hall, William D. Adams and Rebecca E. Waddell; 24, William H. Glaze and Priscilla Jackson; 27, James A. Caswell and Mary A. Clark; 28, Robert B. Green and Susan Odom.

December 1—Joshua J. Pate and Epsy Browning; 4, Robert C. Redding and Martha McLester; 8, Abner Howard and Sarah Glaze; 14, Absalom D. Wooldridge and Lucy A. Green, Charles A. Redd and Eugenie A. Weems, Robert C. Patterson and Hester A. T. Fincher; 15, William J. Coffield and Elizabeth Welch; 22, Benjamin W. Orr and Martha M. McBride, John A. Frazer and Mary Tommy; 25, Israel F. Pickens and Mary Dunning, Henry A. Scott and Virginia A. Lester; 27, Henry R. Toler and Martha J. Nicholson; 28, Aaron Cordery and Sophia Haynes; 29, John A. Jackson and Elizabeth A. Count.

DEATHS.

(FROM THE SEXTON'S REPORTS.)

January 1—Mary Rowe, P. Hancock, and Mrs. Coker's child; 4, W. S. Marble; 9, Clara Wynn; 12, Thomas Spivey; 21, James Collins; 28, Holcomb's child; Mrs. Barrand's child.

February 3—G. Richard's child; 8, Julia A. Richardson; 9, D. G. Upchurch; 10, Clara Frey; A. J. Hall; 13, T. Schley's child; 16, Thomas McKennel; 18, Thomas Kelly; 19, Gammon's child; 25, Mrs. Curry.

March 8—William Alexander; 16, N. P. Foster; 19, C. Schoonmaker; N. Gilmore; 22, G. Redd's child; 28, C. L. Newbery; 30, Mr. Dowd's child.

[N. B.—We presume that all of the dates given in the Sexton's lists are those of the interments of the bodies, not the days of death.]

(FROM THE NEWSPAPERS.)

April 8 (in Albany, Ga.)—Mrs. Barbara Day, of Columbus; 22, Miss Sarah A. Burt; 24, Mrs. Alice Ann McCardel; 25, Warren, child of John G. Dolly.

May 1—James Terrell, infant son of Charles E. McCardel; 18, Mrs. Faunice B. Stoddard, Anne T., daughter of T. M. Hogan; 22, John R. Sturgis, Clerk of the Superior Court; 28, Chipley, son of J. D. Williford; 29, Mrs. Frances Love.

June 7—Patrick B., son of David J. Barber; 12, Samuel Bass, son of Lewis Livingston; 15, Thomas Daniel, son of R. G. Parkman.

July 6—John J. Hickey; 25, Jacob D. Hightower, of Greene county; 31, John Caldwell.

August 14—Sarah Virginia, daughter of R. H. Harris; 25, Joseph J. Ballenger ; 27, John Neal, son of B. F. Griggs ; 28, Mrs. Elizabeth Broadnax ; — John Ward.

September 4—Julia Munro, daughter of Samuel Bonfoy ; 5, (in Montgomery, Ala.,) John B., son of S. B. Harvell of Columbus ; 13, (in South Natick) Mrs. Lucretia M. Curtis, of Columbus ; 19, A. L. Bryan ; —, George S. Carey.

October 6—Mrs. Sarah C. Griggs ; —, Alex. C. Hickey ; 27, Nicholas Ware, son of Dr. R. A. Ware.

November 10—Major Thomas M. Nelson.

December 24—Mrs. Ann J. Bingham.

1854.

Election of Aldermen by their respective Wards, &c.

The city election of this year was held in accordance with the provisions of an act *then pending* in the Legislature, authorizing the election of two Aldermen for each Ward by the voters of their respective wards alone. After the election, an act was passed making it legitimate. The election was held, as usual, on the first Saturday in January, and the most influential question at issue was the ratification of the city's second subscription to the stock of the Mobile and Girard Railroad. Dr. John E. Bacon, the successful candidate for Mayor, had published a card in which he announced that he would not sign the bonds until satisfied that a majority of the people approved the subscription. The vote for Mayor stood—Bacon 469, Morton 303. The following gentlemen were elected Aldermen: 1st Ward, Harvey Hall, E. H. Musgrove; 2d, J. T. Coleman, Wm. Perry; 3d, T. M. Hogan, Thos. K. Wynne; 4th, George I. Pitts, Wm. Daniel; 5th, Joseph Thomas, John Quin; 6th, J. A. Vrooman, H. J. Devon. Marshal, George Gullen; Deputy Marshal, John F. Cleghorn; Clerk, Calvin Stratton; Treasurer, J. L. Howell; Sexton, Thos. Nix.

Council elected Ephraim C. Bandy, Bridge-keeper; R. T. Simons, Clerk of the Market; Edgar G. Dawson, City Attorney; Richard H. Lockhart, City Physician; Mrs. Isabella McGee, Hospital-keeper; Port Wardens—Peter Preer, John C. Calhoun, J. L. Hill, Willis P. Baker, J. M. Everett. Health Officers—J. J. McKendree, J. B. Wright, Daniel McArthur, C. B. Teasdale, E. Dudley, S. Ogletree, Geo. W. Martin, N. J. Peabody, John Durkin, Wm. Matheson. Magazine-keeper— John Whitesides.

Messrs. Bethune & Reynolds, of the *Corner Stone*, were City Printers this year.

A. J. Welsh was in January elected an Alderman of the 1st Ward, vice Ald. Musgrove resigned; and in February J. L. Morton was elected an Alderman of the 5th Ward, vice Ald. Thomas, resigned.

The Treasurer's report showed the total receipts of 1853, $27,096 69, disbursements $24,442 15.

Wm. Holly was in February elected Magazine-keeper, vice John Whitesides, resigned.

The assessors reported the value of real estate in the city this year, $1,894,200.

A tragedy, which caused great excitement in the city, occurred on the 27th of February. Alex. M. Robinson, Deputy Sheriff, attempted to arrest David Wright, jr., and Jack Boyd for disorderly conduct, and Wright, as soon as the officer tapped him on the shoulder, turned quickly and shot Robinson with a pistol. Robinson was conveyed into the *Times* office, and died in a few minutes. Wright and Boyd ran, and were pursued by the city watch and citizens, the watch firing at them several times. Wright was quickly overtaken and brought back; and Boyd was arrested the next day. They were committed to jail. The citizens held an indignation meeting, but did not attempt to take the execution of the law into their own hands. At the August term of the Superior Court, Boyd was found guilty as principal in the second degree in the murder of Robinson, but recommended to the mercy of the Court. The Court, however, sentenced him to be hung on the 27th of September, and his counsel took an appeal. The case of Wright was continued. On the 24th of October Wright escaped from jail, in company with a negro prisoner. The escape was effected by means of a file or saw furnished from without, with which Wright first released himself from his shackles. With a false key he opened the door of his cell, and emerged into the passage. Here the negro man was confined. The two took off the cell door, and with it as a lever the bars of the window were forced apart so as to allow them to escape from the building. A reward of $500 was offered by the Sheriff, and $100 by the Governor, for the re-capture of Wright. He was re-arrested in December in the neighborhood of St. Andrews Bay, Fla., but not without a determined resistance. Mr. Robt. T. Simons ascertained his whereabouts and undertook his arrest. He was accompanied by the Sheriff of Walton county, Florida. Wright fired at both Simons and the Sheriff, wounding the latter in the thigh. Wright was slightly wounded in the face. After several shots had been exchanged Wright surrendered, and was brought back and recommitted to jail on the 30th of December. He was found guilty of murder and sentenced to be hung in September, 1855; but on the night of the 4th of August he set fire to his cell and perished by suffocation. It was supposed that his intention was to escape while the citizens were extinguishing the fire. The flames were extinguished without much damage to the building.

Boyd was first respited by the Governor, and afterwards pardoned by act of the Legislature.

Much correspondence passed this year between the Council and the officers of the Montgomery and West Point Railroad Company on the subject of a location within the city of a depot for that road, and the bringing of it into the city by a bridge across the river. Propositions were made and rejected on both sides. In July, a committee of Council reported a proposition and an unsigned contract for the location of the depot on the North common, north of the square between Oglethorpe and Troup steets, the city also granting the right of way and the privilege to build a railroad bridge, but prohibiting a close connection with any other railroad in the city. This contract was approved by Council, but the Railroad Company declined to accept it unless the city would subscribe $50,000 to the stock of the company.

In October, the Mobile and Girard Railroad Company, through its President, Judge Iverson, again asked the city for an additional subscription of $150,000 to the capital stock of that company. Council resolved to submit the question to a vote of the people; also, at the same time, the question of subscribing $50,000 to the stock of the Montgomery and West Point Railroad Company, so as to secure the bringing of that road and its depot into the city. The subscription to the Mobile and Girard road to be in lieu of the subscription of the same amount voted by the Council of 1853. This election was held on the 4th of December, and resulted as follows: For the Opelika Branch Road subscription, 411, no subscription, 24; for the Mobile and Girard Railroad subscription, 397, no subscription, 35. Council adopted ordinances authorizing these subscriptions on the same day.

A large public meeting of citizens, held on the 13th of September, requested Council to subscribe $100,000 to aid in the construction of a branch of the Mobile and Girard Railroad to Eufaula, if joined by a sufficient subscription from Eufaula and along the line of the proposed road. The Intendant of Eufaula replied to the Columbus committee who addressed him on this subject, that the people of Eufaula were intent on a more *direct* communication with Savannah (only quite recently obtained,) and therefore "received with no favor whatever" the Columbus overture. Pretty plain language, but no doubt true.

Ex-President Fillmore and Hon. John P. Kennedy, his Secretary of the Navy, visited Columbus in April, and received a cordial reception, with the hospitalities of the city. The bill of expense was $1,007.10, of which $728.10 was paid by Council, the balance by the sale of tickets to a soiree.

The extensive "Variety Works" of Wm. H. Brooks & Co., on the river near the Palace Mills, were destroyed by fire on the 24th of July. The Palace Mills and Eagle Factory were in great danger, but were saved without material damage. The loss by the destruction of the "Variety Works" was estimated at $30,000—no insurance. The next week the Eagle Factory was damaged to the amount of near $1,500 by a stroke of lightning, which fired a large quantity of cotton in the Picking room.

INCIDENTS.

A fire company of negroes, organized this year, was voted $200 by Council for equipment, and the members promised fifty cents each for attending and serving at any fire. The fire engine "Columbus" was turned over to them.

The office of Wharfinger was created in May, and Jacob Barrow elected, at a salary of $700 per annum. Mr. Barrow died in July, and Jos. E. Webster was elected.

Richard Jones, who had been appointed by Council to take the city census, reported in August: Number of heads of families in the city, 820; dwellings, 526; stores, 151; Number of white females, 2,232; Number of white males under 21 years of age, 1,127; white males 21 years and over, 1,176; free negroes, 64; slaves, 2,541; total, 7,140.

Permission was this year given to John C. Ruse and others to build a plank road along Randolph street, from its intersection with Front street to the Muscogee Railroad depot on East common. Council also voted to extend to Stewart, Gray & Co., Ruse, Patten & Co., and others, the lease of the plank road from the wharf along the river to Randolph st.

Cotton receipts up to the 1st of June, about 72,000 bales. Prices—in January, 8½ to 8¾c.; in May, 7 to 8c.; in October, 7¼ to 8¼c.; in December, 6½ to 7c.

The yellow fever was distressingly severe in Savannah this year—many people falling victims to it—and much sympathy was felt and expressed in Columbus, by public meetings, by resolutions of Council, and by liberal subscriptions of mate-rial aid. One young man, named John Martin, who con-tracted the disease in Savannah, was sick of it in Columbus in October, but recovered.

The Methodist Episcopal General Conference held its ses-sion in Columbus in May. At this meeting, Drs. George F. Pierce, H. H. Kavanaugh and J. Early were elected Bishops, and the Book Concern located at Nashville.

Winter's Palace Mills were sold in March to a company of gentlemen—Messrs. Mustian & Mott, George W. Winter, Richard Patten and Thomas W. Tallman—for the sum of $50,000.

The Columbus Building and Loan Association organized this year, by the election of Wm. C. Gray, President; Ster-ling F. Grimes, Treasurer; Jordan L. Howell, Secretary; and J. C. Ruse, J. R. Daggers, James Vernoy, M. Barringer, Wm. Daniel and E. Greenwood, Directors.

The first bale of new cotton was received on the 11th of August, from the plantation of David Bussey of Stewart county, and sold at auction at 13¾ cents.

Peter Lynn was shot dead by W. A. Shofner, on the out-skirts of the city, on the 5th of October.

A large frame building on Front street, owned by the Eagle Factory and occupied by a number of its operatives, was destroyed by fire on the 30th of October. Loss $1,200, insured.

The fine residence of Col R. L. Mott, in the upper part of the city, was burned on the 4th of December. The loss was estimated at $5,000.

The location of the powder magazine was this year changed to the East Commons—a new building having been erected there.

P. Gittinger, H. P. Robinson, C. H. Smith, P. Duffy, J. D. Arnold, and R. Robinson rented stalls in the market this year. Their aggregate rents amounted to $279.

The county officers this year were—Sheriff, F. M. Brooks; Clerk Superior Court, David J. Barber; Clerk Inferior Court, A. P. Jones; Tax Collector, Thomas Chaffin; Tax Receiver, D. J. Reese; Surveyor, Philip Lamar; Coroner, J. B. Hicks.

John C. Ruse, H. T. Hall, Thos. P. Larris, R. R. Goetchius, Charles Wise and E. D. Davis were Fire Wardens.

The *Enquirer* of April 4th was in mourning for the death of Mr. John B. Ragland, one of its proprietors.

Seaborn Ogletree was in March elected an Alderman of the 4th Ward, in the place of Ald. Pitts, resigned.

William Matheson was elected, in June, an Alderman of the 6th Ward, in the place of Ald. Devon, deceased.

A. G. Foster was in August elected an Alderman of the 3d Ward, vice Ald. Hogan, resigned.

MARRIAGES.

January 1—John W. H. Latham and Mary A. M. Thomas; 3, Perry A. Browning and Epsy A. Everage; 5, William W. Frazer and Frances J. Kelly; John M. Williams and Elizabeth E. Bailey; 6, William S. Johnson and Louisa M. Durham; 11, Archibald B. Thomas and Frances L. Robinson; 13, Edmund Jones and Amelia C. Cobb; 18, Dred Carraway and Nancy F. Robinson; 19, Thomas Cummings and Martha E. Pool; 22, Benj. Sanborn and Mary E. Dicken; 23 Littlebery Eubanks and Margaret M. Dickson; 26, John Tarver and Charity I. Alston; 28, Charles E. McCardle and Eliza I. Parker; 30, James W. Cartins and Julia F. Lorimer.

February 3—Thomas Pate and Mary Ann Higden; 9, William I. Moss and Margaret A. E. Pry; 10, John T. Rowlin and Mary L. Edwards; 13, John W. Goslin and Sarah A. M. Owens; 15, Wm. G. Andrews and Julia W. Shotwell; 16, Elbert Presley and Susan Smith; William T. Sanders and Eliza S. Morton; Benjamin Simpson and Sarah J. Stafford; 23, Calvin Williams and Jane O. Pry; 28, Jacob W. Shoup and Adaline Hawes.

March 2—Peyton H. Rogers and Mary Alexander; 4, Myrick C. Lunsford and Josaphine Scott; Jasper Hicks and Barthena Bagley; 16, Ransom Covington and Parmelia Dillard; 19, Lafayette Gordy and Henrietta Bray; 26, William T. Holliday and Mary Gammell; 31, Micajah Briley and Mary E. Phillips.

April 4—Robert M. Aldworth and Lucy C. Wheeler; 10, William R. King and Elizabeth Stewart; Lafayette Parkman and Isabella Tillman; 12, Geo. H. Waddell and Celestia Wynne; William Halley and Mary Harris; 15, Jno. Allen and Amanda Tinnent; Joseph D. Norwood and Margaret A. Cook; 18, George Y. Banks and Susan C. Mitchell; 19, Thomas Kennady and Eliza Towns; 20, John Saltmarsh and Caroline J. Luker; William H. Long and

Ann Louisa Tarver; 23, Pickard A. Pike and Eliza A. Brannon; 27, William F. Williams and Julia F. Flewellen.

May 1—Thomas M. Sanford and Amanda V. Wynne; 2, Chas. A. Brooks and Angelina P. Cobb; 9, Littleton Pike and Julia A. Brannon; 14, Nathaniel H. Slaughter and Leacy W. Lamb; 22, I. E. Dickens and Nancy Davenport; 30, David C. Wood and Martha Barton.

June 7—Lewis S. Graves and Georgia Pride; 16, William Corradan and Rosannah Knight; 26, John D. Atkins and Adaline V. Cleve; 29, John C. Kavenaugh and Mary A. A. Naglin; Crawford Coleman and Mary A. Davie.

July 4—Robert R. Owens and Sarah C. Williams; 6, Edward W. Seabrook and Emma C. Dawson; Zachariah Batson and Sarah J. E. Alfred; 13, Riley S. Callaway and Mary Peel; 16, DeWitt C. Daukins and Fannie I. Jones; 19, James Harrill and Ann White; George E. Gager and Virginia B. Salisbury; Calvin E. Johnson and Mary L. Redd.

August 2—Wiley Pollard and Rachel I. Glenn; 4, Wm. Greer and Elizabeth A. Champion; 8, John A. Duke and Epsy A. Bray.

September 7—Alfred A. Livingston and Mary E. Doles; 9, John Ward and Mary McDaniel; 10, Robert Fulford and Catharine Baggett; 15, Archibald I. Smith and Caroline R. Hicks; 17, Benjamin Doles and Martha F. Graybill; 28, Lewis Laury and Emily Conner.

October 5—James A. Witter and Susan Johnson; George Whitten and Elizabeth W. Hunter; Joseph Skinner and Sarah Weed; 10, Thomas G. Wood and Zilphy Cannon; John Peabody and Josaphine L. Chaffin; 12, George W. Crouch and Joanna Rentfroe; 15, Parham D. Redding and Martha Wheelis; 18, Wm. H. Rorie and Susan Stripling; 19, John Hill and Mariah S. Dalton; Alfred Prescott and Emma I. Slade; 31, John H. Davis and Georgia C. Mustian.

November 6—Henry J. King and Mary E. McCook; 7, James M. Bivins and Mary F. Drumright; John H. Bass and Frances E. McGruder; 9, Archibald Cook and Frances A. Lowe; Meredith Hill and Elizabeth W. Dalton; 12, Charles H. Lynch and Martha J. Hudson; 14, James W. Bruner and Melissa A. Decker; 15, Wm. Kirkland and Mary A. Schates; 16, Alfred Munson and Ann Cannon; 21, Bartlett W. Green and Sarah Odom; 21, Edwin R. Goulding and Jane E. Bryan; 23, Lemuel P. Warner and Charlotte F. Matthews; Edmund H. Rees and Sarah Palmer; Andrew I. Putnam and Elizabeth A. Faulkenbury; 26, Stillman Davidson and Nancy A. Decker; Henry Eady and Salina L. Jones; 27, Vincent H. Tennon and Harriet McGehee; 30, Joseph H. Yarborough and Jane E. Thrower.

December 1—James N. Battson and Frances F. Wiseman; 3, John W. Cogbill and Sarah A. Ellison; 5, William Davis and Rebecca Walker; 6, Byrd B. Forsyth and Mary A. Lloyd; 7, James H. Stagg and Elizabeth R. Simpson; 8, Abner Howard and Sarah Glaze; 10, Thomas Sells and Matilda Simmons; 12, Nathaniel C. Ferguson and Mary E. Roberts; 14, James N. Morgan and Margaret J. Rodgers; 16, William T. Jenkins and Nancy Glaze; 18, James Kelly and Mary Dunn; 19, George W. Turner and Amanda C. Key; 20,

Henry D. Cropp and Alice R. Croft ; 21, Robert E. Dixon and Mary A. Mc-Dougald ; 22, Charles Shannon and Caroline Hoxey ; 27, Joel Junman and Rebecca Murphy ; 28, Henry R. Narramore and Louisa W. Huckaba ; Wm. P. Holmes and Lurana Watts.

DEATHS.

(FROM THE SEXTON'S REPORTS.)

January 23—Child of A. K. Ayer ; 26, Mrs. Scroggins ; 29, child of J. A. Bradford ; 31, child of Mrs. Starns.

February 11—Thomas Rhena ; 15, Deborah Paraden ; 22, Mrs. McCall ; 25, child of Mr. Bowers.

March 1—A. M. Robinson ; 3, child of John Clark ; 10, child of Mr. Meredith, child of Mr. Epping, child of Mr. Pike ; 21, child of Samuel Rutherford, Mrs. J. T. Thompson ; 28, Mrs. S. A. Billing ; 30, P. R. Ragland ; 31, child of Mrs. Davenport.

April 3—Mrs. Branham ; 6, child of T. R. Herrendine, Miss Hooper ; 9, Miss Andrews ; 11, T. R. Grossbeak ; 15, child of Mrs. Baggett ; 18, E. B. Fishburn ; 19, Laura Kelton ; 24, Miss Murdock ; 30, Elizabeth Inman.

May 1—Mr. Jackson ; 2, Mrs. Douglass, Barcena Lewis, Mrs. Foley, Mrs. Mary Betz ; 3, Mr. Moat ; 4, child of Mr. Stewart ; 9, Mrs. Adams ; 11, Nancy Piggott ; 13, Anna Mattheson ; 17, Mrs. Elizabeth Thompson, child of Robt. Johnson ; 18, child of George Meredith ; 19, child of Mr. Allen ; 22, child of Clara West ; 23, Catherine Thomas ; 25, child of Mr. Courtney ; 27, child of Mr. Rich ; 30, child of Thomas Hall.

June 2—John Vinson ; 5, child of John Lewis ; 6, H. J. Devon (Alderman ;) 7, child of John Lewis ; 8, child of Mr. Holland ; 10, child of Mr. Flewellen, Mary Sergeant ; 14, Mrs. Mary A. Ayer ; 16, Mrs. Stephens, A. Lammerson. child of Mr. Thompson ; 19, child of John N. Barnett ; 20, Mrs. Brumby ; 22, Miss Sawyer ; 24, Mrs. Moon, Mrs. Mary L. Bonner ; 26, child of Thos. J. Butler ; 26, Frederick Miller, child of Mr. King ; 27, Gibson Tillman ; 28, Fredonia Turner ; 30, Mrs. Catherine Sullivan, Mary Tillman.

July 3—Thomas W. Bowen ; 4, infant of Wesley Barden ; 6, Micajah Anthony ; 7, infant of John Allen ; infant of Mr. Davis ; 16, John A. Morton ; 18, Mrs. Jackson ; 24, Mrs. W. H. Grace ; 25, Jacob Barrow ; 28, child of Wm. H. Grace.

August 1—Miss Anthony ; 3, Elizabeth Coursey ; 4, Mrs. Morn, infant child of E. Dudley ; 7, John Bowers' child ; 8, child of Mrs. Dukes ; 11, Mary Jane Richardson ; 14, daughter of Mr. Meredith, Mrs. Vandenburg, Mr. Stephens ; 21, child of A. McDougald ; 22, Mrs. Draton ; 24, Jackson Kelly ; 27, Miss Meredith ; 31, P. H. Mahone's child.

September 3—Child of Mr. William Garrett ; 4, Miss Lesterjette ; 5, Augustus Thompson ; 9, Miss Brown ; 10, son of Mrs. Chambers, child of Mr. Stephens ; 11, child of John McCarty ; 14, Mary McKenzie, Emma Teal ; 16, Richard Jones ; 18, Mr. Curry ; 19, Miss Cook, child of William Carlisle ; 22, child of S. R. Bonner ; 23, Mr. Lawrence ; 26, child of Elizabeth Brazil.

Five negroes died in July, five in August, and ten in September.

September 11—Sarah Gertrude, daughter of Dr. Jacob Fogle.

October 13—(in Atlanta,) John L. Barringer, of Columbus ; 27, Mrs. Harriet Jefferson ; 31, John Jay, son of John Lloyd.

November 6—Winfield Scott, son of Enoch Willett ; 9, Mrs. Flora McKennell ; 21, Robert Dawson, son of E. G. Thornton ; 23, Susan Jane, daughter of Wm. H. Grace.

December 24—Mansfield Torrance.

There were 25 interments of whites and 11 of negroes during the month of November, but we cannot find the names.

1855.

Financial Difficulties—Sale of City's Stock in Muscogee R. R.

The municipal election, under the new law, was held on the second Saturday in December, 1854 ; but we continue to notice the new government in our report of the events of the year of its administration. Wiley Williams was elected Mayor, and the following gentlemen Aldermen : 1st. Ward, John C. Ruse, J. J. McKendree ; 2d, Henry T. Hall, Wm. A. Bedell ; 3d, Thomas K. Wynne, T. O. Douglass ; 4th, S. R. Andrews, D. A. Ridgeway ; 5th, F. A. Jepson, Israel F. Brown ; 6th, Wm. Daniel, Wm. Matheson. Wm. Mahaffey was elected Marshal ; H. P. Robison, Deputy Marshal ; Calvin Stratton, Clerk ; Isaac Mitchell, Treasurer ; Thos. Nix, Sexton.

. Council elected Robt. E. Dixon, City Attorney ; Enoch Dudley, Bridge-keeper ; Henry M. Harris, Clerk of the Market ; Dr. R. H. Lockhart, City Physician ; Mrs. Isabella McGee, Hospital-keeper. Health Officers—William H. Alston, Wm. Y. Barden, A. F. Brannon, Charles E. Mims, Dr. H. M. Cleckley, A. K. Ayer, William Alley, Wm. G. Andrews, H. J. Smith, O. Danforth, Wm. Brooks, M. L. Patterson. Port Wardens—Edward Croft, A. R. Andrews, William E. Love, J. L. Hill, F. G. Wilkins. Fire Wardens—R. H. Greene,

William Perry, I. G. Strupper, R. R. Goetchius, John A. Frazer, George Hungerford.   Magazine-keeper—William G. Andrews.

The question of raising means to pay $25,000 of bonds issued as subscription to the Muscogee Railroad was a perplexing one this year.   The Finance Committee reported on the 30th of April an ordinance levying a special tax of one-fourth of one per cent. on real estate and one-eighth of one per cent. on slaves; the tax collector to give each tax payer a certificate of stock (divided into whole and half shares) proportionate to the amount of his special tax; which was amended by giving authority to the Mayor to sell a sufficient amount of the stock to make the payment.   As thus amended, the ordinance was adopted.   In June Council passed an ordinance authorizing the hypothecation of $100,000 of the stock owned by the city in the Muscogee Railroad for the loan of $30,000, for this purpose.   On the 25th of June the Finance Committee reported an arrangement with P. J. Semmes, agent of the Bank of the State of Georgia, in accordance with the terms of the ordinance last mentioned; and Council ratified the agreement.

On the 19th of November, Council ratified a contract for the sale of the city's stock in the Muscogee Railroad to Messrs. Richard Patten and John L. Mustian.   It amounted to 1800 shares, and was sold for $151,000—the purchasers assuming the city's liabilities for that amount.   There was some opposition to the sale, and P. J. Semmes, Esq., filed a bill of injunction.   This injunction was dissolved by the Superior Court; Mr. Semmes appealed, and the Supreme Court affirmed the decision dissolving the injunction.   The contest over this question was continued in the next Council.

On the 30th of January the Opelika Branch Road was finished, and the connection of Columbus with Montgomery by railroad was unbroken.   The trains did not then cross the river, but stopped at the depot on the Alabama side.

The assessors appointed to appraise the real estate of the city reported the total valuation at $2,025,000, showing an increase of $140,000 over the previous year.

The river was unusually low during the winter, and steamboat arrivals before April were rare.

John King, an employee of the Muscogee Railroad, was run over by one of the cars, in January, and so badly injured as to cause his death.

D. A. Garrett, who was run over by a train near Atlanta, died in Girard, of the injuries received, on the 5th of March.

The State Medical Convention was held in Columbus in April.

The Rock Island Factory was sold under mortgage, on the 23d of April, and bought by R. L. Mott for $20,250.

The Montgomery Blues and Montgomery Rifles visited Columbus in April, going into camp and remaining several days. They were cordially received and handsomely entertained.

The house of Mrs. Ann Dillon, in the 5th Ward, was burned on the 13th of May.

Among the public entertainments of this spring were well contested races over the Chattahoochee course, and a series of theatrical performances by Mr. W. H. Crisp's Company.

The *Daily Sun* was established on the 30th of July, by Mr. Thomas DeWolf. It was the first daily paper ever published in Columbus. The *Enquirer* and the *Times and Sentinel* then published tri-weeklies.

David Magouirk was shot and killed on the 1st of October, by Zachariah Rogers—they having a difficulty near the polls on the day of the State election.

On the night of the 4th of December, the depot of the Mobile and Girard Railroad, in Girard, was consumed by fire, with about one hundred bales of cotton and some of the papers of the company.

The Opelika Railroad bridge over the river was finished and trains passed over on the 25th of December.

The question of the amalgamation of the Muscogee with the Southwestern Railroad was submitted to a vote of the citizens of Columbus (to determine the action of Council in casting the vote at the stockholders' meeting,) and they voted against it—9 for to 371 against—on the 5th of October.

Receipts of cotton up to the 1st of May, 69,876 bales. Prices —January, 5½@7¼c.; March, 6½@8c.; April, 8½@9c.; May, 9½@9¾c.; June, 11@12c.; September, 8½@8¾c.; October, 7½@8½c.; December, 7¾@8c.

PERSONAL.

Rev. S. H. Higgins was installed Pastor of the Presbyterian Church on the 31st December, 1854.

On the 1st Monday in January, Harvey W. Nance was elected a Judge of the Inferior Court; Thos. Chaffin, Tax Collector; Edward Birdsong, Tax Receiver.

P. J. Semmes was Captain of the Columbus Guards, and Peyton H. Colquitt of the City Light Guards.

J. B. Wright and James Lloyd were Constables of the upper district, and R. T. Simons and Jacob Shoup of the lower district.

Dr. Lockhart resigned, and Dr. W. W. Flewellen was elected City Physician, in July.

David J. Barber, Clerk of the Superior Court, died in September, and on the 2d of October the Judges of the Inferior Court appointed A. S. Rutherford to the office.

Rev. Mr. Dalzell was Rector of the Episcopal Church.

Hon. Walter T. Colquitt died at Macon on the 7th of May.

MARRIAGES.

January 4—John Berrien Oliver and Virginia A. Shorter; Thomas I. Granberry and Emily V. Ferguson; 8, Charles P. Morgan and Sarah E. Horne; 10, Samuel B. Law and Georgia W. Harden; 11, John Harris and Barbary Gammell; Absalom McDonald and Mathena Langey; Samuel R. Brannon and Mary A. Williams; 18, Parker Fisher and Juda W. Clark; 23, Henry B. Nicholson and Sarah A. E. Kemp; 25, Augustus A. Dill and Jackobim Wood; James Phillips and Martha W. Sherwood; 31, Thomas E. Young and Georgia P. Butt.

February 1—David Ennis and Elizabeth Williams; 4, John W. Phillips and

Catharine Wiggins; 11, George W. Blow and Martha A. Heath; 14, John Coleman and Ellen Lyons; 27, Wm. M. Jepson and Cynthia G. Hall; 28, Wm. R. Cobb and Maria R. Hamill.

March 1—Walter S. Clark and Sarepta A. Wood; 3, Henry M. Hames and Martha Little; 8, Charles P. Watt and Sarah P. Eley; Jean B. Beamont and Melvina Moore; 13, Theophilus S. Henry and Sarah I. Edwards; 15, John W. Freeman and Caroline I. Hook; Thomas F. Watt and Minerva Harrell; Jas. E. G. McNeal and Amanda C. George; 19, Joseph Cary and Elizabeth Dukes; 22, John N. Tilley and Mary E. Beauchamp; Henry R. Sedbury and Margaret A. Roper; 28, James Hood and Maria M. Clark; 29, Henry T. Hall and Elizabeth I. Howard; William R. Martin and Jane McCallister; 22, Jackson Harrison and Susan H. Murrell.

April 5—William I. McMillen and Elizabeth Connolly; 8, Aaron D. Brown and Amanda McClesky; 10, William S. Reynolds and Sarah B. Ford; 11, Exton Tucker and Mary T. Speller; Francis O. Goodale and Martha A. Fincher; 21, George W. Scroggins and Nancy I. Dudley; 22, Solomon Belcher and Vicey M. Canline; 23, Joseph B. Ripley and Mary A. Scoonmaker; James Torry and Elizabeth Dickson; 29, George F. Cherry and Mary E. Willingham; 30, Mathew Kenady and Temperance Hudson.

May 8—Thomas W. Camak and Laura A. Ragland; 13, James W. Wellborn and Nancy Davison; 15, James J. Buford and Sarah Bedell; 16, Oliver P. Tillinghast and Mary Jane Thomas; 21, Wm. McMichael and Caroline F. Calhoun; 24, Joseph S. Hood and Caroline Jacobs; 30, John R. Little and Frances L. Ingram.

June 1—Benjamin F. Crittenden and Elizabeth Owen; 5, John P. Cox and Frances Knight; 17, Joseph Cartledge and Martha J. Glenn; 21, William C. Clifton and Clara B. Jones; 26, Moses Simmons and Catharine Kitchens.

July 2—George L. Granberry and Winifred B. Drew; 8, Daniel Odom and Eleanora Pattillo; 19, William C. Bellamy and Fannie H. Lindsey; 22, Jas. Jimmerson and Harriet E. Burton; 24, Wiley J. Howard and Cynthia J. Roach.

August 6—Garland M. Barlow and Sophronia A. R. Lester; James Roe and Jane Wynne; 7, Samuel A. Billing and Ann E. McDougald; 8, Alpha Dinkins and Mahala Johnson; 13, Charles H. Morris and Louisa Olive; 23, John W. Beakley and Martha I. Hawes; 30, William Nance and Eveline Weddington.

September 3—James Y. Boyd and Frances C. Ivey; 6, John W. Worden and Eudoxy Gunn; 7, Henry Wilson and Naome E. McCarty; 8, James McCormack and Angelina R. Seay; 9, James L. Mane and Sarah L. Perry; 12, William L. Head and Frances E. Devon; 15, William H. Radcliff and Matilda Hatcher; 17, Gustavus F. Mertins and Jenny Stahl; 20, Alexander M. Brannon and Julia A. Fuller; Adam J. Livingston and Missouri W. Biggers; 24, Lovick P. Fann and Mary Duke; 25, Benjamin P. Jenkins and Mary E. Ferguson.

October 2—Leander F. Ritch and Eliza A. Graham; 3, David Williams and Lucy C. Henry; 9, George L. Massey and Savannah L. Parkman; 10, William L. Wornam and Sarah E. Hudson; 14, Asbury Hudson and Mary Y. Champion; 16, Robert Flournoy and Eugenie Moffett; 17, Columbus M. Jordan and Mary A. Slack; Benjamin S. Smith and Elizabeth Milner; James Waddell and Elizabeth Parker; 21, Willis Hastings and Martha Lawrence; James Donelson and Patsy Smith; 28, David J. Bray and Ann Benson; 30, Mannering Toles and Elizabeth J. Puckett.

November 4—James V. B. Calhoun and Rachel Hearn; 14, James M. Chambers, Jr. and Mary F. Threewits; 17, Lee Harkness and Malcy Anderson; 28, James Robinson and Eliza Maddox.

December 2—Thomas C. Rees and Martha M. Kimbrough; 4, Benjamin N. Gafford and Martha Speer; William B. English and Harriet L. Weddington; 5, William Davis and Rebecca Walker; 6, James H. Stagg and Elizabeth R. Simpson; 11, William A. Stansell and Sarah C. Passmore; 13, James Sims and Lucretia J. Cross; John N. Sherdon and Martha A. Rodgers; 16, Henry Newsom and Mary E. Abney; 19, George W. Turner and Amanda C. Key; 20, James M. Hughes and Louisiana E. Blankenship; Thomas C. Sutton and Cordelia Wise; Christian Land and Martha Bass; William F. Cropp and Harriet A. Matthews; 27, C. Wyman and Nancy Morris; James A. Granberry and Caroline A. Haynes; James Anderson and Martha A. Tinsley; 31, Neil Wilkinson and Caroline V. Browning.

DEATHS.

(FROM THE SEXTON'S REPORTS.)

January 1—John Sullivan; 12, child of Mr. Stewart, child of Charles Shirley; 14, Miss Moore; 15, James Jackson; 19, Mrs. Martin, Clara Ingraham; 22, child of Mr. Allen; 26, Arabella Eastwood; 27, Elizabeth Balyeu; 29, infant of George Jones. (Most of these were children who died of scarlet fever.)

February 7—Mrs. King; 12, child of Mr. Ford; 15, child of Mr. Biehler; 16, child of Mr. Bailey; 17, Miss Wilson; 18, Mr. Powell, Mr. Coulter; 19, child of Wm. Carlisle; 22, infant of A. Holmes; 24, Mr. Pratt's child; 25, Samuel B. Harvell.

March 4—Child of Benj. Rhina; 8, child of Mrs. Gronbeck; 9, infant of J. H. Daniel; 13, H. Noble; 20, Mitchell Sneed; 21, child of Wm. Deignan; 30, Jane Clayton.

April 2—Child of Richard Warner; 10, Isaac Thornton; 14, Robert Forsyth (child;) 17, child of Wm. Hale; 18, Martha Holmes; 21, Elizabeth Counts, Jordan Odom; 22, child of Mr. Ingram; 27, child of E. W. Starr.

May 4—Mrs. Stubblefield; 6, child of E. Chatterton; 14, Mr. Cox; 15, Mrs. Wood; 17, Mr. Hackney's child, child of Joseph Pranglin; 29, James Lloyd, jr.

June 26—Child of L. Hopkins; 29, daughter of John Kyle; 30, child of Thos. Stubblefield.

July 6—Child of Francis Ray; 10, child of F. C. Johnson; 14, child of —— Walter; 18, son of Mr. Meredith; 20, child of Jane Bowers; 21, child

7

of Mr. Ward; 22, child of Stephen Adams; 29, child of John Lewis; 31, child of J. W. Pease.

August 5—David Wright; 9, child of John Trawick; 13, child of A. Calhoun; 23, child of Elisha Jackson.

September 2—J. Magonigal; 3, George A. Harris; 4, Mrs. Clarady; 8, Hugh McCall; 12, child of Mr. Hicks; Mr. Moore; 17, Mr. Scott; child of Mr. Bowen; child of Mr. Pike; 20, Mrs. Cornelia Daniel; 23, David J. Barber; 25, Mrs. Hicks; Mrs. Townsley.

(FROM THE NEWSPAPERS.)

October 7—Mrs. Mary W., wife of J. Rhodes Browne.

November 12—Leonard Melick.

December 12—Mary Lizzie, infant daughter of R. E. Dixon.

1856.

The City's Indebtedness—Up-Town Bridge—Location.

On the 2d Saturday in December, 1855, the following municipal officers for 1856 were elected: F. G. Wilkins, Mayor. Aldermen—1st Ward, Wm. Y. Barden, J. J. Slade; 2d, W. F. Plane, H. T. Hall; 3d, J. W. Pease, Foster S. Chapman; 4th, Jas. M. Hughes, R. H. Harris; 5th, D. B. Thompson, Jos. J. Jones; 6th, J. E. Mershon, J. Hunley; Marshal, Wm. Mahaffey; Deputy Marshal, H. P. Robinson; Treasurer, Isaac Mitchell; Clerk, Calvin Stratton; Sexton, Thos. Nix.

Council elected Dr. Flewellen, City Physician; John Peabody, City Attorney; E. Dudley, Bridge-keeper; Isabella McGee, Hospital-keeper; Jesse Bradford, Magazine-keeper; Richard Robinson, Clerk of the Market; Thos. Ragland & Co., City Printers. Health Officers—J. J. McKendree, John B. Wright, Lewis Livingston, W. E. Love, Jordan L. Howell, James M. Everett, John Kyle, Jerry Terry, N. B. Love, John T. Walker, S. Ogletree, W. P. Carter. Port Wardens—Clayton, Hill, Calhoun, Duck, Arnold. Fire Wardens—R. Goetchius, George Hungerford, C. Wise, J. C. Ruse, J. B. Strupper, T. O. Douglass.

In January, Wm. M. Lee for the 2d, and James Ligon for the 4th Ward, were elected to fill vacancies occasioned by the resignation of Ald. Plane and Hughes. Ald. Mershon having resigned, John Bunnell was in February elected an Alderman of the 6th Ward.

According to a report of the City Attorney, made in February, the following was the financial condition of the city at that time:

ASSETS.

1,500 shares Mobile and Girard Railroad stock, at $50 per share,	$ 75,000
600 shares Opelika Branch Road, at $80 per share,	48,000
100 shares City Gas Light Company stock, at $80 per share,	8,000
City Bridge,	100,000
City Wharf,	15,000
7 mules, at $175 each,	1,225
Magazine,	600
	$257,825

LIABILITIES.

Bonds for Mobile and Girard Railroad,	$150,000
" for Opelika Branch,	50,000
" Gas Light Company,	10,000
Bills payable to John King,	2,220
	$212,220

The estimate of revenue for the year was $30,740.

The vexed question of the sale of the city's stock in the Muscogee Railroad to Messrs Patten and Mustian continued to perplex Council and distract its deliberations during this year. There were two obstinate parties in the city and in Council, and apparently they were nearly equally divided—a condition that made final agreement and consummation of the sale very difficult. In April Council unanimously passed a resolution to submit to two legal gentlemen, to be chosen by the two parties, the question whether the city was legally bound to consummate the sale, also the sufficiency of the security offered by Patten and Mustian. But at the same meeting of Council the Mayor reported a block in the arrangement arising from a contention about a dividend due and unpaid on the stock. The matter was finally settled by the consummation of the original arrangement and the transfer of the stock to Messrs. Patten and Mustian.

The project of building the "up-town bridge," which had been talked of for some months, was submitted to a vote of the citizens on the 14th of July, and resulted as follows: Bridge 425, No Bridge 282—majority 143. A number of citizens had proposed to build the bridge and give the city control of it—to be tolled or freed just as the lower bridge should be. The location selected was the foot of Bryan street, just above the Howard Factory.

The receipts of cotton this year were very large, being 100,104 bales up to the close of the year, 1st September. Prices—in January, 8@8¼c.; in March, 8¼@9½c.; in September, 10½@11c.; in December, 10½@11½c.

INCIDENTS.

On the 28th of January, a young man named Chisolm, who had occasionally been engaged in the Postoffice as an assistant, was arrested on a charge of abstracting letters from the office. He was examined before Justices and bound over for trial in the sum of $8,000. On the 24th of February, Chisolm, while at large under bond, had a difficulty in the Oglethorpe House with John Wood, the bar-keeper. Wood threw Chisolm to the floor, and Chisolm then drew a pistol and shot Wood, who died the next day. Chisolm fled, but was arrested and committed.

During the last week in January, the steamers Union and Cusseta collided, in a dense fog, on the Apalachicola river, and the Union sunk immediately in fifteen feet water. About fifty bales of cotton was lost. The passengers and crew escaped.

A number of fine horses of the vicinity and from a distance contested for handsome purses over the Columbus Course in March. Among the racing celebrities engaged were Frank Allen, Carolina, Moidore, Gov. Johnson, Jack Gamble, and Floride.

A charter for the Bank of Columbus was passed by the Legislature early this year, and the Bank was organized in April by the election of William H. Young as President, and

John McGough, J. T. Hudson, Wm. Rankin, Wm. H. Young, J. Ennis, R. M. Gunby, S. J. Hatcher, J. P. Illges and J. N. Barnett as Directors.

A fire on the night of the first of April burnt a blacksmith shop and the negro quarters of Wood & Co., on St. Clair street, between Broad and Oglethorpe.

Major Buford, of Eufaula, passed through Columbus on the 4th of April, with a large company of emigrants for Kansas, to assist the South in the sectional struggle then progressing for supremacy in that territory. Some forty or fifty persons joined the company at Columbus, and liberal material aid was afforded here to the expedition.

A Criminal Court for the city of Columbus having been created by act of the Legislature, the election for Judge and Solicitor was held on the 21st of April. P. H. Colquitt was elected Judge and R. E. Dixon, Solicitor.

The Poor House of Muscogee county, about two miles east of the city, was burned on the 18th of April.

A destructive fire on the night of the 24th of April burned the large brick building on Oglethorpe street, owned by Dr. R. A. Ware, and occupied by Thos. DeWolf; also the three wooden buildings between that house and Temperance Hall, two occupied by Mr. Knight and one by Mrs. Aenchbacher. The fire originated in one of the houses occupied by Mr. Knight—cause unknown.

A small boy named William McKay was drowned in the river just below the bridge, on the evening of the 10th of May.

A woman, known as Emma Berry, was shot and killed by a young man named Thaddeus Rees, on the 3d of July. Rees made his escape.

A dispute occurred at the polls in Girard on Tuesday, Nov. 4th, the day of the Presidential election, between two young men named Eli Spivey and Wash. Blackburn, which resulted in Blackburn shooting Spivey twice with a pistol. Spivey died in a day or two afterwards.

The residence of Mr. J. Cole, on Bridge row, was burned on the morning of the 18th of November.

The hull of the steamer Wave, a boat built at Columbus for the navigation of the Chattahoochee, was launched on the 25th of November. It was built under the superintendence of Capt. Charles Blain.

PERSONAL.

Methodist Episcopal appointments for this year: L. Pierce, P. E. Columbus District; Messrs. E. W. Speer and J. H. Harris stationed at Columbus.

County officers this year: Wm. Lamar, Sheriff; A. S. Rutherford, Clerk of the Superior Court; A. P. Jones, Clerk of the Inferior Court; John Johnson, Ordinary; Thomas Chaffin, Tax Collector; I. T. Brooks, Tax Receiver; John B. Wright, Coroner; Phillip Lamar, County Surveyor.

Rev. J. H. DeVotie accepted the pastorship of the Baptist Church in May.

MARRIAGES.

January 3—Stephen Dimon and Lucretia A. Dukes; 8, John W. Hendrix and Elizabeth Hackney; 10, Abram H. DeWitt and Sarah A. Phelps; John F. Pittman and Martha A. George; 19, John Davidson and Martha E. Abner; Samuel S. Cook and Sarah S. C. Bears; 21, John Callihan and Augusta McElrath; 22, Lafayette Martin and Frances Hearn; 24, James S. Tatum and Mary C. Bailey; 31, Wyche J. Palmer and Amanda Weddington, Wm. Fisher and Martha Smith.

February 6—John I. Cumber and Mary Morris; 10, Robt. S. Sherdon and Isabella Buckler; 12, James E. Clark and Mary A. E. Kennady; 13, James T. Taylor and Dorcas M. Hughes; 17, George M. Renfroe and Virginia C. Burton; 20, Daniel D. Cox and Emily O. Luckie; 28, Pleasant S. Shellman and Caroline A. Hoxey.

March 10—Benjamin F. Dalton and Margaret Norris; 13, John H. Weaver and Sarah F. Norris; Jesse Carter and Mary W. Meacham; 16, Enoch Dowdy and Mary E. Mayes; Sterling T. Smith and Rachel R. Canim; John Hatley and Nancy D. Parish; 19, Charles Crichton and Frances Groenbeck; 27, Seymore R. Bonner and Bethia A. Fort; Amos C. Ward and Martha V. Redding.

April 1—John B. Fannen and Sarah A. E. Stanley; Francis A. Byars and Elizabeth W. McMillen; 27, Francis M. Forsyth and Frances M. McCardle.

May 1—Hugh B. Dawson and Eliza Flewellen; 6, William B. Burdim and Mary Ann Wood; 8, Moses Fincher and Martha Easterwood; 13, Lewis W.

Isbell and Franc s A. Redd; 15, George W. Smith and Ann Dillon; Nathan N. Benton and Frances S. Henry; 18, Joshua S. Roper and Frances A. Burrand.

June 5—John Hazleton and Martha V. Lynch; 8, Silas McGuirk and Mary Frazier; 1ɔ, Henry A. Johnson and Sarah Hearn; 25, Isaac I. Moses and Hannah M. Moses; 26, Josiah Mehaffey and Julia Cannon.

July 6—William A. Newsom and Susan E. Stathen; 9, Benjamin Goolsby and Temperance Hudson; 12, Riley Newsom and Martha Williams; 14, James Willox and Delilah McCauley; 24, Washington W. Johnson and Frances E. Gammage.

August 11—William Knight and Mary Frost; 25, Isaac Falkner and Lucy Ann Groff; Vincent D. Tharp and Emily T. Roberts; 29, John Nobles and Georgia A. Cegar.

September 13—Hampton C. Seale and Victoria Gafford; 14, Samuel F. Moon and Eliza Iyatt; 21, Sidney O. Lloyd and Amanda Upton; John Mowell and Franc's Upton; 23, Andrew J. McDonald and Dicy Ann Hall; 25, George W. McGilty and Jane Hinton; 29, James Harris and Frances A. Boyd.

October 2—Alfr d S. Truett and Caroline L. Nicholls; John Mehaffey and Margaret Hendrix 12, James A. McClesky and Eliza Baker; 14, William I. Wood and Leah ٭. Marks; 19, Jean B. Thomas and Nancy McCallister; 21, Wm. H. Baily and Milly A. Christian; Henry V. Horton and Courtney I. Jones; 26, George A. B. Smith and Laura V. Brannon; 28, William E. Hill and Georgia E Nix.

November 4—Luther Gaff and Sarah I. Allen; 5, Albert F. Langford and Christie A. Terry; 6, Peter Preer and Mattie A. Jones; Benjamin F. Bedell and Vanney Burfoil; John M. Faulkenberry and Adaline West; Andrew J. Riddle and Ann P Hunly; 16, James D. Neal and Louisa R. Lawrence; Wm. S. O'Bannon nd May Lloyd; Benjamin I. King and Elizabeth Jackson; 17, Simeon T Hall and Missouri E. Deavers; 20, Jacob W. Cole and Martha A. Lawrenc; David Cannon and Sarah E. Wamock.

December 2—Thomas J. Belcher and Mary A. Allen; John Keller and Rosa Heiman; 3, John P. Mealing and Angelina L. Mealing; 7, John E. W. Henderson and Louisa Murphy; 10, Alexander Peddy and Ann Flemming; Thomas G. Whigha 1 and Ann S. Hickey; 11, Jesse Haddock and Mary A. E. Doles; Henry Voi,ht and Nancy Duncan; 15, James Pridgen and Susan Wilson; 16, Thon is L. Macon and Mary R. Houston; 17, Beauford T. Yarborough and Lo isa Norman; John G. Bunnell and Martha Hodge; Jos. L. B. Wells and P melia C. Stanfield; 18, William A. Hunt and Mary E. Presley; 21, Joseph P. Morris and Malinda C. Eastwood; 23, James Shelton and Cinda Milum; Archibald J. Williams and Elizabeth Stribling; 25, Marion M. Payne and Catharine Teal; 26, James Kimbrough and Mary Johnson.

(FROM THE SEXTON'S REPORTS.)

January 1—Henry Jernigan ; 10, child of Mr. May ; 13, Wm. Matheson ; 18, Mr. Stearns; 20, Mr. Pratt; 21, Mrs. Brady; 23, child of J. C. Rickley; 28, child of J. C. Horlis.

February 4—Child of James Mealer, Mrs. Cavanaugh; 6, child of Andrew Clark; 13, John Clark, child of Mr. Tillman; 22, child of Elizabeth Martin; 24, Joseph Carey, Wm. H. Wood; 28, child of J. Day.

March 14—Ezekiel Davis; 15, Mr. McCorring; 16, child of Mr. Belser; 26, Mrs. A. Mauritzen; 28, Mrs. McGinty; 30, Jackson Tilley.

April 1—Child of Green Beaman; 3, Mrs. Edwards; 8, Mrs. Kennington, child of William Smith; 15, Mrs. Sophia Shorter; 18, Miss Kennington; 25, John I. Ridgway, Mrs. Duncan; 26, child of Martin Harrison.

May 3—Child of H. T. Hall; 9, Mrs. Cofield; 10, Mrs. Clarida; 11, Mrs. Slade; 12, Miss Williams; 13, child of Mr. Duncan, Miss Duncan, William McKay, Nancy Caldwell; 16, child of E. Dudley, son of Mrs. Bailey; 17, Mrs. Tant, Mrs. Foran; 18, Milus Chaffin, Miss Chigg; 21, Miss Bowman; 23, Fanny Forsyth; 26, child of Horace Matthews, child of Martin J. West; 30, child of Mrs. Ingram, child of Mrs. Vickers; 31, Mr. Howard, child of Martin J. West, Narcissa Burran.

June 1—Child of Mr. Cook; 2, child of Susan Foster; 3, child of Mr. Barton; 8, child of Mrs. Kennedy; 10, child of Mrs. M.Gehee; 12, Mr. Kennington; 13, child of Dr. Edwards, child of O. Danforth; 15, child of Patrick Foran; 17, child of Mr. Galespie; 18, Miss Brannon; 20, Miss Boman, David Crumley, child of Mr. Little; 22, child of Wm. F. Luckie; 23, child of John Allen, child of Mr. Dink; 24, child of William Stevens, child of Mr. Kennedy; 26, child of Mr. Howard; 28, child of Mr. Belser, child of John Byard; 29, child of Mrs. Wilson; 30, child of — - McElrath.

July 1—Child of J. J. Slade, child of Mr. Culver, Emma Ortagus; 2, child of Wm. Champion; 3, child of Mrs. Barton, Edward J. Hardin; 4, Martha Arnold; 5, child of John Meredith; 6, child of Mr. McGowen, Mr. Cromley; 7, child of Mrs. Wilson; 8, Louisa Stewart; 10, child of Mrs. Wilson; 12, D. Suddeth; 13, Mr. Kettlebrand; 14, child of G. W. Martin, Mrs. A. Dill; 15, child of L. Wright; 16, Mrs. Sauls; 17, child of J. L Howell; 18, child of Thaddeus Holt, child of Mr. Borders; 22, child of Mr. McMan; 24, child of Mr. St. Ledger, son of Mr. Collins; 26, Mrs. Wm. M. Lee, Cyrus Renfroe; 28, child of A. M. Walker; 29, Charles Gunter, child of Mr. Moat; 31, child of Mr. Lee, child of Sena Day.

[NOTE.—Most of the children named, from April to July, inclusive, died of measles, as did several adults.]

August 1—Mrs. Wayne, Emily Perry; 4, child of Mr. Marchant, child of Mr. Wayne; 5, John Kyle, Thomas Hoxey; 6, Mr. Frazell, Ephraim C. Bandy; 7, Daniel McD. Peabody; 12, Mrs. Warner, Mr Wilson; 16, Mrs. Beaman, child of Mr. King; 18, child of Jas. Kimbrough; 19, Mary R. Moore; 20, child of John Allen; 23, Thomas Shephard; 24, A. Calhoun.

September 1—child of John McCarty; William Owen; 13, child of H. Whitlock; 17, Jane McDaniel; 20, child of Cynthia Phillips; child of James Corcoran; 26, Mrs. Sweet; 28, child of Mr. Marchant.

(FROM THE NEWSPAPERS.)

October 7—(at Columbus Factory) Mrs. Nancy Brown, aged 98; 12, Henry Slade, infant son of Alfred Prescott; 15, (in Girard) Lucius V. Malone.

November 21—(in Bealwood) Mrs. Caroline Matilda Griswold; (in Girard) Stephen D. Phillips, Postmaster; 25, infant daughter of G. W. Ashburn; 28, (in Wynnton) John L., son of James M. Chambers; M. A. Thorn, of Columbia, S. C.

December — Sterling F. Grimes.

1857.

Railroad Connections—Great Sixteen Mile Race.

Col. F. G. Wilkins and Dr. John E. Bacon were the opposing candidates for Mayor at the election in December, 1856. The vote stood—Wilkins 498, Bacon 353. The following gentlemen were elected Aldermen: 1st Ward, William Y. Barden, W. C. Gray; 2d, Wm. Perry, Roswell Ellis; 3d, F. S. Chapman, Dr. T. Stewart; 4th, A. K. Ayer, G. E. Gager; 5th, John Quin, John T. Walker; 6th, Scott Clark, John Durkin. James M. Hughes was elected Marshal; Hugh P. Robinson, Deputy Marshal; Calvin Stratton, Clerk; Isaac Mitchell, Treasurer; Thos. Nix, Sexton.

Council elected Dr. George Davis City Physician—salary $600; Richard Robinson, Clerk of the Market, $150; John G. Bunnell, Bridge-keeper, $700; Isabella McGehee, Hospital-keeper, $300; John Peabody, City Attorney, $150; Jesse Bradford, Magazine-keeper, $75 and fees; City Printer, Jas. N. Bethune of the *Corner Stone*, $300; Port Wardens—J. M. Trawick, Edward Birdsong, J. M. Everett, James L. Hill and U. B. Frost; Health Officers—W. H. Alston, Thos. B.

Slade, M. Barringer, R. A. Ware, H. M. Cleckley, J. L. Howell, R. G. Mitchell, S. R. Andrews, J. L. Morton, W. W. Flewellen, T. V. Rutherford, John Seely.

The policy and convenience of making close railroad connections in Columbus, was a subject of interest this year. A meeting of citizens, held in Temperance Hall on the 10th of June, appointed a committee to confer with the officers of the, railroads and ascertain "the ends to be attained by the proposed connections, and the means and terms of its accomplishment."

The projects of building railroads from Opelika to Oxford, Ala., and from Opelika to Talladega, first engaged the attention of the people of Columbus this year. The *Times* and *Enquirer* suggested the Oxford road, and the *Sun* the Talladega road.

The cars on the Mobile and Girard Railroad were this year running to Guerryton, a distance of thirty-eight miles. Two-thirds of the grading from Guerryton to Union Springs had been accomplished.

The three military companies of Columbus—Columbus Guards, Capt. Semmes; City Light Guards, Capt. Colquitt; and United Rifles, Capt. Wilkins—went to Milledgeville on the 2d of July, to participate in an encampment of the volunteer military companies of the State They returned on the 7th.

Ald. Ellis, of the 2d Ward, having resigned, Peter Preer was in August elected to fill the vacancy.

The receipts of cotton for the year ending Sept. 1, amounted to 80,245 bales. Prices—in January, 11½@11⅝c.; in March, 11@13¼c.; in May, 13¼c. for midling; in September, 14½@15c.; in November, 11@11¼c.; in December, 9¼@9¼c.

INCIDENTS.

There was snow enough on the ground for sleighing in Columbus on the 24th of January.

The "Wave," a new boat built on the banks of the river

at Columbus, under the superintendence of Capt. Charles Blaine, made a successful trial trip on the afternoon of the 9th of February, and started on the 11th on her first trip to Apalachicola.

A fatal duel between two well-known and esteemed citizens of Columbus, on the 23d of February, created a great sensation, and the result was received with universal regret. The parties were Mr. J. P. Hendricks and O. S. Kimbrough. They fought with rifles, on the South Carolina side of the Savannah river, distance forty paces, and Mr. Hendricks was mortally wounded at the second fire.

The new Masonic Hall, on Broad street, was dedicated on the 26th of March. The address was delivered by W. Rockwell, Deputy Grand Master for the Second District of Georgia.

An extraordinary and exciting race, which was run over the Chattahoochee Course on the 4th of April, engaged so much interest at the time and is still so often referred to, that we make particular mention of it here. There were three fine horses entered—all distinguished as among the best racers of the country. They were Puryear & Watson's b. c. Charleston, McDaniel's ch. h. Frankfort, and ——'s m. Sue Washington. The two first named had won well-contested races on previous days of the same meeting, and Sue Washington was celebrated by her fine running and triumphs over many tracks. It was a four-mile race, purses and winnings $2,250. The *Sun's* account was as follows:

The weather was fine, attendance large, and the presence of ladies gave grace to the whole. Each entry had friends, and the wagers ran high. At the call of the bugle all three appeared. And now they are off. Sue has the track, but Charlston takes it the first mile, and leads gallantly off, close hugged by Sue, Frankfort following leisurely. Round they go at a killing pace, and run out in 7:39 ; Charleston 1st, Sue 2d, Frankfort dropping inside the distance.

SECOND HEAT.—Charleston has the track—he sulks—but finally goes off merrily, closely followed by Sue, Frankfort still waiting. The third mile closes, and they enter fourth in the same relative positions. Every eye is strained. See, now, they are coming home—Charleston must win. But lo!

Frankfort awakes, throws off his lethargy, and by a most masterly brush on the last quarter, takes the heat by half a head ; Charleston 2d, Sue near by. Time 7:40.

THIRD HEAT.—'Clear the track!' Now they come up—Frankfort inside. They are gone.   The race now seems to be narrowed down to Sue and Frankfort—Charleston was tired—the mare keeps ahead, and wins the heat in 8:00.   Charleston is now withdrawn ; he shows distress, but has done nobly, and in a two-handed contest would have won the day.

FOURTH HEAT.—The game was now considered sure. The mare took the start and ran through the heat without injury in 8:02.

Frankfort died shortly after the race. It is well for Sue that he lived to make his great brush with Charleston. else had she not won the honors of the day.

RECAPITULATION.

	1st heat.	2d.	3d.	4th.
Sue Washington,	2	3	1	1
Frankfort,	3	1	2	2
Charleston,	1	2	3	withdr'n
Time,	7:39	7:40	8:00	8:02

Distance run, 16 miles, in 31 minutes, 21 seconds.

Charleston was afterwards carried by his owner (Mr. Ten Broeck, we believe) to England, to contend in the great races in that country.   He ran well there, but was not successful in the chief races.   It was said that he was too fat, and exhibited the same sulky disposition at times that he manifested on two occasions on our course.

Provisions were high this year, chiefly because of scant grain crops in the West.   The quotations in Columbus on the 30th of May were as follows: Bacon, 15c. for clear sides; Corn $1.20@$1.25 ; Flour, $7.50@$12 per barrel.

A number of revival meetings held in the M. E. Church in June resulted in about fifty conversions.   Rev. Dr. L. Pierce, Rev. J. E. Evans, and Bishop Pierce were among the ministers who conducted the exercises.

The first bale of new cotton was received on the 28th of August, from the plantation of Rivers Reese, of Chattahoochee county, and sold at 17c.   Another bale of the new crop was received on the same day, from Stewart county, and sold for 17½c.   On the 29th a third bale was received.   It was from the plantation of ames R. Jones, of Russell county, Ala., and was sold by ation at 17½c.

An old man named Lid Gunn was found murdered, with his throat cut, on the nt of the 11th of September, at his house in the suburbs of the city. The coroner's jury found that he was killed by ohn Dozier, who lived with him. The house in which th lived was set on fire and burned the next evening. It v regarded as a den of vice.

Jefferson Parks was lled by Van Ransel Hall, in a difficulty between them ahe house of Patsey Daniel, in the lower part of the city1 the 25th of October. Hall was convicted of manslaug r and sentenced to four years in the penitentiary.

James Garrard stabl and killed Susan Brown, on the night of the 2d of N mber, and then stabbed himself in several places so sever that he died in a few days.

Berry King, in attering to get on a dray loaded with. with wood, fell and wann over, the load crushing and killing him in a few minu.

John Dozier was in vember convicted of the murder of David Gunn, and sented to be hung on the 8th of January.

The outbuildings on ts occupied by J. H. Harris and Mr. Speer, on Jackson str were burned on the 27th of November.

An old man named cAllister, employed in one of the factories, was drowned the river on the 6th of December.

John J. Calhoun wast in several places and killed by James Thompson, in a fficulty between them on the night of the 4th of Decembe Both were young men. Thompson was found guilty o urder, and sentenced to be hung on the 15th of January. ames Guilford, convicted as accessory, was sentenced to hung on the same day. But both these cases, as well as t of Dozier, were appealed to the Supreme Court.

L. P. Rush was this year Presid₤ Elder of the Columbus District, and A. M. Wynn and ₵N. McDonald Methodist preachers for Columbus.

William A. Lawes and Wiley Hutchins were Magistrates of the upper district, and Jn T. Walker and John Quin of the lower; James Lloyd, d Wm. Hale Bailiffs of the upper district, and Jacob W. Slip and Lemuel Lockhart of the lower.

E. Birdsong was County Treasur; J. G. Cook, Tax Collector; J. B. Hicks, Tax Receiver; A. Wales, B. F. Coleman, T. D. West, J. J. McKendree ₤ W. L. Wornum, Justices of the Inferior Court.

Thomas Curry committed suicide on the 6th of January, by taking arsenic.

By a run-off of the train going t of Columbus on the Muscogee Railroad, on the 2d of Aust, John Bryant, fireman, and Patrick Sullivan, wood h₤er, were killed. George Smith, the engineer, had a leg and arm broken.

In October, P. H. Colquitt was e₤ed Senator by a majority of two votes over S. A. Wale₤nd N. L. Howard and R. L. Mott were elected Representa₤es of Muscogee county.

James M. Russell was in October ₤ected Judge of the City Court, vice P. H. Colquitt, resigne₤

MARRIAGE

January 1—John O. Reedy and Georgia Willis; 8, Bartly King and Mary Garrett; 27, James Clem and Eugeni₤mpson; Daniel Cordery and Malvina L. Williams; Thomas J. Kimbrougdd Frances A. L. Biggers; 29, Thomas R. Hall and Ann E. Braughton.

February 2—Richard R. Briggs and Mart₤'. P. Wright; 4, Bolin S. Jeffries and Jane Carrington; 8, Peter K. Ed₤nd Lucinda Hight; William K. Smith and Martha J. Forsyth; Rober₤bson and Elizabeth Howard; 11, Edmund S. Roberts and Mary T. White; 19, Hiram P. Dowdy and Louisa K. McLeroy; 22, John W. Gammel₤d Nancy Barfield; George A. Camrom and Ann V. Sauls; 24, Simeon ₤y and Sarah A. M. Farmer; William C. Wells and Mary E. Beers; Fr₤ M. Pendleton and Sarah V. Ingmire.

March 20—Elijah Couch and a₤d Malinda₤tliff; 24, James M. Harris and Mary Y. Levy; 29, William Garr₤s and Sar₤Bailey; 31, Joseph S. Tinney and Lydia A. Stowe; John T. W₤lker and ₤thia M. Tilley.

April 5—William Webster and Winney I. Almons; 8, Richard A. Dykes and Pernelia V. Byrd; 19, Jeremiah Taylor and Martha Gammell ; John A. Ansley and Missouri Chambers ; 22, Nelson Brittingham and Merilda Youngblood ; 23, Amos C. Ward and Lucy A. Redding ; 26, David P. Russell and Mary E. Slaughter ; 28, William Ratliff and Elizabeth Salter.

May 10—George W. Horne and Catharine W. Bartlett; John F. C. Senn and Josaphine E. Phillips ; 22, James L. Willis and Frances Biggers; 25, Benjamin F. Gardner and Martha A. E. Gilstrap ; 31, James M. McCay and Mary A. L. Harris.

June 2—James M. Williams and Martha E. Seymour ; 7, Charles W. Hewson and Sophronia McAlister; 14, LeRoy J. Hudson and Martha A. Caldwell.

July 1—John N. Gunn and Flora E. Thompson, Roswell Ellis and Ann L. Slade ; 2, Henry Drakeford and Mary A. Terry ; 6, James D. Ferrill and Sarah Hutson ; 15, Thomas S. Tuggle and Sarah E. O'Bannon ; 16, Andrew B. Lawson and Julia I. Bourguine; 26, Thomas I. A. J. Duffee and Susan S. Henly ; 28, Joseph B. Aguero and Eliza I. Abbott.

August 2—Mayberry Hitt and Arena Crouch ; 4, George W. Langford and Mary J. Giddings; 6, David Gunn and Nancy Dees ; 11, William G. Wiley and Mary J. Carnes ; 13, Daniel T. Looney and Martha E. Kirkland ; 18, Harrison Merrill and Olive T. Smith ; 26, John T. Moye and Margaret McGuirk ; 27, George W. Haynes and Victoria E. Broadnax.

September 5—Jackson Rouland and Permelia Lewis ; 6, John I. Bigles and Martha Blakeley ; 7, William K. Jones and Julia A. Goodwin ; 10, John W. Davis and Frances A. McKennell ; 24, Andrew Slagle and Mary Bullock.

October 4—James W. Tillman and Mary A. Senn ; 5, William D. Edwards and Martha E. Hood; 8, Thomas M. Bryant and Martha Clay ; 11, Darius Cox and Roxanna M. Evans ; 29, Adolphus Wittich and Catharine Albrecht.

November 3—Andrew J. Hudson and Nancy M. Perkins ; 7, Charles Markham and Mary J. Wiggins ; 8, Daniel Huff and Eusebia A. Blanchard ; 9, James S. H. Menifee and Rachel M. Hooks ; 11, Henry A. Chapman and Martha G. Wales ; 12, Jack D. Clarke and Mary D. Williams ; John S. Smith and Anna Brassill ; 14,John W. Orun and Harriet E. Hoyde ; 15, David Jones and Elmira Rowe ; 19, Charles B. Mims and Leonora H. Bonner ; George Gullen and Mary E. Smith ; 22, Robert I. Smith and Clarissa A. Tidwell; 25, George A. Kindon and Martha R. Clarke.

December 2—Franklin H. Clark and Martha I. Britt ; 3, Abner A. Evans and Mary E. Lyons ; Thomas G. Perry and Eliza J. Wilson ; Milton J. Glaze and Frances Frazier ; 6, Sylvanus Cherry and Delilah Brassill ; 12, Neal McCary and Martha E. Augle ; 15, Andrew I. Harris and Martha F. Snellings ; 16, Elisha M. Gram and Nancy Thompson ; Edward W. Beers and Sophia V. King ; Alexander L. Smith and Sallie L. Levy ; 17, Encratus Roland and Mary V. Durr; 20, Thomas H. Whitby and Emily M. Gunn ; 22, John McGuire and Nancy Brannon ; Joseph D. Trammell and Mattie C. Sapp ; 23, Daniel Hood and Nancy Edwards ; 24, William Oates and Nancy Newsom ; 27, William Jordan and Mary A. George; 30, John Stringfield and Abigail Hendricks; 31, Joseph Teal and Frances Patrick.

(FROM THE SEXTON'S REPORTS.

January 7—Thomas Curry; 8, John Woods; 11, child of Mr. Foley; 21, child of Mr. Cadman, Miss Tapper; 24, child of Mrs. Summergill; 26, William B. Bacon; 27, Joseph Wise.

February 1—Child of J. A. Bradford; 2, child of Mr. Cadman; 3, Harvill Kent; 8, Mrs. V. R. Tommy; 11, child of Mr. Gayle; 14, Margaret Hudgins, Miss Spencer; 16, child of Mr. Persons; 18, child of Mr. Renfroe; 19, Mrs. Cynthia Cooper; 20, Miss Pettis; 22, child of Mr. Bussey; 24, child of Mr. Garrison, child of Mr. Barden; 27, Mrs. Robinson; 28, Miss Blankenship, Mr. Upton, jr.

March 1—Child of F. C. Johnson; 4, Master Upton, child of Mr. Darling; 6, Mrs. Brown; 9, Mr. Crook; 11, child of Mr. Flynn; 15, child of Mr. Frank; 19, Mr. White; 20, child of Mr. Smith, J. T. Thompson; 21, Mr. Hemphill; 22, child of Mr. McGibbins; 25, child of Elijah Williams; 28, Mr. Cherry; 29, Mr. Knight; 30, Mrs. Buran, Mrs. Dennis.

April 4—Child of Eliza Garven; 5, child of John Vanzant; 7, Mr. McDowall; 13, child of Josephine Champion; 14, William Pride; 16, child of Mr. Lawrence; 18, Mrs. Sheridan; 21, child of Jacob Moore; 22, Caroline McGibbins; Mrs. Louisa Jane Ware, George Murphey.

May 1—Child of John Dunahoe, child of Mr. Sharpe; 2, child of Mr. Brown; 3, child of Mr. Harrington; 7, Jacob Moore, James Moore; 8, Mrs. Sarah McCarty; 9, Hugh Dolan; 10, child of Amanda Rodgers, C. B. Dudley; 12, child of Francis McGehee; 17, child of Thomas King; 20, James M. Mitchell; 21, child of John Dunahoe; 22, child of John Dunahoe, child of A. Dukes, child of —— Hammock, Mrs. David Cropp; 29, Joseph Midway.

June 3—Child of James Caulfield, child of —— Thomas; 4, child of —— Hastings, child of Henry Harris; 5, child of Elizabeth Meredith, Elizabeth Hammock; 8, child of E. Dudley; 9, child of O. Connor; 12, John Allen, Elvira Hopkins; 15, Mrs. Narcissa Boykin; 18, child of Mrs. Porter; 21, Martha Moman; 22, child of Mrs. Ware; 24, Ann Kelly; 25, William Gibson, child of George W. Martin; 26, child of Bryant Duncan, child of Mr. Black; 29, Miss Jones, child of F. G. Wilkins

From July 1st to October 1st (no other date given)—Child of J. K. Maddox, Louisa Adcock, Mrs. Maria Brown, Hugh Farish, child of Dr. Cushman, John Brady, Charles B. Frederick, child of Wm. Davidson, Sarah Brazell, Elvira Williams, Mrs. Hugh Dolan, child of Mr. Collins, child from Hospital, Richard Robinson, child of George Jones, child of Mrs. Shepherd, child of T. Simson, child of W. Barrington, child of John Avery, George Spellman, child of W. Powers, George D. Moss, child of Mrs. Mix, child of Charles Davenport, child of Mr. Smith, Martha Hartz, Mrs. Richard Jones, child of Mr. Ridley, George M. Dickson, child of Mrs. Porter, child of John Avery, child of Dr. Cushman, John Mitchell, child of Wm. Brooks, William Cauley, child of William Getsinger, —— Hyneman, child of Mrs. Griffin, child of Mrs. Garrett, child of Mr. Mix, Miss McGurt, child of Mrs. Upton, child of

P. Finnegan, child of William Jones, child of Mr. Stewart, John Code, sr., child of William Pruden, David Gunn, child of W. H. Hill, child of R. B. Murdock, child of F. M. Gray, Michael Moran, child of A. P. Welsh, child of —— Leggett, child of William Edward, Mrs. George A. Norris, Mr. Manson, child of Mr. Watkins, Mrs. Torrey, Mrs. R. C. Shorter, child of Mr. Brazill, Mrs. Mary Wiseman.

October 1—Mrs. Stahs ; 2, child of Mrs. Edwards, child of Benj. Dellans, child of Ezra Mershon ; 3, child of Mrs. Wells ; child of P. Hollihan ; 7, child of Henry Simmons, child of Mrs. O'Tagus, child of Mr. Harris ; 8, Mr. Bankston, Ann Hamilton ; 9, child of Mr. Jordan, Mary Miller ; 10, Josiah Pranglin ; 11, Mrs. Davis ; 12, child of Mr. Stewart ; 13, Mrs. Geo. W. Dillingham ; 14, Mrs. Paradine ; 16, child of Mrs. Brassill, Mrs. Bray, Miss Parish; 20, Mrs. Seaborn, child of Mr. Browning, Mrs. Josiah Prangle; 21, Mrs. Brady; 22, child of Perry Spencer, Mrs. Brannon; 23, child of Mr. Babbitt, child of Mrs. Meigs; 25, Wm. Fincher; 29, Mrs. McKinnie; 30, Jefferson Parks; 31, Isaac Williams.

November 1—Mrs. Watson, child of Perry Spencer; 2, Mrs. Jas. Kimbrough; 3, Henry Champion, Susan Brown; 4, Mrs. Moman, 6, James L. Garrard; 7, John Riley; 9, child of Mr. Pullam; 11, Miss Holly; 13, Miss Ball, child of James Burem, 15, Thomas Carter; 16, child of Martha Gammon; 19, child of Wm. E. Brooks, Louisa Gilmore; 21, Berry King; 22, child of Martha Ivey; 25, Martha Gunn, Hugh Kirkpatrick.

December 7—John Calhoun, Mrs. Mary McAlister; 8, child of James Bussey; 10, child of John Harney; 13, Mrs. Bussey, Mrs. J. T. Flewellen, child of Jesse Harbuck; 18, Emeline Phole; 20, child of John Kavanaugh; 22, Mrs. Jenny Holtzclaw; 23, James Foley; 25, child of John Hamilton; 27, James Wagner; 28, Mrs. Adams; 30, two children of William Jones.

NOTE.—Both measles and scarlet fever prevailed among the children during this year, and many of them died of those diseases.

1858.

Disastrous Railroad Accident—City Taxes.

This appears to have been a year of considerable business activity and general prosperity for Columbus. The receipts of cotton were large, and the price good, and a heavy trade with the country was done by the merchants. It was also a year of remarkable good health, as the Sexton's reports of interments show. There was a little alarm in November about some cases of fever on the portion of Crawford street known as Battle Row. It was of a malignant type, resembling yellow fever, and the report got out into the country that there was yellow fever in Columbus. Several persons died with it. Whatever may have been the proper name for

8

this fever, it did not spread. Frosts occurred while the first cases were suffering from it, and its course was soon arrested.

The municipal officers for this year were—Mayor, F. G. Wilkins; Aldermen—1st Ward, P. H. Alston, Wm. C. Gray; 2d, Peter Preer, James Vernoy; 3d, Joseph Kyle, J. R. Eastham; 4th, M. Barschall, Joseph Smith; 5th, D. B. Thompson, John T. Walker; 6th, John Durkin, W. R. Brown; Marshal, J. M. Hughes; Deputy Marshal, H. P. Robinson; Clerk, Calvin Stratton; Treasurer, R. G. Mitchell; Sexton, Thos. Nix. These were elected by the people on the second Saturday in December, 1857, except Mr. Wm. C. Gray, Alderman for the 1st Ward, who was elected on the 19th of December, there having been a tie in that ward at the regular election between Wm. C. Gray and D. McArthur.

Council elected N. L. Hutchins, City Attorney; Dr. Ellison, City Physician; J. D. Hughes, Bridge-keeper; W. Tilley, Clerk of the Market; Isabella McGehee, Hospital-keeper; Thos. Ragland & Co., City Printers; Port Wardens—D. L. Booher, J. C. Brewer, L. B. Duck, W. L. Salisbury, John Ligon; Health Officers—Wm. C. Gray, F. J. Abbott, Edward Croft, F. S. Chapman, D. C. Jackson, W. J. Chaffin, J. W. King, A. Ingmire, Wm. Daniel, James M. Everett, John Seely, S. Ogletree.

An act was passed by the Legislature authorizing the Muscogee and the Opelika Branch Railroads to connect their roads by extending them through the City Commons and streets of Columbus, with the assent of the people of the city. Council in March passed an ordinance authorizing the Muscogee Railroad to connect with the Opelika Branch, by extending its road across the North Commons; also to connect with the Mobile and Girard Railroad by extending its road through Thomas street and building a bridge across the river at the foot of Thomas street; the Muscogee Railroad Company to pay into the city treasury for this privilege $2,000 the first year after the making of the connection and $3,000 for every year thereafter. This proposition was submitted to the people at an election held on the 27th of February, and ratified by a vote of 350 to 91. The Muscogee Railroad accepted the proposition, and a contract embodying its terms was approved by Council on the 8th of March.

The following were officers of the Fire Department this year: Chief Engineer, J. L. Morton; Assistant Engineer, J. B. Strupper; Columbus Fire Company No. 1—R. A. Ware, President, J. D. Johnson, Foreman; Vigilant No. 2—Jos. A. Roberts, President, James Vernoy, Foreman; Muscogee No. 3—I. G. Strupper, Foreman, Samuel Lawhon, Assistant.

C. C. Cody was in January elected an Alderman of the 4th Ward, *vice* Joseph C. Smith resigned.

The Financial Committee in a report made to Council on the 15th of March, estimated the expenditures necessary for the year at $51,970. Of this amount $21,000 was for interest on bonds to the Mobile and Girard Railroad, $3,500 for the Opelika Branch Road, and $10,000 for the Gas Company; the balance for ordinary expenses. The receipts were estimated at $19,820, including $2,500 from bonds of the Montgomery and West Point Railroad Company. This estimated income was exclusive of the taxes for 1858, to adjust which to the wants of the city treasury the committee recommended a scale of taxes, as follows: On real estate, 15 cents on the $100 value; on sales of all goods merchandise or other articles not specifically taxed, 15 cents on the $100—this for city purposes; additional tax for railroad purposes, real estate 70 cents on the $100; sales as above 30 cents on the $100. The report of the commitee was adopted with an amendment taxing some other property. Council also resolved to redeem the tax for railroad purposes, when scrip for the same to the amount of $100 should be presented, in stock of the Mobile and Girard Railroad when transferred to the city. Many tax-payers resisted payment of the railroad tax, and a case was carried to the courts by Col. S. Jones and others. Council employed Messrs. Wellborn, Johnson & Sloan as counsel for the city. The collection of the tax being thus suspended, Council borrowed $22,444 from the banks, wherewith to pay the bonds given to the Muscogee Railroad Company. The Supreme Court sustained Col. Jones and others in their resistance to the tax, and Council then asked of the Legislature the passage of an act authorizing a similar tax.

There were four military companies in the city this year, viz: Columbus Guards, Capt. Semmes; City Light Guards, Capt. Colquitt; United Rifles, Capt. Wilkins; and Georgia True Greys, Capt. Andrews.

The new or upper bridge over the river was completed in July, but Council and the company who built it could not agree upon the terms of its acceptance—the company at first asking Council to make a bond to keep it in repair. In November the company threw it open to public use, and Council, in turn, declared the lower bridge free of toll. A committee of Council had reported that the upper bridge was not built in a substantial and satisfactory manner.

John S. Allen was in October elected an Alderman of the 2d Ward, vice Alderman Preer, resigned.

H. P. Robinson having resigned the office of Deputy Marshal, on account of bad health, Henry Riley was elected on the 13th of November.

INCIDENTS.

The river was very high on the 13th and 14th of January, and for a time much apprehension was felt for the bridges, but they were not injured. The bank on the Girard side caved greatly, whole acres falling into the river, taking one or two houses with them. No lives were lost. The Palace Mills sustained considerable damage.

Michael Tracy was shot in the breast and killed by a man named Hinch, on the 7th of February. The affray between them occurred between Bridge and Crawford streets. Hinch was a comparative stranger, having been in the city but a short time. He was arrested and committed.

"Suspension" was this year the terminus of the Mobile and Girard Railroad, and a postoffice was established there in April.

At the Spring Term of Muscogee Superior Court, Samuel Hinch was found guilty of the murder of Michael Tracy, and sentenced to be hung on the 2d of July. James Thompson was re-sentenced to be hung on the same day. Thompson made a speech exonerating Guilford, who, after obtaining a new trial, had plead guilty of involuntary manslaughter and been re-sentenced to three years in the penitentiary. Thompson was hung on the 2d of July, according to sentence. Hinch by appeal, secured a postponement of his execution. He was re-sentenced and he and Dozier were hung on the 17th of December.

A great revival of religion was experienced in Columbus in May and June. On the last Sunday in May about sixty new converts joined the M. E. Church, and a number joined the other churches of the city. On the first Sunday in June about seventy joined the Presbyterian Church. The estimate up to that time was that 170 had joined the Methodist church, 70 the Presbyterian, 60 the Baptist, and 26 the Episcopalian. Many more accessions were afterwards made to each of these churches, making the whole number of converts during the revival over 500.

The M. E. Church in Girard, now in use, was dedicated on the 18th of July by Rev. W. G. Conner, of LaGrange. The same gentleman dedicated a new M. E. Church "in the lower part of the city" (Columbus) on the 1st of August.

The first bale of new cotton was received from the plantation of Mrs. A. E. Shepherd, in Stewart county, on the 30th of July, and sold for 14½ cents.

A new Baptist Church, for the negroes of that denomination, was dedicated on the 22d of August, by Rev. J. H. DeVotie. Its location was the northwest corner of St. Clair and Front streets.

The *Enquirer* commenced the publication of a daily paper on the 24th of September.

A white woman, Mrs. Minchin, was burnt to death by a fire in her house in the southern part of the city on the night of the 13th of November. The fire was extinguished before burning the house.

The Georgia Conference of the M. E. Church was held in Columbus in November—Bishop Pierce presiding.

George D. Prentice of Louisville, Kentucky, lectured in Columbus on the 20th of December, to a good audience.

A terrible railroad disaster, which greatly agitated the city, occurred on the morning of the 31st of December, at the crossing of Randall's creek, about sixteen miles east of Columbus. Heavy rains had fallen, and the creek was very full, washing out some of the foundations of the bridge. The train which left Columbus broke through and was precipitated into the swollen stream. The passenger car was overturned and borne down stream. There were about forty passengers on the train, and twelve or fourteen of them were killed either by the fall or by drowning. Among those lost were Mr. Bouche and Mr. W. H. Snell, train hands, of Columbus; Henry Miller, engineer, of Columbus; two Misses Guise, of Salem, Ala.; a negro man belonging to R. E. Dixon, another belonging to Mr. Mustian, and another belonging to J. M. Russell. Some of the passengers were carried down stream half a mile. Some, after floating or swimming a distance, caught to trees, where they remained for some time before they could be rescued. The person who first brought the news to Columbus was a negro, who thought that he was the only person saved, and his report greatly alarmed the citizens. On the train was Mr. Pryor's noted race horse, Moidore, who was lost.

Another accident occurred about the same hour, in the immediate neighborhood of the city, to the train coming from Macon, and was caused by the sinking down of the track over a culvert, when the engine ran on it. Mr. Jno. Walker, the fireman, was instantly killed; a negro man was caught in the wreck and scalded to death; Mr. George Smith, the engineer, had his jaw broken. The accident blocked up the track and prevented the sending of succor to the sufferers at

Randall's Creek as soon as communication with them would otherwise have been·established.

PERSONAL.

The county officers this year were—F. M. Brooks, Sheriff; A. S. Rutherford, Clerk of the Superior Court; A. P. Jones, Clerk of the Inferior Court; J. B. Hicks, Tax Receiver; Thos. Chaffin, Sr., Tax Collector; Edward Birdsong, Treasurer; J. B. Wright, Coroner; John G. Bethune, Public Administrator; J. E. Lamar, Surveyor.

R. C. Forsyth having resigned the postmastership of Columbus, Dr. H. M. Jeter was in November appointed his successor.

The M. E. appointments for Columbus, for this year, were as follows: For St. Luke, Rev. A. M. Wynn, assisted by Rev. J. M. Austin; Factory Mission, Rev. W. W. Tidwell and Rev. C. L. Hays; Girard Colored Charge, Rev. W. D. Shew.

MARRIAGES.

January 1—John Kingsley and Mary A. Robinson; 5, Joseph Galvan and Mary Ann Bold; 6, Moses H. Phillips and Harriet E. Mims, John Davis and Mary Sperlin; 7, Thomas H. Burch and Charlotte C. Gray, George R. Hays and Mary F. Wood, Joseph Springer and Emily Gettinger, Thomas Bankston and Elizabeth Roberts, Aaron L. Harrison and Mary J. Owen; 10, William Clarida and Sarah W. Kelly; 13, George W. Dawson and Annie J. Sankey; 14, Wesley T. Harm and Mary E. Roland, Wiley S. Green and Eleanor A. Tillman; 20, Willis Spivey and Rachel Shirrer, Jacob G. Burrus and Anna R. Buckler; 21, William H. Hollman and Georgia R. Champion; 24, Edmund B. Ginn and Alley Jane Taff; 26, David I. Britt and Salina A. Wells; 27, Beverly A. Harris and Elizabeth Renfroe; 29, Charles Sinclair and Barbara A. Plymade.

February 2—John G. Jones and Elizabeth A. Plumb; 3, George W. King and Caroline M. English; 4, William B. Watkins and Mary Jones, Lewis S. Jenkins and Sarah R. Pope; 9, Peter T. Bugg, jr., and Elizabeth Wagner; 10, William L. Clark and Anna P. Ridgway; 18, Bird B. Forsyth and Charlotte Creamer; 21, William P. Duncan and Adaline Hackney, James Belcher and Elizabeth Magraff, Jonathan Ward and Mary H. Gilbert; 25, William Dukes and Permelia Walker.

March 5—Lawrence A. Sturgis and Mary D. Forsyth; 7, Charles Cherry and Mary Thompson; 10, Malcolm McNeil and Permelia Edwards; 14, John Flemming and Susan Scroggins; 15, Edward McLesky and Elizabeth Barnes; 22, John K. Moon and Lezina Murphy; John Kirkland and Susan Skates; 30, Jonathan Harralson and Martha E. Thompson; 31, William G. Brown and Frances C. Kent.

April 1—Moses H. Hall and Mary A. Simmons; 6, Barney Veasy and Narsissa Williams; 8, Bartley Smith and Mary Holstead, George R. Clark and Martha A. Johnson; 14, Fielding W. Acee and Martha J. Kirvin; 15, James T. Robison and Susan J Bugg, William Graham, jr., and Mary Davis, Calvin F. Miller and Mary P. Systrythe, James M. Skinner and Martha L. Coleman; 17, David Tunrey and Jane Cobb; 18, Telfair W. Moore and Mary O. Conner; 23, David Perry and Cordelia R. Odom; 24, James Newsom and Martha Thompson; 25, Seaborn Dowdy and Leonora Harris.

May 9—Benjamin Lane and Margaret Holley; 11, Joseph S. Garrett and Virginia E. Heard; 12, Samuel Anthony and Mary A. F. Motley; 13, Wiley G. Roper and Virgiuia A. Beland; Benjamin Yarborough and Eliza Lacy; 17, Francis I. Fagg and Martha E. Smith; 24, George W. Nicholson and Celia A. Haddock; 31, Samuel H. Hill and Rebecca C. Kookogee.

June 3—William H. Smith and Mary A. R. Barnes; 8, William H. Pace and Susan A. Foster; 10, Joseph W. Baker and Arran Coleman; 16, Martin W. Beck and Catharine M. Calhoun; 17, James L. Ware and Susan I. Ware; 18, George W. Jones and Adaline Whitten; 19, Robert Statum and Elvira Abney.

July 1—Horace H. Taft and Sarah A. Bardwell; 4, Stephen B. Freeman and Mary A. Duffel; 8, Hiram A. Gibson and Frances S. Rogers; 15, William I. Davis and Eliza F. Miller; 22, James T. Phillips and Frances Wilkinson; 26, Giles Ivey and Elizabeth Currie.

August 3—Nathaniel A. Nuckolls and Elizabeth P. Kyle; 4, James F. Cooper and Ann Murphy; 6, Hiram F. Williams and Martha A. Harrell; 8, Jesse Lightfoot and Martha Littleton; 9, Archibald M. Kimbrough and Nancy M. Hamer; 10, Jarred L. Reed and Eugenia McDonald; 12, Richard L. Ellison and Lucinda E. Helmes; 22, William Hammock and Sarah A. Davidson; John H. B. Shippey and Georgia A. Askew; 27, William H. Harvey and Mary Gammell.

September 9—Theodore Ewing and Elizabeth Matthison; 15, James M. Duffee and Hetty E. Stringer; Cullen C. Hardison and Fredonia N. Harp; 16, Rice B. Pierce and Martha M. Cowan; 17, William Parish and Caroline Seaborn; 23, Appleton Haygood and Elizabeth C. Martin; James P. Floyd and Martha A. Lloyd; 30, Alfred Hataling and Catharine Cone; Josiah Boland and Susan Hammock; John Hartis and Susan Smith; James Collins and Elizabeth Scott.

October 3—Simeon Smith and Alvania George; 7, Johnson E. T. Stoltz and Mary Davie; 9, John Ingram and Nancy A. Goulding; 12, Lewis Harrison and Rosalie Branch; 14, Samuel C. Rogers and Susan W. Pool; Eothieb N. Acnchbacker and Martha I. Crouch; 17, John W. Skinner and Sarah A. E. Brooks; 20, James M. Crouch and Margaret Clardy; 26, Charles Dudley and Henrietta Jackson; 27, Alexander C. Kirvin and Susan E. Andrews; 28, John Gardner and L. Anna McGinty; James W. Massey and Sarah Yates; 31, Millenton D. Henderson and Sarah D. Green.

November 2—James H. Toole and Mary A. McRea; 11, John F. Ellison and Mary I. Robinson; Floyd Alford and Mary I. Culbreth; 29, John Treadaway and Emily Justice.

December 12—Hillery G. Guy and Elizabeth Turville ; 15, John T. Wright and Sarah Hethcock ; 16, Thomas R. Jones and Mary J. Hargraves ; 17, Perry W. Dalton and Nancy M. M. Jordan; 21, George H. Smith and Mary V. Collins; 22, Samuel E. Smith and Elizabeth Hammonds ; 26, William Smith and Mary Davidson; 28, Robert Garvin and Mary A. Wynne; 30, Leighton. W. Hatcher and Caroline Davis; Henry T. Morris and Sarah E. Camran ; Bryant Barnes and Leviney Marler; Joseph M. I. Tally and Elizabeth A. Jones; George B. Mansel and Jane Creamer; 31, James C. Brooks and Elizabeth Mote.

DEATHS.

(FROM THE SEXTON'S REPORTS.)

January 3—Louisa Lawrence ; 4, child of Mr. Warner; 6, James Ivey; 10, Jane Hall; 11, John Hunley; 15, Leverett Norris; 24, child of Mr. Little ; 26, child of Mr. Langford.

February 3—Child of Joseph Oswalt; 7, Mr. Tracy (killed); 12, Mrs. Paul Long; 13, John Harnett; 14, Micajah Bennett; 17, child of Wm. A. Beach, Mrs. Roswell Ellis ; 28, Miss Rowell (killed by accident.)

March—No deaths.

April 16—John Traywick ; 17, child of D. T. Lunney ; 22, McDonald Brooks, child of Samuel Lewis; 28, Elizabeth Worsham.

May 17—Child of Mr. Wornum, Wm. E. Love ; 20, Abraham Brown; 27, James Harris.

June 2—Child of Amanda Rogers ; 7, George L. McGehee ; 9, child of Mr. Salay ; 16, child of Charles Crichton ; 24, child of J. P. Murray ; 29, Mrs. M. Nance.

July 3—Samuel Brannon, A. K. Ayer; 9, child of Samuel Lewis ; 13, James B. Jones ; 22, Mr. Henley ; 25, child of Mr. Gilbert.

August 1—E. H. Calhoun ; 3, child of John Jones ; 5, Mr. Pitts ; 6, William Douglass ; 9, Ellen Grimsley ; 23, Francis Wilhelm ; 26, Miss Noble ; 27, child of James Fryer.

September 2—Child of Felix McArdle ; 4, child of James Welsh; 12, Thomas G. Moffett, child of Seaborn J. Smith ; 25, Michael N. Clark ; 27, child of Joseph Pranglin ; 28, Daniel M. Barber.

(FROM THE NEWSPAPERS.)

September 28—Hon. S. A. Wales, late Senator, and a Judge of the Inferior Court.

Oct. 11—Patrick McCarthy ; 7, Mrs. Elizabeth Bright Lindsay; 16, Mrs. Olivia M. Harris; 17, Samuel D. Clarke ; 25, (in Girard) Miss Flora Phillips.

Dec. 25—William B. Moore ; 29, (at Apalachicola) John E. Clark, of Columbus.

1859.

Destructive Warehouse Fires—Railroads—Market Ordinance.

The election for municipal officers of this year was held under an amendment of the charter, which required the election of Aldermen by *general ticket*, but Ward representation was still preserved by the requirement that two Aldermen should *live* in each Ward. This is the mode of election still maintained. It met with strong opposition when first proposed, and the Council of 1858 protested against it. The act passed only a few days before the election on the second Saturday in December, 1858.

A leading question in the election of a city government for this year was that of the new bridge. The candidates nominated on the "People's Ticket" were opposed to the Council's receiving the bridge on the terms and conditions proposed by the company that had it built; and this ticket was successful in the election.

The candidates for Mayor were F. G. Wilkins and W. H. Holstead, and the vote between them stood—Wilkins 388, Holstead 353. The following gentlemen were elected Aldermen : 1st Ward, J. J. McKendree, Edward Croft ; 2d, J. W. King, J. A. Urquhart ; 3d, T. O. Douglass, A. C. Kivlin ; 4th, M. Barschall, C. C. Cody; 5th, D. B. Thompson, John Quin ; 6th, S. Ogletree, John Durkin. Dr. Urquhart's name was on both tickets. The vote for the "People's Ticket" ranged from 406 to 476; that for the "New Bridge Ticket" from 214 to 323. J. M. Hughes was elected Marshal; G. W. Haynes, Deputy Marshal; R. G. Mitchell, Treasurer; Calvin Stratton, Clerk ; and Thos. Nix, Sexton.

Council elected John Peabody, City Attorney ; Dr. Ellison, City Physician; W. Tilley, Clerk of the Market; John Bunnell, Bridge Keeper; Mrs. Isabella McGehee, Hospital Keeper ; J. Bradford, Magazine Keeper ; James N. Bethune, City

Printer; Health Officers—M. A. Doney, D. McArthur, A. F. Brannon, Dr. Ware, Jos. Daniel, Thos. Sloan, John Whitesides, John Ligon, W. Daniel, J. T. Walker, Theo. Ewing; Port Wardens—J. R. Eastham, Jas. Everett, W. J. Chaffin, J. F. Howard, Wm. L. Salisbury.

One of the first subjects that necessarily engaged the attention of the new Council was that of the bridges. A committee was appointed to report some arrangement to adjust the difficulty. This committee reported that it had not succeeded in making any satisfactory arrangement with the owners of the new bridge, and offered a resolution re-establishing tolls on the lower bridge. This resolution was rejected. Council resolved to allow the bridge-keeper house rent free temporarily, as compensation for his taking care of the bridge, and in March voted him one dollar per day, up to that time, in addition. No arrangement having been effected with the owners of the new bridge, both bridges remained free of toll.

Thomas M. Hogan was in March elected an Alderman of the 2d Ward, *vice* Alderman Urquhart, resigned.

In March, the Muscogee Railroad Company petitioned Council to release it from the prohibition to connect the Muscogee and Opelika Railraads within the city limits previous to a connection with the Mobile and Girard Railroad, also, and proposed to pay a tax of $1,000 annually for the privilege of connecting the two first-named roads alone—this to include the tax previously levied on the Muscogee Railroad. Council having given consent, the Company advertised on the 26th of March for proposals for the grading and masonry of the connecting section.

The friends of the Opelika and Talladega Railroad and the Opelika and Oxford Railroad, respectively, were quite active this year in urging the claims of these two projects. Columbus was interested in both. A meeting of the citizens, called by the Mayor, was held in the Council Chamber on the 17th of May, at which prominent gentlemen of Tallapoosa and

Chambers counties, Alabama, representing the two enterprises, made interesting addresses. The meeting manifested approbation of both schemes, but did not recommend any immediate aid from Columbus, regarding the progress so far made in obtaining subscriptions as not sufficient to justify a subscription by the city.

The proposition for building a Railroad from Columbus to LaGrange, via Hamilton, was also engaging attention this year. Meetings were held, delegates appointed to railroad conventions, &c., but no progress was made in building the road.

Some of the citizens were greatly opposed to a "Market Ordinance" passed by Council, compelling vendors of country produce to carry their "truck" to the Market House only for sale up to a fixed hour of the day. Gen. Bethune took the lead in opposition to this ordinance, and disregarded it, for which Council undertook to punish him. He carried a case to the Supreme Court, argued it himself, and obtained a judgment that the ordinance was illegal and the action of Council unwarranted. [An amendment of the charter has since given Council the powers then exercised.]

INCIDENTS.

The Georgia Baptist Convention met in Columbus in April, and was largely attended.

A young man named Pittman was shot in the thigh, on the 5th of May, by the accidental discharge of a pistol which he was carrying in his pocket. The accident occurred on Warren street. The ball ranged downward towards the knee, and the wound produced lockjaw; which ended fatally about two weeks after the accident.

An old man named Paradise, a fisherman, was run upon and badly mangled by a train on the Mobile and Girard Railroad, as it was coming in on the 3d of June. He was deaf, and did not hear the train approaching, which could not be checked up entirely until the cow-catcher struck him.

The house of Mr. R. P. Spencer, on Front street near Randolph, was destroyed by fire on the 7th of June.

On the night of the 8th of June, a little after 9 o'clock, one of the most destructive fires that the city ever sustained broke out among the cotton stored in the Alabama Warehouse, then kept by Messrs. King, Allen & Camak. It spread with astonishing rapidity and soon enveloped the whole warehouse, which was well stored with cotton. The heat in a few minutes became too great for the firemen and others to operate inside. The flames soon communicated to the Fontaine Warehouse, kept by Messrs. Hughes, Daniel & Co. Both warehouses were consumed with about eight thousand bales of cotton. A considerable quantity of bagging, bacon, flour, grain, &c., was also burned. The total loss amounted to $500,000 or $600,000, of which the larger portion was not insured. The fire was grand and terrible in its proportions, and the heat was so intense that it could be felt across the river. The origin of the fire was a mystery, and it was by many believed to be the work of an incendiary. It was uncontrollable from the start.

The Israelites of Columbus consecrated a temporary place of worship in June of this year, and were then making an effort to build a Synagogue. There were then about twenty families of Israelites in Columbus, as we learn from a letter of Rev. L. Z. Sternheimer.

Joseph Malone, a sculptor, who worked in the marble yard of T. Kenny, was drowned in the river, into which he went to bathe, on the 7th of August.

The first bale of new cotton was received on the 19th of August, and was sold at 12½ cents. It was from the plantation of W. S. Shepherd, of Stewart County. Another bale was received later in the same day, from the plantation of John M. Sapp, of Chattahoochee county, and sold at 12¼ cts.

The Second Methodist Church in Columbus (now called St. Paul's) was dedicated on the 9th of October. Rev. Dr. Lovick

Pierce preached the sermon for the occasion, and was assisted in the exercises by Rev. Alfred Mann. Dr. Pierce was the first pastor.

PERSONAL.

J. W. Hinton was presiding Elder of Columbus District, and the following were stationed M. E. Preachers in Columbus and Girard: 1st Church, Alfred Mann; 2d Church, Lovick Pierce; Pierce Chapel and Colored charge, O. Driscoll; Factory Mission, W. K. Wardlaw; Girard and Colored Mission, O. W. Landreth.

County officers elected in January: J. L. Howell, Tax Collector; I. T. Brooks, Tax Receiver; E. Birdsong, County Treasurer; T. D. West, a Justice of the Inferior Court.

J. L. Morton was Chief, and T. O. Douglass, Assistant of the Fire Department.

Mr. E. Birdsong, County Treasurer, having died in February, Mr. H. S. Estes was appointed by Governor Brown to fill the vacancy.

MARRIAGES.

January 2—George W. Taft and Mary C. Ginn; 6, Joseph Bambuse and Martha Duncan; 12, James J. Slade and Lelie B. Bonner; 13, James J. Cook and Sarah A. Bozeman; 23, Duncan Smith and Sarah I. Clarke; 24, William I. Blackmon and Sarah I. Collins.

February 3—Leonidas H. Cogbill and Elizabeth Murray; 8, Richard Gill and Rosina I. Hound; Wiley Cannon and Harriet Browning; 12, Charles G. Rush and Emily Horton; 13, Thomas P. Thornton and Mary A. Freeman; 14, Alexander Turner and Charlotte G. Carlton; 15, Erasmus D. Nave and Mary E. Hay; 20, James M. Kelly and Mary Oswalt; 24, Henry Barnett and Maggie A. Williams.

March 3—Neal W. Albrecht and Camilla C. Lightner; 7, John H. Horton and Ellen Garrett; 10, James M. Fletcher and Mary E. Whipple; 13, Wm. F. Hudson and Eliza I. Wellborn; 14, Farley B. Adams and Caroline P. Henry; 17, William I. Webb and Angeline E. Banister.

April 5—James Boyd and Sarah I. Bullock; 7, Thomas Johnson and Lucy Smith; 10, Isaac H. Giles and Matilda Collins; 12, Archibald P. Gentry and Sarah E. Omans; 17, Thomas Ryans and Louisa Smith; 21, James L. Bagley and Sarah A. Riddle; John I. H. Stockdale and Mary I. Cook; Jesse Gulledge and Susan E. Young; Byrd M. Grace and Indiana Barden; 24, Patterson Garrison and Eliza E. Clark; 26, John G. McKee and Georgia M. Smith; 28, Robert Motley and Mary L. Comer.

May 5—Thomas G. Greer and Anna Odom ; 11, Thomas Ellis and Mary Duffell ; 12, Samuel W. Anthony and Mary A. F. Motley ; 24, Franklin C. Johnson and Joanna L. Day ; Alfred M. Greene and Missouri E. McDonald ; 25, Thomas W. Dawson and Anna E. Cody ; Joel W. Blackmon and Louisa Gibson.

June 4—Daniel McDaniel and Mary A. E. Edwards; William Raibun and Harriet Mainyard ; 12, Edmund D. Jones and Emily E. King ; 14, John S. Deer and Nancy W. Crawford; 15, John Lee and Nancy A. Robison ; 16, Berry Doughty and Emily Conters ; David Y. Tinnon and Augustus A. Baxley ; 19, Isaac K. Crawford and Eda A. Clark ; 21, Francis M. Gammell and Frances E. McGee ; 26, Samuel McLendon and Matilda Long ; 28, Hugh H. Parkyn and Isabella R. Mann ; 30, Leander Odom and Nancy L. M. Wallace ; Orlando C. Young and Letha Ann Johnson.

July 3—Zachariah Cohen and Martha McCullers; Joshua Ellis and Mary A. I. Foley ; 4, William S. Lee, jr., and Melissa A. Cook ; James Broughton and Berthena Smith ; 5, Moses Johnson and Harriet Smith ; 7, Geo. W. Driggers and Mary K. Yearty ; William H. Smith and Melvina Ford ; 9, Joseph Hampshire and Frances Ruse ; 12, William H. Thompson and Georgia A. McKay ; 24, John H. Robinson and Catharine Thompson ; 28, James Stringfellow and Elizabeth A. Wallace.

August 2—Grigsby E. Thomas, jr., and Martha B. Slade ; 3, Oliver B. Huckaba and Emma E. Thomas; 6, Robt. E. Baker and Missouri Stephens; 11, Joseph Warlick and Nancy Simpson ; 12, James M. Singleton and Hannah A. Grantham ; 18, Nicholas E. Miller and Triphena C. Dean ; Eugena B. Woodham and Nancy King ; 20, Newett L. Smith and Mary Duke ; 25, John Swinney and Mary A. Collins ; 29, James L. Wells and Martha Lucius.

September 4—Oliver H. Miller and Mary Parker ; 6, Amos McLendon and Mary A. Lanam ; 11, Warren C. Huff and Lizzie M. Odom ; 12, Stephen C. Hyman and Emily A. C. Wood ; 18, Alexander Watson and Mary Dean ; 28, James Shaver and Elizabeth I. Clegg ; 29, Franklin George and Anna Day ; Andrew Jackson and Mary F. Jenkins.

October 5—John H. Butt and Johdgeline Winter ; 6, Sebastian Hoffman and Sarah E. E. Sherly ; Edmund H. Browning and Elizabeth Frier ; 13, Robert G. Johnson and Malvina A. Thompson ; 15, Robert I. Bozeman and Louisa V. Russell ; 16, Edmund I. Kelly and Sarah M. McKenzie ; 17, Richardson Chadwick and Euna V. Falkner ; William H. Dinkins and Martha P. Wicker ; 20, Thomas Turnage and Harriet Burnett ; 22, Robert C. Brooks and Evaline Phillips ; 30, James L. Kimbrough and Mary E. Cashire ; 31, Thomas B. Long and Winnie Seaborn ; Joseph N. Harley and Mary A. Chaney.

November 3—Josiah H. Smith and Carrie C. Enderman ; William E. Ray and Louisa I. McClesky ; 4, Jefferson T. Foster and Elizabeth Godwin ; Samuel C. Watkins and Susan Massey ; 6, Harris W. Freeman and Matilda Sempler ; James F. Warthen and Lydia I. Rhodes ; Frank T. Torbett and Louisa J. Burt ; 15, Thomas L. Kennady and Mary I. Luckie ; 17, Reddick C. Pearce and Mary J. Harrison ; 23, William I. Miller and Cornelia I. Tyler ; Furman W. Mims and Leah F. A. D. Thomas.

December 1—James R. McGehee and Avarilla E. Crawford: 8, William S. Lockhart and Mary A. M. Skinner; Alexander Scott and Caroline C. Wall; Howard W. Finney and Susan E. Smith; 15, Wm. E. Fickling and Martha E. Rogers; Isaac Gammons and Jane A. E. Bozeman; Justin F. Buchanan and Louisa Semple; 18, David N. Morris and Elizabeth Duke; 19, James J. Cherry and Minerva McGehee; 21, Allen G. Burge and Amanda McCay; William I. Baird and Mary A. Whatley; 23, Jackson P. Johnson and Mary Yancy; 24, John I. Lambert and Amanda N. Stephens; 25, Phillip Henly and Susannah Hudson; John Gallaway and Louisa M. Smith; 27, William A. Dunklin and Jennie A. Thompson; 28, Jasper Blackwell and Mary A. Roberson; 31, William M. Allen and Saramantha I. Phillips.

DEATHS.

January 13—Mrs. J. L. Pearce; 21, (in Apalachicola,) Thomas Poitevent, of Girard; 26, E. Birdsong, County Treasurer.

February 1—(in Wynnton,) infant child of J. H. Sikes; —, John E. Clark; 23, (at White Sulphur Springs,) Mrs. Martha A. Mitchell, of Columbus; 26, (in Girard,) John Godwin, builder of the city bridge; 28, (in Girard,) Mrs. Delilah Reed.

March 6—Joseph W. Thomas, former editor of the *Enquirer*: 15, Thos. E. Greenwood.

May 11—Mrs. Temperance Whitesides; 11, (in Wynnton,) James Philip, infant son of John E. Lamar.

June 8—Thomas Emmons, infant son of Thos. S. Spear; 10, Miss Amelia, daughter of James A. Bradford; 11, James McCoy, foreman of the machine shop of the Mobile and Girard Railroad, in Girard; 13, Mrs. A. H. Flewellen; 21, (in Girard,) Green B. Woodson; 19, William Rankin; 28, (in Girard,) Martha Elizabeth, infant daughter of J. C. Harris.

July 6—Reuben Allison, infant son of W. C. Gray; 12, (in Wynnton,) Mrs. Virginia A. Oliver; 21, (in Girard,) William Wommack; 23, (at Warm Springs, Meriwether,) John H. Davis, of Columbus.

August 3—William H. Lamar, Deputy Sheriff; 21, George W. Carey; 26, Miss Adora Rebecca, daughter of Joseph D. Hughes.

Sept. 9—John Joseph, infant son of James M. Everett; —, John M. Flournoy; 18, Miss Laura, daughter of Joseph D. Hughes; —, Dr. Richard H. Lockhart; 27, Mrs. Elizabeth Gammel, aged 115 years.

Oct. 13—(in Linnwood,) Dr. Thos. W. Dawson; 16, Dr. George S. Hardaway; 24, Victor S. Townsley; 9, Dr. Solon M. Grigg; 16, Willie E. DuBose; 30, (in Girard,) Miss Jeannette Phillips.

Nov. 14—Fidel Bachle; 29, John Lloyd.

Dec. 2—Cyprian, infant son of D. F. Willcox; —, Mrs. Ann Gambrill; 15, William H. Huff; 19, (in Richmond, Texas,) Hon. Mirabeau B. Lamar.

1860.

Railroad Projects—Political Excitement—Military Or-
ganizations.

The following was the result of the municipal election on
the second Saturday in December: Mayor, Willis S. Hol-
stead; Aldermen—1st Ward, E. Barnett, J. H. Merry; 2d,
Edward Croft, J. W. King; 3d, James M. Bivins, W. L.
Wornum; 4th, John Ligon, W. L. Salisbury; 5th, John
Quin, D. B. Thompson; 6th, James T. Daniel, John Durkin.
The opponents of Mr. Holstead for Mayor were Wm. Perry
and W. A. Tennille. Jas. M. Hughes was elected Marshal;
G. A. Huckeba, Deputy Marshal; Calvin Stratton, Clerk;
R. G. Mitchell, Treasurer; and Henry Harris, Sexton.

Council elected William Tilley, Clerk of the Market; John
Peabody, City Attorney; F. C. Ellison, City Physician;
Thomas Gilbert & Co., City Printers; Joseph E. Webster,
Wharfinger; C. F. Neuffer, Magazine Keeper; Mrs. Isabella
McGehee, Hospital Keeper. Port Wardens—Jas. M. Everett,
T. O. Douglass, Van Marcus, S. Ogletree, A. M. Kimbrough.

The report of the Treasurer showed that the city was in-
debted for bonds to the Mobile and Girard Railroad $300,000,
bonds to Opelika Branch Road $50,000, bonds to City Gas
Light Company $10,000, Muscogee Railroad stock $1,200,
stock for Opelika Railroad Depot $10,000, and stock for div-
idends in Gas Light Company $2,000.

Council made a contract, in February, with Messrs.
Goetchius & Hodges for the building of a new Market House
on Oglethorpe street, near St. Clair. Some of the citizens
filed an injunction a few days afterwards.

Messrs. J. A. Bradford, M. Barschall and S. R. Andrews,
assessors of real estate in the city, reported in February that

9

they had taken the census of Columbus, and gave the following statistics: White males 2,381, white females 2,394—total whites 4,755; colored males 1,013, colored females 1,328—total colored 2,341; total population 7,116. Value of real estate, $2,966,200. This enumeration included only the city proper, within the incorporated limits.

The *Enquirer* of the 10th of April announced that the Eagle Manufacturing Company had purchased the Howard Factory, and would run both establishments. It added: "We understand that these united Factories run 10,000 cotton and 1,300 woolen spindles; that they have 282 looms weaving cotton and woolen goods; that they consume nine bales of cotton and 1,000 pounds of wool' per day, and employ 500 hands, at an expense of $240 per day for their labor. The capital employed is $375,000."

Work was commenced on the Mobile and Girard Railroad Bridge this year, but was suspended after the construction of two of the piers, and the bridge was not finished until after the war.

S. B. Warnock was on the 30th of June elected an Alderman of the 3d Ward, in the place of Alderman Bivins, resigned. The whole city voted, and the election aroused considerable interest, from the fact that the candidates ran as friends or opponents of the re-election of Maj. Howard as President of the Mobile and Girard Railroad. Mr. Warnock was opposed to Major Howard's re-election, and received 350 votes to 299 for Mr. T. O. Douglas. Council had instructed its delegates to the Convention of stockholders to vote for Major Howard, but after this election it re-considered that vote and instructed them to vote for Wm. H. Mitchel, Esq. At the meeting of stockholders, Mr. Mitchel was elected without opposition.

There were several projects of improvement in whose behalf aid from the city was this year asked. There were the Opelika and Talledega, the Opelika and Oxford, and the La-

Grange Railroads, further aid to the Mobile and Girard Railroad, so as to extend it to Union Springs ; and a system of Water Works for the city. Council adopted an ordinance submitting to a vote of the people, on the first Saturday in July, the question of subscribing not exceeding $150,000 for the introduction of water into the city, and $100,000 to the Opelika and Talladega Railroad (now known as the Savannah and Memphis.) The vote was taken on each proposition separately. The subscription to the Railroad was approved by a vote of 206 to 27. The vote on the Water Works question stood—yeas 38, nays 187. The proposition thus defeated was to bring water into the city from the river above, by means of an aqueduct.

The tax returns of the county, made this year, showed 981 polls, number of slaves 6,164, free negroes 37, number of acres of land—first quality 1,983, second quality 2,568, third quality 27,926, pine land 176,883, value of land $1,800,474, value of city property $2,415,625, value of slaves $4,203,350, amount of money and solvent debts $3,076,128, amount of merchandise $1,078,905, amount of shipping or tonnage $17,-920, all other capital invested in stock of any kind $548,115, value of household and kitchen furniture over $300--$139,200, value of other property not before enumerated $407,796—total $13,687,486. This being the year immediately preceding the war, these statistics are interesting for comparison.

The census taken this year by the Federal authorities showed a white population in Columbus proper (not taking in Wynnton, &c.,) of 5,674, slaves 3,265, free negroes 100—total 9,039. The total population of Muscogee county, by this census, was 17,039.

Party politics ran very high this year, particularly after the election of Abraham Lincoln as President in November. The question of secession engaged the attention of the people of Columbus, as of every other city of the South. The Secession party had a majority in the city, though the co-operationists were pretty strong and made a stout contest. An organization called the "Southern Guard" was formed in Columbus very soon after the November election. It partook of a military character, with a Captain, Lieutenants and other officers. The old military companies of the city joined it. On the night of the 23d of December the city was brilliantly illuminated in honor of the secession of South Carolina. Some of the devices displayed by the arrangement of lights were very pretty and brilliant. It was a beautiful and imposing pageant. There was at the same time a very large meeting in Temperance Hall, which the several military companies attended in uniform. Spirited speeches were delivered. A torch-light procession through the streets, with banners and emblems, was a magnificent sight. Bonfires blazed in the streets, fireworks sparkled and hissed, and altogether it was an extraordinary and most exciting and impressive spectacle. Of the papers of the city, the *Times* advocated secession, the *Enquirer* co-operation, and the *Sun* had two editors, one of whom was a co-operationist and the other a separate State secessionist.

INCIDENTS.

A curious spectacle was presented at the wharf in the early part of January, by the steamers Oswichee and Munnerlyn lying high and dry out of the water. The river fell so rapidly on the night of the 2d as to leave them in that fix. The Munnerlyn was extricated on the 10th of January, without much damage. The Oswitchee was relieved on the 25th of January.

The residence of Joseph Rempert, on Troup street, was burnt on the 18th of January. The house belonged to John Quin.

About one hundred bales of cotton from Macon, en route for Apalachicola, arrived in Columbus on the 20th of January. The river trade was active, and Apalachicola flourishing then.

John H. Dorsett was fatally shot during a fight in the lower portion of the city, late in January. It was said that a man named McCollough shot him in self-defense.

Levi, son of John Rogers, was accidently shot and killed by another youth named George Odom, on the 20th of February, while they were shooting robins near the Muscogee Depot.

Mrs. Allen, wife of John Allen, of Girard, was badly burned by her dress taking fire on the 9th of March, and died two or three days afterwards.

· The jail of Muscogee county caught fire, on the morning of the 19th of March, from a chimney, and was destroyed. There were several prisoners in it, but none were hurt. The fire started inside the building.

The extensive furniture factory of Mr. Walton K. Harris, known as the "Novelty Works," was destroyed by fire on the evening of the 7th of April, with a large quantity of furniture, finished and unfinished. The loss was $14,000 or $15,000, and insurance about $8,000. The stable, kitchen and smoke-house of Capt. McAlister, on the adjoining lot, were also burnt.

A great bank robbery, discovered on the 10th of April, created no little astonishment and interest. It was found that about $45,500 had been stolen from the agency in Columbus of the Marine Bank of Savannah, of which Mr. L. G. Bowers was agent. Mr. Bowers offered a reward of $7,500 for the recovery of the money and the detection of the thief. Early on the morning of the 12th of April, a package containing $30,000 of the money was found on a little bridge in the outskirts of the city, near the Orphan Asylum; and later in the day $13,000 more of it was found secreted under the steps of a house in the same neighborhood. Mr. E. B. Holmes, the teller of the agency, was arrested and gave bond in the sum of $2,500, which was about the amount of the loss of the Bank.

On the night of the 12th of April, the extensive livery stable of Mr. A. Gamell, on Jackson street, was destroyed by fire, with several small buildings in the rear of the stable. Six mules and fifteen horses perished in the flames. The buggies and other vehicles were mostly saved, but 225 bales of hay and a large quantity of corn and fodder were burnt. The loss was not less than $15,000, only partly covered by insurance. The fire was believed to have been the work of an incendiary.

The steamer Oswichee was sunk at Francis Bend, on the 14th of April, while on her way from Columbus to Apalachicola. The passengers and crew all escaped. Most of the cotton floated off and was afterwards picked up.

The kitchens of Mr. F. S. Chapman and Mr. Tillman, on adjoining lots, were burnt by a fire on the night of the 29th of April, with two other small outbuildings.

John O'Brian, who lived in Girard and worked in Columbus, was killed on the Girard end of the bridge, on the 6th of May, by William B. Martin, of Girard. They had a difficulty, O'Brian used brick-bats, and Martin a pistol. The later was bound over in the sum of $2,500, but was never tried.

A young woman named Georgiana Daniel, living on Bridge street, committed suicide by taking laudanum on the 8th of July.

A young man named Louis Keistner, a shoemaker, was drowned in the river, between the falls and the lower bridge, on the 11th of July, while he was bathing.

The first bale of new cotton was received on the 26th of July. It was from the plantation of Col. C. B. Taliaferro, near Girard, and was sold at auction at 12½ cents per pound.

A stranger calling himself John Sley, drew money on a check presented to the agency of the Marine Bank, on the 31st of July, and the genuineness of the check being suspected, he was pursued, when he ran into the river, intending, no doubt, to swim across, but the strong current bore him down and he was drowned. His name was afterwards ascertained to be J. C. Adair.

Mrs. Melvina Morris, a young married lady, committed suicide by plunging into the river on the 4th of August. She had previously exhibited signs of mental derangement.

On the 29th of September, F. C. Johnson for the 2d, and John Hazelton for the 3rd, were elected Aldermen, to succeed Aldermen Croft and Warnock, resigned.

On the morning of the 1st of October, the residence of Mr. E. S. Greenwood, on upper Broad street, was burnt.

The brick building on the west side of Broad street, occupied by Hatcher & McGehee, Harrison & Pitts, and Mims & Perry, was burnt on the morning of the 1st of December.

The new Baptist Church, fronting on Randolph street, was dedicated on the 9th of December—the dedication sermon by Rev. Basil Manly.

PERSONAL.

C. R. Jewett was Presiding Elder of the Columbus District; A. T. Mann, stationed at St. Luke; J. S. Key at St. Paul; W. J. Wardlaw, Factory Mission; L. Pierce and A. G. Haygood, Girard and Pierce Chapel.

The County Officers were—John Hazelton, Sheriff; A. S. Rutherford, Clerk of the Superior Court; John Johnson, Ordinary; A. P. Jones, Clerk of the Inferior Court; Jordan Howell, Tax Collector; I. T. Brooks, Tax Receiver; J. A. Bradford, County Treasurer; William Jordan, Coroner; J. E. Lamar, County Surveyor.

M. G. Watson, Lemuel Lockhart, James Lloyd and —— Brock were constables of the two districts including the city.

Messrs. J. W. Warren and P. H. Colquitt were announced in June as editors and proprietors of the *Times*, Mr. Roswell Ellis having disposed of his interest to Capt. Colquitt, who was the principal editor at the time.

MARRIAGES.

January 1—Wm. M. Allen and Samantha I. Philips; 3, Joseph Mossman and Willhelmina Welding, Robert M. Sacro and Jane Oswalt; 5, James A.

Gun and Eliza Ann Brooks, James .T. Code and Mary E. Casey, Mitchell Blanton and Mary J. Sharp ; 7, Robert C. Miller and Ann M. Osborn ; 8, Thomas Key and Louisa A. Carr ; 12, Haywood L. Spann and Sarah A. Baldwin ; 14, William Clegg and Margaret Shavers ; 16, James Holt and Elizabeth Sanders ; 17, John A. G. Myers and Sarah C. West, Jesse J. Bradford and Mary A. McAlister ; 19, William J. Pittman and Sarah U. Thomas, David Gibson and Sarah Taylor ; 23, George Cane and Malinda Fittz ; 26, Thomas C. C. McEachren and Louisa Hackney ; 30, James Osborn and Rebecca Rentfroe.

February 2—Wm. F. Kelly and Elizabeth Brittain, Thomas Dillard and Frances M. Collins ; 9, James F. Lewis and Louisa J. Foster, Edwin W. Jackson and Mary A. L. Nobles, Levi S. Blake and Mary Megea ; 12, John Mills and Jane M. Glaze ; 13, James P. Blount and Priscilla Chessan ; 14, Alexander Aids and Laura McGraston, Mathew F. Wilson and Temperance Burkes ; 25, George W. Snowden and Susan Maples.

March 4—Norman R. Williams and Mary Barfield ; 10, Geo. W. F. Newsom and Cynthia A. R. Bryan ; 19, George Scroggins and Sarah Yearty ; 24, Augustus L. Forman and Martha V. Hubbart ; 29, Wm. J. Edwards and Mary M. Moore.

April 1—Philo Johnson and Frances Ruse ; 3, Wm. F. Snelling and Bettie A. Lofton ; 4, John B. Scott and Virginia A. Howard ; 5, Samuel W. Fail and Mary A. E. Milton ; 11, Esau Pike and Rebecca Thompson ; 17, Jeremiah B. Broadaway and Elizabeth M. E. Lindley ; 19, George W. Pike and Lucinda Brock ; 22, George Clover and Frances Glaze ; 23, Frederick Franchand and Rosalia A. Sagnet ; 28, Joseph Phillips and Madora Comer ; 29, Isaac Lewis and Mary Lewis.

May 1—Wm. Darden and Mahulda Chadwick ; 2, Samuel Blair and Emily E. Harris ; 10, Anthony Clegg and Mary P. Long ; 12, Benjamin R. Wilson and Margaret Willis, Oliver S. Bennett and Lucy C. Marable ; 13, Nathan Watson and Rebecca Mote ; 15, William L. Tillman and Hattie E. Clements ; 17, Thos. L. Tinnan and Mary L. Hoffman ; 21, William W. Flewellen and Caroline L. Love ; 26, Thos. J. Darden and Mary L. Echols ; 31, Whitford Smith and Jane Allen, John S. Jenkins and Mary Baldwin.

June 4—Thos. Naftel and E. O'Donnell ; 7, Gilbert Watson and Mary C. Blake, James Brooks and Catharine Bryant ; 10, James Price and Harriet Mitchell, John H. Kimbrough and Frances H. Isler, August Michael and Margaret Merkel ; 12, Patrick Foran and Elizabeth McElrath ; 14, George W. Buttan and Louisa Rice ; 15, John T. Stubbs and Emily L. Gerke ; 19, John D. Lewis and Lucinda Thomas ; 25, Moses G. Morris and Melvina Olive, Joseph Williamson and Adaline M. Boyd ; 26, Alex. D. Brown and Mary J. Silva ; 27, Henry H. A. Gabriel and Sarah E. Bankston, Charles W. Stewart and Sarah C. Brown, George R. Flournoy and Julia A. Brown ; 28, James Britton and Lurania Morris.

July 4—Calvin S. Bryant and Mary A. Swetman ; 10, Daniel F. Booton and Martha B. McGruder, Benjamin A. Clark and Virginia S. Kimbrough ; 12,

James Story and Queen Victoria Philips ; 22, Jesse Barns and Mary Fletcher; 25, Simeon D. Pope and Minerva A. Davie ; 26, Benjamin Brock and Malissa Thompson ; 31, John C. Parr and Georgia S. Evans.

August 1—James Covey and Elizabeth Till, James S. Paullin and Sarah E. Borders, James Clegg and Martha R. Layfield ; 2, Anglet Seal and Elizabeth Taylor, James M. Bussey and Mary A. Brannon; 5, Thos. M. Ross and Catharine D. Halley ; 15, Tyra Ramsey and Susan Broadnax ; 21, James Patillo and Sarah Fletcher ; 29, James W. Stanfield and Martha Baird.

September 4—John L. Duffee and Henrietta A. Blackmar, Ellison Conway and Sarah A. Jeffries, Wm. Thompson and Emily Mylan ; 9, James T. Osborn and Laura E. House, David Smith and Celia Smith, Wm. Jackson and Mary Marler ; 10, Frederick Stewart and Fannie J. Guthrie ; 13, Edward W. Blau and Leonora Parish, Thomas Hunt and Mary M. Simpson ; 16, David R. Cox and Mary Sutton; 20, Benjamin F. Hopkins and Sarah B. Davis, Joseph Raily and Josaphine Bellflower ; 22, Ephraim H. Skinner and Mary F. E. Perryman ; 24, Colquitt M. Holland and Frances A. Culverson ; 25, Wm. M. Kelly and Elizabeth Jones ; 30, Andrew J. Edwards and Matilda L. Alford.

October 1—Irvin C. Mabry and Margaret Read; 2, John S. Bryant and Martha J. Johnson ; 5, Zachariah T. Howard and Martha A. E. Green; 8, Elijah F. Pasey and Elizabeth Coulter ; 10, John R. Young and Rebecca E. Knight; 13, John J. McKendree, jr., and Samantha A. E. Folds ; 18, Dr. E. F. Colzey and Mary Hudson ; 21, James M. Frazier and Missouri Smith ; 23, Charles J. Farber and Salina Kendall ; 28, John Milton and Elizabeth S. Simpson, Felix G. Lloyd and Caroline Hackney ; 30, Francis M. Jeter and Julia Lindsey.

November 1—Daniel R. Bize and Mary L. Harris ; 15, Bassil M. Conway and Mary Tillery ; 17, John H. Clegg and Martha A. Smith ; 22, Rolf. S. Sanders and Martha C. Billing, Eli S. Langford and Dorcas A. Gilpin ; 27, William B. Screws and Mary P. Culbertson.

December 4—Thos. J. Hammock and Maria J. Spurlin, Aaron C. Trotman and Anna E. Birdsong ; 6, Aaron Land and Angia Lokey ; 12, Isaac A. Mooney and Hattie M. Jackson ; 13, James M. Crockett and Elizabeth Hill ; 17, Levi D. Philips and Margaret S. Williams ; 20, Giles T. Williams and Anna A. Brown ; 24, Abel Smith and Thirza B. Kirvin ; 25, John Kelly and Frances Page, Wm. H. D. Cram and Emily C. Giddings; 28, John L. Pickett and Mary Crockett ; 30, Joseph Land and Frances Lokey ; 31, Calvin Duffield and Henrietta Russell.

DEATHS.

January 4—Child of Mr. Garrard, Powell Robinson, Mr. McArdle ; 11, Mr. McGee ; 12, child of Mr. Matheson, child of Mr. Horn, child of Mr. Duffy ; 15, Mrs. Brith, Mr. Storckel, Isaac M. Ralls, child of Mr. Wynne, child of Mr. Needham, child of Mr. Horn ; 16, Mr. Watts ; 18, child of Mr. Duffy, Mrs. V. Grice, Mr. Dixon, child of Mr. Booher, Mr. Bright ; 24, child of Mr. Treadwell ; 27, Blake Robinson ; 29, Hampton Horton, child of Mr. Grant.

February 2—James Ligon, Samuel Hall, child of Mr. Brice; 18, child of Mr. Copeland, H. Hurd, William Daniel, Amanda V. Williford, child of Mr. Silver, Patrick Murphy, child of Mr. Sherly, child of A. Picket, ; 25, child of J. B. Starker, child of Mr. Sherman, Mr. Kennedy, child of Mrs. McArdel.

March 6—Child of A. Brannon, child of Mr. Matheson, Mr. Britton, child of Mr. Hunt, child of H. Nance; 10, child of Mr. Martin. Mrs. B. Walker, William Connor, child of Mr. Hicks; 13, child of Mr. Cadman, Mr. McCairn, Mrs. Thomas; 16, child of Mrs. Bonds, Miss Peabody; 17, Lucinda Britt, Wm. McMichael; 18, Emily Coursey, Mr. Mattox.

No reports published for the months intervening between above and the following months:

October 12—Child of Mr. Boyd, child of Mr. Preer; 14, child of Mrs. Delonaugh; 19, child of Mr. Bailey; 20, Leonard Black, Mr. Raiford, Jasper Preer; 25, Mr. Talbot, child of John O'Bryan; 28, child of Jesse Bradford, child of Mr. Bivin.

November 1—Child of Mrs. Emily Moottey; 6, Neil Fulgham; child of Mr. Hall; 7, Harvy Nance; 14, Mr. Paine, child of Mrs. Cooper; 18, Henrietta Wood, Mrs. Moore, Mrs. Murphy, Mr. Bumbush; 19, child of James Smith, child of Mrs. Robison.

(FROM THE NEWSPAPERS.)

April 30—Henry Epping, infant son of S. H. Hill.

May 4—Carolina Lucy, child of L. T. Downing; 7, Victoria Core, infant child of J. W. King; —, James Redd, Jr.; —, Rev. Wm. H. Grace.

June 19—Yelverton, son of John W. King; 27, Mrs. Sarah Ann, wife of Thomas Ragland; 28, Mrs. Martha Irene Abbott.

July 4—Sallie Georgia, daughter of Van Marcus; 9, Mrs. Juliana Hulen; 11, Mrs. Nian W. Chalfant; —, Samuel J. Hicks; —, Isaac T. Cary; 26, Dr. Gilbert Reese.

August 1—Eula, infant daughter of Hatch Cook; 24, L. W. Pryor.

September 5—(near Pine Knot Springs) Thomas, son of Thomas DeWolf; 15, George Van Doren, infant son of James A. Girdner; 24, Charles Henry, infant son of J. H. Weeks.

October 11—Mrs. Mary Lamar.

November 30—Benjamin H. Hurt; —, H. Bishop.

December 18—B. Y. Martin.

1861.

First Year of the War—Military Companies.

The election for municipal officers, on the second Saturday in December last, was contested in a lively manner. There were four candidates for Mayor—D. B. Thompson, F. G. Wil-

kins, W. N. Hutchins and William Perry. The vote stood—
Thompson 300, Wilkins 281, Hutchins 186, Perry 140. The
following gentlemen were elected Aldermen : 1st Ward, G.
W. Dillingham, T. S. Spear ; 2d, J. F. Bozeman, F. C. John-
son ; 3d, J. Hazleton, T. O. Douglass ; 4th, John Ligon, W.
L. Salisbury ; 5th, E. Croft, Van Marcus ; 6th, George Stein,
J. M. Bivins. .James M. Hughes was elected Marshal ; Geo.
A. Huckeba, Deputy Marshal ; George W. Jones, Clerk of
Council ; Jas. D. Johnson, Treasurer ; H. M. Harris, Sexton.

Council elected John Peabody, City Attorney ; Joseph E.
Webster, Wharfinger ; C. F. Neuffer, Magazine Keeper ;
Mrs. Isabella McGehee, Hospital Keeper ; —— Jordan, Bridge
Keeper ; W. R. Jones, Clerk of the Market ; *Times*, City
Printer ; A. Ingmire, James M. Everett, W. S. Holstead, Jas.
M. Denson and Sam'l Law, Port Wardens. Health Officers—
Dr. Flewellen, B. F. Coleman, A. O. Blackmar, Dr. Baird, J.
Kyle, T. H. Sloan, R. W. Denton, Hatch Cook, Joseph Drum-
right, James Kivlin, John Seeley, D. S. Porter.

The political excitement caused by the election of Lincoln
as President continued and increased. The Georgia Legislature had called a State Convention to consider the question
of Secession, and had appointed the 2d of January as the day
for the election of delegates. The two parties in Georgia
were the immediate Secessionists and the Co-Operationists.
The former nominated Hon. H. L. Benning, Jas. N. Ramsey,
Esq., and A. S. Rutherford as their candidates for delegates
for Muscogee ; the Co-Operationists nominated Hon. Hines
Holt, N. L. Howard and Porter Ingram, Esqrs. The Secession ticket was elected by a vote of 944 to 459. Notwithstanding the great excitement and the vast importance of the
issue, the vote of the county was two hundred short of that
cast at the Presidential election in November previous.

The several Military Companies of Columbus were among
the first to signify to Gov. Brown their readiness to respond
to any call for the defence of the State. This they did before
Georgia had seceded.

The Georgia State Convention passed the ordinance of Se-
cession on the 19th of January, and on the night of the 21st
Columbus was brilliantly illuminated in honor of the event.
Cannons were fired, a great torchlight procession, with trans-
parencies and banners, paraded the streets; the Military
Companies of the city then organized—viz: the Columbus
Guards, City Light Guards, Georgia Grays, Muscogee Mounted Rangers, and company D of the Southern Guard, also Fire
Company No. 5, which had assumed a military character,
participated in uniform. The illumination was general and
the whole display was a very imposing and inspiring one.

The "Muscogee Mounted Rangers," a new military company raised by Col. John A. Strother, in view of the probability
of a war between the States, was organized in February.

A Board of Trade was organized in Columbus on the 29th
of March, by the election of the following officers: President,
R. M. Gunby; Vice President, H. S. Estes; Secretary, Geo.
W. Dillingham.

All of the organized military companies of Columbus were
prompt to tender their services to the support of the cause of
the Confederacy. The first one called out was Company "D"
of the Southern Guard, Captain Wilkins. It was called out
by Governor Brown, in response to a requisition by President Davis for two thousand Georgia Troops. This company
left Columbus, to rendezvous at Macon, on the first of April.
The following is a list of officers and members of the company, made out a day or two before its departure. It received several recruits afterwards:

COMPANY "D," SOUTHERN GUARD.

Captain—F. G. Wilkins. Lieutenants—1st, James N. Ramsey; 2d, Geo.
W. Atkinson; 3d, W. R. Turman. Sergeants—1st, Lawrence W. Wall; 2d,
James W. Dennis; 3d, James M. Wiley; 4th, James J. Lovelace; 5th, Chas.
H. Althiser. Corporals—1st, Peter Key; 2d, Thomas Sweet; 3d, Wm. H.
Thompson; 4th, M. G. Watson.

Privates—William F. Allen, Wilkins Brooks, Reason Banks, Wm. H. Bry-
ant, Chas. W. Baker, Frank Bussey, John Barker, Wm. Baker, James Clegg,
Wm. Benton, Robert H. Clinton, Frank Collier, Luke Conly, George W.
Cooper, Seaborn Cook, Junius Currence, Burwell M. Denson, Richard

Deshaser, Christopher Edwards, Stephen Etchinson, Patrick Foran, J. E. Flynn, Nath. C. Ferguson, William L. Foyle, Jno. Fletcher, Wm. Hall, Moses Hall, James Henderson, John P. Hellings, Jos. B. Hagans, Wm. Holstead, Seaborn L. Jones, Randolph Key, Drewry A. Lawrence, Mat. Murphy, James McElrath, George Magnus, Richard Massey, John C. McCurdy, Milton Malone, Alex. McDaniel, Leva D. Matthews, James H. Nix, Vincent Ogletree, Levi D. Phelps, David Purcell, John Chappel Reese, Aug. B. Ridenhour, T. J. Smith, Lewis Simmons, Jason T. Smith, Thos. Sturdevant, John W. Seats, Isaac Smith, Geo. F. Taylor, J. W. Tucker, Jeptha Wiggins, James Wood, Jacob P. White, Clayton Wilson, Leonard H. Young, A. P. Sanderland, James Lynah, James P. Lawrence—61.

This company was at Macon incorporated into the First Georgia Regiment, of which 1st Lieutenant James N. Ramsey was elected Colonel. The regiment passed through Columbus in a few days after its organization, en route for Pensacola.

COLUMBUS GUARDS.

Capt. P. J. Semmes having been appointed a Brigadier General by Governor Brown, resigned his position as Captain of the Columbus Guards, and on the 15th of April Lieut. Roswell Ellis was elected Captain of that company; W. C. Hodges, 1st Lieut., W. G. Clemons, 2d, and J. M. Everett, 3d. This company left Columbus on the 16th of April for Savannah, the place of rendezvous, with 112 men rank and file. It was there made Company G of Second Georgia Regiment, of which P. J. Semmes was elected Colonel. After a short service on Tybee island, it was ordered to Brunswick, Ga., and thence in July, 1861, to Virginia. The following account of the services of this company during the war, and list of its members and casualties at various times, we copy from Haddock's Directory of Columbus:

This company furnished from among its privates more officers than any other Company, some of them rising to the position of Colonels. In Virginia they were attached to Toombs' Georgia Brigade. They participated in the following engagements, besides numerous skirmishes:

April 16, 1862, siege of Yorktown; June 27, 1862, Garnet's Farm; July 1, 1862, Malvern Hill; Aug. 29, 1862, Thoroughfare Gap; Aug. 30, 1862, Second Manassas; Sept. 17, 1862, Sharpsburg; Dec. 13, 1862, Fredericksburg; May 3, 1863, Siege of Suffolk; July 2 and 3, 1863, Gettysburg; July 25, 1863, Thornton River; Sept. 19, 20, 1863, Chickamauga; Oct. 28, 1863, Lookout Valley; Nov. 16, 1863, Campbell's Station; Nov. 18 to 30, 1863, siege of Knoxville; Dec. 14, 1863, Bean Station; Jan. 17, 1864, Dandridge; May 6, 1864,

Wilderness; May 8th to 14th, 1864; Spottsylvania; May 23 to 26, 1864, Hanover Junction; May 28th to 30th, 1864, Totopotomy; June 1st to 6th, 1864, Second Cold Harbor; June 17, 1864, Bermuda Hundreds; June 18th to 30th, 1864, siege of Petersburg; Aug. 14, 1864, Deep Bottom; Aug. 16, 1864, Fussell's Mills; Sept. 29, 1864, Fort Gilmer; Sept: 30, 1864, Fort Harrison; Oct. 7, 1864, Darbytown; Oct. 13, 1864, Darbytown Road; April 2, 1865, Petersburg; April 9, 1865, Appomattox.

When the war closed, they were few in numbers, most of them having been killed, or died in the service of their country.

Officers:—Capt. Paul J. Semmes, elected Col. 2d Ga., May, '61, promoted Brigadier General December, '61, died from wounds received at Gettysburg, July, 1863.

Roswell Ellis, 1st Lieutenant, promoted Captain May, 1861, and Adjutant General of Brigade December, 1863.

W. C. Hodges, 2d Lieutenant, promoted 1st Lieutenant, May, 1861, and Lieutenant Colonel 17th Georgia, and subsequently Colonel.

W. G. Clemons, 3d Lieutenant, promoted Adjutant, April, 1862, and Major Cumming's Brigade, March, 1863.

J. M. Everett, 4th Lieutenant, promoted 3d Lieutenant May, 1861, and died in Columbus, summer 1863.

J. S. Allen, jr., 1st Sergeant, promoted to Lieutenant, 1862, and Adjutant 2d Georgia.

J. M. Denson, 2d Sergeant. promoted 1st Lieutenant.

Van Marcus, 3d Sergeant, transferred to Quarter Master Department, Columbus.

R. Potter, 4th Sergeant, promoted Lieutenant and killed at Malvern Hill.

J. D. Carter, jr., 1st Corporal.

Wm. Redd, 2d Corporal, transferred and promoted Lieutenant and Adjutant.

J. E: Sanders, 3d Corporal, promoted Sergeant.

T. Chaffin, jr., 4th Corporal, promoted Captain, April, 1862.

Rev. J. H. DeVotie, Chaplain.

Privates:—J. C. Apple; S. R. Andrews, jr., transferred to artillery; W. L. Anderson, G. H. Abercrombie; Wiley Abercrombie, promoted Sergeant Major of Regiment to Gen. Canty's Brigade; O. S. Acee, A. E. Acee; W. A. Barden, promoted Lieutenant Colonel; T. M. Barnard; J. F. Birch, promoted Lieutenant, killed at the Crater, Petersburg, 1864; John Ballard, died near Richmond; J. J. Bradford, transferred and promoted Major 37th Georgia; P. S. Bradford, transferred and promoted Lieutenant Co. B, 37th Georgia; W. Banks, killed at Atlanta, July, 1864; E. Banks, killed at Resaca, July, 1864; E. B. Briggs, promoted Sergeant Major and Captain and aid to Gen. Semmes; C. A. Bailey, killed at Gettysburg, July, 1863; Wm. K. Bedell, J. G. Blalock, J. R. Bedell; H. B. Beecher, Sergeant Major, 2d Georgia; T. E. Blanchard, promoted Captain and transferred to Co. B, 37th Georgia; T. M. Beasley, promoted Lieutenant;

D. B. Booher, promoted Lieutenant and killed at Crater, Petersburg, 1864; Jos. D. Bethune, transferred to Nelson Rangers; John G. Bethune; Wm. A. Brown, transferred to Nelson Rangers; W. B. Butt, transferred to Nelson Rangers; R. A. Bacon; A. A. Coleman, transferred to Telegraph Department; C. Coleman, transferred and appointed drill officer; T. G. Coleman; T. M. Carter, transferred to Nelson Rangers; A. A. Calhoun, transferred to Nelson Rangers; J. C. Calhoun, promoted to Captain and Ass't Q. M.; J. A. Cody, transferred and promoted Captain on Gen. Cumming's staff; J. J. Clapp, O. Cromwell; W. G. Croft, transferred and promoted Lieutenant artillery; J. H. Crowell, transferred and promoted Captain; W. S. Davis, transferred and promoted Lieutenant, killed at Spottsylvania; A. B. Davis; R. A. Daniel, transferred to Nelson Rangers; S. M. Dixon; B. H. Dixon, died in Richmond, Va., 1861; J. G. DeVotie; G. W. Dillingham, promoted Capt., and transferred to Commisary Department, 1863; D. T. Dawson; M. D. Doney, died in Columbus, 1864; James Dubose, J. A. Dunn; Robert Enderman, died from wounds received at Chickamauga; J. A. Fogle; T. T. Fogle, promoted Lieutenant and killed in battle Wilderness; W. F. Fergusson; J. L. Girdner, transferred and promoted Lieutenant; H. H. Hall, W. F Hall, J. C. Hogan; W. R. Houghton, promoted O. Sgt.; R. N. Howard, transferred and promoted Lieutenant; R. M. Howard, J. T. Howard, A. Harris, J. W. Hughes; B. H. Hudson, transferred and promoted Lieutenant; D. C. Henry died in 1863; B. H. Holt, promoted Lieutenant Colonel; J. H. Hicks; W. N. Hawks, Jr., transferred; W. N. Hutchins, transferred, promoted Captain and killed at Chickamauga; Harris Johnson, killed at Wilderness; Arthur Ingmire, acting Q. M. of Company; J. T. Johnson, transferred, promoted and killed at Wilderness; L. Q. Johnson; W. E. Jones, Jr., promoted Sergeant, May, 1861; Boykin Jones; W. Jones; S. L. Jones, transferred to navy and promoted Midshipman; J. E. King; W. D. Kyle, transferred and promoted Captain; B. C. Luckie; E. M. Luckie; J. L. Lindsay; J. B. Lindsay; James R. Lively; W. M. Moses; Allen Matthews; M. J. Moses, transferred and appointed Surgeon; T. H. Muse, killed at Gettysburg; W. A. McDougald, transferred and promoted to Lieutenant; W. A. Martiniere, transferred to Nelson Rangers; J. R. Munn, died 1861; G. W. Mays, promoted Lieut. and killed at Gettysburg; Etter Martin; C. McBride; T. J. Nuckolls, transferred and promoted Lieutenant; J. S. Owens, promoted Lieutenant in Nelson Rangers; W. T. Patterson, promoted Lieutenant and killed at Chickamauga; R. C. Pope; J. O. Perry, died 1861; W. H. Perrine; G. H. Peabody; T. G. Paine; J. T. Park, transferred and promoted Lieutenant; S. R. Pitts, transferred and promoted Lieut.; George Phelps; T. F. Ridenhour; N. L. Redd, promoted Lieutenant; Wm. Redd, promoted Lieutenant; J. K. Redd, Jr., promoted aid to General Semmes, raised a Company and was Captain, killed near Petersburg, 1864; N. B. Roberts; G. G. Ragland, transferred and made Captain Nelson Rangers; A. E. Ragland, transferred and promoted Captain; O. S. Ragland, transferred and promoted Lieutenant; G. G. Rucker; Z. C. Rucker, R. M. Rutherford, transferred and promoted; A. H. Rutherford, transferred and promoted; C. R. Russell, transferred to Company K., promoted Captain 1861; E. S. Shorter, transferred and promoted; L. G. Schuessler; C. V. Smith, transferred and promoted in Wheeler's Cavalry; J. H. Sanders; J. H. Slade, killed at Sharpsburg; W. S. Shepherd, transferred, promoted Captain and Lieutenant-Colonel; E. G. Stewart, promoted Lieutenant and Adjutant; I. C.

Spivey, killed at Sharpsburg ; **D. C.** Seymour, transferred and promoted Captain ; **W.** Walker, transferred ; **J. A.** Weems ; David Ware, transferred and promoted Lieutenant ; **M. W.** Wooten ; C. H. Williams, transferred to 1st Ga.; **M. A.** Williams, transferred to Nelson Rangers ; John Wise ; **A. C.** Wingfield, transferred ; **J. H.** Ware, transferred and promoted Lieutenant, killed at Mechanicsville ; Wm. **A.** Young, transferred.

The following is a list of the members of Columbus Guards present at the final surrender of the army by Gen. R. E. Lee, at Appomattox Court House :

Thomas Chaffin, Jr., Captain ; Eugene Stewart, Lieutenant. W. R. Houghton ; J. C. DuBose ; W. L. Anderson ; T. G. Coleman ; Martin Etter ; J. G. Blaylock ; W. F. Hall ; G. G. Rucker ; G. W. Dillingham ; John O. Payne ; W. M. Moses.

In June, 1873, the company re-organized and received arms from the State, and are now well drilled and in good discipline. The officers elected on its re-organization were : W. S. Shepherd, Captain ; Chas. H. Williams, 1st Lieutenant ; Wm. N. Hawks, 2d Lieutenant ; Thos. W. Grimes, 3d Lieutenant ; Cliff. B. Grimes, 4th Lieutenant. At the present time (1875) the following are the commissioned officers : W. S. Shepherd, Captain ; T. W. Grimes, 1st Lieutenant ; Cliff. B. Grimes, 2d ; J. J. Clapp, 3d.

HOME GUARD.

About the middle of April, a large company called the Home Guard, composed of men from 45 to 70 years of age, was formed, and organized by the election of R. A. Ware, Captain ; John A. Urquhart, 1st Lieutenant ; Hines Holt, 2d Lieutenant ; J. J. McKendree, 3d Lieutenant ; J. M. Hughes, 1st Sergeant. This company numbered upwards of 90 members.

CITY LIGHT GUARDS.

The City Light Guards were the next Columbus company called into active service. They were ordered to report at Norfolk, Va., and left for that place on the 20th of April. The following muster-roll and war-record of this company are also copied from Haddock's Directory :

Enlisted in the Southern Cause, April 19th, 1861, and were sent to Norfolk, Va., while the Navy Yard was still burning. At Norfolk they became a part of 2d Georgia Battalion of Infantry, and on the 20th of May, 1861, were engaged from battery at Sewell's Point with the enemy's vessels, Star of the West and Steam Tug, carrying cannon. In this, the first engagement in Virginia, they succeeded in disabling and driving off the vessels. Remaining at Norfolk eleven months, they were ordered to Goldsboro, and afterwards to Wilmington, North Carolina. Here they were re-organized May, 1862, by the election of Lieutenant C. J. Moffett, Captain, and were ordered to Petersburg, Va., from that time becoming part of the

Great Army of Northern Virginia, taking part in the battles around Richmond, Fredericksburg, Chancellorsville, Wilderness, Gettysburg, Petersburg, Warmville, &c., suffering severely in every campaign, and finally surrendered with Gen. R. E. Lee, at the fatal Appomattox Court House, the first and only time the Company was surrendered during the entire war between the States. The members of this Company having gained an enviable reputation in the service of their country, when the smoke of battle was over returned with equal energy to the quiet pursuits of life, and are all to-day active, useful members of society, endeavoring to place themselves and section in their former condition of prosperity.

P. H. Colquitt, Captain afterwards Colonel of 46th Ga. Reg. 1st Infantry, and killed at Chickamauga. Charles J. Moffett, 1st Lieutenant, elected Captain at the re-organization in 1862, promoted to Major 2d Ga. Battalion Infantry after battle of Gettysburg, Pennsylvania. J. A. Shingleur, 2d Lieutenant, in 1862 went upon staff of Gen. S. G. French, afterwards promoted to Major on staff. F. S. Chapman, 2d Lieutenant, resigned 1861, raised a Company and joined Georgia Regiment. H. M. Sapp, elected 1st Lieutenant at re-organization May,1862, and subsequently Captain. R. B. Lockhart, ensign. Rev. Thos. H. Jordan, Chaplain; V. H. Taliaferro, surgeon. W. H. Williams, 1st Sergeant, promoted Brevt. 2d Lieutenant, May, 1861; A. M. Luria, 2d Sergeant, promoted Lieutenant, and killed at battle Seven Pines, June, 1862; E. V. White, 3d Sergeant, promoted to engineer on Steamer Merrimac; W. D. Mathews, Corporal; J. J. McKendree, Jr., Corporal. John Cook, Quartermaster, discharged from disability. Geo. B. Young, Commissary, promoted Lieutenant of Artillery, December, 1861.

PRIVATES—S. W. Alexander, transferred; R. Bugg; H. Brown, killed at Chancellorsville, May, 1863; J. G. Brown, transferred; E. L. Bailey, killed near Gettysburg, July, 1863; Scott Bussey, died in Richmond, December, 1862; G. M. Bryan, transferred; R. A. Chambers, promoted Adjutant 2d Ga. Battalion, afterwards Captain General Canty's staff; Henry W. Chapman; James Cargill, wounded at Petersburg, June 1864. O. C. Cleveland, James J. Carnes; H. H. Colquitt, promoted to Lieutenant, General Colquitt's staff; C. C. Dunn, killed at Petersburg, June, 1864; T. L. Devore, discharged from disability, December, 1861; G. W. Doles; Mark Daily, detailed to Q. M. department; T. Deaton, killed at Gettysburg, July, 1863; T. T. Edmunds; Z. M. Estes, transferred to Q. M. department, Richmond; J. S. Esler, transferred to Q. M. department, Richmond; W. S. Freeman, transferred to cavalry and promoted Sergeant; Jas. Fricker, Thomas J. Garrison, E. Goldman, J. D. Godwin; S. Lowther, wounded at Petersburg, June 1863; J. H. Loeb; C. C. McGehee, transferred to Q. M. department, Columbus; M. Metzga, discharged by substitution; E. McDonald, discharged from disability; W. W. Martin; Z. N. Mayo, died since war; W. McKendree; J. B. O'Neil, killed at Fredericksburg, December, 1861; Wm. Nesbitt transferred to Ala. Regiment; J. B. Oliver, transferred to Q. M. department, Columbus; J. T. Odom, missing; Albert Porter, discharged; R. Z. Rucker; W. S. Robinson, promoted to Adjutant 2d Ga. Battalion; J. J. Reese, J. P. Ryan, discharged from wounds at Gettysburg; M. Riley; W. C. Seats, discharged; P. T. Schley, Jr.; Ed. B. Schley, detailed to surgeon department; G. P. Shepperson, missing; L. C. Strong, discharged from disability; Isaac Sterne; R. Sheridan; C. A. Shivers, transferred to Signal corps; G. E. Thomas, promoted to Ordnance Sergeant, department Petersburg; H. M. L. Torbett, promoted Sergeant; C. F. Taliaferro, discharged from disability; V. H. Taliaferro, promoted to surgeon 2d Ga. Battalion, May, 1861, and Colonel of Cavalry, 1862; M. Thweatt, discharged; S. T. Thweatt, died in Richmond, December, 1864; W. J. Underwood, transferred; D. D.

Updegraf; W. C. Vincent, transferred; E. P. Wagner, killed at Culpepper C. H., August, 1863; T. Waldren, transferred to signal corps; W. R. Wilkerson; A. M. Kimbrough, promoted 2d Leutenant, died Jan'y, 1865; G. J. Peacock, promoted 2d Lieutenant. March, 1863; W. J. Mims; A. Young, promoted Captain of Artillery, 1861; J. Adams. discharged from disability, since dead ; — Sullivan, transferred to artillery, killed ; Henry Henes, transferred to scout duty, died since the war ; W. J. Alston ; J. C. Brown ; J. C. Calhoun ; James Davis ; H. Fields; B. E. Ledbetter ; George Stovall ; D. Saxon ; L. A. Roberts ; R. Johnson ; James Williams ; — Huff ; C. C. Shepperson, promoted Sergeant ; B. S. Shepperson ; W. H. Mims ; Thos. D. Threwitts, died since the war.

The following were the members present at the surrender of Gen. R. E. Lee, 9th April, 1865 :

Maj. C. J. Moffett, commanding 2d Georgia Battalion ; G. J. Peacock, Lieutenant commanding ; H. M. L. Torbet, 3d Sergeant ; J. P. Parker, 3d Corporal.

PRIVATES—Chas. E. Booher, Thos. F. Brown, James J. Carnes, H. W. Chapman, John M. Coleman, George W. Doles, P. J. Golden, Thomas M. Golden, George W. Henderson, J. E. Jenkins, B. E. Johnston, Grigsby T. Long, Uriah P. Mitchell, Wesley A. Oliver, Ben. S. Shepperson, George W. Stovall, Charlton Thompson, W. R. Wilkerson.-

In 1872 the company re-organized, and elected the following officers : Captain, C. J. Moffett ; W. H. Williams, 1st Lieutenant ; G. J. Peacock. 2d Lieutenant; F L. Brooks, 2d Brev. Lieut. At the present writing (1875) the following are the commissioned officers : W. A. Little. Captain ; F. L. Brooks, 1st Lieutenant ; A. W. Brantley, 2d Lieutenant ; John C. Cheney, 2d Brevet Lieutenant.

GEORGIA GRAYS.

The Georgia Grays took their departure from Columbus on the 7th of May, for Macon, the place of rendezvous of the 5th Georgia regiment, of which they were made a part. Of this regiment, John K. Jackson was elected Colonel, and W. L. Salisbury, Major. It was first sent to Pensacola, and afterwards did gallant service in opposing Rosecrans and Sherman —suffering severely at Murfreesboro and Chickamauga, and remaining in the service to the close of the war. We again copy from the Directory :

Officers—John F. Iverson, Captain, promoted Colonel in December, 1862. W. E. Sandeford, 1st Lieutenant, resigned 1861. W. L. Salisbury, 2d Lieutenant, elected Major, 11th May, 1861. L. M. Burrus, Bvt. 2d Lieutenant, promoted Captain, 1862. W. J. Dillon, Sergeant, elected Lieutenant, 1861, discharged, May, 1862. W. R. Wood, Sergeant. J. N. M. Reese, Sergeant, elected Lieutenant, 1861. A. T. Calhoun, Sergeant, elected Lieut., 1862. W. I. Strupper, Corporal, promoted 5th Sergt., 1861. T. Ribero, Corporal, killed at Chickamauga, September 19th, 1863. John Barber, Corporal, discharged. M. V. Cook, Corporal, wounded at Murfreesboro.

Privates—R. Anthony; John Avery, missing; Eli M. Averett, elected Lieutenant in 1862; G. Banks, wounded and discharged Dec. 31, 1862, at battle Murfreesboro; W. Banks; A. J. Boland, transferred to 2d Ga. Battallion; T. Brown, killed at Chickamauga, September 19, 1863; J. Baxley; Richard Brannon; T. Carrol, discharged, August, 1862; J. P. Chapman; W. Carington, discharged, lost leg at Murfreesboro; J. Courtney, discharged from wounds; William Clark, discharged from wounds; Henry Clay, discharged; Sidney Crow; J. Davies, transferred; J. M. Dennis, discharged; Charles Dever, discharged; Thornton Dukes, died at Pensacola, Fla.; —— Ellis; John Everitt, wounded at Murfreesboro; Thomas Everett, first killed from Columbus, October 9th, 1861, at battle Santa Rosa, Fla.; George Fackler, discharged from severe wounds at Murfreesboro, Dec. 31, 1862; George Hammond, discharged; —— Hammock, died; Daniel Hoopaugh, missing; L. P. Jepson, transferred to artillery; J. D. Johnson, died at Tazewell, Tenn.; A. S. Johnson, discharged; J. Jefferson, discharged; T. J. Jones, discharged; T. Jones, discharged; J. W. Jones, discharged; Jack Keenan, discharged; —— Kemp, died; Joseph Little, discharged; Milton Long, died; George Lapham, transferred; J. C. Leslie, transferred and killed at Petersburg, 1864; Asa Lynch; P. H. Madden, discharged; J. Maddox, transferred to engineer corps; E. McEachren, transferred; J. Marler, died; Tom Nobles; Wm. Newman; J. T. Ogletree, transferred to Company A, 2d Battallion Sharp Shooters, and promoted 1st Lieutenant; F. M. Parkman; Julius Prager, missing; John Quin, transferred to engineer corps; Martin Riley, transferred to 2d Battalion Georgia Sharp Shooters; W. H. Robarts; J. Robinson; T. C. Robinson, discharged, April 1862, and joined 1st Bat. Georgia Sharp Shooters; J. M. Robinson, transferred to Washington Artillery, Feb., 1862; Jasper Rooke, died; Lewis Sheline, missing; G. W. Shearer, wounded at Murfreesboro, December 31, 1862; James Short, killed at Chickamauga, 19th September, 1863; G. Smith, discharged; J. Smith, missing; Jep Smith, transferred to 2d Battalion Ga. Sharp Shooters; George Snell, discharged; Larry Sturges, discharged; Martin Surles, died; L. B. Townsley; —— Taylor, transferred to Sharp Shooters; —— Vandenberg; Barney Veasey, died at Chattanooga, 1863; Hamp Wagner, transferred orderly to Gen. Hardee; W. Ward, killed at Murfreesboro, Dec. 31, 1862; —— Willis, discharged; R. A. Wood, transferred and elected Capt. 41st Georgia; Joseph Wood; Jason Yarbrough, transferred to 2d Georgia Battalion Sharp Shooters; Needham Averitt; L. P. Aenchbacker, promoted Corp'l, wounded at Chickamauga, September 19th, 1863; Joseph Barnes, deserted; Chas. Kendall, discharged; John Crouch; John E. W. Henderson; A. H. Allen; J. H. Almonds, died; J. L. Baskin, died; Cornelius Bachelor; J. Bradford, died; W. S. Bradford, killed at Chickamauga, 19th September, 1863; A. J. S. Brooks, died from wounds at Chickamauga 19th September, 1863; Maynard Corley; J. J. Davis; A. L. Davis; J. K. Freeman; U. L. Guthrie, killed at Chickamauga, Sept. 19th, 1863; H. R. Hannah; R. L. Hern; W. A. Jackson; J. A. Lovelace; F. M. McHugh; M. L. McKee; John G. Merck, died;

John Ogle, died; J. D. Pittman; R. Rumsey.; T. J. Roe, died; J. E. Smith; J. E. Stockwell; U. R. Taylor; J. Taylor; A. J. Widner; LeGrand Guerry, wounded at Murfreesboro, Dec. 31, 1862; A. Jones; Wesley Gilbert.

The following were battles of the war in which the Georgia Grays were engaged:

Santa Rosa Island, Florida, October 9, 1861; Perryville; Murfreesboro, December 31, 1862; Chickamauga, September 19, 1863; Resaca; on Lookout Mountain; Bentonville; Port Royal, before Bentonville.

"CONFEDERATE STATES SENTINELS."

The "Confederate States Sentinels," Captain R. R. Hawes, took their departure from Columbus, for Richmond, Va., on the 23d of May, making the fifth Columbus company sent to join the Confederate army. This company numbered 71 members, some of whom were from Columbus, but the larger portion from the surrounding county. We regret that we cannot find its muster roll. The officers elected at the time of its organization, on the 26th of April, were—R. R. Hawes, Captain; C. S. Pryor, 1st Lieutenant; S. E. Taylor, 2d Lieutenant; Joseph B. Wynn, 3d Lieutenant.

COMPANY G. OF SOUTHERN GUARD.

The sixth Columbus Company—being Co. G. of the Southern Guard—left Columbus for the seat of war on the 28th of May. The following was its muster roll:

Officers—Captain, John A. Jones. Lieutenants—1st, Van Leonard; 2d, F. M. Brooks; 3d, C. S. Hart. Sergeants—1st, C. B. Mims; 2d, T. H. Smith; 3d, Wm. Bond; 4th, J. T. Scott. Corporals—1st, B. Daniel; 2d, Arthur McArdle; 3d, W. A. Wales; 4th, D. B. Castleman.

Privates—Alex Aides, Levi Blake, John W. Bozeman, D. M. Crenshaw, Owen Casey, R. S. Crane, A. K. Crane, J. L. O. Davis, Daniel Davis, Thos. Durham, Peter Edgar, William Frazier, Erastus Flemming, J. H. Frampton, James A. Gue, Daniel Grant, Fleming Hodges, George Henderson, James Hodges, Henry Henderson, Calvin Hearn, G. M. Henley, Jesse J. Halton, W. A. Hill, J. E. Jones, William R. Jones, G. W. Jarrett, J. Leonard Jones, Leroy Kilgore, Alfred H. Kimbrough, Thomas H. Knowles, John Lassiter, James Lanning, John T. Moye, George W. Massey, James Manning, John C. Morgan, Amos Murphy, Josiah Murphy, Jack Milton, John McPhatter, A. N. McCarra, Henry W. Martin, John Ousley, J. R. Posey, J. R. Park, James Rivers, Hiram Riley, James P. Russell, John Shores, Patrick Shandley, Wm. Sherrer, James Smith, W. C. Thomas, William Waytor, James A. Williams, Ransom W. Wood, Hampton Wilson, Pat. A. Weatherford, W. O. M. Whitehurst, Stephen G. Wilson, R. C. Yarbrough.

The "Border Rangers," Captain J. A. Strother, was the next Company that left Columbus for the Confederate service. It left on the 13th of June, and was a fine body of men, numbering 106 who left on that day. It was raised chiefly in Muscogee and Harris counties, with a few from Russell county, Ala. We have not been able to obtain its muster roll. The Lieutenants were H. C. Mitchell, J. A. Granberry, J. T. Scott, Hardy Cornett.

COLUMBUS GUARDS.

The Columbus Guards, while stationed at Brunswick, Ga., were on the 9th of June divided into two companies by order of Col. Semmes. They were designated as Columbus Guards, Companies A and B. The following officers for the two companies were elected: Company A—Roswell Ellis, Captain; John S. Allen, jr, 1st Lieutenant; W. G. Clemons, 2d; Richard Potter, 3d; A. A. Calhoun, 1st Sergeant; J. M. Denson, 2d; Van Marcus, 3d; J. J. Clapp, 4th. Company B—W. C. Hodges, Captain; J. M. Everett, 1st Lieutenant; T. M. Barnard, 2d; Thos. Chaffin, jr., 3d; B. H. Holt, 1st Sergeant; W. A. Barden, 2d; R. M. Rutherford, 3d; J. A. Cody, 4th. But this division was overruled by superior authority, and as neither the division of the company, nor the increase of its members to over 114 men would be permitted, a squad of recruits who had gone to Brunswick to join it returned to Columbus on the 26th of June.

"INDEPENDENT LIGHT INFANTRY."

The "Independent Light Infantry," Captain R. A. Hardaway, took their departure from Columbus for the seat of war on the 15th of June.

"MUSCOGEE RIFLES."

On the 18th of June, the "Muscogee Rifles," Capt. T. B. Scott, making the tenth company, left Columbus for the Confederate service. This company had 63 men in its ranks when it left, and Lieut. Sikes left in a few days afterwards with some privates unavoidably detained. The company comprised many young men of promise and standing. The following was its muster roll in July, when in camp near Richmond :

Captain, Thaddeus B. Scott.   Lieutenants—James A. Whitesides, 1st; Jesse H. Sikes, 2d ; James K. Deckrow, 3d.   Sergeants—Wm. L. Robinson, 1st; Augustus M. Green, 2d ; Patrick H. Thornton, 3d ; Hiram A. Gibson, 4th.   Corporals—Joseph W. Holmes, 1st; Sidney C. Lloyd, 2d ; James Simmons, 3d ; George W. Cooper, 4th. Commissary—J. P. Floyd.

Privates—John Wm. Allen, John Anderson, A. J. Autry, Wm. W. Autry, Isham R. Brooks, Joseph H. Brooks, James C. Brooks, John H. Britt, Wm. R. Britt, Amos R. Blackmon, Bryan Burns, Jacob Bluhm, W. V. Bartlett, Jeptha Bergamy, M. A. Bryan, Moses Clay, R. P. Camlino, Smith Colter, B. M. Colter, William Cherry, S. E. Cornett, J. W. Curenton, Henry Dunn, Joseph H. Davie, Joseph Davis, J. W. Davis, James H. Dawson, James J. Dukes, John T. Dean, Joshua Ellis, Howell W. Freel, A. J. Giddens, John C. Griffin, George Gaddis, Calvin L. Grant, Alfred Harris, Achibald B. Hobbs, Wm. L. Hill, Calvin Jernigan, Wm. Knight, Albert Kilgore, Patrick Kelley, John Kirkland, Isaac Lynn, Julius Lipman, J. W. H. Latham, Richard Lewis, Lewis W. Motley, Lewis P. Mosely, F. M. Mitchell, Hugh McTigue, John C. Milton, Wm. H. Miller, W. N. Marchant, Wm. Mooney, R. Clay McCoy, Sowell W. Markham, Gardner Moye, Robert J. Orr, Wm. Omily, N. W. Pittman, Joseph Putnam, Jesse Quick, David Roland, Timothy Smith, Whitford Smith, James L. Smith, James Smith, Josiah M. Smith, D. D. Singleton, B. J. Stonaker, Wm. W. Skates, Lewis A. Taylor, C. J. Woulfe. Drummer, George Blankenship. Fifer, W. G. Slaughter. Total number present, 4 officers and 85 rank and file—89.

The "Jackson Avengers" left Columbus for Virginia on the 21st of July. The following was its muster roll :

Captain—J. J. Bradford. Lieutenants—1st, Wm. H. H. Phelps ; 2d, W. A. McDougald ; 3d, Thomas E. Blanchard.   Sergeants—1st, P. S. Bradford ; 2d, John Schnell ; 3d, James R. Lively ; 4th, John C. C. Walker. Commissary—Chas. E. Johnson.   Corporals—1st, D. D. Adlington ; 2d, H. T. Huff ; 3d, W. C. Kelly ; 4th, Paul Haller.

Privates—Job Alford, M. Blanchard, R. B. Brookins, Jerry Broadaway, J. C. Broadaway, J. C. Brooks, P. A. Browning, Charles Chaffin, James Compton, G. W. Culpepper, E. M. H. Duke, Joseph Ellison, A. Everidge, H. Everidge, jr., Joseph Everidge, Thomas Ellis, Calvin Evers, J. W. Evans, John Gardner, Thomas Garrett, George Greer, J. M. Gray, John Heratt, John Helton, John Hoffman, J. H. Harald, William Hudson, John Jones, Leroy Kilgore, M. Kenny, A. L. Kinsey, George Kirle, James Kilcrease, James Lambert, Benjamin Logan, J. B. Morgan, J. C. McCarty, George McGee, J. N. McKenney, A. B. McCrary, John W. Mainor, B. F. Mainor, Jas. Martin, James Norris, B. F. O'Neal, Wiley Percy, Pink Pike, George Pike, Esaw Pike, Henry Pike, Littleton Pike, John Phelps, James Powers, W. W.

Peddy, J. C. Peddy, B. Raiford, P. T. Smith, W. B. Smith,Thos Thompson, Wm. Thompson, Frank Veach, John Wade, M. M. Wadkins, C. Williams, H. Williams, R. Williams, Wm. Wells, James Wooten. Musician—Wm. Quinn.

"IVEY GUARDS."

The "Ivey Guards," a fine company commanded by Capt. John R. Ivey, left on the 21st of July. The following was its muster roll:

Captain—John R. Ivey. Lieutenants—1st, Wiley N. Hutchins; 2d, Thomas S. Fontaine; Brevt. 2d, S. B. Cleghorn. Sergeants—1st, Charles L. Williams; 2d, Aug. O. Garrard; 3d, Joshua S. Roper; 4th, Wm. D. Miller. Corporals — 1st, James H. Moore; 2d, James Broderick; 3d, James S. Williams; 4th, Elias N. Beall.

Privates—R. O. Allen, H. T. Armstrong, E. Armstrong, David J. Adams, T. J. Alford, Lawrence W. Anderson, Solomon Belcher, James Burran, Stephen Blackmar, Hiram F. Bailey, George W. Brodie, Henry Coy, Jesse Crosby, Edw. C. Daniel, Wyatt L. Dalton, Daniel C. Foster, John Fox, John W. Forby, Christopher C Farr, Simon Farrell, Jackson Grimes, Alex. Gerald, Dennis Govey, Joseph A. Howard, Saul Huey, Robert A. Huey, Henderson Henley, Enoch J. Hodge, John F. Jordan, William H. James, Jefferson James, William James, William H. Lantern, Michael Leddy, Elisha Marlow, Thomas Moore head, Thomas Morgan, Alex. C. Morton, Samuel T. McKenzie, Joseph C. Mc-Kenzie, Absolom McDaniel, Joseph McMillan, William McElrath, Thomas McEchern, M. D. Odom, William D. Ogletree, Andrew J. Odom, James Pike, Andrew J. Ragland, Charles M. Russell, John Riley, H. S. Riley, Joshua A. Reams, John Rembert, Wm. Rotenberg, Erastus V. Sevell, Walter Stewart, William Simmons, John Singon, William C. Thomaston, John S. Thomaston, Joseph Thornton, John F. Underwood, Shepherd Welch, Reuben B. Wilkerson, Theophilus Wilson, John W. Wills, Wm. H. Woodruff, William C. Williford, John M. Wallace, John Wheeler, James Yarbrough.

"SEMMES GUARD."

The "Semmes Guard," Captain William S. Shepherd, left on the 24th of July. The following was its muster roll of officers and of the privates from Muscogee county:

Captain—Wm. S. Shepherd. Lieutenants—R. N. Howard, 1st; Charles R. Russell, 2d; Wm. Redd, Jr., Brevet, 2d. Ensign—J. J. Jones.

Privates from Muscogee county—J. A. Weems, J. D. Bethune, W. A. Barker, W. Lynch, J. B. Hopkins, O. E. Ligon, David Lyons, G. W. Ainchbacker, H. Oliver, Rolin A. Russell, D. G. Russell, J. Greenwood, L. Green.

"COLUMBUS VOLUNTEERS."

The "Columbus Volunteers," Captain F. S. Chapman, and the "Georgia Guards," Captain D. B. Thompson, left Columbus on the 14th of August for Atlanta, where they formed part of a regiment of which Hon. H. L. Benning was elected Colonel. It was the 17th Georgia Volunteers. The following account of the services of the Columbus Volunteers, and its muster roll and casualties, are taken from the Directory:

The Columbus Volunteers arrived with the regiment, (17th Ga.,) at Manassas after the first battle of that memorable field, and went into camp near by. Soon after they went into Prince William's county, and there built winterquarters. Early the Spring following they moved with the army of North Virginia before McClellan's advance, and pitched tents for some time at Orange C. H. Thence they were ordered to the Peninsula, passing through Richmond and taking steamer for King's Landing on the James. Here they confronted the enemy at Warwick river, and began one of the most severe campaigns in the history of the war, occupying during the day, water-filled muddy trenches, and being relieved every other night, to rest a short distance away in the wet swamp. The retreat to Richmond shortly followed, and after a short respite before that city, occupying a portion of the time on Garnett's farm, occasionally skirmishing with the enemy, and took part in the memorable and glorious Seven Days battles. From this period the Company followed the fortunes of General Longstreet's corps, taking part in battles, campaign and march, till at last the sad surrender of the gallant remnant was made by Gen. Lee.

This Company was made up of young men from Columbus, Marion, Chattahoochee and Upson; many of them are sleeping their last sleep on the fields of honor in Virginia and Pennsylvania.

Officers—F. S. Chapman, Captain. Lieutenants—1st, J. J. Grant; 2d, J. R. Mott, promoted Adjutant and Capt. on Gen. Benning's staff. L. E. O'Keefe. Brevt. 2d Lieut., transferred to Trans-Mississippi department and promoted Captain and Adjutant Lewis' Brigade. Sergeants—1st, A. D. Brown; 2d, J. H. Brown, missing; 3d, W. H. Dickerson, promoted Lieutenant and killed at Gettysburg; 4th, S. R. Jaques, promoted to Orderly. Corporals—1st, Matt Underwood, killed at second battle Manasses; 2d, Douglass Moore, killed by railroad accident at Reynold's creek; 3d, James C. Garrett, promoted Sergt.

Privates—James G. Brown; Wm. S. Brown, killed Gettysburg, July, 1864; William Beck; Isaac Beckwiths; N. Barrett; William Bentley; Berry Bentley; Mark Bentley; J. J. Boswell; Robert Beeman, killed; Wm. C. Cousens, promoted to Captain, lost leg and resigned; W. D. Chapman; Henry Chapman, killed; Jeff. Culpepper; Joel Culpepper; John Culpepper, killed; Jasper Culpepper, killed at 2d battle Manassas; William Culpepper; George Corbet; Martin Clark; William J. Chaffin; C. Carpenter; James W. Dickey, promoted Commissary Sergeant; W. H. Dickey; M. Frank; C. C. Fickling, wounded and discharged; William Fickling, died; John Fickling, died; James Gorham, killed; Wm. Harbuck, died; James Hollman; T. B. Howard, transferred and promoted Major; Joshua Jones; W. B. Johnson, died; Clark Jenkins;

Lewis Jenkins, died ; J. W. Jack ; John Key ; Hugh Key, killed at Gettysburg; J. II. Lawrence, promoted Sergeant ; J. F. Lowe, killed at Manasses ; H. C. Lowe, transferred and promoted Hospital Steward; Benjamin Ledbetter, transferred ; J. C. Lightfoot, missing ; John Lindsay, killed ; A. C. McCord, promoted Captain ; J. B. Moore, promoted Major ; Jasper Majors ; T. J. Majors, promoted Sergeant, killed at Fort Gilmore ; Henry Moore, lost an arm and discharged ; D. D. Munn, killed at Gettysburg ; J. McCulloch ; Frank McGehee, died ; William Martin ; L. Meyer, discharged, ; Valentine Martin, died ; William Norton ; Robert Noles ; Cyrus Northrop ; J. H. Patterson ; J. D. Patillo ; —— Pearce, died ; Dan. Pope ; Jack Pope ; S. E. Robinson, promoted Sergeant and Adjutant ; Jacob Revier; Isaac Rice ; Newton Royals ; B. P. Shaw, killed at 2d Manassas ; A. L. Short, killed at Gettysburg ; Willis J. Skinner, killed at Gettysburg ; John Skinner, died ; Isaac Simmons ; — Snead, killed ; John Sutton, died ; J. A. Sellars, promoted 1st Sergeant ; T. J. Story ; O. T. Thweatt ; John Thom, lost arm and discharged ; Allen Talbot ; H. Talbot ; Joseph Terry, transferred to engineer corps; Isaac Wineberger ; S. F. Walker, killed at battle of Wilderness ; Henly Williams, died ; E. L. Wells, promoted Sergeant ; —— Watson, died ; T. J. Young ; A. Young, died.

GEORGIA GUARDS.

The following was the muster roll of the Georgia Guards :

Officers—Captain, D. B. Thompson. Lieutenants—1st, Henry McCauley; 2d, Charles A. Klink ; Brevet 2d, P. Gittinger, jr. Sergeants—1st, Thos. J. Cay; 2d, Thomas Sweet ; 3d, John H. Weeks ; 4th, George Potter. Corporals—1st, Frank Goldsmith ; 2d, A. J. Snipes ; 3d, J. R. Horton ; 4th, W. J. Langston. Quartermaster—J B. Aquem. Commissary—John H. Madden.

Privates—C. Arnold, M. J. Anthony, William J. Bird, James Brock, J. A. Boswell, J. W. Cone, Willis Cook, H. Cannon, William Cone, F. Curtem, T, Comer, Henry Corry, W. M. Davis, J. Davis, Thomas Donnovan, R. P. Falford, Peter Finnigan, John Foran, E. A. Gossette, Thomas Graves, W. M. Hally, S. W. Hall, H. H. Hall, George Hall, J. W. Hall, C. Hargroves, Jas. M. Jones, C. Johnson, J. H. Jones, Henry Jones, Henry Langley, J. B. Lewis, A. Murphy, J. Martin, W. McMichael, J. T. Mullins, L. Maddox, William Murray, D. Purcell, Charles Owens, W, Riley, G. B. Ragan, J. Riley, A. Smith, William Singleton, J. Turner, P. Wry, M. T. Walker, G. W. Lavar.

Mayor Thompson having entered the service, Dr. J. F. Bozeman filled the position of Mayor until the regular election.

A meeting of Ladies of Columbus, held on the 21st of May, formed the "Ladies' Soldier's Friend Society," the object of which was to furnish clothing and other comforts for the soldiers. The following officers were elected : Mrs. A. H.

Chappell, President; Mrs. Robt. Carter, Vice President; Mrs. J. A. Urquhart, Secretary ; Mrs. R. Patten, Treasurer.

The City Council, at its meeting held on the 6th of May, passed resolutions expressing regret for the resignation of Alderman Salisbury, who was about to go with his company to "the front," and declaring "that each member of this Board will imitate his gallant example whenever necessity may require it." Council, at the same meeting, also passed a resolution appropriating $200 for the benefit of the Georgia Grays, and promising a like sum to each company recruited out of and by citizens of Columbus for the Confederate army.

"GEORGIA LIGHT INFANTRY."

The "Georgia Light Infantry," a fine company of young men, Captain Apollos Forrester, left Columbus for the Confederate service on the 7th of October.

"TERRELL ARTILLERY."

The "Terrell Artillery," Captain Edgar Dawson, 1st Lieut. John W. Brooks; 2d, Charles Wright; 3d, T. M. Barnard, left on the 17th of October.

"COLUMBUS MINUTE MEN."

The "Columbus Minute Men," Capt. Hatch Cook—a company formed for coast defence in the service of the State—left for Savannah on the 29th of October.

"COLUMBUS FLYING ARTILLERY."

The "Columbus Flying Artillery," a large and well appointed company, raised by Captain Ed. Croft, left Columbus for Savannah on the 23d of December.

We cannot find the muster rolls of these companies, all of which were composed of volunteers partly from Columbus and partly from the surrounding country, both of Georgia and Alabama.

The war, while it drew off so many valuable citizens, stimulated many industries, and built up some new ones, in Columbus. The Factories were pushed with work, a very large portion of their fabrics being made for the Confederate and State authorities, for clothing the soldiers in the field. The Columbus Foundry and Machine Shops had to enlarge and increase their working force to supply the demand for machinery and materials of war. The Quartermaster's establishment, under the chief management of Colonel F. W. Dillard, gave employment to a large number of women and girls, most of them wives or daughters of soldiers. Among the new industries were a Cap Manufactory by Samuel Thom, and a Sword Factory by Haiman & Co. The ladies had a Soldier's Aid Society, which afforded valuable aid in clothing and sending comforts to the soldiers in the field.

The prices of many commodities advanced greatly even during this first year of the war, and some became so scarce that the people generally had to do without them and to look out for "substitutes." Salt was one of the first articles of prime necessity whose scarcity and high price were severely felt. We make the following quotations of prices for December: Bacon 25 to 30c.; Flour $10 to $12; Coffee 67½c.; Sugar 10 to 12c.; Salt $10 per sack; Corn 85c. to $1; Wheat $2; Prints 15 to 25c.; Osnaburgs 17 to 20c.; Flannels 75c. to $1.25; Shirtings and Sheetings 15@20c.

INCIDENTS.

Mr. John W. G. Gorden, an old conductor on the M. & W. P. Railroad, was found dead in the lower part of Columbus on the morning of the 15th October. It was supposed that he died of heart disease.

A member of the Columbus "Flying Artillery," named Jas. Smith, was stabbed by Isaac Harrell, on the night of the 10th of November, and died in a few minutes. Smith was from Chambers County, Alabama. The killing took place in a liquor shop in Wamackville. Other members of the company burned the shop and the dwelling of the owner.

The extensive tin and hardware establishment of Capt. D. B. Thompson was destroyed by fire on the night of the 2d of December. The stock was very large, valued at $50,000 or $60,000, and insured to only a small amount.

At the State election in October, Dr. A. I. Robison and Col. J. A. L. Lee were chosen Representatives of Muscogee county.

Capt. Jacob G. Burrus was killed on the 8th of April, in a difficulty with John and Thomas Redd. He was shot with a pistol, on "Triangle street."

Ed. Croft was in May elected an Alderman of the 4th Ward *vice* W. L. Salisbury, resigned.

Osborne, a little son of Mr. Wm. Douglass, was drowned in one of the brick yard holes on the 18th of May.

A special election on the 14th of June for one Alderman each for the 1st and 5th Wards, resulted in the choice of Jno. B. Wright for the 1st, and John Peabody for the 5th.

James Gibson, a youth of about thirteen years, was drowned near the upper bridge, while bathing in the river, on the 6th of June.

The Eagle Manufacturing Company, in June, adopted resolutions tendering to the Confederate Government, in exchange for its bonds, the sum of one thousand dollars per month until the end of the war; also appropriating one hundred dollars per month as a contribution in aid of the city fund for the support of families of volunteers.

Aleck Lamar, a youth connected with the *Sun* office, was drowned in the river above the railroad bridge while bathing on the 23d of June.

The Bank of Columbus, in June, subscribed $75,000 to the Confederate loan, which was in addition to $60,000 previously subscribed, and to $35,000 loaned the State of Georgia.

Capt. James Abercrombie, an old and prominent citizen of Russell county, Alabama, living in the vicinity of Columbus, who had removed to Pensacola, Fla., died there on the 2d of July. His remains were brought to Columbus for interment.

A deplorable accident to the train conveying the Columbus Volunteers and Georgia Guards to Atlanta occurred on the evening of the 14th of August, near Randall's Creek. Several of the cars were precipitated into a broken culvert.

Mr. Douglas C. Moore, of the Columbus Volunteers, and a negro boy belonging to Mr. Edward Croft, were instantly killed. Several other persons were wounded.

The first new cotton was brought in on August 30th, being two bales from the plantation of Mr. George Hernden, of Marion county. It classed strict middling, and was sold at 10⅝ cents. Very heavy and long continued rains fell during the first three weeks in August, badly damaging all crops, and preventing the maturity and picking of cotton.

A shock of earthquake was felt in the city on the 31st of August, doing no damage.

The receipts of cotton for the year ending August 31st, amounted to 83,166 bales. Stock on hand 1st Sept., 2,234 bales.

Wm. Butler, the engineer, was killed on the 11th of Sept., by the running off the track of his train on the Mobile and Girard Railroad, at Station No. 6.

Work on the common passenger shed for the several Railroad Companies was suspended in January, on account of the pressure of the times.

Miss Ann Rankin was killed on the 8th of January, being thrown from a buggy in which she and another lady were riding, a few miles from the city.

The stores on the west side of Broad street, occupied by T. B. Scott and Mr. Fischacker, were burned on the night of the 20th of January. They were owned by B. Wells & Co.

PERSONAL.

John Quin and F. M. Brooks were Magistrates, and J. B. Hicks and D. Crockett Constables of the Lower District, and W. H. Brannon and John G. Bethune were Magistrates, and John Lloyd Constable for the Upper District.

Wm. A. Lawes was elected Sheriff of Muscogee county, on the 9th of March, to fill the unexpired term of J. Hazleton, resigned.

January 4—Elias B. Presley and Rebecca J. Stinson; 15, Thomas J. Wynne and Arry M. J. Fincher, Henry C. Mitchell and Rowena Gunby, William H. Gibson and Gussie Greenwood; 16, Alexander P. Pryor and Mary J. Sneed; 22, George W. Gafford and Elizabeth Chatman, Wm. Rodgers and Frances Champion; 24, Joseph Ellison and Ellenora Garrett, James S. Tatum and Sarah Tatum; 28, Wm. Lawrence and Ellen Silas; 29, William T. Griffin and M. F. Thompson, George McDaniel and Sarah Pritchard, John Turner and Martha Cooper.

Februay 10—Daniel H. Wynne and Mary A. Morrison; 14, Thos. J. Willis and Elvira E. Jones; 16, George W. Clay and Caroline Hines; 19, Daniel Grant and Mary E. Hungerford; 25, Wm. Sills and Elizabeth James; 26, John C. Martin and Mary Pittman.

March 1—Wm. T. Merchant and Sarah McMullen; 3, Monroe M. Belcher and Martha Clegg; 5, Alexander C. Morrison and Mary E. Williamson, Wm. Pike and Winnie Thompson; 6, Wm. H. Russell and Mary E. Tomlin; 10, Geo. M. Venable and Susan P. Davis, James B. West and Louisiana Prather; 12, James T. Redding and Martha B. Hardaway; 16, Wm. J. Webb and Adaline Williams; 21, Phineas Gray and Rachel Gray; 24, James T. Owens and Rachel R. Hoffman.

April 1—Alfred I. Young and Clara Wildman; 9, Edward J. Holley and Elizabeth Wynne; 16, Isaac T. Tichnor and Emily C. Boyken; 20, George B. Young and Mary J. Norton; 25, Edward A. Kleber and Mary B. Barden.

May 3—Jesse Schnider and Kate Corbally; 5, Thos. F. Ridenhour and Charlotte T. Davis, Lawrence M. Burns and Mary A. Harris; 9, James Hearn and Elizabeth Corlie; 10, Milton J. Walker and Ella G. Rowe; 26, Thomas McAlister and Nancy Fletcher; 29, Robert C. McIntyre and Martha L. Murdock; 30, Edward Bozeman and Nancy Robinson.

June 2—Mathew H. Pool and Sarah A. Skinner; 5, George R. Clark and Rhoda A. Odom; 6, Conrad Bravogle and Mary A. A. Barry; 14, Williford Cherry and Susan Turner; 18, Robert E. O'Brien and Mariah A. Brown, Harvey Jones and Mary B. Rhodes; 20, Green L. M. Thompson and Sarah Morris; 23, Daniel D. McDuffie and Elizabeth Ham; 27, Richard J. Hunter and Anna C. V. Howard.

July 1—David E. Moody and Mary D. Upton; 14, Wm. J. Langston and Mattie E. Parr.; 18, Walter Stewart and Elizabeth M. Rembert; 25, Wm. M. Foster and Susan Barker; 28, James M. Willis and Nancy J. King.

August 2—John J. Kemp and Emaline Moody; 4, Joseph Pittman and Mary Bradley; 14, Wm. Amos and Lucy P. Cox; 17, Jesse C. Ousley and Elizabeth P. Evans; 25, Wm. R. Green and Antionett V. Vanzant.

September 5—James C. Huckaba and Nancy L. Thomas; 8, James Belcher and Elizabeth Newsom; 15, Franklin J. Johnson and Alice A. Mealing; 17, Wm. S. Tooke and Lucy A. Bussey; 22, Andrew Grande and Lizzie Wynne; 24, James A. Shingleur and Martha E. Flewellen, Lewis Scott and Winney Hurst; 26, James W. Doles and Mary T. Jones.

October 6—Thos. P. Lunsford and Anna J. King ; 8, Charles E. Brooks and Virginia E. Barden ; 15, Benjamin A. Stripling and Ann E. Champion ; 24, Lovick Goodwin and Malinda Rodgers, Peyton H. Colquitt and Julia P. Hurt ; 31, Amory D. Barnett and Sarah A. Turner.

November 5—Lemuel Lockhart and Cally A. E. Vinson ; 12, James C. Edwards and Ann McIntyre ; 17, E. J. Mathews and Susan Colter ; 21, James C. Gartman and Sarah T. Hobbs.

December 1—James V. Averett and Mary R. Skinner ; 3, Thos. C. Parham and Eugenia T. Womack ; 8, Wm. Odom and Elizabeth R. Patrick ; 9, John Livingston and Elizabeth Tadlock ; 10, Wm. A. Speris and Narcissa J. Robinson, Francis J. Abbott and Mary A. Dutton ; 15, John Olive and Melvina Hatton ; 18, Wm. C. Cooke and Clara W. Abercrombie ; 24, Cincinatus B. Kendrick and Mary Holcomb ; 26, Alexander Frazier and Rena Smith ; 31, William A. Teal and Sarah E. Brittain, Frederick F. Coulter and Emaline A. Hill.

DEATHS.

Jan. 31—Horace H. Taft.

Feb. 1—(in Girard,) Jesse Hays ; 12, (drowned at Mobile,) Rev. Noble DeVotie ; 19, Charles Markham.

March 7—Infant daughter of H. H. Epping ; 23, (in Wynnton,) Mrs. Eliza, wife of Hu. B. Dawson ; 28, Charles D. Wales.

April 3—Samuel B. Harvell, Neil G. Smith ; 10, Samuel J. Hatcher ; 15, Dr. Alphonso C. Kivlin ; 24, James Lawrence Hill.

May 9—Child of Dr. Tichnor ; 22, Mrs. O'Bannon ; 31, Dr. LeRoy Holt.

June 5—John C. Wakefield ; 6, infant son of Jesse Cox ; 17, Eva, daughter of G. H. Peabody ; 18, Thos. S. Allen ; 23, infant daughter of F. J. Clemons ; 22, Alex. B. Lamar ; 24, infant daughter of J. P. Murray ; 30, infant son of Geo. C. Renfroe.

July 1—Mrs. James D. Code ; 3, Mrs. R. L. Mott ; 8, Mrs. Bradford ; 22, Mrs. Sallie L., wife of Rev. A. Wright ; 25, J. D. Baldwin ; 30, Miss Sarah E. Crews.

August 2—Col. Van Leonard, Mrs. Nancy Fields ; 7, infant son of Rev. H. H. Parks ; 15, Wm. J. Caraway.

Sept. 3—Infant son of E. M. Clarke ; 5, infant son of James M. Chambers ; 8, E. J. King ; 13, Mary S. Fackler ; 14, Margaret Sanders ; 23, H. B. Dixon, (in Richmond.)

Dec. 1—(in Augusta) George W. Winter, formerly of Columbus ; 24, (at Motgomery) A. S. Rutherford, Clerk of the Superior Court of Muscogee.

1862.

Second Year of the War—Military Feeling, &c.

The municipal election in December last resulted in the choice of Dr. J. F. Bozeman as Mayor; George W. Jones, Clerk; Jas. D. Johnson, Treasurer; no election for Marshal; George A. Huckeba, Deputy Marshal; Henry M. Harris, Sexton. Aldermen—1st Ward, J. J. McKendree, Dr. Flewellen; 2d, J. W. King, F. C. Johnson; 3d, John Hazleton, T. O. Douglass; 4th, John Ligon, J. T. Daniel; 5th, John Quin, W. S. Holstead; 6th, J. M. Bivins, F. M. Gray.

The City Council elected the following officers: Bridge-keeper, Jno. Bunnell; Hospital keeper, Mrs. McGehee; Magazine keeper, Peter Anderson; Wharfinger, W. H. Alston; City Printers, Thos. Gilbert & Co.; City Physician, Dr. A. C. Wingfield.

On the 7th of January, John C. Lovelace was elected Marshal.

A very large, earnest and enthusiastic meeting of citizens was held in Temperance Hall on the 27th of February, at which resolutions were adopted pledging all the resources of the people to the carrying on of the war of defence; declaring that the people of Muscogee will cheerfully and promptly respond to the late and all other calls for volunteers; also requesting the Inferior Court to make provision for the support of volunteers until they shall be received into the service, and calling upon that Court to levy a tax sufficient to support the families of volunteers during their absence. The meeting also appointed a Committee of Public Safety, composed of 21 prominent citizens, and a committee to go through the country and collect all the guns that could be spared, and to call on the people for contributions of money, provisions, clothing, &c.

Two more volunteer military companies—the "Muscogee Volunteers," Capt. Cooper, and the "Price Volunteers," Capt. Bedell—left Columbus on the 12th of March for the rendezvous at Griffin, where they were incorporated into new regiments for the Confederate service. The "Muscogee Volunteers" were made Company C of the 46th Georgia Regiment, of which Peyton H. Colquitt was elected Colonel. He was killed on the 20th of September, 1863, in the battle of Chickamauga. The following was the muster roll of the "Muscogee Volunteers:"

Officers—A. H. Cooper, Captain, killed Sept. 20th, 1863, at Chickamauga. Lieutenants—1st, F. C. Tillman, promoted Captain, killed June 20th, 1864, at Kennesaw; 2d, W. R. Bedell, appointed Adjutant 46th Georgia Regiment, 1862; 3d, J. T. Daniel, promoted to Captain, June 20th, 1864, and surrendered in North Carolina, April 26th, 1865. Sergeants —1st, Charles Neuffer, died at Charleston, S. C., 1862; 2d, A. J. Floyd; 3d, J. W. Huff, elected Lieutenant; J. S. Acee, promoted to Lieutenant of Artillery, 1864; G. G. Cartledge, promoted to Orderly Sergeant, and killed at Franklin, Tenn., 1864. Corporals—1st, Isham R. Brooks, promoted to Orderly Sergeant; 2d, J. R. McGee; 3d, T. J. Skinner; 4th, Thomas Harrison, promoted to Sergeant.

Privates—W. M. Allen; J. L. Anthony; S. W. Anthony, discharged; J. F. Aldmond, died since war; Hezekiah Bedell; T. H. Banks; J. H. Bartlett; W. R. Bartlett; C. C. Bize, promoted Corporal and killed, 1864; D. R. Bize; Thomas Boles, killed, 1864; John R. Brooks; R. C. Brooks, died 1863; P. J. Bigers; William Brown; John Bussey; William Bussey; Wm. Champion, wounded at Jackson, Miss.; J. L. Duffee, discharged 1864; M. R. Edward; W. D. Edward, killed 22d July, 1864; A. J. English; Henry Fleming; John Fleming, discharged, 1864; J. F. Fletcher; J. M. Fletcher, promoted to Sergeant; J. B. Ford; J. H. Galaway; F. M. Gammel; Joseph Hartong; L. J. Haynes; W. C. Henderson; E. J. Horn, killed at Jackson, Miss., 1863; West Horn, died 1862; H. J. Horn; J. D. Holt; E. D. Jones, captured at Chickamauga, 1863; Thomas Kennedy; Jeremiah King, killed; O. K. Land, killed at Chickamauga, September 20th, 1863; William Langford; E. Langford; P. L. Lewis; A. J. Livingston, killed at Chickamauga, Sept. 20, 1863; James Lockhart; William Lockhart; Henry Long; Julius Long; Aaron Long; W. H. H. Lokey, killed at Nashville; Jinks Low; M. T. Lynn; L. J. McGehee; J. W. Massey; B. F. McCrary, wounded and discharged, 1864; N. E. Miller; O. H. Miller, discharged; Silas McGuyrt, discharged, lost arm; John McGuyrt; N. B. Morrill; Spencer Motley; J. D. Moy; J. H. Morrison; James Mooney; J. C. Myers; J. A. Parker; G. E. Parker; Wm. Parker; H. P. Parkman; William Peddy, killed; Elisha Phillips; J. P. Phillips, died; E. P. Phillips, died; F. X. Profumo; W. H. H. Robison, died; G. M. Rogers, killed at Jonesboro, Ga., 1864; John Rogers, died;

11

J. L. Roberts; W. H. Russell; F. P. Scott; C. A. Shivers; J. H. B. Shippey, discharged; H. T. Simmons; D. A. Skinner; J. W. Skinner; C. B.
Sperlin; W. A. Spires; J. M. Thompson; J. N. Thompson, deserted; W.
R. Thompson, deserted; J. W. Thompson, deserted; T. W. Schoonmaker,
transferred to 32d Ga. Regiment, 1863; John Hawkin, transferred; L. I.
Harvey, transferred; Robert Motley, died 1863; J. N. Took; J. J. Took;
R. C. Treadaway; James Turnage, died; W. A. Waters; J. M. Watkins,
killed; Jonathan Watson; Simeon Wilden, killed, 1863; B. T. Willis, killed,
1864; N. C. Willis; E. P. Willis; L. J. Williams, killed 1863; G. W. Wiseman; Robert Wiseman; Neal Wilkerson; Wm. Wilkerson; Lewis Wilkerson, died; Wm. Wragg; J. A. Wynn; T. Jeff. Willis, promoted to Sergt.
and killed at Chickamauga, 20th September, 1863.

A military organization for home defence was effected at a
meeting held in the Court House on the 26th of March. Six-
ty-one volunteers then enrolled themselves, and organized by
electing John L. Mustain, Captain; John Peabody, James
Broadnax, and Frank W. Golden, Lieutenants; R. T. Simons,
Jacob Burrus, John Durkin, and Peter Roman, Corporals;
George A. Huckeba, H. R. Sedberry, J. W. Bishop, and Jos.
Roper, Sergeants; R. S. Stockton, Secretary and Treasurer.

A fine cavalry company, raised by Captain Robert Thompson, left Columbus early this year for the Confederate service, but we cannot find the date. It was made Company A
of the Third Georgia Cavalry, of which M. J. Crawford was
Colonel; R. E. Kennon, Lieutenant Colonel; Howard Johnson, Major; J. P. C. Winder, Adjutant; E. F. Colzey, Surgeon; —— Moulkey, Assistant Surgeon; Harry J. DeLauney, Serg't Major; J. W. Hinton, Chaplain; R. W. Denton,
Quartermaster; J. A. Frazier, Commissary. Most of these
regimental officers were from Columbus. The officers of Co.
A were: Robert Thompson, Captain (afterwards promoted
Colonel of the regiment); Chas. Phelps, 1st Lieutenant; Wm.
Howard, 2d; John Klink, 3d, afterwards 1st Lieut.; Lawrence Wall, O. S., afterwards 3d Lieutenant.

The officers of Company B of the same regiment were: B.
A. Thornton, Captain; Howard Johnson, 1st Lieutenant,
afterwards promoted Major of regiment; Hamp Park, 2d
Lieut.; John Manley, 3d; Thomas King, O. S., afterwards
Lieutenant.

Company, I of the same regiment: John. W. Hurt, Captain; J. S. Pemberton, 1st Lieutenant, afterwards Captain; B. B. Fontaine, 2d Lieut., afterwards Captain; Woolfolk Walker, 3d Lieut.; James Dennis, O. S., afterwards Lieutenant.

The "Columbus Rebels" were mustered into service in April, 1862, at Atlanta, as Company C, 9th Georgia Battalion of Artillery. We copy its roll and record from Haddock's Directory:

This Company was sent to Abingdon, Va., and in the Fall of that year crossed the Cumberland Mountains at Pound Gap, and took part in the Kentucky campaign. After the battle of Perryville, and the withdrawal of Gen. Bragg from Kentucky, retreated with General Humphrey Marshall's command to Southwestern Virginia, where they remained during the Winter. In May, 1863, were ordered to Knoxville, Tenn., and in June of that year assisted in defending the city against the enemy, under General Saunders and Col. John Brownlow. In August of this year, marched with Buckner's corps to join Gen. Bragg, and participated in the operations in McLemore's Cave and the battle of Chickamauga. After the battle was placed in General Wofford's brigade, which composed the advance of our army in the march on Chattanooga. Was sent with Longstreet to East Tennessee, and participated in the engagement at Campbell's Station and the assault on Knoxville. Passed the Winter in East Tennessee and Southwest Virginia, and in June, 1864, was ordered to Lynchburg and assisted in defending that place against the enemy under Gen. Hunter, and after his repulse and retreat went with Earley's corps in pursuit and remained with Gen. Early during his subsequent operations in the Valley of Virginia, after which they were ordered to Richmond, taking part in its defense and surrendering with Gen. Lee's army at Appomattox Court House. The following is an imperfect roll of the company as it is given wholly from memory by an active member of the company. Of the 95 or 100 members some 20 or 25 surrendered with the company at Appomattox Court House:

Officers—George W. Atkinson, Captain, resigned in June, 1863, and was discharged by substitution. Lieutenants—1st, Thos. O. Douglass, resigned in May, 1863, on account of physical disability. 2d, Lieut., A. M. Wolihin, promoted to captaincy in June, 1863, and surrendered at Appomattox Court House. 3d Lieut., P. L. Key, promoted to 1st Lieutenant in June, 1863, surrendered at Appomattox Court House. Sergeants—1st, Geo. A. B. Smith, discharged in May, 1863, by substitution. 2d Sergt., John S. Cargill, promoted in May, 1863, to 1st Sergeant, afterwards Adjutant to General. 3d Sergeant, Wm. Hall, promoted to 2d Lieutenant. 4th Sergt., J. R. Hillings, surrendered at Appomattox Court House. 5th Sergt., B. F. Bussey, promoted to 1st Sergeant, surrendered at Apomattox Court House. Corporals—1st, James McElrath; 2d, John F. Barker, dead; 3d, Luke Conley; 4th, J. A. Fassell, surrendered at Appomattox Court House; 5th, Pat. Foran.

Privates—John Allen, died in 1863; Frank Allums, B. F. Barnes, B. F. Brittain, Wm. Barker, E. C. Beers; H. Bussey, died in 1863; — Brooks, died in 1862; John F. Brown, discharged on account of disability; W. A. Bozeman, discharged by order President Davis; Robert Bozeman, discharged on account of disability; Alfred Bennett; S. P. C. Clark, deserted in September, 1862; Jason Crawford, David Crawford; Jno. T. Cousford, detailed in Government Works at Columbus; W. C. Duffield; Nat. C. Fergerson, promoted to Sergeant in 1863; John Fussell; M. W. Ford, promoted to 3d Lieutenant in 1863 and resigned; J. A. Foster, Wm. Foster, Henry Foster; M. C. Gilbert, discharged by substitution in 1863; John W. Gay, N. B. Gay, John G. Grant,,John Henderson, Toney Henderson, Wm. Hill; A. B. Hudson, dead; Robert Hudson, John A. Johnson, L. W. Keeling, Thos. Lasseter, James J. Littleton, James R. Lawrence; John Landers, promoted to Corporal and discharged in 1863; M. H. Lee, discharged by substitution in 1863; James F. Lewis; R. G. Lynn, wounded in hand and discharged; Allen Mann; James Mann, discharged from disability in 1863; Wm. H. Morgan, Thomas Morgan; George M. Morgan, promoted to Corporal in 1863; Wm. McElrath; M. W. Murphy, promoted to Sergeant, one of the bravest and most effective gunners in the battalion; Wm. Odom, transferred to 46th Georgia Regiment; James Oswall, died in 1862; Leander Odom, promoted Corporal in 1864; D. M. Posey, promoted to Sergeant in 1864; Wm. Price, Robert Powell; Reuben Powell, disabled by wound in hand and discharged; Wm. Reegan, deserted in 1862; Wm. W. Ridenhour, promoted to Sergeant Major in 1862 and 1st Lieutenant and Adjutant in 1863, and died September, 1863, of typhoid fever; Jonas D. Russell, dead; James Russell; John R. Short, promoted to Lieutenant in 1865; Thomas J. Smith, Wm. Smith, James Sanderlin; R. R. Sanderlin, killed at Jeffersonville, Va., in 1863; J. M. Sizemore, B. G. Sikes; Richard Sikes, died in 1862; Aaron Sperling, Wm. Tolson; George W. Tomberlin, discharged on account of disability; J. W. Turnage, L. S. Turnage, Thos. S. Turnage, Wm. Tooke; Jas. M. Williams, promoted to Sergeant in 1864; John Weldon, died in 1862; John C. Wallace; T. B. Wallace, died 1864; W. H. Washington; W. H. Webb, discharged by substitution in 1863; A. J. Wood; R. W. White, promoted to Sergeant in 1863; Brad Wall, died in 1863; George W. Wall, James Wall, Nathan Young.

The "Columbus Minute Boys," a company that had been in the State service for six months, re-organized for the Confederate service on the 19th of May, and elected the following officers: Hatch Cook, Captain; A. V. Boatrite, 1st Lieutenant; John Beasley, 2d; Jas. E. Butt, Brevet 2d.

A fine company of Mounted Partisan Rangers, raised and commanded by Capt. J. H. Sikes, left Columbus for rendezvous at Wilson, N. C., on the 11th of August. The following were the officers elect: J. H. Sikes, Captain; P. A. S.

Morris, 1st Lieutenant; Dr. L. W. Phillips, 2d; J. W. Ware, 3d; John C. Reedy, 1st Sergeant. This command was afterwards increased to a battalion, of which Captain Sikes was elected Major.

The following statistics are obtained from the tax returns of Muscogee county for this year (values in Confederate money): No. of polls 1,166; No. of acres of land 198,902, aggregate value $1,710,035; No. of slaves 6,510, value $3,493,830; value of city property $2,428,175; merchandise $620,961; aggregate value of whole property $13,131,656; number of acres in cotton 2,335, do. in corn 31,882.

W. S. Lee and F. M. Jeter were on the 11th of October elected Aldermen for the 3d Ward, to fill vacancies.

On the morning of the last day of December, before daylight, one of the most destructive fires with which the city was ever visited broke out in the warehouse of Messrs. Greenwood & Gray, corner of Randolph and Front streets. The flames spread with great rapidity, and the whole mass of cotton was soon enveloped in a sheet of fire, giving a brilliant light which illuminated the whole neighborhood of the city. By the exertions of the firemen, the conflagration was confined to the warehouse, but it was with much difficulty that the adjoining auction house of Messrs. Ellis & Livingston, and the Baptist Factory Chapel on the opposite side of Front street, were saved. The amount of cotton in the warehouse was about six thousand bales, belonging in part to planters and in part to buyers. All of it was consumed. The building and a portion of the cotton were insured. The fire was believed to have been the work of an incendiary.

The following were quotations of prices in December: Corn $1.60@$1.80; sweet potatoes $1; peas $1.25@$1.80; sorgo syrup $2.50 per gallon; N. O. sugar 50c. per lb.; salt 50 to 58c. per lb.

INCIDENTS.

The new Presbyterian Church, (corner of Oglethorpe and

St. Clair streets,) was dedicated on the 2d of February—dedication sermon by the pastor, Rev. S. H. Higgins.

The Chattahoochee rose to a great height in February. On the night of the 18th the upper bridge was swept away. It fortunately broke up in passing the rapids, before reaching the lower bridge, and therefore failed to carry off the latter with it. The flood almost reached the flooring of the lower bridge. The banks of the river caved in greatly, particularly on the Alabama side, and the factories were "drowned out" for several days.

Wm. Curran, an Irishman, was shot and killed by Jos. H. Daniel on the 11th of March. The testimony showed that Curran was about to make an attack on Daniel, at the latter's own house, and Daniel shot him in self-defence.

A freshet in April washed away the creek bridge in Girard on the 9th of that month.

Mr. A. G. Lawrence, of Columbus, was killed by a fall from a hotel window in Atlanta on the 26th of August.

An operative in Grant's Factory, named Nickles, was stabbed and killed by another workman, Pickett, on the 29th of August.

Mr. Troup Banks, a son of Col. John Banks, committed suicide by shooting himself with a shot gun, in Wynnton, on the 25th of November. Bad health had affected his mind.

On the night of the 15th of December, the house of Mr. Hughes, in Girard, was burned, and Mrs. Jane Britton, a relative of the family, perished in the flames.

Mrs. Kinsley, wife of John Kinsley, fell from the river bluff on the night of the 26th of December, and was killed by the fall.

PERSONAL.

The Methodist Episcopal appointments for Columbus for the year 1862 were as follows: C. R. Jewett, P. E.; H. H. Parks, St. Luke and Pierce Chapel; Arminius Wright, St. Paul; W. J. Wardlaw, Girard and Factory.

The following county officers were chosen at the election

of January: James G. Cook, Sheriff; F. M. Brooks, Clerk of the Superior Court; A. P. Jones, Clerk of the Inferior Court; J. L. Howell, Tax Receiver and Collector; Thos. Chaffin, Treasurer; J. B. Hicks, Coroner; J. E. Lamar, Surveyor.

Jos. L. Morton was Chief of the Fire Department, and Samuel Lawhon Assistant. Dr. H. M. Jeter was Postmaster of Columbus.

MARRIAGES.

January 1—Martin E. Costan and Ann J. Barber; 9, Amenius U. Bailey and Harriet C. Gregory; 16, Thomas J. Stone and Ursule Taylor; 21, Henry S. Wright and Caroline G. McCrary; 23, John J. Wynne and Martha A. McGehee.

February 2—Joseph Shaw and Emma McGinty, Asa Rabun and Charity Tennell; 4, Wm. J. Gordon and Mary C. W. Baker; 5, John E. Ballou and Mary J. Lamar; 9, James E. Warren and Mary E. Steen, George L. Lapham and Helen Chaffin; 18, Thos. J. McMicken and Margaret Mason; 25, Gustavus A. Koehn and Henrietta Rosenbaum; 26, William Brown and Frances A. Clark.

March 1—Andrew J. Tyler and Rebecca E. Stagg; 6, Elbert J. P. Collier and Sarah A. C. Clark; 9, Jas. Grantham and Matilda Eady; 10, Wm. W. Hall and Nancy L. Hood; 12, Robt. B. Lockhart and Emma J. Rankin; 13, Jas, E. McGrath and Martha J. Olive; 21, Allen Yaughn and Rachel Barentine; 27, Wm. Bryant and Cornelia A. Harris.

April 8—John R. Hortan and Elizabeth McClam; 13, Edmund Mann and Frances M. Morgan, James K. Deckrow and Sarah J. Glenn; 17, Robert R. Thweatt and Mary T. Wales; 21, Andrew J. Brassell and Josaphine F. Sneed, John H. Ward and Mary J. Stephens.

May 1—John L. Preddy and Sarah Braunon; 7, Thos. F. Jones and Sarah J. Johnson; 27, Charles Cogle and Isabella McGehee; 28, Uriah B. Harrold and Mary E. Fogle; 29, W. W. Livingstone and Mary Blair.

June 3—Walter H. Weems and Ella R. Ingram; 8, Pleasant F. Statham and Adaline Duncan; 10, Thos. L. Bagley and Mary C. Rice, John F. Wilding and Sophia Kercheimer; 22, David Ellison and Sarah Upton; 27, Clemens Batestine and Sarah A. Dean.

July 6—Wm. L. Ogle and Savastia T. Teal; 14. Wm. Love and Elizabeth Kearn; 16, Harper J. B. Jones and Catharine B. Spigener; 21, Andrew J. Clark and Jane T. Griggs; 97, Wm. F. Winslett and Elmira C. Pitts; 29, George A. Gammell and Elizabeth C. Smith.

August 4—John Mullins and Elizabeth Copeland; 10, Miles E. Bloodsworth and Martha Cook; 11, Frank Chevers and Ellen Linnehan; 12, Wm. Comer and Abigail Williamson, James B. Sanderlin and Sarah A. Trice; 13, George M. Bryan and Leonora C. Hardison; 17, Felix Roselly and Mary F. Wynne; 18, Geo. T. Hutchins and Barbara A. Baker; 20, Edward T. McCormack and Rebecca Long; 25, James T. Camp and Cecilia Moore; 28, Michael Fagan and Sarah Allen, George Hammond and Georgia Pickett.

September 2—Arthur Lipsey and Catharine Jenkins ; 9, Wm. Letford and Sarah E. Stewart ; 13, John Linnehan and Martha Tillman.

October 7—Joseph Santoin and Lucy E. Echols; 9, Frank Landon and Fannie L. Day ; 15, James Jordan and Georgia A. Clark ; 16, Joseph U. Dickinson and Fannie C. Bridges ; 26, Eugene Arbore and Fannie Trice.

November 1—Robert M. Howard and Alex. C. Lindsey; 16, Henry J. Jones and Sarah J. Henry ; 17, Henry Smith and Mary Ann Dillon; 20, Geo. W. Powell and Jane C. Rodgers ; 25, William R. Turman and Harriet E. Boykin, Thos. E. Blanchard and Sarah E. McDougald ; 26, Albert R. DePoe and Sarah V. Pendleton.

December 1—Charles F. Taliaferro and Lucy H. Bass ; 4, Joel L. Allen and Frances E. Hamilton, Armenius Wright and Sarah A. Taft ; 18, James B. Gladney and Augustus Davis ; 23, Wm. H. Robinson and Mary J. Harris ; 24, John W. Churchhill and Almedia H. Castan ; 28, Charles Tyler and Laura Bolling ; 31, Francis Lewis and Martha Ryals.

DEATHS.

January 1—Anna, daughter of J. Kivlin; 15, (in Beallwood) Dr. Henry Lockhart.

Feb. 3—Gen. Chas. J. Williams; 10, Mrs. Edward Brannon.

March 29—W. Wilkins Brooks.

April 2—Samuel R. Andrews, Miss Mary M., daughter of M. W. Thweatt; 3, D. F. Frederick ; 5, Major John H. Howard; 18, John Fontaine, jr.   -

May 15—Child of Jos. W. Woolfolk; 29, (in Girard) Mrs. Margaret Gifford; 23, Mrs. Narcissa F. Sapp.

June 7—Alderman John Hazleton; 23, R. Watson Denton ; —, (at Columbus, Miss.,) Lieut. James Chambers; 26, (in Girard) Charles B. Lloyd.

July—Adjt. James Ware; 17, Capt. Van Leonard, died of wound in battle near Richmond ; 22, infant son of Rev. W. J. Wardlaw.

August 11—Miss Clara E. Clapp; 14, Mary Augusta Crichton.

Sept. 4—Infant daughter of Solomon M. Crew; 9, Duncan McDougald ; 21, Mrs. Mary M. Dawson.

Oct. 17—Infant daughter of J. A. Shingleur; 26, infant daughter of L. R. Redding; 24, Mrs. Mary V. Hamilton.

Nov. 6—H. P. Albrecht; 17, Henry, son of H. T. Hall; 20, Charles L. Phelps ; 26, child of James M. Chambers, jr.

Dec. 8—George T., son of Alfred Prescott; 11, (in Girard,) Emma, daughter of Lieut. T. Jeff. Bates.

(FROM THE SEXTON'S REPORTS.)

Oct. 2—Child of J. H. Daniel; 3, child of Mrs. Bullook; 4, Mrs. Smith ; 4, Mr. Wright, Peter Boyce; 7, child of Mr. Albright; 9, Mrs. Ballard, —, B. P. Burdet, soldier, Miss Woodruff, child of Mr. Woolfolk; 12, Henry Frone, soldier; 16, child of Dr. Boswell, Mrs. Fox, Miss Rhodes; Mr. Yarn, soldier; 21, Mr. Baugh, Mr. Baugh's child; 22, child of Mr. Culpepper; 25, child of Capt. Humphries; 26, Mrs. Flournoy.

Nov. 1—Child of Mr. Redd, Mrs. Spinks; 3, child of Mrs. Jemison ; 4,

Miss Ann Kirkley; 6, child of Mr. Lawrence; 9, child of Amanda Rogers, child of Mrs. E. Rogers, child of Mr. Couch, child of Mr. McCarvin; 10, child of V. Ogletree, child of Mr. Pike, child of Mr. Smith; 12, child of Mr. O'Bannon; 14, Mrs. Shirley; 15, child of Mr. Furdle, 17, Mrs. Bullock, child of Mr. Weeks, child of Mrs. Conner; 19, Mrs. Britt; 22, Mr. Bullock, Mrs. Harvell; 24, Mrs. Howard; 27, child of Mr. Colquitt, child of Mr. Chambers; 28, H. Montgomery, S. Jones.

Dec. 4—Child of Mr. Montgomery; 8, Benj. Sergureur; 9, child of Mr. Barr; 10, J. E. Jones; 11, child of Maj. Humphries, Mr. Starr.

1863.

Destructive Fires—Local Defence, &c.

The municipal election in December resulted as follows: Mayor, Col. F. G. Wilkins; Aldermen—1st Ward, J. J. Mc-Kendree, W. W. Flewellen; 2d, Chas. E. Mims, J. W. King; 3d, Wm. S. Lee, Frank M. Jeter; 4th, J. A. Bradford, John Ligon; 5th, F. A. Jepson, Wm. Douglass; 6th, James M. Bivins, John Durkin. The vote for Mayor stood—Wilkins 238, F. M. Brooks 207, John Quin 121.

The new Council, at its first meeting, elected the following city officers: Marshal, Thos. Callier; Deputy Marshal, John C. Lovelace; Clerk, George W. Jones; Treasurer, James D. Johnson; Attorney, Wiley Williams; Physician, John B. Baird; Sexton, Wm. H. Harris; Bridge-keeper, Robert Davis; Keeper of Hospital, Mrs. McGehee; Magazine-keeper, Peter Anderson; Wharfinger, Philip H. Alston; City Printer, Thomas Ragland of the *Enquirer*. The salaries of the city officers were raised to correspond with the expenses of living.

Health Officers—P. H. Hartman, B. F. Coleman, Dr. Bozeman, J. K. Redd, Dr. Cleckley, John Johnson, Felix Burrus, W. M. Jepson, John Quin, Charles Wise, F. M. Gray, John Kinsley.

Mrs. McGehee declined to serve as Hospital-keeper with the allowances made, and Mrs. Stringfield was elected.

On Monday night, the 19th of January, the large brick building on the corner of Oglethorpe and Randolph streets— the lower rooms of which were occupied as the Post-office, and the upper story as the boarding-house of Mrs. Teasdale— was consumed by fire. The most valuable matter in the Post-office was saved, but a few mail-bags were burnt. Mrs. Teasdale lost nearly all her household effects. The building belonged to Seaborn Jones, Esq., and had long been used as the Post-office. The fire was no doubt accidental. The Post-office was removed to the corner of Randolph and Broad streets, then known as the Manley & Hodges corner.

Another great fire occurred on the morning of the 3d of February, breaking out in the boot and shoe store of Peter Biehler on Randolph street. It burnt all the houses on the south side of Randolph street from two doors west of the *Enquirer* office to the corner of Broad, and all on the east side of Broad street to and including Dr. Ware's drug store. This included four brick buildings on Randolph street, and five on Broad street. The parties burnt out on Randolph street were P. Biehler, the jewelry establishments of K. Saylor and G. Jordan, the barber shop of Wm. Paine and Weems, the office of Dr. Fogle, dentist. On Broad street, the drug stores of Messrs. Brooks & Chapman and Dr. R. A. Ware, and three dry goods stores were burnt, with a portion of the goods in each of them. Over the burnt stores on Broad street were the law offices of L. T. Downing and John Peabody, Esqs., and the offices of Dr. J. L. Cheney, and Drs. Lee & Phelps. The supply of water was very limited, and to this cause was due the wide-spread destruction by the fire. Four of the buildings on Randolph street were owned by H. H. Epping, also two on Broad street. Dr. Ware, Mr. Downing, and Mr. Morris Kopman each owned one of the burnt buildings.

At a special election held on the 7th of February, Thomas Brassill for the 2d, and Wm. H. Griswold for the 3d, were elected Aldermen to fill vacancies caused by the resignation of Aldermen King and Jeter; and on the 28th of February, II. M. Jeter was elected an Alderman of the 1st Ward to fill a vacancy caused by the resignation of Ald'n McKendree. Alderman McKendree was re-elected in March to fill a vacancy caused by the resignation of Alderman W. W. Flewellen.

A large company was formed to go to the defence of Savannah, then threatened, on the 21st of February. The following officers were elected: F. G. Wilkins, Captain; Jas. M. Everett, 1st Lieutenant; P. J. Phillips, 2d; D. B. Thompson, 3d; James F. Bozeman, 4th. The services of the company were tendered to Gen. Mercer, commanding at Savannah.

A company was formed in Columbus in March, to join Col. Evans' regiment for the Florida service. It organized on the 16th of that month by the election of N. W. Garrard, Capt.; J. F. Burch, 1st Lieutenant; D. B. Booher, 2d; and Stewart Kelly, Brevet 2d.

On account of the presence of the enemy's vessels in the bay, river connection with Apalachicola was suspended this year. Boats ran from Columbus to Chattahoochee, about the mouth of the Flint river.

In July, at the request of Confederate officers in local command, Council instructed the Mayor to have all the citizens of Columbus capable of bearing arms to be enrolled for any emergency requiring local defence. In accordance with this call, there was a general enrollment in the city and county, and seven or eight companies met at the Court-house on the 18th of July, and formed a regiment, electing F. G. Wilkins, Colonel; J. R. Ivey, Lieutenant Colonel; and Jerry Slade, Major. But this organization appears to have been superseded by a regular requisition made by President Davis upon Gov. Brown for the enrollment of 8,000 men for local defence in Georgia. In response to this last call, a regiment was formed at Columbus on the 22d of August, of companies from Muscogee, Harris, Talbot, Taylor, Marion, Chattahoo-

chee and Stewart counties.   W. L. Salisbury was elected
Colonel; Flynn Hargett, Lieutenant Colonel; Capt. Curley,
Major.   The Columbus and Muscogee companies in this reg-
iment were Co. A City Guards, Capt. J. M. Everett; Co. B
City Guards, Lieutenant Brannon; Ivey Guards, Capt. Park;
Chattahoochee Defenders, Capt. Russell.

An "Independent Home Guard" Company of seventy-five
men, composed of men over forty-five years of age, was also
organized—Dr. J. A. Urquhart, Captain; Dr. R. A. Ware,
F. C. Johnson and Wm. B. Langdon, Lieutenants; F. M.
Brooks, W. A. Douglass, B. S. Hardaway, John S. Allen and
Charles Mims, Sergeants; N. L. Howard, W. L. Stapler, C.
E. Johnson and J. I. Lovelace, Corporals; H. Middlebrook,
Treasurer; R. P. Spencer, Secretary.   Two cavalry companies
for the same service, under command of Captains Strother
and Cheney, were also formed.

The news of the death of Gen. Paul J. Semmes, Col. John
A. Jones, and many other officers and privates, killed in the
disastrous battle of Gettysburg, caused much sorrow in Columbus.   Council passed resolutions expressing the deepest
regret for the death of General Semmes and sympathy for his
family, and calling a meeting of citizens to make arrangements for the suitable reception and burial of his remains.
The meeting was held on the 16th of July, and suitable arrangements made to pay the last sad honors to the deceased
citizen and soldier.

Council in November appropriated $5,000 additional to
regular appropriations to assist needy and indigent families
of absent soldiers in the payment of their house rent.

A registration of voters of the city was this year made in
accordance with law, and the total number registered was
365. This number was evidently short of a full registration,
though so many citizens were absent, being in the Confederate service.

Quotations of prices in July : Salt, 30@35c. per ℔; Flour,
25@30c. per ℔,; Pork, 50@60c. per ℔.; Bacon, $1@$1.25 per

℔.; Lard, 90c.@$1; Beef, 40@45c.; Sugar, $1.20@1.25 per ℔.; Syrup, $7@$8 per gallon; Rice, 12½@14c. per ℔.; Butter, $1@$1.25 per ℔. Most of these articles were scarce and hard to get at these prices.

INCIDENTS.

A sensation was created in the city, in April, by news of the death of Robert Emmet Dixon, of Columbus, at Richmond. He was clerk of the Confederate House of Representatives, and was shot by R. E. Forde, of Kentucky, an assistant clerk.

Among the new industries created by the war was a Nail Factory established in Girard by Messrs. D. H. Fowler & Co., of New Orleans. It was run very actively, and turned out a great deal of work of fair quality.

Mr. Robert Davis, bridge-keeper, was found dead on the river bank, on the 4th of September. He had left his house in apparent health but a short time before the finding of his body, which bore no marks of violence or external injury.

On the 13th of October, about one o'clock p. m., there was a general jail delivery. The prisoners rushed upon the jailor as he was opening the door to leave the jail, overpowered him, and succeeded in making their escape. Six or seven white men, confined for counterfeiting and other offences, escaped.

A woman named Smith, living in the lower part of the city, was shot and killed on the 14th of October, by a soldier named Joe Overton, from Arkansas. He was arrested.

The M. E. Conference met in Columbus on the 25th of November—Bishop Early, presiding.

PERSONAL.

J. L. Morton was Chief Engineer, and S. E. Lawhon, Ass't Engineer of the Fire Department.

The election in October resulted in the choice of Col. Jas. M. Chambers as Senator for the District, and Jas. M. Russell and R. R. Hawes as Representatives of Muscogee.

Rev. C. K. Jewett was Presiding Elder of the Columbus

District; Rev. E. W. Speer, Pastor of St. Luke M. E. Church; Rev. Joseph S. Key, of St. Paul; Rev. W. J. Wardlaw, Factory Mission and Colored Charge; Rev. J. H. DeVotie, pastor of the Baptist Church; Rev. S. H. Higgins, of the Presbyterian.

MARRIAGES.

January 1—Chandler M. Pope and Hazeltine Brown; 4, Wm. Freeney and Mary Coker; 7, Joseph Barns and Georgia A. Cary; 15, Thacker B. Howard and Antionette V. Williams, John McCree and Margaret Burnside, Joel W. Moore and Louisa Petty; 20, Wm. R. Hill and L. Nance; 21, Holmes Smith and Mary Welch.

February 1—Donat' Alphonze and Nancy McElmore, Eli Davidson and Martha Belcher; 3, Robert L. Hagler and Catharine Cook; 5, Robert L. Jones and Ophelia Hulsey; 8, White Youngblood and Mary Clark; 9, Francis Collier and Sarah Pigott; 10, Lloyd R. Hoopes and Mary E. Barnard; 11, John Gomer and Nancy Cram; 13, Hugh L. McElvy and Sallie J. H. McElvy; 26, Seaborn J. Howard and Annie P. Schley, Louis Harris and Ella Harris.

March 2—John G. Bush and Ellanora Harris; 3, Eugene Ballamy and Caroline E. Lewis; 5, Daniel L. Wilson and Rosannah A. Calhoun; 10, Wm. M. Chipman and Mary Jane Nealy.

April 5—William A. Davis and Martha Bruce; 9, Joseph B. Pappy and Louisa C. Henry; 18, Robert L. Freeman and Mollie Jackson; 19, James N. Nix and Sarah J. Morgan; 21, Isaac Etheridge and Martha J. Johnson; 23, John B. Lindsey and Helen R. Slade, Wm. Sims and Sarah Jones; 29, Gilbert McDonald and Susan Langford, Isaac C. Ginn and Sarah C. Cordery.

May 1—Henry C. Mann and Laney A. Mixon; 21, Charles M. Smith and Mary M. Hays; 22, James McCarty and Margaret Heagerty.

June 3—Wm. March and Francis R. Brooks; 9, Charles Allard and Mary Alsabrooks; 14, Arthur Montgomery and Mariah McDaniel; 29, Mathew C. Wooten and Lucy M. Taliaferro.

July 2—Charles S. Shorter and Sarah A. Shepherd; 5, Stephen Hamey and Catharine McDonald, Wm. L. M. Smith and Isabella Walker; 7, Johnston Halliman and Zilley Moate; 9, Walter T. Mitchell and Rosannah Kennedy; 12, James M. Parnell and Nancy A. French; 15, A. C. Wingfield and M. W. O'Bannan; 16, Wm. R. Giquilliat and Janet. E. Slade; 22, Jasper Wall and Emaline Taylor; 23, James Searcy and Martha Hamilton, John S. Esler and Elizabeth Thomas; 27, Lyman P. Cowdery and Jane H. Lewis, Wm. F. Winslett and Elmina C. Pitts.

August 5—George M. Dews and Sophronia T. Woodruff; 6, Thos. L. Tinnon and Hennie Roper; 8, Simeon Wooton and Mariah Frost; 9, John G. McKenzie and Martha F. Rentfroe; 12, Jonathan G. Norman and Angeline Duke; 20, Thos. Bird and Clarissa S. West, Fleming Culver and Elvira D. Davis; 23, Lucius Cody and M. L. Akhurst, James M. Williams and Epsey Ann Reid; 27, John Collins and Susan M. Mahone; 28, Thos. E. Reynolds and Elizabeth Taff.

September 1—Norburn T. N. Robinson and Susan R. Bethune; 8, James Mayberry and Susan Murphy; 9, John Wise and Lizzie Wakefield, Elbert L. Wells and Lizzie C. Wise, William H. Baker and Virginia J. Goslin; 12, Thomas Hamilton and Margaret Clark; 14, John Feunty and Sarah Lloyd; 17, Charles A. Terrell and Eliza Parr, Wm. H. H. Blankenship and Josaphine Hallenbeck; 22, Francis A. O'Neal and Amelia F. Boyken; 23, James Laming and Nancy Allen.

October 8—John B. Austin and Margaret Flournoy; 12, Josaphine Echols and Rowena M. Lockhart; 14, John W. Johnson and Caroline M. King, Caleb W. Hughes and Mary J. English; 15, James Jinnett and Elizabeth Folsom; 19, Samuel E. Norton, jr., and Jane Burch; 22, John R. Gregory and Mary B. Rodgers; 28, James F. Waddell and Adelaide V. DeGraffenreid; 29, James H. Farr and Sarah A. Vinson.

November 5—John Schnell and Frances E. Sauls; 15, Zachariah Weisenbergher and Helen Kenny; 18, Lazarus Kohns and Hermenia Straus; 19, S. Davis Tonge and Anna Hochstrasser; 21, Wm. E. Ingram and Sarah F. Bevil; 22, James Herndon and Sarah Knight; 26, John C. J. Ellison and Frances M. Vickers; 28, John Fox and Elizabeth Gale.

December 1—Thomas G. Coleman and Adona Williford; 3, Moses Welch and Mary McCarty, Joseph J. Maddox and Susannah Blackburn; 4, James N. McLester and Anna Sims, Peter K. Edgar and Rebecca C. Aenchbacher; 6, J. J. Tillery and Nancy F. Clegg; 10, Joseph Simmons and Missouri Carey; 14, Emanuel Lopez and Ann V. Pickett; 15, William C. Brooks and Elizabeth Foster, Abner Wilkinson and Rosaline Kent, Isaiah F. Young and Sarah Pickett; 17, John W. Connell and Frances Baldwin; 20, Western Harvell and Tempay Maloney; 23, Wm. B. Free and Elizabeth M. Whitten; 24, George W. Harris and Nancy C. Edwards; 30, Donaldson Huff and Adelia DuBose; 31, Warren R. Kent and Amanda S. Bradford, John R. Mott and Annie E. Chapman.

DEATHS.

(FROM THE SEXTON'S REPORTS.)

Jan. 1—Lt. Col. T. B. Scott; 2, child of Lou. Mayfield; 4, child of John Keller; 5, Mrs. Mary C. Perry; 6, Wm. T. Smith; 9, child of James A. Gue; 10, child of Isabella Kemp; 12, child of F. O. Goodale, child of Wm. H. Chambers, B. F. Lassiter; 13, child of Isabella Kemp; 15, child of James Rumsey, Elizabeth Anders, Louisa W. Thompson; 16, Archibald Burden; 18, step-daughter of J. J. Kemp, S. F. Wiggins; 20, child of Enoch Dudley; 21, L. M. Gager, child of A. H. DeWitt; 22, Stephen Howard, child of Mrs. Smith; 26, child of Mrs. E. J. King, Miss E. A. Young, child of A. Gammel; 27, Mrs. Jane J. Sturgis, child of G. Aenchbacher, child of Adam Smith; 28, Mrs. G. A. Sherwood, child of G. R. Lawrence; 30, Miss J. W. Tilley.

Feb. 2—Mrs. Jane Williams, child of M. A. Blackwell, James Hudson; 6, child of E. E. Adams, L. Decatur Johnson; 7, Mrs. Mary Echols; 8, child of J. H. Dyer, child of W. T. Barnes; 9, John Sullivan; 11, J. Dolan; 15, Miss Mary L. Slade, child of John Maxey; 17, Jett Howard; 20, Cook

Lewis, James M. Chambers, jr.; 21, Margaret Shean; 24, Jordan Broadaway; 25, Samuel Clark, Mrs. N. A. Nuckolls.

March 1—Mrs. Elizabeth Milan; 2, child of J. Lambertson, Peter Holihan; 4, child of J. C. Lovelace; 5, child of J. S. Colbert; 8, child of D. H. Morris, John Barnes; 10, Charles Cleghorn, Major M. W. Perry; 12, Isaac Ellis; 18, two children of W. T. Smith; 19, child of Peter Knowles; 20, child of H. B. Lockett, child of F. C. Humphreys; 24, child of Margaret E. Foley; 25, Thomas Manning, child of H. M. Jeter, John Bowen; 28, child of Nancy Milliner, child of W. H. Hughes; 29, child of W. J. Harper; 31, R. A. Sikes, John W. Allen.

April 3—Child of L. S. Smith; 6, child of M. J. McElrath; 11, child of Mrs. Bradford; 12, child of Lewis Coleman; 13, John P. Sinclair; 16, Patrick Duffy, Moses L. Hann (soldier,) Miss H. M. Cato; 21, Mrs. Julia A. Flournoy, child of Mrs. Charles J. Williams, J. K. Smith (soldier,) Arthur B. Davis; 23, child of David Turner; 27, R. E. Dixon.

May 1—Child of Wm. Bell; 3, child of B. T. Chapman; 8, John H. Mealing, James Wallace; 9, Nollee (soldier,) Miss Mary B. Hannay; 10, Miss Laura A. Greenwood; 12, child of Martha Carnes; 13, child of Mrs. Cook, child of Moses Morris; 14, child of Etna Ellis, child of William Anderson, John Nelson (soldier;) 16, Mrs. Susan C. Young; 18, child of Rebecca Hall, child of Epsy J. Hearn; 20, Major A. M. Gordon, Mrs. Mary Puryear: 22, child of W. H. Chitman, Mrs. W. B. Harris, Mrs. Mary J. Walker; 23, child of Thomas Summergill; 24, child of Josiah Wentry, Jerry Felton; 25, child of Mary E. Shoemaker; 26, Miss Sarah A. Copeland, child of U. H. Shoemake, 27, child of John Isham, Dennis Sullivan, child of Henry Riley; 29, child of J. H. Dyer, Mrs. Mary A. Patterson; 30, child of William McElrarn.

June 2—Cornelius Duffy; 4, child of Eliza Horton, child of Senn; 5, Telitha Frazier; 7, Francis Shoemake; 10, child of Mary E. Shoemake; 11, child of B. Dolin; 16, child of B. Dolin; 17, G. M. Stansel, (soldier;) 19, child of John Rikely, child of William Walker, child of Caroline Hatcher; 20, child of J. S. Smith, child of J. B. Hill; 21, child of Susan Phillips, child of J. M. Young; 25, Mrs. Ann Hull, child of B. A. Berry; 26, child of Eliz. Meredith, J. Pressly (soldier;) 28, child of David Sergeant; 29, W. F. Serrell child of Michael Sullivan, child of Phillip Eifler, child of Mary Ellis, child of James McGirr; 30, George W. Jones.

July 2—Child of Captain Warner, Nancy Mott; 3, child of C. A. Redd, child of J. A. Girdner, Mrs. Louisa Tinnon, child of John Dynon; 4, child of George W. Britton; 5, child of F. M. Boland; 7, Diana Russell; 10, child of Elizabeth Moss; 11, child of Mrs. Allen, child of G. Howard, child of G. W. Langford; 12, child of Dr. T. J. Word, James McCarty; 13, child of Albert Ravenscroft; 14, child of Robert Baldwin, N. B. Drake; 17, child of Wm. Robinson; 19, Emily Bugg; 20, child of Henrietta Mote; 21, child of Simeon Mote, child of Jason Lewis; 24, child of J. H. Smith; 26, child of Francis Williams; 27, child of B. F. Marshall, Mrs. Mary Stewart, child of J. H. Giles, child of Winnie Shepherd; 28, child of Edward Martin, child of John Mote; 31, Mrs. Elizabeth Ligon, child of T. J. Wynn, child of John Tilly.

August 1—Child of Epsy Hearn, Edward Brannan; 3, Miss S. A. Harris, child of Martin Clark; 4, child of R. H. Briggs, child of Simeon Mote; 6, child of C. A. Carpenter, child of Mrs. Allen; 8, Joseph Daniel, child of Robert Kyle; 10, child of D. S. Bullock; 11, child of W. T. Bankston; 12, child of Sarah Morris, child of A. Kaufman, child of Mary Metz, child of Hamilton Raiford, Frank Boykin; 13, child of Delia Bell; 15, J. C. Osborn (soldier;) 17, M. W. Heath; 18, child of T. K. Miller; 19, Mrs. M. A. Ogletree, John Warren; 20, Miss Frances C. Bush, child of W. S. Lloyd; John Gibbons, child of Joseph Nix; 22, Mrs. Mary M. English; 23, child of Geo. Meredith; 24, Delia Bell; 25, child of Frank Rothschild; 26, Mrs. E. B. Chapman; 27, child of Lafayette Watson; 28, child of Sidney Lloyd, child of Mary Willis; 29, August Mitchel, child of Temple Brooks; 30, Elizabeth Walston; 31, Esquire Brock.

Sept. 3—Mrs. Elizabeth Maddox; 4, Y. Johns (soldier;) R. R. Davis, child of N. N. Curtis; 5, child of Mary Copeland; 7, Sarah Morris; 8, child of Thomas Bush; 9, child of Mary Robinson; 10, child of C. Kaufman, child of Samuel Eads, Samuel Kelton; 13, Mrs. M. E. Fleming; 14, Miss Elvira Bowen; 15, Andrew Hagerty, child of J. Rhodes Browne; 16, Mrs. Jane Kendall, Mrs. Jane McGinty; 17, child of Martha Sullivan, Captain G. E. Walker; 18, William Gohian; 19, child of E. W. Nix, John N. Birch, child of Nicholas Howard; 20, James Church; 22, F. W. Allen (soldier;) 26, Mrs. Mary J. Thweatt, child of William Getsinger, child of Jordan L. Howell, Mrs. Sarah Stapler; 28, Francis Wilson, Miss A. A. Switzer; 30, child of Mrs. Hall, Robert J. Emerson (soldier.)

October 3—Child of David Elder; 5, child of Henry T. Hall, Mrs. Shehane; 8, child of Felix McArdle; 9, child of J. S. May; 11, child of L. J. Honsville, child of Mrs. R. Holmes; 12, John Kinsley, Captain Philip Gittenger;* 13, Mrs. Sarah B. Smith, child of J. A. Smith; 14, Patrick Deignan; 15, Amanda Smith, John Tilley; 16, Joseph B. Hughes, O. P. Patterson (soldier;) 19, Georgia Kaufman; 21, child of Dr. Cramp; 23, John S. Arnold, —— Dunaway; 24, Dr. A. I. Robison; 25, John M. Bates (soldier,) W. C. Baker (soldier;) 26, Mrs. Mary Russell; 27, Charles Chapman; 28, W. W. Ridenhour, Frances Short; 31, Julia A. Cooley.

November 1—Mrs. L. A. Reese; 2, child of L. Linsey, child of Henry Mobley; 4, child of Emeline Hudson, Mary A. Wheeler; 7, W. H. Coate (soldier;) 10, child of John Adams; 11, Howard Jones; 12, Mrs. E. M. Saunders; 15, Duncan Martin (soldier;) 17, child of Mary Robinson; 21, child of W. L. Clark, child of A. J. Welch; 23, Edward Bozeman; 25, W. H. Hughes, sr., T. Murphy (soldier;) 26, John Warden, child of Louis M. Collier.

December 3—Miss F. A. Davis, child of Nancy Hooper; 4, Miss Frances Branham, Benjamin Stevens; 5, child of Thomas DeWolf, child of Dr. J. L. Ware; 8, Mrs. Catherine Ford; 9, child of J. M. Baggett; 13, Hamilton Barschall; 18, J. M. Youngblood (soldier;) 22, Thomas Dallard; 23, child of S. Roland, child of Mrs. Wheeler; 24, D. E. Jones (soldier;) 26, William Killcrease; 28, H. C. Harges (soldier,) John Robinson (soldier.)

*Killed in battle, or died of wounds received in battle.

1864.

Condition of Columbus the year precedin ythe close of the War—

Gen. Rosseau's Raid.

This appears to have been a year of few local incidents of an exciting character. But it was a year of unusual business activity in Columbus, and of much feverish excitement caused by the events of the war. A great many residents were absent in the army, or in the prosecution of other public duties, but the city was filled by a transient population, mostly working in the factories, foundries, and other establishments doing work for the Confederate Government or to supply those fabrics usually imported but now cut off by the state of war. The Factories were kept very busy, working all day and all night, employing for that purpose two sets of hands. Among the immense industrial establishments of the city was the Confederate Naval Works, under military command, engaged chiefly in the manufacture of articles needed for the prosecution of the war. This establishment built and furnished two gun-boats for the government, but neither of them rendered any efficient service. One sunk and the other was burned by the enemy. Sometimes work in the large establishments of the city was prosecuted on Sunday, so great was the demand for the public service. The city was full of hospitals for sick and wounded soldiers. The Court-house, among other buildings, was this year devoted to that purpose.

Prices of everything ran up to figures which before the war would have been considered impossible. This was caused by both their scarcity and the great depreciation of the Confederate currency. The pay for work of all kinds was also very high, but still the expenses of living were so great as to impose extraordinarily hard fare on most of the population.

In accordance with an amendment of the acts of incorpora-
tion, made on the 7th of December, 1863, the Clerk, Marshal,
Deputy Marshal and Sexton were elected by the people, and
the following was the result of the election held on the 12th
of December preceding for municipal officers for 1864: F. G.
Wilkins, Mayor; M. M. Moore, Clerk; Thomas P. Callier,
Marshal; J. C. Lovelace, Deputy Marshal; W. H. Harris,
Sexton. Aldermen—1st Ward, H. M. Jeter, J. J. McKendree;
2d, F. S. Chapman, J. M. Dillon; 3d, W. H. Griswold, John
King; 4th, W. R. Brown, J. A. Bradford; 5th, John Quin,
W. L. Salisbury; 6th, J. M. Bivins, John Durkin. The Aldermen were elected by the voters of their respective wards,
and the other officers, named above, on a general ticket.

Council elected J. D. Johnson, Treasurer; Peabody & Bran-
non, City Attorneys; Dr. John B. Baird, City Physician; W.
H. Alston, Wharfinger; William Stringfield, Hospital-keeper.
The *Enquirer* was re-elected City Printer.

Council in April appropriated $5,000 for the relief of the
deserving poor of the city, the number of families needing
and worthy of such aid being reported at one hundred and
fifteen, and afterwards increased to one hundred and fifty.

Columbus was thrown into considerable excitement, in
July, by the approach of a large raiding force under command of General Rosseau. This force, supposed to consist of
1500 or 2000 mounted and picked men, came down through
north-east Alabama, by way of Talladega, struck the Montgomery & West Point Railroad between Notasulga and Auburn, and thence followed the railroad in the direction of Columbus as far as Opelika. The companies organized in
Columbus for local defence, consisting of old men, workmen
in the shops, foundries, factories, etc., were sent out to oppose
their march, and took positions commanding the Crawford
and Salem roads, about a mile and a half west of the city.
This force of undisciplined and poorly armed troops, numbering perhaps six or eight hundred, were under command of
Col. DeLagnel in the field, with the supervision of Major

Dawson, commandant of the post. It occupied the position named during the week ending the 23d of July, when, it having been ascertained that the raiding party had left the railroad at Opelika, striking north-east, the local companies returned to the city. The raiders struck across the country through Chambers county, Alabama, and made their way through to Gen. Sherman's lines above Atlanta.

B. F. Coleman was on the 20th of August elected an Alderman of the 1st Ward, to fill a vacancy caused by the resignation of Alderman Jeter.

Council in August appropriated $5,000 to the Columbus Ambulance Corps, for the benefit of sick and wounded soldiers.

A number of exiles from Atlanta, after the capture of that city, reached Columbus, and in September Council appropriated $5,000 for their relief.

INCIDENTS.

The Eagle Factory company exhibited another instance of its liberality and patriotism by opening a free school for poor children, early this year.

We find the following quotations of prices in April: Flour $350 per barrel; Bacon $4 per pound; Sugar $8 per pound; Coffee $20 per pound; Meal $10 per bushel.

We find the following prices mentioned in October: Imported French Brandy $100 per bottle; Calico $15 per yard; Shoes $100 to $200 per pair.

The Annual Council of the Protestant Episcopal Church of the Diocese of Georgia met in Columbus on the 5th of May—Bishop Elliott presiding.

The residence of Dr. H. M. Jeter, corner of Jackson and Bridge streets, was struck by lightning on the 3d of September, set on fire, and entirely consumed; and on the 6th of September, the stable and outbuilding on the premises of Col. John A. Jones, deceased, were in like manner burned by lightning.

The new steamer Shamrock, built entirely at Columbus, left the city on her first trip to Chattahoochee on the 8th of November.

The residence of Dr. C. T. Cushman, corner of Randolph and McIntosh streets, was entirely consumed by fire on the morning of the 23d of November.

Washington Donally, an employee of the Eagle Mills, was caught by the belting and killed, on the 29th of November.

Frank (or Henderson) Henley was shot and killed by William Dillon, near the corner of Jackson and Few streets, on the morning of the 18th of November, before day.

A gunboat called the Muscogee, built at Columbus for the Confederate Government, was launched on the 22d of December. Mr. Chas. Blain superintended building of the hull. This boat was burnt by the Federal troops under Wilson, while he held possession of Columbus.

PERSONAL.

The M. E. ministers in Columbus for this year were the following: James E. Evans, P. E.; W. P. Harrison, St. Luke; Jos. S. Key, St. Paul; W. J. Wardlaw, Factory Mission; J. T. Ainsworth, colored charge; W. W. Robison, Girard.

The county officers, elected in January, were—John Ligon, Sheriff; F. M. Brooks, Clerk of the Superior Court; John Johnson, Ordinary; James M. Hughes, Tax Receiver; Jordan L. Howell, Tax Collector; D. B. Barnes, Coroner; Thos. Chaffin, Treasurer; J. E. Lamar, Surveyor; G. W. Rosette, Clerk of Inferior Court.

Wm. H. Harris, City Sexton, died on the 13th of May, and E. S. Dennis was appointed to the position temporarily; and at a special election held on the 4th of June, R. T. Simons was chosen to fill out the term.

MARRIAGES.

January 1—Isaac Brigman and Samantha Sizemore, John McFarland and Mary J. Williams; 6, John S. Bridges and Jeffersonia A. Abbott, Daniel O'Brien and Annie Kenny: 7, John W. Pearce and Emma L. Fairwether;

13, George H. Smith and Lurany Byse; 17, Robert H. Noyes and Sarah R. Lamar; 19, Malcom McNeal and Jacintha S. Cooper; 27, Andrew J. Snipes and Sarah J. Simmons, Wm. J. Weeks and Ophelia A. Osborn; 28, Barney Boggs and Susan Harrell; 30, Henry M. Newsom and Permelia Page, Martin V. Cook and Mary S. Bray; 31, Wm. A. Cobb and Martha V. Hazzleton.

February 7—Henry N. C. Pike and Anna L. C. Gentry; 8, John Taylor and Tempy Ann Philips; 9, Young M. Irwin and Martha A. Campbell; 23, Thomas H. Dennis and Evaline E. Wilson; 25, Cautius C. Lyons and Lucy A. Copeland; 28, Madison Upton and Mary R. Littleton.

March 3—Morgan J. L. Fuller and Elizabeth Lowe, Henry T. Williams and Susan Blackstock; 6, John T. Reams and Mary A. Cook; 13, Wm. T. Hinds and Julia Turner' Wm. Cherry and Elizabeth Isham, Henry Lancaster and Mary A. Haddock; 20, James B. Moore and Dora P. Young, John L. Philips and Lucinda Baldwin; 24, John S. Cargill and Julia Kivlin; 25, William Howard and Mary Folsom; 26, John H. Parnell and Frances Streetman; 29, John C. Davis and Frances Ellison; 30, Micajah F. Cooper and Lucinda E. Harris; 31, Garrett B. L. Kirk and Josaphine Farmer, John H. Powers and Angeline Farmer.

April 3—John Wiggins and Elizabeth Higgins; 18, John Beasley and Alice L. Laney; 23, John Robinson and Elizabeth Gordon; 28, George H. Neill and Alabama E. Lindsey.

May 1—Simon G. Glenn and Martha A. Osborn; 4, Pendleton E. Bedell and Christina M. Norman; 10, V. W. Wynne and Emma L. Moffett, James B. Collins and Nettie V. Howard; 13, Robert R. Philips and Mary A. Hagler; 19, James F. Hooten and Mary A. Murphy; 24, Eli Stringer and Catharine Stratford; 26, Robert S. Sherdon and Mary E. Henderson; 29, Bentley Martin and and Matilda Graves, James Kelly and Ann Harrison; 30, Thomas L. Thomas and Mary E. Etheridge.

June 7—John B. Beard and Martha J. Spinks; 12, John W. Lord and Nancy A. Smith; 13, Henry H. Washburn and Fannie McFarland; 14, John M. Kirkland and Amanda Spinks; 16, Julius J. Clapp and Mary E. Dawson; 21, George W. Mays and Sarah Meeks; 26, William Byrd and Lucinda Culbert; 30, Stephen M. Dixon and Fannie E. McDougald.

July 4—John T. Taylor and Lucinda Kilcrease; 6, William T. Crouch and Frances E. Goins; 10, James T. Smith and Henrietta Smith, Benjamin M Tolbert and Evaline Snowden; 20, James C. Cole and Elizabeth A. Beck; 21, Jasper N. Hart and Fannie Gordy; 22, James H. Pulley and Mary Harvey; 24, James L. Quin and Mattie Smith; 26, Lemuel G. B. Wiggins and Mary A. Biggers.

August 2—Thomas J. Jackson and Virginia Miller; 5, John Russell and Sarah A. McLemore; 10, Wm. M. Hogan and Rebecca James; 16, Wm. L. Kingsbury and Frances R. Gilmer; 17, J. W. Williams and Fannie McFarland, Thomas J. Morgan and Martha Davidson; 21, Hillery Wall and Jane Burks; 23, George Darby and Mollie Ballou.

September 1—Wm. Green and Mary A. E. Higgins, B. N. Patrick and

Frances Frederick; 3, Benjamin N. Taylor and Ellen Lewis; Samuel Scofield and Sarah Garris; 13, Andrew J. Cooper and Fannie Cooper; 15, Wm. A. Muncus and Jane Bridwell; 20, Alexander Thompson and Mary Collins.

October 4—John Grant and Margia Phelps; 6, Thos. A. Flannigan and Fannie Gibson; 11, Henry R. Smith and Mozelle Steeley; 12, Albert F. Dasher and Mollie H. Brooks, Robert Hill and Cynthia A. Henderson; 13, George Guess and Letitia Fonhana ; 19, John C. Wolf and Mary C. Caldwell; 20, Wm. M. McAlister and Eleanor M. Lamb; 25, Henry C. Ivey and Mary A. Williams.

November 2—Alvey N. Elliott and Lucinda Blackstock; 3, Louis Harris and Mary Ann Sommers, James W. Sappington and Rebecca E. Stanley; 6, Eskin S. Franklin and Elvania E. Williams, Wm. H. H. Compton and Sarah M. Cooper; 8, Jacob H. Faulkenberry and Missouri Baker; 10, Joseph B. Sewell and Levicy A. McLemore, John K. Filchett and Catharine Anthem, Sutton S. Scott and Lula M. Hurt ; 13, James H. H. Mann and Martha Pattillo ; 16, Wm. T. Tharpe and Mary Ashley; 20, Morgan J. Moore and Sarah A. Clarida; 24, Thompson Rodgers and Cynthia Womak ; 30, John Daster and Ann Braxton.

December 1—Alexander Shelton and Jannette Prince; 4, Andrew J. McCum and Sarah A. Davis; 6, Thos. J. Cox and Emma L. Nuckolls, Gabriel Bass and Mary Ann Thomason, Wm. H. Bradford and Matilda A. Wilson; 8, James E. Torrey and Nancy Linge; 14, Marcellus C. Tarver and Sallie C. Grant; 15, Oliver H. P. Poe and Edna L. McGruder, David G. Little and Sarah Hardin; 22, Thomas Gilbert and Fannie E. Johnson, Benjamin L. Wyman and Victoria Hoxey, L. P. Aenchbacher and Mattie S. Morris; 25 Robert B. Stegall and Matilda C. Murphy; 27, Job N. Harrison and Louisa Howard.

DEATHS.

January 1—Mrs. C. Boyd, Walter M. Gunby; 2, T. W. Reid;* 3, Jos. A. Sanders; 4, Lewis W. Griswold, Anderson Walker; 5, Eddie Gunbe; 6, Miss Minnie Lowther; 8, Mrs. Laura Spencer, Mrs. Sarah E. Phelps, child of James Wells; 11, child of Lafayette Walker, child of Mrs. Yancy ; 16, child of Mrs. Gasoway ; 18, child of Lucinda Phelton, Ben. Brock; 19, W. Jones,* — Howard; 20, child of A. D. Brown, jr.; 21, child of G. W. Chase, E. L. Lawson ;* 24, Matt Watson; 25, child of Mrs. C. Caldwell; 26, M. L. Benning; 27, child of James Rowe, Miss Fannie Brooks, Mrs. M. M. Crouch; 29, G. W. Rehay ;* 30, Mrs. Ann Lewis; 31, C. W. Stewart.

February 2—J. E. Ferrell,* G. W. Adkins ;* 4, Miss Mary E. Lanier ; 6, child of R. M. Gray; 7, child of N. N. Curtis, Mrs. A. A. Fortunbury, Capt. W. E. Jones; 9, child of Leonard Bates ; 14, John Sanders, child of W. M. Allen;* 15, child of Nancy Roland; 16, Myra V. Gray ; 20, Mrs. Mary Silvers, J. M. Moon; 21, Mrs. Catharina Bulger, Wm. Catlet ;* 22, Emma Buffington, Lewis Milan; 24, A. J. Lions; 25, W. G. Miles ;* 26, Mrs. Mary Williams; 27, child of John Madden ; 29, Mrs. Mary Tilmon, Mrs. Augusta Calahan, child of F. O. Goodale.

*soldiers.

March 1—Child of George Stain, Z. E. Linnahan; 5, Allen O. Jefferson, Isaac Heard, child of H. G. Ivey, Noah Gordy; 9, Miss Amanda Baugh, Mrs. Jane M. Ogletree; 10, Andrew Johnson; 11, child of Mrs. S. C. Stewart; 12, Mrs. Elizabeth Harris; 13, Mrs. Mary B. Lawrence; 18, Miss Mary L. Allen; 19, child of John R. Biggers; 20, Col. Seaborn Jones, child of J. M. Crouch; 21, Miss Mary A. Williams; 23, child of A. J. Putnam; 24, child of J. A. Gunter; 27, child of H. T. Snead; 29, Hugh A. Cooper; Dr. John M. James.

April 2—Mrs. Freeman; 3, E. Huskey; 12, J. L. Daniel;* 13, Fred G. Adams; 17, Miss Caroline Tapper; 18, child of R. M. Aldworth, child of T. J. Bradey; 19, William White;* 21, Mrs. C. M. Merry, J. H. Merry; 22, child of Drewry Goins; 24, child of D. H. Fowler; 25, Mrs. L. V. Salisbury; 27, child of John H. Bass, child of Mary Rogers; 31, child of Porter Ingram.

May 1—Child of H. M. Jeter; 3, Mary E. Hall; 5, Thomas H. Lassiter; 6, Mrs. Julia Hudson; 7, H. E. Wright; 10, James Wooten; 11, Miss Mary E. McCarley, child of G. Sauls, child of Mrs. Harris; 16, William W. Lawrence, Mrs. Lucy E. Cairnes; 17, Mrs. L. Harris; 18, Mrs. Ann Thomas; 20, Mrs. C. A. Sappington; 21, J. T. Standmire;* 22, M. A. C. Burns;* 23, child of Dr. H. M. Jeter, J. C. Blue;* 24, child of E. W. Blau, Captain Walker Anderson; 27, Mrs. M. Moughan, Mrs. Mary Colzey; 31, child of W. Raulsan, H. A. James.*

June 1—William R. Cooper; 2, child of P. M. Stathan, J. W. Edge;* 3, child of Thomas Hunt; 4, child of Martha Costan, R. Freeman;* 5, Samuel Fuller; 8, Margaret Gray; 12, child of Joseph Blunt, child of Mrs. E. Smith, child of Alfred Prescott; 13, S. H. Blackmon; 15, William Young; 16, child of T. G. Holt; 18, child of J. Crich, John Crogan, child of Mr. Baggett, child of F. C. Johnson; 19, Robert Chambers, child of James Crouch; 22, Narcissa Goslin; 24, Margaret Reedy; 27, child of W. H. Hall, M. L. Matthews, child of N. Hightower; 28, Capt. F. C. Tillman;* 29, child of Z. Pike, child of Emeline Collins; 8, Joel Reeves,* Isaac Youngblood,* B. Powell;* 9, F. B. Gaston,* R. F. Ingle,* Sergeant Wiley Carmiter,* B. H. Alderman,* Charles Spidle,* Martin Wittinger,* W. A. Mullin,* William Hartsden;* 26, L. P. Goforth.*

July 1—Child of J. H. Warner; 3, child of Docia Allen; 4, child of J. Blakely, child of Mollie Bass; 7, W. J. Williams, child of Mariah McClary; 9, J. G. Perryman; 10, child of Wm. McElrath, child of Mary Seaborns, child of Susan Manuel; 12, Mrs. Strother; 13, child of Rebecca Vickory, child of Francis Ingram; 15, child of Elizabeth Dunaway, Richard O. Hearn; 16, child of T. G. Holt, child of Jeff Mormon; 17, child of Martha Torbet; 20, O. C. Young, Joseph Echols, Mary Powell; 23, child of — Freeldes; 24, child of J. A. Walls; 25, child of Sidney Butler, Elizabeth King; 26, child of Louisa Butler; 27, James Britton, John Cullin, B. A. Sorsby, John Inglish; 31, child of Mr. Babat; 31, child of Mary French, Martha Giboon.

August 2—Child of Caroline Stowers; 3, Capt. W. D. Banks, child of Thomas Tinnon; 5, child of W. D. Atkins; 7, Mrs. Mosman; 8, child of

*Soldiers.

Lunnar Linarey, Paul Hanly, Camden Evans; 9, child of Wain Dukes, Temperence Reedy; 10, child of Mr. Comer; 12, Jacob Mormon, Watkins Banks; 15, Mrs. M. C. Murrell, child of W. C. Kennedy, Miss Mary E. Moore, child of B. N. Powell, Mrs. Bridget McHall, Martha Martin; 19, child of J. K. Hainny; 20, W. Y. Spencer, W. J. Kellet; 21, child of Sarah Bauderman, John E. Davis, Thad. Ruse, Wm. Knight; 22, J. M. Wright, child of J. M. Nobles; 23, child of E. N. Bradshaw, Miss N. Reames; 25, Miss Caroline Fuller, S. K. Hodges; 26, D. H. Fowler; 28, child of J. Landhan, Frank Jones; 29, Miss Susan A. Hawks; 31, child of George Gammel, J. N. Cobb, child of A. P. Rood, Mrs. Margaret Bozeman.

September 1—Child of J. C. Gateman; 2, Crawford Smith, child of Catharine Fusell; Rev. G. W. Stickney, John N. Sanders; 4, Lt. M. Blanchard; 5, child of Thomas DeWolf, Joseph W. Woolfolk; 7, Mrs. Mary Burns, child of R. W. Evans, Mary Mays; 8, L. Y. Mansford, Mrs. Elizabeth Sledge, Mrs. E. C. Ticknor; 9, W. T. Abbott, Joseph Oswall; 10, Mrs. Martha C. Goins, J. R. Bedell, James H. Wilson; 12, child of Martin West, Elizabeth Dunn, B. S. Williams, child of J. R. Banks; 13, two children of Mrs. J. Noles, child of L. Lindsey; 14, W. J. Laster, Paul Hanly, child of D. F. Wadsworth; 15, child of Jennie Lewis, T. M. Williams, James Comer, Henry Burrell, Berry Wilson, Elijah Cook, child of Thomas Names; 18, Mrs. Pittman, Mary Harper, child of Col. Roode, child of Thomas McFarland; 19, child of A. Cadman, Francis Binnion; 20, child of William Rynehart, Mrs. Lucinda Shelton; 21, Mrs. Goodson; 25, Miss Eliza Whitten; 26, child of Robert Kigler; 27, Charles H. Stewart, child of Jasper Teal; 28, Vinson Ogletree; 29, E. F. Powell.

SOLDIERS.—John C. Carroll, F. M. Price, R. J. Medower, A. L. Murry, R. McCulloch, M. Humply, R. Fulling, H. Lockhart, A. Stansel, W. Butler, R. H. Lee, N. Sawyer, L. M. Stephens, John Ferrell, F. M. Nix, B. Reid, A. P. Glaston, J. McKinny, J. C. Croker, R. J. Roberts, A. Weaver, J. D. Ledbetter, T. Ware, A. C. Hudson, C. A. Dean, E. Turner, R. Nickols, C. S. Elmore, C. Glasscock, E. Jenkins, J. J. Scoot, H. Chowing, M. C. Rembert, B. Elmore, John Nobles, J. R. McCullin, Fowler Phillip, H. Gates.

1865.

Last Year of the War—Confederate Prices—Wilson's Raid.

The municipal officers of 1864 were re-elected, with the exception of a few changes of Aldermen. The candidates for Mayor were F. G. Wilkins and B. F. Coleman, and the former was re-elected. Thos. P. Callier was re-elected Marshal; J. C. Lovelace, Deputy Marshal; M. M. Moore, Clerk; and R. T. Simons, Sexton. Aldermen—1st Ward, J. J. Mc-Kendree, W. W. Robison; 2d, F. S. Chapman, F. C. Johnson; 3d, John King, W. H. Griswold; 4th, J. C. Porter, J. McIl-henny; 5th, John Quin, J. M. Everett; 6th, J. M. Bivins, John Durkin.

Council elected J. D. Johnson, Treasurer; Jos. E. Roper, City Physician; Peabody & Brannon, City Attorneys; W. H. Alston, Wharfinger; Mrs. McGehee, Hospital Keeper; —— McKenzie, Bridge Keeper.

Notwithstanding the now feverish excitement in reference to the war, the steady advance of the enemy, the waning prospects of the Confederacy, the constant withdrawal of the working men of the city to meet passing or apprehended raids, and the scarcity and high prices of all the comforts of life, Columbus still presented a busy appearance and had a large transient population. The factories and workshops were kept running busily, and all their fabrics not made for or taken by the Government, found a ready sale. Employment was given by these establishments and by the Quartermaster's Department and other agencies, to large numbers of people who otherwise would have suffered much. Never did a people, on the verge of such spoliation and humiliation as soon followed, more nobly display the virtues of patience and heroism.

A line of fine steamers was in January and February plying regularly between Columbus and Chattahoochee, making almost daily trips. They were the Jackson, Capt. Dan Fry; the Indian, Capt. C. D. Fry; the Shamrock, Capt. W. Wingate; the Mist, Capt. A. Fry; and the Munnerlyn.

We quote some auction prices (Confederate currency) in January: Cow and calf, $360; fine brood mare, $4,500; negro boy 21 years of age, $3,950; negro girl of 18, $3,700; Augusta shirting $6 per yard; salt 85 to 88c. per lb.; pink satin $70 per yard; cooking stove $1,500; cow $500; cloth shoes $30; blankets $70; dinner plates $82.50 per set; sugar $6 to $7.75 per lb.; silver coin $1 for $45.

Frank, a promising son of Mr. Brad.˙Chapman, was killed by the accidental discharge of his gun, while he was hunting on the Alabama side of the river, on the 14th of January.

Capt. C. D. Fry fell from the hurricane roof of the steamer Indian, at Johnson's Landing, on the 25th of January, and received injuries which resulted in his death.

John Smith, living on the Alabama side near the upper bridge, was shot and killed by his step-son, William Wright, on the 11th of February. The difficulty originated in a disput growing out of family matters. Wright fled.

An incident that caused great sensation and excitement in the city was the killing, on the 18th of February, of private John Lindsey, of the 17th Georgia regiment. He was shot by Bob Bennett, one of the Provost Guard of Columbus. Young Lindsey was accused of creating a disturbance of some kind, and the guard was endeavoring to arrest him. He had mounted his horse to go home, when Bennett fired and shot a ball through his head, killing him instantly. A large crowd soon gathered, and demanded the delivery of Bennett, who had sought the protection of the military authorities. Col. Von Zinken, commandant of the post, promised to deliver Bennett to the civil authorities, but it was afterwards announced that he had escaped. John Lindsey was a young man much beloved for his generous and manly character, and was a brave soldier. Bennett belonged to an Arkansas regiment, and had been assigned to light duty on account of severe wounds. Col. Von Zinken was arrested, a few days afterwards, by the civil authorities, on the charge of the murder of young Lindsey. A court-martial was also ordered by Gen. Beauregard to investigate the charge. The civil trial was before Judges McKendree, Quin, Thompson and Salisbury, of the Inferior Court. Messrs. Peabody, District Solicitor, Johnson and Holt conducted the prosecution, Gen. Howell Cobb and Major R. J. Moses the defense. The charge against Col. Von Zinken was that he was accessory to the murder. The court. after a patient investigation of several days, in which a number of witnesses were examined on both sides, and able arguments made by the counsel, acquitted him of the charge.

Two boys, named John Madden and William McElrath, were killed at the Naval Iron Works on the 21st of February, by the explosion of an old shell which they had found in the yard and were trying to open.

Mr. Robert Aldworth was accidentally killed on his place near Columbus, on the 22d of February. He struck a negro, with whom he had some difference, with the butt of his gun, and the shock discharged it, the load passing into his body and killing him in a few minutes.

Cotton sold in February at 75 to 80 cents, Confederate money. The following quotations of other articles are copied from the *Sun* of Feb. 26th: Bacon $4 to $5 per lb., Pork $2 75 to $3 50, Lard $3 75 to $4 50, Butter $5 to $6, Eggs $3 50 to $4 50 per dozen, Beef $2 to $2 50 per lb., Corn $14 to $16 per bushel, Sweet Potatoes $12 to $16 per bushel, Salt $1 10 to $1 25 per lb., Chickens $4 to $5 each, Osnaburg $6 per yard, Sorghum Syrup $12 to $16 per gallon, Cane do. $16 to $20, Sugar $7 to $10 per lb., Sole Leather $14 to $15 per lb.; Irish potatoes $50 to $60 per bushel.

On the 8th of March, the stable and carriage house of Mr. William Beach, on Randolph street, and the residence of Mr. Peter Preer, adjoining, were destroyed by fire.

About the first of April a difficulty occurred on the streets between Dr. A. C. Wingfield, a physician of established reputation and much respected citizen, and Dr. —— Rossey, in which pistol shots were exchanged, and Dr. Wingfield was killed. Dr. Rossey was acquitted on the ground of justifiable homicide. He was only a transient resident of Columbus.

PERSONAL.

The M. E. preachers for this year were—A. Wright, P. E.; W. P. Harrison, St. Luke's; Jos. S. Key, St. Paul's; J. R. Littlejohn, Girard; J. T. Ainsworth, Factory Mission; W. W. Robison, Colored charge.

At the County election held on the 4th of January, the following Judges of the Inferior Court were chosen: J. R. Ivey, J. J. McKendree, John Quin, D. B. Thompson.

W. A. Brannon and F. M. Brooks were Justices of Upper District, and J. A. Whiteside and R. W. Milfoed of the Lower. George Meredith and J. Shoup, Constables.

MARRIAGES.

January 1—George W. Allen and Bethany Higden; 2, Christopher C. Collins and Jessie A. Bridges; 3, Ephraim M. Tilton and Winney Long; 8, James D. Malam and Martha E. Johnson; 10, Newton A. Horn and Sarah Bell; Henry Sillman and Nancy Halley; 12, William T. Hill and Polly Peck; 15, John W. Jones and Sarah Jane Bertram; 17, William Smith and Sarah I. Caffs; 18, William J. Slatter and America S. Greenwood; 19, James Baet and Louisa Jane Blake; Julius Emerich and Hannah Finiler; 29, David Ballard and Eliza Ginn.

February 1—Thomas K. Wynn and Mary Lucinda Shelby; 6, James Corden and Sarah J. Allen; 12, Charles F. Duncan and Mary E. Campbell; 15, John W. Wright and Mary L. Hardaway; Marcus Fish and Rosa Taylor; 16, James H. Ames and Lucy A. Smith; James K. Hughes and Julia A. Coleman; 20, Redd G. Williams and Permelia Ann Biggers; 23, William A. Foster and Martha L. Skinner; George W. King and Nancy Horton; Thomas A. Power and Elizabeth McSwain; David C. Stratten and Emily Crawford.

March 2—David W. Stubbs and Nelly C. Miller; 5, William B. Holmes and Laura J. Maxwell; Andrew J. McDonald and Ann Manning; 6, Samuel E. Wells and Mary Ann Florence; 9, Richard M. Goodroe and Rebecca J. Smith; 12, Francis Hewson and Caroline C. Mahan; 13, James W. McDonald and Puss Mobley; 19, John Finney and Mary Benton; James B. Hathcock and Sarah J. Cattle; 23, Thomas R. Guice and Vernie McJunkin; William C. McCarty and Fannie P. Butt; William D. Amyet and Jarusha Simmons; John S. Stephens and Rebecca Pilkinton; 26, Thomas C. Preddy and Sarah J. Kelly; Peter R. Hyatt and Sarah Lascar; Solomon Clark and Minerva Patillo; 28, Francis W. Jenkins and Mary Ann Ward; Charles W. Lefler and Mary A. Ward; 30, Fleming Hodges and Martha A. Bozeman; 31, A. W. Humphries and Elizabeth L. V. Taylor.

April 2—Josiah Coskins and Lucinda Gardner; 5, John S. Smith and Sallie C. Hanks; 9, LeRoy Kilgore and Martha Goodale; Frank Lindsey and Laura Leake; 13, A. H. Chandler and Mary E. Pullum; 18, John W. Goodloe and Eliza A. Lewis; 29, James A. Clegg and Frances Blackstock; Charles F. Reese and Mattie A. Wade; 30, William J. Wolf and Sarah Ann Jones.

In April, news of the approach through Alabama of a large
Federal raiding party under command of General Wilson,
caused a sensation in Columbus, which was quickened into a
state of alarm and excitement when the enemy reached and
captured Montgomery. Many refugees from that city and
other parts of Alabama fled to Columbus. The local military
authorities organized all the available forces for defense.
The preparation was hasty, troops mostly wholly inexperienced, and the arms generally very inferior. The military
authorities determined with these to attempt a defence of the
city. The enemy arrived in sight of Columbus, on the Alabama side of the river, on Sunday, the 16th of April. We
copy from the *Enquirer*, of June 27th, (which was the first
number of a paper issued in the city after the raid,) an
account of the attack and capture of the city:

On Sunday, the 16th of April, the last battle of the war, on this side of the
Mississippi river, was fought in Girard, Alabama, opposite this city.

The Confederate troops consisted of two regiments of the Georgia State
Line, Waddell's battery, some of the forces of Gens. Buford and Wofford, a
small number of the Georgia reserves, the organized companies for local defense in this city, besides a number of citizens of Columbus and a few hastily
collected reserves of Russell county, Alabama—numbering in all, perhaps,
two thousand men. The outer fortifications, that had been constructed for
the defense of the city, were abandoned for the want of men to defend so long
a line, and the troops were drawn into a line of rifle pits, extending from Dr.
Ingersoll's hill to the "upper bridge," over the Chattahoochee; this line embracing the Opelika railroad and the upper bridges, and two fortifications
near the ends of the trenches, in which batteries were placed. A considerable portion of the excavation and embankment forming this line of defense
was thrown up on the morning of the day of battle. The lower, or "city
bridge," was not encircled within the line, but the plank on the Girard end
had been torn up on Saturday evening, and on Sunday morning every preparation was made to fire and destroy this bridge in the event of an attempt
by the enemy to force its passage.

The first appearance of the Federal forces was about two o'clock, P. M.,
when their advance drove in the Confederate pickets on the Hurt's bridge or
lower Crawford road. It appears that at Crawford the advancing forces had
divided and took the two roads from Crawford to this city, and that the column on the upper and shorter road awaited the arrival of the other to make the
first demonstration. The Confederate pickets, or scouting party, retreated into
the town, closely followed by the Federals, who were within good rifle range

and firing briskly at the retreating party. This advance was met by a fire from a small Confederate force near the creek bridge in Girard, and from the battery on the red hill near the upper bridge, and was soon compelled to retire. A portion of this party, however, made a dash at the lower bridge, firing through it when they found their passage stopped by the tearing up of the flooring. The order was then given to fire the bridge, which was quickly carried out, and it was soon wrapped in flames. In the execution of this order, Capt. C. C. McGehee, of one of the Naval Iron Works companies, acted with conspicuous gallantry. In this first brush two or three men on each side were killed and several wounded.

From two o'clock until dark no attack was made by the Federal troops, though it was evident that they were arriving in considerable numbers and were preparing for the conflict. They showed themselves in small squads on most of the hills commanding a view of the city and of the Confederate line of defense, and the men and their horses took shelter behind these hills and in the small timber along the western suburbs of Girard. The Confederate batteries, meantime, were engaged in shelling the eminences on which these demonstrations were made, and the general conviction in the city was that the Federals were making preparations for shelling Columbus at night. All the Federal forces, we believe, were mounted men, and the sequel proved that they had but two or three, if so many, pieces of artillery with them on Sunday afternoon.

Thus matters continued until night had fairly set in. It was a clear but dark night. About eight o'clock the Federals, dismounting their men, made a vigorous charge upon a portion of the Confederate line. It was met steadily by the Confederate forces, and the musketry firing was for some time sharp and rapid. The batteries also opened upon the assailants, and to those unused to the din of battle it appeared as if the destruction of life must necessarily be great. The attack was repulsed. Again and again the Federal forces, deepening their columns, advanced under cover of the night, to the assault, and again they met by a continued roll of musketry, at close quarters, and by the bellowing cannon in the fortifications. But the Confederate line of defenses was a long one to be manned by so small a force, and a single line of raw troops, even in trenches, could not be expected long to hold out against the constantly compacting and reinforced columns of their assailants. Before the line had been broken, however, it was discovered that a squad of the Federal troops had by some means made their way to the Girard end of the upper bridge and were actually holding the bridge at that end, in rear of the line of defense! How they gained this position is not yet fully known. It is generally supposed that it was by making their way, either in disguise, or under the shelter of some ravines and the darkness of the night, through the line in the neighborhood of the railroad bridge, and coming down on the bank of the river. This successful manœuver proved very embarrassing to the further defense of the city. Orders from headquarters in Columbus were intercepted on their way to the battle-field in Girard, and no communications could be kept up, nor any general understanding of the progress of the fight obtained. In a short time there was a promiscuous rush for the bridge. Friend and foe, horsemen and footmen, artillery wagons and ambulances, were crowded and jammed together in the narrow avenue, which was "dark as Egypt," or "Erebus," for that bridge had no gas fixtures and was never lighted. How it was that many were not crushed to death in this tumultuous transit of the Chattahoochee, seems incomprehensible. The Confederates had no reserved forces, except a few squads for guard duty, in the city, and very little resistance was made after the Federals had crossed the bridge. But nearly all the known casualties on the Confederate side nevertheless occurred on this side of the river. The chivalric and lamented Col. C. A. L. Lamar fell while gallantly endeavoring to rally a squad of Confederates at the city end of the bridge. So did the noble and much-regretted young Alexander W. Robison, who was killed at the bridge. Judge Waddell, of Russell county, was shot and mortally wounded on the upper part of Broad street. Mr. J. J. Jones, the local editor of this paper, and Mr. Evan Jones of Apalachicola, were also killed on Broad street. Capt. S. Isidore Guillet, Col. Von Zinken's chief-of-staff, was killed on the Girard side, while gallantly doing his duty. If there were any other Confederates killed on that side of the river, we have not been able to learn their names. Mr. —— Smith, a watchmaker of this city, and an Englishman by birth, was killed on Broad street; and we hear that two young men, whose names are unknown to us, were killed near the brickyard, in the eastern suburbs of the city. These are all the deaths on the Confederate side of which we have any knowledge.

We have no means whatever of making an estimate of the Federal loss in this fight. The darkness of the night prevented any view of the ground while the battle was going on, and the victors held the field and all access to it afterwards. Had the attack been made in the day time the loss of the assailants must have been much greater than it really was, and there is every reason to believe their casualties were quite numerous.

Northern papers state that Gen. Wilson telegraphed that he captured about one thousand prisoners. The Confederate troops that escaped were scattered in every direction, some on either side of the river, and the organization so hastily collected to defend the city was dispersed to as many quarters as those from which it had been brought together.

Maj. Gen. Howell Cobb was the ranking officer of the day, but the direct command of the troops in the field was assigned to Col. Leon Von Zinken, whose coolness and intrepidity were conspicuously displayed and acknowledged as well by the Federals as the Confederates.

The fight was gallantly maintained on both sides. The Union troops have made ready acknowledgment of the courage with which the Confederates, for mostly raw troops and all hastily thrown together, stood their ground; and the attack of the Federals was made and followed up with an unquailing spirit.

It is plain that an error was committed in making the line of defense too long. Had the railroad bridge been partially destroyed, and the line shortened and doubled around the upper bridge, a much stouter and more prolonged resistance could have been made. But the Federal force would have taken the city in spite of the best dispositions made with our limited means, for they could have sent a large body of troops to cross the river either above or below the city, and have entered it from the Georgia side while they were making demonstrations against the force in Girard.

A very large quantity of cannon, small arms, ordnance and commissary stores fell into the hands of Gen. Wilson, and were destroyed.

We have called this the last fight east of the Mississippi. There was a sharp fight at West Point on the same day, but earlier in the day. There may possibly have been a brush or two in Western North Carolina after the 16th of April, but nothing like a battle of any importance. A fight occurred two or three weeks later in Western Texas, near the old Palo-Alto battle ground, in which the Confederates were successful; and this closed the fighting of the civil war, so far as we have any advice.

GEN. WILSON'S REPORT.

We make on next page extracts from Gen. Wilson's report of his raid through the South, including the capture of Columbus. Only two or three statements call for notice here, either because of their incorrectness, or because they serve to explain some incidents about which there was doubt. Gen. Wilson admits a loss of twenty-five men killed and wounded in the attack on the Confederate position on the Alabama side of the river. He states that his advance, which dashed through Girard about two o'clock p. m. on the 16th, would have captured the lower bridge had the Confederates not fired it. This seems to settle the disputed question as to the propriety of firing the bridge at that time, because Gen. Wilson's assertion shows that Gen. Upton's advance had orders to make an attack on the bridge, whether they would then have captured it or not. The report does injustice to the Confederates in not stating that their line of defence around the upper bridge, &c., was a single one and long drawn out, and that the four or five hundred Federal troops, for whom he claims the honor of breaking through the Confederate lines, did not really encounter one-half their own force. It also confirms the statement that the Federal forces had, in some manner not yet clearly explained, obtained possession of the

13

bridge in the rear of the Confederates before the line of the latter was broken through.

Gen. Wilson's statement of the work of destruction by his orders at Columbus is evidently only approximately correct. In some respects it exaggerates, and in others falls short of the extent of the vandalism. The general estimate of the amount of cotton destroyed puts it at but little over one-half of his statement. He burnt two printing offices (those of the *Sun* and *Times*) and some private buildings, of which he makes no mention. It was claimed that the private buildings were unavoidably burnt because of their contiguity to establishments operated in aid of the Confederacy. There was only one paper mill (the Rock Island) in this section, and therefore only one could have been destroyed.

CAPTURE OF MONTGOMERY.

In the march from Selma, LaGrange's Brigade of McCook's Division was given the advance. The recent rains had rendered the roads quite muddy, and a small body of Rebel cavalry, in falling back before LaGrange, destroyed several bridges, so that our progress was necessarily slow.

At seven a. m., April twelfth, the advanced guard reached Montgomery, and received the surrender of the city from the Mayor and Council. Gen. Adams, with a small force, after falling back before us to the city, burned ninety thousand bales of cotton stored there, and continued his retreat to Mount Meigs, on the Columbus road. Five guns and large quantities of small arms, stores, etc., were left in our hands and destroyed.

Gen. McCook assigned Col. Cooper, Fourth Kentucky Cavalry, to the command of the city, and immediately began the destruction of the public stores. Major Weston, of the Fourth Kentucky, with a small detachment of his regiment, made a rapid march to Wetumpka, swam the Coosa and Tallapoosa rivers, and captured five steamboats and their cargoes, which were taken to Montgomery and destroyed. Early on the fourteenth the march was resumed. I instructed Brevet Major General Upton to move with his own division directly upon Columbus, and to order LaGrange, with his brigade, to make a rapid movement upon West Point, destroying the railroad bridges along the line of march. I hoped to secure a crossing of the Chattahoochee at one or the other of these points.

Minty followed Upton by the way of Tuskegee. McCook, with a part of his division, remained a few hours at Montgomery to complete the destruction of public stores. Shortly after leaving his camp, near Montgomery, La-Grange struck a force of rebels under Buford and Clareton, but drove them in confusion, capturing about one hundred and fifty prisoners.

About two p. m. of the sixteenth, General Upton's advance—a part of Alexander's brigade—struck the enemy's pickets on the road and drove them rapidly through Girard to the lower bridge over the Chattahoochee at Columbus. The rebels hastily set fire to it and thereby prevented its capture. After securing a position on the lower Montgomery road, Gen. Upton detached a force to push around to the bridge of the factory, three miles above the city. He then made a reconnoisance in person and found the enemy strongly posted in a line of works covering all the bridges, with a large number of guns in position on both sides of the river.   He had already determined to move Winslow's Brigade to the Opelika or Summerville road and assault the works on that side without waiting for the arrival of the Second Division.

I reached the head of Winslow's Brigade of the Fourth Division at four o'clock, and found the troops marching to the position assigned them by General Upton.   Through an accident, General Winslow did not arrive at his position till after dark, but General Upton prepared to make the assault in the night, and coinciding with him in judgment, I ordered the attack.

Three hundred men of the Third Iowa Cavalry, Col. Noble commanding, were dismounted, and, after a slight skirmish,· moved forward and formed across the road under a heavy fire of artillery. The Fourth Iowa and Tenth Missouri were held in readiness to suppprt the assaulting party.   At eight and a half o'clock, p. m., just as the troops were ready, the enemy at a short distance, opened a heavy fire of musketry, and with a four gun battery, began throwing canister and grape.   Generals Upton and Winslow in person, directed the movement ; the troops dashed forward, opened a withering fire from their Spencers, pushed through a slashing abatis, pressed the Rebel line back to their outworks, supposed at first to be their main line.   During all this time the Rebel guns threw out a perfect storm of canister and grape, but without avail.

Gen. Upton sent two companies of the Tenth Missouri, Capt. Glassen commanding, to follow up the success of the dismounted men and get possession of the bridge.   They passed through the inner line of works, and, under cover of darkness, before the Rebels knew it, had reached the bridge leading into Columbus.

As soon as everything could be got up to the position occupied by the dismounted men, Gen. Upton pressed forward again, and swept away all opposition, took possession of the foot and railroad bridges, and stationed guards throughout the city.

Twelve hundred prisoners, fifty-two field guns in position for use against us, large quantities of arms and stores fell into our hands.   Our loss was only twenty-five killed and wounded.   Col. C. A. L. Lamar, of Gen. Cobb's staff, formerly owner of the "Wanderer," (slave trader) was killed.

The Rebel force was over three thousand men.   They could not believe they had been dislodged from their strong fortifications by an attack of three hundred men.

When it is remembered that these operations gave to us the city of Columbus—the key to Georgia, four hundred miles from our starting point, and that it was conducted by cavalry, without the inspiration from the great events which had transpired in Virginia—it will not be considered insignificant, although shorn of its importance.

Gen. Winslow was assigned to the command of the city.

CAPTURE OF WEST POINT.

After much sharp skirmishing and hard marching, which resulted in the capture of fourteen wagons and a number of prisoners, LaGrange's advance reached the vicinity of West Point at ten A. M., April 16th, with Beck's Eighteenth Indiana Battery and the Second and Fourth Indiana Cavalry. The enemy were kept occupied till the arrival of the balance of the Brigade. Having thoroughly reconnoitered the ground, detachments of the First Wisconsin, Second Indiana, and Seventh Kentucky Cavalry dismounted and prepared to assault Fort Tyler, covering the bridge. Col. LaGrange describes it as a remarkably strong bastioned earthwork, thirty-five yards square, surrounded by a ditch twelve feet wide and ten feet deep, situated on a commanding eminence, protected by an imperfect *abattis* and mounting two thirty-two pounders and two field guns.

At one P. M. the charge was sounded and the brave detachment on the three sides of the work rushed forward to the assault, drove the Rebel skirmishers into the fort, and followed under a withering fire of musketry and grape to the edge of the ditch. This was found impassable ; but without falling back, Col. LaGrange posted sharp-shooters to keep down the enemy and organized parties to gather material for the bridges. As soon as this had been done he sounded the charge again ;. the detachment sprang forward again, laid the bridges and rushed forward over the parapet into the work ; capturing the entire garrison—in all, two hundred and sixty-five men. Gen. Tyler, its commanding officer, with eighteen men and officers killed, and twenty-eight severely wounded. Simultaneously with the advance upon the fort the Fourth Indiana dashed through the town, secured both bridges over the Chattahoochee, scattering a superior force of cavalry which had just arrived, and burned five engines and trains. Col. LaGrange highly commends the accuracy and steadiness of Capt. Beck in the use of his artillery.

Col. LaGrange destroyed at this place two bridges, nineteen locomotives, and two hundred and forty-five cars loaded with quartermaster, commissary and ordnance stores. Before leaving he established a hospital for the wounded of both sides, and left with the Mayor an ample supply of stores to provide for all their wants.

Early on the morning of the seventeenth he resumed his march toward Macon, passing through LaGrange, Griffin and Forsyth, and breaking the railroads at those places. He would have reached his destination by noon of the twentieth, but for delay caused by an order to wait for the Fourth Kentucky Cavalry, which had gone through Columbus.

DEPARTURE FROM COLUMBUS.

The afternoon of the seventeenth I directed Col. Minty to resume his march with his Division on the Thomaston road toward Macon, and to send a detachment forward that night to seize the Double bridges over Flint river. Capt. Van Antwerp, of my staff, accompanied this party. By seven o'clock A. M. the next day he had reached the bridges, fifty miles from Columbus, scattered the party defending them, and took forty prisoners.

Before leaving Columbus, Gen. Winslow destroyed the rebel ram Jackson, nearly ready for sea, mounting six seven-inch guns, burned fifteen locomotives, two hundred and fifty cars, the railroad bridge and foot bridges, one hundred and fifteen thousand bales of cotton, four cotton factories, the navy yard, foundry, armory, sword and pistol factory, accoutrement shops, three paper mills, over a hundred thousand rounds of artillery ammunition, besides immense stores, of which no account could be taken. The rebels abandoned and burned the gun-boat Chattahoochee, twelve miles below Columbus.

COLUMBUS AS SHE NOW IS.

With the capture and partial destruction of Columbus by
the Federal forces in 1865, ends our continuous history of the
city. Much as other Southern cities suffered by the war, the
loss of Columbus was probably greater than that of any
other, for the reason that the great industrial establishments
that afforded work and support to so many of her citizens
were wholly destroyed, and all the cotton which the planters
of the surrounding country had stored here, and which constituted their only available means of raising money wherewith to continue their work, was burnt. But her recupera-
tion since that time has, under all the circumstances, been
most encouraging, if not surprising. Her cotton manufacturing business—her great distinctive industry—is now larger
than it was at the time of the raid, embracing five distinct
factories, running 1,020 looms and about 35,000 spindles. The
Eagle and Phenix Factory—an immense establishment,

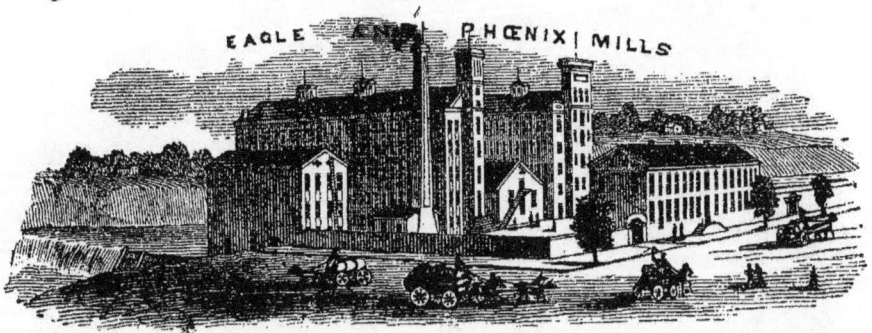

EAGLE AND PHŒNIX MILLS

with three large factory buildings and a capital of $1,250,000
—alone runs about 800 looms and 25,000 spindles. Besides
the Eagle and Phenix, are the Columbus Factory, with 116

Muscogee Mills.

looms; the Muscogee, with 80; A. Clegg & Co.'s, with 30; and the Steam Cotton Mill, which has spindles only. These several manufacturing establishments consumed 8,500 bales of cotton for the year ending Sept. 1st, 1875, besides a large quantity of wool.

In addition to these manufactories, Columbus has several foundries, one of them having the largest iron works attached, south of Richmond; also several sash factories, one gin factory, two furniture manufactories, a very large agricultural implement factory, one stove manufactory, two flour mills, one kerosene oil refinery, and one railroad machine shop. Four railroads terminate at Columbus. One of them, the North and South railroad, when completed, will add new business to her trade, and will furnish a new and competing line to the West and the sea. Upon its line and upon the line of the Savannah and Memphis road, are the richest coal fields in the South, and iron beds of superior ore practically inexhaustible. The latter road will be, when completed to the Tennessee river, the shortest line from the northwest to the Atlantic. Arrangements have been effected which guarantee its early completion. When these two roads are built, Columbus will no doubt add to the busy whirr of her cotton spindles the ruddy glow of a dozen rolling mills.

With the advance of cotton manufactories there will spring up industries for the production of every description of machinery used therein, and in a dozen years this interest alone should double the population of Columbus. Its growth will be forwarded by the fact of its excellent health and remarkable freedom from epidemics, which have year after year scourged many of its neighboring cities. Its public schools are annually attracting population. They are justly the pride of the city. Extensive gas works have been in operation for many years. Columbus, already the largest city in western Georgia, enjoys a commercial importance which is annually increasing. From four railroads and her river, Columbus receives an immense business from as reliable a population as resides in Alabama, Georgia or Florida. Her business men have the facilities offered by four banks of deposit—one National and three State, to-wit: Chattahoochee National Bank, Merchants and Mechanics Bank, Georgia Home Savings Bank, Eagle and Phenix Savings Bank. There are also two daily and weekly papers—the *Enquirer-Sun,* being a consolidation of the old *Enquirer* and *Sun and Times;* and the *Times,* more recently established.

Columbus also has one of the largest and most popular Fire Insurance Companies in the State—the "Georgia Home," which ranks second in amount of its policies, and is

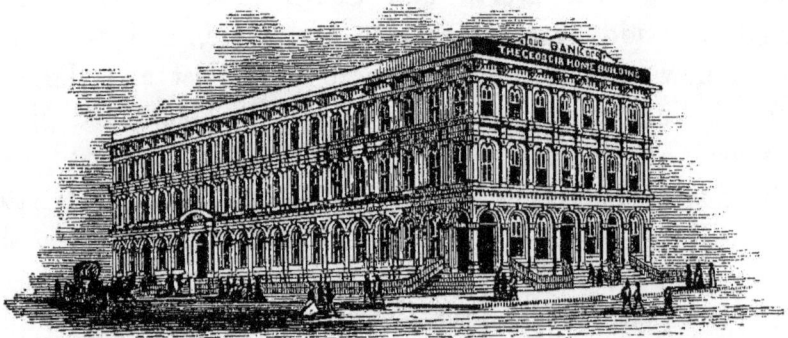

justly regarded as one of the most responsible institutions of the kind in the South.

Nearly every denomination has erected houses of worship. The Baptist, Episcopal, Presbyterian and Catholic, have each commodious churches, and the Methodist three. In addition, the colored people have constructed four comfortable churches. The Fire department consists of two steam and two hand engines, and one hook and ladder company. The city government is conservative, and is economically administered. The police are handsomely uniformed and effective, and law, order and quiet are enjoyed by all classes of citizens.

The population of the city and its suburbs (embracing an area within a mile of the court-house in every direction) is not less than 15,000—all of whom do business or trade in the city.

The immense unused water power of Columbus constitutes one of her great resources of future growth and prosperity. In this respect no city of the Union surpasses her. In his report of an instrumental survey made by Col. L. P. Grant, who is recognized by the profession as one of the ablest civil engineers in the South, that gentleman says:

"The total fall of the Chattahoochee, between West Point and the foot of the fall at Columbus, is three hundred and sixty (360) feet. The fall is not uniform, but occurs in successive shoals, separated by stretches of comparatively slack water. About one-third (one hundred and twenty (120) feet,) of this descent occurs in three and a half miles, terminating at Columbus."

The single power available immediately at COLUMBUS, (120 feet,) affords *fall and water enough*, with improved application of power, and the use of improved machinery, TO DRIVE ONE AND A QUARTER MILLION SPINDLES, *affording employment for nearly sixty thousand* (60,000) *people*, and forming a basis for *a population of about half a million people.*

With these great natural advantages, and with the start already secured in cotton manufacturing—taking the lead of any other city of the South in this respect—we may proudly hope that the "new era" of Columbus, which we date from the close of the late sectional war, will be more progressive and prosperous than her career of 37 years before that event.

APPENDIX.

HISTORY OF MASONRY IN COLUMBUS.

Columbian Lodge, F. and A. M., was organized under dispensation granted October 9, 1828, by Wm. Y. Hansell, Deputy Grand Master, upon petition of Luther Blake and eleven others.   Luther Blake was appointed W. M., E. E. Bissell S. W., and Thos. G. Gordon J. W., and the first meeting was held October 22d, 1828.

A charter was granted by the Grand Lodge in December, 1828, and No. 28 assigned it.   At the time of the Federal raid in April, 1865, the charter was lost, and its present charter was issued October 27, 1865, by the Grand Lodge in lieu of the one lost, no minute of the original having been recorded so that a duplicate could be obtained of it.   Its number, 28, was retained until October, 1838, when it assumed number 8, and that, in December, 1849, was exchanged for number 7, which it still retains.

Oglethorpe Lodge was organized and had its first meeting December 4, 1845, with O. J. H. Dibble as W. M., V. R. Tommy S. W., and J. J. Sutton J. W.   The exact date of dispensation, or by whom issued, is not found of record.   The charter was issued by the Grand Lodge October, 1846, and No. 47 given it.

Lovick Pierce Lodge was organized under dispensation from A. W. Redding, Deputy Grand Master, dated February 11, 1865, upon petition of F. M. Brooks and thirty-nine others.   F. M. Brooks was appointed W. M., W. E. Sandeford S. W., and H. S. Smith, jr., J. W., and the first meeting held February 16, 1865.   It was regularly chartered by the Grand Lodge in October, 1865, as No. 250.

In 1867 the three Lodges above named, upon consultation among themselves, agreed to unite their whole membership in one Lodge, retaining the name of the oldest, Columbian No. 7, and the charters of Oglethorpe No. 47, and Lovick Pierce No. 250 to be surrendered to the Grand Lodge.   In pursuance of such action Oglethorpe and Lovick Pierce Lodges held their last meetings on 30th November, 1867, when their books and rolls were ordered turned over to Columbian Lodge, and they are now (1875) working harmoniously, under John King as W. M., A. M. Brannon S. W., and D. Wolfson J. W., with a membership of about 150.

James Kivlin, one of our oldest residents, was the first Mason who affiliated with Columbian Lodge after its organization, June 13, 1829.   But few of those who received the degrees in the earliest periods of its history are now living, though its records show some who are still alive in this vicinity.

Darley Chapter, Royal Arch Masons, was organized under dispensation from Wm. Schley, Grand High Priest, dated May 24, 1841, on petition of Philip T. Schley and eight others. Philip T. Schley was appointed H. P., Rhodam A. Greene, King, and Abraham Levison, Scribe, and the first meeting was held June 5, 1841. Its charter was granted June 20, 1842, and it designated as No. 7.

Hope Council No. 4, R. & S. M., had its records and property destroyed by fire on 9th of October, 1846, and the time and name of its organization is not definitely known. It is supposed to have been organized about 1842, soon after Darley Chapter. Its first meeting after the fire was April 17th, 1847. It is now working under Hiram Middlebrook, T. I. G. M.; A. Wittich, I. H. T., and L. G. Scheussler, I. H. A.

St. Aldemar Commandery No. 3, K. T., was organized under dispensation issued December 1st, 1857, by W. B. Hubbard, Grand Master of Templars in U. S., upon petition of M. N. Clark and eleven others. Michael N. Clark was appointed E. C.; Phillip T. Gittinger, Generalissimo, and James M. Bivins, Captain General. The Charter was authorized to be issued by the Grand Encampment in September, 1859, but was only issued January 23d, 1860, and the intervening time was caused by dispensation from B. B. French, Grand Master, dated January 10th, 1860.

Adoniram Lodge of Perfection was organized October 28th, 1870, under authority from Melchisedec Consistory No. 3, with M. M. Moore as Th. Pu. Grand Master, and twenty-four members.

Melchisedec Consistory No. 3 was organized July 19th, 1866, under dispensation dated July 9th, 1866, with John King as Ill. Commander in Chief, and fourteen members. It was regularly chartered May 4th, 1868, by the Supreme Council at Charleston.

LOVERS' LEAP.

This is one of the most noted and romantic spots in the vicinity of Columbus, and still possesses an interest for both residents and transient visitors; on account of its natural grandeur and the Indian legend connected with it. The following is the description of the locality and legend connected with it:

This romantic locale is a high and ragged cliff, which terminates an ascending knoll of dark rocks, and projects boldly into the Chattahoochee River. Its summit commands one of the most magnificent displays of river scenery which Nature could present, or which Art could picture. On the left the river pursues its downward course to Columbus, in a straight line. Its flow is rapid and wild, broken by rocks, over which the water frets and foams in angry surges. The bed of the stream is that of a deep ravine, its walls lofty and irregular cliffs, covered to their verge with majestic forest growth. From this point the city of Columbus is but partially visible. At the "Leap," the river makes a sudden turn and forms an angle with its course below, flowing in a narrow channel so regularly lined with rocks on both sides and of such uniform width as to resemble a canal. A short distance above it makes another right angle and resumes its old course.

In the early part of the present century, this region was inhabited by two powerful tribes of Indians. Rivals were they, and, with numbers equal, and alike proud names, well they vied with each other. There was no tribe among all the powerful nation of the Creeks who boasted of their powers before a Cusseta or a Coweta. But they were not friends, for who of those proud red men would bend before the acknowledged superiority of the other? It may have been a small matter from which their jealousy sprung, but the tiny thing had been cheerished, till a serpent-like hatred hissed at the sound of the other's name.

The proud Chief of the Cussetas was now become an old man, and much was he venerated by all who rallied at his battle-cry. The boldest heart in all his tribe quailed before his angry eye, and the proudest did him reverence. The old man had outlived his own sons. One by one had the Great Spirit called them from their hunting grounds, and in the flush of their manhood they had gone to the spirit-land. Yet he was not alone. The youngest of his children, the dark-eyed Mohina, was still sheltered in his bosom, and all his love for the beautiful in life was bestowed upon her,—ah, and rightly too, for the young maiden rivalled in grace the bounding fawn, and the young warriors said of her that the smile of the Great Spirit was not so beautiful. While yet a child she was betrothed to the young Eagle of the Cowetas, the proud scoin of their warrior Chief. But stern hatred had stifled kindly feelings in the hearts of all save these two young creatures, and the pledged word was broken when the smoke of the calumet was extinguished. Mohina no longer dared to meet the young Chief openly, and death faced them when they sat in a lone, wild trysting-place, neath the starry blazonry of midnight's dark robe. Still they were undaunted, for pure love dwelt in their hearts, and base fear crouched low before it, and went afar from them to hide in grosser souls. Think not the boy-god changes his arrows when he seeks the heart of the red man. Nay, rather with truer aim and finer point does the winged thing speed from his bow, and deeply the subtle poison sinks in the young heart, while the dark cheek glows with love's proper hue. The deer bounded gladly by when the lovers met, and felt he was free, while the bright-eyed maiden leaned upon the bosom of the Young Eagle. Their youthful hearts hoped in the future, though all in vain, for time served but to render more fierce that hostile rivalry, more rank than deadly hatred, which existed between the tribes. Skirmishes were frequent amid their hunters, and open hostilities seemed inevitable.

And now it was told by some who had peered through the tangled underwood and matted foliage of those dim woods, that the Coweta had pressed the maiden to his heart in those lone places, and that strange words and passionate were even now breathed by him to her ear. Then the hunters of the Cussetas sprang from their couches and made earnest haste to the dark glen. With savage yell and impetuous rush they bounded before the lovers. They fled, and love and terror added wings to their flight. For a while they distanced their pursuers. But the strength of Mohina failed her in a perilous moment, and had not the Young Eagle snatched her to his fast-beating heart, the raging enemy had made sure their fate. He rushed onward up the narrow defile before him. It led he forgot whither. In a few moments he stood on the verge of this fearful height. Wildly the maiden clung to him, and even then, in that strange moment of life, his heart throbbed proudly beneath his burden. The bold future alone was before him; there was no return. Already the breath of one of the pursuers, a hated rival, came quick upon his cheek, and the bright-gleaming tomahawk shone before him. One moment he gazed on him, and triumph flashed in the eye of the young Chief, and then without a shudder he sprang into the seething waters below. Still the young maiden clung to him, nor yet did the death struggle part them.

The mad waves dashed fearfully over them, and their loud wail was a fitting requiem to their departing spirits. The horror-stricken warriors gazed wildly into the foaming torrent, then dashed with reckless haste down the declivity, to bear the sad tidings to the old Chief. He heard their tale in silence. But sorrow was on his spirit, and it was broken. Henceforth his seat was unfilled by the council fire, and its red light gleamed fitfully upon his grave.

AN OLD REMINISCENCE.

We make below an extract from Gen. Thos. S. Woodward's "Reminiscences of the Creek or Muscogee Indians." It is older than any of the events referred to in our history of Columbus, but refers to localities and people mentioned therein and familiar to our older citizens, and may therefore be interesting in this connection:

The entry of Gen. LaFayette into Alabama was the most imposing show I witnessed while I lived in the State. In 1824, I think it was, LaFayette was looked for in Alabama. I was the first and oldest Brigadier General in Alabama, (after it became a State.) Gen. Wm. Taylor, I think, was the oldest Major General; and Israel Pickens was Governor. There may have been his equal, but there never has been his superior in that office since Alabama became a State. At the time LaFayette was expected, Gen. Taylor was absent, I think, in Mobile. The Indians were a little soured, from a treaty that had been, or was about being made with the Georgians. Gov. Pickens requested me to take an escort and conduct LaFayette through the nation. The Hon. James Abercrombie then commanded the Montgomery Troop, and Gen. Monroe of Claiborne, commanded the Monroe Troop, both of whom volunteered their services. Before the escort left Alabama, (which then extended only to Line Creek,) Gen. Taylor arrived and took the command.

That was before the day of platforms and conventions—men lived on their own money. You must guess then there was some patriotic feeling along, for there were between two and three hundred persons, all bearing their own expenses. Some in going and coming had to travel 400, and none less than 200 miles. Besides the military, there were a number of the most respectable citizens of Alabama—among whom were Boling Hall, ex-member of Congress, ex-Gov. Murphy, Jno. D. Bibb, Jno. W. Freeman and Col. Jas. Johnston, one of the best men that ever lived or died. If there are any such men these days, I have not had the pleasure of their acquaintance. Our trip to the Chattahoochee was pleasant indeed. We made our headquarters three miles from Fort Mitchell, on big Uchee Creek, at Haynes Crabtree's. Had that been a war, and if it had continued to the present day, all of that crowd that's now living would be soldiers. After some three or four days' stay at Crabtree's we learned that Gen. LaFayette had passed White Water, and we knew at what time he would reach the river. The Indians seemed to take as much interest in the matter as the whites. All hands mustered on the west or Alabama side, where we could see the Georgia escort approach the east bank of the Chattahoochee, with their charge. On the east bank, Gen. LaFayette was met by Chilly McIntosh, son of the Indian Gen. McIntosh, with fifty Indian warriors, who were stripped naked and finely painted. They had a sulky prepared with drag-ropes, such as are commonly used in drawing cannon. The General was turned over by the Georgians to the Indians. That was the greatest show I ever saw at the crossing of any river. As the ferryboat reached the Alabama side, the Indians, in two lines, seized the ropes, and the General seated in the sulky, was drawn to the top of the bank, some eighty yards, where stood the Alabama Delegation. At a proper distance from the Alabama Delegation, the Indians opened their lines, and the sulky halted.

Everything, from the time the General entered the ferry, till this time, had been conducted in the most profound silence. As the sulky halted, the Indians gave three loud whoops. The General then alighted, took off his hat, and was conducted by Chilly McIntosh, a few steps, to where stood Mr. Hall, with head uncovered, white with the frosts of age. I knew Mr. Hall from my boyhood. He always showed well in company; but never did I see him look so finely as on that occasion—he looked like himself—what he really was—an American gentleman. As McIntosh approached Mr. Hall, he said, "Gen. LaFayette, the American friend"—"Mr. Hall, of Alabama," pointing to each as he called his name. Mr. Hall, in a very impressive manner, welcomed LaFayette to the shores of Alabama, and introduced him to the other gentlemen. Dandridge Bibb then addressed the General at some length. I heard a number of persons address LaFayette on his route through Alabama—none surpassed Dandridge Bibb, and none equaled him, unless it was Hitchcock and Dr. Hustis at Cahaba. I have always been looked upon as rather dry-faced; but gazing on the face of the most distinguished patriot that it had ever fallen to my lot to look upon, and the feeling remarks of Mr. Bibb on that occasion, caused me, as it did most others that were present, to shed tears like so many children.

After the address at the river, all marched to Fort Mitchell hill, where there was an immense crowd of Indians, the Little Prince at their head. He addressed the "French Captain," through Hamley, in true Indian style. I could understand much of his speech, but cannot begin to give it as Hamley could. The Prince said that he had often heard of the French Captain, "but now I see him, I take him by the hand, I know from what I see, he is the true one I have heard spoken of; I am not deceived—too many men have come a long way to meet him. He is bound to be the very man the Americans were looking for." The Prince, after satisfying the General that he (the Prince) was satisfied that the General was the true man spoken of and looked for, then went on to say, that he had once warred against the Americans, and that the French Captain had warred for them, and of course they had once been enemies, but were now friends; that he (the Prince) was getting old, which his withered limbs would show—making bare his arms at the same time—that he could not live long; but he was glad to say, that his people and the whites were at peace and he hoped they would continue so.

But he had raised a set of young warriors, that he thought would prove worthy of their sires, if there should ever be a call to show themselves men; and that as a ball play was, outside of war, the most manly exercise that the Red Man could perform, he would, for the gratification of the General and his friends, make his young men play a game. The old man then turned to his people, and said to them—they were in the presence of a great man and warrior; he had commanded armies on both sides of the Big Water; that he had seen many nations of people; that he had visited the Six Nations, in Red Jacket's time, (the General told the Indians that he had visited the Six Nations,) that every man must do his best—show himself a man, and should one get hurt he must retire without complaining, and by no means show anything like ill humor. The speech ended, about two hundred stripped to the buff, paired themselves off and went at it. *It was a ball play sure enough*, and I would travel farther to see such a show than I would to see any other performed by man, and willingly pay high for it, at that. The play ended, and all hands went out to headquarters at Big Uchee, where we were kindly treated by our old friend Haynes Crabtree.

There was a man, then living among the Indians, Capt. Tom Anthony, who long since found a last resting place in the wilds of Arkansas. He was a man of fine sense and great humor. There was also an Indian known as Whiskey John. John was the greatest drunkard I ever saw; he would drink a quart of strong whiskey without taking the vessel that contained it from his lips, (this is Alabama history, and there are plenty now living that have seen him do it.) To see John drink was enough to have made the fabled Bacchus look out for a vacancy that frequently occurs among the Sons of Temperance. Capt. Anthony told John that all hands had addressed the French Chief, and that it was his duty to say something to him on behalf of those that loved whiskey. John could speak considerable English in a broken manner. It so happened that the General and others were walking across the Uchee Bridge when John met them. John made a low bow, as he had seen others do. The General immediately pulled off his hat, thinking he had met with another Chief. John straightening himself up to his full height, (and he was not very low,) commenced his speech in the manner that I will try to give it to you. "My friend, you French Chief! me Whiskey John," (calling over the names of several white persons and Indians;) "Col. Hawkins, Col. Crowell, Tom Crowell, Henry Crowell, Billy McIntosh, Big Warrior Indian, heap my friends, give me whiskey, drink, am good. White man my very good friend me, white man make whiskey, drink him heap, very good, I drink whiskey. You French Chief, Tom Anthony say me big Whiskey Chief. You me give one bottle full. I drink him good." The General informed John that he did not drink whiskey, but would have his bottle filled. John remarked "Tom Anthony you very good man, me you give me bottle full. You no drink, me drink all, chaw tobacco little bit, give me some you." Now the above is an Indian speech, and no doubt will appear silly to some who have not been accustomed to those people. Should it, however, fall under the eye of those who were along at that time, they will recognize John's speech, and call to mind our old friends, Capt. Anthony and Col. James Johnson, who was the life of our crowd.

We remained that night at Crabtree's and the next day reached Fort Bainbridge, where an Indian countryman lived, by the name of Kendall Lewis, as perfect a gentleman, in principle, as ever lived in or out of the nation, and had plenty, and it in fine style. The next day we started for Line Creek.

It fell to my lot to point out many Indians, as well as places, for we were stopped at almost every settlement to shake hands, and hear Indian speeches. Among many things and places that were pointed out to the General, was the place where Lot was killed, the old "Lettered Beech," at Persimmon swamp, the old Council Oak, Floyd's battle ground, the grave of James McGirth, the place where McGirth made peach brandy, many years before, and many other things. That night we reached Walter B. Lucas'. Everything was "done up" better than it will ever be again; one thing only was lacking— time—we could not stay long enough. The next morning we started for Montgomery. Such a cavalcade never traveled that road before or since.

On Goat Hill,* and near where Capt. John Carr fell in the well, stood Gov. Pickens, and the largest crowd I ever saw in Montgomery. Some hundred yards east of the Hill, was a sand flat, where Gen. LaFayette and his attendants quit carriages and horses, formed a line and marched to the top of the hill. As we started, the band struck up the old Scottish air, "Hail to the Chief." As we approached the Governor, Mr. Hill introduced the General to him. The Governor tried to welcome him, but, like the best man the books give account of, when it was announced that he was commander of the whole American forces, he was scarcely able to utter a word. So it was with Gov. Pickens. As I remarked before, Gov. P. had no superior in the State, but on that occasion he could not even make a speech. But that did not prevent Gen. LaFayette from discovering that he was a great man; it only goes to prove what is often said, that many who feel most can say least, and many who have no feeling say too much.

*The site of the present Capitol of Alabama.

Full Name Index
to
"Columbus, Georgia 1827—1865"

PART II

ABBOTT
A. J., 35
Eliza I., 99
Francis J., 53, 147
F. J., 23, 102
Jeffersonia, 169
Mrs. Martha Irene, 126
W. T., 173

ABERCOMBIE
Anderson, 12
Everard, 52
James, 12, 43

ABERCROMBIE
Capt. James, 144
Clara W., 147
G. H., 130
James, 194
Wiley, 130

ABNER(Y?)
Martha E., 90

ABNEY
Elvira, 108
Mary E., 85

ACEE
Fielding W., 108
J. S., 149
O. S., 130

ADAIR
J. C., 123

ADAMS
C. A. M., 40
David J., 139
D., 13
Eliza, 16
E. E., 163
Farley B., 114
Fred G., 172
Gen., 182
Harriet S., 16
John, 165
J., 134
Mary, 25
Mrs., 79, 101
Mrs. Ebenade, 33
Pat, 63
P., 20, 54, 55
Stephen, 86
Wiley, 11, 46
William, 70
William E., 40

ADCOCK
Louisa, 100

ADDINGTON
D. D., 138

ADKINS
G. W., 171

ADOU
Mrs., 53

AENCHBACHER
G., 163
L. P., 171
Mrs., 89
Rebecca, 163

AENCHBACKER
Eothieb N., 108
L. P., 135
Samuel, 32

AFFLECK
Georgiana M, 15

AGUERO
Joseph B., 99

AIDE
Alex, 136

AIDS
Alexander, 124

AINCHBACKER
G. W., 139

AINSWORTH
J. T., 169, 177

AKHURST
M. L., 162

ALBRECHT
Catharine, 99
H. P., 156
Neal W., 114

ALBRICHT
Fredericka N., 25

ALBRIGHT, 156

ALDERMAN
B. H., 172

ALDMOND
J. F., 149

ALDWORTH
Robert, 176

Robert M., 77
R. M., 172

ALEXANDER, 183

ALEXANDER
Joseph, 33
Mary, 77
Miss A. B., 15
Miss C. W., 15
Robt. B., 53, 67
R. B., 13, 31, 39, 44
S. W., 133
William, 67, 70

ALFORD
Floyd, 108
Job, 138
Mary A., 52
Matilda L., 125
T. J., 139
Whitman C., 33
William H., 32

ALFRED
Sarah J. E., 78

ALGOOD
Julia, 52

ALLARD
Charles, 162

Allen, 14, 79, 85

ALLEN
A. H., 135
Docia, 172
Euphemia, 16
F. W., 165
George W., 177
Jane, 124
Jesse W., 40
Jno., 77
Joel L., 156
John, 79, 92, 100, 121, 152
John S., 18, 104, 160
John S.(Jr.), 137
John Wm., 138
John W., 164
J., 12
J. S.(Jr.), 130
Lewis C., 9, 18, 26, 36, 38
L. C., 14, 34
Martha, 69
Mary A., 91
Miss Mary L., 172
Mrs., 121, 164, 165

Nancy, 163
R. O., 139
Sarah, 155
Sarah I., 91
Sarah J., 177
Thos. S., 147
William, 128
William M., 116
Wm., 32
Wm. M., 46, 123
W. M., 149, 171

**ALLEN-KING & CAMAK,
113**

ALLEY
William, 80

ALLUM
Frances, 52

ALLUMS
Frank, 152

ALMONDS
J. H., 135

ALMONS
Winney I., 99

ALPHONZE
Donat, 162

ALSABROOKS
Mary, 162

ALSTON
Ann A., 16
Charity I., 77
Philip H., 157
P., 23
P. H., 102
Wm. H., 80
W. H., 93, 148, 167, 174
W. J., 134

ALTHISER
Chas. H., 128

AMES
James H., 177

AMOS
William, 18, 29
Wm., 9, 14, 31, 146

AMOS & JONES, 20, 31

AMYET
William D., 177

ANDERS
Elizabeth, 163

ANDERSON, 29

ANDERSON
Captain Walker, 172
Gen., 43
H. C., 7, 54
James, 85
John, 138
Lawrence W., 139
Maley, 85
O., 47
Peter, 148, 157
William, 164
W. L., 130, 132

ANDREWS, 29

ANDREWS
A. R., 80
Capt., 104
Caroline M., 40
Dr., 44
Mary E., 24
Miss, 79
Samuel R., 48, 156
Sarah Ann Elizabeth, 16
Susan E., 108
S. R., 14, 26, 39, 42, 80, 94, 117
S. R.(Jr.), 130
Wm. G., 77, 80, 81
W. G., 7, 23, 63

ANSLEY
John A., 99

ANTHEM
Catharine, 171

ANTHONY
Capt., 196
Capt. Tom, 195
J. L., 149
Micajah, 79
Miss, 79
M. J., 141
Rev. S., 51
R., 135
Samuel, 39, 108
Samuel W., 115
S., 45
S. W., 149
Tom, 196

ANTWERP
Capt. Van, 185

APPLE
J. C., 130

AQUEM
J. B., 141

ARBORE
Eugene, 156

ARMSTRONG
E., 139
Jane Elizabeth, 24

ARNOLD, 86

ARNOLD
C., 141
John D., 31
John S., 165
J. D., 38
Levinia C., 69
Martha, 92

**ARNOLD & ROBERTSON,
51**

ARNOLD & ROBINSON, 68

ASHBURN
G. W., 93

ASHLEY
Mary, 171

ASKEW
Georgia A., 108
Mary, 16

ATKINS
John D., 78
W. D., 172

ATKINSON
America, 61
George, 151
Geo. W., 128
Littleton, 25

AUBRY
William P., 47

AUGLE
Martha E., 99

AUSTIN
Bethany, 33
John B., 163
Nancy M., 61
Rev. J. M., 107

AUTRY
A. J., 138
Wm. W., 138

AVERETT
David, 33
Eli M., 135
Elizabeth, 69
Harriet, 40
James V., 147
Vincent L., 61

AVERITT
Needham, 135

AVERY
John, 100, 135

AYER
A. K., 15, 19, 55, 79, 80, 109
Mrs. Mary A., 79
Rudolph H., 47
Wm. H., 47

AYERS
James B., 32

BABAT, 172

BABBITT, 101

BACCHUS, 195

BACHELOR
Cornelius, 135

BACHLE
Fidel, 116

BACKER
A., 54

BACKMAN
Samuel, 45

BACON
Dr. John E., 71, 93
R. A., 131
William B., 100

BADKINS
Robert, 69

BAET
James, 177

BAGGETT, 172

BAGGETT
Catharine, 78
James M., 16
J. M., 165
Louisa, 32
Mrs., 79

BAGLEY
Barthena, 77
James, 114
Martha, 24
Thos. L., 155

BAILEY, 85, 126

BAILEY
Amenius U., 155
C. A., 130
Elizabeth E., 77
E. L., 133
Gen. S. A., 44
Hiram F., 139
James, 45
Mary C., 90
Mrs., 92
Sarah, 98
S. A., 23, 31

BAILY
John W. C., 45
Wm. H., 91

BAIRD
Dr., 127
Dr. John B., 167
John B., 157
J. B., 31
Martha, 125
William I., 116

BAKER
Barbara A., 155
B., 12
Chas. W., 128
Eliza, 91
John G., 15
Joseph W., 108
Mary A. E., 70
Mary C. W., 155
Missouri, 171
Robt. E., 115
William H., 163
Willis P., 72
Wm., 128
W., 10
W. C., 165
W. P., 44

BALDWIN

Frances, 163
J. D., 147
Lucinda, 170
Mary, 124
Robert, 164
Sarah A., 124

BALL
Mary, 52
Miss, 101

BALLAMY
Joseph, 162

BALLARD
David, 177
Frances, 16
John, 130
Mrs., 156
Thomas W., 16

BALLENGER
Joseph J., 70

BALLOU
John E., 155
Mollie, 170

BALSH
Alonza, 32

BALYEU
Elizabeth, 85

BAMBUSE
Joseph, 114

BANDY
Ephraim, 71
Ephraim C., 63, 92
E. C., 14

BANISTER
Angeline, 114

BANK
Col., 25

BANKS
Capt. W. D., 172
Col. John, 154
E., 130
George Y., 77
G., 135
John, 5
J. R., 173
Reason, 128
Troup, 154
T. H., 149
Watkins, 173

W., 130, 135

BANKSTON, 101

BANKSTON
Sarah E., 124
Thomas, 107
W. T., 165

BARBAREE
Catharine, 46
William W., 32

BARBARRA
John, 32

BARBER
Ann J., 155
Daniel M., 109
David J., 70, 77, 83, 86
John, 134
Patrick B., 70

BARDEN, 100

BARDEN
Indiana, 114
Mary B., 146
Mrs. Eliza J., 33
Virginia E., 147
Wesley, 79
William Y., 93
Wm. Y., 33, 56, 63, 80, 86
W. A., 130, 137
W. Y., 26, 34, 42

BARDEN & RIDGWAY, 14

BARDWELL
R. N. R., 7, 17
Sarah A., 108

BARENTINE
Rachel, 155

BARFIELD
Mary, 124
Nancy, 98

BARKER
John, 128
John F., 151
Robert, 45
Susan, 146
Wm., 152
W. A., 139

BARLOW
Garland M., 84

James, 24

BARNARD
E., 63
E. & CO., 14
Mary E., 162
T. M., 130, 137, 142

BARNARD & SCHLEY, 19

BARNES
Barney, 52
Bryant, 109
B. F., 152
D. B., 169
Elizabeth, 107
John, 164
Joseph, 135
Mary A. R., 108
W. T., 163

BARNETT
Amory D., 147
E., 117
Henry, 114
John N., 79
J. N., 26, 89
Lucy A., 26
Wm. Henry, 26

BARNETT & KYLE, 19

BARNS
Jesse, 125
Joseph, 162

BARR, 157

BARRAND
Mrs., 70

BARRENGER
J., 48

BARRETT
N., 140

BARRINGER
John L., 80
J., 68
J. L., 55
Matthias, 47
M., 68, 76, 94
Sarah, 53

BARRINGTON
W., 100

BARRON
Amanda S., 69

BARROW
H. H., 62
Jacob, 75, 79
Lucien Strawn, 62

BARRY
Mary A. A., 146

BARSCHALL
Hamilton, 165
M., 102, 110, 117

BARSCHALL & GETTINGER, 68

BARSCHALL & GITTINGER, 31

BARSHALL & GITTENGER, 20

BARTLETT
Burrill, 69
Catharine W., 99
Cosam Emir, 47
J. H., 149
Sarah A., 46
William A., 70
W. R., 149
W. V., 138

BARTLEY
Burrill, 70
Eliza, 70

BARTON, 92

BARTON
Martha, 78
Mrs., 92

BARTWELL
Burton, 40

BASKIN
J. L., 135

BASS
Gabriel, 171
John H., 78, 172
Lucy H., 156
Martha, 85
Mollie, 172
R. L., 15

BATES
Emma, 156
John M., 165
Leonard, 171

Lieut. T. Jeff, 156

BATESTINE
Clemens, 155

BATSON
Zachariah, 78

BATTSON
James N., 78

BAUDERMAN
Sarah, 173

BAUGH, 156

BAUGH
James L., 62
Martha F., 40
Miss Amanda, 172
Mrs. Nancy, 62

BAXLEY
Augustus A., 115
J., 135

BAZEMORE
Pauline S. E., 60

BEACH
William, 176
Wm. A., 16, 109

BEAKLEY
John W., 84

BEALL
Benjamin, 69
Dr. W. E., 6
Elias N., 139

BEAMAN
Green, 92
Mrs., 92

BEAMONT
Jean B., 84

BEARD
John B., 170

BEARS
Sarah S. C., 90

BEASLEY
B., 13
John, 152, 170
T. M., 130

BEASLY

B., 8

BEAUCHAMP
Mary E., 84

BEAUREGARD
Gen., 175

BECK, 184

BECK
Charles, 25
Elizabeth A., 170
Emily M., 51
Martin W., 108
William, 140

BECKWITH
William G., 45

BECKWITHS
Isaac, 140

BEDELL
Benjamin F., 91
Hezekiah, 149
J. R., 130, 173
Pendleton E., 170
Sarah, 84
Wm. A., 80
Wm. K., 130
W. R., 149

BEDSALE
Stephen, 40

BEDSOLE
Charlotte, 45

BEECHER
H. B., 130

BEEMAN
Robert, 140

BEERS
Edward W., 99
E. C., 152
Mary E., 98

BELAND
Virginia A., 108

BELCHER
James, 107, 146
Martha, 162
Monroe M., 146
Solomon, 84, 139
Thomas J., 91

BELER
Frances P., 41

BELL
Delia, 165
Harriet R., 46
James A., 53
Julia Ann, 25
Mary, 16
R. D. S., 34, 45
Sarah, 177
Wm., 164

BELLAMY
William C., 84

BELLFLOWER
Josephine, 125

BELSER, 92

BENNETT
Alfred, 152
Bob, 175
Micajah, 109
Oliver, 124

BENNING
Augusta P., 61
H. L., 127, 140
M. L., 171

BENSON, 47

BENSON
Ann, 85

BENTLEY
Berry, 140
Mark, 140
William, 140

BENTON
Elizabeth, 45
George C., 16
Mary, 177
Nathan N., 91
Wm., 128

BERGAMY
Jeptha, 138

BERGE
Thomas, 40

BERMINGHAM
Rev. T., 51

BERNHARD
Edward H., 51

BERRY
Benj. A., 24
B. A., 164
Emma, 89
Mary, 46

BERTRAM
Sarah Jane, 177

BETHUNE, 68

BETHUNE
Cornelia C., 40
Gen., 112
Gen. James N., 39
James N., 110
Jas. N., 93
John, 18, 23
John G., 107, 131, 145
John M., 13, 15
Jos. D., 131
J. D., 139
Mrs., 15
Susan R., 163

BETHUNE & REYNOLDS,
72

BETZ
Geo. H., 18
Mrs. Mary, 79

BEVIL
Sarah F., 163

BIBB
Dandridge, 194, 195
Jno. D., 194

BICKLEY
Simon P., 15

BIEHLER, 85

BIEHLER
Peter, 158

BIG WARRIOR INDIAN, 196

BIGERS
P. J., 149

BIGGERS
Frances, 99
Frances A. L., 98
James J. W., 53
John R., 172
Mary A., 170
Missouri W., 84

Permelia Ann, 177

BIGLES
John I., 99

BILLING

, S. A., 18
Dr. S. A., 7
Martha C., 125
Mrs. S. A., 79
Samuel A., 84
S. A., 26, 42

BILLING & BOSWELL, 15

BILLUPS
Mrs. E. A., 47

BINGHAM
Mrs. Ann J., 71

BINNION
Francis, 173

BIRCH
John N., 165
J. F., 130

BIRD
Daniel B., 46
Thos., 162
William J., 141

BIRDSONG
Anna E., 125
Edward, 55, 68, 83, 93,
107
Ed., 39
E., 18, 63, 98, 114, 116

BIRDSONG & SLEDGE, 14

BISHOP
H., 126
James, 54
J. W., 150

BISSELL
E. E., 190

BIUS
Elizabeth, 40

BIVIN, 126

BIVINS, 118

BIVINS
James M., 78, 117, 157,

191
J. M., 127, 148, 167, 174

BIZE
Charles, 51, 68
Charles G., 20
C. C., 149
Daniel, 125
D. R., 149

BLACK, 100

BLACK
Leonard, 126

BLACKBURN
Susannah, 163
Thomas Wilson, 25
Wash., 89

BLACKMAN
Eliza Jane, 25

BLACKMAR
A. O., 127
Henrietta A., 125
Stephen, 139

BLACKMON
Amos R., 138
Elizabeth, 69
Joel W., 115
S. H., 172
William I., 114

BLACKSTOCK
Frances, 177
Lucinda, 171
Susan, 170

BLACKWELL
Jasper, 116
M. A., 163

BLAIN
Capt. Charles, 90
Chas., 169

BLAINE
Capt. Charles, 95

BLAIR
Mary, 155
Samuel, 124

BLAKE
Col. S. R., 31
Levi, 136
Levi S., 124
Louisa Jane, 177

Luther, 190
Mary C., 124

BLAKELEY
Martha, 99

BLAKELY
J., 172

BLALOCK
J. G., 130

BLANCHARD
Eusebia A., 99
Lt. M., 173
M., 138
Thomas E., 138
Thos. E., 156
T. E., 130

BLAND
Enoch, 69

BLANDFORD
M. H., 7

BLANKENSHIP
Ellen, 61
George, 138
Louisiana E., 85
Mary, 52
Miss, 100
Susan A., 45
Wm. H. H., 163

BLANTON
Mitchell, 124

BLAU
Edward W., 125
E. W., 172

BLAYLOCK
J. G., 132

BLOODSWORTH
Miles E., 155

BLOW
George W., 84

BLUE
J. C., 172
Rev. Oliver R., 32

BLUHM
Jacob, 138

BLUNT
Joseph, 172

BOATRITE
A. V., 152

BOBITT, 54

BOGGS
Barney, 170

BOLAND
A. J., 135
F. M., 164
James, 40
Jno. W., 24
Josiah, 108
Manilton, 61
Sarah E., 46

BOLD
Mary Ann, 107

BOLES
Thomas, 149

BOMAN
Miss, 92

BOND
James, 70
Wm., 136

BONDS
Mrs., 126

BONFOY
Julia Munro, 71
Samuel, 71

BONNELL
Ann Jane, 32

BONNER
James, 52
Lelie B., 114
Leonora H., 99
Mrs. Mary L., 79
Seymore R., 90
S. R., 79

BOOHER, 125

BOOHER
Chas. E., 134
D. B., 131, 159
D. L., 102

BOOHER & WESSON, 14

BOON
Robert H., 24

BOOTON
Daniel F., 124

BORAW
Samantie, 24

BORDERS, 92

BORDERS
Sarah E., 125

BORING
Mary, 46
Rev. Jesse, 23

BOSTWICK
Thos., 47

BOSWELL
Dr., 156
Dr. J. J., 35
J. A., 141
J. J., 140

BOSWELL & BILLING, 15

BOSWORTH
John F., 16
Wm. M., 63

BOUCHE
Mr., 106

BOULTER
J., 11

BOURGUINE
Julia I., 99

BOURT
James G., 40

BOWEN
E. C., 39
Frances, 52
John, 164
Miss Elvira, 165
Thomas W., 79

BOWER
John, 79

BOWERS, 79

BOWERS
Jane, 85
L. G., 121

BOWMAN

Miss, 92

BOYCE
Peter, 156

BOYD, 73, 126

BOYD
Adaline, 124
Frances A., 91
Jack, 72
James, 114
James Y., 84
Mrs. C., 171
Robert, 31
Sarah Salina, 33
Wesley, 24
William, 53

BOYDEN, 15

BOYKEN
Amelia F., 163
Emily C., 146

BOYKIN
Frank, 165
Harriet E., 156
Mrs. Narcissa, 100

BOZEMAN
Dr., 157
Dr. J. F., 23, 141, 148
Edward, 146, 165
James F., 51, 159
James H., 45
Jane A. E., 116
John W., 136
J. F., 42, 48, 127
Martha A., 177
Mrs. Margaret, 173
Robert, 152
Robert I., 115
Sarah A., 114
W. A., 152

BRADEY
T. J., 172

BRADFORD
Amanda S., 163
James A., 116
Jas. A., 15
Jesse, 86, 93, 126
Jesse J., 124
J., 110, 135
J. A., 79, 100, 117, 123, 157, 167
J. J., 138
Martha, 32

Miss Amelia, 116
Mrs., 147, 164
P. S., 130, 138
Wm. H., 171
W. S., 135

BRADLEY
Mary, 146
Wm. J., 24

BRADSHAW
E. N., 173

BRADY, 92

BRADY
Charles, 61
John, 100

BRAGG
Gen., 151
John N., 61

BRANCH
Rosalie, 108

BRANHAM
Miss Frances, 165
Mrs., 79

BRANNAN
Edward, 165

BRANNON
Alexander M., 84
A., 126
A. F., 80, 111
A. M., 190
Edward W., 61
Eliza, 78
Julia A., 78
Laura V., 91
Lieutenant, 160
Mary A., 125
Mathew, 47
Miss, 92
Mrs., 101
Mrs. Edward, 156
Nancy, 99
Richard, 135
Samuel, 109
Samuel R., 83
Sarah, 155
T. A., 14, 39
W. A., 177
W. H., 145

BRANNON & PEABODY, 167, 174

BRANTLEY
A. W., 134

BRASSELL
Andrew J., 155

BRASSILL
Anna, 99
Delilah, 99
Mrs., 101
Sarah, 52
Thomas, 158

BRAUGHTON
Ann E., 98

BRAVOGLE
Conrad, 146

BRAXTON
Ann, 171

BRAY
David J., 85
Espy A., 78
George T., 69
Henrietta, 77
Mary S., 170
Mrs., 101

BRAZELL
Sarah, 100

BRAZIL
Elizabeth, 79

BRAZILL, 101

BRENZIER
Harriet E., 25

BREWER
Joseph C., 45
J. C., 42, 48, 102

BRICE, 126

BRICE
Richard T., 54
R. T., 27

BRICE & PATTEN, 37

BRICKHOUSE
Cornelia, 62
Nathan M., 45

BRIDGES
Fannie C., 156
Jessie A., 177

John S., 169
Jonathan, 22, 31, 57

BRIDWELL
Jane, 171

BRIGGS
E. B., 130
Richard R., 98
R. H., 165

BRIGHT, 125

BRIGMAN
Isaac, 169

BRILEY
Micajah, 77
Sarah Ann, 40

BRITH
Mrs., 125

BRITT
David I., 107
James D., 52
John H., 138
Lucinda, 126
Martha I., 99
Mrs., 157
Wm. R., 138

BRITTAIN
B. F., 152
Elizabeth, 124
Sarah E., 147

BRITTENHAM
John, 46

BRITTINGHAM
Nelson, 99

BRITTON, 126

BRITTON
George W., 164
James, 124, 172
Mrs. Jane, 154

BROADAWAY
Jeremiah B., 124
Jerry, 138
Jordan, 164

BROADNAX
Frances, 15
James, 150
Jas. E., 25
Mariah E., 52

Mrs. Elizabeth, 71
Susan, 125
Victoria E., 99

BROCK, 123

BROCK
Benjamin, 125
Benj., 171
Esquire, 165
James, 141
Lucinda, 124

BRODERICK
James, 139

BRODIE
George W., 139

BROECK
Ten, 96

BROKAW & CLEMONS, 14

BRONSON
Mary Emma, 17

BROOKE
W. Wilkins, 156

BROOKINS
R. B., 138

BROOKS, 152

BROOKS
A. J. S., 135
Charles E., 147
Chas. A., 78
Dr. T. J., 63
Eliza Ann, 124
Francis R., 162
F. L., 134
F. M., 34, 42, 68, 77, 107,
136, 145, 155, 157, 160,
169, 177, -

???
Isham R., 138, 149
I. T., 90, 114, 123
James, 124
James C., 109, 138
John, 53
John G., 61
John M. S., 47
John R., 149
John W.,, 142
Joseph, 26
Joseph H., 138
J. B., 34

J. C., 138
Miss Fannie, 171
Mollie H., 171
Nancy A., 69
Robert C., 115
R. C., 149
Sarah A. E., 108
Stephen S., 32
Temple, 165
Wilkins, 128
William, 18
William C., 163
William D., 69
William E., 69
Wm., 8, 19, 48, 55, 56,
63, 80, 100
Wm. E., 101
WM. H. & CO., 75

BROOKS & CHAPMAN, 158

BROUGHTON
James, 115

BROWN, 39, 100

BROWN
Aaron D., 84
Abraham, 109
Alex. D., 124
Anna A., 125
A. C., 6
A. D., 140
A. D.(Jr.), 171
Benjamin, 52
Caroline, 53
Delila E., 15
Eliza, 32
Elizabeth, 61
Fannie, 69
Governor, 128, 129
Gov., 127, 159
Hazeltine, 162
H., 133
Israel F., 80
James G., 140
John, 54
Julia A., 124
J. C., 134
J. G., 133
J. H., 140
Mariah, 146
Matilda M., 16
Miss, 79
Mrs., 100
Mrs. Elizabeth, 41
Mrs. Maria, 100
Mrs. Nancy, 93
Oscar V., 32
O. V., 62

Robert Parham, 62
Sarah Ann, 24
Sarah C., 124
Sarah J., 46
Silas R., 24
Susan, 41, 97, 101
Thomas J., 52
Thos. F., 134
T., 135
William, 149, 155
William G., 107
William R., 52
Wm., 53
Wm. A., 131
Wm. S., 140
W. R., 102, 167

John F., 152

BROWNE
J. Rhodes, 86, 165
Mrs. Mary W., 86

BROWNING, 101

BROWNING
Adaline, 60
Caroline V., 85
Edmund H., 115
Elizabeth, 51
Epsy, 70
Harriet, 114
Isabella, 69
Perry A., 77
P. A., 138

BROWNLOW
Col. John, 151

BRUMBY
Mrs., 79

BRUNER
James W., 78

BRUNETTE
James, 24

BRUNO & VIRGINS, 14

BRUNSON
Joseph, 32

BRYAN
A. L., 71
Cynthia A. R., 124
George M., 155
G. M., 133
Jane E., 78
Louisa M., 24

M. A., 138
Nancy Caroline, 16
William E., 61

BRYANT
Benjamin, 32
Calvin, 124
Catharine, 124
James, 54
John, 98
John S., 125
Mrs. Milly, 25
Seaborn, 52
Thomas M., 99
Wm., 155
Wm. H., 128

BRYLEY
Eliza, 32
Martha Ann, 16

BUCHANAN
Abner, 16
Justin F., 116

BUCKLER
Anna R., 107
Isabella, 90
Sarah, 51

BUCKNER, 151

BUCKNER
Judith Ann, 17

BUFFINGTON
Emma, 171

BUFORD, 182

BUFORD
Gen., 178
James J., 84
Major, 89
Vanney, 91

BUGBEE
Ellen Octavia, 24

BUGG
Cecilia, 45
Emily, 164
Martha, 52
Peter T.(Jr.), 107
R., 133
Susan J., 108

BULGER
Mrs. Catharine, 171

BULLOCK, 157

BULLOCK
D. S., 165
Mary, 99
Sarah I., 114

BULLOOK
Mrs., 156

BUMBUSH, 126

BUNNELL
Jno., 148
John, 51, 87, 110
John G., 91, 93

BURAN
Mrs., 100

BURBEE, 54

BURCH
Jane, 163
J. F., 159
Thomas H., 107

BURDEN
Archibald, 163

BURDET
B. P., 156

BURDIM
William B., 90

BUREN
James, 101

BURGE
Allen G., 116

BURKES
Temperance, 124

BURKS
Jane, 170

BURNES
Ida, 69

BURNETT
Harriet, 115
Sarah A., 32
W., 12

BURNS
Bryan, 138
Lawrence M., 146
Mary, 15

Mrs. Mary, 173
M. A. C., 172
Sarah E., 45

BURNSIDE
Margaret, 162

BURRAN
James, 139
Narcissa, 92

BURRAND
Frances A., 91

BURRAYS
James, 61

BURRELL
Henry, 173

BURREN
Narcissa, 32

BURRUS
Capt. Jacob G., 144
Felix, 157
Jacob, 150
Jacob G., 107
Jake, 11
L. M., 134

BURT
Louisa J., 115
Martha, 25
Mary Jane, 25
Miss Sarah A., 70
Richard, 8
R., 13

BURTON
Caroline, 53
Harriet E., 84
Virginia C., 24, 90

BUSBEE
Jane, 54

BUSH
Epsy A., 52
John G., 162
Mary, 32
Mason A., 45
Miss Frances C., 165
Thomas, 165

BUSSEY, 100

BUSSEY
B. F., 151
David, 76

Frank, 128
H., 152
James, 101
James M., 125
John, 149
Lucy A., 146
Mrs., 101
Scott, 133
William, 149

BUTLER
Elizabeth, 70
James, 45
Jones, 22
Louisa, 172
Sidney, 172
Thos. J., 79
Wm., 145
W., 173

BUTT
Captain Moses, 33
Fannie P., 177
Georgia P., 83
Jas. E., 152
John H., 115
J. H., 31
Mary V., 46
Richard L., 16
Sarah A., 25
W. B., 131

BUTT & HOLT, 15

BUTTAN
George W., 124

BUTTS
John, 69

BYARD
Amanda, 47
John, 46, 54, 92

BYARS
Francis A., 90

BYRD
Permelia, 99
William, 170

BYRNE
John, 15

BYSE
Lurany, 170

BYUS
Martha, 15

CADMAN, 100, 126

CADMAN
A., 173

CADWALLADER, 14

CADY
V. H., 23, 35
V. S., 18

CAFFEY
James A., 69

CAFFS
Sarah I., 177

CAIRNES
Rev. Mr., 6
Rev. W. D., 10

CALAHAN
Mrs. Augusta, 171

CALDWELL
John, 70
Martha A., 99
Mary C., 171
Mrs. C., 171
Nancy, 92
Samuel, 32

CALHOUN, 86

CALHOUN
A., 11, 86, 92
A. A., 131, 137
A. T., 134
Caroline F., 84
Catharine M., 108
Col. J. S., 30
Eldridge H., 61
Elizabeth, 62
E. H., 68, 109
James V. B., 85
John, 101
John C., 55, 72
John J., 97
J. C., 63, 131, 134
J. S., 7, 13, 23
Martha Ann, 32

CALLAWAY
Riley S., 78

CALLIER
Thomas P., 167
Thos. P., 173

CALLIHAN
John, 90

CALLOWAY
Mary F., 61

CAMAK
Thomas W., 84

CAMAK-ALLEN & KING,
113

CAMLINO
R. P., 138

CAMP
James, 155

CAMPBELL
J. W., 11
Martha A., 170
Mary E., 177

CAMRAN
Sarah E., 109

CAMROM
George A., 98

CANE
George, 124

CANIM
Rachel R., 90

CANLINE
Vicey M., 84

CANNON
Ann, 78
David, 91
H., 141
Julia, 91
Wherry M., 61
Wiley, 114
Zilphy, 78

CANTY
General, 133
Gen., 130

CARAWAY
Wm. J., 147

CAREY
George S., 71
George W., 116
Joseph, 92
Missouri, 163

CARGILL
James, 133
John S., 151, 170

CARINGTON
W., 135

CARLILE
Nancy, 61

CARLISLE
William, 79
Wm., 85

CARLTON
Charlotte G., 114

CARMITER
Sergeant Wiley, 172

CARNES
James J., 133, 134
Julia C., 61
Martha, 164
Mary J., 99
Sarah E., 40

CARNS
Rev. Dr., 36

CARPENTER
C., 140
C. A., 165
Gillum, 33

CARR
Capt. James, 196
Eleanor, 24
Louisa, 124
Rufus, 46

CARRAWAY
Dred, 77
Hardy B., 24

CARRINGTON
Jane, 98

CARROL
T., 135

CARROLL
John C., 173

CARRTER
Samuel M., 46

CARTER
Col. Farish, 34
James H., 16

Jesse, 90
J. D.(Jr.), 130
Martha A., 61
Mrs. Robt., 142
Robert, 14, 31
Thomas, 101
T. M., 131
W. P., 86

CARTHIDGE
Ann E., 32

CARTINS
James W., 77

CARTLEDGE
Edmund, 69
G. G., 149
Joseph, 84
Priscilla, 69
Walker, 69

CARY
George S., 47
Georgia A., 162
Isaac, 126
Joseph, 84
Mary S., 53

CASEY
Mary E., 124
Owen, 136

CASHIRE
Mary E., 115

CASTAN
Almedia H., 156

CASTELLO
Martin, 15

CASTILLO
Permelia, 61

CASTLEBERRY
James, 60

CASTLEMAN
D. B., 136

CASWELL
James A., 70

CATLET
Wm., 171

CATO
Miss H. M., 164

CATTLE
Sarah J., 177

CAULEY
William, 100

CAULFIELD
James, 52, 100

CAVANAUGH
Mrs., 92

CAY
Thos. J., 141

CEGAR
Georgia A., 91

CHADWICK
Mahulda, 124
Richardson, 115

CHAFFIN
Charles, 138
Helen, 155
Josaphine L., 78
Milus, 92
Thomas, 77, 90
Thomas(Jr.), 132
Thos., 83, 107, 155, 169
Thos.(Jr.), 137
T.(Jr.), 130
William J., 140
W. J., 102, 111

CHALFANT
Mrs. Nian W., 126

CHALMERS
George, 62

CHAMBERS, 157

CHAMBERS
Col. Jas. M., 161
Evaline A., 51
James M., 93, 147
James M.(Jr.), 85, 156, 164
John L., 93
Lieut. James, 156
Missouri, 99
Mrs., 79
Robert, 172
R. A., 133
Wm. Henry, 24
Wm. H., 44, 163

CHAMPION
Ann E., 147

Frances, 146
Georgia R., 107
Henry, 101
Josephine, 100
Lucinda, 69
Mary, 85
Rachel A., 78
William, 33
Wm., 92, 149

CHANDLER
A. H., 177
Ebenezer C., 25
Isaac C., 46
I. C., 45
William B., 17

CHANDLER & WYNN, 14

CHANEY
Mary A., 115

CHAPMAN, 53

CHAPMAN
Annie E., 163
Asa W., 61
Brad, 175
B. T., 164
Captain F. S., 139
Charles, 165
Foster S., 86
Frank, 175
F. S., 93, 102, 122, 133, 140, 167, 174
Henry, 140
Henry A., 99
Henry W., 133
H. W., 134
James, 13
J. P., 135
Lurany C., 25
Maria S., 33
Mary A., 51
Mrs. E. B., 165
Nancy A., 45
Sarah F., 52
William J., 53
W. D., 140

CHAPMAN & BROOKS, 158

CHAPPELL
Mrs. A. H., 142

CHASE
G. W., 171
Hannah E., 53
Martha Ann, 33

CHATMAN
Elizabeth, 146

CHATTERTON
Eldred A., 60
E., 85

CHENEY
Capt., 160
Dr. J. L., 158
John C., 134

CHERRY, 100

CHERRY
Charles, 107
George F., 84
George W., 61
James J., 116
Lemuel, 40
L., 13
Mrs. Lemuel, 26
Sylvanus, 99
William, 138
Williford, 146
Wm., 170

CHEVERS
Frank, 155

CHIGG
Miss, 92

CHILDS
Green S., 53

CHISHOLM
M., 14
W. A., 31

CHISOLM, 88

CHISOLM
J., 62
J. F., 62
Ninetta L., 16

CHITMAN
W. H., 164

CHOWING
H., 173

CHRISTIAN
Edward, 16
Geo. A., 46
Milly A., 91
Thomas W., 25
Wm. B., 47

-50-

CHRISTMAS
Martha E., 40

CHRISTOPHER
Francis Marion, 33

CHURCH
James, 165

CHURCHHILL
John W., 156

CLAPP
Julius J., 170
J. J., 131, 132, 137
J. R., 36
Miss Clara E., 156

CLARADY
Mrs., 86

CLARDY
Margaret, 108

CLARETON, 182

CLARIDA
Mrs., 92
Sarah A., 171
William, 107

CLARK, 38

CLARK
Abraham, 47
Andrew, 92
Andrew J., 155
Benjamin A., 124
Benj. W., 31
Eda A., 115
Eliza E., 114
Frances, 155
Franklin H., 99
George R., 108, 146
George W., 45
Georgia, 156
Gilbert, 54
James E., 90
John, 52, 62, 79, 92
John E., 109, 116
Juda W., 83
Margaret, 163
Maria, 84
Martin, 140, 165
Mary, 162
Mary A., 70
Michael, 48
Michael N., 109, 191
M. N., 8, 30, 55, 191
Patrick, 53

R. H., 31
Samuel, 164
Sarah, 53
Sarah A. C., 155
Scott, 93
Seaton Ira, 25
Solomon, 177
Susan, 69
S. P. C., 152
Walter S., 84
William, 135
William L., 107
W. L., 165

CLARKE
David M., 47
E. M., 147
Jack D., 99
Martha R., 99
M. N., 12, 13
Samuel D., 109
Sarah I., 114

CLAY
George W., 146
Henry, 135
Jesse, 16
Martha, 99
Moses, 138

CLAYTON, 86

CLAYTON
Jane, 85
P. A., 19, 20, 26, 34, 39, 44

CLECKLEY
Dr., 157
Dr. H. M., 80
Hervey M., 60
H. M., 94

CLEGG
Anthony, 124
A. & CO., 187
Elizabeth, 115
James, 125, 128
James A., 177
John H., 125
Martha, 146
Nancy F., 163
William, 124

CLEGHORN
Charles, 164
John, 68
John F., 71
S. B., 139

CLEGHORN & MOTT, 58

CLEM
James, 98

CLEMENTS
Hattie E., 124

CLEMONS
F. J., 147
W. G., 58, 129, 130, 137

CLEMONS & BROKAW, 14

CLEVE
Adaline V., 78

CLEVELAND
O. C., 133

CLIFTON
Dr. A. S., 17
William C., 84

CLINTON
Robert H., 128

CLOVER
George, 124

CLOWERS
Thos. M., 15

COATE
W. H., 165

COBB
Amelia C., 77
Angelina P., 78
Creecy A., 53
Gen., 183
Gen. Howell, 175
George W., 46
James M., 40, 52
Joshua G., 69
J. N., 173
Louisa, 45
Lucinda, 40
Maj. Gen. Howell, 180
Susan I., 40
Susan J., 60
Thomas J., 60
Wm. A., 170
Wm. R., 84

COCHRAN
William H., 61

CODE
James T., 124

John, 11
John(Sr.), 101
J., 11
Mrs. James D., 147

CODY
Anna E., 115
C. C., 103, 110
J. A., 131, 137
Lucius, 162

COFFEE
Rebecca E., 32

COFFIELD
William J., 70

COFIELD
Mrs., 92

COGBILL
John W., 78
Leonidas J., 114

COGLE
Charles, 155

COHEN
Zachariah, 115

COKER
Mary, 162
Mrs., 70

COLBERT
J. S., 164

COLE
Jacob W., 91
James C., 170
J., 90

COLEE
Leah, 69

COLEMAN
Arran, 108
A. A., 131
Benj. F., 17
B. F., 7, 26, 35, 44, 98,
127, 157, 168, 173
Crawford, 78
C., 131
Elizabeth L., 24
John, 84
John M., 134
John T. W., 45
Julia A., 177
J. T., 71
Lewis, 164

Martha L., 108
Thomas G., 163
Thomas J., 70
T. G., 131, 132

COLLIER
Elbert J. P., 155
Francis, 162
Frank, 128
Louis M., 165

COLLINS, 92, 100

COLLINS
Christopher, 177
Emeline, 172
Frances M., 124
James, 70, 108
James B., 170
James S., 32
Jere., 54
John, 162
John J., 52
Mary, 171
Mary A., 115
Mary V., 109
Matilda, 114
Sarah I., 114

COLQUITT, 157

COLQUITT
Capt., 94, 104
Emily L., 46
H. H., 133
Judge, 38
Peyton H., 83, 147, 149
P. H., 89, 98, 123, 133
Walter T., 83
W. T., 31, 54

COLTER
B. M., 138
Frederick F., 147
Smith, 138
Susan, 147

COLYER
Martha, 25

COLZEY
Dr. E. F., 125
E. F., 150
Mrs. Mary, 172

COMER
Frances A. E., 33
James, 173
Madora, 124
Mary L., 114

Mr., 173
T., 141
Wm., 155

COMPTON
James, 138
Wm. H. H., 171

CONE
Catharine, 108
J. W., 141
William, 141

CONLEY
John, 12
Luke, 151

CONLY
Luke, 128

CONNELL
John W., 163

CONNER
Emily, 78
Mary Ann, 33
Mrs., 157
Rev. W. G., 105

CONNOLLY
Elizabeth, 84

CONNOR
William, 126

CONOWAY, 62

CONTERS
Emily, 115

CONWAY
Bassil M., 125
Ellison, 125

COOK, 92

COOK
Archibald, 78
Barnabas, 25
Capt. Hatch, 142
Catharine, 162
Elijah, 173
Eula, 126
Hatch, 126, 127, 152
James G., 155
James J., 114
John, 133
J. C., 13, 22, 39
J. G., 98
J. M., 31

Margaret A., 77
Martha, 155
Martin V., 170
Mary, 114
Mary A., 170
Melissa A., 115
Miss, 79
Mrs., 164
M. V., 134
Parshamia L., 70
Rebecca J., 61
Rhoda Amelia, 25
Samuel S., 90
Seaborn, 128
Susan, 69
Willis, 141

COOKE
Wm. C., 147

COOLEY
Julia A., 165
Leonard R., 51

COOPER, 43

COOPER
Alexander H., 32
Andrew J., 171
A. H., 6, 37, 45
Capt. A. H., 149
Col., 182
Ezekiel, 40
Fannie, 171
George W., 128, 138
Hugh A., 172
Jacintha S., 170
James F., 108
Martha, 146
Mary A., 16
Micajah F., 170
Mrs., 126
Mrs. Cynthia, 100
Sarah, 46
Sarah M., 171
William R., 172
Willis, 62
Wm. C., 48, 55, 63
W. C., 42

COOPER & HOGAN, 14

COPELAND, 126

COPELAND
Elizabeth, 155
John T., 24
Lucy A., 170
Mary, 165
Miss Sarah A., 164

Nancy, 52
Susan, 68

CORBALLY
Kate, 146

CORBET
George, 140

CORCORAN
James, 93

CORDEN
James, 177

CORDERY
Aaron, 70
Daniel, 98
Harriet, 52
Jonathan, 47
Jonathan P., 45
Mary A., 51
Sarah C., 162

CORDRY
Jonathan, 16
Nancy, 15

CORLEE
Mary, 69

CORLEY
Maynard, 135

CORLIE
Elizabeth, 146

CORNETT
Hardy, 137
S. E., 138

CORRADAN
William, 78

CORRY
Henry, 141
Mary Ann, 53

COSKINS
Josiah, 177

COSTAN
Martha, 172
Martin E., 155

COUCH, 157

COUCH
Elijah, 98

COULTER, 85

COULTER
Elizabeth, 125

COUNT
Elizabeth A., 70

COUNTS
Elizabeth, 85

COURSEY
Elizabeth, 79
Emily, 126
Mary Ann, 22

COURTNEY, 79

COURTNEY
J., 135

COUSENS
Wm. C., 140

COUSFORD
Jno. T., 152

COVEY
James, 125

COVINGTON
Elizabeth J., 40
Mary A., 41
Ransom, 77

COWAN
Martha M., 108

COWART
Allen, 33
Salina, 24

COWDERY
George W., 62
Geo. W., 24
G. W., 42
Lester L., 15
Lyman P., 162
L. L., 14

COX, 85

COX
Alanson M., 15
Ann B., 46
A. M., 11
Bartley M., 24
Daniel D., 90
Darius, 99
David R., 125

Eliza A., 32
Jeremiah, 24
Jesse, 147
John P., 84
Lucy P., 146
Mary E., 32
Mary F., 24
Miss Martha Jane, 41
Robert D., 32
Thos. J., 171
Wm. E., 32

COY
Henry, 139

CRABTREE
Haynes, 194, 195

CRAIG
Eliz. E., 46

CRAIG & WIDMAN, 15

CRAM
Nancy, 162
Wm. H. D., 125

CRAMP
Dr., 165

CRANDALL
Caroline, 15
Luke, 16

CRANE
A. K., 136
R. S., 136

CRANSBY
Thomas, 16

CRAWFORD
Avarilla, 116
David, 152
Emily, 177
Gov., 6
Isaac K., 115
Jason, 152
M. J., 150
Nancy W., 115
Priscilla, 61

CREAMER
Charlotte, 107
Jane, 109

CRENSHAW
D. M., 136

CREW

Solomon M., 156

CREWS
Emeline, 53
Miss Sarah E., 147

CRICH
J., 172

CRICHTON
Charles, 90, 109
Mary Augusta, 156
Peter, 18

CRISP
W. H., 82

CRITTENDEN
Benjamin F., 84

CROCKETT
D., 145
James, 125
Mary, 125

CROFT, 123

CROFT
Alice R., 79
Captain Ed., 142
Edward, 80, 102, 110,
117, 145
Ed., 144
E., 127
W. G., 131

CROGAN
John, 172

CROKER
J. C., 173

CROMLEY, 92

CROMWELL
J. H., 131
O., 131

CROOK, 100

CROPMAN
Salathal N., 15

CROPP
Henry D., 79
Mrs. David, 100
William E., 85

CROSBY
Jesse, 139

John, 16

CROSS
Lucretia, 85

CROSSMAN, 62

CROSSMAN
Caroline, 17

CROUCH
Arena, 99
Elizabeth, 45
George W., 78
James, 172
James M., 108
John, 135
J. M., 172
Martha I., 108
Mary A., 61
Mrs. M. M., 171
William T., 170

CROW
Samuel J., 25, 54
Sidney, 135

CROWELL
Col., 196
Henry, 196
Tom, 196

CRUMLEY
David, 92
Rev. W., 60
Rev. W. M., 51

CRUMWELL
Henry, 62

CUBBAGE
Barbary C., 15

CULBERT
Lucinda, 170

CULBERTSON
John, 41
Mary P., 125

CULBRETH
Mary I., 108

CULLIN
John, 172

CULPEPPER, 156

CULPEPPER
Adaline, 46

David, 16
David (Jr.), 70
Eliza, 47
Elizabeth, 40
G. W., 138
Jasper, 140
Jeff., 140
Jeremiah, 40
Joel, 140
John, 140
Margaret J., 46
William, 140

CULVER, 92

CULVER
Fleming, 162
Martha A., 15

CULVERSON
Frances, 125

CUMBER
John I., 90

CUMMING
Gen., 131

CUMMINGS
Thomas, 77

CUMMINS
Benjamin S., 69

CUNNING
Margaret L., 46

CURENTON
J. W., 138

CURETON
Sarah, 31

CURLEE
Solomon, 54

CURLEY
Capt., 160

CURRAN
Wm., 154

CURRENCE
Junius, 128

CURRIE
Elizabeth, 108

CURRY, 79

CURRY
Abram, 47
Mrs., 70
Thomas, 98, 100

CURTEM
F., 141

CURTIS
Mrs. Lucretia M., 71
N. N., 165, 171

CUSHMAN
Charles T., 46
C. T., 15
Dr., 100
Dr. C. T., 169

CUSHMAN & FOGLE, 19

DADE
Mary E., 17

DAGGERS
J. R., 76

DAILY
Mark, 133

DALLARD
Thomas, 165

DALTON
Benjamin F., 90
Elizabeth W., 78
Mariah S., 78
Perry W., 109
Septamus W., 40
Wyatt L., 139

DALZELL
Rev. Mr., 83

DAMILL
John, 46

DANERLY
Wm., 55

DANFORTH
Oliver, 45
O., 63, 68, 80, 92

DANIEL
B., 136
Edw. C., 139
Frances J., 40
Georgiana, 122
James T., 117

Joseph, 165
Jos., 111
Jos. H., 154
J. H., 85, 156
J. L., 172
J. T., 148, 149
Martha Ann, 16
Mrs. Elizabeth N., 41
Patsey, 97
R. A., 131
William, 126
William C., 52
Wm., 41, 63, 71, 76, 80, 102
W., 111

DANIEL-HUGHES & CO., 113

DARBY
George, 170

DARDEN
Elizabeth, 24
Thos J., 124
Wm., 124

DARLING, 100

DART
Mrs. Elizabeth M., 32

DASTER
John, 171

DAUKINS
DeWitt, 78
Mary A. E., 47

DAVENPORT
Charles, 100
Charles J., 46
Mrs., 79
Nancy, 78

DAVIDSON
Eli, 162
John, 90
Martha, 170
Mary, 109
Sarah A., 108
Stillman, 78
William, 69
Wm., 100

DAVIE
Joseph H., 138
Mary, 108
Mary A., 78
Minerva A., 125

Nancy, 25

DAVIES
J., 135
L. J., 11, 14
Mrs., 11
Mrs.L. J., 11

DAVIS, 79

DAVIS
Arthur B., 17, 164
A. B., 131
A. L., 135
Caroline, 109
Caroline P., 16
Catharine, 16
Charlotte T., 146
Daniel, 136
Davie, 46
Dr. George, 93
Elvira D., 162
Ezekiel, 55, 92
E. D., 77
George S., 45
James, 134
John, 107
John C., 170
John E., 6, 23, 173
John H., 27, 32, 54, 78, 116
John W., 99
Joseph, 138
J., 141
J. J., 135
J. L. O., 136
J. W., 138
Kinsey, 69
Lewis, 20
Mary, 108
Miss F. A., 165
Mrs., 101
Mrs. A. B., 11
Mrs. Martha Ann, 54
President, 128, 152, 159
Richard R., 32
Robert, 157, 161
R. R., 165
Sarah A., 171
Sarah B., 125
Susan P., 146
William, 85
William I., 108
Wm., 12, 78
W. M., 141
W. S., 131

DAVISON
Nancy, 84

DAWSON
Captain Edgar, 142
Dr. Thos. W., 116
D. T., 131
Edgar G., 63, 71
Emma C., 78
George W., 107
Hugh B., 90
Hu. B., 147
H. C., 13
James H., 138
John R., 5, 62
Major, 168
Mary E., 170
Mrs. Eliza, 147
Mrs. Mary M., 156
Rev. J. E., 36
Thomas W., 115

DAWSON-HILL & CO., 11, 14

DAY
Anna, 115
Fannie L., 156
Joanna, 115
John I., 69
J., 92
Mary E., 40
Mrs. Barbara, 70
Sane, 92
Wiley L., 16

DEAN
Alsey, 25
Aquilla A. V., 61
C. A., 173
David, 45
Elizabeth, 61
John T., 138
Mary, 115
Mary E., 52
Sarah A., 155
Stephen B., 46
Triphena, 115

DEATON
T., 133

DEAVERS
Missouri E., 91

DEBLOIS
J. A., 55
Nathaniel, 60

DEBLOIS & HALL, 19

DECKER
Elizabeth, 41

George H., 60
John T., 25
Mary, 60
Melissa A., 78
Nancy A., 78

DECKROW
James K., 138, 155

DEER
John S., 115

DEES
John, 40
Nancy, 99

DeGRAFFENREID
Adelaide V., 163

DeGRAFFENRIED
B. B., 14
E. M., 15

DEIGNAN
Patrick, 165
Wm., 85

DeLAGNEL
Col., 167

DeLAUNEY
Harry J., 150

DELLANS
Benj., 101

DELONAUGH, 126

DENNARD
John E., 61

DENNIS
Elizabeth, 53
E. S., 169
James, 54, 151
James W., 128
J. M., 135
Lucinda, 46
Mary F., 47
Mrs., 100
Thomas H., 170

DENSLOW
A. A., 14

DENSON
Burwell M., 128
Jas. M., 127
J. M., 130, 137

DENT
  Robert L., 40

DENTON
  R. Watson, 156
  R. W., 127, 150

DePOE
  Albert R., 156

DESHASER
  Richard, 129

DESSAU, 19

DESSAU
  Mrs., 15

DEVER
  Charles, 135

DEVON, 77

DEVON
  Frances E., 84
  H. J., 71, 79

DEVORE
  T. L., 133

DeVOTIE
  J. G., 131
  Rev. J. H., 90, 105, 130, 162
  Rev. Noble, 147

DeWITT
  Abram H., 90
  A. H., 163

DeWOLF
  Thomas, 82, 126, 165, 173
  Thos., 89

DEWS
  George M., 162

DEXTER
  Charles E., 69

DIBBLE
  O. J. H., 190

DICKEN
  John, 25
  Mary E., 77

DICKENS
  I. E., 78

DICKERSON
  W. H., 140

DICKEY
  James W., 140
  W. H., 140

DICKINSON
  Joseph U., 156

DICKSON
  Elizabeth, 84
  George M., 100
  Margaret M., 77

DIFFLEY
  Peter, 15

DILL
  Augustus A., 83
  A. A., 34, 42, 48
  Mrs. A., 92

DILLARD
  Colonel F. W., 143
  Parmelia, 77
  Sealy, 32
  Susan, 24
  Thomas, 124

DILLINGHAM
  Geo. W., 128
  G. W., 127, 131, 132
  Mrs. George W., 101

DILLMAN
  Mary Ann, 32

DILLON
  Ann, 91
  J. M., 167
  Mary Ann, 156
  Mrs. Ann, 82
  William, 169
  W. J., 134

DIMON
  Caroline E., 16
  Joseph, 62
  Stephen, 90

DINK, 92

DINKINS
  Alpha, 84
  William H., 115

DISMUKES
  J. S., 7

DIXON, 125

DIXON
  B. H., 131
  H. B., 147
  Mary Lizzie, 86
  Robert Emmet, 161
  Robert E., 79
  Robt. E., 80
  R. E., 86, 89, 106, 164
  Stephen M., 170
  S. M., 131

DODSON
  Peggy, 47
  Sam'l C., 32

DOLAN
  Hugh, 100
  J., 163
  Mrs. Hugh, 100

DOLES
  Benjamin, 78
  Benjamin F., 62
  Francis M., 40
  George W., 134
  G. W., 133
  James W., 146
  Mary A. E., 91
  Mary E., 78
  Stephen A., 24
  Walton, 51

DOLIN
  B., 164

DOLLY
  John G., 70
  Warren, 70

DONALLY
  Washington, 169

DONELSON
  James, 85

DONEY
  M. A., 111
  M. D., 131

DONNOVAN
  Thomas, 141

DORSETT
  John H., 121

DOUGHERTY
  Wm., 15

C. S., 173

ELRED
Arabella T., 16

EMERICH
Julius, 177

EMERSON
Robert J., 165

ENDERMAN
Carrie, 115
Robert, 131

ENGLISH
A. J., 149
Caroline M., 107
Eliza A., 46
Mary J., 163
Mrs. Mary M., 165
William B., 85

ENNIS
David, 83
J., 89
Nancy A., 41
Sarah Ann, 46

ENNIS & CO., 14

EPPING, 57, 79

EPPING
Barbara Catherine, 17
Henry H., 15
H. H., 43, 55, 147, 158

EPPING & WINTER, 14

ESLER
John S., 162
J. S., 133

ESTES
H. S., 114, 128
Z. M., 133

ETCHINSON
Stephen, 129

ETHERIDGE
Isaac, 162
Mary E., 170

ETTER
Martin, 132

EVAN
Col., 159

EVANS
Abner A., 99
Ariadna A., 52
Camden, 173
Elizabeth P., 146
Georgia S., 125
James E., 169
J. W., 138
Rev. J. E., 13, 60, 96
Roxanna M., 99
R. W., 173

EVERAGE
Epsy A., 77

EVERETT
Capt. J. M., 160
Elizabeth A., 40
James M., 86, 102, 116, 127
Jas., 111
Jas. M., 55, 117, 159
John Joseph, 116
J. M., 63, 72, 93, 129, 130, 137, 174
Thomas, 135

EVERIDGE
A., 138
H.(Jr.), 138
Joseph, 138

EVERITT
John, 135

EVERS
Calvin, 138

EWING
Theodore, 108
Theo., 111

EYRE
James, 61

E. Y. TAYLOR & CO., 15

FACKLER
George, 135
Mary S., 147

FAGAN
Michael, 155

FAGG
Francis I., 108

FAIL

Samuel W., 124

FAIRCHILD, 54

FAIRWETHER
Emma L., 169

FALFORD
R. P., 141

FALKNER
Isaac, 91

FANN
Lovick P., 84

FANNEN
John B., 90

FANSETT
William B., 61

FARBER
Charles J., 125

FARISH
Hugh, 100

FARLEY
James A., 45

FARMER
Angeline, 170
Josaphine, 170
Sarah A. M., 98

FARR
Christopher C., 139
James H., 163

FARRAR
Peter, 39

FARRELL
Simon, 139

FARRIOR
Mrs. Frances, 41

FASSELL
J. A., 151

FAULKENBERRY
Jacob H., 171
John M., 91
Martha, 62

FAULKENBURY
Elizabeth A., 78
Jacob H., 52

Mary A., 40

FAULKNER
Euna V., 115

FAUN
Lovie P., 69

FELTON
Jerry, 164

FERGERSON
Nat. C., 152

FERGURSON, 45

FERGURSON
Aaron, 39
James, 51

FERGUSON
Emily V., 83
Mary E., 84
Nathaniel C., 78
Nath. C., 129

FERGUSSON
W. F., 131

FERRELL
John, 173
J. E., 171
Wm. B., 15

FERRILL
James D., 99

FEUNTY
John, 163

FICKLING
C. C., 140
John, 140
William, 140
Wm. E., 116

FIELD
Charles, 69
Mary, 25

FIELDS
H., 134
Mrs. Nancy, 147

FILCHETT
John K., 171

FILLMORE
President, 3, 74

FINCHER
Arry M. J., 146
Hester A. T., 70
Martha A., 84
Mary Ann, 17
Moses, 90
William P., 45
Wm., 101

FINCHIN, 62

FINILER
Hannah, 177

FINNEGAN
P., 101

FINNEY
Howard W., 116
John, 177

FINNIGAN
Peter, 141

FISH, 67

FISH
Marcus, 177

FISHBURN
E. B., 79

FISHER
Charles, 60
George W., 52
Henry P., 45
Parker, 83
Wm., 90

FISHHACKER, 145

FITNER
Martha E., 45

FITTZ
Malinda, 124

FLANNIGAN
Harriet A., 60
Thos. A., 171

FLEMING
Ellen A., 46
Henry, 149
John, 149
Mrs. M. E., 165

FLEMMING
Ann, 91
Erastus, 136

John, 107
Samuel J., 47

FLETCHER
James M., 114
Jno., 129
J. F., 149
J. M., 149
Martha, 46
Mary, 125
Mauria, 68
Nancy, 146
Sarah, 125

FLEWELLEN, 68, 79

FLEWELLEN
Abner C., 61
Abner H., 46
Alex., 53
Ann Lane, 24
A. H., 31
Dr., 86, 127, 148
Dr. W. W., 83
Eliza, 90
James T., 40
Julia F., 78
Martha E., 146
Mrs. A. H., 116
Mrs. J. T., 101
Nancy J., 53
William W., 124
W. W., 94, 157, 159

FLORENCE
Mary Ann, 177

FLOURNOY
George R., 124
John M., 116
Margaret, 163
Mrs., 156
Mrs. Julia A., 164
Robert, 85
Samuel W., 34
S. W., 14, 26

FLOYD, 12

FLOYD
Andrew J., 61
A. J., 149
Gen., 196
James P., 108
J. P., 138

FLYNN, 100

FLYNN
John, 46

J. E., 129

FOGLE
Anna Rosina, 41
Dr., 158
Dr. Jacob, 80
Jacob, 41
J., 15
J. A., 131
Mary E., 155
Sarah Gertrude, 80
T. T., 131

FOGLE & CUSHMAN, 19

FOLDS
Samantha A. E., 125

FOLEY, 100

FOLEY
James, 101
Margaret E., 164
Mary A. I., 115
Mrs., 79

FOLSOM
Elizabeth, 163
Mary, 170

FONHANA
Letitia, 171

FONTAINE, 10, 113

FONTAINE
B. B., 151
Henrietta, 40
John(Jr.), 156
J., 36
Thomas S., 139

FORAN
John, 141
Mrs., 92
Patrick, 92, 124, 129
Pat., 151
Rosannah, 61

FORBY
John W., 139

FORD, 85

FORD
J. B., 149
Melvina, 115
Mrs. Catherine, 165
M. W., 152
Sarah B., 84

FORDE
R. E., 161

FORMAN
Augustus, 124

FORRESTER
Captain Apollos, 142

FORSYTH, 39

FORSYTH
Bird B., 107
Byrd B., 78
Captain, 37
Fanny, 92
Francis, 90
John, 6, 23, 57, 58
Martha J., 98
Mary D., 107
Robert, 85
Rosa M., 47
R. C., 68, 107

FORT
Bethia A., 90

FORTSON
Thomas D., 52

FORTUNBURY
Mrs. A. A., 171

FOSTER
Adam G., 48
Amanda, 24
A. G., 15, 26, 39, 42, 77
Col. Thomas F., 33
Daniel C., 139
Elizabeth, 163
Henry, 152
Jefferson T., 115
J. A., 152
Louisa J., 124
Martha, 24
N. P., 13, 30, 70
Susan, 92
Susan A., 108
Whitby, 29
William A., 177
Wm., 152
Wm. M., 146
W., 27

FOUNTAIN
David, 24
Jane, 32

FOWLER

D. H., 161, 172, 173

FOX
John, 139, 163
Mrs., 156
R. W., 14

FOYLE
William L., 129

FRAMPTON
J. H., 136

FRANCHAND
Frederick, 124

FRANCIS
Jas., 16

FRANK, 100

FRANK
M., 140

FRANKLIN
Eskin S., 171

FRAZELL, 92

FRAZER
John A., 70, 81
William W., 77

FRAZIER
Alexander, 147
America A., 69
Frances, 99
James M., 125
J. A., 150
Mary, 91
Telitha, 164
William, 136

FREDERICK
Charles B., 100
D. F., 156
Frances, 171

FREE
Wm. B., 163

FREEL
Howell W., 138

FREELDES, 172

FREEM
Robert L., 162

FREEMAN

Harris W., 115
Jno. W., 194
John W., 84
J. K., 135
Mary A., 114
Mrs., 172
R., 172
Stephen B., 108
Wm., 32
W. S., 133

FREENEY
Wm., 162

FRENCH
Gen. S. G., 133
Mary, 172
Nancy A., 162

FRENCH CAPTAIN, 195

FRENCH CHIEF, 196

FREY
Clara, 70

FRICKER
Jas., 133

FRIER
Elizabeth, 115

FRONE
Henry, 156

FROST
Eli, 52
Joseph, 54
J. W., 13, 26, 42, 48, 63
Mariah, 162
Mary, 91
U. B., 93

FROST & JOHNSON, 14

FRY
Capt. A., 174
Capt. C. D., 174, 175
Capt. Dan, 174
Daniel, 40

FRYER
James, 109

FUCH
Chas., 10

FUDGE
Mary, 69

FULFORD
Robert, 78

FULGHAM
Neil, 126

FULLER
Caroline, 173
Julia A., 84
Morgan J. L., 170
Samuel, 172

FULLING
R., 173

FURDLE, 157

FUSELL
Catharine, 173

FUSSELL
Aaron, 69
Enoch, 45
Jacob, 41
James N., 53
John, 152

FUSSILL
Benjamin A., 53

GABRIEL
Henry H. A., 124

GADDIS
George, 138

GAFF
Luther, 91

GAFFORD
Benjamin N., 85
George W., 146
Victoria, 91

GAGER
George, 78
L. M., 163

GALAWAY
J. H., 149

GALE
Elizabeth, 163

GALESPIE, 92

GALLAWAY
John, 116

GALLOPS
Caleb, 16

GALLUPS
Isham, 60

GALVAN
Joseph, 107

GAMBRILL
Mrs. Ann, 116

GAMMAGE
Frances E., 91

GAMMEL, 47

GAMMEL
A., 163
F. M., 149
George, 173
Mrs. Elizabeth, 116
Zachariah, 16

GAMMELL
A., 122
Barbary, 83
Elizabeth, 51
Francis M., 115
George A., 155
Jeremiah, 52
John W., 98
Martha, 99
Mary, 77, 108
Thomas A., 40

GAMMON, 70

GAMMON
Martha, 101

GAMMONS
Isaac, 116

GARBIN, 62

GARDNER
Benjamin F., 99
John, 108, 138
Lucinda, 177

GARGROVES
C., 141

GARNETT, 140

GARRARD
Aug. O., 139
James, 97
James L., 101

N. W., 159
YONGE & HOOPER, 10

GARRETT, 100

GARRETT
D. A., 82
Elisha F., 53
Elizabeth, 61
Ellen, 114
Ellenora, 146
Frances, 52
James C., 140
Jno. R., 24
Joseph S., 108
Martha Ann, 24
Mary, 98
Mary Emeline, 40
Thomas, 138
William, 79

GARRIS
David, 61
Sarah, 171
William, 98

GARRISON, 100

GARRISON
Martha G., 53
Patterson, 114
Sarah, 15
Thomas J., 133

GARTMAN
James C., 147

GARVEN
Eliza, 100
Robert, 25

GASKEY
Andrew, 52

GASOWAY
Mrs., 171

GASTON
F. B., 172

GATEHOUSE
Geo., 6

GATEMAN
J. C., 173

GATES
H., 173

GAY

John W., 152
N. B., 152

GAYLE, 100

GEER
Charles L., 46

GELLEN
Patrick, 47

GENTRY
Anna L. C., 170
Archibald, 114

GEORGE
Alvania, 108
Amanda C., 84
Franklin, 115
Lucinda, 52
Martha A., 90
Mary A., 99
Samantha, 54

GERALD
Alex., 139

GERKE
Emily L., 124

GERRARD & HOOPER, 15

GESNER
Wm., 63

GETSINGER
William, 100, 165

GETTINGER
Emily, 107

**GETTINGER &
BARSCHALL, 68**

GIBBONS
John, 165

GIBBS
Sarah, 60

GIBOON
Martha, 172

GIBSON
David, 124
Fannie, 171
Hiram A., 108, 138
James, 144
Louisa, 115
Martha, 46

Robert, 98
William, 100
William H., 146

GIDDENS
A. J., 138

GIDDINGS
Emily C., 125
Jane Ann, 16
Mary J., 99

GIFFORD
Mrs. Margaret, 156

GILBERT
Eliza, 53
Mary H., 107
Mr., 109
M. C., 152
Sarah, 24
Thomas, 171
Thos., 148
Wesley, 136

GILES
Isaac H., 114
J. H., 165

GILL
Richard, 114

GILLESPIA
Patrick, 25

GILLEY
Louisa Matilda, 24

GILMER
Frances R., 170

GILMORE, 67

GILMORE
Louisa, 101
N., 70

GILPIN
Dorcas A., 125
Stephen, 54

GILSTRAP
Martha A. E., 99

GINN
Edmund B., 107
Eliza, 177
Isaac C., 162
Loveless S., 40
Mary C., 114

GIQUILLIAT
Wm. R., 162

GIRDNER
George Van Doren, 126
James A., 126
J. A., 164
J. L., 131

GIRRARD, 125

GITTENGER
Captain Philip, 165

GITTENGER & BARSHALL,
20

GITTINGER
Philip, 38
Phillip T., 191
P., 51, 76
P.(Jr.), 141

GITTINGER & BARSCHALL,
31

GLADNEY
James B., 156

GLANTON
John H., 52

GLASS
Louisa, 25

GLASSCOCK
C., 173

GLASSEN
Capt., 183

GLASTON
A. P., 173

GLAWN
Nancy J., 40

GLAZE
Frances, 124
Milton J., 99
Nancy, 78
Sarah, 70, 78
William H., 70

GLENN
Martha J., 84
Nancy A., 45
Rachel I., 78
Sarah J., 155

Simon G., 170

GODWIN
Elizabeth, 115
John, 116
J., 12
J. D., 133

GOEN
Frances, 52

GOETCHIUS
R., 86
R. R., 18, 35, 63, 77, 81

GOETCHIUS & HODGES,
117

GOFORTH
L. P., 172

GOHIAN
William, 165

GOINS
Drewry, 172
Frances E., 170
Mrs. Martha, 173

GOLDEN
Frank W., 150
P. J., 134
Thomas M., 134

GOLDMAN
J., 133

GOLDSMITH
Frank, 141

GOMER
John, 162

GOODALE
Francis O., 84
F. O., 163, 171
J. H., 15
Martha, 177

GOODLOE
John W., 177

GOODROE
Richard M., 177

GOODSON
Mrs., 173

GOODWIN
Jesse, 61

Julia A., 99
Lovick, 147

GOOLDSBY
Wootson, 61

GOOLSBY
Benjamin, 91

GOOSUCH
Charles A., 70

GORDEN
John W. G., 143

GORDON
Elizabeth, 170
Major A. M., 164
Thos. G., 190
Wm. J., 155

GORDY
Fannie, 170
Lafayette, 77
Noah, 172
Sarah R., 61

GORHAM
James, 140

GOSLIN
John W., 77
Narcissa, 172
Virginia J., 163

GOSS
Cassa A. F., 69

GOSSETTE
E. A., 141

GOULDING
Dr., 15
Edwin R., 78
Elizabeth G., 16
E. R., 7, 23
Henrietta, 52
Mrs. Eloise, 41
Nancy A., 108
Rev. Thomas, 33
Thos. B., 41

GOUTER
Permelia, 15

GOVEY
Dennis, 139

GRACE
Byrd M., 114

Mrs. W. H., 79
Rev. Wm. H., 126
Susan Jane, 80
Wm. H., 79, 80

GRAHAM
Eliza, 84
William(Jr.), 108

GRAM
Elisha M., 99

GRANBERRY
George L., 84
James A., 85
J. A., 137
Thomas I., 83

GRANDE
Andrew, 146

GRANT, 125

GRANT
Aug. L., 14
A. L., 39
Calvin L., 138
Col. L. P., 189
Daniel, 136, 146
Elza C., 32
John, 171
John G., 152
J. J., 140
Sallie C., 171

GRANTHAM
Hannah A., 115
Jas., 155

GRAVES
Benjamin F., 52
Lewis S., 78
Matilda, 40, 170
Thomas, 141

GRAVIN
Robert, 109

GRAY
Charlotte C., 107
Francis M., 16
F. M., 68, 101, 148, 157
J. M., 138
Margaret, 172
Myra V., 171
Phineas, 146
Rachel, 146
Reuben Allison, 116
Richard M., 33
R. M., 171

Wesley, 16
Wm. C., 56, 76, 102
W. C., 93, 116

GRAY & GREENWOOD, 38, 153

GRAYBILL
Martha F., 78

GRAY-STEWART & CO., 75

GREEN
Alexander C., 15
Augustus M., 138
Bartlett W., 78
Jos. B., 14
J. R., 17
Lemuel A., 40
Lucy A., 70
L., 139
Martha A. E., 125
Matilda, 41
Robert B., 70
R. H., 26
Sarah D., 108
Wiley S., 107
Wm., 170
Wm. R., 146

GREENE
Alfred M., 115
Caroline, 33
Eliza E., 40
J. R., 27
Rhodam A., 191
Robt. D., 24
Robt. H., 36
R. H., 27, 34, 80

GREENWOOD, 37

GREENWOOD
America S., 177
E., 76
E. S., 13, 123
Gussie, 146
H. T., 27
J., 139
Miss Laura A., 164
Thos., 116

GREENWOOD & CO., 15

GREENWOOD & ELLIS, 14

GREENWOOD & GRAY, 38, 153

GREER, 14

GREER
Elisha P., 40
George, 138
Mary Jane, 25
Thomas G., 115
Wm., 78

GREGORY
Harriet C., 155
John R., 163

GRESHAM
Harrison, 32

GREY
Missouri Ann, 16

GRICE
Mrs. V., 125

GRIFFIN, 100

GRIFFIN
Daniel, 23, 41, 58
Gasoline, 46
James, 32
John C., 138
William T., 146

GRIGG
Dr. Solon M., 116

GRIGGS
B. F., 71
Jane T., 155
John Neal, 71
Mrs. Sarah C., 71
Wm., 47

GRIMES
Cliff. B., 132
Dr. T. W., 26, 30
Jackson, 139
Joseph, 26
Sterling, 93
Sterling F., 54, 76
S. F., 41
Thos. W., 132

GRIMSLEY
Ellen, 109

GRISWOLD
Horace, 33
Lewis W., 171
Mrs. Caroline Matilda, 93
Mrs. Elizabeth, 33
Wm. H., 24, 40, 158
W. H., 33, 167, 174

GROENBECK
Frances, 90

GROFF
Lucy Ann, 91

GRONBECK
Mrs., 85

GROSSBEAK
T. R., 79

GUE
James A., 136, 163

GUERRY
LeGrand, 136
Major LeGrand, 25

GUESS
George, 171

GUICE
Thomas R., 177

GUILFORD
James, 97
Mr., 105

GUILLET
Capt. S. Isidore, 180

GUISE
Miss, 106

GULLEDGE
Jesse, 114
Martha, 45

GULLEN
George, 19, 26, 34, 42,
48, 71, 99

GUN
James A., 124

GUNBE
Eddie, 171

GUNBY
Rowena, 146
R. M., 37, 55, 89, 128
Walter M., 171

GUNN, 11

GUNN
David, 34, 69, 97, 99,
101

Emeline, 40
Emily M., 99
Eudoxy, 84
George W., 69
John N., 99
Joseph, 54
Martha, 101
Permelia E., 61

GUNTER
Charles, 92
J. A., 172

GUTHRIE
Fannie J., 125
U. L., 135

GUY
Hillery G., 109

HACKNEY, 85

HACKNEY
Adaline, 107
Caroline, 125
Elizabeth, 90
Louisa, 124
Mary, 45

HACKREY, 62

HADDOCK, 151

HADDOCK
Celia A., 108
Jesse, 91
Mary A., 170

HADLEY
Jesse D., 16

HAFF
Donaldson, 163

HAGANS
Jos. B., 129

HAGERTY
Andrew, 165

HAGLER
Mary A., 170
Robet L., 162

HAIMAN & CO., 143

HAINNY
J. K., 173

HALE
Nancy, 69
William M., 52
Wm., 85, 98

HALL, 14, 126

HALL
Alexander, 52
Annetta J., 61
A. J., 70
Boling, 194
Cynthia G., 84
Dicey Ann, 91
Elizabeth, 24, 47
Epsy J., 69
E. L., 13
George, 141
Harvey, 22, 26, 31, 34,
44, 71
Henry, 16, 156
Henry T., 18, 38, 57, 58,
80, 84, 165
Hugh, 61
H., 53
H. H., 131, 141
H. T., 23, 27, 44, 48, 55,
63, 77, 86, 92, 156
James C., 69
Jane, 109
Jas., 16
J. W., 141
Mary E., 172
Moses, 129
Moses H., 108
Mrs., 165
Mrs. A. J., 66
Rebecca, 164
Repsey Ann, 25
Rutha, 70
Samuel, 126
Simeon T., 91
S. W., 141
Thomas, 79
Thomas R., 98
Van Ransel, 97
Wm., 129, 151
Wm. W., 155
W. F., 131, 132
W. H., 172
Zilpha, 53

HALL & DEBLOIS, 19

HALL & MOSES, 14, 18,
19

HALLENBECK
Josaphine, 163

HARP
Fredonia N., 108
Lafayette, 41
Ruhama, 51
Samuel D., 45
Sophronia E., 46

HARPER
Elizabeth, 61
Mary, 173
W. J., 164

HARRALSON
Jonathan, 107

HARRELL
Isaac, 143
Martha A., 108
Minerva, 84
Susan, 170
William J., 52

HARRILL
James, 78

HARRINGTON, 100

HARRIS, 101

HARRIS
Alfred, 138
Andrew I., 99
A., 131
Beverly A., 107
Cornelia, 155
Eliza C., 32
Ella, 162
Ellanora, 162
Emily E., 124
Felix M., 40
Frances Jane, 31
George A., 86
George W., 163
Henry, 100, 117
Henry M., 80, 148
H. M., 127
James, 91, 109
James M., 98
Jasper, 17
John, 83
J. C., 116
J. H., 90, 97
J. N. & CO., 11
Leonora, 108
Louis, 162, 171
Lucinda E., 170
Martha D., 40
Martha Elizabeth, 116
Martha W., 17

Mary, 77
Mary A., 146
Mary A. L., 99
Mary J., 156
Mary L., 125
Miss S. A., 165
Mrs. Elizabeth, 172
Mrs. L., 172
Mrs. Olivia M., 109
Mrs. W. B., 164
R. H., 70, 86
Sarah Virginia, 70
Walton K., 121
William H., 52
Wm. H., 157, 169
W. B., 12, 43
W. H., 167

HARRISON
Aaron, 107
Ann, 170
Ann H., 25
Chas. S., 32
Jackson, 84
Job N., 171
Lewis, 108
Martin, 92
Mary J., 41, 115
Thomas, 149
Vincent H., 16
W. P., 169, 176

HARRISON & PITTS, 123

HARROLD
Hannibal, 60
Uriah B., 155

HART
C. S., 136
Jasper N., 170

HARTIS
John, 108

HARTMAN
P. H., 157

HARTONG
Joseph, 149

HARTSDEN
William, 172

HARTZ
Martha, 100

HARVELL
Ann, 16
John B., 71

Mrs., 157
Samuel, 85
Samuel B., 147
Susan, 46
S. B., 71
Western, 163

HARVEY
Benjamin, 32
Mary, 170
William H., 108

HARVILL
S. B., 54

HASKIN
Mary J., 69

HASTER
Nancy, 32

HASTINGS, 100

HASTINGS
Willis, 85

HATALING
Alfred, 108

HATCHER
Caroline, 164
Leighton W., 109
Matilda, 46, 84
Samuel J., 147
S. J., 39, 89

HATCHER & McGEHEE, 123

HATCHER & PITT, 19

HATCHER & PITTS, 29

HATCHER-LEARY & CO., 29

HATHCOCK
James R., 177

HATLEY
John P., 90

HATTON
Melvina, 147

HAUSLER
Charles A., 69

HAWES
Adaline, 77

HERN
R. L., 135

HERNDEN
George, 145

HERNDON
James, 163

HERNE, 62

HERRANDYNE
T. R., 42

HERRENDINE
T. R., 79

HERVEY
C. P., 6

HETHCOCK
Sarah, 109

HEWELL
John W., 46
Joseph A., 61

HEWSON
Charles W., 99
Francis, 177

HIATT
Mrs., 62

HICKEY, 54

HICKEY
Alex. C., 71
Ann S., 91
John J., 40, 70

HICKS, 86, 126

HICKS
Amos, 25
Caroline R., 78
Dorcas, 25
Emma L., 45
James B., 31
Jasper, 77
J. B., 13, 45, 60, 77, 98,
107, 145, 155
J. H., 131
Samuel J., 126

HIGDEN
Bethany, 177
Mary Ann, 77

HIGGINS
Elizabeth, 170
Mary A. E., 170
Rev. S. H., 83, 154, 162

HIGHT
Lucinda, 98

HIGHTOWER
Charnel, 17
Jacob D., 70
Jordan, 17
N., 172

HILL, 86

HILL
Elizabeth, 125
Emaline A., 147
Henry Epping, 126
James Lawrence, 147
James L., 93
John, 78
J. B., 164
J. L., 72, 80
J. S., 63
Meredith, 78
Mr., 196
Robert, 171
Samuel H., 108
S. H., 126
Thos. C., 24
William, 32
William E., 91
William T., 177
Wm., 152
Wm. L., 138
Wm. R., 162
W. A., 136
W. H., 101

HILLIARD
Calvin, 25

HILLINGS
J. R., 151

**HILL-DAWSON & CO., 11,
14**

HINCH
Mr., 104
Samuel, 105

HINDS
Wm. T., 170

HINES
Caroline, 146
Mary A., 33

HINSON
William H., 46

HINTON
Jane, 91
J. W., 114, 150
Margaret E., 40
Mary A. E., 68

HITCHCOCK
Mr., 195

HITT
Mayberry, 99

HOBBS
Archibald B., 138
Sarah T., 147

HOCHSTRASSER
Anna, 163

HODGE
Enoch J., 139
Martha, 91

HODGES
Clara M., 69
Fleming, 136, 177
Henrietta S., 69
James, 136
Mary, 17
S. K., 6, 173
W. C., 6, 23, 129, 130,
137

**HODGES & GOETCHIUS,
117**

HODGES & MYGATT, 14

HOFFMAN
John, 138
Mary L., 124
Rachel R., 146
Sebastian, 115
S., 11

HOGAN, 77

HOGAN
Ann T., 70
J. C., 131
Thomas, 111
Thomas M., 33
Thos. M., 48, 55
T. M., 18, 27, 35, 42, 63,
70, 71
Wm. M., 170

HOGAN & COOPER, 14

HOLCOMB, 70

HOLCOMB
Elizabeth J., 62
Mary, 147

HOLDEN, 18

HOLEHAN
Patrick, 24

HOLIHAN
Peter, 164

HOLLAND, 79

HOLLAND
Colquitt M., 125
Dennis, 6

HOLLEY, 62

HOLLEY
Edward J., 146
Margaret, 108
William, 70

HOLLIDAY
William T., 77

HOLLIHAN
P., 101

HOLLMAN
James, 140
William H., 107

HOLLY
Isabella, 54
Miss, 101
Sarah, 54
Wm., 72

HOLMES
Anderson H., 61
A., 85
E. B., 121
Joseph W., 138
Martha, 40, 85
Mrs. R., 165
William B., 177
Wm. P., 79

HOLSTEAD
Mary, 108
Willis, 63
Willis S., 41, 48, 117

Willis T., 17
Wm., 129
W. H., 110
W. S., 7, 26, 34, 127, 148

HOLT, 175

HOLT
B. H., 131, 137
Col. Hines, 41
Dr. LeRoy, 147
Edgar Perry, 62
Eva, 41
Hines, 15, 41, 62, 127, 132
James, 124
J. D., 149
Leroy, 14
Sarah Ann, 47
Thaddeus, 92
T. G., 172
W. C., 6

HOLT & BUTT, 15

HOLTZCLAW
Mrs. Jenny, 101
William, 47

HONSVILLE
L. J., 165

HOOD
Daniel, 99
Henry, 69
James, 84
Joseph S., 84
Martha E., 99
Nancy L., 155

HOOK
Caroline I., 84

HOOKER
Hiram, 15

HOOKS
David W., 32
Rachel M., 99

HOOPAUGH
Daniel, 135

HOOPER
George C., 53
George Pendleton, 33
Miss, 79
Mrs., 47
Nancy, 165
Richard, 33

R., 54
YONGE & GARRARD, 10

HOOPER & GERRARD, 15

HOOPER & RIDGWAY, 15

HOOPES
Lloyd R., 162

HOOTEN
James F., 170

HOPKINS
Benjamin F., 125
Elvira, 100
J. B., 139
L., 85

HORLIS
J. C., 92

HORN, 125

HORN
Emily G., 45
E. J., 149
H. J., 149
Newton, A., 177
West, 149

HORNE
George W., 99
Sarah E., 83

HORTAN
John R., 155

HORTMAN
John G., 46

HORTON
Eliza, 164
Emily, 114
Hampton, 125
Henry V., 91
John H., 114
J. R., 141
Nancy, 177

HOTI
Howell, 32

HOUGHTON
W. R., 131, 132

HOUND
Rosina I., 114

HOUSE

D. C., 102
Edwin W., 124
Elisha, 86
Elisha A., 51
Elizabeth, 91
Hattie, 125
Henrietta, 108
H. R., 6
James, 85
John, 46
John A., 70
John K., 134
J. J., 31
Mary Jane, 24
Miss, 54
Mollie, 162
Mrs., 79
Priscilla, 70
Thomas J., 170
Wm., 125
W. A., 135

JACOBS
Caroline, 84
Phillip, 40

JAMES
Dr. John, 172
Elizabeth, 146
H. A., 172
Jefferson, 139
Rebecca, 170
William, 139
William H., 139

JAMES BRADFORD & CO.,
9

JAMSEY
Israel H., 17

JANNEY
Israel H., 15

JANNY, 9

JAQUES
J. B., 15
S. R., 140

JARDIN(?)
Edward J., 92

JARRETT
G. W., 136

JEFFERSON
Allen O., 172
Ann M., 32
Benj., 39

J., 135
Mrs. Harriet, 80

JEFFRIES
Bolin S., 98
Sarah A., 125

JEMISON
Lucy A., 69
Mary J., 52
Mrs., 156

JENKINS
Benjamin P., 84
Catharine, 156
Clark, 140
E., 173
Francis, 177
John S., 124
J. E., 134
Lewis, 141
Lewis S., 107
Mary F., 115
William T., 78

JEPSON
Esther, 62
F., 63
F. A., 13, 34, 44, 80, 157
L. P., 135
Wm. M., 84
W. M., 31, 157

JERNIGAN
Amanda C., 61
Calvin, 138
Eliza D., 60
Henry, 92
Lewis, 67
P. N., 54

JETER, 159, 168

JETER
Dr. H. M., 107, 155, 168
Francis, 125
Frank M., 157
F. M., 153
H. M., 164, 167, 172
J. M., 159

JEWELL
John, 45

JEWETT
C. R., 123, 154
Rev. C. R., 161

JIMMERSON
Jas., 84

JINNETT
James, 163

JOCKMASS
John, 39

JOHN
James H., 61
Lovey L., 25

JOHNS
Sarah A., 60
Y., 165

JOHNSON, 175

JOHNSON
Amanda, 53
Andrew, 172
Axupershanee, 16
A. S., 135
Calvin E., 78
Caroline, 25
Charlotte T., 60
Chas. E., 138
Col. James, 196
C., 141
C. E., 160
Elizabeth S., 16
Epsy, 61
Fannie E., 171
Franklin C., 115
Franklin J., 146
F. C., 6, 85, 100, 123,
127, 148, 160, 172, 174
Harris, 131
Henry, 61
Henry A., 91
Howard, 150
Jackson P., 116
James, 16, 18
James D., 38, 157
James W., 15
Jane, 61
Jas. D., 127, 148
Jno., 26
John, 13, 18, 25, 38, 60,
90, 123, 157, 169
John A., 152
John W., 163
J. D., 27, 103, 135, 167,
174
J. T., 131
Letha Ann, 115
L. Decatur, 163
L. Q., 131
Mahala, 84
Martha A., 52, 108
Martha E., 177

Martha J., 125, 162
Mary, 91
Mary C. R., 61
Moses, 115
Mr., 103
Nancy, 25
Philo, 124
Priscilla, 32
Robert, 53
Robert G., 115
Robt., 79
R., 134
Sarah F., 61
Sarah J., 155
Sarah M., 32
Susan, 78
Thomas, 114
Washington W., 91
William S., 77
Willliam D., 69
W. B., 140

JOHNSON & FROST, 14

JOHNSTON
B. E., 134
Col. Jas., 194
John A., 40
M., 15

JOINS
Sarah, 69

JONES, 42

JONES
Adam P., 70
A., 136
A. P., 60, 77, 90, 123, 155
Boykin, 131
Capt. W. E., 171
Clara B., 84
Colonel, 11, 65
Colonel Seaborn, 38
Col., 104
Col. John A., 160, 168
Col. Seaborn, 63, 172
Col. S., 103
Courtney I., 91
David, 51, 53, 99
Dr. Jos., 40
D. E., 165
Edmund, 77
Edmund D., 115
Elizabeth, 53, 69, 125
Elizabeth A., 109
Elvira E., 146
Emeline, 16
Eugene, 17

Evaline, 61
Evan, 180
E. D., 149
Fannie I., 78
Frank, 173
George, 85, 100, 127
George W., 31, 108, 148, 157, 164
Harper J. B., 155
Harvey, 146
Henry, 32, 141
Henry J., 156
Howard, 165
James B., 109
James H., 69
James R., 97
Jasper, 32
Jas. M., 141
Jno. M., 16
John, 7, 15, 109, 138
John A., 17, 136
John B., 53
John G., 107
John M., 60
John W., 177
Joseph J., 52
Joshua, 140
Jos. J., 86
J. E., 136, 157
J. H., 141
J. J., 139, 180
J. Leonard, 136
J. W., 135
Lurany, 51
Marcus D., 9
Martha F. B., 52
Mary, 107
Mary Ann, 40
Mary C., 69
Mary F., 40
Mary T., 146
Mattie A., 91
Miss, 100
Mrs. Richard, 100
Randal, 23
Rhisa, 40
Richard, 75, 79
Richard E., 53
Robert L., 162
Salina L., 78
Sarah, 162
Sarah Ann, 177
Sarah A. E., 24
Seaborn, 158
Seaborn L., 129
S., 157
S. L., 131
Thomas R., 109
Thos. F., 155
T., 135

T. J., 135
Uncle Dabney, 50
Valina B., 45
Walker P., 46
William, 52, 101
William K., 99
William R., 136
Willis H., 60
Wm. R., 12, 26, 38, 51
W., 131, 171
W. E., 39
W. E.(Jr.), 131
W. R., 127

JONES & AMOS, 20, 31

JORDAN, 101, 127

JORDAN
Columbus, 85
Emeline, 54
G., 158
James, 156
John F., 139
Mahulda, 52
Martha, 46
Mary, 40
Nancy M. M., 109
Rev. Thos. H., 133
Rev. T. H., 60
Thomas, 69
William, 99

JORDON
William, 123

JOSEPH COLWELL & CO., 15

JUNMAN
Joel, 79

JUSTICE
Emily, 108

KALE
Mary, 69

KAUFMAN
A., 165
C., 165
Georgia, 165

KAVANAUGH
Dr. H. H., 76
John, 101

KAVENAUGH
John C., 78

KEARN
Elizabeth, 155

KEELING
L. W., 152

KEENAN
Jack, 135

KEINER
Evaline, 53

KEISTNER
Louis, 122

KELLER
John, 91, 163

KELLET
W. J., 173

KELLETT
Wm. J., 45

KELLEY
Patrick, 138

KELLOGG
Jas., 6

KELLY
Ann, 100
Edmund, 115
Elizabeth, 70
Frances J., 77
Georgia A., 60
Jackson, 79
James, 78, 170
James M., 114
John, 47, 125
Michael, 33
Mrs. Mary Ann, 33
Sarah J., 177
Sarah W., 107
Stewart, 159
Thomas, 70
Thos. W., 63
Wm. F., 124
Wm. M., 125
W. C., 138

KELSEY
Morton, 15

KELTON
Laura, 79
Samuel, 165

KEMP, 135

KEMP
Isabella, 163
John J., 146
J. J., 163
Sarah A. E., 83
T., 12

KENADY
Mathew, 84

KENDALL
Charles, 10
Chas., 18, 135
H., 23
Mrs. Jane, 165
Salina, 125
T. H., 13

KENDRICK
Cincinatus B., 147
Martin J., 53

KENNADY
Mary A. E., 90
Thomas, 77
Thomas L., 115

KENNEDY, 92, 126

KENNEDY
John P., 74
Mrs., 92
Rosannah, 162
Thomas, 149
W. C., 173

KENNINGTON, 92

KENNINGTON
Miss, 92
Mrs., 92

KENNON
R. E., 150

KENNY
Annie, 169
Helen, 163
M., 138
T., 113

KENT
Elizabeth, 33
Frances C., 107
Gilbert, 52
Harvill, 100
Henry, 40
Rosaline, 163
Sarah A., 52

Susan, 47
Tabitha Olive, 16
Warren R., 163

KERBO
Rebecca, 52

KERCHEIMER
Sophia, 155

KETTLEBRAND, 92

KEY
Amanda C., 78, 85
Hugh, 141
John, 25, 141
Joseph S., 45
Jos. S., 169, 176
J. S., 123
Madison T., 24, 61
Peter, 128
P. L., 151
Randolph, 129
Rev. Joseph S., 162
Thomas, 124

KIDDER
Charlotte, 53

KIGLER
Robert, 173

KILCREASE
James, 138
Lucinda, 170

KILGORE
Albert, 138
Leroy, 136, 138, 177

KILLCREASE
William, 165

KILLIAN
Salitha Ann, 24

KILPATRICK
Emily, 17

KIMBROUGH
Alfred H., 136
Archibald M., 108
A. M., 26, 117, 134
James, 91
James L., 115
Jas., 92
John H., 124
Martha M., 85
Martha W., 32
Mary J., 52

Mrs., 47
Mrs. B., 26
Mrs. Jas., 101
Mr. Thomas, 26
O. S., 95
Sarah J., 69
Thomas J., 98
Virginia S., 124
Wm. H., 47

KINDON
George A., 99

KING, 47, 54, 79, 92, 159

KING
Anna J., 147
Barry, 97
Bartly, 98
Benjamin I., 91
Berry, 101
Callie, 41
Caroline, 163
Charles, 16
Charles P., 41
Elizabeth, 172
Emily, 115
E. J., 147
George W., 107, 177
Harvey, 25
Henry J., 70, 78
Jeremiah, 149
Jesse, 53
John, 23, 33, 61, 82, 87,
167, 174, 190, 191
John W., 52, 126
Joseph, 23, 26, 34, 46
Jos., 6
J. E., 131
J. W., 43, 48, 102, 117,
126, 148, 157
Lucinda, 60
Maria, 46
Mrs., 85
Mrs. E. J., 163
Nancy, 115
Nancy J., 146
Sam. W., 44
Sarah A., 52
Sarah E., 69
Sophia V., 99
Thomas, 100, 150
William N., 41
William R., 77
Yelverton, 126

KINGSBURY
John, 16
Wm. L., 170

KINGSLEY
John, 107

**KING-ALLEN & CAMAK,
113**

KING. J. W., 110

KINSEY
A. L., 138

KINSLEY
John, 154, 157, 165
Mrs., 154

KIRK
Garrett B. L., 170

KIRKLAND
John, 107, 138
John M., 170
Martha E., 99
Wm., 78

KIRKLEY
Miss Ann, 157

KIRKPATRICK
Elizabeth Susan, 25
Hugh, 101

KIRKSEY
Elisha F., 17
Jared Irwin, 17

KIRLE
George, 138

KIRVIN
Alexander C., 108
J. H., 39
Martha J., 108
Thirza B., 125

KITCHENS
Catharine, 84

KITE
Susan, 32
Susan Ann, 52

KIVLIN
Anna, 156
A. C., 110
Dr. Alphonso C., 147
James, 14, 17, 33, 36,
127, 190
Julia, 170
J., 10, 26, 156
Mary Dillard, 33

KLEBER
Edward A., 146

KLEIN
Samuel, 61

KLINK
Charles A., 141
John, 150

KNIGHT, 89, 100

KNIGHT
Frances, 84
Mathew, 32
Matthew, 16
Rebecca E., 125
Rosannah, 78
Sarah, 163
William, 91
Wm., 138, 173

KNOWLES
Peter, 164
Rebecca, 24
Robert, 53
Thomas H., 136

KOCHN
Gustavus A., 155

KOHNS
Lazarus, 163

KOOKOGEE
Rebecca C., 108

KOPMAN
Morris, 158

KROMER
Francis, 25

KURKIN
John, 110

KYLE
D., 14
Elizabeth P., 108
John, 26, 35, 48, 63, 85,
86, 92
Joseph, 18, 26, 35, 42,
102
Jos., 55
J., 14, 127
Robert, 165
R. B., 6
W. D., 131

KYLE & BARNETT, 19

LACY
Eliza., 108

LAFAYETTE
Gen., 193, 194, 196

LaGRANGE, 182

LaGRANGE
Col., 184

LAIRD
O. P., 15

LAMAN
John, 61

LAMAR
Aleck, 144
Alex. B., 147
Col. C. A. L., 180, 183
Henry J., 45
James Phillip, 116
John E., 116
J. E., 107, 123, 155, 169
Mary J., 155
Mirabeau B., 116
Mrs. Mary, 126
Philip, 60, 77
Phillip, 90
P., 13
Sarah R., 170
William H., 116
Wm., 90

LAMB
Eleanor M., 171
Eliza Ann, 32
Leacy W., 78

LAMBERT
James, 138
John I., 116

LAMBERTH
Slakely, 17

LAMBERTSON
Allen, 69
J., 164

LAMING
James, 163

LAMMERSON
A., 79

LANAM
Mary A., 115

LANCASTER
Henry, 170

LAND
Aaron, 125
Christian, 85
Joseph, 125
Julia A. L., 45
Moses, 40
O. K., 149

LANDERS
John, 152

LANDHAN
J., 173

LANDON
Frank, 156

LANDRETH
O. W., 114

LANE
Benjamin, 108

LANEY
Alice L., 170
Robert, 38

LANGDON
Wm. B., 160

LANGEY
Mathena, 83

LANGFORD
Albert F., 91
Eli S., 125
E., 149
George W., 99
G. W., 164
Jeremiah E., 24
Mr., 109
Susan, 162
William, 149

LANGLEY
Henry, 141
Lucinda, 46

LANGSTON
Wm. J., 146
W. J., 141

LANIER
Clark P., 52

Mary A., 69
Miss Mary E., 171
Sophy A. F., 52

LANNING
James, 136

LANTERN
William H., 139

LAPHAM
George, 135
George L., 155

LARRIS
Thos. P., 77

LARUS
Thos. L., 44
T. P., 48

LASCAR
Sarah, 177

LASSETER
Thos., 152

LASSITER
B. F., 163
John, 136
Thomas H., 172

LASTER
W. J., 173

LATHAM
John W. H., 77
J. W. H., 138

LAURY
Lewis, 78

LAVAR
G. W., 141

LAW
Samuel B., 83
Sam'l, 127

LAWES
William A., 98
Wm. A., 145

LAWHON
Claudius S., 32
Samuel, 103, 155
S. E., 161

LAWRENCE, 79, 100, 157

J. L., 131
S. C., 13, 26

LINDSEY
Alabama, 170
Alex. C., 156
Fannie H., 84
Frank, 177
John, 175
John B., 162
Julia, 125
L., 173
Martha, 32
Virginia, 45

LINES
Lawrence, 24

LINGE
Nancy, 171

LINNAHAN
Z. E., 172

LINNEHAM
Ellen, 155
John, 156

LINSEY
L., 165

LIONS
A. J., 171

LIPMAN
Julius, 138

LIPSEY
Arthur, 156
Sarah, 69

LITTLE, 92

LITTLE
David G., 171
John R., 84
Joseph, 135
Martha, 84
Mr., 109
W. A., 134

LITTLE PRINCE, 195

LITTLEBERY
Eubanks, 77

LITTLEJOHN
J. R., 177

LITTLETON

James J., 152
Martha, 108
Mary R., 170

LIVELY
George W., 56
James R., 131, 138

LIVINGSTON
Adam J., 84
Alfred A., 78
A. J., 149
H., 13
John, 147
Lewis, 63, 70, 86
L., 42
Samuel Bass, 70
William A., 16

LIVINGSTON & ELLIS, 153

LIVINGSTONE
W. W., 155

LLOYD, 39, 62

LLOYD
Caroline E., 52
Charles B., 156
Felix, 125
James, 68, 83, 98, 123
James(Jr.), 85
John, 50, 80, 116, 145
John Jay, 80
Martha A., 108
Mary A., 78
May, 91
Miss Mary Jane, 33
Sarah, 163
Sidney, 165
Sidney C., 138
Sidney O., 91
W. D., 165

LOCHABY
John, 7

LOCKETT
H. B., 164

LOCKHART
Dr., 83
Dr. Henry, 156
Dr. Richard, 116
Dr. R. H., 80
Ellen J., 52
H., 173
James, 69, 149
Lemuel, 98, 123, 147
Richard, 46

Richard H., 72
Robt. B., 155
Rowena M., 163
R. B., 133
Sarah, 45
William, 149
William S., 116

LOCKLIER
Elizabeth, 52

LOEB
J. H., 133

LOFTON
Bettie A., 124

LOGAN
Benjamin, 138
John, 17

LOKEY
Angia, 125
Frances, 125
Mary T., 69
Sarah J., 61
W. H. W., 149

LOMAX
T., 60

LONG
Aaron, 149
Grigsby T., 134
Henry, 149
Julius, 149
Mary, 54
Mary P., 124
Matilda, 115
Milton, 135
Mrs. Paul, 109
N. W., 12
Rebecca, 155
Richard A., 54
Thomas B., 115
William H., 40, 77
Winney, 177

LONGSTREET, 151

LONGSTREET
General, 140

LOONEY
Daniel T., 99

LOPEZ
Emanuel, 163

LORD

John W., 170

LORIMER
Julia, 77

LOT, 196

LOVE
Caroline, 124
Mrs. Frances, 70
N. B., 86
William E., 80
Wm., 155
Wm. E., 109
W. E., 86

LOVELACE
James J., 128
John C., 148, 157
J. A., 135
J. C., 164, 167, 174
J. I., 160

LOVERING, 15

LOVETT
George W., 52

LOVING
Nancy, 62

LOW
Jinks, 149

LOWE
Elizabeth, 170
Frances A., 78
General, 38
H. C., 141
J. F., 141

LOWTHER
Alexander A., 40
Alex., 42
A. A., 48, 55
Miss Minnie, 171
S., 133

LUCAS
George M., 61
Walter B., 196

LUCIUS
Martha, 115

LUCKIE
B. C., 131
Emily O., 90
E. M., 131
Mary I., 115

Wm. F., 53, 92

LUKER
Caroline J., 77
Elizabeth A., 46
James M. C., 69

LUNNEY
D. T., 109

LUNSFORD
Myrick C., 77
Persilla, 25
Thos. P., 147

LURIA
A. M., 133

LUTHER
W., 12

LYNAH
James, 129

LYNCH
Asa, 39, 135
Charles H., 78
Martha V., 91
W., 139

LYNN
Isaac, 138
M. T., 149
Peter, 76
R. G., 152

LYONS
Cautius C., 170
David, 139
Ellen, 84
Mary E., 99

MABRY
Irvin C., 125

MACK
John, 24

MACON
Thomas L., 91

MADDEN
Henry, 54
John, 171, 176
John H., 48, 55, 141
Mary, 52
P. H., 135

MADDOX

Eliza, 85
Joseph J., 163
J., 135
J. K., 100
Louisa, 45
L., 141
Mrs. Elizabeth, 165
Sarah, 45
Sileta, 24
Thomas, 62

MADDUX
Samantha, 24

MADOX
Lycurgus, 52

MAGNER
Mrs., 62
Wm., 38

MAGNUS
George, 129

MAGONIGAL
J., 86

MAGOUIRK
David, 15, 82

MAGRAFF
Elizabeth, 107

MAGUIRT
John O., 45

MAHAFFEY
Wm., 48, 49, 80, 86

MAHAN
Caroline C., 177

MAHONE, 79

MAHOUE
Susan M., 162

MAINOR
B. F., 138
John W., 138

MAINYARD
Harriet, 115

MAJORS
Jasper, 141
Mary Ann S., 40
T. J., 141
Winnifred, 32

MALAM
James D., 177

MALONE
B. F., 13, 27, 35
Joseph, 113
Lucius V., 93
Milton, 129
William P., 41

MALONE & HUDSON, 35

MALONEY
Tempay, 163

MANE
James, 84

MANGHAM
B. S., 12
Colonel, 38
Frances A., 32
Henry, 61

MANLEY
John, 150

MANLY
Rev. Basil, 123

MANN
Allen, 152
A. T., 123
Green J., 52
Henry C., 162
Isabella, 52
Isabella R., 115
James, 152
James H. H., 171
Rev. Alfred, 114
Sarah, 16

MANNING
Ann, 177
James, 136
Thomas, 164
Walter, 46

MANSEL
George B., 109

MANSFORD
L. Y., 173

MANSON, 101

MANUEL
Susan, 172

MAPLES

Susan, 124

MARABLE
Lucy C., 124

MARBLE
Wentworth S., 53
W. S., 70

MARCH
Wm., 162

MARCHANT, 92, 93

MARCHANT
W. N., 138

MARCRUM
Georgian, 15
Lettia B., 68

MARCUS
Sallie Georgia, 126
Van, 117, 126, 127, 130,
137

MARDIS
John W., 53

MARINER, 9, 47

MARKHAM
Charles, 99
Sowell W., 138
Timothy, 45

MARKRUM
Benj. F., 46

MARKS
Jane L., 53
Leah, 91
R. T., 23

MARLER
J., 135
Leviney, 109
Mary, 125
Wm., 24

MARLOW
Elisha, 139

MARSHALL
B. F., 164
General Humphrey, 151

MARTIN, 126

MARTIN

Anthony, 52
Bentley, 170
B. Y., 126
Dr. Alexander L., 32
Duncan, 165
Edward, 165
Edward S., 46
Elijah, 69
Elizabeth, 92
Elizabeth C., 108
Etter, 131
George S., 51
George W., 100
Geo. W., 72
Henry L., 62
Henry W., 136
Jas., 138
John, 32, 46, 76
John C., 146
J., 141
Lafayette, 90
Martha, 173
Mrs., 85
Valentine, 141
William, 141
William B., 122
William R., 84
Wm. W., 13, 18, 26, 34,
42, 48, 55
W. W., 133

MARTIN & DUDLEY, 66

MARTINIERE
W. A., 131

MASON
Frank L., 45
Margaret, 155
Martha A., 61
Mary J., 69

MASS
Nancy Artimus, 24

MASSEY
Eliza A., 51
George L., 85
George W., 136
James W., 108
Jane, 45
Jeremiah, 15
John H., 25
J. W., 149
Richard, 129
Susan, 115

MATHESON, 56, 125, 126

MATHESON

William, 77
Wm., 55, 63, 72, 80, 92

MATHEWS
B. J., 44
E. J., 147
Horace, 53
W. D., 133

MATHEWSON
Wm., 35, 48

MATTHESON
Anna, 79

MATTHEW
Henry, 10

MATTHEWS
Allen, 131
B. J., 27, 38
Charlotte F., 78
Harriet A., 85
Harvey, 24
Henry, 26
Horace, 92
Leva D., 129
M. L., 172

MATTHEWSON
W., 42

MATTHISON
Elizabeth, 108

MATTOX, 126

MAUN
Edmund, 155

MAURITZEN
Mrs. A., 92

MAXEY
John, 163
William, 25

MAXLEY
William M., 51

MAXWELL
Laura J., 177

MAY, 92

MAY
John, 7
J. S., 165
William P., 25

MAYBERRY
James, 163

MAYES
Mary E., 90

MAYFIELD
Lou, 163

MAYNOR
Eliz., 46

MAYO
Z. N., 133

MAYS
Alsey W., 60
George, 170
G. W., 131
Mary, 173

McALISTER, 14

McALISTER
Capt., 121
Mary A., 124
Mrs. Mary, 101
Sophronia, 99
Thomas, 146
Wm. M., 171

McALLISTER, 97

McARDEL
Mrs., 126

McARDLE, 125

McARDLE
Arthur, 136
Felix, 109, 165

McARTHUR
Daniel, 35, 39, 72
D., 26, 102, 111

McBRIDE
C., 131
Martha M., 70
William J., 16

McCAIRN, 126

McCALL
Hugh, 86
Joseph, 46
Lewis S., 46
Mrs., 79

McCALLISTER

Jane, 84
Mary, 52
Nancy, 91

McCANDLESS
William, 69

McCARDEL
Charles E., 70
Eliza, 24
James Terrell, 70
Mrs. Alice A., 70

McCARDLE
Charles E., 77
Frances M., 90

McCARLEY
Miss Mary, 172

McCARRA
A. N., 136

McCARTHY
Patrick, 109

McCARTY
James, 162, 164
John, 62, 79, 93
J. C., 138
Mary, 163
Mrs. Sarah, 100
Nancy, 54
Naome E., 84
Thomas, 11, 53
William C., 177

McCARVIN, 157

McCARY
Neal, 99

McCAULEY
Delilah, 91
Henry, 141

McCAY
Amanda, 116
James M., 99

McCLAIN
Eliza Caroline, 32

McCLAM
Elizabeth, 155

McCLARY
Mariah, 172

McCLELLAN, 140

McCLESKY
Amanda, 84
James A., 91
Louisa I., 115

McCLURE
Martha J., 15

McCOLLOUGH, 121

McCONNEL
S. M., 6

McCONNELL
Wm., 16

McCOOK, 182

McCOOK
Mary E., 70, 78
Sarah C., 45
Wright, 51

McCORD
A. C., 141

McCORMACK
Edward T., 155
James, 84

McCORRING, 92

McCOY
James, 116
R. Clay, 138

McCRARY
A. B., 138
B. F., 149
Caroline G., 155

McCREE
John, 162

McCULLERS
Britton, 67
Eliza, 41
Jas. W., 16
Martha, 115

McCULLIN
J. R., 173

McCULLOCH
J., 141
R., 173

McCUM
Andrew J., 171

McCURDY
John C., 129

McDANIEL, 95

McDANIEL
Absolom, 139
Alex., 129
Daniel, 115
George, 146
Jane, 93
Mariah, 162
Mary, 78

McDONALD, 98

McDONALD
Absalom, 83
Andrew J., 91, 177
B. F., 6
Catharine, 162
Elizabeth A., 25
Eugenia, 108
E., 133
Gilbert, 162
James R., 52
James W., 177
Missouri E., 115

McDOUGALD
Ann E., 84
A., 79
Duncan, 156
D., 9
Fannie E., 170
General, 23
Mary A., 79
Sarah E., 156
W. A., 131, 138

McDOWALL, 100

McDUFFIE
Daniel D., 146

McEACHREN
E., 135
Thomas C. C., 124

McECHERN
Thomas, 139

McELMORE
Nancy, 162

McELRAIN
William, 164

McELRATH, 47, 92

McELRATH
Augusta, 90
Elizabeth, 124
James, 129, 151
M. J., 164
William, 24, 139, 176
Wm., 152, 172

McELVY
Hugh L., 162
Sallie J. H., 162

McFARLAND
Fannie, 170
John, 169
Thomas, 173

McGAR
Peter, 13

McGEE, 125

McGEE
Frances E., 115
George, 138
Isabella, 86
J. R., 149
Mrs. Isabella, 72, 80

McGEHEE
Capt. C. C., 179
C. A., 18
C. C., 133
Francis, 100
Frank, 141
George L., 109
G. S., 14
Harriet, 78
Isabella, 93, 102, 110, 155
James R., 116
L. J., 149
Martha A., 155
Mary V., 45
Minerva, 116
Mrs., 8, 92, 148, 157, 158, 174
Mrs. Isabella, 117, 127
Stephen F., 60

McGEHEE & HATCHER, 123

McGIBBINS
Caroline, 100

McGIBBONS, 100

McGIBONY

J. C., 25
R. A., 7

McGINTY
Emma, 155
L. Anna, 108
Mrs., 92
Mrs. Jane, 165

McGIRR
James, 164

McGIRTH
James, 196

McGITTY
George W., 91

McGLAUN
Elizabeth J., 61

McGLAWN
Edmond, 24

McGOUGH
John, 89

McGOWEN, 92

McGOWEN
Mahulda, 53
M., 62

McGRADY
Mary C., 61

McGRASTON
Laura, 124

McGRATH
Jas. E., 155

McGRUDER
Edna L., 171
Frances E., 78
Martha B., 124

McGUIRE, 68

McGUIRE
James, 48, 55
John, 99

McGUIRK
Margaret, 99
Silas, 91

McGUIST
Mary Ann, 32

McGURT
Miss, 100

McGUYRT
John, 149
Silas, 149

McHALL
Bridget, 173

McHUGH
F. M., 135

McILHENNY
J., 174

McINTOSH
Billy, 196
Chilly, 194
Indian General, 194

McINTYRE
Ann, 147
Robert C., 146

McJUNKIN
Vernie, 177

McKAY
Georgia A., 115
William, 89, 92

McKEE
H. C., 15
John G., 114
M. L., 135

McKENDREE, 159, 175

McKENDREE
Caroline Eliza, 33
Henry C., 33
John J., 33, 68
John J.(Jr.), 125
J. J., 17, 20, 39, 58, 72,
80, 86, 98, 110, 132, 133,
148, 157, 167, 174, 177
W., 133

W., 133

McKENNEL
Thomas, 70

McKENNELL
Frances A., 99
Mrs. Flora, 80

McKENNEY
J. N., 138

McKENNIE
Milledge G., 52

McKENZIE, 174

McKENZIE
Andrew J., 46
Ann, 62
Elizabeth, 51
John G., 162
Joseph C., 139
Kenneth, 5, 38, 39
Kennith, 31
K., 13
Mary, 79
Samuel T., 139
Sarah M., 115

McKINNIE
Mrs., 101

McKINNY
J., 173

McLAREN
P., 13, 14

McLEMORE
Levicy A., 171
Sarah A., 170

McLENDON
Amos, 115
Lucinda J., 47
Samuel, 115

McLEROY
Louisa K., 98

McLESKY
Edward, 107

McLESTER
James N., 163
Martha, 70
Nelson, 16, 47

McMAN, 92

McMICHAEL
Sarah M., 32
Wm., 84, 126
W., 141

McMICKEN
James H., 52
Thos. J., 155

McMILLAN

Joseph, 139

McMILLEN
Elizabeth W., 90
Neil, 52

McMILLEN. William, 84

McMULLEN
Sarah, 146

McMURRAY
Cornelia A., 45

McNAUGHTON
Frances, 46
Tabitha, 40

McNEAL
Jas. E. G., 84
Malcom, 170
Mary J., 52

McNEEL
Anda, 16

McNEIL
A. H., 14, 18
Malcolm, 107
Nancy B., 25

McPHATTER
John, 136

McQUEEN
Harry H., 39
H. H., 52

McRAE
Dawson A., 40

McREA
Mary A., 108

McROBINSON
N., 15, 42

McSWAIN
Elizabeth, 177

McTIGUE
Hugh, 138

McVAY
Cinthia, 33

MEACHAM
Mary A., 69
Mary W., 90

MEAD
Mentoria E., 16

MEALER
James, 92

MEALING
Alice, 146
Angelina L., 91
Georgia E., 52
John Henry, 25
John H., 164
John P., 91
Susan R., 69

MEASLES
Jas., 69

MEDOWER
R. J., 173

MEEKS
Susan, 170

MEGEA
Mary, 124

MEHAFFEY
John, 91
John W. B., 68
Josiah, 91

MEIDNER
E., 14, 18
M., 14, 18

MEIGS
Henry D., 36
Mrs., 101
Mrs. Clara, 41
Prof. Josiah, 41

MEINHEM & CO., 18

MELICK
Leonard, 86

MENIFEE
James S. H., 99

MERCER
Gen., 159

MERCHANT
Wm. T., 146

MERCK
John G., 135

MERDITH

Miss, 79

MEREDITH, 79, 85

MEREDITH
Elizabeth, 100
Eliz., 164
George, 79, 177
Geo., 165
John, 92
Joseph, 53

MERKEL
Margaret, 124

MERRILL
Harrison, 99

MERRITT
John R., 46

MERRY
J. H., 14, 44, 117, 172
Mrs. C. M., 172

MERSHON, 87

MERSHON
Ezra, 101
J. E., 86

MERTINS
Gustavus F., 84

METTS
Adolphus, 52

METZ
Mary, 165

METZGA
M., 133

MEYER
L., 141

MICHAEL
August, 124

MIDDLEBROOK
Hiram, 191
H., 160

MIDDLEBROOK & WADE,
14, 18, 19

MIDWAY
Joseph, 100

MILAM

Amelia, 69

MILAN
Lewis, 171
Mrs. Elizabeth, 164

MILES
William, 32
W. G., 171

MILFOED
R. W., 177

MILLER
Abraham, 16
Calvin F., 108
Eaton P., 33
Eliza. F., 108
Frederick, 79
Henry, 106
Mary, 101
Nathan, 32
Nelly C., 177
Nicholas, 115
N. E., 149
Olive H., 115
O. H., 149
Robert C., 124
Tabitha A., 45
T. K., 165
Virginia, 170
William, 33
William D., 69
William I., 115
Wm. D., 139
Wm. H., 138

MILLINER
Nancy, 164

MILNER
Elizabeth, 85

MILTON
Bassill M., 61
Jack, 136
John, 125
John C., 138
Mary A. E., 124

MILUM
Cinda, 91

MIMS
Charles, 160
Charles B., 99
Charles E., 41, 80
Chas. E., 157
C. B., 136
C. E., 27

Furman, 115
George W., 41
Harriet, 107
Lerry C., 24
Martha, 53
W. H., 134
W. J., 134

MIMS & PERRY, 123

MINCHIN
Mrs., 105

MINTER
Anna Lewis, 17
L. D., 17

MINTY, 182

MIRTIN
G. W., 92

MITCHEL
August, 165
Wm. H., 118

MITCHELL
F. M., 138
Harriet, 124
Henry C., 146
H. C., 137
Isaac, 15, 44, 55, 80, 86, 93
James M., 100
John, 100
Lewis S., 40
Mrs. Martha A., 116
Robt., 24
R. G., 7, 13, 94, 102, 110, 117
Sarah E., 52
Susan C., 77
Uriah P., 134
Venona, 15
Walter T., 162

MIX, 100

MIX
Mrs., 100

MIXON
Lancy A., 162

MOAT, 79, 92

MOATE
Zilley, 162

MOBLEY

Ellen, 47
Henry, 165
Puss, 177

MOFFETT
Charles J., 133
C. J., 132
Emma L., 170
Eugenie, 85
Maj. C. J., 134
Thomas G., 109

MOHENA, 192, 193

MOMAN
Martha, 100
Mrs., 101

MONKEY
Rebecca E., 41

MONKUS
Mary, 69

MONROE
Gen., 194

MONTGOMERY
Arthur, 162
H., 157

MOODY
Emaline, 146
Lewis, 46

MOODY & DURR, 14

MOON
Benjamin W., 16
John K., 107
J. M., 171
Mijamon, 46
Mrs., 79
Rhoda A., 52
Samuel F., 91

MOONEY
Isaac, 125
James, 149
Wm., 138

MOOR
Woody A., 25

MOORE, 14, 86

MOORE
Cecilia, 155
Douglas, 145
Douglass, 140

Harriet, 52
Henry, 141
Jacob, 100
James, 100
James B., 170
James H., 139
Joel W., 162
J. B., 141
Mary Ann, 24
Mary M., 124
Mary R., 92
Melvina, 84
Miss, 85
Miss Mary E., 173
Morgan J., 171
Mrs., 47, 126
M. M., 167, 174, 191
William B., 109

MOOREHEAD
Thomas, 139

MOOTTEY
Mrs. Emily, 126

MORAN
Michael, 101

MORFELL
E., 12

MORGAN
Charles P., 83
Christopher C., 46
Elijah, 52
Frances M., 155
George M., 152
James, 32
James N., 78
John C., 136
J. B., 138
Martha, 16
Mary E., 45
Sarah J., 162
Thomas, 139, 152
Thomas J., 170
William W., 46
Wm. H., 152

MORMAN
Jane, 40

MORMON
Jacob, 173
Jeff, 172

MORN
Mrs., 79

MORRELL

Cynthia A. E., 53
Daniel Y., 61

MORRILL
N. B., 149

MORRIS
Ann, 46
Charles H., 84
David N., 116
D. H., 164
Frances E., 51
Henry M., 61
Henry T., 109
Joseph P., 91
Joseph W., 69
Josiah, 35
Lurania, 124
Mary, 90
Mattie S., 171
Moses, 164
Moses G., 124
Mrs. Melvina, 123
Mrs. Thomas, 25
Nancy, 85
P. A. S., 153
Sarah, 146, 165
Sarah A., 45
Thomas L., 69

MORRIS & HANSERD, 15

MORRISON
Alexander C., 146
J. H., 149
Mary A., 146

MORTON, 14, 22, 71

MORTON
Alex C., 139
Alex. C., 45
Eliza S., 77
John A., 79
Jos. L., 155
J. L., 7, 17, 20, 26, 28,
35, 48, 55, 58, 59, 63, 72,
94, 103, 114, 161

MOSELY
Lewis P., 138

MOSES
Hannah, 91
Isaac I., 91
Major R. J., 175
M. J., 131
W. M., 131

MOSES W. M., 132

**MOSES & HALL, 14, 18,
19**

MOSEY
John, 15

MOSMAN
Mrs., 172

MOSS
Elizabeth, 164
Eliz. P., 46
George D., 100
William I., 77

MOSSMAN
Joseph, 123

MOTE
Elizabeth, 109
Henrietta, 164
John, 165
Rebecca, 124
Simeon, 164, 165

MOTLEY
Lewis W., 138
Mary A. F., 108, 115
Robert, 114
Sarah, 25
Spencer, 149
Thomas E., 52

MOTT
Col. R. L., 76
John R., 163
J. R., 140
Mrs. R. L., 147
Nancy, 164
R. L., 82, 98

MOTT & CLEGHORN, 58

MOTT & MUSTIAN, 36, 76

MOUGHAN
Mrs. M., 172

MOULKEY, 150

MOUNGER
J. C., 31

MOWELL
John, 91

MOY

J. D., 149

MOYE
Gardner, 138
John T., 99, 136

MULFORD
Davis, 13

MULLANY
Barney, 24

MULLENS
Jeremiah, 17

MULLIN
Parmilla Ann, 25
W. A., 172

MULLINS
John, 39, 155
J. T., 141

MUNCUS
Wm. A., 171

MUNN
D. D., 141
John, 42, 43, 48
J. R., 131

MUNRO
R. W. B., 14
Wm. H., 45

MUNSON
Alfred, 78

MURDOCK
Ann, 47
Martha L., 146
Miss, 79
R. B., 101

MURPHEY
George, 100
Rebecca, 79

MURPHY
Amos, 136
Ann, 108
A., 141
Catharine, 61
Gov., 194
Josiah, 136
Lezina, 107
Louisa, 91
Mary A., 170
Matilda C., 171
Mat., 129

Miss, 62
Mrs., 126
M. W., 152
Patrick, 126
Susan, 163
T., 165

MURRAY
Elizabeth, 114
J. P., 109, 147
William, 141

MURRELL
Mrs. M. C., 173
Susan H., 84

MURRY
A. L., 173
Mary Ann, 25

MUSE
T. H., 131

MUSGROVE, 72

MUSGROVE
E. H., 47, 68, 71
Mary Jane, 47

MUSTAIN
John L., 150

MUSTIAN
Col. J. L., 21
Georgia C., 78
John L., 81
Mr., 106

MUSTIAN & MOTT, 36, 76

MUSTIAN & PATTEN, 87

MYERS
John A. G., 124
J. C., 149

MYGATT & HODGES, 14

MYLAN
Emily, 125

NAFTEL
Thos., 124

NAGLE
Emma A., 45

NAGLIN
Mary A. A., 78

NAMES
Thomas, 173

NANCE
Harvey W., 83
Harvy, 126
H., 126
L., 162
Mrs. M., 109
William, 84

NAPIER, 54

NAPIER
Benjamin, 54
Frances A., 53
Lucretia J., 46

NAPPIER
Mary A., 69

NARRAMORE
Henry R., 79

NAVE
Erasmus D., 114

NEAGLE
Jacob, 52

NEAL
James D., 91

NEEDHAM, 125

NEEDHAM
Mrs. Jane, 25

NEILL
George H., 170

NELSON
Amos R., 52
Anderson B., 31
Belsy A., 61
Catharine, 46
C. H., 23
John, 164
Leonard P., 31
Major Thomas M., 71

NESBITT
Wm., 133

NEUFFER
Caroline L., 16
Charles, 149
C. F., 117, 127
John, 47

NEWBERRY, 53

NEWBERRY
Benjamin F., 61
Charnot, 67
C. L., 70
Franklin, 24
John, 46
Rebecca A., 51

NEWBY
Jordan, 62

NEWMAN
Wm., 135

NEWSOM
Asa, 45
Elizabeth, 146
Geo. W. F., 124
Henry M., 170
James, 108
Mary A., 46
Nancy, 99
Riley, 91

NEWSOME
Henry, 85
William A., 91

NEWSON
Carter, 24

NICHOLLS
Caroline L., 91

NICHOLSON
George W., 108
Henry B., 83
Martha J., 70

NICKLES, 154

NICKLESON
William O., 40

NICKOLS
R., 173

NILES
Jonathan, 17
J. T., 39

NISBETT
Mary A., 16

NIX, 39, 62

NIX

Ambrose, 46
Edward W., 16
Elizabeth C., 69
E. W., 165
F. M., 173
Georgia E., 91
James H., 129
James N., 162
Joseph, 165
Sarah A. F., 69
Thos., 42, 48, 55, 71, 80,
86, 93, 102, 110
Wm., 68

NOBEL
Col., 183

NOBLE, 45, 68

NOBLE
Hezekiah, 36
H., 51, 60, 85
Miss, 109

NOBLES
John, 91, 173
J. M., 173
Mary A. L., 124
Tom, 135

NOLEN
Sarah, 54

NOLES
Mrs. J., 173
Robert, 141

NOLLEE, 164

NORMAN
Christinia M., 170
Emily, 45
James T., 52
Jane Ann, 31
Jonathan G., 162
J. S., 10
Louisa, 91

NORRIS, 62

NORRIS
G. A., 39
James, 138
Leverett, 109
Margaret, 90
Mrs. George A., 101
Sarah F., 90
Susan, 16
Thomas B., 61

NORTHINGTON
Elafan, 70

NORTHROP
Cyrus, 141

NORTON
Mary J., 146
Mrs. Mary A. E., 41
Samuel E.(Jr.), 163
William, 141

NORWOOD
Joseph D., 77

NOYES
Robert H., 170

NUCKOLLS
Emma L., 171
Mrs. N. A., 164
Nathaniel A., 108
Thomas J., 59
T. J., 131

NUNNELEE
Benjamin F., 61

OATES
William, 99

ODOM
Abraham, 46
Andrew J., 139
Anna, 115
Cordelia, 108
Daniel, 84
Delilah, 46
Frances, 40
George, 121
Jordan, 85
J. T., 133
Leander, 115, 152
Lizzie M., 115
Maria N., 40
Mary, 40
M. D., 139
Pleasant, 51
Rhoda A., 146
Sarah, 78
Susan, 70
Wm., 147, 152

OGLE
John, 136
Wm. L., 155

OGLETREE
J. T., 135

Mrs. Jane M., 172
Mrs. M. A., 165
Seaborn, 77
S., 72, 86, 102, 110, 117
Vincent, 129
Vinson, 173
V., 157
William D., 139

OLIVE
John, 147
Louisa, 84
Martha J., 155
Melvina, 124

OLIVER
Francis D., 32
H., 139
John Berrien, 83
John J., 61
J. B., 133
Mrs. Virginia A., 116
Orman, 46
Wesley A., 134

OMANS
Sarah E., 114

OMILY
Wm., 138

ORR
Benjamin W., 70
D. W. & CO., 11, 14
Isaac W., 25
Robert J., 138

ORTAGUS
Emma, 92
Gregory, 15

ORUN
John W., 99

OSBORN
Ann M., 124
Elizabeth, 16
James, 53, 124
James T., 125
J. C., 165
Martha A., 170
Ophelia A., 170
Rebecca J., 46

OSTEEN
Caroline, 51
Louisiana J., 51
Sidney A. F., 53

OSWALL

James, 152
Joseph, 173

OSWALT
Jane, 123
Joseph, 109
Mary, 114

OTT
Edward S., 16

OUGLE
Lucinda, 46

OUSLEY
Andrew J., 46
Jesse C., 146
John, 136

OVERTON
Joe, 161

OWEN
Davis, 61
Elizabeth, 84
Martha A., 61
Mary J., 107
William, 93

OWENS
Charles, 141
Frances Elizabeth, 25
James T., 146
J. S., 131
Laney, 69
Rebecca, 32
Robert R., 78
R. A., 62
Sarah A. M., 77
William, 11
William C., 17

O'BANNAN
M. W., 162

O'BANNON, 157

O'BANNON
Mrs., 147
Sarah E., 99
Wm. S., 91

O'BRIAN
John, 122

O'BRIEN
Daniel, 169
Robert E., 146
T., 13

O'BRYAN
John, 126

O'CONNER
Mary, 25

O'CONNOR, 100

O'DONNELL
E., 124

O'HARA
Mary Jane, 17
Miss, 14
Mr., 14

O'KEEFE
L. E., 140

O'NEAL
B. F., 138
Francis A., 163
Mahala A., 24

O'NEIL
J. B., 133

O'QUIN
Eliza A., 53

O'STEIN
Wm. L., 16

O'TAGUS
Mrs., 101

PACE
Cynthia A., 60
Nancy A. F., 25
William H., 108

PACKMAN
H. P., 149
Matilda, 53
Mrs., 54

PADGETT
Elijah, 16

PAGE
Frances, 125
Permelia, 170

PAINE, 126

PAINE
T. G., 131
Wm., 158

Henry N. C., 170
James, 139
Jane, 33
Littleton, 78, 138
Mary Ann, 16
Pickard A., 78
Pink, 138
William F., 69
Wm., 146
Z., 172

PILKINTON
Rebecca, 177

PITCH
Lucinda, 32

PITT & HATCHER, 19

PITTMAN, 112

PITTMAN
John F., 90
Joseph, 146
J. D., 136
Mary, 146
Mrs., 173
N. W., 138
William J., 124

PITTS, 77

PITTS
Elmina C., 162
Elmira C., 155
George, 17, 55, 63
George L., 71
Mr., 109
S. R., 131

PITTS & HARRISON, 123

PITTS & HATCHER, 29

PLANE, 87

PLANE
W. F., 86

PLEDGE
Miss Julia H., 47

PLUMB
Elizabeth, 107

PLYMADE
Barbara A., 107

POE
Oliver H. P., 171

POITEVENT
Thomas, 116

POLK
Mrs., 38
President James K., 37

POLLARD
Charles T., 65
Wiley, 78

POMEROY
Mary A., 52

POND
Asa, 9, 38, 39
Cornelia F., 40
Thomas G., 69
Thos. G., 15

POND & WILCOX, 14

POOL
Elizabeth A., 33
Martha E., 77
Mathew H., 146
Sarah T., 24
Susan W., 108
Thos. J., 24

POPE
Chandler M., 162
Dan., 141
Jack, 141
Miles G., 39
R. C., 131
Sarah R., 107
Sarah V. C., 41
Simeon D., 125

PORTER
Albert, 133
A., 44, 48
D. S., 127
J. C., 174
Mrs., 100

POSEY
D. M., 152
J. R., 136

POTTER
George, 141
Richard, 137
R., 130

POWELL, 85

POWELL

B., 172
B. N., 173
E. F., 173
Geo. W., 156
Mary, 172
Reuben, 152
Robert, 152
Wade H. T., 17

POWER
Thomas A., 177

POWERS
James, 138
John H., 170
W., 100

PRADEN
Wm. H., 18

PRAGER
Julius, 135

PRANGLE
Mrs. Josiah, 101

PRANGLIN
Joseph, 85
Josiah, 16, 101
Jos., 109

PRATHER
Louisiana, 146

PRATT, 85, 92

PREDDY
John L., 155
Thomas C., 177

PREER, 126

PREER
Alderman, 104
Jasper, 126
Peter, 72, 91, 94, 102, 176

PRENTICE
George D., 106

PRESCOTT
Alfred, 78, 93, 156, 172
D. B., 41
George T., 156
Henry Slade, 93

PRESLEY
Elbert, 77
Elias B., 146

John R., 32
Mary E., 91

PRESSLY
J., 164

PRICE
F. M., 173
James, 124
Nancy, 40
Wm., 152

PRICKETT
Ann, 17

PRIDE
Georgia, 78
William, 100

PRIDGEN
James, 91

PRINCE
Ann S., 40
Jannette, 171

PRITCHARD
Sarah, 146

PROCTOR
Susan, 46

PROFUMO
F. X., 149

PRUDEN
Jos. S., 57
William, 101
Wm. H., 6

PRUETT
John T., 69
Mrs. Mary A., 24

PRY
Jane O., 77
John T., 52
Margaret A. E., 77

PRYOR
Alexander P., 146
C. S., 136
L. W., 126
Mr., 106
Sarah, 47
S. C., 58

PUCKETT
Elizabeth J., 85

PULLAMI, 101

PULLEY
James H., 170

PULLUM
Mary E., 177

PURCELL
David, 129
D., 141

PURPLE
Rosa E., 24
S. B., 14

PURYEAR
Mrs. Mary, 164

PURYEAR & WATSON, 95

PUTNAM
Andrew I., 78
Ann, 24
A. J., 172
Joseph, 138
Martha, 61

QUICK
Jesse, 138

QUIN, 175

QUIN
James L., 170
John, 7, 11, 18, 31, 55,
68, 71, 117, 120, 135, 145,
148, 157, 167, 174, 177

QUINN
Col. John, 39
John, 98
Wm., 139

RABUN
Asa, 155

RADCLIFF
William H., 84

RAGAN
A. B., 20
G. B., 141
Mrs. Cynthia, 26

RAGLAND, 68

RAGLAND
Andrew J., 139
A. E., 131
G. G., 131
John B., 77
Laura A., 84
Mrs. Sarah Ann, 126
O. S., 131
P. R., 79
Thomas, 63, 126, 157
Thos., 102
William, 25

RAIBUN
William, 115

RAIFORD, 126

RAIFORD
B., 139
Hamilton, 165

RAILY
Joseph, 125

RALLS
Isaac, 125

RAMSAY
Susan, 16

RAMSEY
James N., 128, 129
Jas. N., 127
John, 60
Tyra, 125

RANDALL
Elvira A. R., 61
Newsom, 45

RANDALL'S CREEK, 106

RANKIN, 10

RANKIN
Emma J., 155
Miss Ann, 145
William, 11, 116
Wm., 14, 89

RATLIFF
Malinda, 98
Penelope C., 45
William, 99

RAULSAN
W., 172

RAVENSCROFT
Albert, 164

RAWL
Sarah, 16

RAWSON
Martha E., 16

RAY
Benjamin F., 61
Francis, 85
Riley F., 41
Sarah, 40
William E., 115

READ
Elizabeth, 69
J. M., 31
Margaret, 125

REAMES
Miss N., 173

REAMS
John T., 170
Joshua A., 139

RED JACKET, 195

REDD, 156

REDD
A. G., 6
Charles A., 70
C. A., 164
Frances A., 91
G., 70
James(Jr.), 126
John, 144
J. K., 39, 63, 157
J. K.(Jr.), 131
Martha T., 17
Mary C., 16
Mary L., 78
Miss Eliza J., 33
Mrs. E. A., 47
N. L., 131
Thomas, 144
Thos. Y., 6
Wm., 130, 131
Wm.(Jr.), 139
Wm.(Sr.), 47

REDD & CO., 19

REDDING
A. W., 190
James A., 16
James T., 146

Lucy A., 99
L. R., 156
Martha V., 90
Parham D., 78
Robert C., 70

REED
Barbara A., 61
Erastus, 23
Jarred L., 108
Mrs. Delilah, 116
Murry, 15

REEDY
John, 153
John C., 98
Margaret, 172
Temperance, 173

REEGAN
Wm., 152

REES, 68

REES
Cinthia J., 32
D. J., 24, 44
Edmund H., 78
Frances, 46
Henry, 46
James Franklin, 33
Thaddeus, 89
Thomas C., 85

REESE
Charles F., 177
Dan J., 60
Dr. Gilbert, 126
D. J., 39, 77
Frances A., 52
John Chappel, 129
J. N. M., 134
Mrs. L. A., 165
Rivers, 96

REEVES
Augusta F., 16
Joel, 172
Wiley M., 33
Willis M., 47
W. M., 44

REHAY
G. W., 171

REID
B., 173
Eleanor A., 53
Epsy Ann, 162
E., 9

Luke, 11
M., 13
Robert, 69
Templeton, 15, 54
T., 9
T. W., 171
WM. A. & CO., 14

REIGHLEY
Sarah Ann Margaret, 32

REMBERT
Elizabeth M., 146
John, 139
M. C., 173

REMPERT
Joseph, 120

RENFORE
George M., 90

RENFROE, 54, 100

RENFROE
Cyrus, 92
Elizabeth, 24, 107
Geo. C., 147
James H., 45
Jno. E., 16
J. M., 39
Mary, 46

RENTFROE
Emily, 51
Joanna, 78
Martha F., 162
Rebecca, 124

REVEL
Mary M., 40

REVIER
Jacob, 141

REYNOLDS
Arabella A. A., 52
Mrs. A, P., 25
Nancy F., 53
Phil., 10
Thomas, 53
Thomas H., 46
Thos., 7
Thos. E., 162
William, 84

REYNOLDS & BETHUNE, 72

RHENA

Thomas, 79

RHINA
Benj., 85

RHODES
Lydia I., 115
Mary B., 146
Miss, 156

RIBERO
T., 134

RICE
Isaac, 141
Louisa P., 124
Mary C., 155
William C., 69

RICHARD
G., 70

RICHARDSON
Geo. W., 40
Julia, 70
Lucinda A., 24
Mary Jane, 79

RICHEY
David, 70

RICKLEY
J. C., 92

RIDDLE
Andrew J., 91
Sarah A., 114

RIDENHOUR
Aug. B., 129
Mary E., 45
Thos. F., 146
T. F., 131
Wm. W., 152
W. W., 165

RIDGEWAY
Cordelia A., 60
D. A., 80

RIDGILL
W. J., 39

RIDGWAY
Anna P., 107
John I., 92
J. I., 14, 22

RIDGWAY & BARDEN, 14

RIDGWAY & HOOPER, 15

RIDLEY, 100

RIKELY
John, 164

RILEY
Henry, 104, 164
Hiram, 136
H. S., 139
John, 101, 139
J., 141
Martin, 135
M., 133
Sarah, 69
Sarah A., 54
W., 141

RIPLEY. Joseph B., 84

RITCH
James J., 32
Leander F., 84

RIVERS
James, 136

RIVES
James T., 62

ROACH
Cynthia J., 84
Nancy Amanda, 16

ROAN
Henry, 40

ROBARTS
W. H., 135

ROBBINS
Milton, 50

ROBERSON
Mary A., 116
Richard, 20, 31

ROBERTS
Edmund S., 98
Elizabeth, 107
Emily T., 91
Jos. A., 103
J. L., 150
L. A., 134
Mary E., 78
Nancy, 32
N. B., 131
R. J., 173
Susan J., 52

ROBERTSON
Alex. W., 51
A. M., 55
Richard, 51

**ROBERTSON & ARNOLD,
51**

ROBINETTE
Granville L., 32

ROBINSON, 14, 44, 68

ROBINSON
Alex. M., 72
A. J., 14
A. M., 63, 79
Blake, 125
Eliza, 53
Elizabeth H., 53
Frances L., 77
George W., 33
Hugh Peyton, 40
Hugh P., 93
H. P., 76, 86, 102, 104
Isaac, 69
James, 85
John, 165, 170
John H., 115
Josephine, 24
J., 135
J. M., 135
Laney, 46
Lewis, 70
L. T., 42
Margaret F., 40
Mary, 61, 107, 165
Mary I., 108
Mrs., 100
Nancy, 146
Nancy F., 77
Narcissa J., 147
Norburn T. N., 163
N. Mc., 43, 48, 54
N. M. C., 7
Powell, 125
Richard, 68, 86, 93, 100
Sarah J., 52
S. E., 141
T. C., 135
William, 60
Wm., 164
Wm. B., 63
Wm. E., 53
Wm. L., 138
W. S., 133

ROBINSON & ARNOLD, 68

ROBISON, 54

ROBISON
Alexander W., 180
A. I., 63
Dr. A. I., 55, 144, 165
George, 62
H. P., 80
James T., 108
Mrs., 126
Nancy A., 115
N. M. C., 34
Perry, 53
Richard, 38
W. H. H., 149
W. W., 169, 174, 177

ROCKMORE
Jno. J., 17
Susan E., 25

ROCKWELL
C. S., 15
W., 95

RODGERS
Amanda, 100
Anthony F., 61
Caroline, 62
Hugh R., 45
James R., 69
Jane C., 156
Malinda, 147
Margaret J., 78
Martha A., 85
Mary B., 163
Mary M., 61
Rachel, 46
Thompson, 171
Wm., 146

ROE
James, 84
T. J., 136

ROGAN
Dr., 11

ROGERS
Amanda, 109, 157
Edward F., 52
Elizabeth J., 16
Frances S., 108
G. M., 149
John, 121, 149
Levi, 121
Margaret Elizabeth, 24
Martha, 32
Martha E., 116
Mary, 172

Mrs. E., 157
Peyton H., 77
Samuel C., 108
Zachariah, 82

ROLAND
Catharine, 69
David, 138
Eucratus, 99
Martha, 16
Martha C., 70
Mary E., 107
Nancy, 69, 171
S., 165

ROLEN
James W., 61

ROLLING
Laura, 156

ROMAN
Peter, 150

ROOD
A. P., 173

ROODE
Col., 173

ROOKE
Jasper, 135

ROONEY & SAMMIS, 14, 18, 19

ROPER
Hennie, 162
Joshua S., 91, 139
Jos., 150
Jos. E., 174
Margaret A., 84
Wiley G., 53, 108

RORIE
Wm. H., 78

ROSCOE
Scilla, 69

ROSECRANS, 134

ROSELLY
Felix, 155

ROSENBAUM
Henrietta, 155

ROSETTE
G. W., 169

ROSS
Thos. M., 125

ROSSEAU
General, 167
Gen., 166

ROSSEY
Dr., 176

ROTENBERG
Wm., 139

ROTHSCHILD
Frank, 165

ROULAND
Jackson, 99

ROUNDS
Martha Ann, 32

ROWE
Ella G., 146
Elmira, 99
James, 171
J., 10
Mary, 70

ROWELL
A. H., 68
Elizabeth, 40
Margaret, 51
Martha A., 61
Mary, 45
Miss, 109

ROWLIN
John T., 77

ROYALS
Newton, 141

ROYSTON
Cyrus, 61

RUCKER
G. G., 131, 132
R. Z., 133
Z. C., 131

RUDLEDGE
Mary E., 52

RULE
Eveline, 15

RUMSEY
James, 163

R., 136

RUS
Elizabeth M., 61

RUSE, 37

RUSE
Frances, 115, 124
Francis N., 17
John C., 18, 35, 75, 77, 80
J. C., 7, 29, 76, 86
Thad., 173

RUSE-PATTEN & CO., 15, 75

RUSH
Charles G., 114
L. P., 98

RUSSELL
Capt., 160
Charles, 139
Charles R., 139
C. R., 131
David P., 99
Diana, 164
D. G., 139
Henrietta, 125
James, 152
James M., 98
James P., 51, 136
Jas. M., 161
John, 170
Jonas D., 152
J. M., 106
Louisa V., 115
Mrs. Mary, 165
Rolin A., 139
Wm. H., 146
W. H., 150

RUTHERFORD
A. H., 131
A. S., 60, 83, 90, 107, 123, 127, 147
Col. A. S., 24
Frances Eliza, 17
R. M., 131, 137
Samuel, 79
T. V., 94

RUTLEDGE
John W., 70

RYALL
William, 32

RYALS
Martha, 156

RYANS
Benjamin, 53
Thomas, 114

RYNEHART
William, 68, 173

SACRO
Robert M., 123

SAGNET
Rosalia A., 124

SALAY
Mr., 109

SALISBURY, 142, 160, 175

SALISBURY
Mrs. L. V., 172
Private, 59
Virginia B., 78
William, 41
Wm. L., 111
W. L., 48, 102, 117, 127, 134, 144, 167

SALTMARSH
John, 77

SAMMIS
Phebe Jane, 33

SAMMIS & ROONEY, 14, 18, 19

SANBORN
Benj., 77

SANDEFORD
W. E., 134, 190

SANDERLAND
A. B., 129

SANDERLIN
James, 152
James B., 155
R. R., 152

SANDERS
Abey E., 70
Allen W., 25
Doctor H., 16
Elias, 46
Elizabeth, 47, 124

John, 171
John N., 173
Jos. A., 171
J. H., 131
J. R., 130
Lucinda, 45
Margaret, 147
Rolf. S., 125
Sarah, 62
Shadrack, 62
T., 10
William T., 77

SANFORD
Thomas M., 78

SANKEY
Annie J., 107

SANTHALL
Eliza, 25

SANTOIN
Joseph, 156

SAPP
H. M., 133
John M., 113
Mattie C., 99
Mrs. Narcissa F., 156
Teresa E., 69

SAPPINGTON
James W., 171
Mrs. C. A., 172

SARTWELL
F. W., 11
Simon, 24
S., 11

SAUL
Elizabeth A., 41

SAULS
Ann V., 98
A. M., 7
Frances E., 163
G., 172
Mrs., 92
Sarah H., 52
Wm., 46

SAUNDERS
General, 151
Mrs. E. M., 165

SAVAGE
James, 62

SEMPLE
Louisa, 116

SEMPLER
Louisa, 61
Matilda, 115

SENN, 164

SENN
Isabella A., 61
John F. C., 99
Mary A., 99

SERGEANT
David, 164
Mary, 79

SERGUREUR
Benj., 157

SERRELL, 45

SERRELL
Wm. F., 31, 39
W. F., 164

SESSIONS
Mary E., 69

SEWELL
Joseph B., 171

SEYMOUR
D. C., 132
Martha E., 99
Nathan, 25

SHAAF
Mary C., 40

SHAEFFER, 10

SHAFFER
F., 15

SHANDLEY
Patrick, 136

SHANNON
Charles, 79

SHARP
Mary J., 124

SHARPE, 100

SHAVER
James, 115

SHAVERS
Margaret, 124

SHAW
B. P., 141
James, 13, 53
Jane, 46
Joseph, 155
William, 41
Willis J., 141

SHAY
Harriet E., 16

SHEAN
Margaret, 164

SHEARER
G. W., 135

SHEHANE
Mrs., 165

SHELBY
Mary Lucinda, 177

SHELINE
Lewis, 135

SHELLMAN
Pleasant S., 90
Rebecca, 46

SHELTON
Alexander, 171
James, 91
Mrs. Lucinda, 173

SHEPHARD
Thomas, 92

SHEPHERD
Captain William S., 139
Mrs., 100
Mrs. A. E., 105
Sarah A., 162
Sarah T., 61
Winnie, 165
W. S., 113, 131, 132

SHEPPERSON
Ben. S., 134
B. S., 134
C. C., 134
G. P., 133

SHERDON
John N., 85
Robert S., 170

Robt. S., 90

SHERIDAN
Mrs., 100
R., 133

SHERLY, 126

SHERLY
Sarah E. F., 115

SHERMAN, 126, 134

SHERMAN
Gen., 168

SHERRER
Wm., 136

SHERWOOD
George, 53
Martha W., 83
Mrs. G. A., 163

SHEW
Rev. W. D., 107

SHINGLEUR
James A., 146
J. A., 156

SHIPPEY
Elizabeth, 61
James H. B., 108
Joseph J., 61
J. H. B., 150
Martha E., 24
Sarah V., 61
William T., 33

SHIRLEY
Charles, 85
Mrs., 157
Richard, 69

SHIRRER
Rachel, 107

SHIVERS
C. A., 133, 150
Robet M., 54
Thomas J., 54
Thos. J., 13

SHOEMAKE
Francis, 164
Mary E., 164
U. H., 164

SHOEMAKER

Mary E., 164
T., 7

SHOFNER
Salina, 46
Wm. A., 15
W. A., 76

SHORES
John, 136

SHORT
Frances, 165
James, 135
John R., 152
J. A., 141
Nathan H., 32

SHORTER
Charles S., 162
E. S., 131
James H., 14
J. H., 8
Mrs., 31
Mrs. James A., 11
Mrs. R. C., 101
Mrs. Sophia, 92
Reuben, 10
Reuben C., 48
R. C., 39, 42, 48, 55
Virginia A., 83

SHOTWELL
Julia W., 77

SHOUP
Jacob, 83
Jacob W., 77
J., 177

SHYLOCK, 29

SIKES
Capt., 153
Capt. J. H., 152
Jesse H., 138
J. H., 116
Lieut., 137
Richard, 152
R. A., 164
R. G., 152

SILAS
Ellen, 146
Sarah, 70

SILLMAN
Henry, 177

SILLS

Wm., 146

SILVA
Mary J., 124

SILVER, 126

SILVERS
Mrs. Mary, 171

SIMMONS
Elizabeth, 41
Henry, 101
H. T., 150
James, 138
James M., 68
Jarusha, 177
Joseph, 163
Lewis, 129
Martha, 52
Mary A., 108
Matilda, 78
Moses, 84
R. T., 169
Sarah J., 170
William, 139

SIMONS, 36

SIMONS
Robt. T., 68, 73
R. T., 18, 71, 83, 150,
174

SIMPSON
Benjamin, 77
Catherine, 17
Elizabeth, 125
Elizabeth R., 78, 85
Eugenia, 98
Mary, 16
Mary M., 125
Nancy, 115

SIMS
Anna, 163
Geo. H., 24
James, 85
R., 31
Wm., 162

SIMSON
T., 100

SINCLAIR
Ann M., 53
Charles, 107
John P., 164

SINGLETON

D. D., 138
James M., 115
William, 141

SINGLEUR
J. A., 133

SINGON
John, 139

SIZEMORE
Henry H., 69
J. M., 152
Richard D., 40
Samantha, 169
Wiley, 16

SKATES
Susan, 107
Wm. W., 138

SKINNER
D. A., 150
Ephraim, 125
James M., 108
John W., 108
Joseph, 78
J. W., 150
Martha L., 177
Mary A. M., 116
Mary R., 147
Sarah A., 146
Sarah M., 62
Thomas J., 69
T. J., 149

SLACK
Mary A., 85

SLADE
Ann L., 99
Emma I., 78
Fanny Blount, 33
Helen R., 162
James J., 68, 114
Janet E., 162
Jerry, 159
J. H., 131
J. J., 86, 92
Martha B., 115
Miss Mary L., 163
Mrs., 92
Rev. Thos. B., 33
Thomas B., 48
Thos. B., 15, 55, 94

SLAGLE
Andrew, 99

SLATTER

SPEAR
Lucy Ann, 40
Thomas Emmons, 116
Thos. S., 116
T. S., 127

SPEARS
Mary Ann, 40

SPEER, 97

SPEER
E. W., 90
Martha, 85
Rev. E. W., 162
Thos. C., 31

SPELLER
Mary T., 84

SPELLMAN
George, 100

SPENCER
Lambert, 15
Miss, 100
Mrs. Laura, 171
Richard P., 56
R. P., 39, 113, 160
W. Y., 173

SPERIS
Wm. A., 147

SPERLIN
C. B., 150
Mary, 107

SPERLING
Aaron, 152

SPIDLE
Charles, 172

SPIGENER
Catharine, 155

SPINKS
Amanda, 170
Martha J., 170
Mrs., 156

SPIRES
W. A., 150

SPIVEY
Eli, 89
E. B. W., 51
I. C., 132

Thomas, 70
Willis, 107

SPRINGER
Joseph, 107

SPURGERS
William H., 17

SPURLIN
Maria J., 125

STAFFORD
Mrs., 62
Sarah J., 77

STAGG
James H., 78, 85
Rebecca E., 155

STAHL
Jenny, 84

STAHLS
Mrs., 101

STAIN
George, 172

STALLINGS
Frances M., 16

STANDMIRE
J. T., 172

STANFIELD
Irene, 61
James, 125
Parmelia C., 91
Sarah A. E., 45

STANFORD
Dr. F. A., 48
Lieutenant, 37

STANFORD & ELLIS, 14

STANLEY
Rebecca E., 171
Sarah A. E., 90

STANSEL
A., 173
G. M., 164

STANSELL
William A., 85

STAPLER, 14

STAPLER
Mrs. Sarah, 165
W. L., 160

STARKE
Sarah J., 61

STARKER
J. B., 126

STARNS
Mrs., 79

STARR, 157

STARR
E. W., 85

STATHAM
Pleasant, 155
Sherard, 69

STATHAN
P. M., 172

STATHEN
Susan E., 91

STATON
Abraham, 32

STATUM
Robert, 108

STEARNS, 92

STEARNS
Nancy, 25

STEEN
Mary E., 155

STEGALL
Robert B., 171

STEIN
Caroline, 53
George, 52, 127

STEPHENS, 79

STEPHENS
Amanda N., 116
Artamesia, 52
A., 13
Betsey, 46
Elizabeth, 61
Janet, 52
John S., 177
L. M., 173

Martha A., 52
Mary J., 155
Missouri, 115
Mrs., 79
M., 47
Nehemiah, 41
Rosannah E., 61
Thomas J., 69
William, 40
William B., 32

STERN
Simon, 61

STERNBERG
Frederika E., 70

STERNE
Isaac, 133

STERNHEIMER
Rev. L. Z., 113

STEVENS
Benjamin, 165
William, 92

STEWART, 79, 85, 101

STEWART
Charles, 173
Charles D., 36
Charles W., 124
C. W., 171
Dr., 7, 8
Dr. T., 55, 93
Elizabeth, 77
Eugene, 132
E. G., 131
Frederick, 125
George, 36
Louisa, 92
Mrs. Mary, 164
Mrs. S. C., 172
Rosannah, 62
Sarah E., 156
Theopholis, 50
Theo., 42
Walter, 146
William W., 52

STEWART-GRAY & CO., 75

STICKNEY
Rev. G. W., 173

STINSON
Rebecca J., 146

STOCKDALE

John I. H., 114

STOCKS
Thomas, 58

STOCKTON
R. S., 18, 39, 150

STOCKWELL
J. E., 136

STODDARD
Mrs. Faunice B., 70

STOLTZ
Johnson E. T., 108

STONAKER
B. J., 138

STONE
Thomas J., 155

STORCKEL, 125

STORY
James, 125
T. J., 141

STOVALL
George, 134
George W., 134

STOWE
Lydia A., 98

STOWERS
Caroline, 172

STRATFORD
Catharine, 170

STRATTEN
David C., 177

STRATTON
Calvin, 14, 18, 26, 42, 48, 55, 63, 71, 80, 86, 93, 102, 110, 117
C., 8, 34

STRAUS
Hermenia, 163

STREETMAN
Frances, 170

STRIBLING
Elizabeth, 91

STRINGER
Eli, 170
Elizabeth, 33
Hetty E., 108

STRINGFIELD
John, 99
Mrs., 158
William, 167

STRINGFLLOW
James, 115

STRIPLING
Benjamin A., 147
Susan, 78

STRONG
L. C., 133

STRONG & WOOD, 14

STROTHER
Captain J. A., 137
Capt., 160
Col. John A., 128
Mrs., 172

STRUPPER
George, 29
I. G., 10, 14, 27, 81, 103
John, 18
John B., 29
J., 14
J. B., 10, 23, 35, 44, 48, 55, 86, 103
W. I., 134

STUBBLEFIELD, 85

STUBBLEFIELD
Mrs., 62
Thos., 85

STUBBS
David, 177
John J., 124

STURDEVANT
Thos., 129

STURGES
Larry, 135

STURGIE
Judge, 13

STURGIS
John, 68
John R., 62, 70**

Lawrence, 107
Lucy E., 32
Mrs. Jane J., 163
Thad S., 13
Thad., 48

ST.LEDGER, 92

SUDDETH
D., 92

SUGGS
John W., 61

SULLIVAN, 134

SULLIVAN
Catherine, 79
Dennis, 164
James, 11
Jas., 14
John, 85, 163
John James, 41
Martha, 165
Michael, 164
Patrick, 62, 98
P., 11
Robert H., 52

SUMMERGILL
Mrs., 100
Thomas, 52, 164

SURLES
Martin, 135

SUTTON
Benj., 47
Jesse T., 51
John, 141
John A., 40
J. J., 190
Mary, 125
Thomas C., 85

SUVELL
Edward W., 33

SWANN
William C., 15

SWEET
Mrs., 93
Thomas, 128, 141

SWETMAN
Mary A., 124

SWINNEY
John, 115

SWITZER
Lovick, 54
Miss A. A., 165

SYSTRYTHE
Mary P., 108

TADLOCK
Elizabeth, 147

TAFF
Alley Jane, 107
Elizabeth, 162
Richard, 69

TAFT
George W., 114
Horace H., 108, 147
Sarah A., 156

TALBOT, 126

TALBOT
Allen, 141
H., 141

TALIAFERRO
Charles, 156
Col. C. B., 122
C. F., 133
Lucy M., 162
V. H., 133

TALLMAN
Thomas W., 76

TALLY
Joseph M. I., 109

TANNER
R., 15

TANT
David K., 32
Mrs., 92

TAPPER
Miss, 100
Miss Caroline, 172

TARBOROUGH
Richard, 47

TARBOT
J. M. & CO., 14

TARBOX
J. M., 18, 29, 35

TARBUTTON
William, 11
Wm., 47

TARVER
Ann Louisa, 78
Henrietta, 53
John, 77
Marcellus, 171

TATUM
James, 146
James S., 90
Sarah, 146

TAYLOR, 135

TAYLOR
Benjamin N., 171
Elizabeth, 125
Elizabeth L. V., 177
Emaline, 162
E. T., 22, 37
Gen., 194
Gen. Wm., 193
Geo. F., 129
Greene, 32
James T., 90
Jeremiah, 99
John, 170
John T., 170
Julia A., 32
J., 136
Lewis A., 138
Matilda, 60
Nancy J., 52
Rosa, 177
R. H., 27
Sarah, 124
S. E., 136
Ursule, 155
U. R., 136
William, 40
William M., 52

TEAL
Catharine, 91
Emma, 79
Jasper, 173
Joseph, 99
Malinda R., 16
Savastia, 155
William A., 147

TEASDALE
C. B., 72
Henry, 54
H. S., 7
Mrs., 15, 158

TIDWELL
  Clarissa A., 99
  Rev. W. W., 107

TIERVEY
  Patrick, 47

TILL
  Elizabeth, 125

TILLERY, 44

TILLERY
  J. J., 163
  Mary, 125
  Presley, 46
  William, 46

TILLEY, 10

TILLEY
  Cynthia M., 98
  Jackson, 92
  John, 165
  John N., 84
  Mary M., 45
  Miss J. W., 163
  William, 117
  W., 102, 110

TILLINGHAST
  Oliver P., 84
  O. P., 13

TILLMAN, 92, 122

TILLMAN
  Capt. F. C., 172
  Eleanor A., 107
  F. C., 149
  Gibson, 79
  Isabella, 77
  James W., 99
  Martha, 156
  Mary, 79
  William L., 124

TILLY
  Elizabeth Emily, 15
  John, 68, 165
  W., 8

TILTON
  Ephraim M., 177

TINNAN
  Thos. L., 124

TINNET

Amanda, 77

TINNEY
  Joseph S., 98

TINNON
  Celia A., 53
  David Y., 115
  Mrs. Louisa, 164
  Mrs. Mary, 171
  Sarah J., 53
  Thomas, 172
  Thos. L., 162

TINSLEY
  Martha A., 85

TIPPER
  Thos. J., 16

TIPTON
  Emily, 45

TOBY
  Frederick, 18, 28
  F., 8, 39

TOBY & WELLS, 10

TODD
  James J., 41

TOLBERT
  Benjamin M., 170

TOLER
  Henry R., 70

TOLES
  Mannering, 85

TOLSON
  Wm., 152

TOMBERLIN
  George W., 152

TOMBLIN
  Frances, 24

TOMLIN
  Mary E., 146

TOMLINSON
  Elizabeth, 16

TOMMEY
  Sarah A., 46
  V. R., 31

TOMMY
  Mary, 70
  Mrs. V. R., 100
  V. R., 190

TONGE
  S. Davis, 163

TOOK
  J. J., 150
  J. N., 150

TOOKE
  Sarah, 46
  Wm., 152
  Wm. S., 146

TOOLE
  James H., 108

TOOMBS, 129

TORBET
  H. M. L., 134
  Martha, 172

TORBETT
  Frank T., 115
  H. M. L., 133

TORRANCE
  Mansfield, 80
  M., 42

TORREAN
  Chas., 13

TORRENCE
  Mansfield, 18, 26, 48

TORREY
  James E., 171
  Mrs., 101

TORRY
  James, 84

TOWLER
  Thomas M., 46

TOWNS
  Eliza, 77

TOWNSEND
  Wm. W., 24

TOWNSLEY
  Lyman B., 52
  L. B., 135
  Mrs., 86

Victor S., 116

TRACY
Michael, 104, 105
Mr., 109

TRAMMELL
Joseph D., 99
Thomas J., 61

TRAWICK
I., 13
John, 86
John M., 48
J. M., 93

TRAYWICK, 43

TRAYWICK
John, 46, 109
J. M., 42

TREADAWAY
John, 108

TREADWAY
R. C., 150

TREADWELL, 125

TREADWELL
Henry B., 40
Thomas, 10

TRICE
Fannie, 156
Sarah A., 155

TROTMAN
Aaron C., 125

TRUAX
John L., 69

TRUETT
Alfred, 91

TUCKER
Exton, 84
James O. A., 53
J. W., 129

TUGGLE
Thomas S., 99

TULLIS
Martha Irvin, 24

TUNREY
David, 108

TUREAN, 10

TURMAN
William R., 156
W. R., 128

TURNAGE
Henry, 24
James, 45, 150
J. W., 152
L. S., 152
Mary Ann, 15
Thomas, 115
Thos. S., 152

TURNER
Alexander, 114
Clara, 40
David, 164
E., 173
Fredonia, 79
George W., 78, 85
Isham, 52
John, 146
Julia, 170
J., 141
Liomel H., 24
Sarah A., 147
Susan, 146

TURRENTINE
George W., 18, 47
G. W., 8, 26
Lucy C., 40

TURVILLE
Elizabeth, 109

TWILLEY
James, 16
Mary E., 32

TWITTY
Anna L., 69

TYLER
Andrew J., 155
Charles, 156
Cornelia I., 115
Gen., 184

ULDRICK
Hiram, 41

UNDERWOOD
John F., 139
Matt, 140
W. J., 133

UPCHURCH
D. G., 70

UPDEGRAFF
D. D., 134
Joseph, 67
Judith, 69

UPTON, 100

UPTON
Amanda, 91
Frances, 91
Gen., 181, 182, 183
Madison, 170
Sarah, 155

UPTON(Jr.), 100

URQUAHART
John A., 48

URQUHART, 111

URQUHART
Caroline L., 41
Dr. J. A., 160
John A., 132
J. A., 39, 42, 110
Mrs. J. A., 142

VAN, 62

VAN VECHTEN, 14

VAN VECTEN
Captain, 37

VAN VEICHTON
Capt., 29

VAN VEIGHTEN
H. W., 18

VANDENBERG, 135

VANDENBURG
Mrs., 79

VANPITT
John S., 32

VANSANT
John, 62

VANZANT
Antoinett, 146
John, 100

VEACH
Frank, 139

VEANEMAN
Jennette, 54

VEASEY
Barney, 135

VEASY
Barney, 108

VENABLE
Geo. M., 146

VERNOY
James, 40, 76, 102, 103

VERSTILLE
Henry W., 52

VICKERS
Elijah, 52
Eliza, 68
Emily, 16
Frances M., 163
Mrs., 92

VICKERY
John B., 32
Joseph S., 32

VICKORY
Rebecca, 172

VIGAL
Henry C., 69

VINCENT
W. C., 134

VINSON
Cally A. E., 147
John, 79
Luther T., 69
Sarah A., 163

VIRGINS & BRUNO, 14

VOIGHT
Henry, 91

VonZINKEN
Col., 175
Col. Leon, 180

VROOMAN
J. A., 71

WADDELL, 178

WADDELL
Geo. H., 77
James, 85
James F., 163
Judge, 180
Rebecca E., 70

WADE
Jane, 15
John, 139
Mattie A., 177

WADE & MIDDLEBROOK,
14, 18, 19

WADKINS
M. M., 139

WADSWORTH
D. F., 173

WAGNER
Elizabeth, 107
E. P., 134
Hamp, 135
James, 101

WAKEFIELD
John C., 147
Lizzie, 163

WALDREN
T., 134

WALES
A., 98
Charles D., 147
Martha G., 99
Mary T., 155
Senator S. A., 109
S. A., 98
W. A., 136

WALKER
Anderson, 171
A. M., 39, 92
Captain G. E., 165
Isabella, 162
John C. C., 138
John T., 28, 86, 93, 98,
102
J. T., 111
Lafayette, 61, 171
Milton J., 146
Mrs. B., 126
Mrs. Mary J., 164
Mr. John, 106

M. T., 141
Permelia, 107
Rebecca, 78, 85
Sophronia E., 40
S. F., 141
William, 16, 164
Woolfolk, 151
W., 132

WALL
Angelina, 47
Brad, 152
Caroline, 116
Enoch J., 33
George W., 152
Hiller, 170
James, 152
Jasper, 162
Jesse, 46
Lawrence, 150
Lawrence W., 128
Mary Ann, 16
Susan A., 61

WALLACE
Benjamin F., 53
Elizabeth A., 115
James, 164
John C., 152
John M., 139
Nancy L. M., 115
Susannah, 61
T. B., 152

WALLS
Jane, 45
J. A., 172
Shadrack, 15

WALSINGHAM
John H., 53

WALSTON
Elizabeth, 165

WALTER, 85

WALTERS
Martha, 16
Matilda Catharine, 32
Michael L., 47
Michael S., 32
Young E., 32

WALTON
Joseph, 11

WAMACH
Wiley, 33

WAMOCK
Sarah E., 91

WARD, 86

WARD
Amos C., 90, 99
John, 53, 71, 78
John H., 155
Jonathan, 107
Laura A., 61
Mary Ann, 177
Mary A., 177
W., 135

WARDEN
John, 165

WARDHAW
W. K., 114

WARDLAW
Rev. W. J., 156, 162
W. J., 123, 154, 169

WARE
David, 132
Dr., 111
Dr. J. L., 165
Dr. R. A., 44, 71, 89, 158, 160
James, 156
James L., 108
J. H., 132
J. W., 153
Mrs., 100
Mrs. Louisa Jane, 100
Nicholas, 71
Robt. A., 43
R. A., 14, 23, 27, 31, 42, 48, 94, 103
Susan I., 108
T., 173
W. A., 132

WARLICK
Joseph, 115

WARNER
Brady F., 16
Captain, 164
J. H., 172
Lemuel P., 78
Mrs., 92
Mr., 109
Richard, 85
Richard A., 25

WARNOCK, 123

WARNOCK
S. B., 118

WARREN
James, 46
James E., 155
James W., 62
John, 165
J. W., 41, 123
Louisa, 15
Louisiana F., 52
Mary D., 45
Mrs. Sarah Vivian, 62

WARTHEN
James F., 115

WASHBURN
Henry H., 170

WASHINGTON
W. H., 152

WATERS
Elsey, 46
Mary E., 46
William, 53
W. A., 150

WATKINS, 101

WATKINS
Harriet, 61
Irving, 46
John W., 51
J. M., 150
Martha, 25
Samuel, 25
Samuel C., 115
Washington, 52
William B., 107

WATSON, 141

WATSON
Alexander, 115
Daniel G., 53
Gilbert, 124
Jas. F., 14
Jonathan, 150
Lafayette, 165
Matt, 171
Mrs., 101
M. G., 123, 128
Nathan, 124

WATSON & PURYEAR, 95

WATT
Charles P., 84

Lucy H., 24
Thomas, 69
Thomas F., 84

WATTS, 125

WATTS
Lurana, 79
William M., 61

WAYNE, 92

WAYNE
Mrs., 92

WAYTOR
William, 136

WEATHERFORD
Pat. A., 136

WEATHERS
Martha, 16

WEAVER
A., 173
Eliza, 25
John H., 90
Matilda, 32
Samuel, 32
Sarah A., 70

WEBB
Eliza, 32
Haner A. M., 47
John H., 61
Maranda A., 32
Pyrene C., 15
Sandel, 24
William I., 114
Wm. J., 146
W. H., 152

WEBSTER
Joseph E., 18, 117, 127
Jos. E., 75
J. E., 39, 54
Mrs., 62
Mrs. E., 11
Washington Irving, 33
William, 99
William T., 53

WEDDINGTON
Amanda, 90
Eveline, 84
Harriet L., 85

WEED
Sarah, 78

WEEKS, 157

WEEKS
B., 11, 26
Charles H., 126
John H., 141
J. H., 126
Wm. J., 170

WEEMS, 68, 158

WEEMS
Edward M., 69
Eugenie A., 70
J. A., 132, 139
Lock, 31
Locke, 47
Mrs. M. F., 47
S., 14
Walter, 155

WEISENBERGHER
Zachariah, 163

WELCH
Andrew Jackson, 24
A. J., 165
Catharine, 31
Elizabeth, 52, 70
George W., 25
Harriet, 52
James, 45, 53
Mary, 162
Moses, 163
Sarah, 31
Shepherd, 139
William, 46

WELDING
Willhelmina, 123

WELDON
John, 152
Simeon, 52

WELLBORN
Eliza I., 114
James W., 84
John C., 24
John S., 69
Marshall J., 31
Mr., 103

WELLS
B., 11
B. & CO., 14, 145
Elbert L., 163
E. L., 141
E. & CO., 11

James, 171
James B., 7, 40
James L., 115
John B., 13
Joseph Wiggins, 18
Jos. L. B., 91
L. W., 18, 29, 35, 44
Mrs., 101
Salina A., 107
Samuel E., 177
S. G., 13
William C., 98
Wm., 139

WELLS & TOBY, 10

WELSH
A. J., 72
A. P., 101
James, 109

WENTRY
Josiah, 164

WESSON & BOOHER, 14

WEST
Adeline, 91
Clara, 79
Clarissa S., 162
James B., 146
Joseph, 25
Martha, 173
Martin G., 45
Martin J., 92
Sarah, 124
T. D., 98, 114

WESTMORELAND
Charles W., 45

WESTON
Maj., 182

WHATLEY
Allen, 25
Mary A., 116

WHATLY
Levi, 45

WHATSEY
William, 24

WHEELER
John, 139
Lucy C., 77
Mary A., 165
Mrs., 165

WHEELIS
Martha, 78

WHIGHAM
John M., 40
Samuel A., 41
Thomas G., 91

WHIPPLE
Augusta Ann, 33
James, 60
William W., 68

WHIPPLER
Mary E., 114

WHISKEY CHIEF, 196

WHISKEY JOHN, 195, 196

WHITBY
Thomas H., 99

WHITE, 100

WHITE
Ann, 78
Eveline, 33
E. A., 15
E. V., 133
Jacob P., 129
R. W., 152
William, 172

WHITEHURST
Bartlett W., 41
W. O. M., 136

WHITESIDE
J. A., 177
Mary T., 98

WHITESIDES
James A., 138
John, 10, 72, 111
Mrs. Temperance, 116

WHITLOCK
H., 93

WHITMAN
Michael W., 25

WHITTAKER
Samuel, 61

WHITTELSEY
Jabez Hamlin, 32

WHITTEN

Elizabeth, 146
Jane, 84
John J., 155
Lizzie, 146
Mary A., 109
Mary F., 155
Thomas J., 146
Thomas K., 80
Thos K., 71
T. K., 34, 42
V. W., 170

WYNN'S HILL, 49

YANCY
Mary, 116
Mrs., 171

YARBOROUGH
Beauford T., 91
Benjamin, 108
Joseph H., 78

YARBROUGH
Francis A., 61
James, 139
Jason, 135
R. C., 136

YARN, 156

YATES
Sarah, 108

YAUGHN
Allen, 155

YEARTY
Mary K., 115
Sarah, 124
Wm., 45

YONGE, 15

YONGE
GARRARD & HOOPER, 10
W. P., 10

YOUNG
Alfred, 146
A., 134, 141
Dora P., 170
Dr., 10
George B., 146
Geo. B., 133
Isaiah, 163
John, 24
John R., 125

J. M., 164
Leonard, 129
Miss E. A., 163
Mrs. Susan C., 164
Nathan, 152
Orlando C., 115
O. C., 172
Susan E., 114
Thomas E., 83
T. J., 141
William, 172
William H., 88
Wm., 132
Wm. H., 89

YOUNG EAGLE, 192, 193

YOUNGBLOOD
Isaac, 172
J. M., 165
Merilda, 99
White, 162

YOUNGER
John, 69

www.ingramcontent.com/pod-product-compliance
Lightning Source LLC
Chambersburg PA
CBHW031115020426
42333CB00012B/93